JAMES K. POLK
A POLITICAL BIOGRAPHY

JAMES K. POLK

A POLITICAL BIOGRAPHY

BY

EUGENE IRVING McCORMAC, Ph.D.

NEW YORK

RUSSELL & RUSSELL · INC

1965

FIRST PUBLISHED IN 1922
REISSSUED, 1965, BY RUSSELL & RUSSELL, INC.
L. C. CATALOG CARD NO: 64-66402

PRINTED IN THE UNITED STATES OF AMERICA

TO
THE MEMORY OF
MY MOTHER

PREFACE

In the two standard sets of American biographies—namely, the *American Statesmen Series* and the *American Crisis Biographies*—the name of James K. Polk does not appear in the list of titles. Evidently the editor of the first set did not consider Mr. Polk to have been a statesman worthy of serious consideration, and the editor of the second set seems to have been unaware that Polk had played a conspicuous part in any of the crises of American history.

Although it is not my purpose to criticize the selection made by these editors, I believe that the character and success of Polk's political career entitled him to a place in either series. I believe that the following pages will show Mr. Polk to have been a constructive statesman—a statesman possessed of vision, sound judgment, and unusual executive ability. Surely he was a "crisis" President. He extended our national boundaries to the Pacific Ocean and determined the political destinies of the future population of the vast area lying west of the Louisiana Purchase. His request for an appropriation with which to conduct negotiations with Mexico called forth the Wilmot Proviso; and this proviso precipitated the "irrepressible conflict," which was one of the greatest crises in American history.

When nominated for the Presidency in 1844, Polk was neither unknown nor inexperienced in national affairs. He had been selected to conduct Jackson's bank war in the House of Representatives, and he had performed this task to the entire satisfaction of the President and the Democratic party. As Speaker of the House of Representatives, he had displayed alertness of mind, sound judgment, and ability as a party leader. And when, in 1844, Van Buren announced his opposition to the annexation of Texas, General Jackson urged that Polk be nominated, for, as he said, Governor Polk was the ablest exponent of Democratic doctrines and the one who would be most capable of carrying them into successful operation. The General did not overrate the political ability of his protégé. As President, Polk formulated his policies with precision and confidence; and despite many obstacles, he succeeded in carrying them into effect.

It has not been my purpose to write a personal biography. Therefore this volume deals almost entirely with Polk's political career. In the discussion of the events of his administration I have attempted to show the part played by the President in formulating the policy of the nation. In the field of foreign relations I have been concerned mainly with the President's foreign policy and with the motives, viewpoints, and exigencies which led to the adoption of that policy. For this reason the history, policies, and motives of other countries concerned have been treated incidentally only. Polk's policies were influenced by what he believed to be the facts concerning those countries, and not by the facts which have subsequently been found to be true. For example, I did not feel that a biography of President Polk called for an exhaustive discussion of conditions in Mexico, either before or during our war with that nation. For similar reasons, the discussion of the Oregon question is confined to the official acts of Great Britain and to the interpretation of those acts by the government of the United States.

The material used in the preparation of this volume has been gathered mainly in the University of California Library, the Tennessee State Library, and the Library of Congress. I am indebted to Dr. John W. Jordon, Librarian of the Historical Society of Pennsylvania, for placing at my disposal the Buchanan Papers, and to Professor St. George L. Sioussat for assistance of various kinds. I am under especial obligation to Dr. Gaillard Hunt and Mr. John C. Fitzpatrick, of the Manuscripts Division of the Library of Congress. Their never-failing courtesy and valuable suggestions facilitated my research work in many ways.

Dr. Justin H. Smith's valuable work entitled "The War with Mexico" was published soon after the manuscript of my volume had been completed. Although it appeared too late to be used in the preparation of my manuscript, I am gratified to note that on most points covered by the two works we have arrived substantially the same conclusions.

BERKELEY, CALIFORNIA,
December, 1919.

CONTENTS

[ix]

[x]

CHAPTER I

ANCESTRY AND EARLY LIFE OF JAMES K. POLK

The pedigree of the Polk family has been traced back to 1075—to Fulbert, who was born in the reign of Malcolm III, of Scotland. In 1153 Fulbert was succeeded by his son Petrius, who took the surname Pollok from the estate which he inherited. In 1440 Sir Robert de Pollok, a "younger son" of the family, inherited an Irish estate and removed to Ireland. By common usage the name of this branch was soon contractd into Polk. Sometime between 1680 and 1687[1] Robert Bruce Polk, or Pollok, second son of Sir Robert II, left Ireland with his wife, six sons, and two daughters, and settled in Somerset County, Maryland. Their oldest son, John Polk, married Joanna Knox and established that branch of the family whence came our subject, James K. Polk.

William Polk, the only son of John and Joanna, after living for a time in Carlisle, Pennsylvania, removed with his family to Mecklenburg County, North Carolina. Colonel Ezekiel Polk, the seventh child of William, married Mary Wilson, and the fourth child of this union was Samuel Polk, the father of the future President. The President's mother was Jane Knox, a great-grandniece of John Knox, of Scotland. Her father, James Knox, of Iredell County, North Carolina, was a captain in the Revolution. Mrs. Polk was a rigid Presbyterian, and a woman of keen intellect and high character. From her James inherited many of his well-known traits. She lived to witness the whole of his successful career, and to assist, during his last moments, in preparing him for "a future estate."[2]

---

[1] Authorities differ as to the date.

[2] Garrett, *Pedigree of the Polk family*. Richardson, *Messages*, IV, 371. Nelson, *Memorials of Sarah Childress Polk*, 150 and *passim*. Chase, *History of the Polk Administration*, 475.

James Knox Polk, oldest of the ten children of Samuel and Jane Knox Polk, was born on November 2, 1795, in Mecklenburg County, North Carolina.[3] The Polk family had settled in this frontier region some time before the Revolution, and tradition has credited Polk's ancestors with a leading part in promulgating the much-mooted Mecklenburg Declaration of Independence. His grandfather, Colonel Ezekiel Polk, whom the Whigs in 1844 accused of Toryism, was an officer in the Revolutionary army.

James's father, Samuel Polk, was a plain but enterprising farmer. At an early age he had been thrown upon his own resources and had met with the hardships incident to frontier conditions. With the hope of improving his fortunes, he followed the trend of emigration westward, and in the autumn of 1806 settled in the valley of the Duck River, Tennessee. He was one of the first pioneers in a region then a wilderness; but the valley proved to be fertile and Mr. Polk in time was rated as a prosperous farmer. He was an ardent supporter of Jefferson, and his faith in the soundness of Republican doctrines was inherited by his son James. The correspondence in the Polk Papers indicates that the entire family, including the President's mother, took a keen interest in politics and that all of them were firm believers in the maxims of Jefferson.

James was but eleven years old when his father located in Tennessee. Had he possessed a strong physique, doubtless he would have shared the fate of the average eldest son and have been trained to cultivate the family estate. But he was not strong[4] and his first years in Tennessee were spent in making

---

[3] On November 2, 1846, Polk noted in his diary: "This is my birthday. According to the entry in my father's family Bible I was born on the 2nd day of Nov., 1795, and my mother has told me that the event occurred, as near as she could tell about 12 o'clock, Meridian, on that day." (*Diary*, II, 216.)

[4] "I closed my education at a later period of life than is usual, in consequence of having been very much afflicted and enjoyed very bad health in my youth. I did not commence the Latin Grammar until the 13th of July, 1813." (Polk, *Diary*, IV, 160.)

good use of such limited educational advantages as were afforded in a pioneer community.

Young Polk was studious and ambitious, but Fate seemed determined to deprive him of the opportunity for satisfying his desire for an education. His health did not improve, and his father, believing that a more active life than that of a student would be conducive to health, determined to make a business man of his son. Accordingly, much to the son's disgust and over his protest, he was placed with a merchant to learn the business. After remaining but a few weeks with the merchant, however, the earnest appeals of the son overcame the resistance of the father, and in July, 1813, James was permitted to continue his education under the guidance of Reverend Robert Henderson at a small academy near Columbia, Tennessee. For about a year Polk "read the usual course of latin authors, part of the greek testament and a few of the dialogues of Lucian," and, according to the testimony of his preceptor, he "was diligent in his studies, and his moral conduct was unexceptionable & exemplary."[5] After spending nine months at Murfreesborough Academy, where his "literary merit and moral worth" won the approval of the rector, Samuel P. Black,[6] James entered the University of North Carolina at Chapel Hill in the autumn of 1815. He was naturally drawn to the university of his native state, and the fact that his cousin, Colonel William Polk, had for many years been one of its trustees, may have been an additional reason for selecting this institution.

At college Polk manifested those peculiar traits which later characterized his career as a statesman. Eschewing the less profitable, but usually more attractive, side of college life, his time was occupied with hard and well directed study. "His ambi-

---

[5] A recommendation dated December 31, 1814. MS in Tenn. Hist. Soc. Library.

[6] Recommendation dated October 5, 1815. MS in Tenn. Hist. Soc. Library.

tion to excel," wrote one of his political friends,[7] "was equalled by his perseverance alone, in proof of which it is said he never missed a recitation nor omitted the punctilious performance of any duty." Numerous remarks in the diary written while he was President show that, in Polk's own opinion, time spent in mere pleasure was so much time wasted. He seems to have been equally serious-minded during his college days. Neither at college nor at a later time did Polk deceive himself or attempt to deceive others by assuming great native brilliancy. He never posed as one whose genius made it easy for him to decide great questions offhand. He never attempted to conceal the fact that his conclusions were reached as the result of unremitting labor. And if his conclusions were sometimes attacked as unsound, he was, on the other hand, spared the embarrassment of ridicule, which often fell to the lot of his more brilliant competitors during his long political career.

Polk was graduated from the university in 1818 and enjoyed the distinction of being awarded first honors in both mathematics and the classics. He was very fond of both subjects, as each appealed to his taste for industry and precision. Of his classical training he retained the substantial and discarded the ornate. "So carefully," wrote the friend above cited, "has Mr. Polk avoided the pedantry of classical display, which is the false taste of our day and country, as almost to hide the acquisitions which distinguished his early career. His preference for the useful and substantial, indicated by his youthful passion for mathematics, has made him select a style of elocution, which would perhaps be deemed too plain by shallow admirers of flashy declamation."

After his graduation Polk returned to Tennessee with health impaired by close application, and early in 1819 began the study of law in the office of Judge Felix Grundy. A warm personal and political friendship resulted, which was severed only by the death

---

[7] *Democratic Review*, May, 1838. Polk says that this sketch was written by J. L. Martin, later *chargé d'affaires* to the Papal States (*Diary*, IV, 132).

of Grundy in 1840. The pupil studied hard, and late in 1820 he was admitted to the bar. He immediately began the practice of law at Columbia, in his home county of Maury, among friends and neighbors whose confidence in his ability assured him, from the beginning, a profitable practice. "His thorough academic preparation, his accurate knowledge of the law, his readiness and resources in debate, his unswerving application to business, secured him, at once, full employment, and in less than a year he was already a leading practitioner."[8] His account books show that he continued to enjoy a lucrative practice although much of his time was spent in public service.[9]

For three years the young attorney's time was occupied exclusively in the practice of his profession. His only active participation in politics was to serve for one term as clerk of the state senate. In 1823, however, he was chosen to represent his county in the state legislature, and, having thus entered the political arena, he continued in a very active, and for the most part successful, political career to the close of his term as President. He spent two years in the legislature, where he soon established a reputation for business capacity and for superiority in debate. He took an active interest in all measures for developing his state and gave special attention to the providing of better educational advantages. He enjoyed the personal and political friendship of General Jackson, and it afforded him much pleasure to assist by his vote in sending that military hero to Washington to represent the state in the Senate of the United States. Few acts of his life gave him, in later years, greater pride than his participation in launching Jackson in his political career; and, as the General was ever mindful of the welfare of his political supporters, this incident was no impediment to Polk's own political advancement. His friendship for Jackson was natural, although the two men differed widely in personal characteristics and in

---

8 *Dem. Rev., sup. cit.*
9 His account books are in the Library of Congress.

their attitude toward authority. From early youth Polk had been an ardent advocate of republicanism. He was a firm believer in the teachings of Jefferson and shared with his patron an unbounded faith in individual freedom. Pioneer conditions also are conducive to a strong belief in practical democracy, and Jackson seemed to be a leader who understood the people's desires and sympathized with them.

On January 1, 1824, Polk married Sarah Childress, whose father was a prosperous farmer near Murfreesborough, Tennessee.[10] Mrs. Polk was a lady of refinement and ability. Her sound sense and personal charm aided materially the political fortunes of her husband and later caused her to be regarded as one of the most popular ladies of the White House. Many who rated her husband as inferior, even contemptible, joined in the unanimous verdict that Mrs. Polk was a lady of culture and attractive personality. This fact is attested by numerous private letters. Judge Story was "thunderstruck" to hear of Polk's nomination in 1844, but he admired Mrs. Polk. When her husband was leaving Washington in 1839 to enter the campaign for the governorship of Tennessee, Story expressed his admiration for Mrs. Polk in a poem written in her honor.[11]

One of the young men who attended Polk on his wedding day was his law partner, Aaron V. Brown, later United States senator and governor of Tennessee. Their friendship continued to the end, and to no one else, except Cave Johnson, did Polk more frequently confide his usually well concealed political plans.

Two years in the state legislature increased the young attorney's natural taste for politics, and his success in that field made him determine to seek a wider opportunity for satisfying his political ambitions. In 1825 he offered himself as a candidate, and in August of that year was chosen to represent, his district in Congress. When elected, he was not quite thirty years of age,

---

[10] Nelson, *Memorials of Sarah Childress Polk,* 17.
[11] *Ibid.,* 54.

and on entering Congress, he was, with one or two exceptions, the youngest member of that body.

Mrs. Polk did not accompany her husband on his first trip to Washington. The journey was made on horseback, in company with several other members of Congress. At Baltimore they took the stagecoach, leaving their horses until their return in March.[12] On his second journey to Washington, Mrs. Polk accompanied him in the family carriage. The money paid to members as mileage in those early days was small compensation for the hardships encountered on a journey from remote western states. Still, the pioneer statesmen endured such hardships without complaint; they even extracted pleasure from these tedious overland journeys.

There was little ostentation in Washington in this early period. The life of the average congressman's family was extremely simple. It was customary for two or more families to rent a single house for the season and "mess" together.[13] Among the "messmates" of the Polks were Hugh L. White, of Tennessee, and John C. Calhoun, of South Carolina, both of whom later became Polk's bitter political enemies.

Although in politics a disciple of Jefferson and an ardent supporter of Jackson, Polk was wholly unlike either man in personal peculiarities. Jefferson was a born leader of men, and his exuberant optimism and personal charm attracted hosts of disciples. He advertised his democracy by extreme informality and slovenly garb; and he delighted in shocking the "well born" by disregarding the rules of social etiquette. Jackson, also, was a born leader of men. He commanded the multitude because he insisted upon doing so,[14] but the "plain people" approved him

---

12 *Ibid.*, 27–28.   13 *Ibid.*, 30–31.

14 Judge Catron has given such an excellent description of Jackson's will to command that it seems desirable to rescue his letter from oblivion in spite of its length. It was written on the day after the General's funeral.

"One thing may be safely said of Gen¹ Jackson—that he has written his name higher on the Temple of fame, than any man since Washington,

mainly for the reason that they regarded him as one of themselves. Polk, on the contrary, had few intimate friends. His associates recognized his ability, but he lacked that magnetism which alone can attract a wide personal following. He was naturally formal and punctilious, and he seldom sacrificed his dignity in the pursuit of popular applause. While he was

of those belonging to History in this country. And what is more remarkable in him than any other American is, that he maintained his power from seventy to *eighty,* when he had nothing to give. This he did by the force of will and courage, backing his thorough out & out honesty of purpose. His intuitive faculties were quick and strong—his instincts capitally good. The way a thing should be done struck him plainly—& he adopted the plan. If it was not the best, it would still answer the purpose, if well executed. Then to the execution he brought a hardy industry, and a sleepless energy, few could equal—but this was not the best quality he brought to the task. He cared not a rush for anything behind—he looked ahead. His awful *will,* stood alone, & was made the will of all he commanded; & command it he would and did. If he had fallen from the clouds into a city on fire, he would have been at the head of the extinguishing host in an hour, & would have blown up a palace to stop the fire with as little mis-giving as another would have torn down a board shed. In a moment he would have willed it proper—& in ten minutes the thing would have been done. Those who never worked before, who had hardly courage to cry, would have rushed to the execution, and applied the match. Hence it is that timid men, and feeble women, have rushed to onslaught when he gave the command—fierce, fearless, and unwavering, for the first time. Hence it is that for fifty years he has been followed, first by all the timid who knew him—and afterwards by the broad land, as a matchless man—as one they were ready to follow wherever he led—who with them never was weary—and who could sweep over all opposers abroad or at home, terrible and clean as a prairie fire, leaving hardly a smoke of the ruin behind. Not even death could break the charm. The funeral yesterday was a great mass meeting—of women, children, men, black, white colored—of every grade, mixed up by the House crammed within. There was not a loud word nor a smile so far as I heard or saw. See him they would and did—nay they would see the cof[f]in cased in lead. It was just possible to have room for the soldiers, (a rather tedious process) they claimed it as a *right* to see the thing done. The [illegible] crowd followed him to the Tomb; a stone grave by the side of Mrs. Jackson's—laid there in 1828—covered with a copper roofed canopy some ten feet high resting on stone pillars. He was tediously put in, and the tomb-stone left off, so all could look once more. It was a scene for a painter to see the dense crowd at the particular spot—the slave women in an agony of grief laying their heads on the shoulders and backs of the lady friends of their old master; leaving laces wet with tears—nor did the circumstance elicit a single remark so far as I heard. Death did not make all equal, more completely than did this funeral'' (Catron to Buchanan, Nashville, June 11, 1845, *Buchanan Papers*).

Speaker of the House, a press correspondent gave the following sketch of his personal appearance:

I have never seen a man preside over a popular legislative body with more dignity and effect than Mr. Polk. In person he is rather below the middle size, and has a firm and upright carriage which gives great self-possession and command to his manner. His head is finely formed, with a broad and ample forehead, and features indicative of a character at once urbane and decided. He is scrupulous in his dress and always appears in the chair as if he were at a dinner party.[15]

[15] *United States Magazine*, quoted by Nashville *Union*, July 17, 1839.

CHAPTER II

OPPOSITION MEMBER OF CONGRESS

On questions of governmental policy which divided the people of his day Polk entered the political field, as he left it, a consistent Jeffersonian Republican. Like his illustrious patron, however, he found, when entrusted later with the highest executive responsibilities, that theories, however good, must sometimes yield to the practical solution of the problem in hand. On such occasions, as in his expansion policy, he did as Jefferson had done; he assumed far-reaching power for the executive branch of the central government, leaving himself thereby open to the same criticisms which he and Jefferson had hurled at the Federalists.

Polk began his career in Congress as an opponent of the existing administration, and republicanism is always most vigorous when relieved of responsibility. During his first years in Congress his republicanism could have free play. He took a definite stand at once on the side of the states and the people, and vigorously assailed the autocratic powers alleged to have been assumed by President Adams, as well as the centralizing tendencies of that administration.

At a later day Polk's political opponents ridiculed him as being Jackson's *alter ego* and asserted that he had ascended the political ladder on the coat-tails of the "old hero." However effective such allegations may have been as campaign arguments, the fact remains that as early as 1825 Polk's political views were already freely promulgated in Congress, while those of Jackson on most questions were yet unformulated, or at least unannounced. As to the tariff, the only important question on which the General seems at that time to have formed a definite idea, the two men differed widely. That Polk, like others, humored the whims of General Jackson for political reasons need not be denied, that he profited by his friendship is beyond question; but priority in advocating measures later championed by both men would seem to absolve Polk from the charge that his opinions were derived ready-made from his more conspicuous chief. It does not appear that he gripped more firmly to the General's coat-tails than did others of his party.

Since the Tennessee land question was the theme of Polk's first formal speech in Congress, and since this subject was destined to acquire great political significance, it seems desirable to give a summary of its history in order to show its political importance.[1]

North Carolina, the former owner of Tennessee, when ceding this territory to the United States, had reserved the right to dispose of certain lands included in the ceded area. Other tracts were reserved for the Indians. These reservations necessarily limited the amount of land left at the disposal of Tennessee. Under the so-called compromise agreement of 1806, much of the Indian land was procured for the state, and one-sixth of it was to be reserved for educational purposes. In 1821, however, the provision relating to school lands was found to be invalid. As a result, the Tennesseans decided to ask Congress for certain government lands (in Tennessee) which might be disposed of for educational purposes. As the lands in question were those which settlers had declined to purchase at the price asked by the federal government, they were commonly called "waste" lands, although they were far from being worthless.

Although the legislature considered the subject as early as 1821, no definite action was taken until 1823, when it was referred to a select committee of which Polk was made chairman. From

---

[1] For a more detailed account, see Professor Sioussat's interesting article, "Some Phases of Tennessee Politics in the Jackson Period," *Am. Hist. Rev.*, Oct., 1908.

this committee the chairman reported resolutions which, in addition to asking Congress to grant the lands in question, requested the senators and representatives from Tennessee to work for this end.[2]

In 1825, Polk was transferred from the state legislature to the federal House of Representatives. Realizing that the school land question was of prime importance to the people of his state[3] he embraced the earliest opportunity (January 23, 1826) to call up the Tennessee memorial—which he had prepared in 1823—and moved that it be referred to a select committee rather than to the Committee on Public Lands; and despite considerable debate this course was followed. Polk was made chairman of the new committee.[4] The bill which he reported soon afterward failed to pass the House. As will appear later, however, this Tennessee land question was revived from time to time by both Polk and "Davy" Crockett, and it was one of the rocks on which the Jackson party in Tennessee split into fragments.

Questions less local in character soon presented themselves. All of Jackson's supporters asserted, and doubtless many of them believed, that their hero had been virtually, even if not legally, cheated out of the Presidency in 1824 by "bargain and corruption" on the part of Adams and Clay. The well-known fact that the House of Representatives, whenever it might be called upon to select the chief magistrate, was intended by the Constitution to

2 Printed copy of the resolutions in *Colonel Wm. Polk Papers.*

3 "You cannot be too industrious," wrote one of his constituents a year later, "in endeavoring to effect the object contemplated in your Report of the last session on the subject of those govr n ment lands. To get this matter through 'is a consumation devoutly to be wished' for it will in a great measure disarm the opposition." The writer told Polk that the press did not tell the people very much about his work in Congress, and he advised Polk to send personal communications to many friends to counteract any assertions by enemies that he is inefficient. He also urged Polk to make a "thundering speach" against Haynes' bankrupt bill. "I do not know what your sentiments are on this subject but I think I know what your *interest* is" (Jim R. White to Polk, Dec. 30, 1826, *Polk Papers*).

4 *Register of Debates*, 19 Cong., 1 sess., 1075–1077.

have a free choice, irrespective of the popular vote, did not in the least appease their wrath. They resolved at once on two lines of policy—to alter the Constitution of the United States in order to deprive the House of the privilege of choosing a President in any case, and in the meantime to make it as uncomfortable as possible for the one who had been so chosen. It is not easy to determine the degree of their sincerity in the first part of their program, but in the second part they were in deadly earnest.

The first move toward altering the Constitution was made by McDuffie, of South Carolina. On December 9, 1825, he offered resolutions which were referred to the Committee of the Whole House. His resolutions declared that the Constitution ought to be so amended that in electing the President and Vice-President of the United States "a uniform system of voting by Districts shall be established in all the States," and in no case should the choice of these officers devolve upon the respective houses of Congress. The resolutions provided also that the subject should be referred to a select committee "with instructions to prepare and report a joint resolution embracing the aforesaid objects."[5] On December 29, Cook, of Illinois, offered resolutions much like those of McDuffie, but providing in addition that the voters in the districts should vote directly for both officers. If by employing this method no election resulted, the choice should "be made by States" from the two highest on the list.[6] The last part was not clear, for it did not specify the manner in which the states should make the choice.

The resolutions of McDuffie and Cook caused considerable debate, and afforded an opportunity for others to air their views on constitutional questions. Some thought that the people were already intrusted with more power than they could use with intelligence, while others vigorously expounded the doctrine of *vox populi vox dei.* McDuffie was not, he said, "one of those visionary

---

[5] *Register of Debates,* 19 Cong., 1 sess., 797.
[6] *Ibid.,* 866.

advocates of the abstract rights of man, that would extend the power of the people further than is conducive to the happiness of the political society.'' Patriotic intentions, he admitted, would furnish no adequate security for the wise selection of a chief magistrate, in the absence of sufficient intelligence. ''It would be a vain and delusive mockery, to invest them with an elective power, which they could exercise to the destruction of that which is the end of all government—the national good.''[7]   Although McDuffie himself believed that the people were sufficiently intelligent to make a proper choice, the conservatives could not be convinced that he was not playing with fire.

Polk spoke to the resolutions on March 13, 1826.[8]   He apologized for departing from his usual custom of giving a ''silent vote,'' and for extending a debate already prolonged. But as the subject was national in scope and vital in character, he could no longer remain silent. He attempted no flights of oratory, but he displayed at once more than ordinary ability as a debater. His remarks were clear and incisive, both in declaring his own views and in refuting the arguments of others. Jefferson himself never gave more unqualified endorsement to the doctrine of majority rule. The resolutions involved, said Polk, the question of the people's sovereignty. *''That this is a Government based upon the will of the People; that all power emanates from them; and that a majority should rule;* are, as I conceive, vital principles in this Government, never to be sacrificed or abandoned, under any circumstances.'' In theory, all ''sound politicians'' admit that ''the majority should rule and the minority submit,'' but the majority, in his opinion, did not always prevail under the existing system of elections.

In his zeal for the popular cause Polk attempted to refute an assertion made by Storrs, of New York, that it was not intended by the framers of the Constitution to intrust the choice of

---

7 Feb. 16, 1826. *Abridg. of Debates,* VIII, 992.

8 *Abridg. of Debates,* IX, 8–16.

dent and Vice-President to direct popular vote. He made the rather astonishing statement that, if Storrs were right, "I am free to admit that I have been wholly mistaken, and totally wrong, in my conceptions upon this subject." With a shade of sophistry he held that it was not reasonable to suppose that the people, having "recently broken the chains of their slavery, and shaken off a foreign yoke," should in drafting their Constitution have voluntarily disfranchised themselves. In spite of well-known facts to the contrary, he tried to prove his contention by quoting parts of the preamble,[9] and rather unsuccessfully from the *Federalist*, Randolph, and Monroe, to show that election by the people had been intended by those who framed the Constitution. He was on surer ground when he asserted that it mattered little whether Storrs were right or wrong, inasmuch as the question before them did not concern elections under the present provisions of the Constitution but an amendment for changing the present method of selecting a President.

In Polk's opinion, there were several good reasons why the President should never be chosen by the House of Representatives. He is not an officer of the House. He is the chief magistrate of the whole people and should therefore be responsible to them alone, and dependent upon them for reëlection. Election either by the House or the Electoral College always makes choice by a minority possible, and there is danger that such elections will become more frequent. Representatives are chosen a long time before, and not for the purpose of selecting a President. A Representative may be ignorant of the wishes of his constituents, or he may willfully ignore their preference. The long period between the election of Representatives and their choice of a President affords ample time to influence their votes by bribery or by executive patronage.

Election by districts, as proposed in the resolutions, was, Polk believed, better than a continuation of the present system under

---

[9] "We, the People etc. do ordain and establish this Constitution."

which some electors were chosen by state legislatures, others by districts, thereby making it possible for one-fourth of the people to elect a President. But he concurred with Livingston, of Louisiana,[10] who preferred to dispense with electors altogether. "Let the people vote directly for the President without their intervention . . ." then ". . . there can be no division between contending candidates for elector, in favor of the same candidate, and the majority of the people of each district can control and give the vote of that district . . . the sentiment of each mass of the community throughout the Union, composing a district, is fairly elicited, and made to have its due and proportional weight in the general collected sentiment of all the districts in the Union."

Although he offered no resolution embodying his ideas he suggested one[11] for the committee's consideration. His suggestions were more explicit and covered the ground more completely than the resolutions already before the House. Some of his arguments on this subject were partisan and sophistical; but in no case did he indulge in such absurdities as did one of his opponents, Edward Everett, who tried to convince his fellow-members that any attempt to amend the Constitution was itself unconstitutional. Each member, said the sage from Massachusetts, had taken an oath to support the Constitution as it is, and could not propose to alter it without violating that oath.[12] Neither George III nor John Tyler could plead a more tender conscience nor display a greater respect for oaths of office than Everett did on this occasion. No wonder Polk asked if "the gentleman [were] serious in this puerile conception?"

---

[10] McDuffie favored this also.

[11] Each state was to be divided into as many districts as it had members in both houses of Congress. The people in each district were to vote directly for President and Vice-President, without the intervention of electors, and a plurality in each district was to count as one vote. If no election should result, the matter was to be referred back to the people, who were then to select from the two highest on the list (*Abridg. of Debates*, IX, 16).

[12] *Ibid.*, 18.

In attempting to show that members of the House were not the proper persons to elect a President, Polk supported the extreme democratic view which would divest a member of Congress, even as a legislator, of his representative character and make him a mere delegate. "It has been openly avowed upon this floor," said he, "that there is no connection between the Representative here, and his constituent at home; that the Representative here is not bound to regard or obey the instructions of those who send him here. For myself, I have never entertained such opinions, but believe, upon all questions of expediency, that the Representative is bound to regard and obey the known will of his constituent." Any other view would intrust the rights of the people to "the accidental interest, or capricious will of their public servants." He no doubt had Jefferson's inaugural in mind when he added: "Shall *we* assume to ourselves the high prerogative of being uncontaminated and incorruptible, when the same attributes are denied to all the rest of mankind? Is immaculate purity to be found within these walls and no other corner of the earth?" Whether representatives endowed with "immaculate purity" or "angels in the form of kings"[13] can be intrusted with the government of their fellows may be open to question, but both Jefferson and Polk must have known that the framers of the Constitution had consciously placed more reliance on the discretion of the public officials than on the efficacy of a count of heads.

A remark made by Everett gave Polk an opportunity to pay tribute to General Jackson as the champion of the people. If the government were ever destroyed, said Everett, "it would not be by a President elected by a minority of the people, but by a President elected by an overwhelming majority of the people; by some 'military chieftain' that should arise in the land." "Yes, sir," answered Polk, "by some 'military chieftain,' whose only crime it was to have served his country faithfully at a period

---

[13] See Jefferson's inaugural address.

when that country needed and realized the value of his services.''
If the government were ever destroyed, it would be, in his opinion,
by ''the encroachments and abuse of power and by the alluring
and corrupting influence of Executive patronage.'' This was
intended, of course, as a thrust at President Adams; but in lending his support to the elevation of the ''old hero,'' Polk was helping to hasten the demoralizing influence of patronage which he
so much feared.

Some of the northern members objected to the proposed
amendment on the ground that under it slaves would be represented. During his whole political career, slavery was a subject
which Polk avoided whenever possible. It is interesting to note,
however, that his opinions now expressed for the first time in
Congress were never substantially modified. He regretted exceedingly ''that scarcely any subject of general concern can be
agitated here, without having this important subject of slavery,
either collaterally, or incidentally, brought into view, and made
to mingle in our deliberations.'' His views now expressed were
reiterated in substance when he had to deal with the Wilmot
Proviso. Both now and later he was unable to see why this
irrelevant topic should be dragged into discussions of public
policy.

In answering his opponents Polk declared his firm belief in
state rights. Storrs and others had alleged that the proposed
amendment would tend to consolidate the people of the Union.
Polk denied this and said that he would oppose the amendment
if he had any idea that it would produce any such result. ''No
man,'' said he, ''deprecates more than I do, any violation of
rights secured to the States by the Federal Constitution,'' and
no one more fears ''the yawning gulf of consolidation.''[14]

Polk always referred to himself as a Republican, but it is
plain that he was not a believer in true representative govern-

---

[14] ''When I speak of State rights, I mean, as I understand the constitution to mean, not the rights of the Executives of the States, but I mean
the rights of the people of the States.''

ment, and was in fact a democrat.[15] His remarks show clearly
the influence of Jefferson's teaching. He was an admirer of General Jackson, and used his influence both publicly and privately[16]
to promote the General's interests, but there is no evidence that
he relied on Jackson for political opinions. On the contrary,
Jackson read with approval Polk's speech on the constitutional
amendment and assured him that it was well received by his
constituents and would give him a strong claim to their future
confidence. "I agree with you," wrote the General,[17] "that the
District System is the true meaning of the Constitution, but as
this cannot be obtained any uniform System ought to be adopted
instead of leaving the election of President to Congress."

As a critic of the Adams administration Polk did not rise
above the political claptrap of the day. All that can be said in
his favor in this respect is that he spoke less frequently than
did some of his colleagues. Even his private letters are tinctured
with a bias and a bitterness that do him no credit. A letter
written to Colonel William Polk concerning the subserviency of
the Speaker and of congressional committees is of special interest,
for in it Polk makes the same charges which were later made
against himself when he became the leader of the administration
forces. "The 'factious opposition' as they are termed," said
the letter,[18]

who really consist of the friends of the Constitution, & who do not support
upon the fashionable doctrine of *faith* every measure emanating from the
administration, merely because it is an administration measure, are to the
extent of the power of the administration, and its friends literally
proscribed."

Senate committees have been "arranged for effect," although
there is but a small administrative majority in that body.

---

[15] There was, of course, no Democrat party at this time.

[16] For example, in a letter to Colonel William Polk, Dec. 14, 1826, he
urged the latter to induce the legislature of North Carolina to give some
public expression in favor of Jackson on January 8 (*Colonel Wm. Polk
Papers*).

[17] Jackson to Polk, May 3, 1826, *Polk Papers*.

[18] Polk to Col. Wm. Polk, Dec. 14, 1826, *Colonel Wm. Polk Papers*.

"Studied majorities in favor of the administration have been placed on each, regardless, it would seem in some instances, of qualifications, talents, or experience. The selections were no doubt made, in conformity to a previous secret understanding, among the favorites at Court."

In the House, also, "some remarkable changes have been made in committees by the Speaker. They too have all been arranged for effect." The power of patronage, he continued, is corruptly used to "sustain an administration, who never came into power by the voice of the people." How could a man who felt thus, within three short years, give his unqualified support to the administration of General Jackson? The answer is simple. Polk was, despite his ability and generally sound judgment, above all a party man.

At the close of his first term in Congress, Polk, in his appeal to his constituents for reëlection, laid special stress on his opposition to the Panama mission. Soon after taking his seat, he said it became his duty to act upon a proposition emanating from the executive, "as novel in its character as it was believed to be in consequences."[19] Not believing in entangling alliances, "I was opposed to the Mission in every possible shape in which it could be presented, believing, as I did, that the United States had nothing to gain, but much to lose, by becoming members of such an extraordinary Assembly." The administration, lacking popularity, was trying to extend the powers of the federal government "to an inordinate and alarming extent . . . and substitute patronage for public will." He was reëlected without difficulty and was, at the beginning of the next session of Congress, made a member of the Committee on Foreign Affairs.[20]

Throughout the Adams administration Polk corresponded with General Jackson. He not only supplied the hero of the Hermitage with information on passing events, but offered welcome suggestions and advice. "I feel greatly obliged to you," wrote

---

[19] Polk's circular letter to his constituents, dated March 4, 1827. Printed copy in *Colonel Wm. Polk Papers*.

[20] *Jour. of H. R.*, 20 Cong., 1 sess., 25.

Jackson on one occasion,[21] "for the information contained in your letter [on internal improvements] . . . and I truly appreciate those feelings of friendship which dictated the communication."

When, in the spring of 1828, the subject of Jackson's execution of the six militia men was under investigation in Congress, Polk and Judge White procured and published a statement from General Gaines and a copy of Governor Blount's orders to Jackson.[22] It was Polk who first notified Jackson of his vindication by a committee, and it was to Polk that the General forwarded additional documents to be used in case it should become necessary.[23] Jackson approved Polk's advice that the attack of the opposition relating to this subject should be met by an active campaign of refutation, but that there should be no defense on the Burr episode until there had been some definite charge.[24] To another letter from Polk offering advice on political matters, Jackson answered: "I have read your letter with great interest & attention—the reasons therein contained leaves no reason to doubt of the correctness of your conclusions, it is such as I had long since concluded to pursue."[25] It is evident that the General already recognized the soundness of Polk's judgment and his shrewedness as a practical politician.

During the session of 1828–29 the Tennessee land bill again became the subject of animated discussion in the House. When he first introduced it, in 1825, Polk had the unanimous support of the people of Tennessee, and of the entire delegation in Congress from that state. But it now met with opposition from an

---

[21] Jackson to Polk, Dec. 4, 1826, *Polk Papers.*

[22] Polk to Jackson, April 13 and 15, 1828, *Jackson Papers.*

[23] Jackson to Polk, March 23, 1828, *Polk Papers.*

[24] The six militia men are made a hobby by the opposition, said Jackson, by which they "can impose upon the credulity of the ignorant. . . . The plan there that you have suggested is the only one that can fairly meet, and effectively put down their hobby." "I think your reflections on the Burr business is correct, no defence, without a charge" (Jackson to Polk, May 3, 1828, *ibid.*).

[25] Jackson to Polk, Sept. 16, 1828, *ibid.*

unexpected quarter—an opposition which resulted in a bitter political feud. The eccentric David Crockett, for reasons best known to himself, had come to the conclusion that the "waste" lands, instead of being sold at a higher price for the support of schools, should be given or sold at a nominal price to poor settlers. He therefore offered an amendment to effect this purpose, and thus assumed the rôle of champion of the poor, as opposed to the rich who, as he said, could alone afford to take advantage of schools. Whatever his motives may have been, his opposition to a bill which he had ardently supported at the last session was at once attributed to the influence of Jackson's political enemies. The Tennessee delegation, wrote Polk,[26] were mortified to think that Crockett "should have coöperated with some of our bitterest and most vindictive political enemies, men, some of them of 'coffin hand bill' and 'six militia men' memory, and joined them in denouncing the Legislature of his state on the floor of Congress." Gales and other "Adamsites," Polk continued, are urging him on and reporting speeches that he never made, while he, it is said, will vote for Gales and Seaton for public printers and against Duff Green. They are making a tool of Crockett in order to deal a blow at Tennessee. Other members of the Tennessee delegation, said Polk, will furnish evidence against Crockett, but prefer not to do so, because the people might regard such action as persecution.

Crockett differed from his colleagues not merely on the land question; he opposed, also the attempt made by the Jackson party to introduce *viva voce* voting in the House so that they might brand the unfaithful. Several members, including Polk, Judge White, R. Desha, and J. C. Mitchell prepared statements concerning the boasts and the conduct of Crockett, and addressed them to Pryor Lea, one of their colleagues. The statements were based largely on assertions made by Crockett at White's lodgings in the presence of the men who had prepared them. Crockett

---

26 Polk to McMillan, Jan. 16, 1829, *ibid.*

there produced his amendment and boasted that it would be adopted. When asked if he were willing to imperil the entire land bill by insisting upon his amendment, he replied in the affirmative. His constituents, he said, wished the land bill to be killed, for so long as the land continued to be property of the United States the people might use it free of charge. He went so far as to avow that, regardless of his instructions from the legislature, he would support the measures of any man who would vote for his amendment. All agreed that he had been fraternizing with Adams men in an effort to procure their votes. To Mitchell, Crockett openly admitted that Gales had printed— under Crockett's name—a speech which had never been delivered, so that the latter might distribute it among his constituents.

As a result, it was thought, of Crockett's opposition, the House laid the entire land bill on the table. Not satisfied with his victory, however, the incorrigible "Davy," after returning to his district in western Tennessee, continued his attacks upon his colleagues. In public addresses he told the people that the land bill, had it passed, would have sacrificed the interests of the poor settlers. He was especially enraged by what he termed Polk's "officious interference" in the affairs of West Tennessee.[27] Apparently, Polk retaliated by publishing articles hostile to Crockett in a local paper of the latter's congressional district.[28]

Although Crockett did not succeed in his efforts to obtain cheap land for his constituents, he nevertheless had the pleasure of blocking the attempt made by his colleagues to procure school

[27] Adam R. Alexander to Polk, April 25; Polk to Alexander, May 1, 1829; ibid.

[28] In volume 80 of the *Polk Papers* is a series of five undated articles in Polk's handwriting headed "Col. Crockett & his course in Congress." They are signed "Several voters," and as Crockett is spoken of as "our immediate representative," it is evident that they were to be understood as coming from his constituents. They were probably written for publication in some West Tennessee newspaper. They point out that Crockett had been elected as a friend of General Jackson, but that he has been supporting the old Adams-Clay party, "under the orders of Daniel Webster" and other Hartford Convention Federalists. He has been absent from duty in the House and has done "literally nothing" for the poor settlers of his district.

lands for their state.[29]   Until his defeat by Adam Huntsman in
1835 he remained in Congress and continued to oppose all measures championed by the followers of Jackson.   The importance of
his defection lies in the fact that it was the first breach in the
solidarity of the Jackson party in Tennessee.   One of the chief
critics of Crockett's apostasy in 1829 was Judge White, a man
destined ere long to become the center of a political storm that
would overthrow Jackson's supremacy in his state and seriously
weaken it in the nation.   For the time being Crockett stood practically alone.   Tennesseans generally were proud to uphold the
standard of their warrior hero.

As General Jackson entered the White House the specter of
executive usurpation vanished through the window and Polk,
like other critics of President Adams, now became a loyal supporter of executive policies.   In a letter to his constituents, dated
February 28, 1829,[30] Polk congratulated them on the recent
political victory, and dwelt at length on the significance of that
victory.   The contest had been ''between the virtue and rights
of the people, on the one hand and the power and patronage of
their rules [rulers] on the other.''   The people, said he, have
spoken with a voice of warning to future aspirants who may seek
to elevate themselves by bargain and intrigue.   The country is
still destined to be divided into political parties, and already
there is evidence that the partisans of Adams and Clay are preparing under the leadership of the latter to oppose the incoming
administration.   But Jackson has nothing to fear from his
enemies.   ''He is expected to produce reform, correct abuses, and
administer the Constitution in its purity, and upon Republican
principles contemplated by its wise framers.''   He has been chosen
by the people, and his administration will be both prosperous and
popular.

---

[29] By the acts of 1841 and 1846 Congress finally granted these lands to
Tennessee (Sioussat, ''Some Phases of Tennessee Politics in the Jackson
Period,'' *Am. Hist. Rev.*, 1908, 58).

[30] Pamphlet in Tenn. State Library.

Having pronounced this encomium on the new régime, Polk reminded his constituents that he had contributed his "feeble aid" to the Jacksonian cause because he believed the General's principles to be orthodox and his purpose to be to serve the whole Union. According to others, however, the aid which he had contributed was not so *feeble* as his modesty had led him to assume. The Adams men in Tennessee gave him "grate credit" for compassing their mortifying defeat, and resolved, on that account, to defeat him if possible at the next election.[31]

Despite efforts of his enemies Polk was re-elected by a large majority. On his return to Washington he soon became leader of the administration forces in the House and, as will appear in the following chapter, acted as Jackson's aide-de-camp in the war on the Bank of the United States. With his customary discretion he declined to join with those who felt impelled to give unsolicited advice to the President regarding his social and his executive duties. Toward the end of Jackson's first year in office, and after political Washington had been arrayed in hostile camps by the crusade against Mrs. Eaton,[32] certain members of Congress met, by invitation of C. A. Wickliffe, of Kentucky, for the purpose of discussing the situation. Some of those who attended proposed that the President should be urged to remove Eaton from the cabinet, and that he should be advised to hold regular cabinet meetings. When consulted, Polk, White, Grundy, and other members from Tennessee declined to participate. They even refused to enter into a correspondence with Wickliffe concerning the subjects which had been discussed at the meeting.[33] By thus declining to assume the rôle of guardian over the President, Polk and his associates retained his confidence and good will. While each did his part in supporting Jackson's legislative program, Polk, more than any other, aided in his war against the Bank of the United States.

---

[31] Yell to Polk, Sept. 9, 1829, *Polk Papers.*
[32] See Parton, *Life of Andrew Jackson,* III, chap. xvii.
[33] Letters from Wickliffe to White, Grundy, Polk *et al.,* Dec. 24, 1831. Also other letters on this subject in the *Polk Papers.*

CHAPTER III

POLK AND THE BANK OF THE UNITED STATES

In the bank controversy of Jackson's administration, which Sumner has called "one of the greatest struggles between democracy and the money power,"[1] Polk bore a prominent and difficult part. It was a part which required a thorough knowledge of the subject, alertness of mind, industry, and sound judgment. It required, also, an intimate knowledge of the plans and purposes of the President, and a certainty on Jackson's part that his confidence would not be misplaced. As this is a biography of Polk, not of Jackson, no attempt will be made to treat the bank war in all of its phases. Yet it seems necessary to consider certain aspects of this controversy in order to make clearer the part played by Polk as a member of the Committee of Ways and Means.[2]

It is generally held by historians that Jackson, when he became President in 1829, harbored no special hostility to the Bank of the United States, but that he was later won over by his friends, who had grievances of their own against the bank. But if Jackson's memory may be relied upon, this belief is contrary to the facts in the case. In 1833, in reply to a letter of inquiry from Polk, Jackson stated that the original draft of his inaugural address, written at the Hermitage, contained a paragraph giving his views on the bank, and another, his views on surplus revenue. After he had reached Washington, he said, he was persuaded by friends to omit both of these paragraphs, as it was thought that the subjects were better suited to an annual message to Congress.

---

[1] Sumner, *Andrew Jackson*, 227.

[2] The summary of the beginnings of the bank war, unless otherwise noted, is drawn largely from Sumner.

"Every one knows," he added, "that I have been always opposed to the U. States Bank, nay all Banks."[3]

In his first annual message Jackson questioned both the constitutionality and the expediency of the existing bank, and vaguely suggested the desirability of a bank "founded on the credit of the government and its revenues." This part of the message was referred by each house to a regular committee. In the Senate, Smith, of Maryland, reported from the Committee on Finance in favor of the bank. In the House, April 13, 1830, McDuffie, of South Carolina, reported from the Committee of Ways and Means, also in favor of the bank. McDuffie declared that the constitutionality of the bank had already been settled by decisions of the Supreme Court, that its expediency was beyond question, and that a bank modeled on the President's suggestions would be both inexpedient and dangerous. On May 10, the House, by a vote of eighty-nine to sixty-six, tabled resolutions which declared that the House would not consent to renew the charter of the bank, and on May 29 it likewise tabled resolutions calling for a report of the proceedings of the bank. It was evident that Congress would not support the President in his opposition to the bank. The defection of McDuffie, who had taken a leading part in the attack of the Jackson forces on the Adams administration, made it necessary for the President, when the time came for forcing the bank question to an issue, to look elsewhere for a leader on whom he could rely.

In his message for 1830, Jackson again proposed a bank as a "branch of the Treasury Department." This seemed to indicate a desire for something like the sub-treasury which was later recommended by President Van Buren. But Jackson's suggestions were vague and Congress gave them little serious consideration. An attempt of the Secretary of War, in July, 1831, to remove the pension funds from the New York branch of the bank,

---

[3] Polk to Jackson, Dec. 23, 1833. Jackson's reply is undated and written on the back of Polk's letter (*Polk Papers*).

met with opposition and failure. By the end of 1831 the President's message was more pacific in tone, and the report of his Secretary, McLane, even spoke in favor of the bank.

The tone of the message only encouraged his political opponents, who were already making plans for the next Presidential election. The bank took the initiative by addressing a memorial to Congress, asking that the bank be rechartered. On January 9, 1832, this memorial was presented in the Senate by Dallas and in the House by McDuffie, both "bank Democrats."[4] The committees of the two houses to which the subject was referred both reported in favor of a new charter, but with certain modifications. The Jackson supporters now determined to fight a recharter with every possible weapon and demanded a searching investigation of the bank's conduct. On February 23, Clayton, of Georgia, presented a motion in the House asking for the appointment of a select committee to conduct the investigation. Technical objections were raised by friends of the bank, but Polk met their objections point by point and defeated them with their own weapons.[5] In a speech delivered on this occasion, Polk condemned the bank for having the audacity to ask for a charter and then trying to prevent an investigation. The inference to be drawn from such shrinking from scrutiny, said he, was that there was something "rotten in the state of Denmark." In justification of his motion for a select committee, Clayton presented two lists of charges, which had been prepared for the purpose by Benton.[6] The first specified seven instances of charter violation, involving forfeiture; the second gave fifteen instances of abuse, which required correction, though not involving forfeiture. The investigating committee which the Speaker selected submitted three reports (that of the majority unfavorable to the bank), but our present purpose does not warrant a discussion of either the reports or the charges.

---

[4] *Register of Debates*, 22 Cong., 1 sess., 54.

[5] Benton, *Thirty Years View*, I, 236.

[6] *Ibid.*, 237. The charges are given on the next page.

In the Presidential campaign of 1832, Clay, seeing the *availability* of the bank question, made it a leading issue. In so doing he acted contrary to the better judgment of many friends of the bank, including its president, Nicholas Biddle. A bill passed Congress, providing for a recharter of the bank, and Jackson must now either admit defeat or kill the bill by his veto. He accepted the challenge, vetoed the bill, and appealed to the people to sustain him. He was reëlected by a large majority. Jackson's triumph at the polls was not in reality an endorsement of his veto, but he so regarded it and resolved to exterminate the "monster."

When the bank question first became prominent, the opinions of the administration party were not yet clearly defined. This party "was still only that group of factions which had united in opposition to Adams."[7] A large number of Jackson's most enthusiastic supporters were friends of the bank. Some of the political leaders, including Van Buren, had even signed petitions for the establishment of branch banks. Many politicians, as Niles said, had to "turn a short corner," when Jackson came out against the bank. More independent spirits, like McDuffie, refused to see the light and braved the executive wrath. Opposition in Congress made Jackson only the more determined to wage a relentless war upon the "corrupt institution," but his success would depend, to a considerable degree, on the orthodoxy and ability of the leaders of the administration forces in that body. Obviously the administration program could not be intrusted to the recently converted, whose past record would surely be held up to embarrass them. The fight must be led by those whose record was unassailable. Such was James K. Polk, of Tennessee, the friend and neighbor of the President. He gave to the administration his unqualified support, and, to quote his eulogist,[8] "in

---

[7] Sumner, *Andrew Jackson*, 248.

[8] Eulogy delivered at the time of Polk's death, by L. M. Smith, Newman, Ga. (*Papers of Mrs. Polk*, I).

the hour of darkness and danger, was unquestionably its chief reliance.''

When Congress convened in December, 1832, Polk was transferred from the Committee on Foreign Affairs to the Committee of Ways and Means. A confidential letter written by Jackson to Polk on December 16 discloses the temper of the President as well as the intimate relations of the two men:

> The president with his respects to Col. J. K. Polk, of Congress, encloses him a note from Mr. Page of Philadelphia, a man of high character & in whom confidence may be placed. This is done to add to the information heretofore given the Col. *to show* him that the hydra of corruption is only *scotched, not dead,* and that the intent is thro' Wolf's recommendation, to destroy the vote of the people lately given at the ballot boxes & to rally around the recharter the present Session of Congress *two thirds.* . . . Call upon the Sec. of the Treasury who must agree with me that an investigation by Congress is absolutely necessary.

A postscript instructed Polk to have Sullivan, a government director, brought before the committee, and ended with a peremptory order ''Attend to this.''[9] Polk did ''attend'' to it, and the Secretary of the Treasury seems to have been persuaded that an investigation was necessary.

Though Jackson in his annual message, December 4, 1832, informed Congress that the report of the Secretary of the Treasury ''will exhibit the national finances in a highly prosperous state,'' nevertheless he advised the sale of all corporation (bank) stocks held by the government. He also urged that the safety of public deposits in the Bank of the United States was worthy of ''serious investigation'' by Congress. In response to these suggestions, the Committee of Ways and Means, of which Polk was a member, undertook an investigation of the charges which had been brought against the bank. The directors were summoned to Washington and examined upon oath,[10] and other testimony was taken to supplement the information which had

---

9 *Polk Papers.*
10 *Dem. Rev.,* May, 1838.

been gathered by the President. Reuben M. Whitney, the political scavenger of the administration, wrote to Polk from Baltimore, February 9, 1833, urging him to hasten the investigation, and warning him that Adams and Sergeant had been consulting with members of the committee. On February 11 Whitney wrote from Philadelphia advising Polk that the bank relied much on the ability of Verplanck[11] to outgeneral his opponents on the committee. While the investigation was in progress, Polk, on February 13, reported a bill to sell the bank stock owned by the government, but it failed in the House by a vote of one hundred and two to ninety-one. On March 1, Verplanck, for the majority of the Committee of Ways and Means, reported the bank to be sound and the public deposits safe, although it was admitted that in interfering with the plan of the government to pay off the three per cent securities the bank had exceeded its lawful powers. This report was adopted by the House. The *Globe* charged the majority with forcing the adoption of its report without having considered or presented the evidence which had been collected by its minority members. Many members, it said, who were not in favor of the bank had voted for adoption because, on the showing of the majority report, they could not conscientiously say that the bank was *not safe*.[12] Anticipating the character of the majority report, Polk prepared and submitted a minority report for himself and two other members of the committee. After criticizing the majority of the House for wishing to force the adoption without adequate consideration of evidence, and intimating with some justice that the committee had passed lightly over certain damaging testimony, Polk went with considerable detail into the question of the "three per cents." These were securities bearing three per cent interest issued by the government

---

[11] Chairman of Ways and Means Committee and a friend of the bank. Whitney urged Polk to see that Gilmore, another member of the committee, should not be tampered with. Verplanck, he said, was not to be trusted and should not be permitted to have access to the testimony already taken, unless accompanied by "one of our friends" (*Polk Papers*).

[12] Washington *Globe,* March 6, 1833.

in 1792 for accrued interest on the Revolutionary debt. The government had decided to pay off about $6,500,000 of these, and on March 24, 1832, the Secretary of the Treasury notified the bank of his intention to pay this amount on the first of July. Biddle requested the government to postpone payment until October 1 and agreed to reimburse the treasury for the extra three months' interest. To this the government agreed. When asking for postponement, Biddle based his request largely on two special reasons, neither of which implied that the bank wished any accommodation for itself. The assigned reasons were: (1) that $9,000,000 of duty bonds would be payable on July 1, and merchants would be inconvenienced should the three per cent debt also fall due on that date; (2) should the much feared cholera appear, business would be deranged, and if, in addition, the bank should have to call in its money loaned to merchants, in order to pay off the three per cents, great distress would result.

The government having agreed to delay payment, the bank made secret but unsuccessful attempts to arrange with Thomas W. Ludlow, New York agent of foreign holders, to postpone payment of part of this debt. It then sent General Cadwallader, a director of the bank, to Europe. He made an agreement with Baring Brothers & Co., of London, by which the Barings were to arrange with certificate holders to postpone payment for one year. The Barings were to pay all holders who were unwilling to wait and themselves to assume the debt to that amount. As a result of Cadwallader's agreement adjustments were made to the extent of nearly five million dollars. Every effort was made to keep the transaction a secret, but it leaked out, and an account of it was published in a New York paper. Biddle then disavowed the arrangement.

In his minority report Polk showed conclusively that the real reasons for the bank's desire for postponement could not have been those assigned by its president. He gave a very clear analysis of the evidence which had been collected by the committee and made it plain that the bank had no intention of applying any of its money to the purpose for which it had said it desired these funds. He reached the inevitable conclusion that the bank had desired postponement because of its own weakness.

In his entire report, but especially in his arraignment of Biddle, Polk displayed those qualities which ever distinguished him in debate, and which fully justified the confidence reposed in him by General Jackson. His preparation was exhaustive and his arguments clear cut and logical. His language was well chosen and dignified, but at the same time scathing and merciless. "When the President of the Bank," said Polk, "not only induces the board to act for reasons unknown to themselves, but conceals even from the committees acts done in their names, something stronger than doubt almost seizes on the mind. When, to the consideration that the committees know little of the proceedings had in their names, is added the fact that every Government director is excluded from even that little, by being excluded from every committee, the Government at least has grounds to doubt whether its interests are safe in such keeping. When a show of the strength of the Bank is made, consisting of sums in specie and amounts in exchange, while the debts are secretly contracted, which have enabled the Bank to accumulate these funds, are concealed even from those who make the exhibition, there is just ground to doubt whether there be soundness in the institution, or proper precaution and responsibility in its management."[13]

When, in the spring of 1832, Benton prepared his catalogue of charges against the bank for Clayton to present in the House, he strained his imagination in order to make his list as long and as formidable as possible. Such a course may have been effective for campaign purposes, but many of Benton's charges were easily shown to be exaggerated or unfounded. For this reason his arraignment lost force and failed to convince the doubtful. Polk, on the contrary, confined his denunciation to points on which the

---

[13] *Reports of Committees*, 22 Cong., 2 sess., No. 121.

bank could offer no legitimate defense of its conduct. His arguments were then, and are today, unassailable.[14] Polk well knew
that neither his report nor his arguments on the floor would have
much weight in the House, as a majority of the members were
resolved to stand by the bank in spite of its faults. He was
speaking to a wider audience and may have been already seeking
popular support for the impending executive assault on the bank.
However this may have been, he significantly pointed out that
the institution might be reached by the executive without any
assistance from Congress. "Whether the existing facts," said
Polk in his report,

> are sufficient to justify the Executive in taking any steps against the
> Bank, authorized by its charter, is a matter for the decision of the proper
> officers, acting upon their own views and responsibility: any opinions by
> Congress can make it neither more nor less their duty to act. Whatever,
> therefore, the opinions of the members of this committee might be as to
> the justice or policy of any Executive action, they deem it unauthorized
> and improper to express them officially.

In other words, it was for the executive alone to determine
whether the bank had violated its charter or had been guilty of
mismanagement, and, if so, to apply the remedy.

Whether, at the time Polk made his report, Jackson had resolved upon·a removal of the deposits from the bank as a proper
remedy, we are unable to say.[15] If he had, Polk, who was certainly in his confidence, was doubtless aware of the fact. Polk's
remarks on executive responsibility and his indifference to the
opinions of Congress seem to indicate that such was the case.
He may even have suggested removal of the deposits to the President, but of this there seems to be no direct evidence. It is

---

[14] "Its facts and reasonings," said the *Globe* (March 6, 1833), "are
perfectly irresistible. It exposes the subterfuges and self-contradicted
testimony under which that corrupt and corrupting institution has shel-
tered itself, in a manner so clear and convincing, that it must satisfy
every honest man who reads it, of the utter profligacy of its management."

[15] To quote Sumner on this point: "Lewis says that he does not know
who first proposed the removal of the deposits, but that it began to be
talked of in the inner administration circles soon after Jackson's second
election" (Sumner, *Jackson*, 297).

worthy of note, however, that the well-known paper of September 18, 1833, in which Jackson announced to his cabinet his intention to remove the deposits, makes use of many of the same facts and employs much the same reasoning that Polk had already used in his minority report.

The minority report arrayed against its author all the power and the venom of the bank party, and measures were taken to prevent his reëlection to Congress. Friends of the bank held a meeting at Nashville and denounced his report. He was accused of destroying credit in the West by proclaiming that the people were unworthy of mercantile confidence. Handbills signed "Muhlenging" were circulated, alleging that Polk as a member of Congress had been opposed to pensioning Revolutionary soldiers.[16] Polk met the issue squarely as a foe of the bank, and during the campaign stress was laid on the bank affiliations of Bradford, his opponent. Under the circumstances, Polk's success or defeat was regarded as of more than local importance. "Your friends here," wrote Donelson from Washington, "take a deep interest in your election and are all well apprised of the instruments which are employed to defeat you."[17] Donelson showed his own interest by inclosing in his letter evidence to be used against Bradford. In 1827 Bradford had applied to Adams for an appointment as marshall. His friends had sent letters of recommendation representing him to be a friend of Adams and an opponent of Jackson. From the files in the State Department, without the knowledge of the Secretary, Donelson had copied extracts, and now sent them to Polk, to be used at his discretion so long as Donelson's name was not mentioned. A speech made by Bradford in the Tennessee Senate in 1831, in favor of rechartering the bank, was also reprinted and circulated among his constituents. It was a spirited contest, but Polk was reëlected by a majority of over three thousand votes.

---

[16] *Dem. Rev.*, May, 1838. Polk's "Circular Letter" to his constituents.

[17] A. J. Donelson to Polk, May 30, 1833, *Polk Papers*. The letter was marked *"Private and for your eye alone."* There is nothing to indicate whether Jackson was cognizant of Donelson's act.

As soon as he was safely elected, Polk, with the assistance of Cave Johnson, began a quiet campaign for the Speakership.[18] He received encouragement from his political friends, but the expected vacancy[19] did not occur and he continued his labors as a floor member.

The adoption by Congress of Verplanck's report did not in the least alter Jackson's opinion of the character of the bank. On August 31, 1833, he[20] sent Polk a confidential letter in which he inclosed a report of the bank directors. Polk was authorized to use the facts contained in the report, but not to divulge that they had come from the President. Jackson regarded these facts as proof positive that Biddle had been using the people's money for purposes of corruption.

By September Jackson was ready to carry into effect his plan to deprive the bank of the use of government money. Duane had in May succeeded McLane in the Treasury Department and was expected to do the bidding of the President. On September 18, Jackson read to his cabinet the well-known paper in which he asserted that the deposits ought to be removed. Among the reasons assigned for the proposed action were the political activities of the bank, its attempt to postpone payment of the three per cents, and the fact that it had come into existence by an unconstitutional law. He would not, he said, dictate to the Secretary, but the President himself, assuming all responsibility, had

---

[18] This subject will be considered at length in another place.

[19] Stevenson was expected to accept a foreign mission and not be a candidate for reëlection. He resigned later for this purpose.

[20] The signature is cut off, but the letter is in Jackson's unmistakable hand. He says: ''You will find from the inclosed that I have at last thro the Government Directors got a *Small peep* into their expense account, and the corruption on the morals of the people.

''In two years $80 odd thousand expended to corrupt the people & buy a recharter of that mamoth of corruption. I think when these scenes of corruption are made known to the people and that by an order of the board of directors, the whole funds of the Bank are placed at the disposal of Mr. Biddle to appropriate as he pleases [cut out with signature] most bold specious of corruption ever practiced by any body of people in the most corrupt governments'' (*Polk Papers*).

decided that, after October 1, government money should no longer be deposited in the bank, and that all money there on that date should be drawn out as needed. Duane declined to give the necessary order to effect Jackson's purpose and later refused to resign. He was dismissed and Attorney General Taney commissioned to take his place, September 23, 1833.[21] Taney gave the order, and the "hydra of corruption" was at last more than "scotched."

Jackson's high-handed act produced much excitement throughout the country. The bank issued a paper[22] in reply to the President's charges, and a bitter conflict was inevitable as soon as Congress should assemble. "At such a crisis it became important to have at the head of the Committee of Ways and Means a man of courage to meet, and firmness to sustain, the formidable shock. Such a man was found in Mr. Polk, and he proved himself equal to the occasion."[23]

Congress met on December 2, 1833, and, as a result of the recent election, the administration forces were in unequivocal control of the House. Jackson's message, dealing among other topics with his removal of the deposits, and accompanied by a report of the Secretary of the Treasury on the same subject, was sent to Congress on the third of December. A contest at once arose over the reference of both message and report. Friends of the bank wished them referred to the Committee of the Whole House, where the enormity of the President's conduct might be discussed without limit. The Jackson supporters, on the other hand, wanted them referred to the Committee of Ways and Means, of which Polk had recently been made chairman. On the tenth, McDuffie succeeded in carrying a resolution to refer Taney's report to the Committee of the Whole. On the eleventh, Clay, of Alabama, presented a resolution to refer that part of the President's message relating to finance to the Committee of Ways and Means, but to this McDuffie and others offered vigorous

objections. On the same day, Polk moved a reconsideration of
the vote which had referred Taney's report to the Committee of
the Whole, and he was at once accused by the opposition of aiming to have it referred to his own committee so that he could
smother the question. Chilton, of Kentucky, who was especially
opposed to a reconsideration, did not wish to see "the whole
weight of this massive Government imposed on the shoulders of
his friend from Tennessee,"[24] and urged that the question ought
to be left with the larger committee so that all might discuss it.

Discussion was the last thing which Polk desired, and precedent supported his contention that the reference made under
McDuffie's resolution had been entirely irregular. Never before,
he said, had a great subject of national policy been referred, in
the first instance, to the Committee of the Whole on the state of
the Union. The course which he advocated was simply the usual
one. In the argument Polk was the equal of any of his opponents.
When they told him that the Secretary's reasons had been stated
in his report, thereby making investigation by a committee unnecessary, Polk replied that the report contained various statements of fact which might involve the bank's charter, and that
these facts should be carefully investigated. He also reminded
them of their assertions that the state banks in which the President had deposited public money were unsafe, and that the public
faith had been violated. "Is it not proper, then, for a committee
of the House to inquire by which party the contract was violated?"[25] After much discussion the House, on December 17,
decided, by a yea and nay vote of one hundred and twenty-four
to one hundred and two, to reconsider its vote on McDuffie's
resolution.

Having won on the question of reconsideration, Polk now
fulfilled Chilton's prophecy by moving that Taney's report be

---

24 *Cong. Globe*, 23 Cong., 1 sess., 24. All arguments made in the House,
unless otherwise noted, are taken from the *Globe*, and may be found under
dates mentioned in the text.

25 *Ibid.*, p. 25, Dec. 12, 1833.

referred to the Committee of Ways and Means. McDuffie immediately moved that Polk's committee be instructed to "report a joint resolution providing that the public revenue hereafter collected be deposited in the Bank of the United States, in conformity with the public faith pledged in the charter of the said bank." It is not at all likely that McDuffie expected his motion to carry, but he gained what was doubtless his main object—an opportunity for a discussion of all phases of the question. This move on the part of the opposition brought from the President a letter instructing Polk to make a short reply and then to call for the previous question;[26] but two long months of debate had yet to elapse before Polk's committee would be able to consider the Secretary's report, unhampered by annoying instructions.

Binney, of Pennsylvania, interrupted the discussion on December 18 by presenting a memorial from the bank. The substance of this document was a declaration that the bank was entitled to the deposits unless Congress should decide otherwise. On Polk's motion, the memorial was referred to his committee. On the same day, Chilton moved to instruct the Committee of Ways and Means to report a joint resolution directing the Secretary of the Treasury to restore the deposits to the bank, but, on the request of McDuffie, this motion was withdrawn.

On the main question of referring the Secretary's report with instructions to Polk's committee, McDuffie made the opening speech (December 19). The gist of his remarks was that removal of the deposits was illegal because the President had usurped authority in performing it. Even the President, he said, had admitted that the authority rested with the Secretary, and, if so, Jackson could not lawfully assume it. On December 30, Polk replied in defense of the administration. As usual he had thoroughly prepared himself for his task. He was ready with authorities and precedents to support his own contentions as well as to refute those of his opponents. So thorough and

---

[26] Jackson to Polk, Dec. 18, 1833, *Polk Papers.*

inclusive was his array of facts and arguments that, although the debate lasted nearly two months longer, there was little for any other administration member to add. Every opposition member who spoke to the question devoted most of his time to answering the arguments of Polk. He was regarded by all as the chief supporter, in the House, of the President and his policies. Jackson himself, on his next visit to Tennessee, told the people of Nashville that "Polk for the hard service done in the cause deserves a Medal from the American people."[27]

So far as a reference of Taney's report to the Committee of Ways and Means, as well as the attempt to instruct that committee, were concerned, Polk showed without difficulty that the opposition members were clearly in the wrong. The memorial of the bank setting forth its grievances, and likewise the charges of the government directors against the bank, had, after full deliberation, been referred by the House to the Committee of Ways and Means; there was consequently no good reason why the Secretary's report should not be sent to the same committee. Polk intimated that the real reason for this attempt to interrupt the normal procedure was the desire of his opponents to "flood the country with inflammatory speeches," telling the people that panic must result from the removal of the deposits. Should the committee be compelled, said Polk, to act under the instructions proposed by McDuffie, it would be prejudging the question; investigation would be superfluous, and a report made under such instructions would be absurd. The task of justifying the arbitrary conduct of the President was more difficult. By many, Polk's argument on this subject may not be regarded as convincing.[28] But whether Jackson had acted within his rights or had

---

[27] Robert M. Burton to Polk, Aug. 27, 1834, *Polk Papers.* Polk's speech may be found in *Cong. Deb.*, X, 2.

[28] When Polk was a candidate for the Presidency, the *National Intelligencer* (Sept. 21, 1844) said: "Throughout the whole of Mr. Polk's course in Congress in relation to the Bank of the United States, there was exhibited a zeal not only without knowledge, but often, we must think, against conviction."

been guilty of gross usurpation, no one could have defended his course more ably than did the chairman of the Committee of Ways and Means. A slightly new turn was given to the discussion by the motion of Jones, January 14, 1834, to substitute instructions for those submitted by McDuffie. McDuffie's instructions, as Polk had pointed out, prejudged the whole question, and were mandatory as to the findings of the committee. Those now offered by Jones simply instructed the committee to ''inquire into the expediency of depositing the revenues hereafter collected,'' not in the Bank of the United States, but in state banks.[29] It was now a question of compulsory restoration of the deposits, on the one hand; on the other, discretion for the committee as to its findings, after the expediency of deposit in state banks had been investigated.

While the question of reference with instructions was being debated, memorials from groups of individuals, some for and some opposed to the bank, were sent to the House. One came from the Maine legislature, upholding Jackson and pronouncing the bank unconstitutional. Efforts were made to refer some of the memorials to select committees, but, usually, on Polk's motion, they were all sent to the Committee of Ways and Means. Polk and his committee were therefore the objects of much criticism and even abuse. The sole purpose of both Taney and Polk, according to Binney, was to sustain the administration, without thought of the country's welfare. Polk's object in wishing to get possession of Taney's report, in the opinion of Moore, of Virginia, was to stifle debate, to put the stamp of approval on the report, and then to send it forth to deceive the people and prejudice them against the bank. A motion made by Hubbard to refer to Polk's committee the President's message on the re-

---

[29] On February 19, Mardis, of Alabama, offered a resolution, ''That the Committee of Ways and Means be instructed to inquire into the expediency of reporting a bill requiring the Secretary of the Treasury to deposit the public moneys of the United States in State banks.'' There was much debate on this resolution, but, as it was later withdrawn by the mover, it will not be considered in the present discussion.

fusal of the bank to surrender its books and papers as pension
agent, caused Watmough, of Pennsylvania, to think that "the
Committee of Ways and Means have got a voracious appetite,
and seem desirous to devour all that comes before the House."
It was a question of law, he said, and should be referred to the
Judiciary Committee. He was supported by Barringer, of North
Carolina, who asserted that Polk's committee was trying to grasp
all important legislation so that it might be shaped in the administration mold. But oppositon was futile; the message went
with the memorials to appease the "voracious appetite" of Polk
and his colleagues. There, too, went Taney's report, the main
subject of discussion. On February 18, 1834, the two months'
debate was closed by invoking the previous question, and Polk's
original motion (of December 17, 1833) to refer to his own committee Taney's report on the removal of the deposits was at last
carried by a yea and nay vote of one hundred and thirty to
ninety-eight. All motions to instruct the committee had already
been voted down, and the House now refused to hear new resolutions for this purpose. The victory of the committee was complete, and it could proceed, unhampered, to perform its part in
the executive program. Polk's successful defense of the administration brought him letters of commendation from all parts of
the country, and especially from his own state. Governor Carroll
wrote from Nashville to compliment Polk on his "temperate, able
and successful vindication of the President," and added that
"this is almost the universal sentiment here."[30]   Polk's services

---

[30] Governor Carroll to Polk, Jan. 23, 1834, *Polk Papers*. John H. Dew,
member of the Tennessee legislature, wrote to Polk, Jan. 21: "Your
argument in defence of the Executive for the exercise of an ordinary
power, expressly conferred on him by the Constitution of the U. S. and
fully sanctioned by precedent & custom evinces a most intimate acquaintance with the multifarious movements that have been made upon the
great American political *Chess board* from the organization of the Government to the present *Crisis*. You have shown most incontestibly, from
laborious research into public records and documents that the President
and his Cabinet have in all things acted strictly within the sphere of their
Constitutional duty and rule of action." There are many similar letters
among the *Polk Papers*.

as guide in the proposed constitutional convention of his state were eagerly sought, and he was much talked about as a desirable candidate for Governor of Tennessee, and for Speaker of the national House of Representatives. Even your enemies say, said a letter from his home town, that "you could be elected for anything in Maury."[31]

Before the vote on the reference of Taney's report had been taken, the Committee of Ways and Means had already made it quite clear that nothing favorable to the bank might be expected from them. On February 11, Polk reported for the committee on Jackson's message against the bank—the message in which the bank was denounced for not surrendering the books and money held by it in its capacity as pension agent. Polk fully sustained the President and refuted every contention of the bank. "The committee," so read the report, "cannot condemn, in terms too strong, the conduct of the bank in this transaction." He reported a bill to the effect that, in future, pensions should be paid by officers of the government, and not left in "the hands of an irresponsible corporation."

By March 7, the committee was ready to submit its opinions on the removal of the deposits. These opinions were placed before the House on that date, and it was generally understood that they had been drawn up by the chairman. They held that both the removal of the deposits and the placing of this money in state banks were unquestionably legal. The committee believed the bank to be unconstitutional, but, even if it were not, its conduct had been such that it ought not to be rechartered, and therefore, the deposits ought not to be restored. They expressed full confidence in the competence of state banks to perform all necessary services for the government, and revived Jefferson's well-known arguments to prove that such an institution as the Bank of the United States had never been contem-

---

31 T. H. Cahal to Polk, Jan. 2, 1834, *Polk Papers*. Maury was Polk's county.

plated by the framers of the Constitution. For his own reputation, Polk might well have stopped here; but he repeated the
arguments of the day that "none can doubt the power of the
bank to create embarrassment," and he proceeded to show that
this had been done by loaning money at a given place during one
month, and then calling it in during the next. Such action may,
indeed, have been within the power of the bank, but banking
institutions seldom resort to that form of amusement. This may
have been one of the occasions noted by the *National Intelligencer*[32] on which Polk's zeal was not supported by either
"knowledge" or "conviction." However this may be, Polk had
not been found wanting in his defense of the President. His
services as a party leader of the House were none the less efficient because history may pronounce some of his arguments
untenable.

The House, on March 12, suspended the rules so that Polk
might have his report made a special order and thereby hasten
its adoption. This action was denounced by Adams, who said
that Polk, acting under royal prerogative, would soon close all
debate by the previous question and deprive the minority of its
constitutional right of discussion. But Adams could not very
well complain, as Polk pointed out, because Adams himself had
voted for the previous question when the bill to recharter the
bank had been forced through the House.

Polk did not, however, immediately call for the previous question, and his critics made the most of the opportunity afforded
them. Instead of reporting on Taney's reasons for removing the
deposits, said Wilde, of Georgia (March 19), the committee had
reported an argument—that the bank ought not to be rechartered. They had "gone beyond the President and the Secretary,
in claiming power for the Executive." Harden, of Kentucky,
admired the "master-stroke of policy" of the committee in pronouncing against recharter when that question was not before it,

---

[32] *National Intelligencer*, Sept. 21, 1844. See above, note 28.

but it had given no information except a reëcho of Taney's report. McDuffie criticized Polk for shutting off debate, but he gave him full credit for acting "with a tact and skill and zeal worthy of a better cause."[33] McDuffie concluded his argument on April 4, Mason called for the previous question, and the debate on Polk's report was closed. Resolutions prepared by the committee, providing among other things for a select committee to investigate the bank, were quickly adopted. The new committee, appointed by the Speaker on the seventh, repaired at once to Philadelphia whence Mason, one of its members, kept Polk informed of its proceedings by confidential letters.[34] But the bank refused to submit its books for examination, and the special committee soon (May 22) reported that it had been unable to perform the duty assigned to it by the House. While investigation thus ended in failure, nothing was left undone which in any way depended upon the vigilance or activity of Polk. On June 13, he succeeded in sending to the table two joint resolutions from the Senate: one, disapproving of the removal of the deposits; the other, directing that the deposits be restored to the Bank of the United States.

By adopting Polk's report the House had put its stamp of approval on the President's act in removing the deposits, but the question of depositing this money in state banks had still to be considered. Jackson's opponents had always contended that, without the authority of Congress, the President had no right to intrust public money to such banks. On April 22, 1834, Polk reported from his committee a bill for regulating these state deposit banks. It was based on the report of the Secretary of

---

33 McDuffie said he had criticized Jackson in the hope of bringing out Jackson's supporters. "The honorable member from Tennessee did come out boldly and manfully, took his position, and, whatever views I may entertain of his generalship, I am ready to bear testimony that the position which he has assumed is the only one he could assume, without leaving unprotected and undefended the very part which it was his duty to defend" (April 3, 1834). I have converted this into direct discourse. It is reported *indirectly* in the *Cong. Globe.*

34 Mason to Polk, May 5 and May 10, 1834, *Polk Papers.*

the Treasury. Adams (June 7) attempted to filibuster by moving a resolution to call on the Secretary of the Treasury to lay
before the House the names of officers and stockholders of such
banks, as well as numerous unimportant details. Polk promptly
met this by moving an amendment which required a similar
statement from the Bank of the United States. A request made
by Adams (June 13) that Polk should withdraw his amendment
gave the latter an opportunity, not only to defend the administration, but to employ that sarcasm and scorn which ever made
him feared as a debater. It was far more necessary, Polk believed, to require information from the old bank than from the
new banks, because the government was a stockholder as well
as a depositor in the Bank of the United States. It was also
more necessary, he said, because that bank

had set itself up in antagonistic position to the Government, had denounced the Executive as a tyrant, usurper, and despot, and more recently,
had denounced and insulted the representatives of the people, because they
had sustained him in his measures. But, according to the gentleman, this
immaculate and inoffensive Bank of the United States must not be looked
into, though the affairs of the State banks must be thoroughly probed.[35]

Polk's bill for regulating the deposits in state banks passed the
House, June 24, 1834, by a vote of one hundred and twelve to
ninety, but it was now near the end of the session and the Senate
at its last meeting, June 30, laid the bill on the table. In the
House, at least, the friends of the bank had been defeated on
every point, and the acts of the President had been fully vindicated. The completeness of this vindication was due, in no small
measure, to the industry and vigilance of the chairman of the
Committee of Ways and Means.

---

[35] Polk here read from the *National Gazette* an article in which the
bank directors had denounced Jackson and the House.

CHAPTER IV

POLK-BELL CONTEST FOR THE SPEAKERSHIP

During his canvass for reëlection to Congress in 1833, Polk seems to have decided to become a candidate for the Speakership in the event of his success at the polls. Public attention had recently been called to this office by a rumor that the Speaker of last session, Andrew Stevenson, was to be given a diplomatic appointment and would therefore not be a candidate for re-election.

Whether Polk's idea of becoming a candidate originated with himself or was suggested to him by friends is uncertain. There are among his papers letters which show that, soon after his election early in August, he began to sound his friends on the subject. Other letters make it equally clear that he was being considered for the office by men who knew nothing of his own initiative in the matter. Cave Johnson, his most intimate friend, aided him by soliciting the support of their political associates.

His first campagn for the Speakership was soon abandoned, for Stevenson did not go abroad as soon as had been expected. However, his aspirations met with some encouragement. In answer to a letter from Polk on the subject, C. C. Clay, of Alabama, wrote: "Should the vacancy, of which you speak, occur, I know of no other member, whose election to fill it would be more agreeable to my own feelings than yours." On the same day Clay said in a letter to Cave Johnson: "I am pleased with your suggestion of Polk as the successor of Stevenson, and hope we may be able so to manage, as to effect the object."[1] A week later Leavitt, a member from Ohio, informed Polk of Stevenson's

---

[1] Clay to Polk, Aug. 19, 1833; same to Johnson, same date, *Polk Papers*.

rumored appointment to a foreign mission. He did not know, he said, whether Polk had been approached, but he hoped that he would be chosen to fill the vacancy.[2] Other letters of similar import were received; one from Cave Johnson[3] said that he had been writing letters to members of the House in an effort to bring about concerted action in Polk's behalf.

At this early date Jackson seems to have taken no special interest in Polk's political promotion, although he was ready to give it his approval. Having corresponded with the President on the subject, Grundy informed Polk[4] that he had "received an answer from the highest quarter of the most satisfactory & encouraging character." He advised Polk to induce his friends to write to members of the House, but to avoid writing such letters himself. James Walker, a brother-in-law of Polk, went to Washington in October in quest of a mail contract. After an interview with the President in relation to Polk's aspirations, Walker reported that "*he gives in to them I think decidedly and frankly.*"[5] Jackson told Walker that some persons believed it would not "look very modest" to solicit the Speakership for Tennessee, as well as the Presidency. The President himself ridiculed this objection and assured Walker that Polk's election would in no respect embarrass the administration. Walker got the impression, however, that William B. Lewis was in favor of Bell. Here may have been the beginning of Polk's intense dislike for Lewis. Another interview with Jackson convinced Walker that the President was not only willing but eager to have Polk chosen Speaker of the House. He was charmed with the Vice-President and advised Polk to make it known to Van Buren that he would support him for the Presidency.[6]

---

[2] H. H. Leavitt to Polk, Aug. 26, 1833, *ibid.*

[3] Johnson to Polk, Aug. 26, 1833, *ibid.*

[4] Grundy to Polk, Sept. 13, 1833, *ibid.*

[5] Walker to Polk, Oct. 22, 1833, *ibid.*

[6] Walker to Polk, Nov. 7, 1833, *ibid.* From Yell, also, came a letter (Dec. 1) stating that in his opinion Van Buren could throw the Speakership to whom he pleased.

The twenty-third Congress convened on December 2, 1833, and Stevenson was reëlected Speaker on the first ballot—virtually without opposition. As Polk's candidacy had been contingent upon Stevenson's refusal to stand for reëlection he accepted the party program without evidence of disappointment. The committees were announced on the ninth, with Polk at the head of the Committee of Ways and Means—the appointment having been made, it was said, upon the suggestion of General Jackson. The chairmanship of this committee is an important position under normal conditions. At this time, when the President was preparing for his last and greatest contest with the bank, it was undoubtedly the most responsible position in the House. But Polk was not the man to shirk responsibility, and his success in outgeneraling the bank party soon demonstrated that the administrtaion had been fortunate in its choice of a leader.

Polk had scarcely accepted his new appointment when letters came from friends at home urging him to become a member of the proposed Tennessee constitutional convention. "A great number of people," wrote James Walker,[7] "will be satisfied in no other way than for you to be in the Convention."

While there seems to have been a general desire for Polk's services in the convention and a feeling that he of all men in the state was best fitted to draft a new constitution, yet some, even among his friends, appear to have doubted his ability to cope with his new duties in Congress. His brother-in-law, A. C. Hayes, wrote from Columbia, Tennessee, that Polk's friends were pleased, and his enemies mortified, by his elevation to the chairmanship of the Committee of Ways and Means. But he added: "I have, however, heard it suggested by some of your *good friends*, that you may not leave the present congress with the same reputation with which you entered—'they fear, that there is too great weight of talent against you on the Bank Question.' "[8]

---

[7] Walker to Polk, Dec. 18, 1833, *Polk Papers*.
[8] Hayes to Polk, Jan. 10, 1834, *ibid*.

Polk himself had no such fears, for self-confidence was one of his chief characteristics; difficulties never appalled him when party services were to be performed. He was already occupied with his committee and therefore declined to serve in the convention.

On June 2, 1834, Speaker Stevenson presented to the House his long expected resignation. On the same day John Bell, of Tennessee, was chosen to succeed him. On the first ballot Polk received forty-two votes to Bell's thirty. Both men gained as the balloting proceeded, but Bell's gains—due to accessions from the anti-Jackson camp—were larger than those of his rival. When the tenth ballot was counted the tellers reported that Bell had received one hundred and fourteen votes—more than enough to elect—while his nearest competitor, Polk, had received but seventy-eight.

The brief official record of this day's proceedings which one finds in the *Congressional Globe* gives not the slightest hint of the heartburnings and bitterness which were associated with this choice of a Speaker. From this election, however, resulted a political feud which split the Jackson party in Tennessee, and materially weakened it in other states. From this day forth Polk and Bell were uncompromising enemies—each determined to overthrow the political power of the other. As the opponents of the President had helped to elect Bell, the new Speaker was forced to ally himself more and more with this element. His endorsement of Judge White's candidacy aroused the ire of the President. Regarding both men as apostates and traitors, Jackson resolved to employ every means at his disposal for the purpose of crushing them. Polk profited much by this new turn of affairs. He was already fighting the battles of the President in the war on the bank. He had always enjoyed the confidence and good opinion of Jackson; but Bell's defection still more identified the Speaker's rival, Polk, with the party of the President. In a greater degree than ever was Polk now regarded as the administration leader of the House.

The antecedents of the Speakership election and the attitude of Polk and Bell toward adhering to a party program are told in a statement prepared, at Polk's request, by Cave Johnson. Johnson was, of course, one of Polk's closest friends, but his statement seems credible and is corroborated by the testimony of other members of the House. It reads as follows:

> It was supposed many months before the vacancy actually happened, that it would take place & several individual friends of the administration were spoken of as suitable to fill the vacancy, among the number you & Col. Bell were esteemed the most prominent. None seemed to doubt that if so many friends of the administration were run, that the election would be finally settled by the votes of the opponents of the administration, who would of course cast their votes upon the man least acceptable to the President & his friends. This was a result the friends of the administration wished to evade—and therefore it was proposed, that the friends of the administration should have a meeting that the strength of the several candidates should be ascertained, that the strongest should be run as the candidate of the administration party & the others should yield their pretensions & support him. You unhesitatingly determined, that you was willing to have the election submitted to the friends of the administration & let them decide who should be the candidate & that you would support the man thus selected. You was considered I believe finally by all parties as the administration candidate & so far as I knew, heard or believe every vote which you received except one was given by the friends of the administration. . . . I understood, from members who conversed with Col. Bell upon the subject whose names I can give if necessary, that he refused to submit his claims to the Speakers chair to the friends of the President, & in consequence of his refusal no such meeting was holden. He received the votes of the opponents of the administration & was elected by them in conjunction with a few votes received by him among the friends of the administration.[9]

In a similar statement,[10] John McKintry, of Alabama, charged Bell with having refused to submit his claims to Jackson's friends and with having stated "that he did not expect to be elected by the administration party in the House, that he did not expect to get of that party more than 25 or 30 votes, [and] that he was supported by the opposition & elected by them." McKintry was

---

[9] Johnson to Polk, Sept. 12, 1834, *ibid.*
[10] McKintry to Polk, Aug. 13, 1834, *ibid.* C. C. Clay, of Alabama, in a letter to Polk (Sept. 13) says that Bell was generally considered to be an opposition candidate.

equally positive that Polk had readily consented to submit his claims to his party friends and to abide by their decision.

Up to the time that Bell became a candidate for Speaker, he was considered to be a loyal supporter of General Jackson. He was so regarded in his own state as well as in the House of Representatives. When the rumor that Stevenson would not be a candidate for reëlection was first circulated, it will be remembered that Jackson was consulted as to his attitude toward Polk's candidacy. Although the President was willing to give his approval, he did not appear to have any special interest in Polk's elevation. There is no evidence that the General, at that time, harbored any ill feeling toward Bell. Indeed, James Walker gathered from various conversations that Major Lewis preferred Bell for Speaker. But Bell's conduct during his recent campaign for the office changed all this. He was first distrusted, then openly denounced, by the President and his friends.

Congress adjourned shortly after the election of a Speaker, and in the final rush of legislation little attention was given to the contest between the two candidates. It was not apparent at the time that the controversy would have any vital significance in national politics. The first important result of the victory of Bell over Polk was its effect upon the influence of the two men in their home state.

For some time past Polk had been considered a desirable candidate for governor, and after his defeat by Bell his friends in Tennessee renewed their offer to support him for this office. His ever loyal brother-in-law, James Walker, began on his own initiative to agitate Polk's claims to the office and to assure him of the certainty of success. He informed Polk[11] that he had not lost prestige on account of his recent defeat, and that he could beat any man in Tennessee if he would consent to run. Letters offering support and encouragement came from Cave Johnson and other party leaders of the state. James Standifer assured

---

[11] Walker to Polk, June 30, 1834, *Polk Papers.*

Polk that he had not "seen the first man but what says they would rather have James K. Polk's standing than John Bell's Speaker's place and all, the people are for the man that stands up boldly for the President and his measures, they are for no other sort of man these times."[12] The sentiment expressed in this letter was becoming general in Tennessee, namely, that Polk and Grundy were the administration leaders in the state, and that Bell had deserted to the enemy. This view was impressed upon the President, who was then spending his vacation at the Hermitage, and it was about this time that he declared Polk to be deserving of a medal for "the hard service done in the cause."

Much resentment was aroused in Middle Tennessee by a speech delivered by Bell at Murfreesborough on October 6, 1834. The circuit court was then in session and Bell took advantage of the occasion to address the people there assembled. There are conflicting reports as to the substance of this speech, but in general the account of it given to Polk in a letter from his brother-in-law, John W. Childress, seems to be corroborated by the testimony of many who heard the speech delivered. According to this letter[13] Bell was very severe in his criticism of all who had questioned the propriety of his course in Congress, particularly during his contest for the Speakership. He asserted that all his competitors except one had treated him in a gentlemanly manner, leaving it to be inferred that Polk had not. "He vaunted greatly," said Childress,

his adherence to principle, his unwavering support of the president, and said distinctly, and in these words, that had he not been true and firm to the administration, he could have changed the small majority in the house upon the Bank question by going over and taking his friends with him and thereby have defeated all the measures of the President.

His enemies, he said, had managed to delay Speaker Stevenson's appointment to a foreign mission in the hope of weakening his

---

[12] Standifer (member of Congress from Tennessee) to Polk, Aug. 25, 1834, *ibid.*

[13] Childress to Polk, Oct. 7, 1834, *ibid.*

(Bell's) prospects and strengthening their own (i.e., Polk's), but of this the President was of course not aware. He alleged that although other tricks had been employed in an effort to defeat him, he still had the confidence of the entire party except six or seven individuals. He said

that he was willing to give Jackson's experiment [state banks] a fair trial and if it did not answer the wants of the people, that then he *might* be in favor of a National Bank. That he had no idea that a metalic currency would answer the purpose of a circulating medium and almost said it was Demagoguic in any one that would say so.

W. R. Rucker, another brother-in-law, said in a letter[14] that the speech was "most intemperate and ill advised" and that many of Bell's friends did not approve such "abuse" of Polk and General Jackson.

Under the circumstances, Bell's speech was certainly ill advised, even if every assertion made in it had been true. Moreover, even though reports of the speech may have exaggerated its abusive character, yet certain remarks attributed to the speaker were of such a nature that, if skillfully used, they would arouse the ire of General Jackson against the man who had uttered them. Protestations of loyalty to the administration had an unwelcome ring in the General's ears when accompanied by boasts of Bell's great influence over party members and of the ease with which he might have defeated administration measures in the House. The truth of such an assertion would make it all the more galling to a man of Jackson's temperament. One can imagine his exclaiming: "By the Eternal, I'll show John Bell!" Then, too, Bell's remark concerning the President's *experiment,* and his *quasi* endorsement of a national bank, were most unfortunate for any man who wished to retain the friendship of "the old hero."

Polk's answer to Rucker indicated clearly the use that was to be made of Bell's speech. If the address has been accurately reported, said Polk, "it places him clearly and unequivocally at

---

14 Rucker to Polk, Oct. 12, 1834, *ibid.*

issue with the policy of the administration.''[15] He wished the speech to be reported accurately and published to the world; then he would be fully prepared to meet its author on the issues which it had raised.

Before Bell's Murfreesborough speech had been delivered, Polk, as we have seen, had already been collecting statements from his friends concerning Bell's conduct in Congress. Both men had also been exerting themselves to get control of the press in Middle Tennessee. Local newspapers at that time wielded great influence, and the success of a politician depended in a great measure on his control over the reading matter of his constituents.

Polk's home was in Columbia; therefore the *Observer,* a local paper of that place, supported its townsman and criticized Bell's maneuvering in the late Speakership election. The two leading papers of Nashville at that time were the *Republican* and the *Banner.* The *Republican* defended Bell, and many of Polk's friends promptly administered the customary punishment of canceling their subscriptions to that paper. One of these was Colonel Archibald Yell, an ardent admirer of Polk and an orthodox party man. In answer to his protest, Allan A. Hall, editor of the *Republican,* defiantly predicted that Polk would soon lose the friendship of Jackson, Grundy, and Governor Carroll, and would be driven from power if he should dare to persist in his opposition to Bell.[16]

Bell succeeded in getting control of the *Banner,* also. Until the middle of September, 1834, this paper had been edited by

---

[15] Polk to Rucker, Oct. 16, 1834, *ibid.*

[16] Yell to Polk, Sept. 25, 1834, *ibid.* One part of Hall's letter, as quoted by Yell, read: ''and now mark me Yell for a prophet in less than six months there will be a split between Carroll & Polk nay there will be a split between Polk & the President!! Coming events cast their shadows before. Col. Polk by no earthly possibility can continue to maintain his present *position,* in the event of Certain future Contingencies which are *obliged* to take place.'' Yell took this to mean that Polk was to be driven from the chairmanship of the Committee of Ways and Means. Carroll denied that he was hostile to Polk (Carroll to Polk, Dec. 19, 1834).

Samuel H. Laughlin, a friend of Polk, but who, unfortunately for both men, had been made extremely unreliable by a passion for strong drink.[17]　His contract as editor expired at this time and the proprietor, Hunt, formed a partnership with Bell.　A new editor was installed and the paper henceforth championed the cause of the Speaker.[18]　For the time being Polk had to rely mainly on the support of the Columbia *Observer* and the Murfreesborough *Monitor*.

Bell seems to have become somewhat alarmed at the result of his Murfreesborough speech, for both of his Nashville papers maintained that he had been misquoted, and that he was still a loyal follower of General Jackson.　Thereupon, William Brady, of Murfreesborough, set about collecting statements from various persons who had heard Bell deliver the address.　These Brady published in an extra number of the *Monitor*.　Copies of this number were sent to the President, to members of Congress, to leading political journals, and to prominent individuals, for the purpose of removing the ''veil which now covers the political hypocrite [Bell].''[19]

Polk and his associates saw the necessity of establishing in Nashville a paper which would promulgate their own views.　''I think it more desirable,'' wrote A. C. Hays, of Columbia,[20]

that a Newspaper should be established in Nashville, that will fearlessly speak the sentiments of the people of the State, at this time than it has ever been, because I believe that the Press is at this time more under the influence of the *Bank & Bell & Foster* faction than it has *ever been*.

Laughlin had offered to serve as editor of an administration journal, but Brady[21] was not alone in thinking that ''poor Sam'' had already proved himself to be a total failure.　''The trouble

---

17 One becomes accustomed to reading in private letters: ''Laughlin has been drunk for a week.''

18 John W. Childress to Polk, Sept. 18; Wm. Brady to Polk, Dec. 26, 1834, *Polk Papers*.

19 Brady to Polk, as cited above.

20 Hays to Polk, Dec. 24, 1834, *Polk Papers*.

21 Brady to Polk, as cited above.

is,'' said he, ''Sam lacks moral courage; and when the sound of the Bugle is heard—and the enemy shall appear in force—Sam's in the straw.'' In Brady's opinion, some editor ought to be found who would be ''wholly *de Nashvilleized*,'' who would stand by the President and support Van Buren as his successor.[22] For his own purposes, said Brady, Bell is putting Judge White forward to succeed Jackson, with the hope of succeeding White in the Presidential chair.

Bell's success in getting control of the Nashville papers was disconcerting enough to Polk's Tennessee friends, but they were still more chagrined because the Washington *Globe* seemed also to be lending its support to the Speaker. ''How is it with the Globe?'' wrote Brady in the letter above cited,

if that print is with the President and his friends, to me it has an awkward way of shewing of it. It is true that Blair sanctions the President personally, and in the main the measures of his administration; but how is it, that every apologetic article, which has appeared in the Nashville papers or elsewhere, in relation to Bell's election to the Speaker's chair, or his Murfreesboro Speech have found their way into the columns of the Globe?

Brady thought that Blair ought to give both sides or neither; Polk should compel him to show his colors by presenting for publication in the *Globe* the account of Bell's speech which had appeared in the extra *Monitor*. ''Why is the Globe either silent— or giving support to Bell?'' asked Childress.[23] People in Tennessee, he added, are beginnig to believe that the President prefers Bell to Polk; this is what Bell's adherents claim, and the attitude of the *Globe* lends color to their assertions. By all means, urged Childress, Polk must have his side of the argument published.

By courting the enemies of the administration and by subsequent indiscretions, Bell had engendered feelings of distrust

---

[22] On December 28 General Samuel Smith, in a letter to Polk, dwelt on the necessity of starting a new paper. Many in Tennessee, said he, whom Jackson believes to be his friends are in reality against him.

[23] Childress to Polk, Dec. 20, 1834, *Polk Papers*. Polk received other letters of similar character.

and hostility that were destined to involve others in serious political difficulties. Polk was a man who did not easily forget, and
by lending aid to Bell in 1834 Blair was paving the way for his
own downfall, when Bell's rival became President ten years later.
Polk's friends believed that they saw the sinister as well as
successful influence of the Speaker in every quarter. Polk himself alleged that Bell's exertions in behalf of Judge White were
not due to any love for the judge, but for the sole purpose of
promoting his own political advancement.[24]

The project of founding an administration newspaper in
Nashville now absorbed the attention of party leaders. As no
really suitable man could be found to edit such a paper, Laughlin
was considered, although not without misgivings.[25] Many politicians who had hitherto shouted for Jackson had deserted to
White, and nearly all of the papers of Middle Tennessee, including even the Columbia *Observer*,[26] had come out for the
judge. This fact made it all the more necessary to have an
orthodox journal which would *enlighten* the people, and Laughlin,
despite his weaknesses, was a loyal party man. After many
tribulations capital was collected, an outfit purchased, and in
March, 1835, Laughlin was installed as editor of the Nashville
Union. Polk and Grundy were the guiding spirits of the new
paper, and to them and Cave Johnson "poor Sam" appealed for
aid in increasing his subscription list. He reported to Polk that
the editor of the *Banner* was "wallowing in the mire," entirely
under the influence of Bell and Foster; and that efforts were
being made to retard the progress of the *Union*."[27]

During the excitement which was created by Bell's Cassedy
letter, Laughlin—being "himself again"[28]—with his "sharp pen"

24 Polk to James Walker, Dec. 24, 1834, *Polk Papers*.

25 Sam'l G. Smith to Polk, Jan. 6, 1835, *ibid*.

26 James Walker to Polk, Jan. 17, 1835, *ibid*.

27 Laughlin to Polk, April 17, 21, 1835, *ibid*.

28 Grundy to Polk, June 25, 1835, *ibid*. For the Cassedy letter, see
p. 84.

did effective service for Polk by heaping odium upon Bell. "That Cassedy letter," wrote Grundy to Polk, "will make you Speaker, I think."[29] It did, indeed, contribute to this result, but in Tennessee the combined influence of Bell and White could not be overcome. In spite of heroic efforts on the editor's part, the *Union* could not pay expenses, and the list of political "apostates" was steadily growing. Although Laughlin labored without salary, he was not without hope,[30] and his pungent editorials undoubtedly aided Polk in his campaign for reëlection.

President Jackson viewed with alarm the disintegration of the administration party in his home state. He was especially interested in the election of members of Congress. From his retreat at the "Rip Raps" he asked Polk[31] for reliable information concerning the political situation, and directed him to coöperate with Grundy and Cave Johnson in combating the schemes of Judge White and John Bell. He was able to get some news from the *Union,* although it came irregularly; "the other Nashville papers, like base coin, circulate freely, but they have become the mere echo of Duff Green & other opposition prints."

White's candidacy had irrevocably split the Jackson party in Tennessee. The President now considered White, Bell, and all their supporters to be his political and personal enemies. Polk, Grundy, and Johnson were to a greater degree than ever looked upon as the administration leaders in the state. It was certain that Polk would have the President's backing in his next contest with Bell for the Speaker's chair. From Washington, Donelson[32] wrote to congratulate Polk on his triumphant

---

29 *Ibid.*

30 "I am now fairly in a State of belligerancy with my worthy neighbors. I have them, I think, in a good way if I can keep them so. A gradual but sure work of reformation in public sentiment is in progress here, and I hope the same work is going on throughout the State" (Laughlin to Polk, July 5, 1835, *ibid.*).

31 Jackson to Polk, Aug. 3, 1835, *ibid.*

32 Donelson to Polk, Aug. 28, 1835, *ibid.*

reëlection in spite of the "intrigues" of Bell, and he reported the President to be in good spirits, notwithstanding the defeat of Governor Carroll. Donelson had, he said, conversed with many politicians, all of whom wished Polk to be chosen Speaker.

In Nashville, Laughlin, through the columns of the *Union* and by letters to individuals, was doing his utmost to discredit Bell and to present Polk's claims to reward for his loyalty to General Jackson. Polk had been the intended victim of Bell's "treachery," wrote Laughlin, and therefore "ought to be made the instrument of his defeat."[33]

While the rivalry between White and Van Buren was of greater interest in national politics, yet administration leaders in all parts of the Union had come to feel that Bell—the alleged instigator of the party schism—was, after all, more guilty than White, and consequently deserving of punishment. Polk, on the other hand, was clearly entitled to the support of the administration forces in Congress. As chairman of the Committee of Ways and Means he had borne, in the House, the brunt of the President's war on the bank. In his home state he had done more than any other, with the possible exception of Grundy, to oppose the Bell-White coalition and to uphold the standard of General Jackson.

When Congress convened in December, Polk's election to the Speaker's chair was practically assured, and he was chosen on the first ballot by a majority of thirty-nine votes. His triumph over Bell was regarded by all as a distinct party victory. A

---

[33] Laughlin to Polk, Aug. 30, 1835, *ibid.* He quoted several reasons which he had assigned when urging Polk's election, among them:

"That your election will prostrate Bell and the White influence in this State, by showing to the people the true position of Bell, and how his position is received by the Republican party every where else, and that they are only sustained now by the false opinion which prevails that they are friends of Gen. Jackson.

"That your election will unmask the White party and exhibit them as the opponents of the Administration.

"That much is due to you. That you have stuck when others failed. . . . That your confidential relation to the President ought to be considered both as a merit and as a necessary qualification in a Speaker &c &c."

"White" member of the Tennessee legislature, when writing to congratulate Polk on his election,[34] said that, although Bell's own friends hardly expected him to win, they did not think that he would be beaten so badly; they "attribute Mr. Bell's defeat to the influence of the President." Although a White supporter, the writer said that Polk had gained by his firm stand and that he was now stronger in his district than either White or Van Buren. "The election of Speaker," wrote Judge Catron,[35] "had an uncommonly great effect on the country people. They had been lead to believe great strength existed elsewhere—this is now admitted to be a mistake, and what must follow [defeat of White] is certain, as I believe." Bell himself had not been sanguine. He predicted his defeat by Polk before Congress had convened.[36]

Before proceeding with Polk's career as Speaker of the House of Representatives it seems desirable to retrace our steps in order to consider, in the following chapter, Judge White's unsuccessful campaign for the Presidency. The rivalry between White and Van Buren was the dominant factor at the time in both state and national politics. It played an important part in making Polk the presiding officer of the House, and it helped to shape many of the issues with which Polk, as Speaker, had to deal.

---

[34] H. M. Watterson to Polk, Dec. 21, 1835, *Polk Papers.*

[35] Catron to Polk, Jan. 8, 1836, *ibid.* "The effect of the news [Polk's election] upon the White cause," wrote Nicholson, December 20, "has been blighting." Many White men, said he, now think that their candidate should be withdrawn.

[36] W. H. Polk to J. K. Polk, Dec. 21, 1835, *Polk Papers.* He had seen a letter written by Bell to Judge Kennedy before the opening of Congress.

CHAPTER V

JUDGE WHITE AND THE PRESIDENCY

No biography of a statesman of the thirties—particularly of a prominent Tennessean—would be complete that did not include a chapter on the far-reaching effect of Judge White's decision to become a candidate for the Presidency. The importance of this decision lay in the fact that General Jackson had made other plans. In the parlance of the day, "King Andrew" had decreed that the "little magician" must be his successor, regardless of the will of the subjects—the "consent of the governed." When, therefore, the friends of White brought him forward as a rival to Van Buren, harmony in the Jackson camp was at first threatened, and finally destroyed. "Davy" Crockett had driven the first wedge into the solidarity of the Jackson domination of Tennessee; the White movement split it asunder. The result was the birth of the Whig party and a national political realignment.

When White was first mentioned in connection with the Presidency, Jackson's feelings were those of regret that his old friend should have been deluded by designing politicians; but when the judge was found to be a willing victim—independent even to the point of defying the President's wishes—the old-time friendship changed to bitter hatred. It was soon made apparent to politicians that they could not support Judge White without forfeiting all claim of loyalty to General Jackson. Assurances on their part that the two things were not incompatible availed nothing; all were forced to choose between the two men.

It is not easy to determine just when and by whom Judge White was first brought forward as a candidate for President, but his nomination for that office was considered by the Tennessee legislature as early as December, 1833. Up to this time, so far as Tennessee politics were concerned, Judge McLean, of Ohio, seems to have been regarded as Van Buren's most formidable rival. Some of the local papers had hoisted the McLean banner, with either Governor Carroll or Judge White for Vice-President.[1] But before adjourning in early December, 1833, the legislature seriously considered the feasibility of presenting a Presidential candidate from their own state. A resolution to nominate White was actually drawn up; but it was made known by a member that White opposed such a proceeding, and the matter was dropped. None of the members manifested any interest in nominating either Van Buren or McLean.[2]

Several causes coöperated in fixing the attention of politicians on White as a possible candidate. It was well known that Jackson had decreed that the Vice-President should succeed him; in spite of this, however, Van Buren had never been popular in Tennessee. Many of the President's most loyal supporters did not, and could not, share his admiration for the "heir apparent." State pride caused many to feel that, if possible, another Tennessean should be chosen to fill the office, and, next to Jackson, White was generally conceded to be the most able and popular son of the state. It is probable that Jackson's preference for Van Buren would have been sufficient to cause a split in the party as soon as the White movement assumed serious proportions, but the rivalry between Polk and Bell, and the support of White by the latter, lent an added bitterness and political significance to White's candidacy. The plan to nominate White was alleged to have been conceived by Bell for the purpose of advancing his own political fortunes in both state and national politics. Whether this allegation was true or false is a matter difficult to determine; but whatever Bell's motives may have been,

---

[1] Yell to Polk, Dec. 1, 1833, *Polk Papers*.

[2] A. O. P. Nicholson to Polk, Dec. 5, 1833, *Polk Papers*. Orville Bradley to White, Aug. 23, 1836 (Scott, *Memoir of Hugh Lawson White*, 302).

it seems clear that White's conduct was at all times aboveboard and commendable. He was too honest to seek political preferment by underhand methods, but he was, also, too brave and independent to step aside simply because General Jackson willed that he should do so.

Up to the time when White and Van Buren had been formally nominated and party lines definitely drawn, there was quite a diversity of opinion in Tennessee, even among Jackson's friends. On December 22, 1833, A. V. Brown wrote to ask Polk "the signs as to the 'successorship to the throne,' " and spoke of McLean's popularity. "Personally," said Brown, "I like McLean myself but *politically* I fear he is *too far off* from us in the South—and how will Van Buren help that matter in the least?" Between Clay and Van Buren, he continued, "might not one find refuge in the personal worth & virtue of McLean, although he would prefer some other than either, if chance or destiny had not thrown him too far in the rear of probable success?"[3] Other passages in the letter indicate that it was Calhoun to whom he referred. Generally, however, those of Polk's correspondents who were "not satisfied" with Van Buren were of opinion that White was the only man who would bring success to the party.[4]

On June 2, 1834, Bell defeated Polk in the contest for the Speakership. He was supported by many who were openly opposed to the administration. In the House Polk had, during the entire session, been leading the battle against the bank, and when Congress adjourned on June 30 he had won a signal victory for the administration. In his defeat by Bell, Polk could easily be made to assume the rôle of a martyr who had suffered for his loyalty to the President and the party. He seems sincerely to have regarded himself as a victim of the treachery of Bell, who had solicited opposition votes.

---

[3] *Polk Papers.*

[4] E.g., John W. M. Breazeale to Polk, March 21, 1834, *Polk Papers.*

As soon as Congress had adjourned, both men returned to Tennessee to air their grievances on the platform and in the public press. Polk, as we have seen, applied to his congressional friends for statements which would prove the perfidy of Bell, while Bell proceeded to get control of the Nashville papers, the *Republican* and the *Banner,* in order to defend himself and to overthrow the influence of Polk. Many of Polk's friends were desirous of nominating him for Governor, but he preferred to continue in national politics.

General Jackson, also, spent his summer vacation in Tennessee. The bank question was uppermost in his mind, and in a speech delivered in Nashville he made it clear that any new federal bank would be quite as objectionable as the one now in existence. As yet he seems to have taken no active interest in the quarrel between Bell and Polk, but he naturally felt grateful to the latter for his loyal support of the administration during the last sesssion. It was at this time that he declared Polk to be deserving of a medal from the American people for his services in Congress. Bell had not yet broken with the party and gave the President new assurances that he would continue to support the administration.[5] Indeed after Jackson's return to Washington there was, as we have seen, complaint in Tennessee that the *Globe* seemed to show a preference for Bell.[6] But during the fall of 1834 the political situation in Tennessee became such that the interests of Polk and the President were closely identified, while Bell cast his lot with the opponents of the administration. The main cause of the party cleavage was the renewed effort to nominate Judge White for the Presidency.

While Jackson was still in Nashville a caucus was held in that city—by friends of the bank, it was said—for the purpose of considering the nomination of White.[7] White was informed that

[5] Gen. Sam'l Smith to Polk, Sept. 20, 1834, *Polk Papers.*

[6] See above, p. 57.

[7] Burton to Polk, Aug. 27, 1834, *Polk Papers.*

the President threatened. to denounce him should he express a willingness to become a candidate.[8] Jackson doubtless noted many evidences of the popularity of White and of the unpopularity of Van Buren, but at this time it is probable that he had hopes of preventing disaffection.

While the President was passing through East Tennessee on his way to Washington, Orville Bradley, a member of the legislature, told him of the attempt made by the assembly in 1833 to nominate White — an attempt which Bradley, acting under White's directions, had been able to defeat. He told the President, also, that two-thirds of the legislature had been unfavorable to Van Buren. Jackson vigorously defended Van Buren. He said "that White could hardly get a vote out of Tennessee, and that Tennessee must not separate from the rest of his friends." He was willing to compromise by supporting White for Vice-President, and it would be time enough for White to run for President after Van Buren had retired.[9]

Jackson did not at this time harbor bitter feelings toward White, personally. These did not come until later, and even then, as will appear, he regarded the judge more as a dupe of political intriguers than as his personal enemy. His feeling in 1834 was one of annoyance that White should be made the instrument in an attempt to thwart the plans he had made for Van Buren.

White and Jackson had long been close personal friends. The judge had loyally supported the "old hero" in his campaigns for the Presidency and during the first part of his administration was regarded as one of his most able advisers.[10] But White was no sycophant, and he was too independent to follow any man's program, even though the man might chance to be

---

[8] White to Polk, Aug. 26, 1834 (Scott, *Memoir of Hugh Lawson White*, 254).

[9] Bradley to White, Aug. 23, 1836 (Scott, *Memoir of Hugh Lawson White*, 302).

[10] See letters of Jackson, Overton, Coffee, Polk *et al.*, in Scott, *Memoir of Hugh Lawson White*, 267–269.

General Jackson. As early as 1831, when Jackson was recon-
structing his cabinet so that Van Buren might, under the President's own rule,[11] be made eligible to succeed him, he had invited
White to become Secretary of War, while Eaton, the outgoing
Secretary, was to have White's place as Senator from Tennessee.[12]
The judge declined the offer, and although no breach between
the two men resulted, White was henceforth made to feel that
he was no longer in good standing in administration circles.[13]

Jackson was irritated by various manifestations of White's
independence, and especially so by his disregard of the President's wishes when Clay's compromise tariff bill was before the
Senate in 1833. The Senate had voted to refer Clay's bill to
a select committee. Before White, their presiding officer, had
appointed the committee, he was invited to a conference with
the President. Preferring Clay's bill to one which had been sent
to the House by the Secretary of the Treasury, and anticipating
that Jackson had sent for him for the purpose of dictating the
membership of the committee, White, before going to see the
President, selected a committee which he thought would support
Clay's measure. A majority, which included Clayton, of Delaware, were rated as anti-administration men.[14] The President
was much "mortified" and told Grundy in a letter that "it is an
insult to me, & the Sec. of the Treasury that such a man as

---

[11] This rule was that none of his cabinet should succeed him if he
could prevent it.

[12] White's testimony before the House Committee (Scott, *Memoir of
Hugh Lawson White*, 299; Washington *Globe*, May 25, 1831).

[13] "The true reason why nothing I have said is noticed in the Globe,
I have no doubt is, because I have never assured any man that as soon as
Gen. Jackson's terms of service are at an end, I will use all my endeavors
to elect the favorite of those who direct the operations of the paper. I am
for Gen. Jackson; but am not either a Calhoun Jackson man, or a Van
Buren Jackson man, and therefore it is pleasing to the Globe and Tele-
graph not to notice favorably anything I can say or do; and as I am
opposed to Mr. Clay, his papers will of course speak disrespectfully of
me." White to F. S. Heiskell, editor of the Knoxville *Register*, May 18,
1832 (Scott, *Memoir of Hugh Lawson White*, 269).

[14] Testimony of Judge White before the House Committee (Scott,
Memoir of Hugh Lawson White, 299).

Clayton should be upon it [the committee]."[15]　Nevertheless, Jackson held White in high esteem, and, despite this "insult" and other similar vexations, the two men continued amicable relations.　White was still rated as a Jackson man, and, in the judge's opinion, it was not until the President visited Tennessee in 1834 that he became convinced that White would not support his political program.[16]　Jackson was willing to compromise by letting White have the Vice-Presidency, but the judge must not stand in the way of Van Buren.

Up to the time that Polk returned to Washington for the opening of Congress, there is nothing in his correspondence, except his letter to White, to indicate that he took an active interest in the movement to nominate Judge White.　His thoughts were centered on Bell, and the suggestion made by C. C. Clay[17] to *"take good care to put your adversary in the wrong"* was entirely superfluous.　His task was made comparatively easy by the indiscretions of the adversary himself.　Bell's Murfreesborough speech[18] proved a boomerang to its author, for in it he had criticized the President and given quasi support to the national bank.　Then, too, Hall, of the Nashville *Republican,* had boasted that there would be "a split between Polk and the President," and that Polk would be driven from power[19] by the political influence of Bell.　Such arrogance, when duly reported to the President, was sufficient to arouse his resentment, and, when it soon developed that Bell was one of the most ardent supporters of White, he was denounced as a political apostate.

The determination of White's Tennessee friends to nominate him, and Jackson's strenuous opposition to such a nomination, placed Polk in an awkward position.　White's friends have always

---

15 Jackson to Grundy, Feb. 13, 1833, *Am. Hist. Mag.,* V, 137.

16 "He no doubt believed that whenever he and those he could control changed their creed, I would change my creed likewise, and he was never convinced to the contrary, until after his attempt upon me through Mr. Bradley, which was in the autumn of 1834." White to the "Freemen of Tennessee" (Scott, *Memoir of Hugh Lawson White,* 320).

17 Clay to Polk, Sept. 23, 1834, *Polk Papers.*

18 See above, p. 53.　　　　19 Yell to Polk, Sept. 25, 1834, *Polk Papers.*

assumed that Polk treacherously turned against White simply to please General Jackson, and White himself appears to have held this view. Even now, after Polk's entire correspondence has become available, it is difficult to determine to what extent this charge is true. His friendship for Judge White he never attempted to conceal, and that he desired the support of Jackson is beyond question; but after his defeat by Bell the political situation, both in Tennessee and in Congress, was such that for reasons of his own, and irrespective of Jackson's wishes, he could not support a candidate whose chief sponsor was his rival, John Bell. He liked White and, like many of his Tennessee friends, he probably did not share the President's admiration for Van Buren; but he was a firm believer in party loyalty; and besides, the men who were taking the lead in promoting White's interests were at the same time endeavoring to undermine Polk himself.

Polk's habitual reticence adds to the difficulty of determining his thoughts and motives. If possible, he always avoided controversies which did not immediately concern himself, and to his best friends he was guarded in expressing his opinions. When, in 1831, there was discord in Jackson's cabinet, Polk discreetly declined to participate in the effort to force Eaton from the cabinet, or even to discuss the matter in writing.[20] When the break between Jackson and Calhoun occurred, he forwarded Calhoun's "defense" to his friends, but without disclosing his own views. One of his closest friends complained that " I write you my opinions freely as I am not disposed with you to conceal my views, but I must acknowledge that you have been more *prudent* with yours for I am not able to even conjecture how your feelings are after all your long letters."[21]

---

[20] Several letters to C. A. Wickliffe declining to discuss the subject (*Polk Papers*).

[21] A. Yell to Polk, March 13, 1831, *Polk Papers*. Yell expressed his own opinions freely enough. He believed Calhoun's defense to be honest and sincere, and that Crawford was a scoundrel. He had a "bad impression" of Van Buren and hoped that he would not be nominated as Jackson's successor. The attempt to force Van Buren on the people would only aid "Prince Hal."

Polk and White had long been personal and political friends. There is nothing to indicate that their friendship had been in any degree affected by the coolness between White and the President. To this White's comments on Polk's defeat by Bell in 1834 bear witness. "Both are to me like children;" he wrote[22] "therefore I took no part in the contest." Polk's expression of "surprise and astonishment"[23] in September, 1834, when informed of Jackson's threat to denounce White, should he consent to become a candidate, was no doubt unfeigned. He was frequently evasive or noncommittal, but he was not given to flattery.[24]

Polk returned to Washington to assume his duties in the House in December, 1834. Up to this time there appears to have been no connection between his quarrel with Bell and Jackson's opposition to White. But he had not been in Washington long before these two controversies became merged by an effort on the part of Polk's opponents to bring White out as a candidate. Polk's own version of his attitude toward the judge's nomination is stated in a *"confidential"* letter to his brother-in-law, James Walker. As his motives in opposing White have often been questioned, it seemes desirable to insert this letter in spite of its length.

I have been so busily engaged in preparing the appropriation bills— and those connected with the Banks that I have not heretofore taken leisure to write to you. I have had nothing to do with the management—and undercurrents which I understand have been going on here in regard to the next Presidency. I have considered that it was my first duty to attend to the important measures committed to the committee of which I am a

[22] To editor of Knoxville *Register* (Scott, *Memoir of Hugh Lawson White*, 253).

[23] Polk to White, Sept. 2, 1834, *ibid.*, 254.

[24] White's biographer in commenting on this letter (of *September, 1834*) makes the rather astonishing statement that as soon as Polk ascertained "the sentiments of Gen. Jackson in regard to his successor" he shaped his "course according to the President's wishes, although motives of personal policy . . . decided him not to define his position until after his reëlection the ensuing August." She then goes on to show that Polk and Cave Johnson "had determined to pick a quarrel" with White in February, 1835!

member. This I have done and shall continue to do, and I am sure my
constituents will appreciate my services more than if I were engaged in
the intrigues of politicians with a view to my own personal advancement.
I have no doubt that my constituents feel and think as I do, upon the subject of the succession,—but still they have not commissioned me here—
either to engage their votes, to commit them upon the subject or to express
their opinions. As a citizen I shall have a right to my own opinion,—and
whenever there shall be occasion shall certainly exercise it. In regard to our
countryman Judge White I have said this,—that there was no man to
whom personally—I have ever had kindlier feelings, and that if he was
brought forward, or taken up and run by our political party, it would give
me pleasure to support him,—but at the same time I think that the party
now dominant in the country, who have recently achieved so signal a victory,
have fought the battle to little purpose, if in the moment of this triumph,
they permit themselves to be divided & distracted about men, and thereby
perhaps enable our political adversaries to take advantage of our divisions,—
throw the election into the House, when there is danger that the money of
the Bank and the patronage of the Government,—would corrupt & purchase
votes enough to carry the election against us. It must certainly be the desire
of our party, who are emphatically—from the policy we advocate, the party
of the country,—if possible to continue united and not divide about men.
I think the party should unite if it be possible and run but one man, and
it would assuredly give me pleasure should Judge White be that man. Suppose we divide and select more than one candidate,—and suffer the friends
of our respective candidates to become irritated & exci[ted] against each
other; may not the opposition, and will they not take advantage of such a
state of things, and at a moment when it shall be too late for us to retrace
our steps, and re-unite our friends in favor of any one, suddenly push out a
candidate of their own, defeat an election before the people, throw the election into the House and thus stand a fair chance to come into power
against the popular will. To meet such a state of things I repeat we
should continue united and if possible run but one man. Should Judge
White be the man upon whom the party unite, none would support him
with more pleasure than myself. Upon this subject, the present moment
may be an important crisis. As soon as Congress assembled,—many of the
opposition members expressed wishes that Judge White should be brought
out and announced their intention to support him,—if he was &c. Their
motive for this, the game they will play hereafter or the subject they hope
to effect, I know not except—that they would doubtless do any thing in
their power to divide & scatter us. That portion of our delegation in W^t
Tennessee, who manifested such unprovoked hostility to me during the past
summer—I mean the Speaker, Dickinson &c. probably think they can make
something out of this state of things to my prejudice, and for their own
purposes,—have been zealous, or pretended to be so, to bring Judge White

out at once, and at all events, without waiting to consult any portion of the democratic party—residing in other states with whom we have so long acted,—and who have so long acted with us in supporting the administration of the present Chief Magistrate. Ought they not to be at least consulted before such a step is taken? But that portion of our delegation probably think that by taking this course they will gain an advantage of me in Tennessee and that by uniting with the opposition Mr. B[ell] may be enabled to retain his place here at the next Congress, in the same way he originally obtained it. The East Tennessee part of our delegation very honestly and sincerely desire to see Judge White elected. On the day before yesterday I was informed by Col. Standifer that there was to be a meeting of the delegation,—on the night following (last night) upon the subject and was requested to attend. On yesterday Mr. Lea spoke to me on the subject & told me the meeting was to be at *Peyton's* room and urged us to attend. I told him that my attending or not attending was a matter of no consequence;—that neither my own opinions or that of my constituents of Judge White would be changed,—whether I attended or not; that I had no commission from my constituents to speak for them; that, that was a matter they would attend to for themselves, when the time came for them to act; that I was very laboriously engaged in the discharge of my public duty as a member of the House; and that I did not regard the proposed meeting as any part of that duty. I told him furthermore that I could not but suspect that, that portion of our delegation who are, without cause given by me so exceedingly hostile to me, were prompted in this movement more in the hope of injuring me, than for any love they had for Judge White. And furthermore I told him, that what was conducive against my attendance was this— that I could not without losing all self-respect go into a consultation upon any subject,—(unless public duty required it,) with that portion of our delegation,—who had during the past summer through their organs and tools so unjustly and wantonly assailed me, and especially when I was informed that the meeting was to take place at the room of a colleague[25] who was certainly unfriendly in his feelings towards me, and had never invited me to come to it. For these reasons I declined and did not attend. The meeting was held, Grundy, Blair & myself absent. Johnson attended— but will probably communicate to the delegation his views in writing; they entirely accord with mine. I understand that *Dunlap* (though I have not talked to him) agrees in his views with Johnson and myself. I write you very confidentially—that you may be apprised of what is going on here. From the unfairness with which I have been treated in other things I have reason to suspect that letters may be written home misrepresenting me upon

---

[25] Peyton, who was White's nephew, had opposed Polk in the Speakership election and had given as his reason, according to Cave Johnson, that Polk had worked with the Nullifiers! (Johnson to Polk, July 15, 1834, *Polk Papers*).

this;—probably representing from my absence from the meeting, that I am
unfriendly to Judge White &c.—and I look for nothing else than to see
some misinformation in regard to it, through the Nashville papers. I write
you to put you in possession of the facts,—that you may in the proper way,
and without using my letter publicly be enabled to put the matter right.
I wish you to take so much of your time from your business—which I know
to be pressing upon your time, as to write me your opinion fully & freely
upon the subject;—and whether you think I have acted prudently or not.
I have acted upon my convictions of what was proper,—and with feelings of
most perfect friendship for Judge White. Can I be affected by it?

James Walker, Esq.,
    Columbia, Tenn.

Very sincerely,
Yr friend,
James K. Polk[26]

This letter seems to give ample reasons why a man of Polk's
well-known belief in party loyalty should not support the apparently hopeless cause of Judge White. It is not fair to assume,
as the friends of White have done, that those who did not come
out for the judge were necessarily the abject creatures of General
Jackson. There was only one man whose support could, by any
possibility, have elevated White to the Presidential chair. That
man was Jackson himself; and neither Polk nor those who acted
with him could hope, even if they had so desired, to alter the President's determination to aid Van Buren. To support White, as
Polk pointed out, would result in splitting the party and endang-
ering its success, without benefiting the judge in any particular.
It was too much to ask of Polk to coöperate with men whom he
both distrusted and despised as he did Bell and Peyton in supporting a candidate who would inevitably be defeated. There
is no reason for questioning the sincerity of Polk's belief that
Bell was flirting with the opposition, as he had done when he
was a candidate for Speaker. The assertions made by Polk,
Grundy, and Johnson that they would gladly support White if
he could procure the party nomination were said by their opponents to be pure cant and of course there was no possibility of his

---

[26] The letter is dated Dec. 24, 1834, *Polk Papers*.

procuring such a nomination unless Jackson should change his mind—but there is nothing in their private correspondence to indicate that they did not really prefer White to Van Buren.

On the day after the above letter was written Polk wrote[27] another *"confidential"* letter to Walker. Alluding to the former letter he said:

Since then the fact that a meeting took place and the objects of it has been communicated to ———— ————[28] and my course is highly approved. The meeting has attracted attention and things as they *really are in Tennessee*, are beginning to be well understood here. He says that if Judge White should be united upon and be a candidate of the party—that then he should be supported by the party—but any portion of those professing to be the friends of the administration who would bring him or any one else out—without consulting the wishes of the friends of the administration in other States, will eventually not only destroy him but themselves. The storm I apprehended is to burst upon us, and we in Tennessee must be prepared to meet it. Whatever our personal preferences for men may be, as patriots we should go for the good of the country,—and to that end should avoid divisions—and preserve if possible the integrity of the party.

The portion of the letter just quoted clearly indicates that Polk declined to attend the meeting without having a consultation with the President. Continuing, he told Walker that the person to whom he has alluded (Jackson ?)

says he has already heard that it has been dropped out by some one of the opposition, that the plan of their operation, is upon the *Bell* system, alluding to the Speaker's election. I will not be hasty or imprudent in this matter,— but may venture to communicate what is passing *to you*.[29]

He wished to know whether Tennessee would probably send delegates to the national convention of the party. He instructed

---

[27] Polk to Walker, Dec. 25, 1834, *Polk Papers.*

[28] Blanks in the copy in the Polk collection, but evidently mean Jackson.

[29] Cave Johnson, Polk told Walker, had written to the Tennessee delegation stating that he would not support White ''if he is to be run by the opposition Nationals and Nullifiers,—aided by a small portion of the Jackson party.'' Polk, Dunlap, and Blair felt the same way, and ''Grundy is more excited than I have almost ever seen him,—and seems almost ready to come out and denounce the whole movement,—as calculated to divide and destroy the party.''

Walker to prevail upon the Columbia *Observer* to support the regular nominee in case its favorite should fail to procure the nomination. To this Walker replied[30] that he preferred White if he could be nominated by the party, but he feared that a split would make success doubtful. He promised to induce the *Observer,* if possible, to support the national ticket whoever might be nominated.

In a formal statement prepared by Polk[31] several items concerning the meeting of the Tennessee delegation in Washington are related which are not mentioned in his letters to Walker. According to this account, on the Sunday night before Congress convened, while Polk was calling on Grundy, Duff Green came in and urged that the Tennessee members should come out for White. Green expressed his own readiness to support the judge. Polk remained silent, but Grundy replied that he was not prepared to act on this subject. Although Polk had declined to meet with the other delegates, Lea, of Tennessee, came to the House a few days after the meeting had been held and handed Polk a letter which the delegation had prepared to send to Judge White. There were no signatures attached and Lea explained that the delegation had desired to have Polk sign it first. Polk replied

---

[30] Jan. 12, 1835 (*Polk Papers*). Walker had already written on January 7 that it had been reported in Tennessee that Bell and others intended to run White whether he is chosen by the national convention or not. "I believe Judge White is the most popular man in Tennessee except Gen. Jackson, but I do not think it is certain that even he can get the vote of Tennessee in opposition to the regular nomination of the Republican party—it looks like suicide—and how can we mix with such men as Poindexter and others of the same stamp?" He hopes that White will not lend his name to the scheme.

[31] It is addressed to J. B. & Co. (John Bell & Co.), but is changed into a letter to Cave Johnson. It is dated January 20, but relates to events that occurred as late as March 26. It probably is the first draft of his statement addressed to Johnson under date of March 26. In another letter to Johnson, dated March 28, Polk gives his reason for addressing him instead of Bell. Bell's criticisms of Polk had been contained in a letter written to Johnson, and, as Polk had received no communication directly from Bell, he could not write to him; or, if he should do so, Bell would not publish the letter. So it was sent to Johnson for publication at the proper time.

that he had nothing against White, but would not act with a portion of the party. A few days later Hubbard, of New Hampshire, informed Polk that Green was trying to interest members of Congress in the establishment of a White paper in Washington. Bell had tried to convince Hubbard that it would benefit New Hampshire to join with the South and West in forming a new party, but Hubbard declined to coöperate with him. May, of Illinois, told Polk that he had "stumbled on a caucus" composed of Bell, Peyton, and other Tennessee members. To May's protests against dividing the party, Bell replied that he saw no sacrifice of principle in winning opposition votes. In all of this Polk saw—or, at least, pretended to see—a plot of Bell, Green, and Crockett[32] to use Judge White for the purpose of overthrowing the Republican party.

The other side of the story is told in letters written to Cave Johnson by other members of the Tennessee delegation. These, White's biographer has published for the purpose of showing the "duplicity of Johnson and Polk."[33] The essential difference between these letters and those of Polk above quoted is that they state that Polk and Johnson had expressed a preference for White over any other man and had agreed to support him "under any circumstances that he, Judge White, would permit his name to be used," while Polk maintained that he had promised support only in case White should be nominated by the party. Which of the two statements is correct we are unable to determine with absolute certainty, but Polk's version accords with his invariable practice of conforming to the party program.[34]

While Polk was declining to meet with Bell, his friend Brady was sending to Jackson and to members of Congress copies of the

---

[32] Crockett had signed the letter to White.

[33] Scott, *Memoir of Hugh Lawson White*, 259–262.

[34] Standifer asserted that the meeting of the delegation held for the purpose of considering White's nomination "was a project of my own without being prompted by any one." Both Polk and Grundy, he said, after ascertaining that Bell would be there, declined to attend the meeting (*ibid.*, 260–262).

Murfreesborough *Monitor* containing Bell's Murfreesborough speech. He also urged upon Polk the necessity of establishing an administration paper in Nashville.[35] The plan of the bolters, he said, was White for eight years, and then "the Speaker will graciously condescend to take upon himself the burthens of State."

There is abundant evidence that Polk's Tennessee friends really believed that Bell and his adherents were plotting to divide the party. Daniel Graham of Murfreesborough wrote[36] that, while he preferred White to any other man, he distrusted his supporters. "No one here doubts," wrote Polk's brother-in-law, W. R. Rucker, "that he [Bell] is a thorough Bank man and at heart (though a dissembling hypocrite) one of Gen¹ Jackson's bitterest enemies."[37] In the opinion of James Walker, another brother-in-law, Van Buren was the only man who could lead the party to victory. "We justly esteem and appreciate Judge White, but cannot consent to become the tools of the opposition, or to be associated in political feeling with such as Poindexter & others."[38] A. V. Brown, one of Polk's closest friends, preferred White as a successor to Jackson but asked the question,

Do the Whigs really mean to do something finally for him—or is it a part of their policy to make a *present shew* in his favor to effect division in the Jackson ranks & so weaken Mr. Van Buren & then finally press some favorite of their own & so throw the Election in the House?[39]

Childress informed Polk[40] that it was rumored in Nashville that Bell and his friends were confident of throwing the election into the House, where White would have a majority, and that they

---

[35] Brady to Polk, Dec. 26, 1834, *Polk Papers*.

[36] Graham to Polk, Jan. 2, 1835, *Polk Papers*.

[37] Rucker to Polk, Jan. 5, 1835, *Polk Papers*. "Don't misunderstand me," he added, "I like White as well as any of these people, but I don't like these intriguing friends of his." He urged Polk to inform Jackson of the intrigues.

[38] Walker to Polk, Jan. 15, 1835, *Polk Papers*.

[39] Brown to Polk, Jan. 15, 1835, *Polk Papers*.

[40] Childress to Polk, Jan. 23, 1835, *Polk Papers*. Childress was Mrs. Polk's brother.

were equally confident of defeating Polk and Cave Johnson at the coming election.

The anomalous situation in Tennessee was aptly put by another of Polk's correspondents.

The more I reflect on the posture of affairs, the more am I provoked at the success of iniquity. Almost every man in the community who takes part in or cares for public doings, finds himself occupying a false position which he is compelled to defend. I shall find myself opposed to Judge White, which is not true, so of Doct Rucker & thousands of others—whilst thousands will find themselves opposed to Genl Jackson who are sincerely with him. Furthermore Genl Jackson & Judge White will find themselves in hostile attitude before the scene closes, whatever may be their hopes and expectations now.[41]

All agreed that John Bell was the man who had created this embarrassing predicament.

No doubt the intriguing of White's supporters was greatly exaggerated, but it seemed real enough to those who were striving to preserve party solidarity. Jackson's determination to force upon the people an unpopular candidate was after all the main cause of the difficulty, for many could not pass White by and support Van Buren without sacrificing their principles. Party loyalty alone kept others from espousing White's cause, and for some time many of Jackson's friends had hopes that he might yet drop Van Buren and acquiesce in White's nomination.[42]

The President, however, had no thought of abandoning his favorite. He vehemently condemned the activities of the Tennessee delegation, and he was beginning to regard Bell as an enemy.[43] Back of the encouragement given to White by political opponents was seen the hand of Henry Clay, who was believed to be ready to seize any advantage that might result from throwing the election into the House.[44]

---

[41] Daniel Graham to Polk, Jan. 29, 1835, *Polk Papers.*

[42] Gen. Sam'l G. Smith to Polk, Feb. 3, 1835, *Polk Papers.*

[43] Polk to Walker, Jan. 18, 1835, *Polk Papers.*

[44] Copy of a letter from Polk to somebody in Tennessee, dated February 7, 1835, *Polk Papers.* The letter was probably written to James Walker; see Walker to Polk, Feb. 24, *ibid.*

After the meeting of the Tennessee delegation, White of course realized that the members had divided on the question of supporting him. He regretted the discord that had arisen but nevertheless declined to forbid the use of his name.[45] On December 29, 1834, the delegation had addressed him a letter asking if he would accept a nomination, and he replied in the affirmative.[46] He said afterwards that he would never have consented to become a candidate but for Jackson's threat to make him "odious to society" if he did.[47]

Outwardly, at least, the judge remained on friendly terms with the Tennessee members of Congress who had opposed his nomination until a controversy arose over a question of patronage. Polk and Johnson had recommended, and Jackson had appointed, a district attorney for West Tennessee without consulting Senator White. In a letter to the two men[48] White intimated that there had been "secret contrivance" to bring about the appointment. If, as White's biographer asserts, these two Tennesseans "had determined to pick a quarrel with Judge White," they now had their opportunity—and they certainly made the most of it. They replied in a very caustic letter in which they repelled what they regarded as insinuations against themselves and the President. White's rejoinder was equally caustic, and the break was complete.[49]

It is quite possible that Polk may have welcomed such an excuse for openly breaking with the judge. The time had arrived when he must take a definite stand for one side or the other, inasmuch as it was now certain that the opposition intended to

[45] White to Alexander, Jan. 12, 1835 (Scott, *Memoir of Hugh Lawson White*, 255).

[46] Correspondence in Scott, *Memoir of Hugh Lawson White*, 329–331.

[47] Speech at Knoxville, Aug. 1, 1838 (Scott, *Memoir of Hugh Lawson White*, 359).

[48] Dated Feb. 24, 1835 (*Polk Papers*).

[49] The correspondence may be found in the *Polk Papers* under dates of February 24–26. Part of it is printed in Scott, *Memoir of Hugh Lawson White*, 256–259.

use White for the purpose of defeating the nomination of an administration candidate—that is a regular Republican nomination.[50] Such being the case, both self-interest and party loyalty beckoned in the same direction, for he could expect no favors from the men who were promoting the campaign for White's nomination. Bell was his personal enemy and political rival; many letters warned him that the White adherents were scheming, as one put it, "to get White & the people upon one side & Van Buren & my friend Col. Polk on the other."[51] Having made the inevitable choice, Polk endeavored, through James Walker and other local leaders, to hold his constituents in line for the administration, but White's popularity was already playing havoc with party solidarity.[52] At a political meeting held in Columbia on February 12, Walker, by resolution, tried to pledge the meeting to the "party candidate." The resolution was defeated by the aid of many who had hitherto been averse to White's nomination.[53] Not long after this Walker felt certain that White would carry Tennessee and he cautioned Polk that "non interference may be your true position."[54]

Nearly all the newspapers in Tennessee favored White's nomination. Bell controlled both Nashville papers, and late in February F. K. Zollicoffer, of the Columbia *Observer*, hoisted the White banner. Polk and his friends in Middle Tennessee were without an organ of influence until they established, a month later, the Nashville *Union*, which White, in a speech in the Senate,

---

[50] Polk to —— (probably Walker), Feb. 7, 1835, *Polk Papers.*

[51] James H. Thomas to Polk, Feb. 12, 1835, *Polk Papers.* J. W. Childress wrote (Jan. 23) that Polk and Johnson had been marked for defeat. Similar information came from Gen. Smith (Feb. 13), W. G. Childress and James Walker (both Feb. 14), *ibid.*

[52] Some in Tennessee, said W. G. Childress in his letter of February 14, "seem to think or to say that Jackson, the Jackson party and Jackson administration will soon be no more, that the whole will be swallowed in the White party."

[53] "The small politicians are all on the scent and expect to rise on the White excitement" (Walker to Polk, Feb. 24, 1835, *Polk Papers*).

[54] Walker to Polk, Feb. 28, 1835, *ibid.*

called a "vehicle of slanders and falsehoods, gotten up in this city [Washington]" for the purpose of distorting the truth.[55] This paper was edited by Samuel H. Laughlin; its policy was directed by Polk, Grundy, and Judge Catron, who were mainly responsible for its financial support.

Polk returned home after Congress had adjourned, only to find White's prospects daily growing brighter. In a speech delivered at Columbia, April 20, he justified his refusal to join other members of the delegation in asking White to run on the ground that he had not been sent to Washington for the purpose of making presidents. His personal preference had been for White, he said, if he could have been nominated by the Republican party.[56] Grundy approved this speech, but as to any further discussion of the subject his advice to Polk was that "the judicious course is a plain one—say nothing."[57]

In Washington, General Jackson was eagerly awaiting news from Tennessee. He was now fully convinced of Bell's "perfidy," but apparently he did not yet realize the strength of the White movement. In a long letter[58] he expressed a fear that Polk's promised communication had been delayed by illness, " for I am sure the little noise, and various meetings, got up by the instrumentality of Mr. Bell and Co. cannot have alarmed you." After delivering a homily on the iniquity of abandoning principles, and citing Clay, Calhoun, and Burr as horrible examples, he said that "Mr. Bell, Davy Crockett & Co. has placed Judge White in the odious attitude of abandoning principle & party for office," and with the association of the nullifiers

The eyes of the people soon were opened to this wicked plan, to divide and conquer the Democracy of the union, prostrate the present administration by making it odious by crying out corruption and misrule, and being supported by office holders, and corruption, thereby to bring into power the

[55] Scott, *Memoir of Hugh Lawson White*, 292.
[56] Speech printed in the Washington *Globe*, May 29, 1835.
[57] Grundy to Polk, May 11, 1835, *Polk Papers*.
[58] Jackson to Polk, May 3, 1835, *ibid.* The letter was marked "private for your own eye—it is wrote in haste."

opposition, recharter the United States Bank, destroying the republican government & substitute in its stead, a consolidated government under the controle of a corrupt monied monopoly.

After scanning this doleful picture of a future possibility, Polk must have felt relieved when he read further on that ''Mr. Bell & Co. have not succeeded—Virginia is erect again.'' ''Surely,'' continued the President, ''Tennessee will never put herself in the false position of joining the piedbald opposition of Whiggs, nullifiers, blue light federalists, and Hartford convention men. It cannot be—heaven and every principle of virtue and republicanism forbid it.'' Had White remained with his party, said Jackson, he might have procured the Vice-Presidency, but

he has been placed by Mr. Bell & Co. as the candidate of the opposition under the odious imputation of abandoning his old republican principles & party, for office, and whether he has or not the world has taken up that opinion, and he never can regain the confidence of that party again. The opposition never intended that he should be elected, they meant to divide, that they might conquer for Mr. Clay who, you may rely, is to be their candidate at last.

He had hopes that ''judge White's eyes may be opened and he will *now* see that he is in a false position and abandon Bell, Davy Crockett & Co., and withdraw himself from the odious attitude intriguing apostates have placed him [in].''

It was doubtless pleasing news that Jackson thus fixed the blame for disrupting the party upon Polk's own enemies, Bell and Crockett. Equally pleasing must it have been to read that

You and Grundy, (by the true Republicans in Congress) are looked to, to take a firm and open stand in favour of the republican principles, a *national convention* by *the people,* and in toto, against nullification & disunion—and against *little* caucuses, of a few apostate members of congress, & preserve Tennessee from the disgrace of uniting with the piebald opposition to put down my *administration, and my fame* with it, and give the reigns of Government into the hands of those who have recently conspired to recharter the Bank.

In this fight for principles, said the President, all must take a definite stand; ''do your duty (as you have done here) *at home,* and you will stand high with the republicans everywhere.'' Saving Tennessee proved to be a more difficult task than Jackson had anticipated, but, by attempting to do so, Polk and Grundy earned his undying gratitude.

In the President's opinion, two mutually antagonistic factions had joined forces for the purpose of destroying the Republican party. While Bell and Clay were aiming at consolidated government, Calhoun and his friends were using White's name ''to build up a Southern confederacy and divide the union.'' The President still spoke of White with regret more than anger. He did not charge him with being either a consolidationist or a nullifier, and he still had hopes that the judge would free himself from the influence of evil associates.

Jackson was much encouraged by the success won by his party in Virginia, Rhode Island, and Connecticut. As to Tennessee he had fears, but he also had hopes. ''Can it be,'' he said in closing his letter,

that Tennessee will abandon republican principles and be ranked with apostates, nullifiers & bluelight Federalist—Tristam Burges says she will—*forbit it virtue, forbit it heaven*—Tennessee has sustained me thus far, and I trust she never will abandon her principles for any person.

In another long letter written to Polk on May 12, Jackson vented his wrath upon those who held political control of the state for their refusal to participate in the national nominating convention.[59] ''How it is,'' he asked, ''that there is no man in the Republican ranks to take the stump, and relieve Tennessee from her degraded attitude?'' This question may have been intended as a hint for a more aggressive stand on Polk's part. ''If I was a mere citizen of Tennessee again,'' he continued, ''and wanted

---

[59] For example, the Nashville *Banner,* denouncing the national convention, said: ''So long as we live and breathe American air, we will resist the insidious proposition (whensoever and wheresoever it may originate), to lay at the feet of village politicians and placemen, who most usually fill *conventions,* the inestimable privilege of thinking and acting for ourselves in the choice of our rulers.'' Quoted in *Niles' Register* (March 28, 1835), XLVIII, 58.

everlasting fame, I would ask no other theatre to obtain it than
before the people of Tennessee."[60] In this letter Jackson spoke
of the seceders as "White Whiggs," and although both White
and Bell still claimed membership in the Republican party, the
press of both parties was beginning to class them as Whigs.[61]
It was becoming the custom to apply this name to the National
Republicans, of whom Clay was a recognized leader; they, with
the White supporters, constituted the new Whig party.[62]

The desire of the Jacksonites to identify White and Bell with
the Clay faction of the Whigs was aided materially by the discovery of Bell's "Cassedy" or "Bedford" letter of May 11,
1835.[63] There is nothing particularly damaging to either man
in the letter itself, but as construed and placed before the people
by their opponents, it was said to be a pledge that White, if
elected, would not veto any law for rechartering the bank. The
latter part of it was construed as a suggestion that Polk's

---

60 In *Polk Papers*. Jackson's signature has been cut from this letter.

61 "Elected, if elected at all, by the votes of the Whigs, he [White]
will naturally and necessarily select his councillors from their ranks, and
modify his measures according to their views." Richmond *Whig*, quoted
by Richmond *Enquirer*, and reprinted in Washington *Globe*, May 4, 1835.

62 In his letter of May 3 to Polk, above quoted, Jackson spoke of
"modern Whiggs." He often omitted the h, and invariably used the
double g.

63 It was written to Charles Cassedy of Bedford County, Tennessee,
and read as follows:

"Dear Sir: You will receive enclosed, the manifesto of the White
cause and party. I think it contains our principles and the argument upon
which they may be sustanied briefly set forth.

"You will see by my letter all I know of Judge White's views about
the Bank. He doubtless never will swerve from them, but it would be
most unprecedented, and do him, and very justly too, a great injury, to
be declaring before hand, that he would put his veto upon any measure
whatever. It would be said to be an electioneering declaration, and besides Mr. Van Buren has given no such pledges.

"To defeat me for the Speaker's chair, is the main interest which
Mr. Polk and Johnson have in this whole contest, as I believe.

"It would not do to ask Polk to vote for me against himself, but he
might be made to pledge himself to go for me against any other candidate.
My course in appointing him chairman of the Committee of Ways and
Means could be used to show that I have not been influenced by personal
considerations against him, when the country is concerned.

"Yours truly,   "JOHN BELL."
Printed in Nashville *Union*, April 5, 1839.

constituents should pledge him to cast his vote for Bell in the election of a Speaker. Between the lines there was seen a threat to defeat Polk in his campaign for reëlection to Congress unless he should give such a pledge. The rumored contents—before its publication—were far worse than the letter itself, and its appearance in print failed to counteract the effect which the rumors had produced.[64]

Knowing that the people still believed in Jackson despite their loyalty to Judge White, Bell, who was himself a candidate for reëlection, published a long letter in the Nashville *Republican* denying that he had "brought White out" in the sense and for the reasons claimed by the Democrats. "I am not against Jackson or his administration," he wrote, "but I am opposed to Mr. Van Buren."[65] As a blow at Polk, however, he published in a McMinnville paper extracts from the correspondence which had passed between Cave Johnson and the Tennessee delegation at the time that White had been invited to become a candidate. Bell's adversaries now published the entire correspondence in the Nashville *Union,* and that journal highly commended the course which had been pursued by Polk, Grundy, and Johnson. From T. J. Pew, of Kentucky, Laughlin, the editor, learned that during the previous autumn Bell had urged Col. R. M. Johnson to become a candidate on the bank ticket[66] and this paper now claimed to have conclusive proof of Bell's affiliations with the bank. His "Cassedy" letter was published in the *Union* on June 26, and Grundy confidently assured Polk that "that letter will make you Speaker, I think."[67]

During this same month (May 20) Van Buren was nominated for the Presidency by the Baltimore convention, and a bitter

---

[64] A similar letter was written by Bell to a man in Giles County (Kincannon to Polk, June 1, 1835, *Polk Papers*). Kincannon said that he had seen the letter.

[65] Copied by the Washington *Globe*, May 28, 1835.

[66] Laughlin to Polk, May 30, 1835, *Polk Papers*. Pew said that he had seen Bell's letter to Johnson.

[67] Grundy to Polk, June 25, 1835, *ibid.*

national campaign was waged in Tennessee simultaneously with the contest for supremacy between Polk and Bell. Although Jackson had, in his "Gwin letter,"[68] asserted that it was to be a convention "fresh from the people" to whose will all in the party ought to submit, it was well known that this body had been called together for the sole purpose of ratifying the "appointment" already made by the President. His letter to Gwin had failed to produce the desired effect, for Tennessee did not even send delegates to the convention at Baltimore. Still unwilling to believe that the people of his state could fail to do his bidding, Jackson caused a statement to be circulated to the effect that the contest was really between himself and White, and not between the judge and Van Buren.[69]

There was much vituperation on either side during the months which preceded the congressional elections in Tennessee. Both parties seemed to realize that, if elected, Polk would be chosen Speaker of the House. Polk was popular in his district and many of the "White Whigs" remained loyal to him. Toward the close of the campaign, the Bell forces became more moderate in their criticisms, for it had become apparent that by indulging too freely in denunciations they had strengthened both Polk and Van Buren.[70]

Confident of victory, Jackson, from his retreat at "Rip Raps," was already planning work for Polk to do as soon as he had been reëlected.[71] Polk, Grundy, and Johnson were to get up meetings which would instruct Representatives in Congress to vote against the chartering of any bank. They were also to induce the state legislature to instruct the Senators from Tennessee to vote

---

[68] *Niles' Register*, XLVIII, 80–81.

[69] Scott, *Memoir of Hugh Lawson White*, 335.

[70] Polk to Jackson, Aug. 14, 1835, reporting his victory at the polls, *Polk Papers*.

[71] Clay, said the President, is the real candidate of the opposition, and Bell will sacrifice White and try to get votes for himself in the Speakership election. "The Judge will be left politically prostrate as ever Aron Burr was, and as few to sympathize with him on his downfall."

for Benton's expunging resolution and against a bank charter. In order to preclude the charge of persecution, he advised that the local meetings should draft their instructions before the legislature had convened and before either Bell or White had been nominated for reëlection as members of Congress. In any event, Bell's "Cassedy letter" would be a sufficient answer to any such charge.[72] And yet the man who wrote this letter vehemently denied that he ever interfered with the free choice of the people!

Some of the party politicians[73] were inclined to doubt the wisdom of having the members of Congress instructed by local meetings. They were not given much choice, however, in the matter of instructing Senators, for the President himself prepared an outline of instructions, which he sent to Governor Carroll. Major Guild was selected to present the instructions in the legislature. Jackson sent to Carroll, also, two volumes of the *Extra Globe* which contained Benton's speeches and other materials that might be useful for reference. He instructed Polk to repair to Nashville before the meeting of the legislature for the purpose of arranging everything for prompt action.[74] He also urged Polk to be in Washington a few days before the opening of Congress, and "there must be a meeting of the friends of the administration & select the candidate for Speaker and elect him the first ballott." He did not state explicitly that Polk would be that candidate, but his assurance that "the New England states will sustain you" indicates that Polk was the President's own choice for the office.[75]

---

[72] Jackson to Polk, Aug. 3, 1835, *Polk Papers.*

[73] For example, A. V. Brown (Brown to Polk, Aug. 27, 1835, *Polk Papers*).

[74] "You must be in Nashville some days before the Assembly meets, every arrangement ought to be made, and as soon as the House is formed the resolutions ought to be offered, or the opposition will forestall you by a set prepared for their own pallate be prompt and do not permit yourselves to be outgeneraled, the first blow is half the battle, and as they are preparing to elect a Senator, these resolutions will strike terror & confusion in their ranks—produce a panic, and blow up all their digested arrangements, and will add all the doubting members to your ranks."

[75] Jackson to Polk, Sept. 15, 1835, *Polk Papers.* "When you read & note burn this" was his final instruction.

Even if there had not already existed a strong personal friendship between Polk and the President, their common desire to overthrow the Bell-White faction was sufficient to identify their political interests.

For the next two months Polk kept Jackson well informed on passing events in Tennessee. With Donelson, also, he kept up a separate correspondence, concerning which they did not always take the President into their confidence.[76] Donelson did not share Jackson's belief that the legislature would adopt the Guild resolutions to instruct the Senators from Tennessee.[77]

In October, while the legislature was in session, Judge White visited Nashville and other nearby towns, where public dinners were given in his honor. Without assigning any reasons, Polk curtly declined to attend any of these, but he reported to the President that White had taken advantage of the occasions to electioneer for himself and to censure Polk, Grundy, and other supporters of the administration. Jackson was much incensed by this information, but he still believed that the effect of the judge's speeches would be counteracted by the debate in the legislature on the expunging resolutions. "Mark these words," he wrote to Polk, "have the yeas & nays taken upon them, and all who votes against them will be taught by the people of Tennessee that they have misrepresented them."[78] White, in Jackson's opinion, could not be too severely condemned for attacking Polk and other members of Congress; "rouse Grundy & Johnson into action, and I will vouch for the virtue of the people."[79]

The President's wish for prompt action on the expunging resolutions was doomed to disappointment; a wearisome discussion

---

[76] Both suspected that Bell had a spy in the President's household by whom he was supplied with administration secrets, but they give no clew as to whom they suspect (Donelson to Polk, Sept. 24, 1835, *Polk Papers*).

[77] Donelson to Polk, Oct. 20, 1835, *ibid.*

[78] "I cannot yet believe," he continued, "that the democratic republicans of Tennessee can be so unjust to me, as to unite with Clay & the opposition in condemning me for preserving the constitution."

[79] Jackson to Polk, Oct. 20, 1835, *Polk Papers*.

followed the introduction of the subject. On the other hand, the legislature very promptly nominated White for the Presidency, even before Jackson's above-quoted letter had reached Tennessee. In his letter of acceptance, White declared emphatically that his political principles had undergone no change; that the administration forces, and not he, had deserted the traditional party standards and become "a mere *faction.*"[80] After the formal nomination had been made the people regarded the campaign as a contest between Jackson and White, and the Presidency was the principal topic of discussion at every local gathering. The country people generally stood loyally by the President, while those living in towns were more apt to favor White.[81]

After the congressional delegation had set out for Washington—Polk to be elected Speaker over his arch enemy, Bell, and Johnson to frighten his friends by his near approach to a duel with the much hated Bailie Peyton[82]—the legislature continued the acrimonious debates on Jackson's expunging resolutions. To add variety, the White supporters in the legislature were accused by their opponents of fraud in connection with the public printing. While the debate was in progress, Jackson sent appeals for support to members of the legislature, and it was said that Polk had prepared the list to be thus solicited. White, also, corresponded with some of the members. He made no attempt to influence their votes, but his exposure of the methods employed by the President to defeat him undoubtedly brought him support. Strong language was used by both sides, and members did not hesitate to call General Jackson a "dictator" or to accuse him of trying to appoint his successor.[83]

---

[80] The documents relating to White's nomination are printed in Scott, *Memoir of Hugh Lawson White*, 331–334.

[81] J. W. Childress to Polk, Nov. 22, 1835, *Polk Papers.*

[82] Laughlin to Polk, Dec. 1; J. W. Johnson to Polk, Dec. 9, 1835, *Polk Papers.*

[83] A. O. P. Nicholson to Polk, Feb. 4, 1836, *ibid.* "It is declared every day & by the leaders, that to Mr. Van B's personal character they do not object—but their great objection is, to Prest Jackson nominating his successor" (Catron to Polk, Jan. 8, 1836, *ibid.*).

Both Jackson and Bell were said to have flooded the state with "franked" political literature for the purpose of influencing both the legislature and the people. But the command of the "old hero" was no longer as of yore. The legislature which had so recently nominated Judge White now declined to instruct him to vote for Benton's expunging resolution[84]

Polk was elected Speaker of the House by a large majority, and both in Washington and in Tennessee the defeat of Bell for that office was expected to injure White's prospects in his own state. "It was urged by the faithful," wrote White,

that by the election of Polk, the vote of Tennessee would be changed. The course of Alabama,[85] it was said, will be followed by the legislature of Tennessee, and in a very short time my name will be dropped everywhere. . . . Everything which can be done to my injury, within their power, is done by Grundy and Johnson, from my own State, and probably by Polk, also.[86]

Party leaders in Tennessee undoubtedly believed that White would now withdraw from the race, or that in any case Van Buren would carry the state. Polk received many letters expressing this opinion.[87] Their hopes of defeating the judge were somewhat disturbed by the refusal of the legislature to instruct him on the expunging resolutions, but they were revived by the expected effect of White's votes against some of Jackson's appointments and by his arguments and vote in favor of Clay's land distribution bill.[88]

---

84 E. H. Foster to White, Feb. 26, 1836 (Scott, *Memoir of Hugh Lawson White*,. 337).

85 The legislature of Alabama nominated White, but on the condition that he should be "the choice of the republican party throughout the Union."

86 White to Geo. W. Churchwell, Jan. 3, 1836 (Scott, *Memoir of Hugh Lawson White*).

87 Among the rest Nicholson wrote (January 22) that since Polk's election the White men had practically given up the struggle; "all excitement here has subsided, and the election of V. B. is given up by all but Gen. Barrow."

88 Walker to Polk, April 11, 1836. White's vote on the land bill "must seal his fate," wrote Laughlin to Cave Johnson on May 9. One of White's admirers said at a political meeting that he "had followed White to his grave when he [White] voted for the land bill—and that he could not stand to be buried with him" (Herndon to Polk, May 25, 1836). All in *Polk Papers*.

One of the most serious handicaps of the administration party in Tennessee was the weakness of their press. The Bell-White faction had procured control of the leading newspapers in Nashville and elsewhere. The Nashville *Union* was the main Democratic organ and Polk was in constant receipt of letters from Laughlin, its editor, which stated that the paper was approaching bankruptcy. Laughlin himself was enthusiastic but unreliable. Many a letter from Nashville politicians reported to Polk that "Laughlin has been drunk for a week." Near the close of the campaign he became so untrustworthy that Judge Catron was obliged to edit the *Union*.[89]

For our present purpose it is unnecessary to follow in detail the remainder of White's campaign for the Presidency. By splitting the Democratic party and by bringing to Polk the powerful support of General Jackson, it was one of the principal factors in elevating Polk to the Speaker's chair. In his attitude toward White, Polk may have in some degree played the "unscrupulous partisan" which Parton says he was,[90] but the political situation which resulted from White's candidacy left him very little choice.[91] He could not coöperate with Bell, and it would have been political suicide to break with the President.

With the remainder of this campaign Polk's political welfare was not so intimately connected. It will therefore be treated incidentally only, in connection with his career as Speaker of the House.

---

[89] Catron to Polk, Sept. 6, 1836, *Polk Papers.*

[90] Parton, *Life of Andrew Jackson,* III, 617.

[91] That partisan Democrats really believed Judge White to have been made the tool of designing politicians and his own ambition is well indicated by Laughlin's entry in his diary on hearing of the death of White. "So, here is the end of ambition—of the ambition of an old politician who had been betrayed and deceived by his pretended friends, John Bell and others, into a course of intrigue and tergiversation, which had cast him from the Senate, had lost him the esteem of all good men in his state, and had embittered his latter days, and probably shortened his life. What a warning his example ought to afford to all thinking and candid men!" (*Diary,* April 14, 1840). As White carried the state by an overwhelming majority, there must inded have been a dearth of "good men" and a surplus of rascals!

CHAPTER VI

SPEAKER OF THE HOUSE UNDER JACKSON

Following Jackson's advice Polk went to Washington late in November, 1835, in order to prepare the way for his election as Speaker.[1] The twenty-fourth Congress assembled on December 7, and, as the President had planned, Polk was elected on the first ballot. The coveted office was his reward for party loyalty, but he soon discovered that he must also pay the penalty of his success by being the object of more heckling and abuse than had fallen to the lot of any of his predecessors. The Democrats had a substantial majority in the House and were able to carry their measures; but the knowledge of this power only made their opponents more determined to goad the majority by obstructive tactics and by personal vituperation.

The entire period of Polk's speakership was one of political unrest, sectional discord, and personal animosity. Those who had so recently been friends and relentless in pursuing the common enemies, Adams and Tobias Watkins, hated one another all the more cordially now that the party was disintegrating, for each faction believed the other treacherously to have abandoned traditional party principles. On his own account, Polk had to suffer the slings and arrows of his brilliant but censorious rival, and of Peyton, Crockett, and other personal enemies. In addition, all who harbored grudges against the "military chieftain"— whether Nullifiers or Whigs—took keen delight in vitriolic attacks upon the administration, and in making it personally uncomfortable for the Speaker, whom they charged with being the President's creature and obedient slave. To this potpourri of

---

[1] Jackson to Polk, Sept. 15, 1835, *Polk Papers.*

discord was added the battle between Adams and the southern fire-eaters over the abolition petitions. Each side accused the Speaker of unfairness and harrassed him with hairsplitting questions of parliamentary procedure. Fortunately for himself his knowledge of detail, his methodical mind, and his habitual coolness under the most trying ordeals, enabled him to preside over the exciting debates with dignity and success when many a more brilliant man would have met with failure.

The disposition to humiliate Polk was manifested even before he had been elected. As soon as the House had been called to order, the clerk announced the first business to be the election of a Speaker by ballot. To this customary procedure Patton and others objected, and insisted upon a *viva voce* election. Except for showing a disposition on the part of the opposition to resort to annoying tactics whenever possible, this attempt to alter the mode of election was of little importance, for the House proceeded to ballot as usual, and Polk received one hundred and thirty-two votes to eighty-four for Bell—a vote which Benton says "was considered a test of the administration strength, Mr. Polk being supported by that party."[2]

The President's message was sent to Congress on the second day of the session. Evidently descrying the gathering war clouds, Jackson called attention to the dangers that would result from internal dissensions. He again recommended the adoption of an amendment to the Constitution which would prevent the election of a President from devolving upon the House. It is unlikely, however, that he had much hope that his suggestion would be followed.

The standing committees were announced by the Speaker on the fourteenth of December. In forming them, Polk followed the usual custom of placing safe party majorities on those which would have the shaping of important legislation. In so doing he simply followed precedent; but he had, when a minority

---

[2] Benton, *Thirty Years' View*, I, 569.

member, condemned the practice, and by adhering to precedent now he became the object of criticism and abuse.

The first difficult problem which confronted the new Speaker was the disposition of abolition petitions. On December 18, 1835, Jackson, of Massachusetts, presented a memorial in which citizens of his state asked Congress to abolish slavery in the District of Columbia. Hammond, of South Carolina, moved that the petition ''be not received,'' but Polk ruled that such a motion had never before been presented to the House and that under the rules it was not in order. When Hammond offered another motion to ''reject'' the petition, Polk ruled that any petition might be rejected after it had been received. Although his rulings were logical and fair, they were assailed by the contestants on either side. The Speaker's motives were impugned and appeals were taken to the House, but even John Bell admitted that Polk had made the best disposition of a new and debatable question. This particular petition was sent to the table on Decemcember 21; but others like it soon appeared, and the ''right of petition'' became one of the most heated topics of debate. The *Globe* upheld the cause of the petitioners. Should the House, it said, yield to the demands made by Hammond and Wise and refuse to receive such petitions, it would be violating one of the most sacred constitutional guaranties.[3]

Nearly all of the northern members held that all petitions from American citizens must be received and that, after reception, Congress might dispose of them as it pleased. Southern members did not deny the right of petition, in the abstract; they were willing, they said, to receive ''*bona fide*'' petitions. But radicals from that section argued that, inasmuch as the petitioners in question were asking something which did not fall within the power of Congress to perform, there could be no obligation to receive requests to do the impossible.

---

[3] Washington *Globe*, Jan. 1, 1836.

On February 8, Pinckney, of South Carolina, presented a resolution which prescribed a method for dealing with anti-slavery petitions. After its passage by Congress it was popularly known as the ''gag rule.'' It directed that all memorials, already presented or to be presented, praying for the abolition of slavery in the District of Columbia should be referred to a select committee. By the same resolution the committee was instructed to report that Congress possessed no power to interfere with slavery in states and ought not to interfere with it in the District. Regarded as a compromise, the resolution was passed by a large majority, but its provisions did not win the approval of extremists on either side. Slavery restrictionists condemned a measure which to them seemed a combination of cowardice and tyranny, while southern hotspurs like Hammond and Wise were dissatisfied because Congress would not reject all petitions relating to this subject. The recalcitrant members raised endless technical objections and appealed repeatedly from the decisions of the chair, but only in one instance did the House fail to sustain the rulings of the Speaker. Of all the objectors, Wise was the most abusive and unfair. Among other things he accused Polk of trying to force members to ''vote like mules'' without affording them an opportunity to consider the questions to be decided.

Pinckney's resolution did not succeed in precluding further debate on the subject of slavery. Briggs, of Massachusetts, presented another petition on February 15, and, in response to a question put by Wise, Polk decided that the Pinckney resolution applied only to petitions which had already been received. Thereupon Wise moved that the Briggs petition ''be not received,'' and the Speaker ruled the motion to be in order. The ruling was clearly an error on Polk's part, and his decision was overruled by a vote of the House. His apparent concession to Wise was severely criticized by both northern and southern men. Among the latter, Manning, of South Carolina, said that the effect of the Speaker's decision would be to renew the angry

sectional debates which the supporters of the Pinckney resolution
had hoped to obviate; in addition, it was an arbitrary setting
aside of the will of the House. "If the Speaker," continued
Manning, "can by his decision reverse this resolution . . . then
he has power to suspend, alter, or change, any deliberate act of
this House, intended as a rule for its governance."[4] The vote
of the House settled the question for the session at least. The
effect of the reversal of Polk's decision was to apply the "gag
rule" to all petitions that might appear, and to refer them automatically to the select committee. It was, of course, well understood that they would not be considered or reported back by the
committee.

The Nashville *Republican* criticized Polk for being unable to
keep order in the House. It contrasted him unfavorably with
Bell, and *proved* his incompetence by citing numerous appeals
that had been taken from his decisions. The *Globe* replied that
the disorder and appeals were machinations of Bell's henchmen,
who had been purposely trying to discredit the Speaker. It
pointed with pride to the fact that only one of his decisions—a
new rule which Polk had construed in favor of the Bell men—
had been reversed by the House.[5]

The twenty-fourth Congress had not been long in session before the candidacy of Judge White entered into the debates of
the House. On January 2, 1836, the *Globe* charged that Nullifiers, like Wise, and Abolitionists were supporting White for no
other reason than to draw votes from Van Buren. For the same
reason, it said, Webster was urged to run on a ticket of his own.
In turn, Wise embraced every opportunity to attack the President and administration members, including the Speaker, and
to accuse them of engaging in political intrigues.

---

[4] *Cong. Globe*, 24 Cong., 1 sess., App., 145.

[5] "The truth is, Mr. Polk has deserved the confidence of the House by
a firm, faithful, industrious, and able discharge of his duties." This paper
denied that Polk desired or had been offered a place in the cabinet, for
the administration wished him to remain in the Speaker's chair (Washington *Globe*, March 16, 1836).

Such an opportunity was presented when Adams moved that a certain passage of the President's message be referred to a select committee. During the last days of the twenty-third Congress the House had passed, as part of the general appropriation bill, an item of $3,000,000 to be expended for national defense by order of the President. As the two houses had been unable to agree on certain details, the measure was defeated in the Senate. The President in his message deplored the failure of Congress to pass this necessary measure, and again recommended the appropriation. Adams moved that the subject be referred to a select committee for the purpose of ascertaining by whose fault the appropriation had been lost.[6] While debating the question, Wise sarcastically remarked that it was a most important subject, for "the fate of the presidential canvass is in part made to depend upon it." The President, he said, had intended to use the money as a secret service fund; had Cambreleng not refused to accept the reasonable amendments proposed by the Senate, the measure would have carried. He charged Polk with having solicited votes for the appropriation on the plea that the President desired it, and with having requested the members solicited to refrain from mentioning this fact.[7] Scarcely a measure came before the House that was not made by Wise the motif for an assault upon the administration. His criticisms of the Speaker were many and bitter, and frequent though futile were his appeals from the decisions of the chair. Polk's friends thought that Wise and Peyton were trying to provoke the Speaker into fighting a duel; even his own family feared that blood might be shed.[8]

---

[6] The *National Intelligencer* had asserted that the House, not the Senate, had been at fault—a charge which Adams resented.

[7] Jan. 21, 22, 29. *Cong. Globe*, 24 Cong., 1 sess.

[8] James Walker advised Polk to treat their abuse with contempt. No one, he said, would doubt the Speaker's physical courage. The whole matter was, in his opinion, a scheme of Bell to disgrace Polk by drawing him into a duel with either Wise or Peyton (Walker to Polk, March 14, 1836, *Polk Papers*).

Although Bell was less abusive than either Wise or Peyton, he frequently questioned the justice of the Speaker's rulings and accused him of partisan bias.[9] On February 3, 1836, during a debate on the reference of a Senate bill for limiting the terms of certain officers, Bell said that never before had so many things of importance been excluded from the discussions of the House "by forms and decisions upon the rules." His principal speech of the session was delivered while the naval appropriation was being discussed in the House. He had little to say on the subject under consideration, but, having avowed his intention "to indulge the privilege of debate to the utmost limit of parliamentary license," he launched into an extended discussion of "the general policy of the present Administration, as lately developed."[10] He employed the present occasion, he said, because those who were in control of the House took good care to exclude any resolution to which such remarks as he desired to make would be really germane. After twitting the Speaker with having changed his opinions on the subject of patronage,[11] he arraigned the administration party for having abandoned the principles on which General Jackson had been chosen President. It was not surprising, he said, that strange doctrines should appear, inasmuch as the single principle which is common to the present majority is unlimited devotion, not to any particular creed, but to *the party*. He pointed out with remarkable precision the evils of abject partyism, and the inevitable abuses which result from

---

[9] Perhaps, as was later suggested by the Boston *Age* (Aug. 17, 1836), prudence led Bell to refrain from leading the assault and to delegate this function to his two associates. Still, Wise needed little urging, and the fact that Bailie Peyton was a nephew of Judge White was sufficient to account for his animosity.

[10] March 16, 22, 25, 1836. *Cong. Globe*, 24 Cong., 1 sess., App., 722 ff.

[11] "It was, I believe, a private scheme [earlier] of my colleague, who is now the presiding officer of this House [Mr. Polk] to take from the Secretary of State the power of designating the publishers of the laws, and to vest it in the House of Representatives; so important at that day was the purity of the public press regarded by the Jackson party."

personal government by a popular hero.[12] His own speech was
no doubt intended for campaign purposes, but the picture which
he drew of existing evils was none the less accurate on that account. If it lacked in any particular, it was in being too charitable to the President himself, for after all Jackson was the
individual most responsible for perpetuating those evils in the
interest of party discipline. There were other critics of the

[12] ''How has it happened that these abuses have not only been suffered
to exist, but even to increase, under an Administration so decidedly popular and powerful? When this problem shall be solved to the satisfaction
of the public, the remedy will be supplied. The true answer to the question, how these abuses came to exist under such an Administration, is,
because the *Administration is such* as it is, because it is *popular.* Every
man of sound mind and lawful age knows that the President, nor any
other being of created existence, can exercise a personal inspection and
superintendence over all, or even a tenth part of the most important details of the public service. Yet every important transaction connected
with the public service is so managed by the subordinate officers, as to
throw the responsibility upon the President. If the delinquent officers
do not do this themselves, their defenders in Congress and out of Congress
do not fail, in effect, to fix the responsibility there. Whether in Congress,
or in the country, complaint is made of abuse in any branch of the public
service, the answer is, eternally, that the charge is meant as an attack
upon General Jackson! His great name and popularity are the shield and
buckler of every official delinquent, whether from incompetency or infi-
delity, from a clerk to the head of a Department—from the register or
receiver of a land office, or an Indian agent, to a Minister Plenipotentiary!
The name and services of General Jackson, I repeat, are invoked to shield
and cover, as with a mantle, every official transgression or omission, from
the highest to the lowest, whenever it suits the interest of party to avail
themselves of them.
''And the people are called upon to rally round—to stand by and
defend—not the individual arraigned—not the delinquent department, but
the President himself, who it is asserted through a thousand channels, is
intended to be struck at and stabbed through the sides of the accused
officer or Department. The people cannot at once detect the artifices of
party. They are jealous of everything which savors of an attack upon
General Jackson, and they in general act upon that suspicion. Those,
therefore, who dare, here or elsewhere, to find fault with the course of
affairs, upon any ground, instead of finding countenance from those in
power, or from the dominant party—instead of being cheered on in the
ungracious task of reform, are met on the threshold, with the charge of
secret and sinister motives—with anti-Jacksonism! They are told, that
their object is to assail the character of the hero of New Orleans, and the
conqueror of the United States Bank; as if either one or the other of
those victories could be of any worth now or hereafter, except to protect
the Constitution, the country, and its liberties—as if those victories could
be of any value, if as the price of them we are to surrender that very
Constitution, those very liberties—those rich and glorious prizes for which

administration,[13] but none covered the whole ground so thoroughly and so accurately as did Bell.

The attacks made by Wise on the Speaker and the administration were capricious and, to his associates, extremely entertaining. His assertions, however, were more irritating than convincing. His own resolution, which called for an investigation of the method by which state banks of deposit had been selected, gave him an opportunity to vent his wrath upon Reuben M. Whitney, and upon those who had employed Whitney. His time was ill spent; assailing Whitney's reputation was like slaying the dead.

Throughout the session the Presidential campaign was a topic of absorbing interest. Few questions came before the House that did not elicit a discussion of the approaching election. This was natural, perhaps, for Van Buren had been nominated for the avowed purpose of continuing the policies of the present administration, and it was from these very policies that the White element of the party had revolted. On this subject personal animosity increased as the end of the session approached. As

those battles were fought and won. If those who venture to make charges against any department of the public service are not met precisely in this way, they are, at all events, told that General Jackson is the head of the Government—that he is responsible for all the executive branches of the public service, and no attack can be made upon any branch of the public service, therefore, without attacking him, and everybody knows that he does his duty. A most shameful, egregious, and pernicious flattery. But the absurdity of the argument does not prevent it from being constantly interposed. The argument is, that because General Jackson is able, faithful, and patriotic, in the discharge of all his duties, therefore all the subordinate officers of the Government are so likewise. But more: if anyone shall reply to all this, and that he means no attack upon General Jackson, that he is willing to exonerate him from any agency in the abuses which are alleged to exist, he is forthwith denounced as a hypocrite—as a dastardly assailant, who wants the courage and independence to make a direct attack. He is dared to come forward like a man, and assail General Jackson as the author of all these abuses—his pride is appealed to—his feelings are chafed to draw him on to utter the fatal denunciation; and the moment he does so, the myrmidons of the party stand ready to hack him to pieces! These, sir, are the true *causes* of the continued abuses in the public service.''

[13] Robertson, of Virginia, when speaking (April 5) on the same bill, asserted that the administration desired a large appropriation for the navy so that there might be no surplus to distribute among the states.

if to make amends for the moderation displayed in his speech on the naval appropriation bill, Bell, when discussing the river and harbor bill on June 23, severely castigated both the Speaker and the administration. He charged the administration with deliberate extravagance, and said that the Committee of Ways and Means had been purposely organized by Polk "upon a principle of extravagance."[14] His purpose was to show, as Robertson, of Virginia, had tried to show when discussing the naval appropriation bill on April 5 that the administration hoped to nullify the effect of Clay's "distribution bill" by leaving no surplus for distribution among the states. However, it is difficult to see how Polk could have anticipated the passage of this bill when he appointed the Committee of Ways and Means.

Bell had little reason to complain of Polk's committees, for, as Gillet, of New York, pointed out (June 24), they were substantially the same as those appointed by himself.[15] In selecting his committees Polk had given no greater advantage to the majority than was customary, yet it is interesting to recall in this connection that he, too, during the Adams administration, had complained because "studied majorities" had been placed on committees, "in conformity to a previous secret understanding,

---

[14] "I have said that I regard this bill as the result of a deliberate system of extravagance—of a plan for increasing the wants of the Government, and exhausting the Treasury. . . . I affirm that your Committee of Ways and Means of this House was organized upon a principle of extravagance. Look at the composition of that committee, sir, and then tell me it was not constituted with a deep design, and expressly with a view to the largest expenditure for which a pretext could be found, in every branch of the public service. Was there ever such a Committee of Ways and Means appointed in this House? Was there ever a more palpable desertion of the principle of representation—a more shameful abandonment of the interests of the entire interior of the country?" (*Cong. Globe,* 24 Cong., 1 sess., App., 745).

[15] Gillet scathingly denounced Bell's attitude toward Polk. He twitted Bell with not having defended his constituent (the President) when during the last Congress he had been called a *toothless tyrant* by a member of the opposition party. Repelling such attacks upon the President and declining to attend a caucus of the Tennessee delegation were the only crimes, said Gillet, of which Polk could be convicted, and as Speaker, "even his political opponents bear testimony to his capacity, honesty, and impartiality."

among the favorites at Court.''[16] Both men advocated majority rule, yet neither accepted it with good grace when he chanced to be numbered with the minority.

In this same speech Bell reverted to the caucus of the Tennessee delegation, which had been called to consider the nomination of Judge White. He said that the main object of the meeting had been to test the sincerity of certain members and that two of these gentlemen, Polk and Grundy, ''are at this moment in the enjoyment of the rewards of their hypocrisy and their treachery to their colleagues.'' He still spoke with respect of General Jackson and denied that he had ever called the President a tyrant or a crouching sycophant. ''He may be the master of *slaves* and *menials*,'' said Bell, ''but nature has disqualified him from becoming one himself.''

The first session of the twenty-fourth Congress terminated on July 4, 1836. Among its legislative acts were the admission to statehood of Arkansas and Michigan, and the reorganization of the general post-office along lines advocated by Amos Kendall. Another law approved the President's order for removing public deposits from the Bank of the United States, and regulated for the future the method of depositing public money in state banks. As a result of the payment in full of the national debt, Clay introduced in the Senate his well-known measure for distributing among the states the surplus revenue of the federal government. As it was made to assume the guise of a deposit rather than a gift, the bill passed both houses of Congress and was signed— but with reluctance—by the President. On June 7, while the bill was before the House, an attempt was made to refer it to the Committee of the Whole, for the purpose, said the *Globe,* of prolonging the debate and thereby defeating the admission of Arkansas and Michigan. Polk blocked such a reference by casting his ballot in the negative and making it a tie vote.[17]

---

16 Polk to Colonel Wm. Polk, Dec. 14, 1826, *Col. Wm. Polk Papers.*
17 Washington *Globe,* June 10, 1836.

Although the Speakership is the most important and responsible position in the House, and although the Speaker's influence upon legislation is surpassed by few other officers of the federal government,[18] yet, from the very nature of his position, that influence is difficult to trace. By the personnel of his committees, by his decisions, by his control over debate by recognizing or refusing to recognize members who may desire to speak, one may trace in a general way the part played by the Speaker; but necessarily he takes little part in the discussions of the House. Polk did not even avail himself of the privilege of participating in debate when the House had resolved itself into a Committee of the Whole. For this reason his views on the various measures are not readily ascertained, and during this particular period his private correspondence affords little assistance. That he satisfied the party which elected him, there is abundant evidence in the records of the House, and in the public press. That he possessed the necessary knowledge and coolness of temperament to avoid the pitfalls prepared by his adversaries, is equally clear. "Never," said the editor of the Boston *Age,*

> was man more rigidly and constantly assailed by a pack of untiring pursuers, than was Mr. Speaker Polk by his uncompromising assailants. They left no stone unturned that could be moved to his disadvantage. . . . But notwithstanding all the efforts that were made to destroy Mr. Polk, he passed the ordeal unscathed, and ultimately triumphed.

The editor said that he did not like Polk personally, and that he had preferred Bell for Speaker, still "it is but an act of justice to say of him, that he discharged his duties with great ability, promptness, and throughout the session was popular with an immense majority of the members," and self-respect compelled

---

18 Mrs. Polk probably voiced her husband's sentiments when she said, years afterward: ''The Speaker, if the proper person, and with a correct idea of his position, has even more power and influence over legislation, and in directing the policy of parties, than the President or any other public officer.'' Conversation with Samuel J. Randall. Quoted in Nelson, *Memorials of Sarah Childress Polk,* 206.

northern Whigs to support the Speaker in putting down Wise and his friends.[19]

After the adjournment of Congress on July 4, the great problem to be solved by the administration forces was not so much how to elect Van Buren, for that seemed certain, but how to save Tennessee. The prospect of losing the vote of the President's own state was most humiliating to himself and to the entire party. At first Jackson could not believe such a calamity possible; but, as the campaign proceeded, even he began to realize that, if the state could be saved at all, it could be done only by heroic efforts.

As usual, Jackson spent his vacation at the Hermitage, and during the summer he was honored with public dinners at various places. The people of Nashville entertained him with a barbecue to which "all creation" was invited.[20] The press and the platform of the respective parties vied with each other in regaling the people with political gasconade and personal abuse of the opposing politicians. On the President's side were Polk, Grundy, Cave Johnson, and Judge Catron, assisted by many lesser lights who followed their directions. Opposed to them were White, Bell, Peyton, and Foster, aided by a much longer and much abler list of second-rate assistants than could be rallied to the Jackson standard.

The most serious handicap with which the administration leaders had to cope was the want of an influential press. The Nashville *Union,* which had been founded after Bell had obtained control of the other Nashville papers, had never prospered, and was now in the final stages of bankruptcy. Long, the proprietor, had given up in despair and gone to Athens in East Tennessee to edit an obscure Van Buren sheet of precarious existence.[21] Due to drink, Laughlin, the editor of the *Union,* had become so unreliable that Catron, in the heat of the campaign, was forced

---

[19] Boston *Age,* Aug. 17, 1836; copy among *Polk Papers.*
[20] Laughlin to Polk, Aug. 8, 1836, *Polk Papers.*
[21] Long to Polk, Aug. 21, 1836, *ibid.*

to come to the rescue and edit the paper himself.[22]   The Washington *Globe* devoted considerable space to political affairs in Tennessee. It tried to convince the people of the state that White could not by any possibility be elected, and that his nomination had been the work of instruments of Clay and Calhoun, who were conspiring against Jackson and Van Buren and attempting to deceive the people of Tennessee.[23]   Bell, of course, was charged with being the chief conspirator. ''It is painful,'' said the *Globe* on October 7,

> to a fair mind to deal with petty tricks—the offspring of low cunning— of a man educated as a pettifogger, and improved into a political Machiavel by a persevering study of the arts of deception in a seven years' apprenticeship in Congress. John Bell has arrived at a point which entitles him to a diploma as a political imposter

who is trying to deceive the people of Tennessee. As examples of Bell's hypocrisy, it cited his original opposition to White and his attempt to induce R. M. Johnson to run for President on a bank platform.

Much emphasis was placed on White's alleged affiliation with friends of the United States Bank. Bell's ''Cassedy letter'' was said to have pledged White, in the event of his election, to sign a bill for rechartering the bank. In several letters, Van Buren had already stated his unalterable opposition to such an institution, and by so doing furnished an excuse for the catechizing of his rival. In a letter addressed to him by one of the local Democrats, White was asked the definite question whether he, if elected, would sign a bill to establish a bank of discount and deposit, or one of deposit only. It was hoped that the letter would place the judge in an embarrasing position, but this hope was not realized. He met the issue squarely by stating that, while he considered the bank question to be obsolete, he would nevertheless give his

---

[22] After the campaign was over Catron, in a letter to Polk (Nov. 24) said that, while he hated to desert a man for ''that infirmity,'' they must have a reliable èditor.

[23] Washington *Globe*, Aug. 27 and Sept. 5, 1836.

views on the subject. He had always believed, he said, that Congress did not possess the power to authorize any bank to transact business within the states; moreover, even if the power existed, it should not be exercised. This was still his opinion.[24]

In a speech delivered at Knoxville in August, White had already given a very complete statement of the principles for which he stood. He enumerated the doctrines which had been advocated by himself and the President at the time of the latter's first election. For advocating these same doctrines, said he, the President is now "openly denouncing me as a 'red hot Federalist,' having abandoned his Administration and being as far from him as the poles are asunder." The judge claimed to uphold the Republican creed of Jefferson, while the President is on "that side which leads directly to monarchy, although I hope he does not so intend it."[25]

Not even Jackson could shake the faith of Tennesseans in the ability and the integrity of Judge White. Even though the motives of his leading supporters may have been somewhat questionable, nothing that was ignoble or equivocal could be traced to White himself. He carried the state in spite of the misrepresentations of his traducers, and never again during the life of the "hero of New Orleans" was Tennessee to be found in the Democratic column at a Presidential election—although one of her own sons was the candidate in 1844.

The President was greatly mortified by the loss of his state. He declared that White had always been a hypocrite, and that the "morals of society" demanded his exposure.[26] But the mote in

---

[24] Andrew A. Kincannon to White, Sept. 14; White to Kincannon, Sept. 19, 1836, *Polk Papers.*

[25] Speech printed in Scott, *Memoir of Hugh Lawson White*, 346 ff. Excerpts in Washington *Globe*, Sept. 23, 1836.

[26] "Nothing but falsehood appears to be the weapons of our modern new born White Whigs of Tennessee in their late political crusade. White, Bell, Peyton, Murray & Co. appear to have abandoned truth, and now when the election is over, does not wish to be held accountable for their falsehoods . . . should I live to get home, a duty I owe to truth & the morals of society will induce me to expose Judge White, Mr. Bell, Mr. Peyton,

his brother's eye obscured the huge beam in his own own; his unfair treatment of White had been the determining factor in making the Judge a candidate and in winning for him the electoral vote of the state.

Congress reassembled on December 5 and, on the following day, received the last annual message of General Jackson. This document criticized the operation of the deposit act passed at the last session and advised the adjustment of revenue to the actual needs of the government. It informed Congress of the promulgation of the "specie circular" and asked that the policy therein adopted be made permanent by legislative enactment. It urged that the finances of the government should be put on a hard money basis. The tone of the message was optimistic, and indicative of the satisfaction felt by the President with the results of his administration. It contained no hint that he even suspected the country to be already on the verge of one of its most disastrous industrial and financial crises.

To carry the administration program through the House was a task of little difficulty for the Speaker. Polk arranged his committees on a political basis, and there was a safe majority in that body to insure the passage of desired measures. It required both skill and patience, however, to preserve order and to render harmless the assaults of an opposition whose animosity had not been lessened by their recent defeat at the polls.

Early in the session there appeared a new avalanche of memorials in which Congress was asked to abolish slavery in the District of Columbia. Generally, but not always, they were presented by John Quincy Adams. Polk decided that the "gag rule" had

---

Mr. Murray, and their falsehoods, so that the moral part & truth loving portion of the citizens of Tennessee may judge what credit can be reposed in those men, when they make assertions as to the acts & doings of others. I now believe that Judge White has been acting the hypocrite in politics, all his life, and individually to me—that he is unprincipled & vindictive I have full proof—that he will willfully lie, his Knoxville speech amply shows. I can forgive, & will, but I never can forget hypocrisy, or the individual capable of it" (Jackson to Rev. H. M. Cryer, Nov. 13, 1836, *Am. Hist. Mag.*, IV, 242–243).

expired with the last session, and so the whole question was once more open for discussion. After several heated debates, the rule was reënacted in an aggravated form which sent all such petitions to the table as soon as presented, without even the courtesy of a reference to a committee. Southern members looked upon these petitions as the work of fanatics[27] whose sole purpose was malicious mischief. They failed to realize that abolition was simply one among the many manifestations of the birth of a public conscience and of a desire to reform the world. The old idea that governments should not abridge personal privileges, even by eradicating admitted evils, was, during this period, rapidly giving way to a new belief that society as well as individuals possesses rights, and that governments are in duty bound to protect them. It was a period among which "isms" of various sorts flourished, and among the number, *abolitionism.* The most important and permanent product which resulted from this social unrest and striving for the ideal was the emergence of a public conscience and a determination to adjust individual conduct to the standards of public opinion. A feeling of responsibility for existing evil led the troubled conscience to seek power to eradicate it, and in seeking the necessary power the reformers naturally turned to the federal government. Calhoun understood the changed viewpoint far better than did his contemporaries. He realized that, on the subject of slavery, a national conscience had developed, although he may have exaggerated the part played in this development by the Nullification proclamation of General Jackson.[28]

---

27 "Abolition," said Bynum, of North Carolina, Jan. 9, 1837, "is priestcraft [i.e. New England clergy], concocted and brought into existence by their unholy alliance with the superstitious and ignorant of both sexes."

28 Speaking in the Senate on the Oregon bill, Aug. 12, 1849, Calhoun said: "The abolition of African slavery in its old form in the British West India Islands, and the long and violent agitation which preceded it, did much to arouse this feeling at the North, and confirm the impression that it was sinful. But something more was necessary to excite it into action,—and that was, a belief, on the part of those who thought it sinful, that they were responsible for its continuance.

"It was a considerable time before such a belief was created, except to a very limited extent. In the early stages of this Government, while

The enactment of gag rules resulted in more harm than good to the cause which they were intended to benefit. Many who had little sympathy with abolitionists disapproved of this drastic method of stifling public opinion. They regarded the gag laws as a fatal blow to the right of petition, although it is difficult to see why the southern members were not right in their contention that this right extended only to those who would petition about their own grievances, and not those of other persons. The right of the people to petition for a redress of their own grievances was never questioned by the most belligerent of the southern fire-eaters.

Polk was a slaveholder, but he did not let this fact influence his decisions. When objections were raised because Adams insisted upon presenting petitions from states other than Massachusetts the Speaker decided, on February 6, 1837, that "every member had a right to present a petition, come from what quarter it might." Adams thereupon informed the Speaker that he had a petition purporting to have come from slaves and asked if it would fall within the regular rule. The character of the petitioners presented a new point in procedure, which Polk did not attempt to decide; instead, he asked for a ruling by the House. Without seeking to ascertain the nature of the petition—which

it was yet called, and regarded to be, a federal Government, slavery was believed to be a local institution, and under the exclusive control of the Governments of the States. So long as this impression remained, little or no responsibility was felt on the part of any portion of the North, for its continuance. But with the growth of the power and influence of the Government, and its tendency to consolidation,—when it became usual to call the people of these States a nation, and this Government national, the States came to be regarded by a large portion of the North, as bearing the same relation to it, as the counties do to the States; and as much under the control of this Government, as the counties are under that of their respective State Governments. The increase of this belief was accompanied by a corresponding increase of the feeling of responsibility for the continuance of slavery, on the part of those in the North who considered it so. At this stage it was strengthened into conviction by the proclamation of General Jackson and the act of Congress authorizing him to employ the entire force of the Union against the Government and people of South Carolina." Having discovered the extent of *national* power, said Calhoun, the abolitionists have, since 1835, been striving to bring it into operation (Calhoun, *Works*, IV, 517–521).

turned out to be a hoax, and asked for the expulsion of Adams— southern members wasted much time in an intemperate tirade against the venerable ex-President. They at first demanded his expulsion, and, failing in this, asked that he should be censured "for giving color to an idea" that slaves might address a communication to Congress. After Adams had riddled their arguments with sarcasm and ridicule, the House finally ended the matter by deciding simply that slaves had no right to petition. The charge made by Adams that Polk had exercised arbitrary authority in his decisions on the subject of petitions seems to have been wholly unwarranted, for the Speaker accorded him every privilege which the rules of the House permitted.[29]

The Speaker's enemies tried on many occasions to confuse him by propounding unusual and complicated questions, but in this they were invariably disappointed. His thorough knowledge of parliamentary procedure, and his ability to anticipate their designs and to prepare for them, enabled him to render his decisions promptly and correctly. Never frustrated, he was quick to see the bearing of an unusual proposition.[30] Although he safeguarded the interests of the administration whenever possible, yet his rulings were sustained—almost without exception, by a considerable number of his political opponents.

The most severe charge which was brought against Polk during the session arose out of the investigation of Reuben M. Whitney's connection with the Treasury Department. It was alleged that Whitney had given out advance information to speculators

---

[29] Polk's opinion of Adams' conduct and his complaints is recorded in an undated manuscript in the *Polk Papers*. It is an answer to letters written by Adams to the Quincy *Patriot*. "The Speaker carries out and enforces the decisions of the majority & therefore he represents in his letter that the 'Speaker and the majority of the House' have undertaken to exercise 'arbitrary authority.' If Mr. Adams is unwilling to submit to the decisions of the majority of the House, he is unfit to be a member of that body. . . . His complaints that his petitions were not read,— shows either a total ignorance of the rules of the House, or is an attempt to impose on the public" (*Polk Papers*, undated, vol. 80).

[30] For example, Bell's motion of January 10 for leave to bring in a bill to secure freedom of elections.

regarding the purport of Jackson's specie circular, and that he had been a partner in the resulting speculations. It was said, also, that he had levied blackmail upon the state banks which had been selected as depositories for government funds. A majority of the committee which Polk appointed to investigate these charges exonerated Whitney, but, in a minority report, Peyton, of Tennessee, accused the Speaker and the majority of the committee with having deliberately covered the fraud out of subserviency to the President. Nothing better, he said, could be expected from a Speaker who had crawled up to his office and had exchanged principle for power.[31] Even if these charges had been true, Peyton was not the man to throw stones. Hamer, of Ohio, forced him to admit that he had himself solicited for Bell the support of the President on the plea that Bell was a good party man and that Polk had been seeking votes from the Nullifiers.

The short but stormy session was adjourned by the Speaker on March 3, 1837. Although Polk had been severely criticized by some of his enemies, no one—as was done two years later—refused to join in extending to him the customary vote of thanks. The administration and its defenders had been denounced in violent language for alleged interference in elections, abuse of the power of patronage, and derangement of the finances of the country. Investigations had been demanded, and in some cases undertaken, but the charges had not been sustained. Indeed, so long as Polk had the selection of committees, there was small danger that any malfeasance would be *officially* unearthed.

For good or for evil, General Jackson had triumphed over all opposition. Van Buren had been chosen to succeed him, Taney

---

31 "The *price*, in *these days*, which must be paid for *power*, is the *sale* and *prostration* of *every principle* of *honor, patriotism, independence;* and I fear, sir, the day is distant when we shall see the *Speaker* of an *American Congress* dare to appoint investigation committees, a majority of which will be in favor of inquiry, how important soever it may be to the *preservation* of the *institutions* and *liberties* of *this country.* . . . Any man who *crawls* up to that point [Speakership] in *these days,* will never hazard the *consequences* of a *patriotic,* a *generous,* or a *noble* action; it would be fatal to him." March 1, 1837 (*Cong. Globe,* 24 Cong., 2 sess., App., 349–359).

had been confirmed as Marshall's successor, the mortifying censure of the Senate had been expunged, and the Bank of the United States no longer existed as a federal institution. On the last day of the session Congress passed an act which not only carried out another of the President's wishes, but which affected materially the future career of the Speaker of the House. Incorporated in the civil appropriation bill was a clause providing for the outfit of a minister to Texas, which meant, in effect, a recognition of Texan independence. The already approaching financial crisis made Congress unwilling to continue by law the policy of the specie circular, as Jackson had recommended in his message; instead, that body sent him, on the last day of the session, a bill which would virtually annul the celebrated circular. But even in this, "Old Hickory" had his way. He declined to sign the bill on the ground that its provisions were obscure and contradictory.[32]

---

[32] Richardson, *Messages*, III, 282.

CHAPTER VII

SPEAKER OF THE HOUSE UNDER VAN BUREN

Judge White's victory in Tennessee humiliated, and for the time being discouraged, the Democrats of that state. Before the winter had passed, however, their hopes revived and they began to lay plans for the future. They were encouraged by the belief that White would never again be a candidate and that the main cause of defection would therefore be removed. In a letter to Polk, Nicholson said that the opposition leaders were determined to hold the state, and would do all in their power to injure Van Buren. But the people, said he, had gone over to White for purely personal reasons and would return to the Democratic fold.[1] Childress, also, had hopes that the people would renew their allegiance. He believed, on the other hand, that the leaders of the White party would vote for "Theodore Dwight himself" if he were run on the opposition ticket.[2] Still another informant discovered that the White faction was plotting to get control of the legislature for the purpose of ousting Grundy from the federal Senate. They were planning, he thought, to run Bailie Peyton for Governor; and should this be done, no one except Polk or Jackson could defeat him.[3] At the Hermitage Jackson was busily engaged in repelling slanders invented and circulated by the Whigs. One of these slanders was that, as a result of endorsing notes for relatives, the General had become financially ruined and now wanted a national bank. Protesting that he never had and never would favor a bank, Jackson announced his intention

---

[1] Nicholson to Polk, Jan. 22, 1837, *Polk Papers.*

[2] Childress to Polk, Feb. 17, 1837, *ibid.*

[3] J. H. Talbot to Polk, April 21, 1837, *ibid.*

to prepare an article on the subject which he desired Polk to see before its publication.[4]

Democrats were united in their desire to regain control of the state, but opinions differed as to the better method of procedure. Grundy advocated a conciliatory attitude toward the White supporters; this policy was adopted, and was voiced by John O. Bradford, the new editor of the Nashville *Union*.[5] But the seceders did not respond to kind treatment. Dunlap was badly beaten in his campaign for reëlection to Congress, and his district sent only bank supporters to the state legislature.[6] Cave Johnson was likewise unexpectedly defeated by an opponent who was as "bitter and malignant" as John Bell.[7] The result of the election caused a tempest at the Hermitage. Still blind to the real cause of the dissensions within his party, Jackson, in characteristic fashion, denounced the temporizing policy of Grundy and the *Union*.[8]

The outcome of the state elections and the fact that the sub-treasury plan was unpopular in Tennessee[9] led Catron and

---

[4] Jackson to Polk, May 22, 1837, *ibid.*

[5] Catron to Polk, July 7, 1837, *ibid.*

[6] Dunlap to Polk, Aug. 7, 1837, *ibid.*

[7] Johnson to Polk, Aug. 7, 1837, *ibid.* One gets an interesting glimpse of the prevailing professional ethics from his remark that he is going to Mississippi to practice law, for "I cannot charge my friends & my enemies will not employ me." In another letter to Polk, August 14, Johnson tells a story which indicates that election methods in his day were not unlike those of our own: "I was beaten in the last two days by the almost united action of the merchants & iron makers—who as if by concert upon my leaving a county for the last time went to work, under the pretence of collecting their debts, telling the people that they would be compelled to collect in gold & silver if I were elected—the price of property be reduced to almost nothing and the people ruined. Some of the iron makers, told their workmen, that they could not be employed if I was elected."

[8] "Davidson [County] has resulted as I expected, from the imbecile councils, of the Nashville politicians. The Union has been Muzzled by some unseen hands, and has been a great help to the enemy instead of benefit to the republican party. Mr. Grundy will feel the effects, of the combination, which has been produced by supineness & want of courage" (Jackson to Polk, Aug. 6, 1837, *Polk Papers*).

[9] James Walker informed Polk on August 27 that if the Van Buren administration should adopt the sub-treasury plan, it would find itself in

other prominent Democrats to believe that the state could never be regained by pursuing Grundy's conciliatory policy. It was a battle of numbers against wealth, said Catron,[10] and war to the knife was therefore the true Republican policy. He favored the sub-treasury plan, for "the Treasury is the arm of power" and must not be placed in private hands; the possession of government money by private banks "will convert the keepers into Federalists in principle & practice in a few years." Unlike Jackson and Van Buren, he advocated the emission of paper money by the Treasury, for the people want it and "numbers will govern in fact, in Congress, & out of it." Although he approved in general the idea of a sub-treasury, still, after reading the new President's message on the subject, he pronounced the plan there suggested to be sound in principle, but hardly possible in practice. The people, he said, demanded something more tangible, and unless provision were made for issuing paper money, the party would surely go down to defeat.[11] "Strike boldly," was his advice to Polk, "it is your habit, & the means of your elevation; it is expected of you."[12]

The echo of Jackson's farewell address had scarcely died away before the long-gathering financial storm burst upon the country, leaving in its wake the wrecks of shattered banks, ruined business enterprises, and a panic-stricken people. So desperate were

---

the minority in Tennessee, as the plan was too unwieldy and costly. White, he said, had announced that he was not opposed to a bank located in the District of Columbia, with branches in the states. Walker thought that this idea would win in Tennessee if states instead of individuals were made stockholders (*Polk Papers*).

[10] "Open war, & to the knife, has ever been the course for the Republican side—no other position is left for it, nor has there been, since the days of Jefferson. It is the contest of Wealth against numbers; sapped by the statutes of descents when wealth consisted of Estates: but the European policy is here basing itself upon *incorporated* & merchantile wealth" (Catron to Polk, Sept. 2, 1837, *ibid.*).

[11] Catron to Polk, Sept. 10, 1837, *ibid.*

[12] "Go in for 30 or 40 millions, to be circulated fast as may be by the Govt—go for 20ties & over in gradations of tens. Strike out the interest feature—boldly declare that the farmers will hoard the notes bearing 5 per cent" (Catron to Polk, September 27, 1837, *ibid.*).

financial conditions that Van Buren felt constrained to convene
the twenty-fifth Congress in extra session on September 4, 1837,
for the purpose of laying before that body his plans for relief.
His principal recommendation was the establishment of a sub-
treasury; for experience had shown, he said, that depositing public money in state ·banks was little better than leaving it in the
hands of the federal bank. The only safe custodian of the public
funds was, in his opinion, the government itself. As a temporary
remedy, he advised Congress to withhold further deposits with the
states under the distribution act, and to authorize the emission of
treasury notes. Although his recommendations were straightforward and sensible, they were, for that very reason, unlikely
to be followed. Even the members of his own party were divided
in opinion concerning the cause of the trouble, consequently they
did not agree on remedies to be applied. Catron, as we have seen,
was an advocate of paper money, while Jackson and the President
still believed in hard money. Jackson received advance information concerning the character of the message and was delighted
with the news that the President would recommend a separation
of government finances from all banks, and the collection of public
revenues in gold and silver coin.[13]

The members of Congress who had striven so hard to defeat
Van Buren at the polls were not disposed to aid him now by
sympathetic coöperation. In the House they were far more
intent upon making life uncomfortable for the Speaker and the
President than they were on relieving the financial stress of their
fellow-citizens. It was known, of course, that Polk would be
reëlected, and before the ballot had been taken, Mercer, of Virginia, proposed to transfer from the Speaker to the House itself
the power to appoint committees. While the suggestion was not
adopted, Mercer had the satisfaction of insulting Polk by implying
that he could not be trusted. On the other hand, Patton, of
Virginia, wished to have the rules so amended that the Speaker

---

[13] Jackson to Polk, Aug. 6, 1837, *ibid.*

might have a vote on all questions, but his amendment was rejected by the House. As most of the business of the session would necessarily pass through the hands of the Committee of Ways and Means, Polk safeguarded the interests of the administration by selecting seven of its nine members from the ranks of his own party.

Although the President, when convening Congress, had definitely limited the scope of legislation, Adams was more terrified by the possible annexation of Texas than he was by the magnitude of the financial crisis. On September 13, he moved to ask the President whether Texas had offered to join the United States, and, if so, what had been the reply made by our government. Any proposition to annex it, declared Adams, would be unconstitutional—one which neither the President nor Congress "had any right to receive, entertain or consider." It was his firm opinion that "a very large portion of the people of this country, dearly as they loved the Union, would prefer its total dissolution to the act of annexation of Texas." The House, on September 18, curtailed his dissertations on the subject by passing a rule which limited discussions to questions included in the President's message. Adams tried by various devices to inject the subject of Texas into later discussions, but Polk rigorously enforced the rule just adopted.

The rule for limiting discussion did not deter Wise from offering a resolution which provided that a committee be chosen by *ballot* to investigate the causes, delays, and failures of the Florida war. Adams approved this method of selecting committees, for, said he, experience had proved that no real investigation would be prosecuted by any committee selected by the present Speaker.

Having failed in his attempt to deprive the Speaker of the power to make appointments, Wise welcomed the appearance in the House of the Senate bill for creating a sub-treasury. This subject gave him an opportunity to vent his wrath and sarcasm not only upon the "Greatest and Best," as he called General

Jackson, but upon Van Buren and Polk as well. The late and present administrations, he said, "have deliberately and wickedly, with malice aforethought, wrought this mischief" and should be indicted by the people for their crimes. He took special delight in reading one of Jackson's messages which had incorporated a part of Polk's report—as chairman of the Committee of Ways and Means—highly commending the safety and efficiency of state banks. And now we read in the message of Van Buren, shouted Wise, "that *the experiment has failed*"—the great chief, whom all had been taught to regard as a god, was after all a weak mortal whose wisdom was as fallible as that of other men.[14]

Little was accomplished during this brief session. The subtreasury bill was defeated, and Congress contented itself with the enactment of emergency measures. The first three installments paid out under the operation of the distribution act were permitted to remain with the states, but the fourth was postponed and never paid. To meet the immediate needs of the government, the President was authorized to prepare interest-bearing treasury notes to be issued to an amount not exceeding ten million dollars. Having failed to agree upon any permanent financial policy, Congress, on October 19, adjourned until the regular session in December.

Before Congress had adjourned, the Tennessee legislature met in regular session. Governor Cannon assailed with some vehemence both Jackson and his successor. The Whigs began at once to formulate plans which they hoped might insure Polk's political downfall and prevent the reëlection of Grundy. Some of the Democrats were in favor of silently ignoring their critics, but Polk, who was still in Washington, urged the adoption of an aggressive course and the prevention of the election of a Senator, for the present at least.[15] Before he set out for Tennessee, Polk was authorized by Grundy to withdraw his name, as candidate

---

[14] *Cong. Globe*, 25 Cong., 1 sess., App., 318.

[15] Jonas E. Thomas to Polk, Oct. 5; Polk to Nicholson, Oct. 9, 1837; *Polk Papers*.

for Senator, should it develop that the interests of the administration might be promoted by so doing.[16] Grundy was reëlected,
but not without difficulty, for the ranks of the Whigs were
steadily increasing.

The Democrats were alarmed but not disheartened. A new
editor, Cunningham, was put in charge of the *Union;* for to the
moderation of Bradford, under Grundy's guidance, had Jackson
attributed the recent defeats.[17] Most hopeful of all was Jackson
himself; he prophesied that Tennessee would be ''herself again''
in less than two years, in spite of Bell's New England tour,
which was designed to transfer the state to Webster and the
Federalists.[18]

When the twenty-fifth Congress met in December for its
second session, a rather unusual problem was presented to the
House for solution. It was a question of settling a contested
election of members from Mississippi, and, as the decision ultimately devolved upon the Speaker, Polk incurred the enmity of
Sergeant S. Prentiss, a man quite as venomous as Wise or Peyton,
and far more able than either.

In July, 1837, the Governor of Mississippi had called a special
election in order that the state might send members to the extra
session of Congress which had been proclaimed by President Van
Buren. Claiborne and Gholson, the men chosen at the special
election, were, at the extra session, declared by the House to be
members for the entire term of the twenty-fifth Congress. Notwithstanding this decision of the House, Mississippi held another

---

[16] Grundy to Polk, Oct. 17, 1837, *ibid.*

[17] Although removed for the *moderation* of his editorials, Bradford
was, on the other hand, dropped from the roll of divinity students by
the Whig bishop for being so ardent a Democrat. The incident well
illustrates the political intolerance of the period.

[18] ''The course of Mr. Bell in attending the aristocratic, federal &
shin-plaster meetings in Boston & New York, & his speeches at those
meetings, which is a transfer of Tennessee to Mr. Webster & the blue
lights, abolitionists and vagrants, is working well here—it has opened
the eyes of the democracy of Tennessee, and none of his Whigg friends
here will guarantee the sale.'' Jackson to Grundy, Dec. 16, 1837 (*Am.
Hist. Mag.*, V, 138–139).

election in November and chose for Representatives S. S. Prentiss and T. J. Ward. Claiborne and Gholson were supporters of the administration, and their friends in Mississippi, relying on the decision made by the House, took no part in the November election. As a result, Prentiss and Ward were easily elected. Each side now claimed its representatives to have been lawfully elected and appealed to the House for a decision. After prolonged debate the House reversed its former decision and pronounced the election of Claiborne and Gholson void. It then proceeded to ballot on the validity of the second Mississippi election at which Prentiss and Ward had been chosen. On this question the vote stood 117 to 117. Polk cast his ballot in the negative, and the whole matter was referred back to the people of the state, who later reëlected Prentiss and Ward. The "glorious infamy" which attached to the Speaker's vote against him, Prentiss never forgot. In a flight of oratory he told the people of Mississippi that "the still small voice of James K. Polk deprived you of that which a hundred thousand bayonets could not have forced upon you."[19] On his return to Congress he had the supreme satisfaction, not only of harassing the Speaker on every possible occasion, but of opposing the ordinary vote of thanks to Polk on his retirement from the Speakership.

Slade, of Vermont, precipitated a stormy debate on slavery by presenting, on December 20, two memorials which asked for the abolition of slavery in the District of Columbia. After moving that the memorials be referred to a select committee, he entered into a prolonged and scathing discussion of the slavery question in its various phases. Having recognized the member from Vermont, Polk found it difficult to prevent his continuing, since Slade for some time was careful to keep within the bounds of parliamentary rules. When he finally launched into a discussion of slavery in Virginia, a member entered a protest and

---

[19] Clipping from some Philadelphia paper, dated Feb. 7, 1838 (*Polk Papers*).

Polk ordered Slade to his seat.[20] Wise, Rhett, and other southern radicals were choking with rage. Several exhorted their colleagues to leave the hall in a body. After adjournment a meeting was held, and, although threats of disunion were freely made, few members were ready for so drastic a procedure.

On the following day Patton, of Virginia, introduced, as a "concession . . . for the sake of peace, harmony, and union," a gag rule more drastic than its predecessor. It directed that all petitions on the subject of abolition should be laid on the table "without being debated, printed, read or referred," and that no further action should be taken thereon. The rules were suspended, the previous question invoked, and the vote hurriedly taken. When his name was called, Adams shouted that the resolution violated the federal Constitution, whereupon the Speaker forced him to take his seat. Polk then ruled to be out of order the demand made by Adams that his reason for not voting should be entered in the journal. A few days later, Polk even extended the new "gag-rule," by deciding that a resolution of the Massachusetts legislature asking for a repeal of the gag rule also came under the rule itself and could not therefore be considered.[21]

Sectional feeling was still more embittered during this session by the killing, in a duel, of Jonathan Cilley, of Maine, by another member of the House, William J. Graves, of Kentucky. The demands made upon Cilley by Graves and his second, Wise, were held by many to have been extremely unreasonable. By such members the killing of Cilley was regarded as little better than premeditated murder. The appointment of a committee to investigate the circumstances of the duel with a view to punishing members who had taken part, led to a strange alignment in

---

[20] Polk said that, while his position would not permit him to state his own opinions on such agitation of this question, "they might readily be inferred by the House."

[21] January 3, 1838. Polk seems, however, to have felt that he had gone too far in this matter, for on February 5 he ruled to be in order a petition of similar purport from citizens of Massachusetts.

defense of the participants. Friends of Graves and Wise charged
that Polk had "packed" the committee to the prejudice of the
defendants; while Adams, declaring the investigation to be "an
administration measure," not only condemned the committee for
having prepared an opinion, but objected to receiving their
report. So intense was partisan feeling that Sawyer, of North
Carolina, objected to receiving a message from the President
which arrived while the clerk was reading the report of the committee, but Polk promptly decided that the constitutional right
of the President to send a message to the house at any time
transcended the rule which required unanimous consent to its
reception.

Hectoring of the Speaker continued to the end of the session.
On June 23, Adams reached the climax of absurdity by demanding that Polk should reduce to writing some irrelevant remarks
which Adams had made and which the Speaker had declared to
be out of order. On Polk's refusal, Adams appealed from the
decision. Needless to say, the House sustained the Speaker.

While Polk was successfully parrying the shafts of his enemies
in Congress, his friends in Tennessee were compassing the downfall of Bell, as well as formulating new plans for the Speaker
himself. Donelson was indefatigable in his efforts to *expose* Bell's
treachery. From his retreat at the Hermitage "the chief" forwarded documents to the Speaker and requested him to answer
Bell's charges against himself [Jackson], either in Congress or
through the *Globe.*[22] Desirous of representing Polk's district in
Congress, Nicholson saw in the Speaker excellent Vice-Presi-
ential timber, but Polk was inclined to agree with other friends
that he might be able to accomplish more good in the governor's
chair. Ex-Governor Carroll had announced to Polk his willingness to become once more a candidate for the office, and promised
to handle Cannon "without gloves";[23] but the politicians, fearing that he would be defeated, did not rally to his support.

---

22 Doneldson to Polk, Jan. 4; Jackson to Polk, Feb. 2, 1838; *Polk Papers.*
23 Carroll to Polk, Feb. 17, 1838, *ibid.*

Even before Polk had consented to run for governor, each party was striving to strengthen its own position in the state and to weaken the hold of its opponent. In Boston, C. G. Greene, under Polk's direction, collected evidence to prove that Bell, on his New England tour, had been entertained by Hartford Convention Federalists;[24] while in Tennessee, the Whig legislature instructed Grundy to vote against any sub-treasury bill that might come before the Senate. Although the purpose of this move was to force his resignation, he disappointed the Whigs by promptly announcing that he would obey his instructions. Much Whig literature was franked from Washington. White and Bell scattered widely the speech in which Wise had castigated Polk and the President.

From many sources Polk was importuned to accept the gubernatorial nomination, for it was believed that he could regain the state for the Democratic party.[25] Apparently the office was not attractive to him, yet duty to his party seemed to point in that direction. Late in the summer, after mature consideration, he finally consented to become a candidate. Many letters told him of the good effect which his acceptance had produced. One from Cave Johnson reported that in many places "whole neighborhoods" had returned to the Democratic party.[26]

The Democrats were still embarrassed by the weakness of their local papers, for Cunningham had proved to be quite as unsuccessful a journalist as Bradford. When seeking a more competent editor for the *Union*, Polk offered the position to

---

[24] Green to Polk, Jan. 18, 1838, *ibid.*

[25] One correspondent intimated that prospects of success might be better in the state than in Congress. Polk, he said, would redeem the state if any one could, and "If there is any possible chance of the opposition getting the upper hand in the ensuing Congress, perhaps this course might be the prudent one; as your friends would as soon be annihilated at once, as to see that *most* INFAMOUS OF ALL INFAMOUS PUPPIES, John Bell, triumph over you in a contest for the Speaker's chair. Should the opposition succeed in their views, this must and will be the result, as you are now the most dreaded and consequently the most hated by them" (W. S. Haynes to Polk, July 24, 1838, *ibid.*).

[26] Johnson to Polk, Nov. 2, 1838, *ibid.*

several persons in succession. Among the number were Edmund Burke[27] and C. G. Greene, of Boston. It was Greene, who, when declining the offer, suggested Jeremiah George Harris, then editor of the *Bay State Democrat*.[28] For the Democrats this proved to be a most fortunate suggestion. In Harris they found a man in every way suited to Tennessee politics—one who was more than a match for his adversaries of the quill, with the possible exception of Parson Brownlow. The *Union* was enlarged, and on February 1, 1839, the proprietor, J. M. Smith, introduced the new editor to the people of Tennessee. In the same issue Harris announced his policy: namely, to fight for the principles of Jefferson and his Republican successors, and for the overthrow of ''Federalism'' in the state.[29] A week later Smith reported to Polk that a war of words with Hall, editor of the *Banner*, had already begun and that he [Smith] was much pleased with Harris.[30]

The proprietor of the *Union* had no reason to revise his opinion. Harris launched at once into a campaign of vituperation and merciless denunciation of the Whigs which endeared him to his friends and made him dreaded by his opponents. He was the type of editor in whom the people of the West delighted. He and General Jackson became fast friends, but, in the main, it was to Polk that he looked for counsel and guidance. He plunged with zeal into the campaign against Governor Cannon and announced that ''Tennessee has not seen so proud a day since the election of her own Jackson to the Presidency as will that on

27 Burke was later a Representative from New Hampshire. In 1845, Polk put him in charge of the General Patent Office.

28 Greene to Rives of the *Globe*, Dec. 3, 1838, *Polk Papers*.

29 ''That tory federalism of 1798, Hartford convention federalism of 1814, and 'whig' Federalism of this day are identical, so far as they relate to the two grand party divisions of the country, is too susceptible of the clearest letter of proof to admit of a doubt.''

30 ''Mr. Hall of the Banner has commenced the war with the new editor of the 'Union' and if I am not mistaken he will find that he will have a little more to do than he at present imagines'' (Smith to Polk, Feb. 7, 1839, *Polk Papers*).

which the sovereigns of her soil shall by their unbought suffrage call Mr. Polk to the gubernatorial chair.''[31]

This is not, however, the place for a prolonged discussion of Polk's gubernatorial campaign. Reserving this for another chapter, we may follow his career through his last session as Speaker of the House. Selected by the Democrats for the avowed purpose of bringing Tennessee back into the party fold, Polk, as he called to order the third session of the twenty-fifth Congress, was more cordially hated than ever by Bell, Wise, Prentiss, and other enemies of the administration.

Van Buren's message, which reached the House on December 4, 1838, was optimistic in tone. He informed Congress that the rapid improvement of financial conditions and the resumption of specie payment by the principal banks had proved beyond question that a federal bank is not indispensable. Reiterating the belief that a sub-treasury would prove to be the best agency for collecting and disbursing the public revenue, he again recommended its creation by law. He alluded to Swartwout's defalcation and asked for legislation which would make such peculation in future a felony.

The lawmaking body of the nation paid little heed to the President's recommendations. Jockeying for position suited their present mood far better than constructive legislation. Having made gains in recent political contests, the Whigs had high hopes of carrying the next Presidential election. Without as yet announcing any program for themselves, they employed all of

---

[31] Nashville *Union*, Feb. 8, 1839. In the same issue Harris quoted an article from the Pennsylvania *Reporter* in which that paper urged that Polk should be made Vice-President. Concerning Polk's record the *Reporter* said: ''Knowing that the Bank of the United States was about to bring the whole of its mighty influence to bear against the administration of Gen. Jackson, it was deemed of the highest importance to be well fortified at the point where the attack was to be made, and the chairman of the Committee of Ways and Means, as the financial organ of the administration, became the most important position in the House. Col. Polk's known position in opposition to the re-charter of that institution, his intimate acquaintance with its history and transactions, and his powers as a ready and able debater, recommended him for its occupancy. And well did he justify the confidence so reposed in him.''

their energies in heaping odium upon the administrations of Van Buren and his predecessor. In the House the session was stormy from the beginning. When they could enlist the votes of the so-called conservatives, the Whigs were able to outvote the Democrats, and the task of the Speaker was made still more difficult.

On the second day of the session, and before the President's message had been received, Adams fanned the flame of sectional discord by moving that all petitions, remonstrances, and resolutions, for or against the annexation of Texas, should be referred to a select committee. His resolution was laid on the table by a vote of 136 to 61. His solicitude on this subject proved to be unwarranted, for the President in his message assured Congress that all proposals for annexation had been withdrawn. Adams then submitted a resolution which called for a committee to investigate the controversy of Andrew Stevenson, late Speaker of the House and present minister to England, with Daniel O'Connell, a member of Parliament. This also was sent to the table, but it had accomplished its intended purpose of attaching odium to the administration.

Abolition petitions again made their appearance. The persistence of the reformers aroused the fears as well as the wrath of southern members, and slaveholders required guaranties for the protection of their "peculiar institution." On December 11, Atherton, of New Hampshire, submitted a series of resolutions the purport of which was to declare unconstitutional any interference with slavery either in the states or the District of Columbia, and to reënact the gag rule regarding petitions. After a brief debate these resolutions were adopted by the House. The adoption of the gag rule did not, however, eliminate the slavery question. On the thirteenth, Adams tried to introduce a resolution to the effect that no enactment of Congress could add to or deduct from the powers of Congress which had been conferred by the Constitution. On the same day, Wise offered a series of resolutions which were designed to deprive Congress of all power to interfere with slavery. In both cases permission to introduce the resolutions was denied by the House. While Polk applied the gag rule whenever possible, Cushing, of Massachusetts, won applause from the reformers by forcing the Speaker to decide that a protest against the constitutionality of the gag rule, although itself out of order, must be inserted in the *Journal,* if brought up on the following day in the form of a correction of the minutes.[32]

For the Whigs, the news of Swartwout's defalcation was an unusually sweet morsel, for it gave them an excuse to explore with telescope and microscope the administrations of Jackson and Van Buren. And, as the Democrats no longer had a majority in the House, it incidentally gave them a chance to humiliate Polk by depriving him of the power to appoint the investigating committee. In disposing of the questions mentioned in the President's message, Cambreleng had moved that the part relating to the defalcation be referred to the Committee of Ways and Means, of which he was chairman. On December 21, Garland, of Virginia, moved to amend by referring the question to a select committee of nine to be chosen by *ballot.* In a scurrilous tirade, Wise asserted that any committee appointed by the present Speaker would conceal rather than disclose the facts. He had, he said, been chairman of another committee selected by Polk to investigate the affairs of the General Post Office, and all his efforts to ascertain the truth had been defeated. Kendall, the Post Master General,[33] had declined to furnish information on the

---

[32] Dec. 21, 1838. *Cong. Globe,* 25 Cong., 3 sess., 59.

[33] Wise called Kendall ''the President's *thinking* machine, and his *writing* machine—ay, and his *lying* machine! Sir, if General Jackson had been elected for a third term, one great good would have come of the evil—*Amos Kendall would have been worked to death!* Poor wretch, as he rode his Rosinante down Pennsylvania avenue, he looked like Death on a pale horse—he was chief overseer, chief reporter, amanuensis, scribe, accountant general, man of all work—nothing was well done without the aid of his diabolical genius.'' Shielding Kendall, said Wise, was the more reprehensible because Jackson had so relentlessly pursued Tobias Watkins: ''When the *indictments,* the *prosecutions,* were pressed unrelentingly against poor Watkins—when the Administration was crying,

ground that he was responsible to the President alone, and the
majority of the committee had excluded everything that might
reflect upon the administration. "Now, sir," said Wise to the
Speaker,

I propose to show that *your* committee obeyed the will of their master.
Yes, as you had done, by *packing* and stocking the committee. It was *your*
committee—peculiarly and emphatically *yours*—its *appointment*, its *conduct*,
its honor or *infamy*, will forever attach itself, sir, to *your name*. In illustrating the conduct of that committee, I could consume days to show how
the plainest and most obvious and undeniable propositions were voted down;
how resolution after resolution, question after question to witnesses, going
into the very vitals of inquiry, were unblushingly rejected and stifled by
the majority of the committee . . . *you*, the Speaker, the President of the
United States, the heads of Executive Departments, *your* committee, and
your whole party, combined and conspired to stifle investigation.

Some of Wise's friends asked him to yield the floor for a motion
to adjourn. He declined on the plea that he might never get it
again, for, said he to the Speaker, "I distrust you, sir."[34] Polk
bore the onslaught with dignity and composure, and without
interference until Wise referred to Benton as the "monster"
who was to perpetuate the present dynasty. On January 8, 1839,
he again assailed the Speaker and compared him to a gambler
who plays with loaded dice.[35]

It was believed by the Speaker's friends that Wise, Peyton,
and Clay were trying to provoke him into sending a challenge,[36]
for the "murder" of Jonathan Cilly had not been forgotten.

Shylock-like, 'my bond, my bond!' against one of Mr. Adams's default-
ers, then 'general and minute inquiries' were not only lawful, but a
duty; but, sir, the moment the band of investigation touched one of *his*
'little ones,' then inquiry was worse than a 'Spanish Inquisition.' "

[34] Dec. 21, 1838. *Cong. Globe*, 25 Cong., 3 sess., App., 386–387.

[35] "My colleague," said he, "wants the committee appointed by
ballot, in order to avoid imputations on the *Speaker;* I want it appointed
by ballot, to avoid the Speaker himself."

[36] According to a story printed in the *Globe*, August 21, 1844, on the
authority of General Jackson, Clay at one time appeared at the bar
of the House and said to Speaker Polk: "Go home, *G–d d–n you, where
you belong!*" In 1844 this ejaculation was made the theme of a campaign song. During a heated debate in the House, Wise shouted to Polk:
"*You are a damned little petty tyrant; I mean this personally—pocket
it!*"

But Polk treated their insults with silent contempt, and by so doing did much to establish a new precedent in such "affairs of honor." His personal bravery was questioned by none except his bitter enemies, and even the impetuous Jackson commended him for ignoring such flagrant indignities.[37]

The committee was chosen by ballot, and, needless to say, a majority of its members were opposed to the administration. The Democrats asked for the privilege of selecting the minority members, but their request was denied. Both majority and minority reports were tabled by the House on February 27, 1839. The investigation had been successful only in intensifying political discord. In a letter to Polk, Jackson asked for an account of the investigation, and expressed the belief that Swartwout could not have invested all of the million and a quarter which he had taken. "Where is the balance?" he asked, "The Whiggs have it."[38] To Grundy he suggested that William B. Lewis and Daniel Jackson, if put on oath, might tell how Swartwout had invested some of his money.[39]

Defalcations had been both frequent and brazen, and their cause, as Underwood, of Kentucky, pointed out,[40] could be traced to Jackson's policy of filling offices with those "whose subserviency to the will of the President, and devotion to the interests of party, constituted their principal recommendation." But undoubtedly Bynum's statement was equally true—that, when demanding that the select committee be chosen by ballot, the Whigs were less interested in political purity than in blasting Polk's prospects in his gubernatorial campaign.[41]

---

[37] Jackson to W. P. Rowles, Aug. 24, 1840. Printed in Washington *Globe*, July 19, 1844.

[38] Jackson to Polk, Feb. 11, 1839, *Polk Papers.*

[39] "I have no doubt," he continued, "if the truth can be reached, that the Whigg merchants of New York hold in their hands of the revenue chargeable to Swartwout, from $600,000 to $800,000 if not more, and it is suggested that he loaned to our little Whigg printer, Hall of the Banner, some thousands." Jackson to Grundy, Feb. 20, 1839 (*Am. Mag. of Hist.,* V, 141–142).

[40] *Cong. Globe,* 25 Cong., 3 sess., App., 375.

[41] *Idem,* 125.

Unquestionably disintegration of the Jackson party was due in part to the jealousy of ambitious politicians who had failed to obtain what they considered to be an adequate reward for services rendered. But there was a deeper cause for defection—one based on the nature and ends of government itself. For example, a man of Bell's type—one who believed in constitutional government, and one whose penetrating mind enabled him so clearly to see the inevitable results of administering the government according to Jacksonian methods—never logically belonged in the ranks of the party which followed so loyally the dictates of the "old hero." Bell, and all others who viewed things as he did, were constitutionalists, and they gravitated naturally to the party which accepted the precepts of Hamilton, Marshall, and Webster. During Jackson's first term, and to some extent during his second, there was much confusion of thought on governmental principles and functions. Admiration for the man had obscured the vision of many who would otherwise have been quick to detect the inherent evils of Jacksonism. By the time Van Buren became President, the personal element had, to a considerable degree, disappeared from politics. In the party realignment which resulted, personal qualities were not entirely ignored; but of far greater importance was the attitude of statesmen and their supporters toward the fundamentals of government itself. On this question the issue was clear cut.

Several speeches delivered during this session show that their authors fully understood the nature of Jacksonism and its paralyzing influence upon constitutional government. The President in his message had attributed the success of our institutions to the "constant and direct supervision by the people over every public measure." With this as a text, Bell assailed the "democratic tendencies" of which the administration boasted, and made an ardent plea for a return to constitutional government:

The People are told that our ancestors, who framed the Constitution in 1789, were half a century in the rear of the improvements of the present age; that they had not the benefit of the new lights which experience has shed upon the subject of government since that time, and which are now in full blaze around us. The science of government, we are told, has made great strides since our Constitution was framed; and, in deed, that instrument is beginning to be looked upon by many rather as a device of bad men, to advance the interests of the few at the expense of the many, and forming an actual obstruction to that full tide of happiness and prosperity which awaits us when the inventions of modern democracy shall be substituted for it. At all events, it is proclaimed to be the duty of every man who would improve the condition of the human family to strengthen the democratic tendencies of the Constitution, and to disrobe or rather strip it of those limitations and restrictions upon the popular will, with which our unimproved ancestors have thought it necessary to encumber it. . . . In truth, sir, it cannot be disguised that there are a class of politicians in the country at this moment, whose aspirations it does not suit that any restriction, any limitation whatever, shall exist in the practice of the Government upon the will or absolutism of the majority; and, in the estimation of all their followers, our Constitution is defective.[42]

Deploring the attempt to bring about more immediate control by the people, Bell boldly asserted that

according to our system, the People do not, and cannot, exercise any *direct* supervision over any public measure. Their power, their influence, their supervision, can be constitutionally exercised only by petition and remonstrance, and by the utterance of their voice at the ballot-box.

This was but a simple statement of facts; nevertheless, it required temerity to proclaim such a truth in the face of clamor for the exercise of popular will. To Van Buren's declaration that the extension of practical democracy had strengthened the Union, Bell replied that never before had there been such a relaxation of all ties which bind society together.[43] The power of the people, he said, had not in reality been increased, for party discipline had deprived them of all voice in public affairs.[44] The

---

[42] Dec. 26, 1838. *Cong. Globe*, 25 Cong., 3 sess., App., 360–361.

[43] ''At no former period has so general a spirit of opposition to legal restraints or requirements manifested itself throughout the country, when they stand in the way of wilful passions or purposes of any kind. Slight regard for the Constitution and laws, commencing with the Government itself and its administrators, has gradually diffused itself over society.''

[44] ''Such is and has been the power of party discipline—such the despotic principle of party association for years, that the mass of the community have rather stood in the relation of subjects to be governed than the controlling elements of power.''

truth of this statement, however, only made more deplorable the fact that the party which Bell himself had helped to organize should keep up the fiction of popular sovereignty, and even outdo their opponents in catering to the passions of the multitude.

When discussing an appropriation bill, on February 19, 1839, Kennedy, of Maryland, diverged from his subject to give a critical analysis of Jacksonism and to point out its disastrous consequences. Jackson, he said, had been singularly unlucky as a reformer, although he had been an innovator ''in the broadest and worst sense'':

> His administration was one ceaseless change: change, sometimes stealing along in noiseless advance, sometimes bursting forth in bold, open-day achievement; one while sweeping with the breath of spring, at another with the rage and havoc of the tornado. We had ever change of men, change of measures, change of principles. . . . The pervading characteristic of that most anomalous and extraordinary administration was mutation—uncertainty—experiment. It lived in perpetual motion, defying all hope of repose; it rejoiced in turmoil, and revelled in paradox. . . . The idea of political consistency never entered the President's head—he had no perception of the meaning of the term.

Jackson's idol, continued Kennedy, was popularity, and whatever sustained popularity constituted the theory of his conduct. It was not that wholesome popularity based on services rendered, ''but a domineering, wayward, arrogant popularity—an impatient, hectoring assumption of the right to lead, which repudiates all law, despises all observance, and maintains its supremacy by personal and party force.'' Jackson, said he, used his popularity to increase his power; and, in turn, he used that power to increase his popularity.[45]

---

[45] ''The very boldness of his designs seemed to fascinate the public admiration: he dazzled the popular mind by that fearlessness which we were, for a time, accustomed to interpret as a proof of his honesty and uprightness of purpose. . . . . He flattered the People with the address of a practiced courtier, startled and amused them by the thunderclaps of his policy, identified his success with the gratification of their favorite passions, grappled himself with wonderful adroitness to the predominant sentiments, wishes, and prejudices of the great and massive majority—

On February 22, Slade, of Vermont, obtained the floor for the purpose of discussing the general appropriation bill. His time was mainly occupied, however, in a masterful arraignment of Jackson and Van Buren, and of their methods. He attributed the gift of prophecy to Benton, Van Buren, and R. M. Johnson, who, in 1826, had reported to the Senate on the evils of executive patronage. Patronage, they said, would inevitably lead to one man power. By exchanging patronage for votes the President would soon control not only both houses of Congress, but the entire country.[46] "What was prophecy in 1826," said Slade, "has become history in 1839."

Under the caption of the "Pretensions of Democracy," he contrasted the now obsolete Republicanism of Jefferson with

---

and became a monarch, an autocrat, by the sheer concentration of republican suffrage."

Having discussed in detail the methods by which Jackson had arrogated all authority to himself while professing reverence for the Constitution, Kennedy depicted most admirably the effect of Jacksonism, not alone upon the character of the government, but upon society itself. It led not merely to corruption in official circles, but it demoralized the masses, as well. "We lived," said he, "in the midst of convulsions. The public taste was vitiated and fed by the stimulus of constantly recurring political eruptions; it delighted in strange conjectures—the heavings and spasms of that capricious power which displayed itself in such fantastic action at the capital. A spirit of insubordination, of misrule and riot became diffused through the community. Wild and visionary theories of political duty were disseminated abroad and showed themselves, in the most mischievous forms, in the proceedings of the State Legislatures. The most abstruse and difficult problems of political economy—questions of currency, finance, constitutional power—were summarily but authoritatively disposed of by the shallowest pretenders to statesmanship; and the oldest and best institutions of the country attacked and beaten down by political charlatans. Knowledge, deliberation, experience, all were obliged to give way to this newly-inspired intuition; and the greatest pains were taken by party leaders and demagogues to deceive the people into the belief that the profoundest questions of government might be consigned to the decision of men of the lowest scale of qualification in political science" (*Cong. Globe*, 25 Cong., 3 sess., App., 410–412). The whole speech is well worth reading.

46 "We must look forward to the time when the nomination of a President can carry any man through the Senate, and his recommendation can carry any measure through the two Houses of Congress; when the principle of public action will be open and avowed—the President wants my vote, and I want his patronage; I will vote as he wishes, and he will give me the office I wish for. What will this be but the government of one man? and what is the government of one man, but a monarchy?" Quoted from their report by Slade.

the madness of Jacksonian Democracy—"*the* Democracy," as it is called. Its chief characteristic, said he, is sham, and it relies for its success upon fomenting class prejudice.[47] He read the well-known letter to Monroe in which Jackson urged the President to crush the "monster, party spirit," and contrasted the sentiments expressed in that letter with the practice of the administration of its author. Hypocritical as had been the pretensions to political virtue of those who had brought General Jackson forward for the Presidency, Slade did not believe that even they had fully realized the political debauchery upon which they were entering.[48]

The Speaker, to whom this merciless, but for the most part well-merited, arraignment of Jacksonism was officially addressed, listened, undismayed by the perils which were being depicted. None believed more thoroughly in party discipline than he, and few had been more closely identified with the administrations of Jackson and Van Buren. He had effectively served his party in many capacities, from conducting the bank war in the House down to establishing local party newspapers. His enemies fully recognized his skill as a political strategist, even though they denounced him as the tool of those whom he served.

---

[47] "Thus, the rich are made an object of jealousy to the poor. The laborer is excited against the capitalist—the indolent and improvident against the industrious and frugal—the ignorant against the learned and intelligent—and even the vicious and abandoned against the virtuous and upright. Associated wealth, no matter how widely it may embrace men of small means, is declared to be monopolizing and dangerous. Banks, however prudently and safely managed, are denounced as the money making machines of the wealthy, designed only to make the rich richer and the poor poorer. Factitious distinctions are created. Jealousies are excited. An imaginary aristocracy is raised up in the midst of every community; and nothing can be heard but the war-cry—down with monopolies, and down with the aristocracy."

[48] "It seems impossible they should have dreamed that General Jackson, the author of the noble sentiments I have quoted, could ever be brought to enact, in his own administration, an utter falsification of every profession they contained—a falsification so complete, that there should not be, as in truth, there is not, found a single one of his friends whose face does not crimson with blushes at an exhibit of the contrast" (*Cong. Globe*, 25 Cong., 3 sess., App. 323 ff).

Jacksonism was not without its defenders, although they failed to match their opponents in oratorical powers or in logical arguments. Crary, of Michigan, saw in the Supreme Court a political body "of the worst character," and he commended Jackson for having assumed the right to construe the Constitution as he pleased. As soon as men are elevated to that court, said Crary, they apply themselves to the study of British law and British precedents, and "they cannot be operated upon by the healthy influence of a sound public opinon."[49] Rhett, of South Carolina, said that the country had always been divided into two great political parties—one which feared government and another which feared the people. Inasmuch as strength in the government could be attained only at the expense of popular freedom, he believed, like Jefferson, in restricting the functions of government within the narrowest possible limits.[50]

The entire session was characterized by intense party and personal recrimination. The Democratic party was no longer omnipotent. It was reaping the harvest of its own misdeeds, and, in addition, it was held accountable for the distressed condition of the country, although this had resulted from causes economic rather than political. Hope of success added boldness to the attacks of its opponents. Twelve years earlier, an attack upon Jackson and his policies would have meant political suicide for the assailant; it was now one of the surest means of acquiring popularity.

More than any other member of the House, Polk was given credit by one party, and blame by the other, for the success of the legislative part of the Jackson program. Consequently his adversaries were unwilling to permit him to withdraw from national politics without making one more attempt to humiliate him in the eyes of the nation. They had been unsuccessful in their efforts to confuse him in the complexities of parliamentary

---

[49] *Cong. Globe*, 25 Cong., 3 sess., App., 154.
[50] *Idem*, 134.

procedure. Their insulting invectives and their invitations to
personal combat had been received with a dignity and composure
that did credit to the Speaker. Unable to gratify their desire
to injure the Speaker in a more effective manner, his enemies
resorted to the petty and unprecedented course of opposing the
ordinary vote of thanks on his retirement from office. Prentiss,
who had, at a previous session, been deprived of a seat in the
House by Polk's casting vote, was chief actor and stage manager
in this puerile *opera bouffe*. The resolution which thanked the
Speaker for "the able, impartial, and dignified manner" in which
he had presided over the House, Prentiss moved to amend by
striking out the word *impartial*. Prentiss did not "deny the
capacity of the *Speaker*, his dispatch of business, or his full and
thorough knowledge of parliamentary law," but he could not
agree that he had been *impartial*. He argued that the House
had expressed its distrust of the Speaker by taking from him the
appointment of the Swartwout committee. On the other hand,
he frankly admitted that his main objection to the resolution
was the favorable effect it would have upon Polk's gubernatorial
canvass in Tennessee. The Speaker, he said, was "playing a
political game," in which this resolution would constitute an
important part. Reviewing the personnel of the House committees, he condemned the Speaker for having put on all "political
committees" a greater number of administration men than the
small majority of that party would justify. He charged Polk
with being a tool of the President and of the party. "A more
perfectly party Speaker," said he, "one who would be more disposed to bend the rules of the House to meet the purposes of his
own side in politics, never had pressed the soft and ample cush-
ions of that gorgeous chair."[51]

There was little justification for this intemperate arraignment
and for the conduct of the other fifty-six members[52] who cooperated with Prentiss in opposing the customary vote of thanks.

---

[51] *Cong. Globe*, 25 Cong., 3 sess., 251–252.
[52] The vote stood 94 to 57.

When forming his committees, Polk had simply followed precedent. Many Whigs bore testimony to the justness of his decisions. And yet, he could hardly complain because of this partisan attack, for he had himself, on a former occasion, quite as unjustly accused a Speaker of subserviency to "the throne."[53]

Polk's farewell address to the House, in response to the resolution of thanks just passed, did much to destroy the effect of the shafts which had been hurled at him, and to elevate him in the opinion of fairminded men of all parties. He did not descend to answer the charges made against him or to indulge in recrimination. Without boasting, he alluded to his record of "constant and laborious" service,[54] and to the peculiar difficulties which attach to the office of Speaker. All Speakers. said he, have borne testimony to the impossibility of giving entire satisfaction to all, but

it has been made my duty to decide more questions of parliamentary law and order many of them of a complex and difficult character, arising often in the midst of high excitement, in the course of our proceedings, than had been decided, it is believed, by all my predecessors, from the formation of this Government.

Ignoring the minority, he thanked the majority for the evidence of their approbation. With good-tempered adroitness, he belittled the effect of the negative vote by declaring that he regarded the resolution just passed "as the highest and most valued testimony I have ever received from this House," because, under the circumstances, it was not a mere and a meaningless formality.[55] Many who, for partisan reasons, had voted against the resolution, as soon as Congress had adjourned, hastened to assure the late Speaker of their personal good will.[56] Instead of discrediting

---

[53] See pp. 19–20.

[54] "I can, perhaps, say what few others, if any can—that I have not failed to attend the daily sittings of this House a single day since I have been a member of it [14 years], save on a single occasion, when prevented for a short time by indisposition."

[55] *Cong. Globe*, 25 Cong., 3 sess., 252–253.

[56] The Nashville *Union*, March 22, 1839, quoted a letter from a person who had been present when Polk made his farewell address: "I

the Speaker, the minority had really made him an object of interest throughout the Union. Their conduct was generally condemned, while his dignified reply raised him in the estimation of all except the most zealous partisans.[57] His ability as a presiding officer was made still more apparent during the following session by contrasting him with his successor, R. M. T. Hunter, of Virginia. In the opinion of Cave Johnson, Hunter displayed "ignorance of rules and a want of energy & power to command"; he feared that the House had chosen a boy to do the business of a man.[58] J. W. Blackwell likewise reported that Hunter was too young for the position. "While you were Speaker," said he, "your friends praised, and your enemies abused you, but it is now admitted, on all sides, that Jas. K. Polk was the best presiding officer that we have had for many years, and some say— the best we ever had."[59]

At the close of the session Polk set out for Tennessee to engage in an active campaign for the governorship. After fourteen years of service in the House of Representatives, his party had assigned him duties in a new field of labor. Whatever his success in the new field might be, no one even dreamed that the retiring Speaker would next appear in Washington as President-elect.

---

never witnessed more enthusiasm than the Speaker's admirable reply to the vote elicited. Many of those who had voted in the negative expressed their admiration of it, and gave evident signs of shame and regret at the partisan course they had pursued. Even Mr. Graves, of Kentucky, declared to a friend at his elbow that the Speaker had done as well as any one could do under such circumstances, and stepping forward took manly leave of him—as also did most of the members, a few bitter and envious partisans excepted."

[57] For example, the Worcester (Mass.) *Palladium*, an independent paper, said: "The disreputable conduct of the opposition members of Congress, towards the Speaker of the House, at the close of the session, makes that gentleman an object of peculiar interest, at the present moment, to the whole democratic party of the Union. An effort was made, as violent as it was uncourteous, to prevent the passage of the usual complimentary resolution to the Speaker on his retiring from the Chair. But it was an unavailing effort." Quoted by Nashville *Union*, April 8, 1839.

[58] Johnson to Polk, Dec. 21, 1839, *Polk Papers*.

[59] Blackwell to Polk, Dec. 30, 1839, *ibid*.

CHAPTER VIII

POLK VERSUS CANNON, 1839

In May, 1838, shortly before he consented to become a candidate for the governorship of Tennessee, Polk was examined by a phrenologist, who, unless he had made a thorough study of his client beforehand, made some exceedingly shrewd *guesses*.[1] "He is very quick of perception"; so reads the prepared statement,

when he enjoys, he enjoys remarkably well, and when he suffers, he suffers most intently. . . . His is a remarkably active mind, restless unless he has something of importance to do; cannot be idle for a moment, is by nature one of the most industrious of men; loves mental labour & hard study as he does daily food; . . . and is throughout a *positive* character.

The traits pointed out in another part of the statement are manifest throughout Polk's public career, but especially so during the four years of his Presidency: He

thinks well of himself; often asks advice, & does just as he pleases; is one of the firmest of men; slow in committing himself, but once committed, does all in his power to carry through his measures . . . has many acquaintances, few bosom friends . . . has an astonishing command of *facts* and can call to mind with great precision what occurred long ago.

To those who are familiar with Polk's career in national politics only, one part of the phrenologist's statement might seem very wide of the mark. In it, the phrenologist says that Polk would have succeeded on the stage, for he has ability in the use of pungent sarcasm and ridicule and "could 'take off' the peculiarities of others if he would indulge this propensity." During the campaign which followed, Polk indulged this propensity to the full—especially against his opponent and Bailie Peyton—for ridicule and mimicry were among the chief weapons

---

[1] The phrenologist's name was O. S. Fowler, and the statement which he prepared bears the date of May 30, 1838 (*Polk Papers*).

used in assailing his adversaries. He is usually regarded as "a man who never smiled"; however this may have been, he was very successful in the art of amusing others.

There was rejoicing among the Democrats of Tennessee when, in September, 1838, Polk announced that he would enter the contest with Governor Newton Cannon for the highest office of his state. He received many letters in which the writers expressed their delight, promised support, and assured him of victory. It was the general opinion that he alone could restore the state to the Democratic party. It was, indeed, this belief that induced him to abandon his career in the national legislature. The unholy work of White and Bell must be undone; Old Hickory's state must be redeemed.

While he was still in Washington, presiding for the last time over the House of Representatives, Polk received many letters from Tennessee friends urging him to put the chief emphasis of his gubernatorial campaign on national issues and state internal improvements. It was pointed out that the Whigs would confine themselves almost exclusively to an attack upon the national administration and that the people of the state were much interested in internal development. The advice seems to have accorded with his own views. At any rate the topics suggested were the ones on which he placed the most emphasis.

As stated elsewhere, one of the most important events of Polk's campaign against Cannon was the advent of Jeremiah George Harris as editor of the Nashville *Union*. In response to the popular taste of the period, the press of the state had been notorious for extravagance of statement and personal abuse. It now entered upon a campaign of scurrility and abandon that has seldom been equaled; Mark Twain's employer could scarcely have made his editorials more "peppery and to the point."[2] Equipped with a style that was cutting without descending to mere ribaldry, and with a pen dipped in wormwood, Harris goaded his

---

[2] See Mark Twain, "Journalism in Tennessee," in *Sketches New and Old*.

opponents to a frenzy that was unprecedented. Lacking the
ability to imitate his style, his enemies often resorted to coarse
and vulgar abuse. No Whig editor in the state, except the in-
imitable Parson Brownlow, could cope with him in picturesque
invective. Harris had a spread-eagle woodcut prepared, large
enough to cover a considerable portion of the front page of his
paper. As its appearance in the *Union* was always accompanied
by news of Democratic victory, the Whigs expressed their contempt by calling it "Harris's buzzard."[3]

When Harris took charge of the *Union*, February 1, 1839,
A. A. Hall, of the Nashville *Banner*, was already making capital
of the charge made in Congress, by Wise and others, that Polk
had "packed" the committees of the House. The new editor
plunged at once into a vigorous defense of the Speaker and attributed the charges to jealousy of Polk's success and to a desire
to injure him in Tennessee. When the House voted to select the
Swartwout committee by ballot, the *Banner* exultingly heralded
the event as proof positive that the House, having learned by
experience that "Speaker Polk could not be trusted, proclaimed
the fact to the world."[4]

Some of the other Whig papers were even more scurrilous
than the *Banner*. For example, an article in the Knoxville
Register, signed "Curtius," spoke of Polk as "lost to a sense
of honesty, decency and integrity, laboring under insanity and
disgrace, pliant tool, traitor, apostate and tory."[75] The Memphis
Enquirer called him "a crouching sychophant" who lacked even

---

[3] It was said that a leading Whig, who had gone to the Murfreesborough post-office in quest of election news, saw through the window a
package of *"Unions"* and exclaimed in disgust: "It's all over; there is
Harris's infernal buzzard in the mail" (Phelan, *Hist. of Tenn.*, 381).

[4] "He has been tried by his peers and found wanting. A brand is
upon him that no time can efface. He may cry 'Out d—d spot,' but it
will abide with him for life" (Quoted in Nashville *Union*, February 8,
1839.) When criticizing a speech made by Dr. Duncan, candidate for
Congress, the *Banner* called it "the roaring, staving, bellowing, howling
Doctor's fanfaronade of bombast and nonsense" February 13, 1839.

[5] Quoted in *Union*, March 4, 1839.

the sense of shame.[6] A friend had written to Polk that "your election is dovetailed into that of every candidate for Congress in the State."[7] The Whigs apparently believed this, also, and were resolved at all hazard to defeat him.

In April, 1839, Polk formally opened his gubernatorial campaign by publishing a long and argumentative "Address to the People of Tennessee."[8] The address deals almost entirely with national issues, the nature of the government, and the principles of the two great political parties. It was pronounced by the *Banner*[9] to be "a poor enough concern"; but Phelan, with sounder judgment, has called it "the ablest political document which appeared in this State up to the time of the war."[10] For the student of history, it is one of the most interesting documents ever penned by its author, for in it he has stated fully and with clearness the principles and doctrines which he considered to be essential to all just government. It was evidently prepared with great care, and nowhere else does he give so full a statement of his views on so varied a list of subjects.

---

6 "Condemned and spit upon by a majority of the U. S. House of Representatives, in taking from him [Mr. Polk] the power of appointing committees, freely entrusted to all of his predecessors, but which he basely prostituted for the benefit of the party—of locofocoism—plainly told in language of thundering indignation that has been heard even to the shores of the seas, that he was no longer worthy of the confidence of Congress, like a crouching sychophant, instead of resigning his narrowed trust with shame, and disdaining tamely to see his integrity assailed by even those who exalted him, he submits, ignobly bears the rankling contumely, and in hope of political reward for 'self-sacrifice' upon the altar of loco-focoism, he still patiently ministers at its shrine reeking in corruption with a zeal that can only be inspired by a hope of reward." When quoting this, the *Union* replied in the same issue that "the raving of Mr. Prentiss, the ranting of Mr. Wise, and the management of Mr. Bell in reference to the appointment of the 'Swartwout Committee,' were all calculated for *effect* in Tennessee," and would be so regarded by the people (Nashville *Union*, March 4, 1839).

7 A. Balch to Polk, February 21, 1839, *Polk Papers.*

8 A copy in pamphlet form may be found in the *Polk Papers*, vol. 83. It is printed in full in the Nashville *Union*, April 10, 12, 15, 1839, as well as in other papers.

9 Nashville *Banner*, April 11, 1839. On April 17 the *Banner* called it "an elaborate and ingenious production, but characterized by a want of manliness, candor and sincerity."

10 Phelan, *Hist. of Tenn.*, 381.

In stating his reasons for confining his address so largely to national questions, Polk asserted that the chief objections urged against him were based on the principles and policies which he had upheld as a member of Congress. He gave a historical summary[11] of the perennial contest between those who distrusted and ignored the will of the people and those who believed that government should carry into effect the popular will. The popular party, he said, had triumphed in the convention which drafted the Constitution, but Hamilton and his adherents soon procured by construction what they had failed to have embodied in the Constitution. Democracy triumphed under Jefferson, but under J. Q. Adams the

latitudinarian doctrines, with all the consolidating tendencies of the Hamilton school, as practiced under the administration of the elder Adams, were resuscitated and revived. It was publicly proclaimed that the wholesome restraints of the public will on the action of the servants of the people were to be disregarded, and that the 'Representative was not to be palsied by the will of his constituents.' It was declared by the Chief

---

[11] "In the origin of the Government there were two parties. In the Convention that framed the Constitution one party distrusted the power and capacity of the people for self-government, and wished a strong central government. They admired the British Constitution—they were in favor of a President and Senate for life—they were for forming a strong government, far removed from the popular control; they wished to abstract from the power of the States—to restrict the right of suffrage, and to create other influences than the will of the people to control the action of their public functionaries. This party was not successful in the convention, and a constitution was formed which invested the new government with a few delegated and well defined powers, leaving all others to the States and the people, to exercise according to their sovereign will. The parties in the convention were the germ of the two great political divisions, which afterwards contended, and are still contending for the mastery in the Government.

"No sooner was the government put in operation under the Constitution, than the enemies of popular control over public authority, attempted by a latitudinous construction of the Constitution, to make the government in practice what they had in vain attempted to make it in principle and form. Alexander Hamilton, a professed monarchist in principle, and in the Convention the leading advocate of a strong central government, was the first Secretary of the Treasury, and immediately began, by strained and unwarranted constructions of the Constitution, to enlarge the power and influence of the Federal Government, with the view of diminishing the power of popular will over the administration of the Government." Jefferson himself could scarcely have penned a more telling indictment against the Federalists.

Magistrate to be ineffably stupid to suppose that the Representatives of the people were deprived of the power to advance the public weal, thereby substituting the unrestrained discretion of Congress and of the Federal Government for the specific grants of power conferred by a Constitution of limitations and restrictions.

Polk's recital of historical occurrences was accurate and well put; but it was begging the question to imply, as he did, that the framers of the Constitution had intended that representatives should divest themselves of all judgment and become mere automatons for registering the popular will. Custom and a desire for reëlection may prevent members of Congress from exercising their own judgment, but undoubtedly Adams rather than Polk reflected the views of those who drafted the Constitution.

It was thought by many politicians of both parties that Clay would be the candidate of the Whigs at the approaching Presidential election. Polk, therefore, devoted a considerable portion of his address to Clay and the policies which he advocated. The principal achievements of the Federalist administrations were, in Polk's opinion, the grasping of power by the general government and the creation of the money power. Their successors, the Whigs, likewise stood for these evils, and in addition, had adopted Clay's "miscalled 'American System' of high tariff and internal improvements, the result of which combination would oppress the poor and increase the evils of executive patronage.

The administration of Jackson he eulogized without stint. The adherents of White were told that they had supported the judge because he had been represented to be a better "Jackson man" than Van Buren, consequently there was no reason now why they should not return to the party of the people. It was untrue, said he, that Jackson had changed since his elevation to power; his detractors, not he, had deserted to the enemy. "I," continued Polk,

in common with the whole Republican party, am represented to you as one of these changelings. In what have I changed? I opposed Henry Clay on account of his odious Federal doctrines, and his coalition with

Mr. Adams, and I oppose him still. I opposed the high tariff policy, and I oppose it still. I opposed Internal Improvements by the General Government, and I oppose them still. I supported the removal of the deposits, and I have not changed my language or my opinions in relation to that great measure. In fine, what single point is there, involving the principles of the great Republican party, in which my course has not been uniform since 1825, when I was first honored with a seat in Congress, down to the present day?

From a man who had a reputation for concealing his views, this was certainly a most unequivocal declaration. Moreover, it was a true declaration, and it required courage to make it under the existing political conditions in Tennessee. Whether right or wrong, Polk had not swerved from his original political platform, although many of the policies for which he stood had become unpopular in his state. He may have broken with Judge White for personal as well as political reasons, but on national issues he had been consistent. He pinned his faith now, as he had always done, on government by the will of the majority; and however chimerical this may be in practice, his most private correspondence indicates that his belief in its practicability was sincere. Passing lightly over state issues, he asked for approval or condemnation on his record in national politics—a record which was being grossly misrepresented by the Whig papers of the state.[12]

At Murfreesborough, on April 11, 1839, Polk made his first speech of the campaign. Governor Cannon attended and was invited by Polk to speak first, on account of his age and office. This he declined to do, saying that, although he had not come prepared to speak, he might make a reply. Polk talked for two and a half hours, mainly on national issues and in commendation of the Jackson party. He said little on state issues, of which the *Banner* (April 15) ungenerously credited him with knowing "very little more than the man in the moon."

---

[12] "For months past I have been the unceasing and almost exclusive object of their calumnies and misrepresentation."

Cannon in reply said that *he* had never "clung to the coat tail" of General Jackson, and when "danger approached, jumped into his pocket," but, instead, he had had to "stem the buffetings of his wrath." Before the Creek war, according to his own story, Cannon was a member of a jury selected to try one Magnus on the charge of having murdered Patton Anderson, a personal friend of Jackson. When Cannon voted for acquittal, Jackson, pointing his finger at the young juror, exclaimed, "I'll mark you, young man!" Cannon insinuated, also, that, in fulfillment of this promise, Jackson had, during the Creek war, purposely exposed Cannon and a small detachment of troops to almost certain death, while the General himself remained in safety on the other side of the river. He was a "tyrant by nature and education," and no one could be his follower "who would not be his tool and his slave."[13]

In a brief rejoinder Polk, according to the *Union* (April 12), made the "roof ring" with his "power of ridicule." The *Banner,* on the other hand, reported that "the locomotive candidate seemed to feel deeply that he had caught a *Tartar,*" and that Governor Cannon "triumphantly overthrew" him.[14]

Polk's superiority, both in intellect and debating powers, was apparent from the beginning of the campaign. Cannon was slow and prosaic—lacking in force and personal magnetism. He was unable either to hold the attention or to arouse the sympathy of the multitude. He had until recently professed loyalty to Democratic doctrines, and he still seemed uncertain as to whether he had become a full-fledged Whig.[15] There was, on the contrary,

---

[13] Nashville *Rep. Banner,* April 16; Nashville *Union,* April 12, 1839.

[14] The *Banner* made much sport of Polk's "grins and grimaces" in imitation of Bailie Peyton and Henry Clay. "James K. Polk, the narrow minded, superficial, little, grimacing politician attempting to expand his outward man, gesture and voice into something his hearers might take for *Henry Clay!*" He tried, also, it said, to imitate Webster (*Banner,* April 13, 1839).

[15] In his reply to Polk, Cannon said: "I believe I have always been a Democrat. Indeed, they used to call me an Ultra Democrat, a Radical." He claimed to be a Democrat still, but not in favor of Van Buren (*Banner,* April 16, 1839).

no uncertainty about Polk's views, and he knew how to state them most effectively. He was, says Phelan,[16]

the first great "stump speaker" . . . always full of his subject, ready at retort, sophistical, quick to capture and turn the guns of the enemy against him, adroit in avoiding an issue whose result must be unfavorable, thoroughly equipped with forcible illustrations, humorous anecdotes, and a ridicule which ranged through all the changes from burlesque to wit.

With no pretensions to oratory, his strength lay in his ability to state the issues clearly and forcibly, and to argue these issues in language that was simple and convincing.

On April 13, the candidates met again at Lebanon. On state issues they were in substantial agreement, and once more their time was occupied mainly with a discussion of national affairs. At the close of the debate Governor Cannon, pleading important state business, set out for Nashville. Polk informed his wife that the Governor and himself got on "very harmoniously," but there was little harmony in his relations with Bell.

Polk and Cannon had consumed the entire afternoon, and Bell, who was not expected to take part, took the stump at 5:30 in a "rage of passion." He talked until sunset, and then announced that he would continue at the courthouse after supper. His first address, as reported, was most abusive in character.[17] Polk wrote home that even Bell's friends were disgusted by the speech, and that he had no difficulty, in his reply, in putting Bell in the wrong and winning tremendous applause.[18]

Governor Cannon resumed the debates, at McMinnville, on April 18, but shortly after he retired from the stump entirely. At McMinnville, having been taunted with indecision, he at last

---

[16] *Hist. of Tenn.*, 377.

[17] He said that Hopkins L. Turney, Representative from Tennessee, "was not good enough for the Penitentiary—that Amos Lane was a scoundrel—that Dr. Duncan was a moral pestilence—that these were the tools which Col. Polk set forward to make speeches in Congress, instead of coming out and answering him [Bell] on the floor of Congress face to face" (*Union*, April 17, 1839).

[18] Polk to Mrs. Polk, April 14, 1839, *Polk Papers*.

came out squarely for Clay, in the event of his nomination.[19]
Because Polk had declared here and elsewhere that he and Cannon differed little in their views on state questions, the *Banner*
called Polk a "Government emissary" and regarded it as extremely impudent in him to try to depose the Governor for his
dislike of Van Buren.[20]

The people in those days took keen delight in political campaigns. They attended in large numbers, and no debate was
long enough to be tedious if it were spiced with personal recrimination and with what passed for witty retorts. The popular ear
in Tennessee of that day was not attuned to a very high grade
of humor, while, in argument, pungent thrusts rather than logic
won the sympathy of the audience. The festal side of a campaign
was quite as important as the forensic, consequently political
debates were usually held in open air, accompanied by a banquet
or a barbecue. When Polk reached East Tennessee, the Whig
section of the state, special pains were taken by the Democrats
to give his journey the appearance of a triumphal procession.[21]
Even though he could not hope to gain many votes in this section,
the appearance of popularity in a Whig stronghold might aid him
in other parts of the state.

---

19 Nashville *Union*, April 22, 1839.

20 "Is it not a most impudent, unheard of request, then, on his part,
to the people of Tennessee, that they should turn Governor Cannon out
and put *him* in, all because the Governor is opposed to Mr. Van Buren's
election? Is it not apparent that he is a Government emissary, traversing
the State, county by county, with the sole view of revolutionizing it on
the subject of national politics?" (*Banner*, April 19, 1839). On May 22,
the same paper called Polk a deserter from genuine republican doctrines,
"a political changeling—a weather cock, pointing ever in the direction
from whence comes the breath of the President's nostrils—a devourer,
eater-up of his own sentiments, formerly proclaimed in tones of self-
gratification—a palace slave laborer for his master at Washington."

21 The *Tennessee Sentinel* thus described a Polk meeting at Jonesborough on May 17, 1839: "As a means of enhancing the enjoyments of
the day, suitable arrangements were made for a dinner, free to all of
each party, without distinction, who might think proper to participate."
After dinner there were toasts to Washington, Jackson, Van Buren, Polk,
Amos Kendall, *et. al.*,—and one to "*Newton Cannon*—the friend and
supporter of Henry Clay for the next Presidency. Will the freemen of
Tennessee be thus transfererd by *dictation* from the mouth of any *Cannon?*
Cries of No! No!" Quoted in Nashville *Union*, June 3, 1839.

The political contest was by no means confined to the stump and the platform. Wherever a group of people gathered, issues and candidates were freely discussed. Personal encounters not infrequently resulted[22] when arguments had failed to convince. Despite his surroundings, however, Polk always maintained his own dignity; although his language on the stump was often scathing and exasperating, he never descended to vulgarity or mere personal abuse.

Accuracy was not a desideratum in a political newspaper. That editor was most popular who could hurl grotesque epithets at his opponents and who always reported as well as prophesied victory for his own side. Harris of the *Union* fully measured up to the Democratic ideal,[23] and for this reason his paper wielded great political influence.

In June, A. A. Hall, of the *Banner,* caused consternation in Democratic ranks by quoting anti-slavery articles which had been written by Harris while he edited the New Bedford (Massachusetts) *Gazette.*[24] By befogging the issue and heaping abuse upon his accusers, Harris was quite successful in extricating himself from the difficulty. Nevertheless, the charge that Harris had been an abolitionist did Polk some injury in the canvass, for it was he who had been mainly responsible for bringing the editor to Nashville.[25] In order to divert attention from his own past record and to give new impetus to Democratic enthusiasm Harris

---

[22] For example, Polk's brother-in-law, Dr. Rucker, is reported to have thrashed a ''bully'' whom the Whigs had brought to Murfreesborough to provoke a quarrel with him (John W. Childress to his sister, Mrs. Polk, May 27, 1839, *Polk Papers*).

[23] For example, in reporting a debate between Bell and his opponent, Burton, the *Union* said that Bell abused Van Buren, eulogized Clay and called Polk ''the travelling missionary,'' but Burton ''literally dissected his opponent who has been schooled in the sophistries of partizanship, and laid the diseased limbs of Modern Whigism bare to the bone'' (May 27, 1839).

[24] One of them, dated May 13, 1836, in opposing the annexation of Texas, called slavery ''the blackest, the foulest, blot on our national escutchen,'' and said that it would be ''the height of madness'' to extend it over more territory (*Banner,* June 11, 1839).

[25] John W. Childress to Mrs. Polk, June 18, 1839, *Polk Papers.*

printed in the *Union* (June 24) the "Mecklenburg Declaration of Independence" and suggested its ratification on the Fourth of July. He dilated at length on the fact that Polk had been born in Mecklenburg county—a fact which proved that he had come from pure Democratic stock.

The Whigs hoped for good results from a speech made by Judge White in Knoxville, on the Fourth of July. He still professed adherence to Jeffersonian Republicanism, but denounced the Democrats, whose whole creed consisted in "always acting with the *same man,* or set of men." Far from being democrats they were, said he, "in reality *monarchists.*"[26] Harris was horrified because White had talked politics on the Fourth of July, but concluded from the "claptrap" which the judge had uttered that he must be in his "dotage."[27]

White's warning against monarchists did not produce the effect which the Whigs had anticipated, for Polk succeeded in winning back a considerable number of those who had supported the judge in 1836. Before the close of the campaign he received many letters telling of the good results which his canvass had achieved.[28]

Cannon was easily vanquished, and he retired from the stump, but Bell dogged Polk's footsteps, bringing into full play his great ability and oratorical powers. On July 17 he spoke at Nashville "from early candle-lighting until midnight" in an effort to defeat Polk in Middle Tennessee. He was, however, doomed to disappointment. On August 1 Polk was elected by a majority of three thousand votes, and Harris got out his "buzzard" to adorn the front page of the *Union* along with the election returns. The result of the campaign was justly regarded as a great

---

26 Copied from Knoxville *Times* in Nashville *Banner,* July 18, 1839.

27 Nashville *Union,* July 19, 1839.

28 C. W. Hall, writing from Kingsport on July 12, told him that "one of my neighbors said the other day, 'Sir, I did not understand my political position, until I heard Col. Polk, and I then discovered most clearly, *that I was acting with men, who are opposed to my principles,* and I instantly resolved to quit their company'. . . . This is a common observation" (*Polk Papers*).

personal victory for Polk, inasmuch as the Whigs elected seven members of Congress and the Democrats only six.[29] The Democrats elected a majority of the state legislature, which gave them the power to get rid of the Whig Senators by hampering them with obnoxious instructions.

Up to the very last the Whigs of the state seemed confident of victory. They were reluctant to admit defeat even after the election had been held. But the *Banner*, on August 9, mournfully informed its readers that owing to a lack of proper organization in Middle Tennessee[30] the ''Spoilsmen for a season will have the management of affairs in the State.'' Two days before this, prominent Whigs held a meeting in Nashville. Resolutions were passed urging the organization of committees in every county for the purpose of retrieving the state. They invited Clay to visit Tennessee, but he was unable at the time to accept the invitation. Although the *Banner* from time to time reported enthusiastic Whig meetings, it was several weeks before there were signs of recovery from the shock of the recent defeat.

In their elation over Polk's election, the Democrats rather overrated its significance. It has already been noted that they regarded the result as a personal victory for Polk over his enemies; but, in addition, they interpreted it to mean that Tennessee had returned, or at least was returning, to the party of Jackson and Van Buren. Polk had been nominated for the avowed purpose of regaining the state for the national administration; he had made his canvass almost entirely on national issues; and Bell, as well as others, had opposed him on his record as an administration member of Congress. As his friend Maclin said in a letter, more importance was attached to Polk's success than to the election of any other candidate. There was, in his

---

[29] One of these was Cave Johnson. Writing to Polk on August 11 he said that he had been elected by a majority of 1300 votes, and, as he had entered the race only on account of Polk and Grundy, he expected to retire from politics at the end of his term (*Polk Papers*).

[30] On August 13 the same paper attributed the result to bribery and illegal voting.

opinion, but one thing lacking to make the triumph complete—
namely, the success of Burton over John Bell.[31]

To no one did the national effect of Polk's victory appear of
greater importance than to General Jackson. As soon as the
news reached him, he hastened to congratulate Polk and the
country on his election and "the return of old democratic Tennessee to the republican fold again." With customary hyperbole
he predicted that "it will be at least a century before she will
permit herself to be again duped into her late false position by
such jesuitical hypocrites & apostates as Bell, White & Co."[32]
Polk was doubtless well aware of the program that was to be
carried into effect in the event of his election, and presumably
he aided in formulating it; therefore Jackson did not allude to
it in the letter just quoted. In a letter to Van Buren, however,
the General outlined the party plans in characteristic fashion.
As the Democrats have elected both governor and legislature,
said he,

of course Mr. Foster[33] & his gagg law will not any more trouble the U.
States Senate—Judge White must resign, or he will feel the weight of
instructions & a Senator elected over his head—the precedent set by our
last Legislature will justify this proceedure. My own opinion is, White
will resign—Bell being disappointed in going into the Senate to fill White's
vacancy, which was the price of his apostacy, if he is disappointed in getting into the Speaker's chair, will resign or *cut his throat* in despair &
disappointment; and this catastrophy will end the existance of bluelight
federalism in Tennessee.

For so great a triumph, he gave the principal credit to Colonel
Polk and General Robert Armstrong.[34] As will appear in the

---

31 Sacfield Maclin to Polk, August 10, 1839, *Polk Papers*.

32 Jackson to Polk, August 13, 1839, *ibid*.

33 E. H. Foster was elected to the Senate when Grundy resigned.

34 Jackson to Van Buren, August 12, 1839, *Van Buren Papers*s "I
hope," wrote Richard Warner to Polk, September 29, "we shall be able
to adopt such measures as will compel Foster to give up the seat he and
his friends usurped at the last session." The legislature should instruct
the Senators to vote for the sub-treasury bill. If this does not bring
"poor old White" to his senses, it should then be ascertained whether
he is a Senator at all. (On account of ill health, White had tendered his
resignation to Governor Cannon, but it had not been accepted.)

following chapter, the program here outlined, except the suicidal
rôle assigned to Bell, was carried into successful operation.

When the election took place, the "old hero" was sojourning
at Tyree Springs, in Sumner County. After it had been ascertained beyond question that the state had been redeemed, the
leading Democrats of Middle Tennessee, including Polk, Attorney-General Grundy, Judge Campbell, and General Armstrong,
reported, with their ladies, to that place in order to join with
the General in celebrating the victory. Burdens of state as well
as the infirmities of age were, for the time being, forgotten, and
the company once more indulged in the frivolities of youth.
Each morning, after breakfast, a mock court was held, of which
Grundy was Chief Justice and General Jackson, Associate. From
fines levied by this "court," provisions for the day were supplied—a proceeding which seems to have added much to the
enjoyment of the company.[35]

Polk did not remain long within the jurisdiction of this
improvised court. He soon returned to his home in Columbia
to complete his plans for ousting the Whig Senators, and to
prepare for his inauguration. Unlike many who offered him
advice, Cave Johnson believed that the program of persecution
would do the Democrats more harm than good, and therefore
urged Polk to oppose it. "It is essential," he wrote,

to the existence of our party that every selfish consideration be laid aside
& act in concert & no man can do so much to effect this as yourself. . . .
It has struck me with some force, that *our friends* should go to work &
do the business of the State without the slightest interference with Federal
politics—let White and Foster take their course—go to Washington if
they choose—if Foster adopts that course he is forever disgraced—toward
the conclusion of the Session we can instruct.

He did not "wish our party to have the semblance of coercing
either until it is absolutely necessary." He believed that Foster
would resign even without instructions, but however that might
be, "by all means let the necessity for interference be manifest

---

[35] Nelson, *Memorials of Sarah Childress Polk*, 60–63.

before it is done, rather let it be urged upon the Legislature by the people rather than upon the people by the Legislature.''[36] Johnson's advice may have been prompted by political sagacity rather than by a sense of justice, but whatever the motive his recommendations were good.

As will appear in the following chapter, other counsels prevailed, and the Democrats elected to make the most of their political power. Their choice gave them a temporary advantage, although eventually their unfair treatment of the Whig Senators helped to transfer votes from their own party to that of their opponents.

---

[36] Johnson to Polk, Clarksville, September 28. The year is not given. The letter has been put with the *Polk Papers* for 1838, but evidently it was written in 1839.

CHAPTER IX

GOVERNOR OF TENNESSEE

In accordance with an absurd custom, a governor of Tennessee, in the closing hours of his administration, enacted the solemn farce of submitting to the legislature a message in which he made elaborate recommendations for its consideration. This was done with a full knowledge that within a few days a new governor would be inaugurated and that he, in turn, would present entirely different recommendations.

On October 8, 1839, Governor Cannon submitted his final message to a legislature composed of thirteen Democrats to ten Whigs in the Senate, and forty-nine Democrats to thirty-three Whigs in the lower house. It is unnecessary to dwell on his suggestions concerning state affairs, for, needless to say, no heed was paid to them. For political reasons, however, the Democratic majority in the new legislature felt that his severe condemnation of the national administration merited both consideration and rebuke. Unanswered, the Governor's remarks might tend to influence the wavering, and a refutation would afford another opportunity to herald the glorious achievements of the "party of the people."

Among other things the retiring Governor had expressed a hope that "the country will ere long be delivered from the maladministration of the present rulers, with its pernicious train of experiments and spoliations." This part of his message was referred by the legislature to a "Committee on Federal Relations" which was created early in the session. The most active member of the committee was Samuel H. Laughlin, former editor of the Nashville *Union* and a personal friend of both Polk and

Jackson, and it was easy to foretell what the verdict would be. On January 29, 1840, Laughlin reported that his committee had been

wholly unable, from anything contained in said message, or in the past action of the Federal Government, executive, legislative or judicial, during the late or present administrations, which can, in the slightest degree, even by implication, afford the least warrant of authority for the imputations contained in that portion of said message.[1]

The verdict of the committee was approved by the legislature, and little attention was paid to a minority report which upheld the contentions of the former Governor. Laughlin's report served as a vindication of the national administration. In addition, it served as the basis for one of the instructions given to the federal Senators from Tennessee—the instruction to vote against the bill to prevent interference in elections by certain federal officers.

On October 14, 1839, Polk was inaugurated as governor of Tennessee. Among those present to witness the ceremony it gave Harris of the *Union* "great pleasure to notice ex-President Jackson, with health apparently improved." The inaugural address, according to the same writer, was "an effort of great happiness on the part of Gov. Polk." "It was," wrote Old Hickory, "a great address well suited to the occasion—there was a great contrast betwen his and Mr. Cannon's."[2]

On account of its supposed influence on national politics, more importance was attached to Polk's inauguration than is usually the case when a state executive is installed. Levi Woodbury voiced the sentiment of most Democrats when he wrote: "I have seldom known the result of any election to be more triumphant & gratifying over the whole Union than that of yours."[3]

---

[1] *Tenn. Sen. Jour.*, 1839–40, 7, 504.

[2] Jackson to Van Buren, Oct. 18, 1839, *Van Buren Papers.*

[3] Woodbury to Polk, October 20, 1839, *Polk Papers.*

The new Governor's first message was submitted to the legislature on October 22, and the subjects most emphasized in it
were banks and internal improvements. He expressed the belief
that there had been no necessity for the suspension of specie
payments by the banks of Tennessee. On the assumption that
they had suspended such payments simply because eastern banks
had done so, he urged the enactment of measures which would
compel resumption, for "like individual debtors, they should
meet their liabilities honestly and promptly as long as they are
able to pay." Banks often, said he, do their most profitable
business during suspension, while the loss is borne by labor. He
denied that the federal government had been responsible for derangement of the currency or that a national bank could have
prevented it. The main cause of financial distress, he said, was
speculation on borrowed capital. For remedy, therefore, he did
not seek new legislation, but suggested something far more sensible—a remedy which in no degree depended on governmental
action. "The only substantial and permanent relief," said the
Governor,

is to be found in habits of economy and industry, and in the productive
labor of our people. By the observance of these, another crop would more
than liquidate our eastern debt. We must bring our expenses within our
income. Our merchants and traders must cease to indulge in hazardous
and wild speculations which they are unable to meet.

This was very sound advice, far too sound to be widely accepted
in a period when most people believed that the government was
able to dispense or withhold prosperity at will, regardless of their
own reckless speculative ventures.

Another recommendation was that the legislature should, by
law, prohibit the Bank of Tennessee from emitting notes under
twenty dollars, because excessive issues of paper tended to drive
out metal money, and in addition, to facilitate speculation.

Polk declared himself to be strongly in favor of internal improvements made by the state. He asked, however, that existing

laws on that subject should be so modified as to prevent extravagance. For example, the legislature at the preceding session had
enacted a law which required the state to subscribe for one-half
of the capital stock of all railroads, macadamized turnpikes,
graded turnpikes, and sanded turnpikes for which acts of incorporation ''have heretofore been granted or for which acts of
incorporation may be hereafter granted.'' Such a law had great
possibilities for evil, and under it worthless enterprises had
already been undertaken. Polk now urged that the law should
be so modified that subscriptions in future must be limited to
works of real improvement, and that a board of public works
should be created to authorize and supervise such enterprises.[4]

On the whole the Governor's message was a creditable document, although it lacked the vigor and elaboration which usually
characterized his written productions. It was evident that his
interests were national rather than local. His recommendations
were duly considered by the legislature, but even the members
of that body seemed to be more interested in ''doing practical
politics'' for the national party than in enacting laws for the
good of the state. At any rate practical politics was given first
place on their program.

It was well known to all that the main reason for making Polk
the gubernatorial candidate was the belief that he alone could win
the state back to Democratic allegiance. For this same reason
he had consented to make the race. The question which soon
presented itself was: What does he expect as his reward, if he
succeeds? During the campaign the Whigs made the charge that
Polk did not care for the governorship, and that his nomination
had been simply a ruse to win Tennessee for Van Buren and the
Vice-Presidency for himself at the approaching federal election.
In such an event he would, of course, resign in the middle of his
term. The charge was repelled by Polk's friends, but the probability of its truth was so great that many, especially in East

---

[4] *Tenn. Sen. Jour.*, 1839–40, 64–68.

Tennessee, declined to vote for him under the circumstances. He was urged[5] to make an emphatic denial of the charge, but he followed his usual policy of keeping silent. When, therefore, the state senate, within forty-eight hours after his inauguration, began to consider the question of nominating Polk for Vice-President, the *Banner* charged that this had been the sole purpose of making him governor, and that the people had been grossly deceived.[6]

The senate with little opposition passed a resolution nominating Van Buren and Polk, and on October 22, the same day on which it received the Governor's message, the house proceeded to consider this senate resolution. Two amendments were offered by the opposition—one to require the candidates to support a federal bank, another to strike out the name of Polk—but both were promptly rejected. After prolonged and animated debate the house, on November 4, concurred in the senate resolution and formally nominated the two candidates.[7] Until the question had been decided, the local newspapers kept up a war of words on the subject, each trying to surpass its rival in vulgar abuse, which doubtless pleased the readers but which made few converts in the legislature.[8]

In Washington the Democratic members of the Tennessee delegation in Congress were busily engaged in an effort to procure for Polk the second place on the national ticket. His principal competitor was the incumbent, Colonel Richard M. Johnson, of Kentucky. Johnson had the support of the conservative

---

[5] H. W. Anderson, of Brownsville, to Polk, September 10, 1839, *Polk Papers.*

[6] Nashville *Banner,* Oct. 19, 1839. One enthusiastic friend urged Polk not to leave the governorship for the Vice-Presidency: "The plan that I had laid off was for you to be our Governor six years and then Senator Six and at the end of Benton's eight years make you President" (Amos Kirkpatrick, of Meigsville, to Polk, Oct. 17, 1839, *Polk Papers*).

[7] *Tenn. House Jour.,* 1839–40, 68–69.

[8] To quote one sample of their ability in vivid description: The *Union,* on October 16, informed its readers that John B. Ashe, a state senator, "came very near bursting his boiler and collapsing his flue on yesterday," in condemning the *Union.*

element of the party—of the class of people whose main rule of action is leaving well enough alone. But a portion of the party desired a more vigorous candidate, a man who would conduct a more energetic campaign, and a man who would be more acceptable to the southern states. These qualities were especially desired in the candidate for Vice-President in order to offset the want of them in Van Buren, their candidate for President.

The supporters of Polk fully realized that it would be difficult to procure for him the coveted nomination. They knew that there was little genuine enthusiasm for Johnson in any quarter, still they feared that he might be nominated by the national convention simply because that body would not know how to get rid of him. Their only hope seemed to lie either in preventing the calling of a national convention, or in preventing any nomination of a Vice-Presidential candidate if such a convention should be held. A letter outlining the situation was sent to Polk by six Democratic members of Congress from Tennessee.[9] It stated that a national convention had been recommended by New Hampshire, and that it now seemed to be a certainty. If so, it was their opinion that Johnson would probably be nominated, although New England, New York, Virginia, North Carolina and other states preferred Polk. Johnson was a "dead weight" on the party, they said, but it was hard to drop him. It was possible, they believed, that the convention might fail to nominate any one, and break up in confusion, but at all events Tennessee should be fully represented in the convention. In a separate letter (dated February 4) Brown tells Polk that Calhoun is for him on the ground of "your *position,* your *abilities* & your *principles.*"

A few days after the receipt of the above-mentioned letter Polk informed Hubbard, a member of the House from New Hampshire,[10] that his position was "passive"—that he would accept

---

9 The letter was dated at Washington, February 3, 1840, and was signed by Felix Grundy, A. McClellan, H. M. Watterson, H. L. Turney, C. Johnson, and A. V. Brown (*Polk Papers*).

10 Polk to Hubbard, February 7, 1840, *Polk Papers.*

the nomination at the hands of his party, but would not seek it. Such at attitude was in line with his usual adherence to party unity. His passive attitude, however, seems to have been somewhat affected by his unanimous nomination by a Virginia convention. This nomination was made, it was said[11] at the instance of the friends of Calhoun. In response to Polk's letter, Hubbard strongly urged Polk to put aside all delicacy and run. Johnson, he said, was in favor of both tariff and internal improvements, and was unpopular with many in the party. For these reasons, said Hubbard, Democrats should oppose a national convention, and should nominate Polk in some other way; Virginia had done so, and why should other states not follow her example? Should the election eventually devolve upon the Senate, he was certain that Polk would be chosen.[12] In Washington, A. J. Donelson was using his influence to procure Polk's nomination. On March 4 he wrote that, although the South was unequivocally for Polk, yet he feared that the convention would choose Johnson instead.[13]

Polk was willing enough to run, but being a firm believer in party solidarity, he was reluctant to become the candidate of a portion of the party unless it should develop that the party as a whole could not agree upon a choice. Writing to Cave Johnson on March 27, he said that "up to now" he had maintained that he would not run unless nominated by the undivided party. But, said he, the refusal of Virginia and South Carolina to send delegates to the Baltimore convention had changed the situation by making unanimity in any case out of the question; consequently if the convention should fail to make a nomination, in other words, in the event of there being no party nominee, he might in that case consent to run.[14]

---

11 Theophilus Fisk to Polk, Richmond, February 21, 1840, *Polk Papers.* In reporting the news to Polk, Fisk added: "Wherever my paper, the Old Dominion, circulates, and it has a very wide one, the people will hear of no candidate but yourself."

12 Hubbard to Polk, February 23, 1840, *Polk Papers.*

13 Donelson to Polk, March 4, 1840, *ibid.*

14 *Polk Papers.* He wrote a similar letter to Hubbard on April 5, 1840.

Ready as ever to aid his friends, General Jackson used his influence in an attempt to procure Polk's nomination by the national convention. In a letter to Van Buren he said that

A man ought to be chosen that all the republicans in every state would cheerfully unite on, and if this is not done it will jeopardise your election—it ought to be a man whose popularity would strengthen you, not one that would be a dead weight upon your popularity.

Polk, in his opinion had double the popularity of Johnson, and his nomination by the party would insure victory. He was pained to learn from Major Donelson that many in Congress believed it advisable to make no nomination for the Vice-Presidency; "surely our friends have not taken a common sense view of the whole subject."[15]

Before leaving Tennessee, Laughlin and some of the other delegates to the Baltimore convention held a conference in Nashville with Polk, Jackson, and other political leaders. The General was firm in his belief that candidates ought to be nominated for both President and Vice-President, and that Van Buren and Polk should be the nominees. Polk, he repeated, would add strength to the ticket, while Colonel Johnson would be an encumbrance. On the other hand, Polk made it clear to the delegates that in no event would he run as a sectional candidate, as Judge White had done in 1836; should Johnson be nominated, he would earnestly support him. Should no nomination be made at Baltimore, and if within a reasonable time a sufficient number of states had not indicated a preference for himself, he would then take field in support of Colonel Johnson or any other candidate that seemed most likely to bring success to the party.[16]

Laughlin arrived in Washington on April 25, and three days later, after conferences with Tennesseans, he recorded in his diary that "all were now agreed that Gov. Polk could not be nominated—that Johnson could not without New York, and that

---

15 Jackson to Van Buren, April 3, 1840, *Van Buren Papers.*

16 S. H. Laughlin, "Diary," April 14, 15, *Tenn. Hist. Mag.*, March, 1916, 45–47.

the best way, if possible, was to make no nomination. This matter was in treaty between Mr. Grundy and Mr. Wright.'' On the day following, Laughlin reported to Polk that Benton and Buchanan were secretly in favor of Johnson and that ''such creatures as Walker and Sevier are only fit to do mischief,'' but that Calhoun was heartily in favor of Polk's nomination.[17] At a meeting held in Grundy's room on May 1 it was agreed that Polk's only hope lay in preventing any nomination by the convention, and some believed that a refusal by delegates to attend would be the most effective way of procuring the desired result.[18] This plan was not followed, however, and a few days later Laughlin wrote from Baltimore that the convention had nominated Van Buren but, by a vote of one hundred and thirty-two to ninety-nine, had declared it inexpedient to nominate a candidate for Vice-President.

After the convention had adjourned without naming a candidate for Vice-President, Polk prepared a statement in the form of a letter to Grundy and requested him to have it published in the Washington *Globe*.[19] It had been his wish, he said, that the Baltimore convention might nominate a candidate, but, as it had not done so, he still hoped that the opinions of the majority could in some way be ascertained. In that event he would cheerfully support the choice, but, as he had been nominated by some of the states, he would let the party decide whether to settle on one or more. He hoped that some one would be chosen by the electoral college. In answer, Grundy told him[20] that no doubt he would have won if there had been no convention, but as matters now

---

[17] S. H. Laughlin, ''Diary,'' April 28, 29, *op. cit.* Laughlin to Polk, April 29, 1840, *Polk Papers.* In his diary for May 4, Laughlin recorded that ''Mr. Buchanan from hostility to Gov. Polk's future prospects had allied himself to King, and by contrivance, their friends were trying first to effect a compromise with the friends of Johnson and Polk and thereby get King nominated upon the half-way house principle; but if they could not get this done, they united and were to unite with Johnson's friends and press for a nomination.''

[18] Laughlin to Polk, May 2, 1840, *Polk Papers.*

[19] Polk to Grundy, May 27, 1840, *ibid.*

[20] Grundy to Polk, June 1, 1840, *ibid.*

stood, he thought that Johnson would be elected. The Nashville *Union,* he said, had injured rather than aided Polk by calling on the states to declare their preference. As it would not look well to withdraw formally from the race, Grundy advised Polk simply to do nothing.

The contest between Polk and Johnson for second place on the Democratic ticket was more than a rivalry between the two men. Back of it was a party cleavage which four years later was to land Polk in the White House. Despite Jackson's loyalty to Van Buren, many of the General's best friends did not like the ''little magician''; they supported him only from a sense of party duty. Still less did this wing of Democracy like Colonel Johnson, and, if they must support Van Buren, they wished at least to have a Vice-Presidential candidate for whom they could willingly vote. There seems to be no evidence that Polk himself had, up to this time, been opposed to Van Buren, nevertheless he was on very intimate terms with the insurgent faction of the party. This wing of the party was impelled mainly by a desire to promote southern interests, although a revolt against ''old fogyism'' was already becoming a political factor. Its adherents regarded Polk as sound on southern questions, while they had doubts in the case of both Van Buren and Johnson. Party cleavage had existed before Polk had been suggested for the Vice-Presidency, but the apparent hostility of the administration to his candidacy aided in widening it. Although the President himself seems to have expressed no preference, those who were in his confidence and who were supposed to voice his wishes were directly or indirectly supporting Colonel Johnson. Among them were Benton, Buchanan, Kendall, and Blair.[21] For a second time[22] Blair appeared reluctant to give aid to Polk when he was sorely in need of it. These instances alone furnish a very good reason

---

[21] Jackson's attitude toward the candidates had no connection with this party split. He favored Van Buren and Polk, and opposed Johnson, purely for personal reasons.

[22] The first time was when Polk was a candidate for Speaker of the House.

why Polk, when he became President, declined to adopt the *Globe* as his official organ.

Shortly after the Democratic convention had adjourned, Cave Johnson informed Polk[23] that a *Life of Van Buren and Johnson* had appeared and that he believed it had been published at the office of the *Globe*. Blair, he said, had declared himself to be impartial as to Colonel Johnson and Polk, but "I have no faith in that establishment so far as your interests are concerned." For this reason he (Cave Johnson) and his friends were not eager to extend the circulation of Kendall's *"Extra Globes,"* which had been prepared especially for campaign purposes. On May 25, five of the Tennessee delegation[24] addressed a letter to Kendall himself. In it they stated that while they were anxious to advance the cause of the administration, they were unwilling to prejudice the cause of their favorite candidate, and therefore, "before we undertake the circulation of the *Extra Globe,* we are desirous of being informed, whether the *Extra* will take any part, & if any what part, in the election of Vice President." Kendall gave a rather evasive reply[25] in which he stated that, while he thought well of their "favorite candidate," he would attempt to promote the cause of the party by speaking well of any or all candidates as the occasion might require. With this reply, which was regarded as a virtual endorsement of Johnson, they had to be content, but the hostility to Kendall and Blair by no means abated. The element that supported Polk became more and more alienated from Van Buren and his intimates until, in 1844, they succeeded in preventing his nomination.

The other question of a purely political nature that engrossed the attention of the Tennessee legislature was that of forcing White and Foster out of the United States Senate by the use of humiliating instructions.

---

23 Johnson to Polk, May 24, 1840, *Polk Papers.*

24 Cave Johnson, A. V. Brown, H. L. Turney, A. McClellan, and H. M. Watterson.

25 June 9, 1840. Both letters are in the *Polk Papers.*

In White's case another method was first attempted, for the judge was still popular in the state, and, if he could be eliminated without resorting to instructions, less odium would attach to his adversaries. In the fall of 1838 White had, on account of ill health, tendered his resignation to Governor Cannon. The Governor suspended action in the hope that White's health might improve. As it did improve sufficiently to enable him to make the journey to Washington, the resignation, at Cannon's request, was withdrawn without having been accepted.

Rumors of White's letter of resignation had found their way to Democratic ears and suggested the possibility of disposing of the judge by maintaining that by his own action his seat had become vacant. Accordingly, when the legislature convened in October, 1839, the senate by resolution asked Governor Cannon for copies of the correspondence which had passed between himself and White relative to the latter's resignation. Cannon replied that White's resignation had never been accepted and that his letter had been returned; all other correspondence had been personal, not official, and had not been preserved. Attorney-General Grundy wrote[26] from Washington urging that White's successor should be chosen without delay, and expressing the opinion that Foster would resign if instructed to vote for the sub-treasury bill. Such a program, if successful, would give the Democrats an opportunity to choose both Senators, one of whom was to be Grundy himself.

Notwithstanding Grundy's advice, the difficulty of proving that White's seat had become vacant seemed to be so great that, on October 25, Levin H. Coe introduced in the state senate a series of resolutions which instructed the Senators and requested the Representatives to carry out the wishes of the legislature on certain enumerated subjects.[27] While the resolutions were being

---

26 Grundy to Polk, October 17, *Polk Papers.*

27 (1) To vote against the chartering of a United States bank. (2) To vote for the sub-treasury. (3) To vote against any bill for the prevention of interference in elections by certain federal officers, as such a bill would

discussed by the legislature, Judge White wrote to one of the members of the lower house stating that he would resign rather than support the sub-treasury bill.[28] His letter was read to the legislature, and soon afterwards that body, by a strict party vote, passed the resolutions. General Jackson's program was thereby successfully carried into effect, and once more he had the satisfaction of humiliating the man who had dared to run for President against his wishes. It was a contemptible transaction, and those who participated in it are deserving of nothing but condemnation. It remained to be seen, of course, whether the Whig Senators would repudiate their instructions, but there was little doubt that White at least, would resign.

On his way to Washington, early in November, John Bell stopped at Knoxville to deliver a public address in which he scathingly denounced the administration and its supporters. In response to a call from the audience, White addressed the same meeting in language which was reported to have been violently intemperate.[29]

While White was yet on his journey to Washington, Polk, in a letter to Van Buren, congratulated him on recent Democratic victories, and pointed out that they were a good omen for 1840. "Judge White," said Polk, "forgetting the dignity of his station, as well as the former character of which he boasted, descended into the political arena, and became an active partisan and travelling electioneer." He told Van Buren that the legislature

---

violate the Constitution of the United States. (4) To vote against distribution among the states of revenue derived from the sale of public lands—and for reducing the price of such lands. (5) To vote for a repeal of the duty on salt. (6) To support in good faith the leading measures of the present administration (*Tenn. Sen. Jour.*, 1839–40, 77–79; Scott, *Memoir of Hugh Lawson White*, 370).

[28] White to Jacobs, September 5, 1839 (Scott, *Memoir of Hugh Lawson White*, 371).

[29] Lewis P. Roberts to Polk, Nov. 11, 1839, *Polk Papers*. Roberts doubtless exaggerated in reporting that White "characterized the whole of the V. B. party as gamblers and blacklegs" and accused Van Buren of pocketing the money which the people had lost from a derangement of currency.

had instructed the Senators to support the President's measures, and expressed the belief that Foster would resign and White obey the instructions. Grundy, he said, would be the best man to succeed Foster; he therefore urged the President to give up his Attorney-General for the good of the cause.[30]

Foster promptly resigned on November 15, thus leaving one seat in the Senate at the immediate disposal of the Democrats. Catron, who was holding court in Louisville, believed that White, too, would soon be forced to resign. Tennessee, he wrote, must be held loyal to the administration, and the best way of insuring this was to make Polk the candidate for Vice-President.[31]

The legislature by a party vote chose Grundy to fill Foster's unexpired term. As soon as the news reached Washington, however, one of his friends, H. C. Williams, pointed out to him that he was not eligible for the office.[32] The constitution required that a Senator, at the time of his election, must be a local resident, and it was thought that Grundy was not such a resident so long as he remained in the cabinet. He therefore resigned his seat in the Senate, and the technicality was obviated by his reëlection after his return to Tennessee.[33]

On receiving his instructions from the legislature, White decided that instead of resigning at once he would wait until some question had been presented which would compel him either to vote contrary to his principles or to violate his instructions. The Democrats, therefore, hastened to bring forward an obnoxious measure. On January 13, 1840, Silas Wright called up the sub-treasury bill and thereby forced the issue. White rose and explained to the Senate the embarrassment of his position, and then read the letter of resignation which he was about to send

---

[30] Polk to Van Buren, Nov. 11, 1839, *Van Buren Papers*.

[31] Catron to Polk, Nov. 19, (1839 ?), *Polk Papers*.

[32] Williams to Polk, Nov. 28, 1839, *"Most strictly confidential."* On December 1 Cave Johnson gave a similar opinion, and said that Grundy would go to Nashville to look after the matter *(Polk Papers)*.

[33] *Niles' Register*, Jan. 11, 1840.

to the Tennessee legislature.[34] Grundy and others had expected
from the persecuted Senator a bitter arraignment of the administration party. They had come prepared to answer him, but
Grundy himself admitted that White's letter to the legislature
had been "drawn with some ability" and was too respectful to
call for a reply.[35]

While no one questioned the legal right of a state to instruct
its Senators, it was generally felt that the legislature had used
its power for the unworthy purpose of punishing White and gaining a political advantage to which the Democrats were not entitled. A dinner was given in the deposed Senator's honor at
which all of the prominent Whigs were present. His public career
and his loyalty to principle were exalted in toasts and addresses
made by Clay, Preston, and many others.[36] It was his last public
appearance. An attack of pneumonia before his departure from
Washington and the fatigue caused by the journey home greatly
impaired his vitality, and his death occured on April 10, 1840.

White's resignation gave the choice of his successor to the
Democratic majority in the legislature. As the judge was from
East Tennessee, custom required that his successor should be a
resident of the same section of the state. The legislature selected
Alexander Anderson, a lawyer of fair ability but a man without
national reputation.

As noted above, the principal recommendations made by
Governor Polk in his message dealt with banks and internal improvements. To these topics the legislature gave its attention
when it was not too busily engaged with *practical politics*. Like
most banks in the Union those of Tennessee had suspended specie
payments. In response to the Governor's suggestion Yoakum, on
October 28, 1839, presented a resolution which, if adopted, would

---

[34] Both explanation and letter are printed in Scott, *Memoir of Hugh
Lawson White*, 375 ff.

[35] Grundy to Polk, Jan. 13, 1840, and other letters on the same subject in the *Polk Papers*.

[36] An account of this dinner is given in Scott, *Memoir of Hugh Lawson
White*, 395 ff.

compel the Bank of Tennessee and its branches forthwith to resume and continue specie payments on all notes of and under ten dollars. Another resolution moved by Jennings, an opposition member, required the committee on banks to interrogate the president and directors of this bank as to whether financial accommodations were made on the basis of political sentiments. On November 11, Jennings presented a bill which embodied and made more explicit the ideas included in his resolution. The bill required the committee on banks to call on the Bank of Tennessee for the following items of information: (1) whether the choice of officers of the branch banks was influenced by politics; (2) whether contracts were so influenced; and (3) whether politics was considered in making loans. Another bill was proposed by Wheeler the purpose of which was to compel all banks of the state to resume specie payments within thirty days on penalty of forfeiture of their charters. On January 15, 1840, Jennings proposed an amendment to the state constitution the intent of which was to prevent the state in future from becoming the sole proprietor of, or a partner in, any bank, and from raising money on the credit of the state, except for defense.[37]

None of these proposals was enacted into law. The Democrats easily disposed of the political measures of their opponents, but, with the exception of a few minor remedial regulations, they were unable to carry their own. Toward the close of the session Laughlin submitted a report from the committee which had been appointed by the senate to investigate the banks. It stated that no evidence of politics in bank transactions had been discovered and that specie payments would, in the opinion of the banks, be resumed by July 1, 1840.[38] This belief, however, proved to be erroneous.

In response, also, to suggestions made in the Governor's message, the legislature undertook to modify existing laws on the

---

[37] *Tenn. Sen. Jour.*, 1839–40, 85–86, 109, 156–157, 407.

[38] *Ibid.*, Appendix.

subject of internal improvements. Yielding to a popular clamor for state aid, the legislature under Cannon's administration had made it obligatory for the state to become a partner in all improvement ventures regardless of the nature of the enterprise. Wholesale extravagance had been the result; nevertheless it was not an easy matter to eliminate the abuses without doing injury to those who, relying on continued support from the government, had invested capital in various projects.[39] The secretary of state reported to the senate that, under the act of 1836, $2,732,541⅔ had been subscribed by the state to improvement enterprises, and under the act of 1838, $889,500 had been subscribed for turnpikes and river improvements, $65,000 to the Louisville, Cincinnati, and Charleston Rail Road Company, and a similar amount to the Hiawassee Rail Road Company.[40]

In order to save the state in future from such ruinous expenditures, the legislature repealed all laws which had required the governor to subscribe for stock in improvement corporations. In the repealing act provision was made for the withdrawal, so far as possible, from partnerships already formed. By another act, passed on January 28, 1840, the legislature recalled $150,000 in state bonds which had been placed with banks to be sold and the proceeds invested in stocks of improvement companies. This legislation was substantially what the Governor had recommended, and, although there was no remedy for the waste that had already

---

[39] In responding to a vote of thanks at the close of the session, Speaker Coe, of the Senate, stated very clearly the difficulty which confronted the legislature: "In 1836 and 1838 laws were passed for the encouragement of Internal Improvement and works of the most extensive character have been commenced, and are now in progress of erection. If we continued to advance under the law as we found it, many saw in it the germ of a disordered and bankrupt treasury, and a people loaded down with taxes, levied to pay the interest on an onerous State debt—whilst it was asserted by others, with much reason, that the State had voluntarily tendered the right hand of assistance to large bodies of our fellow citizens, and had invited enterprises, having for their object the cultivation and improvement of our common country; and under such circumstances the sudden withdrawal of all aid, would involve individuals in private ruin and consign public works to dilapidation" (*ibid.*, 545–546).

[40] Reports of Luke Lea, secretary of state, Oct. 25 and Nov. 23, *Tenn. Sen. Jour.*, 1839–40, 74, 142.

occurred, so long as Polk remained in the governor's chair care was taken to restrict expenditures and to reduce the state debt.

During Polk's first year as governor of his state, the people of the nation were engaged in the whirlwind Presidential campaign of 1840—the first and most boisterous of its kind. In every state in the Union the contest was waged with unprecedented fury, and especially so in Tennessee. Reason and logical argument were cast to the winds, while noise and caricature became the order of the day. The "stump speech" played a less important part than usual; while both sides, but especially the Whigs, expended their energies in fantastic processions. The greater the din of deafening and discordant noises, the more spectacular or grotesque the banners and other devices designed to excite the emotions of the crowd, the more successful was the pageant considered.

For sentimental reasons, as well as for the importance of her electoral votes, the contest in Tennessee was regarded as of national significance. Failure to redeem "Old Hickory's state" was thought by Democratic politicians to be nothing short of disgrace, while the hope of thus humiliating their opponents spurred the Whigs to untiring effort. But the Whigs had the advantage from the outset. The rank and file of the Democrats did not share the feeling of the party leaders; they could not wax enthusiastic over Van Buren. In the Whig camp, on the contrary, there was unity.

In 1839, as soon as it became known that Polk had been elected, prominent Whigs held a convention in Nashville and arranged for the appointment of local committees throughout the state. These committees were effective engines of agitation, and the *Union* promptly denounced them as "new and strange fermentations in the body politic to be put down by all lovers of peace and social order."[41] Clay was invited to visit Tennessee by a delegation sent to Kentucky for that purpose by the Nashville

---

[41] Phelan, *Hist. of Tenn.*, 384.

convention, but, the sage of Ashland, pleading illness and pressure of private business, declined to make a definite promise
to accept.[42] It was expected, of course, that the legislature
would instruct the Whig Senators and force their resignation,
and the *Banner* was certain that such a course would be of
great advantage to the Whigs in the Presidential campaign.
This paper urged the Senators to remain in office until forced
to resign. In such an event their names were to head the Whig
electoral ticket, and the state was to be "thoroughly and ably
canvassed, in every county and every neighborhood and victory
would be assured."[43]

The national convention of the Whig party met at Harris-
burg, Pennsylvania, on December 4, 1839. Due to prejudice
against national conventions, the Whigs of Tennessee refused to
send delegates, for it will be remembered that opposition to the
convention which nominated Van Buren was a chief factor in the
creation of the "White Whig" party. As their hearts were set on
Clay, they were disappointed, and at first somewhat discouraged,
when Harrison received the nomination. They soon rallied,
however, and throughout the campaign their loyalty and energy
were not surpassed by the Whigs of any other state. Bell was
their most eloquent speaker, although Foster, who canvassed the
entire state, was more successful in winning votes. In this campaign the Whigs appealed more to the eye than to the ear. They
relied more on banners and processions than on oratory or arguments. "The fact is," wrote one of Polk's Democratic friends
after the election, "the people like coonery and foolery better
than good argument."[44]

The great event of the campaign was the Whig convention
held in Nashville on August 17, 1840. Delegations came from
surrounding states, each joining in the spectacular procession

---

42 *Niles' Register*, October 12, 1839.
43 Nashville *Banner*, quoted in *Niles' Register*, September 7, 1839.
44 Isaac Goladay to Polk, November 9, 1840, *Polk Papers*.

and each bearing aloft banners fantastically decorated and
adorned with mottoes designed to win popular applause.[45] The
procession wended its way to a grove in the outksirts of the city,
where the multitude was entertained by speeches made by prominent Whigs of Tennessee and other states. Foster, who was
chairman of the meeting, made the opening address, but the lion
of the occasion was Clay himself, whose personal magnetism and
oratorical flights electrified the audience, although his address
was rather commonplace.

The Democrats were not so well organized as the Whigs and
their speakers were decidedly inferior to those of their opponents.
Their most effective debater, Polk, was prevented by his office
from actively entering into the canvass, although he made a
few speeches in favor of Van Buren, which led to his present-
ment as a "nuisance" by the grand jury of Sevier county,[46] and
the Whig papers circulated the story that the Governor's grandfather had been a Tory during the Revolution.[47] Nicholson met
Bell in debate; Cave Johnson, A. V. Brown, and H. L. Turney did
their utmost to stem the Whig tide; Jackson wrote letters in
which he lauded Van Buren, and denounced Harrison as a Federalist, but the people would not listen as of yore. On the eve
of the election the Democrats tried to brand Harrison as an abolitionist. At the last moment, they distributed handbills on which
they had printed a letter which Harrison was alleged to have
written to Arthur Tappan declaring himself to be such. But
the plot had been discovered, and the *Whig* was ready with
Harrison's denial as soon as the handbills appeared.

Tennessee refused to be "redeemed"; the vote for Harrison
was 60,391, while Van Buren polled but 48,289. It was a signal
victory for the Whigs, and, unlike four years earlier, it could
not be said that voters had supported the Whig candidate simply
because he was a favorite son of the state. Undoubtedly one of

---

45 The parade is described in some detail by Phelan, *Hist. of Tenn.*, 387 ff.
46 *Ibid.*
47 Edwin Polk to Polk, August 27, 1840, *Polk Papers.*

Polk's correspondents was right in saying[48] that many Democrats had refrained from voting because they ''could not be rallied to Van Buren,'' and that the Democratic loss was much greater than the Whig gain. Still, any hopes built on such calculations were illusive, for in national politics the state was irretrievably lost to the Democrats.

Not realizing the real strength of the Whigs, the leading Democrats, almost before the smoke of battle had lifted, began to formulate plans for winning the next state election. First of all, Harrison and his administration must be vigorously assailed, regardless of the course he might pursue. The difficulty of finding anything of sufficient importance to attack caused them no little anxiety. A. O. P. Nicholson put the case frankly in a letter to Polk, written before it had been definitely ascertained that Harrison had been elected. The Democrats, he said, must

keep up a raking fire upon the whole of Harrison's inconsistent and imbecile history. It is unfortunate for us that Harrison's administration (if elected) will not be developed before our August elections, but still enough will probably have transpired to present available points of attack.[49]

And yet the politicians who uttered such sentiments claimed to be followers of Jefferson, one of whose cardinal principles was ''absolute acquiescence in the decisions of the majority.''[50]

Although the Democrats were hopeful and even confident, the Whig victory of 1840 made them realize that Polk's defeat in 1841 was within the realms of possibility. When, therefore, in December, 1840, it was reported in Washington that Grundy could not live, the Democratic members of Congress from Tennessee counselled together and decided that Polk ought to succeed him as Senator from his state. In a letter to Polk,[51] Hopkins L.

---

[48] Samuel P. Walker to Polk, November 4, 1840, *Polk Papers.*

[49] Nicholson to Polk, November 6, 1840, *Polk Papers.* Other letters to Polk also expressed regret that there would probably be little to attack.

[50] See Jefferson's first inaugural address.

[51] Turney to Polk, December 21, 1840. On the same day A. V. Brown wrote a letter of similar purport. Both in *Polk Papers.*

Turney pointed out to the Governor that his reëlection was doubtful and, even if such were not the case, he would stand a better chance of promotion if elected Senator. Both Cave Johnson and A. V. Brown, he said, concurred in this view. Before this letter had reached its destination, however, Polk had appointed Nicholson to succeed Grundy, whose death had occurred on the nineteenth of the month. So gratified was Nicholson by his appointment that, on his arrival in Washington, he saw visions of his benefactor's certain elevation to the Presidential chair. After telling the Governor of his popularity in Washington and of the anxiety for his reëlection, he added: "I shall be disappointed if your success in this contest does not lead on certainly to your elevation to the Presidency."[52]

While the politicians on either side were speculating on the probability of Harrison's calling an extra session of Congress, considerable excitement was caused in Nashville by the shooting of J. George Harris, editor of the *Union,* by Robert C. Foster, a son of the deposed Senator. Harris quickly recovered, but the affair furnished Democrats with something to denounce while they were awaiting further political developments.

In case Harrison, after his inauguration, should call Congress together in extra session, Tennessee would have no representation in the House[53] unless the Governor should see fit to call a special election. Anderson, who had been chosen to fill Foster's unexpired term, would cease to be Senator on March 4, and the official term of Nicholson, who was serving on the governor's appointment, would be automatically terminated should Polk decide to call an extra session of the legislature. Should no extra session be called, Nicholson would continue in office until the regular session which would open in October, 1841. As the probability of a called session of Congress increased, the Democrats differed as to whether it would be wiser to convene the

---

[52] Nicholson to Polk, Jan. 13, 1841, *ibid.*

[53] The terms of present members would expire on March 4 and a regular election would not be held until autumn.

legislature and attempt to elect two Senators, or to be contented with one Senator, Nicholson, leaving the other seat vacant.

When sounded on the subject, Polk expressed himself as opposed to convening the legislature. He gave, as his reasons, economy, and the fear that the Whigs would make political capital of such a procedure. On the other hand, Jackson, who had lost none of his political zeal, strongly favored an extra session in order that two Senators might be chosen and instructed as to how they should cast their votes. "If it can be done with propriety," he advised Governor Polk,

if there is a called session of congress, the Legislature should be convened to give us a full representation in the Senate; and to instruct our senators & request our representatives to vote against a high Tariff, a distribution of the Public Funds, against a national Bank of any kind, or deposits in the State banks, and against a repeal of the sub-treasury act, and, altho last not least, to pass a law to compell our Banks to resume specie payments or wind up.[54]

From Washington, Anderson urged the necessity of a full representation in the Senate.[55] Turney seconded this appeal and once more tried to induce the Governor to become a candidate. Polk, he said, could do much good in the Senate, for since Grundy's death there was no one able to cope with the Whigs. On this same subject Polk received what appears to be his first letter from Andrew Johnson.[56] In it Johnson advises the Governor to convene the legislature for the purpose of electing members of Congress whose terms, unless he is "rong," expire on the fourth of March.

While Nicholson was in Washington, still worrying for fear there would be little in the Harrison administration to assail,[57]

---

[54] Jackson to Polk, Feb. 8, 1841, *Polk Papers.*

[55] Anderson to Polk, Feb. 17, 1841, *ibid.*

[56] At least it is the first letter from Johnson in the Polk collection. It seems that Polk had written to Johnson, stating that either he or Blair must run for Congress. Johnson declined to become a candidate (Johnson to Polk, March 4, 1841, *Polk Papers*).

[57] "I do not calculate that we will be able to make any capital out of the Inaugural; but the Cabinet will be enough for our purposes, if we use

the much-reviled administration of Van Buren passed into history.[58] Ignoring his critics, the "little magician" remained unperturbed and courteous to the end. When his successor arrived in Washington, an invitation to dine was extended by Van Buren and accepted by Harrison, and the Nashville *Union* marvelled that Harrison could take "vermacilla soup from those horrible gold spoons!"[59] The Whig newspapers never tired of contrasting the democratic simplicity and generous hospitality[60] of Harrison with the royalistic pomp and cold exclusiveness of Van Buren. It was unkind of the Whigs thus to purloin from their opponents the very arguments—almost the exact phrases— which had done such effective service in winning popular support for General Jackson. Such utter disregard for the proprietary rights of others fully justified J. George Harris in trying to render harmless the stolen implements of war. Shortly after

---

it with skill." It is rumored, he said, "that Webster will be Secretary of State; Granger, Post-Master-General; Ewing, Secretary of the Treasury; Bell, Secretary of War; Preston, Secretary of the Navy; and Crittenden Attorney-General. What think you now of the Cabinet! I think you may set it down as settled that we are to have an anti-war fed. for Secretary of State, an abolition fed. for Post-Master-General, a uniform fed. for the Treasury, a gag-bill Clay fed. for Atty. Gen., a gag-bill-no party-White Whig fed. for the War, and a Nullification fed. for the Navy. Will not this open the eyes of Tennesseans! If not, then may we surrender at discretion" (Nicholson to Polk, Feb. 12, 1841, *Polk Papers*).

58 "Tomorrow night, at twelve o'clock," said the *Madisonian*, "the administration of Martin Van Buren terminates. That administration, accidental in its beginning, and unfortunate and profitless in its career, will then have gone, with all its powers, its prerogatives, its follies, its malign influence, and with whatever streak of virtue may have been possibly mingled in its texture, to control us, to agitate us, to injure us, no more. Four years it has lived, and its principal achievement has been the passage of the sub-Treasury, by trampling with contempt upon the broad seal of a sovereign State. What good it has done, we are unable to point out. What harm it has accomplished, we may possibly conceive of, by considering the present condition of the Treasury, of our foreign relations, of our Navy, of the Army and the defences, of the Post Office, and of the public morals, and the condition of the people. But we congratulate the country that it has at last come to an end. It is gone" (The *Madisonian*, March 3, 1841).

59 *Union*, March 4, 1841.

60 Under the heading "Hospitality at the White House" an article in the New Haven *Palladium* said: "He [Harrison] keeps his house open to all comers. . . . The servants at the White House find more difficulty

his inauguration, the President had directed Webster to issue a most wholesome order stating that any interference in elections, state or federal, by federal officers, would be regarded as cause for removal. The plain farmer of the Whigs was promptly branded by Harris as a usurper of royal powers and a violator of the rights of states, for "the Autocrat of all the Russias never issued an *Ukase* more potent."[61] But before these unjust charges against the President had been put in type, the career of the "autocrat" had been cut short, and the same issue of the paper which contained them chronicled, also, the news of Harrison's death.

As Polk's campaign for reëlection began as soon as his competitor had been nominated on March 5, 1841, the incidents of the remainder of his gubernatorial term will be treated in the succeeding chapter, which deals primarily with that spirited political contest and with the transfer of Tennessee to the Whigs.

---

in adapting themselves to the change of Administration than any other officeholders. He breaks in on all the elegant aristocratic usages of the palace, and plays the mischief with that systematic courtly etiquette which with the Sub-Treasury constituted the two great radical reforms of the late President. He gets up at sunrise, like a plain farmer as he is, and wants his breakfast within an hour after, (the vulgar man!)—and eats with an appetite of a common day laborer. He gave one of his servants a regular 'blowing up' the other day, for leaving a visitor dripping wet and muddy in a cold 'ante-chamber,' because the President was at breakfast and could not be disturbed, and because the carpet would be injured by the muddy feet of one who came on foot! The President brought the visitor into the breakfast parlor, and insisted on making him comfortable at the fire at once. At all these things the *democracy* are much shocked, and look aghast at this desecration of the 'palace!'" Quoted in Nashville *Banner*, April 5, 1841.

[61] Harris quoted from the *Evening Post:* "this document has added the last insult that can be given to a free and independent people, and will be held up to popular execration by every man who is not disposed to yield his neck to the yoke of party, or who is not a base and degraded slave. It is so insolent in spirit and dictation, breathes an air so vile and debasing, that it is difficult to speak of it without subjecting one's self to an unwonted excitement" (Nashville *Union*, April 12, 1841).

CHAPTER X

DEFEATED BY JONES IN 1841

From the day of their defeat in 1839 the Whigs of Tennessee had been marshalling their forces for the next gubernatorial contest, and the great national victory of 1840 gave them reason to hope for success. It had also, by example, indicated the type of campaign that would be most likely to win that success. Cannon's main weakness as a candidate had been his inability to adjust himself to the guerrilla variety of campaign by which many a less brilliant politician had endeared himself to the people. Capable but painfully serious, Cannon was a shining mark for the shafts of wit and ridicule which Polk had hurled with unerring aim whenever they had met in joint discussion. On the contrary, Polk had demonstrated his adaptability to a degree that surprised his closest friends. Distinguished for his dignified and learned discussions in the national House of Representatives, Polk had, in 1839, discomfited his rival and won the people by a most skilful use of mimicry and sarcasm. The Whigs were therefore familiar with the campaign methods of the Governor as well as the predilections of the people, and the convention which assembled at Murfreesborough on March 5, 1841, displayed political wisdom by nominating the one man in the state who was thought to be capable of "beating the governor at his own game." This man was Major James C. Jones,[1] a "horny-handed" farmer from Wilson County, who had represented his county in the legislature, served as a Presidential elector, and acquired a local reputation as an effective "stump speaker." Tall and ungainly in appearance, Jones possessed many of those grotesque personal

---

[1] Jackson declined to call Jones, major, "for he never was a corporal" (Jackson to Polk, March 20, 1841, *Polk Papers*).

qualities which had made John Randolph famous. Even the
sobriquet "Lean Jimmy," with which his admiring friends had
christened him, served as a valuable asset in a contest so closely
following the "great whirlwind campaign" of 1840. Realizing
that, in knowledge and debating powers, he was no match for his
adversary, Jones resorted to hectoring tactics and relied more
on amusing than on convincing his audience. Nevertheless he
was a man of considerable ability, and he displayed a fair knowledge of the political issues of the day. In spite of the picture
drawn by Phelan and others, there was a serious side to the campaign of 1841. Jones did not devote all of his time to "coonery
and foolery," but at times displayed alertness and skill as a
debater.

As in 1839 the canvass dealt principally with national issues.
In his "Address to the People," Polk stated that his views on
national questions had been given in detail in his address of
1839, and that nothing had since occurred to alter them. He
had, he said, been forced to begin the campaign early because of
the untiring efforts of the Whigs to defeat him.[2]

Each side accused the other of being Federalists, and Harrison's "autocratic" order against interference in elections, and
Van Buren's regal splendor, were offered as evidence to prove
the opposing contentions. The death of Judge White nearly a
year before did not prevent his name from being dragged into
the contest. Jackson, in exhorting Polk to answer the "falsehoods" of Bell and Foster regarding Van Buren's extravagance
in furnishing the executive mansion, provided him with a statement that it was Bell's disappointment at not being made a
member of Jackson's cabinet, on White's recommendation, that
had caused Bell to desert the party and to bring White out for

---

[2] "From the moment of my election in 1839, it had been manifestly an
object of no minor importance with my leading political opponents in the
State, to prostrate and destroy me. Their attacks were constant. Their
presses kept up an incessant war upon me. No calumny or misrepresentation of my political opinions and course had been too gross to fill their
columns" (Nashville *Union*, March 29, 1841).

the Presidency.[3] A friend in Albany[4] furnished Polk with several letters written by Granger, the Postmaster-General which were to be used for the purpose of proving him to be an Abolitionist. Jones and other Whigs tried to counteract the effect produced by these by asserting that Polk's grandfather had been a Tory.

Early in March Jones published a list of his speaking appointments. He opened the campaign at Murfreesborough, where he boasted that he could tell a greater number of anecdotes than the Governor himself.[5] He promptly accepted an invitation from Polk to meet in joint debate whenever possible,[6] and they met for the first time at Murfreesborough on the twenty-seventh of March.

Polk opened the discussion with a spirited attack upon the Harrison administration. He denounced Granger as an Abolitionist, and Webster as a Federalist who, in 1835, had been so unpatriotic as to declare that he would not support a certain bill to appropriate money for defense "though the *enemy* were battering down the walls of the Capitol." Unfortunately for himself, Polk tried, as he had done in the canvass with Cannon, to weaken his opponent by making him an object of ridicule. Among other shafts of sarcasm, he said that his friend Jones was a "promising young man," but "as for his being Governor, that's all a notion."[7] As soon as Jones took the platform, he referred repeatedly to Polk as "my venerable competitor." This he continued to do whenever they met in debate, much to the amusement of the audience, for Polk at that time was only forty-six years of age.

Before the candidates met again, Governor Polk issued a public statement in which he gave his reasons for not convening

3 Jackson to Polk, March 20, 1841, *Polk Papers*.

4 E. Crowell to Polk, March 19, 1841, *ibid.*

5 Yoakum to Polk, March 15, 1841, *ibid.*

6 Polk to Jones, March 15; Jones to Polk, March 18, 1841, *ibid.*

7 Nashville *Union*, March 29, 1841.

the legislature in extra session so that Senators might be chosen in time for Harrison's called session of Congress. He had already called a special election for the purpose of choosing members of the House of Representatives. In declining to convene the legislature, Polk, as we have already noted, disregarded the wishes, not only of General Jackson, but of nearly all of the leading Democrats of the state. It was thoroughly characteristic of Polk to follow his own judgment rather than the wishes of his friends, even of "Old Hickory," and yet he was often charged with being a weak tool of General Jackson.

The main reasons assigned in his public statement for not convening the legislature were unnecessary expense and the impropriety of taking advantage of an accident to strengthen his own party in the federal Senate. The members elected to the legislature in 1839 had not, he said, been chosen with the selection of Senators in view, and "my opinion is that the frank, fair, and honest course, is to leave the choice open for the decision of the people at the next August election." Harrison, he said, had given him an opportunity to disregard the popular will, for it is

certain that if I had availed myself of them that the present General Assembly, if convened, would choose two Democratic Senators. If, however, the President under the influence and control of inflamed partisans, maddened with their late success . . . has committed a capital political blunder, it is no reason why I should commit one also.

He denounced the President for unnecessarily convening Congress, for, as there was plenty of money in the Treasury, the call must have been made for purely political reasons.[8]

---

[8] "Large and extravagant promises which can never be redeemed had been made to the people, and it was doubtless deemed to be necessary to do something, or to *appear* to do something to keep up the public expectation, and thereby possibly to operate upon the elections which are to take place in States during the present year. . . . They probably fear to let the public mind sober down to a state of calm reflection, lest peradventure they may not succeed in their favorite measures of Federal policy, at the next regular session of Congress." Printed in Nashville *Union*, April 1, 1841.

Whether the Governor was influenced solely by a spirit of fairness, no one but himself could know, but, whatever his motives were, he received no thanks from the Whigs for his magnanimity. The *Banner* bitterly assailed him for impugning the motives of the President, and for praising himself. It pronounced his action hypocritical and declared that his forbearance had been due to a knowledge that the legislature would not dare to choose two Democrats in the face of the late election, and to fear that an attempt to make such a choice would injure his own prospects of reëlection.[9] At a debate held at Lebanon shortly after the publication of Polk's statement, Jones won applause by reminding the Governor that his solicitude for the popular will had not prevented him from appointing Nicholson Senator after the people had repudiated him (Nicholson) by refusing to make him a Presidential elector. The Whig paper of the town commended Polk's wit and added that ''he makes as much of it with his face as with his tongue.''[10] Most effective of all were his impersonations of Bailie Peyton, the chief feature of which was what the Whigs called ''Polk's horrible grin.''

The candidates visited the principal towns of the state. From the press notices, one would be led to believe that their time was occupied almost entirely with the relation of humorous anecdotes and the coining of witty remarks. Nevertheless, their printed speeches show that a serious discussion of political issues was by no means omitted. Polk, especially, displayed great power as a debater. He thoroughly understood the questions under

---

9 Nashville *Banner*, April 5, 1841. The most abusive of all papers was Parson Brownlow's Jonesborough *Whig*. In an article addressed to Polk, the editor said that the Governor while ''under the influence of *liquor* or opium, being *half drunk*'' had denounced the *Whig* for criticising his ancestors who had been lying in the tomb for forty years. Brownlow reminded Polk that he had criticized both White and Harrison since their death, and then continued: ''You canting, cringing hypocrite—you demagogue and time-serving politician, you advise mankind as to prudence and moderation!'' Undated in *Polk Papers*.

10 Lebanon *Chronicle*, quoted by Nashville *Banner*, April 5, 1841.

discussion, and few could excel him in clear and logical presentation. Had his opponent attempted to meet the Governor's arguments by a frank and fair discussion, he would have been easily vanquished, for his knowledge of political questions was superficial and limited. To Jones, however, ignorance of the subject was never a cause of embarrassment. By substituting bold assertion for knowledge, he was able to discuss any topic without hesitation, and, so far as his audience was concerned, he had disproved every contention of his adversary. It availed Polk little to demolish these assertions by clear presentation of historical data. Like Douglas in his debates with Lincoln, Jones would calmly reiterate his assertions, no matter how often they had been refuted, or else he would divert the attention of the audience by a humorous anecdote or by a dissertation on the beauties of coon fur. In either case the effect of Polk's argument was entirely lost, while his adversary succeeded in winning the vociferous applause of an uncritical audience. No wonder that a Democrat who heard their debate at Somerville exclaimed in disgust: "Mr. Polk made an ass of himself, talking sense to a lot of d—d fools," and urged that the Governor "ought to get a stick and crack Jones's skull, and end this tomfoolery!"[11]

One of Jones's most exasperating characteristics was his never-failing good humor. As he had declined to become embarrassed by the most complete demonstration of his ignorance, so, also, he refused to be angered by sarcasm or ridicule. At times Polk tried to crush his opponent by belittling his abilities and by holding him up to scorn. In reply, Jones would solicit the compassion of the hearers for his "irascible but venerable competitor." Polk said that he had tried to discuss questions of state in a serious manner and that his opponent had wisely made jest of things which were beyond his comprehension. When he asserted that Jones was better suited to the circus ring than to the Governor's chair, Jones good-naturedly admitted that they

---

[11] Phelan, *Hist. of Tenn.*, 403.

would both do well in the ring—himself as a clown, and the
Governor as "the little fellow that is dressed up in a red cap
and jacket and who rides around on a poney."[12] The Governor
wearied of the travesty, and would gladly have abandoned joint
meetings, but, as they had been undertaken upon his own invitation, there was no way of breaking gracefully with his trifling
antagonist.

The debates attracted attention in all parts of the state, and
everywhere large audiences greeted the speakers. Much importance was attached to their meeting at Nashville, which was not
only the capital, but the political headquarters of the state.
Here, on May 19, they were greeted by a large and enthusiastic
concourse of people, and each candidate according to agreement
spoke for two and one-half hours. "Polk," as Phelan has well
said, "made a speech that would have swept from the stump any
man who had ever been Governor of Tennessee before him, and
any man who was Governor after Jones until Andrew Johnson
came forward."[13] It was a forceful and logical presentation
of the issues, replete with historical data and spiced with humorous illustrations. Jones's address was a compound of sophistry
and nonsense. Intead of answering Polk's arguments he constructed innumerable "men of straw" and then demolished them
to the entire satisfaction of his audience. He misquoted and
distorted everything that the Governor had said, after which
he amused the crowd by poking fun at his opponent and by relating preposterous stories.[14] No man of Polk's training and
dignity could cope with such politcal bushwhacking.

Had the people been really interested in political issues,
Jones could not have commanded a hearing. But since 1840,

12 *Ibid.*, 402.　　　13 *Ibid.*, 404.

14 The *Union* of May 24 thus described him: "Maj. Jones is a floater;
amusing at times, but superficial as a bubble. He drifts along on the surface of today and plays with the uppermost passions and prejudices of his
hearers; trifles with important matters and converts important matters into
trifles. . . . In a word, he is quite possible as an electioneer for his party—
good of the kind, but the quality is none of the best."

the Whigs had abandoned serious discussion and had staked
everything on an appeal to the emotions. For this reason Polk's
training and success were used to prejudice the people against
him. Not only had his grandfather been a Tory, but the Governor himself was said to be an aristocrat, who, at heart, held
the people in contempt. Ignorance, uncouth appearance, and
slovenly dress were regarded as attributes of honest statesmanship, and Jones always emphasized the fact that he had followed
the plow.[15] The Governor, however, deserved little sympathy
on account of these misrepresentations, for with similar weapons
he had aided in "putting down" the able and upright John
Quincy Adams.

Up to the close of the canvass, no one could predict, with
any degree of certainty, what the result would be. The Whigs
did most of the shouting. They made extravagant claims, but
many Democrats could not believe that a majority of the people
would be willing to cast out a man of Polk's ability and reputation and put in his place a man whose sole claim to fame rested
on a grotesque personal appearance and low-grade wit. The
Democrats, however, had overrated the people's sense of propriety, and on that account were doomed to disappointment.
At the election, which was held on August 5, Polk was defeated
by a majority of over three thousand votes, but the *Union* congratulated the Democrats on their "signal TRIUMPH OF PRIN-
CIPLE in sweeping away TEN THOUSAND of the last year's majority."[16] It was generally conceded, even by the Whigs, that
no other man in the party could have polled so many votes, and
instead of losing prestige, Polk was credited by his party with

---

[15] The Knoxville *Register* in contrasting the candidates said that Jones
was "free, manly, undisguised, plain, and carrying conviction with every
sentence." Polk was "hidden, dissembling, artful, shrinking and hypocritical in the extreme" Quoted in Nashville *Banner*, August 2, 1841.

[16] "Never," said Harris, the editor, "did Gov. Polk win for himself
more laurels than he has won in this contest. The Democracy of the whole
Union will appreciate his Herculean efforts at the expense of health to
maintain the principles that he has uniformly supported, the principles
of Jefferson and Jackson" (Nashville *Union*, August 12, 1841).

having won a great personal victory. In a letter to Van Buren, General Jackson rejoiced in the reduction of the Whig majority and said that "Gov. Polk deserves the thanks of the Democracy of the whole union, he fought the battle well and fought it alone, I may say." Strange to say, Jackson commended rather than criticized Polk for having disregarded his advice about convening the legislature. He pointed out to Van Buren that, had the legislature been called, two Democratic Senators would have been elected, but "the Governor threw aside policy, and adopted the real republican creed—that a majority have the right to rule."[17]

In the legislature which was elected with Jones, the Whigs had a majority of three in the lower house. In the senate the Democrats still had a majority of one. But one of their number, Samuel Turney, was regarded as rather independent in politics, and, when the time came for him to take a definite stand with his colleagues, he proved to be weak and vacillating. Nominally, however, the Democrats had a majority of one and thereby possessed the power to block any measure of the lower house that required their separate approval. But on any question which required the joint vote of the two houses the Whigs, by virtue of their majority of three in the lower house, were in a position to outvote their opponents.

In Tennessee, politics had precedence over legislation. Therefore the defeated party began at once to devise ways and means of preventing their opponents from filling the two vacant seats in the United States Senate. The term for which Judge White had been elected, and which since his resignation had been filled by Alexander Anderson, had expired. The other vacancy had been caused by the death of Senator Grundy, and had been filled temporarily by A. O. P. Nicholson, by virtue of the Governor's recess appointment.

Following the election, Polk received many letters, the main object of which was to congratulate him for having reduced the

---

[17] Jackson to Van Buren, Aug. 16, 1841, *Van Buren Papers.*

Whig majority. In these letters several of his friends expressed the opinion that the Democrats ought to demand the privilege of choosing one of the Senators, and that Polk himself should be the man. Among others, Hopkins L. Turney advised such a course. He assured Polk, also, that his brother, Samuel Turney, would vote with the Democrats.[18]

When plotting to force the Whigs to concede them one Senator, Democratic leaders tried to ease their conscience by asserting that in 1840 Whig members of the legislature had threatened, in the event of Polk's convening the legislature, to remain at home and thus prevent an election of Senators. It was further alleged that these threats had been made on the advice of Henry Clay.[19] It was said, also, that, during the recent campaign, when it was believed that the Democrats would elect a majority of the legislature, Jones had boasted that the Whig members would not permit the Democrats to hold an election for Senators.[20] Polk at first was noncommittal, but he soon made it known that he was not a candidate for the office. The reason which he gave for not permitting the use of his name was that he would not accept any office except one conferred upon him by a vote of the people.[21] With Polk out of the race, the politicians turned their attention to other candidates, but nothing could be done, of course, until the meeting of the legislature and the inauguration of a new governor.

---

[18] Turney to Polk, Washington, Aug. 24, 1841 (*Polk Papers*). Laughlin, Huntsman, and others assured Polk that some of the Whigs had agreed to vote for him.

[19] H. L. Turney to Polk, Jan. 2, 1842, *ibid.*

[20] Alex. Anderson to Polk, Aug. 20, 1841, *ibid.* Anderson urged that the Democrats should now practice this plan upon those who had invented it.

[21] Geo. W. Smith, of Memphis, advised Polk not to permit the use of his name for two reasons: (1) possibility of defeat and loss of prestige; (2) it would lend color to the Whig charge that he had never cared for the governorship, and had wished it only as a stepping-stone to a higher office. (Smith to Polk, Sept. 2, 1841, *ibid.*) Polk may have been influenced by considerations of this kind.

As soon as the legislature had convened, Polk, on October 7, submitted his final message as governor.[22] It was a long document and filled with detailed information on various topics, but mainly on banks and internal improvements. For a man who had only a week longer to serve, Polk was surprisingly free with advice and suggestions for the future. He expressed satisfaction with the degree of prosperity which had been enjoyed by the people during the last two years, and he attributed it to corrective legislation and the consequent elimination of extravagant speculation. He regretted that banks had not been compelled by law to resume specie payments, and once more recommended the enactment of such a law. "There is," said he, "no sound principle of ethics or of public policy which should exempt Banks from the moral and legal obligations which rest upon individuals to pay their debts." He pointed out that the bank note circulation amounted to about three million dollars and that the average rate of depreciation was eight and one-half per cent; this unnecessary burden was borne by the people, while the banks were prosperous—even paying dividends. He reported that the law recently enacted which provided for "the reduction of the State debt" had enabled him to recall and to cancel fifteen hundred state bonds of one thousand dollars each. The outstanding internal improvement bonds amounted to $1,816,916.66⅔, while, so far, only one company had paid a dividend to the state—the small sum of $1620. The currency, he said, had been much improved by the law which prohibited the emission of notes under ten dollars; as a further remedy for financial ills, he recommended that commercial houses and improvement companies should be prevented by law from issuing checks designed to circulate as money. The internal improvement board had, in his opinion, accomplished much good by requiring various companies to reduce their stock and to conduct their affairs in a more economical manner. Among other things the retiring Governor

---

22 *Tenn. Sen. Jour.*, 1841–42, 22–42.

recommended that improvements be made in hospitals for the insane, that sexes be segregated in penitentiaries, and that the governor be given power to commute the death penalty to life imprisonment.[23] His recommendations were salutary and sensible. Some of his suggestions indicated grave need for improvement in social conditions.

One paragraph in the Governor's message is especially interesting, for in it Polk expressed his views on the slavery question, a subject which he usually avoided. He informed the legislature that he had, during the past year, received two communications from friends of negroes convened in London, on June 12 to 20, 1840, in which they had asked for the abolition of slavery and the slave trade. Viewing these communications ''as an impertinent and mischievous attempt on the part of foreigners to interfere with one of the domestic institutions of the State,'' he had declined to enter into any correspondence with this convention. Doubtless he was governed more by his belief in state rights than by an interest in the institution of slavery itself; still, he was ready to resent outside interference with the ''peculiar institution.''

On October 14 Polk delivered his valedictory, and on the same day James C. Jones was inaugurated as his successor.[24] While it is true that Polk's interests were national rather than local, yet the state was indebted to him for causing the enactment of beneficial laws. Under his leadership the state had been freed from a ruinous internal improvement policy, and he had done much to check currency inflation and to reduce the debt of the state. His reform measures were all in the line of sound statesmanship, and, if we may judge from the suggestions made in his final message, the people might have profited by continuing him in office.

---

[23] He could now pardon only.
[24] *Tenn. Sen. Jour.*, 1841–42, 78.

CHAPTER XI

POLK IN RETIREMENT

On October 14, 1841, James C. Jones became governor of Tennessee, and on the nineteenth his first message was sent to the legislature.[1] His recommendations differed little from those which had already been submitted by his predecessor,[2] and, also like Polk, he attributed most of the distress of the people to their own fault—to buying more than they could reasonably hope to pay for. In one respect only did Jones differ radically from the former governor. The crisis in the monetary affairs of the country, he said, had been produced by the destruction of the Bank of the United States. Such a statement was naturally to be expected, for some part of a Whig governor's message must needs indicate the change of administration, and the bank was a subject of general interest.

As usual the legislature was far more interested in "practical politics" than in the less sportive business of lawmaking. The paramount question was the election of United States Senators, but first of all, the opinions of both legislators and constituents must be molded so as to accord with those of the leaders. The Democrats were most active in the senate, for in this branch they had, counting Samuel Turney, a majority of one. The leaders in the senate were Samuel H. Laughlin, former editor of the *Union*, and Andrew Johnson, who, at the recent election, had been promoted to the upper house. Johnson had ability and force, but Laughlin excelled him in political cunning and effectiveness as a manipulator. In the Polk-Bell contest, Johnson

---

[1] *Tenn. Sen. Jour.*, 1841–42, 116–125.

[2] Jones was accused of having *borrowed* from Polk's inaugural of 1839, and to prove the claim the *Union* published the two addresses in parallel columns (Laughlin, *Diary*, Oct. 21, 1843).

had supported the latter. Laughlin had ever been subservient and therefore enjoyed the entire confidence of Polk and other prominent Democrats.

On October 18, Laughlin, as chairman of the committee on federal relations, submitted a series of eight resolutions to which four more were added on the fifth of November.[3] The preamble recited the Virginia and Kentucky Resolutions of 1798 and declared that many of the laws enacted by Congress at the late extra session violated the spirit of the Constitution quite as much as did the laws against which those historic resolutions had protested. The first resolution reaffirmed those of 1798 and asserted that they were "universally true at all times and especially applicable to the present crisis and state of affairs." The succeeding seven resolutions condemned the convening of Congress by Harrison and, also, the various measures[4] proposed or enacted by the Whigs at that session. This indictment of the Whigs was intended to prepare public opinion for the items which were to follow—the four resolutions that were added on the fifth of November. The first of these, the ninth of the entire list, declared that the legislature had full power to instruct Senators chosen to represent the state in Congress, and that it was the duty of these officials to obey or resign. The second asserted that it was the duty of candidates for legislative offices to give explicit answers to queries made by citizens or members of the legislature concerning their views on public questions. The third affirmed the right of the people to instruct members of the legislature. The fourth formally instructed the Senators (not yet chosen) and requested the Representatives from Tennessee to conform their votes to the opinions expressed by the foregoing resolutions.

The last four resolutions displayed far more shrewdness than principle. On their face they contained nothing which any

---

[3] The resolutions may be found in *Tenn. Sen. Jour.* under the dates given.

[4] For example, the "bankrupt bill" and the tariff, distribution, and bank bills.

advocate of representative government could very well decline to support. But they were designed, as every one knew, for the purpose of harassing the Whig candidates with embarrassing interrogations and for rendering them ineligible should they decline to answer. By asserting the right of the people to instruct their representatives in the legislature, the Democrats hoped to hold in line their own members who might be inclined to follow their individual judgments. Their party had nothing to lose by obstructive tactics, and, by blocking their opponents at every turn, they might worry the Whigs into conceding one seat in the Senate.

Ephraim H. Foster and Spencer Jarnagin were selected as the Whig candidates and on November 16 the lower house sent to the senate a resolution urging the immediate election of two United States Senators lest delay ''may lead to bargain, intrigue, and management, to the detriment of the public interest.'' As soon as the resolution was read in the senate, Andrew Johnson moved to amend by making it read that delay ''may lead to bargain, intrigue, and management, to the great detriment of E. H. Foster and Spencer Jarnagin, and thereby promote and advance the public interest, by keeping them out of power for the next four and six years.''[5] The Democratic majority in the senate soon came to be called ''the immortal thirteen'' and except for an occasional desertion by Samuel Turney they voted as a body on all questions of party politics.

The customary method of electing Senators in Tennessee was by a joint ''convention'' of the two houses. As the Whigs had a majority of three in the lower house and the Democrats a majority of but one in the senate, it was obvious that if the usual method were to be followed the Whigs would outnumber their rivals in the convention. The Democrats now made the discovery that the usual method was unconstitutional, for, as they alleged, the constitution of the state required that each house should vote

---

[5] Protests against the amendment were made, but it passed the senate by a vote of 13 to 12 (*Tenn. Sen. Jour.*, 1841–42, 227, 232–233).

separately for Senators. For their own purposes it was an important discovery; by no other method could they hope to prevent an election until the Whigs were ready to compromise on choosing one Senator from each party.

Up to November 22 the Democrats were confident of their ability to prevent an election unless the Whigs would yield to their terms. A few days before, Turney had introduced a resolution calling for an election by convention, but he had subsequently voted with the Democrats on the above-mentioned Johnson resolution. On the twenty-second, however, Turney caused consternation in Democratic ranks by announcing that he would call up and support his resolution in favor of a convention election.[6] According to William H. Polk, Turney had, for the last two weeks, "been shivering in the wind," due to the fact that the Whigs had "brought every influence to bear on him within the range of human ingenuity."[7] On November 22 Gardner moved to amend Turney's resolution by fixing the following Saturday as the date on which the Senate would vote *separately* for federal Senators. Turney accepted the amendment, but it was the younger Polk's opinion that, after one trial, Turney would revert to the convention plan. The Democrats offered another *compromise* resolution the purport of which was to declare elected Hopkins L. Turney and Thomas Brown, a Whig from East Tennessee. It was hoped that, having passed the senate, this resolution could be forced through the lower house.[8] On the twenty-third Gardner modified his amendment.

---

[6] "On Saturday last the '13' were safe against the world, and the Whigs considered themselves as beaten. Guess then, what our astonishment was, when coming into the Senate on Monday morning [November 22], Sam Turney announced that he had changed his mind, and would call up and vote for his own resolutions to bring on the Senatorial election at an early day on joint vote in Convention." Turney said that his change of mind was due to letters from his constituents (Laughlin to Polk, November 24, 1841, *Polk Papers*).

[7] W. H. Polk to J. K. Polk, November, 22, 1841, *ibid.*

[8] "My own impression is, that if the resolution passed the Senate, as now amended, declaring Turney and Brown the Senators elect—we *can force* it through the House, by lashing the doubtful men into a redemption of their former pledges . . . . can at least produce a tie" (*Idem*).

The legislature was now asked to choose one Senator from each party on the ground that the popular vote at the recent election had been nearly equally divided. Other modifications were suggested, but these, as well as Gardner's resolution, were rejected. The Democratic majority in the senate succeeded in passing a resolution which named Hopkins L. Turney as Grundy's successor, but, on December 1, the lower house refused to concur in its adoption. On the same day Speaker Samuel Turney joined the Whigs of the senate in making an agreement with the lower house to meet in joint convention on the second and third of December for the purpose of electing Senators. It was understood that each of those days would be devoted to filling one of the vacancies.

On December 2, therefore, Speaker Turney and the twelve Whigs proceeded, according to agreement, to the chamber of the lower house to join with that body in choosing one of the Senators. The other twelve Democratic senators declined to attend the election. When summoned by the doorkeeper, they sent written notice to their speaker (Turney) that they were in the senate chamber, ready for "constitutional business."[9] The joint convention, for want of a quorum, was forced to adjourn. On the morning of the third the lower house again notified the senate that it was ready to receive the senators and to proceed to the election of one of the federal Senators. It had already been arranged to hold the other election in the afternoon and for this reason Speaker Turney deemed it to be unnecessary to join the house in convention twice in one day, inasmuch as both elections could be held during the same half-day. He therefore voted with the Democrats in declining to attend the forenoon session of the convention. This vote so angered the Whig senators that they left the senate chamber in a body. By so doing they gave a distinct advantage to the Democrats, who now adjourned to the following day, thereby nullifying the original

9 *Tenn. Sen. Jour.*, 1841–42, 280.

resolution which had designated December 2 and 3 as the days on which elections by *convention* should be held.

By seceding from the senate the Whigs had committed the tactical blunder of releasing Turney from his agreement. He now blamed them for the failure to elect Senators, and once more became one of the "immortal thirteen."[10] Five of the twelve Democratic senators submitted a written statement of reasons why they had refused to participate in the proposed election. The proposed method of election, they asserted, would violate the Constitution of the United States, which vests the election of Senators in the legislature of the state—not in a convention. It would violate, also, the state constitution, which says that Senators shall be chosen by the concurrent vote of the two houses *"sitting separately"*—not together. Both statements were untrue, and besides, the convention method had been thoroughly established by custom, and up to this time its validity had never been questioned. This new-born solicitude for constitutional limitations was simply a clever bit of pettifogging.

Before any attempt to elect Senators had been made, two interesting resolutions for dividing the state were offered in the senate. The first was introduced by Andrew Johnson, on December 7, and provided that a joint committee of the two houses should be appointed to consider the expediency and the constitutionality of ceding East Tennessee to the United States so that it might be made an independent commonwealth and called the "State of Frankland." The resolution directed Governor Jones to correspond with the governors of Georgia, North Carolina, and Virginia with a view to procuring portions of those states for inclusion within the limits of "Frankland." On December 15, Gardner offered a similar resolution which provided for the

---

[10] Turney's explanation, *ibid.*, 304–305. On December 13, J. Geo. Harris informed Polk by letter that there was no prospect of an election. "Thank God and the immortal thirteen Ephraim's [Foster] fiddle is broke. No more will its dulcet strains minister to the desponding faculties of faction" (*Polk Papers*).

creation of the state of ''Jacksoniana.'' It was to include the ''Western District'' of Tennessee and portions of Kentucky and Mississippi.[11] The senate rejected Gardner's proposal by a vote of eleven to fourteen. Johnson's resolution passed the senate by a vote of seventeen to six (January 18), but after considerable discussion and many futile attempts to amend, this too was finally rejected by the lower house.

In accordance with the Laughlin resolutions,[12] Democratic members of the legislature had addressed queries to all senatorial candidates concerning their views on public questions. Foster and Jarnagin treated these queries with silent contempt. Hopkins L. Turney, the Democratic aspirant, gave satisfactory answers as a matter of course, and so, also, did Thomas Brown, a Whig of Roane County, East Tennessee. On December 20, Laughlin offered in the senate a resolution which differed little from the one previously submitted by Gardner. Whereas, in choosing Senators, the popular will should be consulted, so read the preamble, and, as the recent election had shown the people to be about equally divided in politics, and as neither party was able to choose Senators without the coöperation of the other, it was therefore resolved that Turney and Brown, having responded to all interrogatories, be declared the Senators to represent the state in the Senate of the United States. Turney was to fill the unexpired term of Grundy, and Brown was to have the full term of six years.[13] The resolution passed the senate but failed in the other house, and that body once more invited the senate to join them in an election by convention. The Whigs of both houses refused to coöperate with the Democrats in electing a

---

[11] *Tenn. Sen. Jour.*, 1841–42, 288, 345.

[12] Those which he had introduced on Nov. 5, relating to the interrogation of candidates for office. See above.

[13] *Tenn. Sen. Jour.*, 1841–42, 366–67. ''Some of our friends here are of opinion—that after all our Senators should be elected—if the Whigs can be brought 'to elect one and one' '' (A. V. Brown to Polk, Washington, Dec. 23, 1841, *Polk Papers*). This seems to indicate that the Democrats had counted more on preventing an election than on effecting a compromise.

comptroller and a treasurer unless the Democrats would agree to choose Senators by a joint vote. Of this refusal the Democrats tried to make political capital;[14] by exploiting it they endeavored to divert the attention of the people away from their own obstructive tactics.

Polk kept in close touch with the contest that was being waged at Nashville and from time to time gave directions to his political friends. He was one of the first to doubt the loyalty of his old friend A. O. P. Nicholson, and to suspect him of courting an alliance with Foster for the purpose of procuring their election to the Senate.[15] He was most severe in his denunciation of Nicholson and predicted that he would follow in the footsteps of John Bell.[16] Hearing that some of Bell's friends had made overtures offering to settle the senatorial deadlock by choosing Bell and some Democrat, Polk stated to Senator Maclin[17] that it would never do "to elect *Bell* by Democratic votes. It would not only be placing him in a position to do mischief but it would be rewarding his apostasy." He had heard also, he said, that similar overtures had been made by Foster's friends. "To no man in the State," he continued, "would it be more grating than to myself to be driven to the necessity of making a compromise by which he might obtain a seat in the Senate, and yet it is not

14 ''Our whole object is,'' wrote Wm. H. Polk, who was a member of the lower house, ''to place them [the Whigs] in the position of refusing to elect State officers, necessary and essential to the proper administration of our State Government, because we prevent them from placing in the Senate men who stand *Mum*'' (W. H. Polk to J. K. Polk, Jan. 6, 1842, *Polk Papers*).

15 In answer to one of Polk's letters, J. P. Hardwick wrote from Nashville that ''I have no doubt a great effort is being made to carry out an unholy alliance between F. & N.'' (Hardwick to Polk, Jan. 16, 1842, *ibid.*)

16 ''Every day convinces me more and more that he [N] is now travelling in the broad road—that John Bell travelled for several years before his apostacy—whilst he was making *loud professions* of his adhesion to our principles. We all know where *John Bell* now is, *and mark what I now say to you*, that five years, perhaps not one will pass—before he is where *Bell* now is, unless it shall be his personal interest shall make him *seem* otherwise. *I am not mistaken*'' (Polk to State Senator Sackfield Maclin, Jan. 17, 1842, *Andrew Johnson Papers*, vol. 1).

17 *Ibid.*

impossible that our *safety as a party* in the State might require such a sacrifice."[18] Should an agreement with Foster be made, Polk believed that the Democrat ought to be chosen from East Tennessee; but if any western Democrat was to be selected, it should be Hopkins L. Turney. He preferred a Whig Senator to Nicholson, because he had "more respect for an open opponent than a hypocritical friend."[19] Some of the "immortal thirteen," however, were unwilling to accept any compromise which did not eliminate both Foster and Bell.

On February 7, the last day of the session, Laughlin, probably acting under instructions from Polk, offered a new resolution "in the spirit of harmony, concession and compromise." This resolution authorized the Whig members of the legislature to choose a Senator from any of the three divisions of the state (east, middle or west), and provided that the Democrats should then select a Senator from one of the other divisions. The resolution passed the senate by a strict party vote, but not until an amendment had been added which required that both Senators must be "selected from men who have not been in public life for the last four years." Such a limitation had not been contemplated by either Laughlin or Polk, but some of the *thirteen* would accept nothing less. The lower house would not, of course, agree to the resolution; all hope of compromise was at an end; and the legislature adjourned without having filled either vacancy. On the same day the *thirteen* had the satisfaction of

---

[18] "It would be a *bitter pill*," said Polk, "to take Mr. F. even upon a compromise, and yet if nothing else can be done I have been brought very seriously to doubt, whether we had not better take him with *some good and true Democrat* than to have the State unrepresented in the Senate and thus raise up a perplexing troublesome issue of *Senators or no Senators* in the State, which may and probably will be the test question in our elections in 1843. Before you can compromise at all with him or any other Whig—they must yield to *your mode of elections and agree to obey instructions.* If they will do this and agree to give us a Democratic Senator with him—my conviction is, that it is the course of safety to yield to it."

[19] Polk to James Walker, Jan. 17, 1842, *Polk Papers.* Whether well founded or not, the belief in Nicholson's disloyalty was quite general. H. L. Turney wrote from Washington to Polk, April 25, 1842: "I think A. O. P. N. has put his foot in it. Can it be possible that he can longer deceive the democracy of Tennessee?"

rejecting for a second time a list of persons whom Governor Jones had nominated to be directors of the Bank of Tennessee, and as a result, the Democratic incumbents retained their positions.

In their game of obstruction the Democrats had won a decided victory—much greater than they had any reasonable hope to expect. Had any of the "immortal thirteen" failed them, everything would have been lost, and more than once Samuel Turney had threatened to desert to the enemy. By bad management, the Whigs had failed to take advantage of his willingness to coöperate with them, while the Democrats spared no effort to hold him in line. The tactics employed by the senate to attain its ends were as unscrupulous as they were successful. The aid given by Polk and Jackson was something of which neither man had reason to be proud, but politicians are seldom overscrupulous when party interests are at stake.

Just as the Democrats were rejoicing over their success in thwarting the Whigs, their own party suffered a real loss in the retirement of J. George Harris from the editorship of the *Union*.[20] He had taken charge of the paper when it was bankrupt and impotent, and under his management it had become one of the most influential papers in the state. His style was not always elegant nor his assertions true, but he was peculiarly fitted to perform the task to which he had been assigned. After his retirement the *Union* rapidly deteriorated, until Polk and his associates had to take its rehabilitation in hand during the campaign of 1843.

After the adjournment of the legislature, the thoughts of politicians turned to plans for the future. Although it was an open secret that Polk would, in 1843, again be the candidate for governor, both he and his friends were ever on the alert to promote his prospects for the Vice-Presidential nomination in 1844.

---

[20] In the issue of March 31 Harris announced that he was going to Europe for a few months and that the owners, Hogan and Heiss, would conduct the paper themselves.

The more apparent it became that Van Buren would again head the Democratic ticket, the more necessary it seemed to be to find a running mate that would be acceptable to the South and West. Maclin, of the Tennessee senate, voiced the general sentiment when he told Polk that "Our friends intend to fight the battle with you, and keep Van Buren as much out of sight as possible." In these two sections of the Union, influential leaders fully appreciated Polk's great services to the party and looked with favor upon his nomination for the Vice-Presidency, but, as Maclin frankly told him, it had been urged that he was not well known to the people in other parts of the country.[21]

Politicians of both parties attached much importance to Van Buren's visit to the Hermitage in the spring of 1842. Knowing Jackson's warm friendship for Polk, the Whigs expected and many Tennesseans hoped that the visit would result in a formal agreement between Van Buren and Polk. But, despite the efforts of Polk's friends in his behalf, the New Yorker remained noncommittal to the point of exasperation[22] and left Tennessee without having mentioned to Polk the subject of the Vice-Presidency.[23]

Although Van Buren declined to take any part in promoting Polk's candidacy or even to discuss it, and even though his indifferent attitude during his visit had still further alienated the supporters of Polk, yet both the Whigs and the Calhounites were

---

[21] Maclin to Polk, May 4, 1842, *Polk Papers.* Maclin had just returned from Mississippi, where he had been sounding Polk's praises and urging the people to call a convention for the purpose of nominating Van Buren and Polk.

[22] "I am at a loss to know what to say to you, I can learn nothing. . . . Mr. Van Buren seems disposed to say nothing on the subject we spoke of when I last saw you. I made an effort through Donelson again this evening but it was all *Mum.* . . . It may be that he will say to you what he will not say to another person. The old Genl will *tell him before leaving the Hermitage,* to have a conversation with you" (Gen. R. Armstrong to Polk, May 4, 1842, *Polk Papers*).

[23] Polk himself said in a letter that during Van Buren's visit neither had "mentioned verbally or in writing" the subject which the Whigs say brought him to Tennessee (Polk to Elmore, of South Carolina, June 13, 1842, *Polk Papers*).

certain that an agreement between the two candidates had been effected and that one of its objects was to crush Calhoun.[24] Van Buren was not popular in Tennessee, and many Democrats felt that Polk's election would be more certain if some other than the New Yorker could be nominated for President.[25] Cass was most frequently mentioned by those who held this belief. Others were inclined to await developments. Benton, like Van Buren, had declined to commit himself in Polk's favor, but his denunciation of Richard M. Johnson was regarded by Tennesseans in Washington as a hopeful sign.[26] Realizing the general indifference toward Van Buren in southern states, friends of Calhoun began to entertain hopes that he would be nominated for the Presidency in 1844;[27] but, believing, as they did, that Polk was in agreement with Van Buren, they did not, it appears, seek assistance from his friends. Then, too, the adherents of the great nullifier could hardly hope for the coöperation of a man who was thought to be under the dominating influence of General Jackson.

When the Tennessee legislature convened in the autumn of 1842, another futile attempt was made to fill the vacant seats in the federal Senate. J. George Harris, who had returned to Nashville, reported to Polk that Bell's supporters had offered to make an agreement whereby Bell was to answer the queries which had

---

24 "It is thought," wrote Dixon H. Lewis, "Van has effected his purpose with Polk," while according to Gentry, of Tennessee, no one doubted that Van Buren and Polk would be the Democratic candidates (Lewis to Richard Crallé, May 31, and June 10, 1842, *Crallé Papers*).

25 "I assure you, sir," wrote J. P. Hardwicke, "there is a disinclination to take up Van Buren again. I have taken some pains to arrive at this conclusion at our little caucuses" (Hardwicke to Polk, Nov. 13, 1842, *Polk Papers*).

26 Cave Johnson to Polk, Jan. 29; H. L. Turney to Polk, Jan. 31, 1843, *Polk Papers*.

27 One of the hopeful was Duff Green. He thought that, if the Van Burenites' plan of an early nominating convention could be thwarted, Calhoun would be nominated. "It has now narrowed down," he wrote, "to a choice between Calhoun and Van Buren and the demonstrations are becoming more decided for Mr. Calhoun so that, in my opinion, the concentration in his favor will become so apparent as public opinion develops that the convention will indeed become obsolete" (Green to Crallé, February 8, 1843, *Letters of Duff Green* in Library of Congress).

been ignored by Foster and Jarnagin. Having done this, he was to be elected as one of the Senators, and the Democrats were to fill the other vacancy with a candidate of their own choice. Harris was in favor of such an agreement if Polk would consent to be the Democratic Senator; Foster would be killed, politically, while Bell if properly instructed would be less powerful than at present.[28] Nothing, of course, resulted from the suggestion. Polk had already declined to make any compromise with Bell, and besides, the overtures of Bell's friends were probably made without his knowledge. During this session the Democrats made little attempt to force a compromise, but simply contented themselves with blocking the Whigs from electing their candidates. Their greatest fear seems to have been that Nicholson, by some treacherous agreement with the Whigs, would attempt to promote his own selfish interests.[29]

Feeling that both his own and his party's interests could be best served by defeating Governor Jones, Polk once more entered the race. The campaign was opened by a joint debate at Springfield, March 25, 1843. Jones scathingly denounced the conduct of the "immortal thirteen." Polk retorted by charging that Jones had originated the idea which they had put into practice. The *Union*[30] published letters from Whigs who claimed to have heard Jones boast that, in case the Democrats should have a bare majority on joint ballot, the Whigs would prevent a choice of Senators by refusing to participate in the election. Throughout the campaign the *Union* defended the thirteen for preventing the election of men who refused to be bound by the wishes of their constituents. The refusal of the state senate to confirm Jones's list of bank directors was purely for political reasons. The truth was reprehensible enough, but on the stump Jones

---

[28] Harris to Polk, Dec. 11, 1842, *Polk Papers*.

[29] W. H. Polk to J. K. Polk, February 14, 1843, *Polk Papers*. Andrew Johnson, fearing that his known friendship for Nicholson might be misinterpreted, wrote to Polk that "you have always been my first choice for anything" (Johnson to Polk, February 20, 1843, *ibid.*)

[30] March 31, 1843.

won applause by asserting that the Polk directors were corrupt and time-serving partisans who, for fear of exposure, did not dare to relinquish their offices.

In many respects the campaign was a repetition of that of 1841. There was, perhaps, more argument and less burlesque, although both candidates made use of anecdotes and sarcastic retorts. Polk was not unmindful of his own powers of wit. When writing to his wife of a debate held at Jackson with Milton Brown, he said that his opponent tried to turn the "occasion into a frolic . . . but I turned the laugh upon him & almost laughed him out of the Court House."[31]

In his "Letter to the People"[32] Polk, as usual, emphasized national issues such as the tariff, the national bank, and the general extravagance of the Whigs. Once more Tennessee was regarded as the pivotal state—the index to the approaching Presidential campaign. As it was practically certain that Clay would be the Whig candidate, much of Polk's time on the stump was devoted to Clay and his policies. Incensed by a revival of the old "bargain and corruption" charge of 1825, Clay challenged Polk to a discussion of this question at a time and place to be fixed by the Tennessean himself.[33] Apparently the challenge was not accepted.

Early in the campaign a group of persons in Memphis submitted to the two candidates a list of questions on political topics. Jones replied at once, and among other things expressed the following views. He favored a national bank, but was not fully satisfied with Clay's bill that had been vetoed by Tyler. He believed in a tariff for revenue, with incidental protection to home industries. In his opinion the legislature had full power to choose Senators in any manner which it saw fit. The last

---

[31] Polk to Mrs. Polk, April 4, 1843, *Polk Papers.*

[32] It bore the date of May 17, 1843, and was printed in the *Union,* May 23 and 26.

[33] Typewritten copy of a letter from Clay to Polk dated Ashland, May 20, 1843, *Polk Papers.*

answer did not harmonize very well with his condemnation of the Democratic senate for insisting that each house should vote separately.[34]

In answer to the same queries Polk stated that he believed in the sub-treasury, and in metal money for the nation supplemented by a limited amount of paper issued by state banks. He opposed direct taxes and endorsed tariff for revenue only. Like Jones, he thought that the legislature possessed the right to elect Senators in any manner agreeable to itself. He held, on the other hand, that all candidates for office were under obligation, when called upon, to express their views before election on all public questions. "The chief, if not the only value of the right of suffrage," said he,

consists in the fact, that it may be exercised *understandingly* by the constituent body. It is so, whether the immediate constituency consists of the Legislature, as in the case of the election of United States Senators, or of the people in their primary capacity, in the election of their Executive or Legislative agents. In either case the constituent has a right to know the opinions of the candidate before he casts his vote.[35]

Except on the bank question the views expressed by the two men were very much alike. Indeed, the paramount issue was: Shall Tennessee be returned to the Democratic column in national politics?

Throughout the campaign the Democrats were handicapped by the weakness of their party press. Since Harris's resignation the *Union* lacked both spirit and influence, and was rapidly drifting into bankruptcy. On the other hand, the Whigs had several vigorous papers, the most invincible of which was Brownlow's Jonesborough *Whig*. Polk was condemned for the part he had taken in the administrations of Jackson and Van Buren, and again it was said that he sought the governorship merely as a stepping-stone to the Vice-Presidency. Polk's "Tory"

---

[34] Jones's reply is dated April 24, 1843, and is printed in the Memphis *American Eagle*, May 2, a copy of which is among the *Polk Papers*.

[35] The answer is dated May 15, and is printed in the *Union*, June 2, 1843.

grandfather was again held up to scorn, while a Chattanooga paper charged the Democratic candidate with being an aristocrat who had "refused to eat with some wagoners who were stopping at the same tavern with him some years ago."[36]

Although Polk made a thorough canvass and demonstrated his superiority over his rival, Jones was reëlected by a majority of nearly four thousand votes. This time the Whigs elected a majority of the legislature as well as the governor, and the power of the "immortal thirteen" had been broken. Polk attributed the victory of the Whigs to their success in drawing the attention of the people to local questions and away from great national issues. He was still confident that his party would carry the state in the federal election of 1844.[37]

Soon after the election the defeated candidate's friends once more turned their attention to procuring for him the Vice-Presidential nomination. They were interested of course in his personal advancement, and besides, they had hopes that, with their favorite on the ticket, Tennessee might be restored to the Democratic party. On September 5 the *Union*, in a series of editorials, urged his nomination and declared him to be "one of the ablest men in the democratic party in the Southwest." In a letter to Van Buren, General Jackson expressed the belief that the former President would be nominated—and elected, also, if Polk were put on the ticket with him. Such a ticket, he said, would surely carry Tennessee; Polk would add strength to the party in all of the states, while Colonel Johnson would weaken it.[38]

The new legislature met on October 2, 1843. In the senate the Whigs had fourteen members, the Democrats, eleven; in the lower house the Whigs numbered forty, the Democrats, thirty-five. The two main political questions which confronted the

---

[36] Both articles and a denial are in the *Union*, June 27, 1843.

[37] Polk to Van Buren, August 8, 1843, *Van Buren Papers*.

[38] Jackson to Van Buren, September 22, 1843, *ibid*.

legislature were fixing a permanent location for the state capital, and the election of federal Senators. Although now in the minority, the Democrats planned to prevent the election of Foster and Jarnagin by supporting two other Whigs, A. R. Alexander, of West Tennessee, and Joseph L. Williams, of East Tennessee. Some of the Whigs, especially the Rutherford delegation, were eager to have the capital removed from Nashville to some more central location. The Democrats therefore concocted a scheme by which they hoped to procure a sufficient number of Whig votes to elect Alexander and Williams by offering to vote for the removal of the capital. Polk was then in Nashville and gave his support to the plan.[39] Their plotting was in vain. On October 7 both houses voted to retain the capital at Nashville, and on the seventeenth Foster and Jarnagin were elected Senators, the former to fill Grundy's unexpired term, the latter to succeed Anderson.[40]

Repeated defeats annoyed but did not discourage Democratic leaders. Harmony within their own ranks was the first desideratum, and Laughlin undertook the task of bringing Nicholson and his adherents back into the fold.[41] The task did not seem hopeless, for since the seats in the Senate had been filled by the Whigs there was no reason why Nicholson should not coöperate with his former associates. The "little magician" was the chief cause of embarrassment. Democrats, generally, were ready to support Polk, but from all parts of the state came reports of indifference or hostility to Van Buren.

Laughlin's "missionary" work was not confined to the Nicholson faction. As soon as the question of locating the capital had been settled, it was a foregone conclusion that Foster and Jarnagin would be elected. Freed from the responsibility of

---

[39] S. H. Laughlin, "Diary," October 1–4, 1843.

[40] *Ibid.*, Oct. 17. "*Jonakin* has gone home a Senator—and Ephe is running about, grinning and jumping like a pleased monkey—with just about the dignity of one, at best" (Laughlin to Polk, Oct. 20, 1843, *Polk Papers*).

[41] Laughlin to Polk, Oct. 12, 1843, *Polk Papers*.

manipulating the scheme to defeat this election, Laughlin could devote his entire energy to procuring for Polk the nomination for Vice-President. In letters to influential leaders and newspaper men, he almost demanded that Polk should be taken up by "the press and the People." He proposed that the former Governor should be nominated by the state convention which was to meet in November, and that the Tennessee delegation should go to the national convention "supporting his claims, and uncommitted as to Presidential candidate, but committed to abide its nomination." He told his correspondents that if Polk were put on the ticket with Van Buren or any other good Democrat the party would surely win, "but without Polk's name we would be beaten and tied down in federal chains in Tennessee for the next six or ten years."[42] His remark concerning the national convention seems to be the first indication of the plan, later adopted, to nominate Polk, and to remain noncommittal as to the Presidential candidate. The determination to make no nomination for President was strengthened, no doubt, by a letter written from New York by Harvey M. Watterson to A. O. P. Nicholson. Van Buren was Watterson's own choice, but, fearing that his favorite could not be elected, he did not believe it wise to nominate him. Cass, in his opinion, was the most *available* candidate. He said that "the Van Buren party intend to give Polk the *go by* as to a nomination for the Vice Presidency," and that Johnson would be nominated by the national convention.[43] On October 18, two days after the receipt of Watterson's letter, Laughlin conversed with A. V. Brown. Brown advised serving notice on the New Yorkers that the Tennesseans would support Van Buren if his adherents would agree to support Polk; otherwise they would go for Cass. To this Laughlin and Armstrong assented, and Donelson was selected to state their views to Silas Wright and other friends of Van Buren.[44] Probably this threat

42 S. H. Laughlin, "Diary," Oct. 9, 1843.
43 *Ibid.*, October 16, 1843.
44 *Ibid.*, October 18, 1843.

was not carried into effect.   At any rate Polk later disclaimed any knowledge of a project to drop Van Buren for Cass.[45]   In January, 1844, he asked Heiss to place Van Buren's name along with his own at the head of the political columns of the *Union*,[46] but, for the time being, the editor refused to comply.

The State convention met at Nashville on November 23, 1843. Polk was nominated for Vice-President by a unanimous vote, but no one was named for the Presidency.   The convention simply agreed to support whatever candidate the Baltimore convention might see fit to nominate.   The reason assigned for not nominating Van Buren, as stated to him in letters from both Polk and Jackson,[47] was a fear that the Cass supporters might resist such action, and that a breach in the party would result.

On hearing from Cave Johnson and A. V. Brown that Van Buren was stronger in Washington than Cass and that he would, in all probability, be nominated at Baltimore, Polk advised the editors of the *Union* to come out for the ex-President.[48]   His real feeling toward Van Buren is not easy to determine, but from his silence rather than his words, one always gets the impression that his support of the New Yorker was based, as in this case, on expediency instead of admiration for the man.   It was quite natural that this should have been so, for Van Buren had more than once shown indifference when Polk needed his aid.

Realizing that the party had suffered from the want of a vigorous newspaper, Polk turned his attention to rehabilitating the Nashville *Union*.   Since its purchase by Hogan and Heiss, it had been edited by the senior partner.   He had never been a forceful writer, and of late his health had become so impaired that the paper was practically without an editor.   With the consent of the owners, Polk asked Laughlin to take charge of the

---

45 Polk to Cave Johnson, March 18, 1844, ''Polk-Johnson Letters.''

46 Polk to Heiss, Jan. 21, 1844, ''Heiss Papers.''

47 Jackson to Van Buren, Nov. 29; Polk to Van Buren, Nov. 30, 1843, *Van Buren Papers*.

48 Polk to Heiss, Dec. 21, 1843, ''Heiss Papers.''

paper and promised him financial support from the party. Fearing, however, that he might jeopardize his chances of being elected to Congress (from his home district), Laughlin at first declined to accept the position.[49] His subsequent acceptance and his editorial services to his party will be considered in the following chapter.

---

[49] Polk to Heiss, Dec. 21, 1843, "Heiss Papers." Laughlin to Polk, Dec. 7; Heiss to Polk, Dec. 19, 1843, *Polk Papers.*

CHAPTER XII

SELECTION OF CANDIDATES, 1844

The campaign of 1844 may be said to have opened with the new year. From early in January announcements from prospective candidates, declarations of principles, and notices of nominations made by local bodies, began to occupy leading places in the columns of the party journals. There was little doubt that Clay would be chosen to head the Whig ticket, although, in response to an inquiry from friends, Webster announced his willingness to accept a nomination at the hands of the Whig convention. Tyler had been read out of the Whig party, and, since the Democrats had not shown a disposition to adopt him as their own, it seemed likely that he would enter the contest as an independent candidate. Van Buren's nomination by the Baltimore convention was fully expected by all parties not so much because any considerable portion of his party wanted him, as because there seemed to be no one who had a better claim. He had been left by General Jackson as a legacy to the party, the position he had occupied gave him prestige, and, as Dixon H. Lewis remarked, he had the advantage of *"being considered the candidate of the party."*[1] These influences combined would insure him the nomination unless something should happen before the meeting of the convention to change indifference into active hostility. For some time, of course, there had been active hostility in certain quarters, but this came generally from those who were promoting the interests of some other still more unpopular candidate, such as Calhoun or Tyler, consequently there was little danger from that source. Unless something should occur to cast doubts on

---

[1] Lewis to Crallé, June 10, 1842, *Crallé Papers.*

his orthodoxy or his personal fitness, Van Buren was reasonably certain of the nomination, but unfortunately for him, that something did occur—the unexpected turn in the Texas question. Before the appearance of this firebrand, friends of other aspirants were exerting every effort to weaken his hold on the party and to strengthen that of their favorites. The most active were the supporters of Calhoun and Cass; some were ready to join with the followers of Tyler; and a few, like W. C. Rives,[2] announced that, as Van Buren's nomination seemed assured, they would vote for Henry Clay.

Early in the year, when Van Buren's nomination seemed to be a foregone conclusion, the main topic of discussion in Democratic ranks was the choice for the second place on the ticket. The persons most frequently mentioned were Colonel Richard M. Johnson, of Kentucky, and James K. Polk, of Tennessee. As in Van Buren's case, many were ready to support Colonel Johnson simply because they did not see how the party could drop him gracefully.[3] The Van Burenites favored Johnson, but for this very reason his nomination was vigorously opposed, especially in the South and Southwest. It was felt by many that if Van Buren must be accepted, the Vice-President should be a man more agreeable to the southern wing of the party. For some time the Tennessee Democrats had been urging Polk's claims to this office, and since his second defeat by Jones they were still more determined to procure for him the nomination.

Ardently desiring this office, Polk began as early as the fall of 1843 to ask his friends to use their influence with politicians of other states. In a letter to Donelson he expressed the belief that Van Buren would be made the candidate for President, and if so, "the candidate for the Vice Presidency must come from the West,—and from a slave-holding state." He hoped that the

---

[2] His letter, dated January 1, is printed in *Nat. Intell.*, Jan. 12, 1844.

[3] It was rare to see a person, wrote Cave Johnson, who did not prefer Polk. The main trouble was getting rid of "Old Dick" (Johnson to Polk, Jan. 31, 1844, *Polk Papers*).

press and party leaders would come out early for Van Buren and himself, at least before R. M. Johnson had yielded his "pretensions for the Presidency" and had become his competitor for the second place. Even this early he expressed distrust for the Washington *Globe.*

I do not understand *Blair's* course. . . . I do not think he is inclined to do me justice. Why I know not, unless it be that he has strong attachments for *Col. Johnson,* and looks to his restoration with *Mr. Van Buren.*

The attitude of Ohio and Mississippi, he said in another letter, would go far to settle the question, therefore Donelson and other Tennessee friends should send letters to prominent politicians in those states.[4]

Early in January, 1844, Laughlin and others procured from General Jackson letters to political leaders in various states. These letters were used in an effort to induce state conventions to declare their preference for Polk.[5] A letter signed "Amicus" that appeared in the *Globe* and advocated the nomination of William R. King, of Alabama, gave Cave Johnson and A. V. Brown an opportunity to sound Polk's praises and to urge his nomination. In an article signed "A Tennessee Democrat," they pointed out that King, voluntarily, and Van Buren, under instructions, had voted for the United States Bank, and that it would never do to have two candidates who had endorsed that discredited institution. But, they asked, who does not remember in Jackson's battle against the bank "the unterrified ability displayed by Governor Polk on these trying occasions?" The very fact that Tennessee was a doubtful state was an additional reason for nominating Polk.[6] To a friend in Tennessee Johnson wrote that old-line politicians such as Buchanan, Calhoun, Benton, and Blair were doing their utmost to ruin Polk's prospects, and other

---

4 Polk to Donelson, Oct. 19, Dec. 20, 1843, "Polk-Donelson Letters." The Ohio politicians mentioned were Allen, Tappan, Medary, Dawson, and Medill.

5 Letters of W. H. Polk and Laughlin to Polk (*Polk Papers*).

6 Washington *Globe,* Jan. 15, 1844. Johnson to Polk, Jan. 13, 21, 31, 1844, *Polk Papers.*

letters told Polk that these men feared him as another rival for the Presidency.[7]

In general, conservatives evinced a preference for either King or Colonel Johnson,[8] but the more aggressive element favored Polk. The Mississippi state convention at its Jackson Day (January 8) celebration drank toasts to Polk and nominated him for Vice-President,[9] and in many other states there was growing sentiment in his favor. The attention of the country had recently been called to the state of Tennessee by the introduction in Congress of a bill to reimburse General Jackson for the thousand dollar fine imposed upon him at New Orleans in 1815. William H. Polk moved in the Tennessee legislature to instruct the Senators and request the Representatives from that state to vote for the bill. Although such an action was only to be expected from any Tennessee Democrat, it is not unlikely that Polk had considered the probable effect on his brother's candidacy.[10]

The private correspondence of this early part of 1844 is very interesting in view of the assertion made later that an anti-Van Buren plot had been hatched in Tennessee by the intimate associates of Polk. The letters show conclusively that instead of opposing the ex-President's nomination the leading politicians were trying hard to bring it about. On the other hand, the rank and file of the Democracy of the state cared little for Van Buren and feared that he would be a "dead weight" upon the party. Even Hogan and Heiss, the proprietors of the *Union*, at first declined to place his name at the head of their political column,

---

[7] Levin H. Coe to Polk, Jan. 27, 1844, *ibid.*

[8] In a letter to the editor of the *Globe*, dated January 28, Johnson stated that he had, at various places, been nominated—sometimes for President, sometimes for Vice-President. He would accept either, he said, if ratified by the national convention, but in any event he would support the regular nominees.

[9] Nashville *Union*, Jan. 23, 1844.

[10] When Polk's resolution reached the senate, a Whig member moved that the preamble should be changed to read that the "question is now brought before the American people not with a view to relieve Gen. Jackson . . . but alone for political effect" (Nashville *Union*, Jan. 25, 1844).

although Polk had requested them to do so.[11] Urged by Laughlin
as well as by Polk, the editors finally, though reluctantly, consented. His name appeared for the first time on February 8,
1844, and the editors stated frankly that

in placing Mr. Van Buren's name at the head of our paper, subject to the
action of the National Convention, we assume no new position either in
reference to our views or the preferences of the great body of the democracy in Tennessee.

They would support, they said, the nominee of the convention,
whoever he might be.[12] On March 12, after much urging by Polk,
Laughlin assumed the editorship not only of the *Union* but of
the *Star Spangled Banner,* a weekly campaign journal which
was to be published from the same office.[13] The tone of the *Union*
now became more favorable to Van Buren, and there seemed to
be little doubt that he would be nominated at Baltimore.

Up to the time that Van Buren's Texas letter was published,
there was no indication that influential Tennesseans had any
intention of opposing his nomination. Cave Johnson, who, with
R. J. Walker, was charged later with having instigated the plan
to defeat him at Baltimore, was a hearty supporter of the ex-
President. In a letter written from Washington he told of a
movement in that city to nominate Cass. This movement, he
believed should be vigorously opposed, for "in my opinion *your
only chance* for the position we wish" depends upon the nomination of Van Buren.[14] At a large meeting held at Nashville
on March 15, 1844, to celebrate the anniversary of Jackson's

---

11 "Tell the General," said Polk in a letter to Donelson, December 20,
1843, "that I had an interview with both Editors of the Union, when I
was at Nashville and both agreed to take decided and bold ground for
Van Buren in their paper. If they do not do so, in their next paper, I
will write to them and urge it upon them. The paper here has done so"
("Polk-Donelson Letters").

12 Nashville *Union*, Feb. 8. Polk to Heiss, Jan. 21 "Heiss Papers";
Laughlin to Polk, Feb. 4, *Polk Papers.*

13 Polk's letters to Heiss advising the employment of Laughlin are in
the "Heiss Papers." Various letters of Polk and Laughlin on the subject are in the *Polk Papers.*

14 Johnson to Polk, March 6, 1844, *Polk Papers.*

birth and the remission of his fine by Congress,[15] efforts were made to create enthusiasm for both Van Buren and Polk. While at Nashville Polk answered Johnson's letter and fully concurred in the views he had expressed. A few days later he wrote again on the same subject and said that "the movement which you say is on hand—to profess publicly to support Mr. Van Buren, with a secret intention to attempt to nominate Genl Cass in the Convention,—can receive no countenance." If there is any movement in Tennessee, said he, to couple his name with that of Cass to the prejudice of Van Buren, he is not aware of it, and if discovered, he will not permit it.

It is now settled that the preference of a large majority of the party is for *Mr. Van Buren,* and the whole party should yield to his nomination and make it unanimous. Such men as *Duff Green,* and the discontented in our ranks may attempt to produce confusion by resisting the popular choice of the party, but their movements can receive no countenance or support from me.[16]

Immediately following the Nashville meeting Laughlin sounded the trumpet more vigorously than ever for Van Buren and Polk, and insisted that four-fifths of the Democrats in Congress were in favor of the ex-President's nomination. Although a friend of General Cass, Laughlin deplored the agitation in his behalf. Cass himself, said he, "has frowned upon the design." Those who had come out for Cass had, in Laughlin's opinion, done so for the purpose of dividing the party, and most prominent among them was Duff Green, "a renegade deserter."[17]

On March 20, the day before the appearance of Laughlin's editorial, Polk had declined an unofficial offer of a place in the cabinet of John Tyler. Abel P. Upshur, Secretary of State, and Thomas W. Gilmer, Secretary of the Navy, had been killed in the *Princeton* disaster of February 28, leaving two vacancies in

---

[15] Laughlin submitted a resolution which declared that revenge had led Judge Hall to impose the fine. Polk seconded the resolution and made a speech on political questions (*Union,* March 19, 1844).

[16] Polk to Johnson, March 18, 1844 (''Polk-Johnson Letters'').

[17] Nashville *Union,* March 21, 1844.

the cabinet. Calhoun had been selected to succeed Upshur,[18] but John Y. Mason, who had been invited to take Gilmer's place declined, at first, to accept the offer. At this juncture Theophilus Fisk, former editor of the *Old Dominion* and a friend of the President, sent a letter to Polk asking whether he would accept the navy portfolio ''without any pledge, shackle, or trammel being asked of you, other than is already guaranteed by your exalted character and standing.''[19] Mason, however, changed his mind,[20] and by accepting the appointment left no vacancy to be filled.

Without knowledge of the offer made to Mason, or of his accceptance, Polk had already written to Fisk, stating that he would not accept a place in the cabinet. In a letter to Cave Johnson, which was intended also for the eye of Silas Wright, Polk gave a twofold reason for declining a cabinet position. In the first place, it would seem like withdrawing from the race for Vice-President, and this he had no intention of doing. Again, Tyler's administration was supposed to be hostile to Van Buren; consequently, if he accepted, he would be placed in a false position, for he was heartily in favor of Van Buren. This, in effect, was a notice to the Van Burenites that he was still in the race for Vice-President and that, as he was loyal to their candidate, he expected their support in return. He also called attention to Laughlin's editorial in the *Union* against the attempted movement for Cass. In another passage of the letter he not only declared his own views on the Texas question, but he intimated, also, that he took it for granted that Van Buren would not oppose annexation. Speaking of Calhoun's call to the Department of State, he said:

---

[18] For the circumstances of Calhoun's selection, see Schouler, *Hist. of U. S.*, IV, 455.

[19] Fisk to Polk, March 9, 1844, *Polk Papers*. Fisk said that the idea was his own, but he told Cave Johnson that he was acting by authority of the President (Johnson to Polk, March 10, *ibid.*).

[20] Much to the surprise of both Tyler and Fisk—so said the latter in a letter to Polk, March 13 (*ibid.*).

I think it probable that he will see that it is his interest to co-operate thoroughly with the Democratic party, so heartily for *Mr. Van Buren*, harmonize his friends at the South, and make a great effort upon the Texas and Oregon questions.[21]

At the time that Polk declined to accept a place in Tyler's cabinet, the Texas question was fast approaching its critical stage. Since Polk was soon to become closely identified with this important question, it seems necessary to give a brief summary of its history up to this point and to ascertain, if possible, whether he or his friends had any part in bringing it forward.

The idea of annexing Texas was not new; but since the failure of the first attempt, during Jackson's administration, no party had made annexation an active political issue. That it was made an issue in the campaign of 1844 was due, according to Benton,[22] to the machinations of Calhoun, who hoped by this means to prevent the nomination of Van Buren and the election of Henry Clay. The first move in this direction was made in the winter of 1842–43. At that time a letter, written by Thomas W. Gilmer but inspired by Calhoun, was printed in a Baltimore paper. It advocated the immediate annexation of Texas in order to forestall the designs of Great Britain. The letter, said Benton, was "a clap of thunder in a clear sky," for no one was aware of any such design. Webster left the Department of State in May, 1843, and after the brief term of Legare, was succeeded on June 24 by Abel Upshur, of Virginia. Upshur was a friend of Calhoun and interested in the annexation of Texas. It was probably due to the influence of Upshur and Gilmer that Tyler first became interested in annexation, but before long the President had determined to use it for his own purposes. In his third annual message, which was sent to Congress early in December, 1843,

---

[21] In another letter of the same date which was intended for Brown and Johnson only, Polk made still more explicit the purpose of the first letter, for he pointed out that Wright, if he would, could certainly prevent R. M. Johnson from being nominated (Polk to Johnson, March 21, 1844, "Polk-Johnson Letters").

[22] Benton, *Thirty Years' View*, II, 581 ff.

Tyler alluded to the dangers that might result from continued war between Texas and Mexico, and hinted pointedly at possible annexation.

At this stage of the question Aaron V. Brown, an intimate friend of Polk, became a leading factor in the annexation program. Whether or not he was consciously lending his aid to the Tyler-Calhoun project is not easy to determine. In a conversation with Benton on the first day of the session, Brown spoke of annexation as "an impending and probable event," and he was rebuked by the Senator who said that it was *"on the part of some, an intrigue for the presidency and a plot to dissolve the Union—on the part of others, a Texas scrip and land speculation."*[23] In a "confidential" letter to Polk, Brown alluded to Tyler's message and added: *"But this is not all.* I have reason to suppose it will soon be followed up with some definite and precise proposition—some think a treaty." The Whigs, said he, think that Tyler has brought the question up as a firebrand between North and South in order to gain support for himself, and that nothing will come of it; but however this may be, it is Brown's opinion that neither Whigs nor Democrats of the South and West should commit themselves against annexation.[24]

This was not the first time that Brown had shown an interest in the Texas question. In January, 1843, he had sent to Jackson a copy of the *Madisonian* containing Gilmer's letter and had received in reply the famous letter of February 12 in which the General urged the necessity of immediate annexation. Jackson's letter was not made public until a year later, about three months after Tyler had submitted his message on the subject of Texas. The procurement and the publication of Jackson's letter have been declared by Benton to be links in the chain of events which had been forged by Calhoun and his fellow-conspirators for the purpose of making Texas the leading political issue and Calhoun the candidate, although he does not say that Brown was fully

---

23 *Ibid.*, 583.
24 Brown to Polk, Dec. 9, 1843, *Polk Papers.*

aware of the part he was playing.[25] He has intimated, also, that the letter was purposely dated 1844 instead of 1843; but Brown's own letter—published at the same time—explained the circumstances under which it had been procured and stated explicitly that it had been in his possession for a "long time."[26] However, Benton's interest in Van Buren's nomination and his opposition to annexation seem to have led him to associate events which in reality were not related; on the other hand, Brown's own desire for Texas is sufficient to explain his soliciting the opinion of General Jackson on the subject.

If Brown was a conscious participant in any conspiracy to undermine Van Buren, it is quite evident that his bosom friends, Polk and Cave Johnson, were not aware of the fact. Although Johnson looked with favor on the acquisition of Texas, he was averse to having it made an issue for campaign purposes. At the time that Polk's name was mentioned in connection with Tyler's cabinet, Johnson stated his opinions very explicitly in a letter to Polk:

I fear some secret movements are making here so as to bring up the Texas question here prominently before the Convention meets & to make it operate if practicable agt Van in the Convention & agt Clay in the election—if it can be brought up fairly & properly & with a reasonable prospect of getting it I should have no objection, but if it is designed merely as a political question to operate in the ensuing canvass then I shall deplore it. An effort no doubt will be made to unite the destinies of Oregon & Texas so as to unite the South & West—may you not be identified with these movements if in the cabinet? & if unsuccessful what follows?[27]

The friends of Calhoun confidently expected that their leader would profit from the emergence of the Texas question. Fearing that "being considered a candidate" would, if left unchallenged, procure for Van Buren the coveted nomination, they began at an early date to seek support for their favorite.[28] Due to their

---

25 Benton, *Thirty Years' View*, II, 584.

26 The letters of both Jackson and Brown were published in various newspapers—among others, the Nashville *Union* of April 2, 1844.

27 Johnson to Polk, March 10, 1844, *Polk Papers*.

28 Dixon H. Lewis to Richard Crallé, June 10, 1842, *Crallé Papers*.

efforts the time for holding the national convention was postponed from December, 1843, to a later date, in order that they might have a longer time to educate public opinion; for even before Jackson's Texas letter was written, they were confident that Calhoun would be nominated.[29]

During the summer of 1843 the administration had become convinced that Great Britain was about to interfere in Texan affairs and effect, if possible, the abolition of slavery there. Duff Green was in England gathering information, and his communications were supplemented by reports which came from Texan representatives in London.[30] In December, as we have already noted, Tyler called the attention of Congress to the dangers of foreign interference in Texas, and soon afterwards he began to formulate plans of annexation. The supporters of Calhoun cooperated with the President, and there seemed to be no doubt in their minds that their patron, and not Tyler, would reap the political reward. Their hopes of success mounted high when Calhoun was called to take charge of the Department of State. Like the President they were interested in annexation *per se;* in addition, they fully appreciated its importance as a campaign issue. "It is the greatest question of the *Age,*" wrote Dixon H. Lewis, and he rejoiced that Calhoun was in a position "to direct its force & control its fury."[31] Three days after Lewis had made

---

[29] In a letter written from Washington, February 8, 1843, Duff Green told Crallé that although the Van Buren faction wanted an early convention, he hoped that it could be delayed until June. "It has now," said he, "narrowed down to a choice between Calhoun & Van Buren and the demonstrations are becoming more and more decided for Mr. Calhoun so that, in my opinion, the concentration in his favor will become so apparent as public opinion developes that the convention will indeed become obsolete" (Letters of Duff Green, Library of Congress; Benton, *Thirty Years' View,* II, 585).

[30] Smith, *Annexation of Texas,* chap. vi.

[31] "Every thing depends on the Texas question, which is an element of Power so much stronger than Clay, V Buren & their conventions that it unsettles all calculations as to the future course of men & parties. It is the greatest question of the *Age* & I predict will agitate the country more than all the other public questions ever have. Public opinion will boil & effervesce . . . more like a volcano than a cider Barrell—but at

this assertion Jackson's Texas letter appeared in the Richmond *Enquirer*. No doubt it fitted into the Calhoun program, yet it is not at all certain that this was Brown's motive in having the letter published. Surely General Jackson did not write it for any such purpose.[32]

The emergence of the Texas question was not welcomed by Henry Clay. Early in December, 1843, he stated his opinions on the subject in a letter to John J. Crittenden.[33] There were, he said, already a sufficient number of issues without "adding freak ones" of this character, and he did not think it right to allow John Tyler to make capital out of this exciting topic. In his opinion, annexation, either by treaty or by conquest, was entirely out of the question; however, unless Tyler should present some definite project of annexation he did not feel called upon to make public expression of his views. In the following March, when it was rumored that the President was negotiating with Texas, Clay—with his usual faith in his own ability both to shape and to direct political issues—still felt confident that he could stem the tide of Texas agitation.[34]

last will settle down with *unanimity* for annexation in the South & West & a large majority in the North. It will in the meantime *unite* the *hitherto divided South*, while it will make Abolition & Treason synonymous & thus destroy it in the North.

"The beauty of the thing is, that Providence rather than Tyler has put Calhoun at the head of this great question, to direct its force & control its fury. It is understood by letters from him that he accepts.

"P. S. It is understood the preliminaries of the Treaty have already been arranged & only awaits the special minister who is daily expected." (Lewis to Crallé, March 19, 1844, Crallé Papers). Alexander H. Stephens believed that "the dissolution of the present Confederacy" lay "near Mr. Calhoun's heart" (Stephens to James Thomas, May 17, 1844, *Rep. Am. Hist. Assn.*, 1911, II, 58).

[32] Benton says that Blair declined to publish the letter in the *Globe* (*Thirty Years' View*, II, 587). Later, however, it was printed in that paper, along with Brown's letter explaining his reasons for publishing it.

[33] Clay to Crittenden, December 5, 1843, *Crittenden Papers*.

[34] Writing from Savannah, he said: "I think I can treat the question in a manner very different from any treatment which I have yet seen of it, and so as to reconcile all our friends, and many others to the views which I entertain. Of one thing you may be certain, that there is no such anxiety for the annexation here at the South as you might have been disposed to imagine" (Clay to Crittendon, March 24, 1844, *Crittenden Papers*).

The time was fast approaching when candidates must take a definite stand either for or against annexation. Despite the desire of some of them to eliminate this topic from the issues of the campaign, every day brought the subject more into prominence. Calhoun's position was already well known, for in his letter accepting the cabinet portfolio he had come out strongly in favor of annexation. Clay would probably be nominated by his party no matter what position he might choose to take with respect to the all absorbing topic. Of greater importance, therefore, was the stand to be taken by Van Buren; for on this would depend, in all probability, his success or failure in the nominating convention.

On March 27, 1844, W. H. Hammet, a member of Congress from Mississippi and an "unpledged delegate to the Baltimore convention," addressed a letter to Van Buren asking for his views on the annexation of Texas. In writing this letter Hammet was evidently coöperating with the most loyal friends of Van Buren, and not, as Benton has intimated, with the supporters of Calhoun.[35] After taking ample time for consideration Van Buren on April 20, drafted his reply and sent it to his most intimate friend, Silas Wright. When it reached Wright on the evening of the 26th, it was read to a number of Van Buren's friends, including Fairfield, King, and Benton. They approved it and decided that it should be published immediately in the *Globe*. This course was decided upon before Hammet had even seen the letter.[36] The ex-President began his letter by asserting his belief that the United States had the constitutional right to annex Texas. He then gave a history of the quesion and of his own attempt to purchase it while Secretary of State under Jackson.

---

[35] Benton, *Thirty Years' View*, II, 587.

[36] Wright to Van Buren, Washington, April 29, 1844, *Van Buren Papers*. "Hammet was frightened," said Wright, "and it was with some difficulty that we induced him to our proposition for publication, before he had read it; but he behaved well and himself and the Major remained at the Globe office until about midnight, to examine the proof."

But, said he, as conditions are now, annexation would in all probability bring on a war with Mexico, and

could we hope to stand perfectly justified in the eyes of mankind for entering into it; more especially if its commencement is to be preceded by the appropriation to our own uses of the territory, the sovereignty of which is in dispute betwen two nations, one of which we are to join in the struggle?

He thought not, for ''we have a character among the nations of the earth to maintain.'' He did not believe that there was danger of foreign interference in Texas or that nothing but immediate action could prevent Texas from being lost to the United States.[37]

On the very day that Van Buren penned his answer to Hammet, Cave Johnson sent him a letter from Washington.[38] He informed the ex-President that within two days the Texas treaty would be sent to the Senate, and, from all appearances, would be the controlling factor in the next Presidential election. For this reason he and other friends hoped that Van Buren would favor annexation, because ''they hope such a position will not injure you in the North, whilst it must overwhelm Mr. Clay in the South if he hesitates or equivocates.'' In order to forestall intrigues to prevent his nomination, Johnson urged him to make his position known at the earliest possible date.[39]   Johnson's warning, to be sure, came too late; on the other hand, it seems

---

[37] The letter was published in the Washington *Globe*, April 28, 1844.

[38] Whether Johnson had any knowledge of Hammet's letter to Van Buren, I am unable to say. If he had, Van Buren's long delay in answering probably induced him to write.

[39] ''In the event of your being favorable to the treaty, I entreat you to take the earliest opportunity of giving your views—we have intrigues on hand here if practicable, to supersede you in the Baltimore Convention— and this question is one of the means used to arouse some of the Western & S Western members agt you—from a supposition that you are hostile to it—the delay of the Globe in coming out—your delay and the opinion of some of the N. Y. Democrats—all are urged & I fear with some effect among the members.'' Already, said he, some are expressing fears of Van Buren's ''availability'' and are talking of other candidates, such as Stewart, Dodge, and Cass. He is gratified to learn that Nicholson, who had headed the Cass movement in Tennessee, now says that Van Buren is the only man who can carry that state. Such, also, is the opinion of Governor Polk (Johnson to Van Buren, April 20, 1844, *Van Buren Papers*).

to show that he was sincerely desirous of Van Buren's nomination until the New Yorker had taken a position which would, in all probability, render his election impossible. The sincerity of Johnson's regret when Van Buren's opposition to annexation became known is expressed in a letter to Polk. "Many of us are in rather low spirits today—his course gives great advantage to the discontents over us and they will make the most they can out of it."[40] Two days later he reported that the excitement over Van Buren's letter was not abating, and that the friends of Texas had called a meeting at the capitol over which R. J. Walker had presided. They wanted another candidate—some were looking to Cass, others to Calhoun.[41]

Clay, who was then on a canvassing tour, reached Wahington in the latter part of April. While there his letter on the Texas question, dated at Raleigh on April 17, was given to the *National Intelligencer* for publication. He was decidedly opposed to annexation, because it would surely result in a war with Mexico. Even if Mexico should agree, he believed that it would be inexpedient to admit Texas into the Union.[42] Knowing that Van Buren, whom he supposed would be his opponent, did not favor annexation, Clay had not the "smallest apprehension" in stating his position.[43]

Inquiries were not limited to candidates for the Presidency. Late in March a nonpartisan, anti-Texas meeting assembled in Cincinnati and a committee of five, including Salmon P. Chase, drafted a letter to Polk asking his views on annexation. When the letter reached Columbia, Polk was on his farm in Mississippi,

---

40 "A serious & powerful effort," he continued, "will be made to get a new nomination in which I think most of my democratic colleagues will unite, from the little I can learn. The discontents are moving heaven and earth & will never stop until the Convention is over if they do so then." At present, he said, the desertion is toward Cass, but he does not believe that Cass will get the nomination (Johnson to Polk, April 28, 1844, *Polk Papers*).

41 Johnson to Polk, April 30, 1844, *ibid.*

42 *Nat. Intell.*, April 27, 1844.

43 Clay to Crittenden, April 21, 1844, *Crittenden Papers.*

but as soon as he had reached home his reply to the committee was prepared without hesitation. It bore the date of April 23 and advocated unequivocally "immediate re-annexation."[44] Like Jackson in his letter to Brown, Polk emphasized the point that our original title to Texas had been valid beyond question and that the territory had unwisely been ceded to Spain. He conveniently ignored the fact that the cession had been made by those who possessed the constitutional authority to make it. And however unwise such an action may have been, it is difficult to see the bearing of this lack of wisdom on our subsequent right to re-annex the lost territory. On account of the danger that Texas might become a British colony, Polk maintained that all European countries should be excluded from both Texas and Oregon. "Let Texas be re-annexed," said he,

and the authority and laws of the United States be established and maintained within her limits, as also the Oregon Territory, and let the fixed policy of our government be not to permit Great Britain or any other foreign power to plant a colony or hold dominion over any portion of the people or territory of either.[45]

These remarks on colonization are not without interest, for they are a forerunner of what was later called the "Polk Doctrine."

Polk's letter was written only three days after that of Van Buren and of course without knowledge of its contents. Indeed, as late as May 4, after he had read Clay's anti-Texas letter, he expressed the hope and the belief that Van Buren would "now take ground for annexation."[46] The views which he expressed coincided with those held generally by Democrats in Tennessee. On the very day that Van Buren penned his indictment against annexation, an enthusiastic meeting of Democrats at Nashville

44 "I have no hesitation in declaring that I am in favor of the immediate re-annexation of Texas to the territory and government of the United States. I entertain no doubt as to the power or the expediency of the re-annexation."

45 MS, dated Columbia, April 23, 1844, *Polk Papers*. Printed in Washington *Globe*, May 6, 1844.

46 Polk to Johnson, May 4, 1844, "Polk-Johnson Letters."

passed resolutions in favor of it by a unanimous vote.[47] It is not surprising, therefore, that Van Buren's letter had a "prostrating and cooling effect" upon his supporters in that state or that many who had stuck to him from a sense of duty should now feel relieved from further obligation.[48] Individuals could express their sentiments very freely to one another, but Laughlin, who for some time had been sounding Van Buren's praises, was now in somewhat of a quandary. As editor of the party organ, he must of course make some comment. On May 9, therefore, he pointed out in an editorial that, while Clay's objections to annexation were permanent, those of Van Buren were temporary—objections only until certain obstacles had been removed. Laughlin himself advocated immediate annexation, regardless of consequences; still, if a majority of Democrats should decide to wait, he was ready to acquiesce. This left the way open for continued support of Van Buren. Since taking charge of the *Union*, Laughlin had been bitter in his assaults upon Clay. The Whig candidate had perjured himself by challenging Randolph to fight a duel; he was guilty of Cilly's death, because he had written the challenge for Graves; but neither crime was surprising in a man who had "defrauded Gen. Jackson out of the Presidency, for an office worth $6000 per annum."[49]

Before his treaty with Texas had been consummated, Tyler seems to have given up hope that he might be nominated by the Democrats. His official organ indignantly denied the assertion made by the *Globe* that he was knocking for admission to the Baltimore convention; on the contrary, "the friends of the Veto-Administration intend having a Convention which will represent the Republican party more truly than Mr. Van Buren's

---

[47] Nashville *Union*, April 23, 1844.

[48] "Indeed it has given a pretext for doing that which they have had in their minds to do—to declare against V. B., and a considerable portion of them will never be reconciled to him" (Nicholson to Heiss, May 8, 1844, "Heiss Papers").

[49] Nashville *Union*, March 30, 1844.

Convention, and the nominee will be elected.''[50] Still, the President was ready to welcome assistance from any quarter, for in May his friend Fisk sounded Cave Johnson concerning Jackson's opinion of his administration, and at the same time Polk was being considered for the War Department or the British mission.[51]

Cass was the last of the aspirants to declare himself on the Texas question. In response to a letter from Hannegan, he, too, came out for immediate annexation.[52]

On May 1, four days after Clay's Texas letter had appeared in print, the Whig convention assembled at Baltimore. One day sufficed for nominating the candidates and adopting a platform. Without a dissenting voice, Clay was chosen for the first place, and on the third ballot, Frelinghuysen, of New Jersey, was selected as his running mate. The platform was drawn to suit the candidate. It avoided the Texas and bank questions and emphasized tariff, currency, distribution, and usurpation by the Executive. With one omission—the bank question—Clay took his stand on the traditional Whig policies, and appealed to the people to sustain him.

While the Whigs rallied with enthusiasm to the standard of their chief, harmony within Democratic circles was rendered impossible by the appearance of the "lone star" on the political horizon. The party which had long been distinguished for its effective discipline and its unity of action now appeared to be hopelessly divided on the eve of battle. Even the great "chief" at the Hermitage seemed to be uncertain as to the proper plan of campaign. His commands were ambiguous, for they resulted from conflicting emotions; he longed to see his old friend Van Buren nominated, but his desire for Texas was still stronger. Although few had a definite idea as to the best means of restoring harmony, as the time for the Baltimore convention approached

---

[50] *Madisonian,* April 3, 1844.

[51] Johnson to Polk, May 8, 1844, *Polk Papers.*

[52] His letter was dated at Detroit on May 10. There is a copy in *Niles' Register,* May 25, 1844.

the conviction that Van Buren could not be elected became very widespread. The Virginia Democratic central committee, by resolution, released the delegates of that state from the obligation to obey their instructions, and delegates of other states announced publicly that they would not vote for Van Buren.[53]

Before the appearance of his Texas letter Van Buren had been accepted generally as the candidate; not because he enjoyed a wide popularity, but because a small minority urgently advocated his nomination and the rest of the party, being more indifferent than hostile, simply acquiesced, since they had no substitute to offer. After the publication of his Texas letter, his downfall was brought about by much the same process that had procured his elevation to party leadership. The few who were violently opposed to his nomination had little difficulty in convincing others, and especially the friends of Texas, that he could not possibly be elected. Those who had supported him from a sense of duty only, now had no hesitancy in transferring their allegiance to another candidate who would be more likely to win. Amos Kendall emphasized this point in a letter written to Van Buren. He told him frankly that he had no good news, and that unless some one else could be nominated at Baltimore the southern delegates would put up a third candidate. Kendall did not believe that the pro-Texas feeling was due to any organized movement, but rather to the "continued ding-dong sung in their ears" by a few of the most interested. Van Buren's letters, he said, had appeared at the worst possible time; the guns were being trained on Clay, and Van Buren appeared just in time to get the shot.[54] Cave Johnson reported the political situation as apparently hopeless. Benton and the New Yorkers seemed to

---

[53] Many such details are given in *Niles' Reg.*, LXVI, 162–163.

[54] Kendall to Van Buren, May 13, 1844, *Van Buren Papers.* Hendrick B. Wright, of Pennsylvania, believed that Van Buren could not be nominated—and if nominated, could not be elected, and Wm. R. King, writing from New York, reported it to be generally admitted that the ex-President could not be elected (Wright to Buchanan, May 13; King to Buchanan, May 14, 1844, *Buchanan Papers*).

be determined not to yield; Calhoun and his supporters were equally uncompromising, while each faction claimed a majority of the convention. "I see no hope," said Johnson, "unless some man can be found disconnected with both these fragments of the democratic party & who will yield to the annexation of Texas."[55] Polk, the man to whom this letter was written, fulfilled these requirements; and before the letter had reached its destination, his *availability* had already been discussed at the Hermitage.

The correspondence which passed between Democratic leaders in Tennessee about the middle of May shows an absence of definite plans for the future. On May 10 Donelson[56] summoned Polk to Nashville to consult with General Jackson and others in the hope that they might find some means of preventing a split in the party over the annexation question. "I feel deeply mortified," said he,

that our wise men should differ so much; and particularly that a measure of such vast consequences should have been kept so long in the dark and precipitated with so much haste.

Donelson was fully aware that Jackson's indorsement of annexation would aid Tyler and Calhoun; and, apparently, although his letter is not very clear, he did not approve making Texas a leading issue.[57] Polk accepted the invitation and reached Nashville on the twelfth. On the following day he and General Armstrong repaired to the Hermitage. They were met on the road by Donelson, who was taking to Nashville for publication in the *Union* Jackson's well-known letter which appeared a few days later under date of May 13th. In it, Jackson insisted that Texas must be annexed.

---

[55] Johnson to Polk, May 12, 1844, *Polk Papers*.

[56] Gen. Armstrong and other politicians wrote, also.

[57] "I am particularly anxious that the ground occupied by the Genl. should be thoroughly understood by you. What he may now say if not modified by disclosures recently made will produce important results. If the Texas question is urged as it doubtless will be by Tyler & Calhoun, and Genl. Jackson gives the weight of his name to sustain their views, making it a leading question in the South, the sooner we know it the better. Come and talk over the matter with the Genl. and our friends generally" (Donelson to Polk, May 10, 1844, *Polk Papers*).

When reporting the interview to Cave Johnson,[58] Polk said that

He [Jackson] speaks most affectionately of *Mr. Van Buren*, but is compelled to separate from him upon this great question, and says both he and *Mr. Benton* have by their letters cut their own throats politically. He has no idea that *Mr. V. B.* can be nominated or if nominated that he can receive any Southern support.

Jackson said that the Baltimore convention must select some other candidate and that he should be from the Southwest; and Polk's letter hinted that the General had suggested that Polk himself ought to be placed at the head of the ticket. Polk asserted that he aspired to the second place only, but that his friends might use his name as they might see fit; in any event the party should unite on some *"one candidate"* and he must be in favor of annexation. "I have stood by *Mr. V. B.,*" he continued, "and will stand by him as long as there is hope, but I now despair of his election—even if he be nominated." In another letter written on the following day,[59] Polk was more explicit concerning Jackson's desire to substitute his name for that of Van Buren. The General remarked, said he, that writing the anti-Texas letter was the only vital error ever committed by Van Buren; nevertheless, it would be fatal to his election.

He thinks the candidate for the Presidency should be an annexation man and reside in the Southwest, and he openly expresses (what I assure you I had never for a moment contemplated) the opinion that I would be the most available man; taking the Vice-Presidential candidate from the North. This I do not expect to be effected.

Polk thought it was more probable that some northern man would be nominated for first place, and himself for the second. If Van Buren should be withdrawn, his friends would doubtless control both nominations, therefore great pains should be taken to conciliate them. Nothing, said Polk, could prevent Clay's election except the harmonious selection of a candidate at Baltimore. In offering suggestions for bringing about such harmony

---

[58] Polk to Johnson, May 13, 1844, "Polk-Johnson Letters."
[59] Polk to Johnson, May 14, 1844, *ibid.*

he displayed that shrewedness and attention to detail which made him one of the most astute politicians of his time.[60] Along with this went another letter to Johnson, marked "Highly Confidential."[61] Johnson was authorized to show the first letter to Silas Wright, and we are not left in doubt as to the reason.

Mr. Wright's declaration to you, in the conversation which you detail in your letter of the 8th that I was "the only man he thought the Northern Democrats would support if Van Buren was set aside, because I was known to be firm and *true* to the cause," is precisely the opinion which *Genl J.* expressed to me when I saw him two days ago. The General had previously expressed the same thing to others.

He once more asserted that he had aspired to the second office only and had been loyal to Van Buren; but since the secret attack on the ex-President " 'Fortune is in a frolic,' and . . . there is no telling what may happen." He recommended General Pillow to Johnson as a shrewd and reliable colleague in carrying out all plans.

In Jackson's letter of May 13 to the Nashville *Union,* in which he commented on Van Buren's Texas letter, the General said his old friend evidently was unaware that conditions had changed since he had been President. No difference of opinion could change his confidence in Van Buren, but as to Texas, "Let us

---

[60] "I have but little hope that union or harmony can be restored among the members, but I have hope that the Delegates *'fresh from the people'*—who are not members of Congress—and have not been so much excited can be brought together. Let a strong appeal be made to the Delegates as fast as they come in, *to take the matter into their own hands, to control and overrule their leaders at Washington, who have already produced such distraction, and thus save the party.* The Delegates from a distance can alone do this. I suggest as a practical plan to bring them to act,—to get one Delegate from each State who may be in attendance to meet in a room at Brown's hotel or somewhere else, and consult together to see if they cannot hit upon a plan to save the party. If you will quietly and without announcing to the public what you are at, undertake this with energy and prosecute it with vigor, the plan is feasible and I think will succeed. If the preliminary meeting of a Delegate from each State can agree upon *the* man, then let each one see the other Delegates from his own State, and report at an adjourned meeting the result. This is the only way to secure efficient action when the Convention meets.'' The essential features of this plan were followed, and resulted in success.

[61] Polk to Johnson, May 17 [14], 1844, "Polk-Johnson Letters."

take it now and lock the door against future danger.''[62] His
complimentary remarks about Van Buren were much like an
epitaph for a departed friend. When he penned them he felt
certain that his former protégé was doomed. In a letter written
on the following day he told Benjamin F. Butler that nothing
could restore Van Buren except indorsement of annexation, for
''you might as well, it appears to me, attempt to turn the current
of the Miss[iss]ippi as to turn the democracy from the annexation
of Texas to the United States.''[63]

Texas must be annexed, and Van Buren must be dropped. So
much, at least, was settled; and if Polk could be substituted, so
much the better. The *Union* now began to prepare its readers
for the change. Laughlin had been chosen as a delegate to the
Baltimore convention, and Heiss took charge during his absence.
On May 14, Heiss announced that Van Buren's name had been
placed at the head of the political column because he was thought
to be the choice of the Democracy. It would be left there until
some action had been taken by the convention, although the editor
disagreed with his weak position on the Texas question. On the
18th, Heiss declared further support of the New Yorker to be
hopeless, and by the 23rd he was ready to hazard some ''guesses''
regarding the nomination. The first was that Van Buren would
come out for Texas or withdraw. The second was that one from
a suggested list would be selected as the candidate. Heading
the list was the name of Governor Polk,[64] but since Laughlin was
a member of the pre-convention conference held at Nashville,

---

[62] This letter was dated May 13, and published in the Nashville *Union*,
May 16, 1844.

[63] ''Clay's letter had prostrated him with the Whiggs in the South &
West, and nine tenths of our population had decided in favour of Mr. V.
Buren & annexation of Texas—when this, illfated letter made its appear-
ance and fell upon the democracy like a thunderbolt'' (Jackson to Butler,
May 14, 1844, *Van Buren Papers*. A full copy, also, in *Am. Hist. Rev.*,
July, 1906, 833–834). The letter was carried to Butler by Donelson. Both
men were delegates to the Baltimore convention.

[64] The others suggested were Calhoun, Cass, Stewart, Tyler, and
Buchanan.

the "guess" regarding Polk required no great powers of divination.[65] On May 28, Heiss made another significant statement in the *Union:*

We do not believe Mr. Van Buren will receive one vote from the Tennessee delegation. If he does, that delegate who votes knowingly against the wishes of his constituents, will be marked, hereafter, as a man unworthy of their confidence.

Nearly all the delegates to the Democratic convention gathered in Washington on their way to Baltimore. For what transpired there, we must rely mainly on letters written by Gideon Pillow.[66] Pillow and Laughlin reached Washington on May 21 and began a campaign of interviewing delegates to ascertain their views. Pillow represented Cave Johnson as being rather apathetic and without hope of success. It is true that Johnson was inclined to see the dark side; but he was a shrewd politician and a personal acquaintance of most of the delegates, and it is probable that he exerted fully as much influence as either Pillow or Laughlin.[67]

Pillow reported the party to be hopelessly divided. The insurgents declared that they would not attend the convention unless the two-thirds rule were agreed upon, and that they would not support Van Buren in any event. The Van Burenites were equally insistent on a majority rule.[68] The pro-Texas Democrats

[65] On June 4 the *National Intelligencer* quoted the guesses made by Heiss and remarked that the "inference is irresistible" that the arrangement for dropping Van Buren and bringing Polk forward was made in the neighborhood of Nashville.

[66] Pillow was both conceited and unprincipled; still, if allowance be made for his exaggeration of his own importance, his account is probably authentic. His letters to Polk are among the *Polk Papers.* Copies edited by Professor Reeves are accessible in the *Am. Hist. Rev.,* July, 1906, 835ff.

[67] In his letter of May 24, Pillow said: "I saw your letter to C— J— and noted its suggestions." Evidently he refers to the letter to Cave Johnson, May 14, 1844. See above.

[68] In a letter written from Washington to Van Buren, May 26, Wright said that the Texas men were plotting to defeat him by means of the two-thirds rule. New Hampshire men were told, said he, that Woodbury would get the nomination in case Van Buren should be set aside; the Pennsylvanians were told the same with respect to Buchanan, and the Tennesseans with respect to Polk, *Van Buren Papers.*

tried to commit Polk's friends against Van Buren, but all except a few of the Tennessee delegates maintained a discreet silence on this subject. Two of them, Anderson and Jones, were bitterly opposed to the New Yorker and would not coöperate with their colleagues. Even Andrew Johnson was ready to sacrifice Polk in order to get rid of Van Buren. Pillow was satisfied that two-thirds of the delegates favored Polk for Vice-President; many expressed a preference for him as the candidate for President. No agreements were reached before leaving Washington, yet Pillow was quite certain that Van Buren would be forced to withdraw, and, if so, that his friends would never support Cass. On the other hand, he thought it probable that they would be willing to support Polk. If Polk should be brought forward, it must be done by the North, because it would never do for southerners to suggest his name.

The Democratic convention assembled in Baltimore on May 27, 1844. A large majority of the delegates had been instructed to vote for Van Buren by state conventions which had been held before the publication of his anti-Texas letter—in fact, before Texas had been seriously considered as a political issue. But Tyler and Calhoun had precipitated the question, and many who were bitter opponents of both of them were nevertheless in favor of annexation. Because Van Buren had taken his stand against annexation, many held that their instructions were no longer binding, for the conditions under which they had been framed had changed completely, and Van Buren no longer represented the will of the people. In a few cases, as in Virginia, steps were taken to annul the instructions. Some of the delegates from other states openly repudiated their instructions, and others went to Baltimore prepared to vote for Van Buren on the early ballots and then to use their own judgments. Benton, Welles, and other adherents of the ex-President have asserted that there was wholesale intriguing against their favorite. No doubt there was, but the widespread defection which preceded the convention was not wholly due to intrigue.

The convention selected as its chairman Hendrick B. Wright, of Pennsylvania, and as its secretary William F. Ritchie, whose father was editor of the Richmond *Enquirer*. The friends of Van Buren desired a majority nomination, but his opponents succeeded in adopting the two-thirds rule, which had been used on former occasions. The Van Burenites complained that the rule was now adopted for the purpose of defeating their favorite, but, although the charge was true, the majority merely followed the usual practice of Democratic conventions. In asking for a new rule the New Yorkers were requesting a personal favor for their candidate, which, under the circumstances, they had no right to expect. Van Buren himself had not been overscrupulous about accepting a nomination at the hands of Jackson's "made to order" convention. He had small reason to complain because the advantage was now with his opponents. On the first ballot he received a majority of the votes, but not the necessary two-thirds. In succeeding ballots his vote steadily decreased. After the seventh ballot had been taken, J. L. Miller, of Ohio, moved, by resolution, to declare Van Buren the party nominee, on the ground that he had, on the first ballot, carried a majority of the convention. Hickman, of Pennsylvania, caused much laughter by moving that General Jackson be nominated for President by a unanimous vote. Both motions were ruled to be out of order, and the convention adjourned for the day without having selected a candidate.

The evening of May 28, the second day of the convention, was a momentous one for Polk; and Pillow and George Bancroft are in substantial agreement as to what happened, except that each claims first honors in the transactions which took place. In a letter to Polk, in which he chronicled the events of the day, Pillow said: "I have within the last few minutes received a proposition from a leading Delegate of Pennsylvania and of Massachusetts to bring your name before the Convention for President." Pillow explained to them that if done at all this must be done by the North. "There is, I think a strong probability of your name

ultimately coming up for President. I do not think it prudent
to move in *that* matter now. I want the North to bring you
forward as a *Compromise* of all interests.''[69] The delegate from
Massachusetts was evidently George Bancroft, for, in a letter to
Polk, Bancroft said that after the convention had adjourned on
the second day ''it flashed on my mind, that it would be alone
safe to rally on you.''[70] Carrol and Hubbard, of the New Hampshire delegation, heartily agreed, and likewise Governor Morton,
of Massachusetts.

I then went to your faithful friends Gen. Pillow and Donelson. They
informed me that if we of N. E. would lead off, they would follow with
Mississippi and Alabama. . . . Certain of this, I repaired with Gen. Donelson and Pillow to the house where were the delegates of Ohio and New York,
and I spent the time till midnight in arguing with them.

Medary, of Ohio, was agreeable, and assured Bancroft that Ohio
would go for Polk in preference to Cass. Kemble, of New York,
also agreed to support Polk.

On the morning of the third day, May 29, Tibbatts, of Kentucky, withdrew the name of Richard M. Johnson and, as Pillow
reported to Polk, ''we brought your name before the Convention
for the Presidency.''[71] On the first ballot of the day, the eighth
of the session, Polk received forty-four votes.[72] As soon as the

---

[69] Pillow to Polk, May 28, 1884 (*Am. Hist. Rev.*, July, 1906, 841).

[70] Bancroft to Polk, July 6, 1844 (Howe, *Life and Letters of George
Bancroft*, I, 253). Years afterward Bancroft wrote a still more detailed
account of his activities during that evening. He stated explicitly that
''Polk owed his nomination by the Democratic Convention to me,'' and that
''I was the one who of my own mind and choice, first, on the adjournment
of the nominating convention, for the day, resolved to secure the nomination for Polk'' (Bancroft to I. G. Harris, *Bancroft Papers*, Lenox Library;
cited by Reeves in *Am. Hist. Rev.*, July, 1906, 841). Perhaps, without
realizing it, Bancroft was inspired by Pillow and Laughlin to suggest
Polk's nomination.

[71] Cave Johnson told Polk that John Kettlewell, of Baltimore, was
''the man who first started your name in the Baltimore Convention''
(Johnson to Polk, Jan. 11, 1845, *Polk Papers*).

[72] In his letter of the 29th to Polk Pillow said 42 votes, but the Baltimore *Sun* reported the vote as follows: Van Buren, 104; Cass, 114; Polk,
44; Buchanan, 2; and Calhoun, 2. Polk received 6 from N. H., 7 from
Mass., 2 from Pa., 1 from Md., 9 from Ala., 6 from La., and the 13 votes
of Tennessee.

result had been announced, Frazer, of Pennsylvania, stated that he had at first voted for Van Buren because he had been instructed to do so, and then for Buchanan as the favorite son of his state; but seeing that neither could be nominated, he had cast his vote for "James K. Polk, the bosom friend of Gen. Jackson, and a pure, whole-hogged democrat, the known enemy of banks and distribution." His remarks were greeted with applause and several warm friends of Van Buren now announced that for similar reasons they were ready to unite upon Polk. Governor Hubbard, of New Hampshire, and General Howard, of Maryland, pleaded for Polk and harmony, and Medary pledged the vote of Ohio.[73] Roane took the Virginia delegation out for consultation and returned to announce that its vote would be transferred from Cass to Polk.[74] The ninth ballot had not proceeded far before it became evident that it would be the last. The Polk list became so large that Butler withdrew the name of Van Buren, and many who had supported other favorites now transferred their votes to the Tennessean. In this way his vote was made unanimous, and although South Carolina was not represented officially, Elmore and Pickens were present and pledged the support of their state to the new candidate. Silas Wright, of New York, a warm friend of Van Buren, was nominated for Vice-President; he declined the honor, and George M. Dallas was chosen in his stead.[75] A series of resolutions was adopted, one of which declared in favor of "the re-occupation of Oregon and the re-annexation of Texas at the earliest practicable period." The committee on resolutions had considered the "one term" pledge which had been referred to it by the convention, but reported against such a restriction on the ground that it would

---

[73] Speaking of Bancroft's influence, Laughlin told Polk that "he and old Morton" were mainly responsible for wheeling the "Yankee States" into line (Laughlin to Polk, May 31, 1844, *Polk Papers*).

[74] Bancroft to Polk (Howe, *op. cit.*, I, 254).

[75] The above details, unless otherwise noted, have been taken from the report of the convention published in the Baltimore *Sun*, May 28–30, and *Niles' Register*, June 1, 1844.

be inconsistent to take such action after so many had been instructed to support Van Buren for a second term.

When notifying Polk of his nomination, Pillow[76] was inclined to take all the credit for bringing it about. To be sure, he very modestly said that "I had good help in some *true-men* in the North," but that he "got no help" from "our home people." On the other hand, Bancroft has made it clear that Donelson took a leading part in procuring votes for Polk, and it is unlikely that two such veteran politicians as Laughlin and Cave Johnson were entirely inactive. It appears that the knowledge of Jackson's preference for Polk was by no means confined to Tennesseans,[77] and it would be interesting to know in what degree this fact had a bearing on the ultimate choice of the convention.

From the above account it will be seen that Polk's nomination resulted from a combination of influences originally distinct. Seeing no hope of their own election, both Tyler and Calhoun were ready, for two reasons, to lend their support to the new candidate. In the first place, he believed as they did on the Texas question; in the second, so long as the office was beyond their own reach, they would rather see it go to a new man than to one of the competitors who had so roundly abused them. In the long run the Van Burenites were, for similar reasons, constrained to acquiesce in Polk's nomination and to contribute their support to his campaign. The Calhoun faction and the insurgent element led by R. J. Walker were enemies in other respects, but they agreed on annexation and therefore combined successfully to prevent the nomination of Van Buren. There is plenty of evidence that the Van Burenites had no love for Polk,

---

[76] His letter bore the date May 30, but obviously it was written on the 29th (*Am. Hist. Rev.*, July, 1906, 842).

[77] J. B. Jones, writing from Baltimore to his paper, the *Madisonian*, May 29, said: "It is true I hear it whispered about the streets, that the nomination of Mr. Polk was agreed upon at the Hermitage, Mr. B. F. Butler, in behalf of Mr. Van Buren and the *Globe*, concurring" (*Madisonian*, May 30, 1844).

yet their feeling toward him was indifference rather than hostility. Though they were not strong enough to nominate their favorite, they could at least veto the nomination of an objectionable rival like Cass, and, within certain limits, could determine the choice of the candidate. To Polk they had no specific objection; consequently, if all factions would agree to accept him, his nomination would be less objectionable than that of Cass or Buchanan. Therefore they made a virtue of necessity and reluctantly transferred from Van Buren to Polk. They claimed afterwards that they had been responsible for Polk's nomination, and this was true in the sense that they could have prevented it; still, under the circumstances, Polk had small reason to feel under obligation to men who, after all, had acquiesced in his nomination merely as a choice of evils.

Even before the appearance of his anti-Texas letter, Van Bulean had little real popularity outside of a small circle of friends. After its publication, his defeat at the polls being inevitable, his nomination would have meant party suicide. This fact should have been obvious to his most ardent supporters, and yet they chose to regard his defeat at Baltimore as the result of a series of political intrigues. They did not, of course, have all the information which is now accessible, consequently the motives of many of their contemporaries were misjudged. Benton's version of Van Buren's downfall has already been noted; still more elaborate and equally erroneous is the version of Gideon Welles.

In a history of the contest which he prepared but never published,[78] Welles, like Benton, attributed the shelving of Van Buren to a many-sided intrigue in which Calhoun, originally, was the chief actor.[79] In a "last desperate struggle for the

[78] MS article, "A Review of the Political History of the United States and Presidential Contests" (*Welles Papers*, Library of Congress).

[79] "If Mr. Calhoun was insatiable in his ambition, he was also fertile in his schemes to promote it. They were often visionary and startling, so much so as to forfeit rather than beget general confidence, yet to those

presidency'' he brought forward the Texas question, and, when he entered Tyler's cabinet, he believed that the President would assist him. His main object, up to this time, according to Welles, was to make Van Buren's nomination impossible. But Tyler appropriated the Texas question and resolved to stand for reëlection; and while many Democrats were ready to espouse annexation, they would not rally to the standard of Calhoun. In other words, he had succeeded in weakening Van Buren, but had failed in the attempt to attract support for himself. Robert J. Walker, said Welles, was interested in the annexation of Texas because it offered an opportunity for land-scrip speculation. Working through Mason, Tyler's Secretary of the Navy, Walker had convinced the Richmond politicians that the surest means of defeating the aspirations of Calhoun was the nomination of some other pro-Texas Democrat. The preference of the Virginians, said Welles, was Levi Woodbury, but on arriving at Baltimore they found that New England would not support him.

Up to this point, with some modification as to Walker's motives, Welles's account is apparently accurate, but his statements concerning the promotion of Polk's interests are erroneous in detail and give an unfair impression of the attitude of the Tennessee politicians.

Although Calhoun had announced before the meeting of the convention that he would not permit his name to be presented, Welles believed that he still had hopes of being nominated and that they had been blasted by the nomination of Polk. After asserting that Polk was ''brought forward'' by the friends of Van Buren who, under the circumstances, would not support any of the other competitors, Welles then proceeds to tell how the Tennesseans under the leadership of Cave Johnson and Gideon

---

with whom he was intimate, or who were within the circle of his influence, there was a charm in his plans that was to the adventurous inviting. There were always some one or more prominent points in his intrigues that enlisted ardent supporters, and on these points he concentrated the energies of an intellect of unusual power, and pursued his object with an intensity that had no limits.''

Pillow had, for some time before the meeting of the convention, been playing a "deep and subtle game" to procure Polk's nomination. They "concealed their purpose from Genl Jackson who would give no countenance to the movement"[!]; they "fastened themselves on Wright and Benton as friends and partisans of Van Buren, which they were except in the contingency of securing Polk's nomination," betrayed their confidence and secretly intrigued against Van Buren.[80]

Many of the items in Welles's statement may be true enough, but in one of the main clauses the terms are inverted. He contends that the Tennesseans were ready to support Van Buren *unless* they could nominate Polk; whereas, they desired to nominate Polk *because* Van Buren's nomination, or his election at any rate, was no longer possible. Their efforts in Polk's behalf were made not only with Jackson's knowledge, but at his instigation. Under the circumstances, neither he nor they considered these efforts to be a betrayal of Van Buren. Surely Jackson had made it clear to both Van Buren and Butler, as well as to Benton, that he favored the nomination of some pro-Texas candidate. So successful, however, were the Tennessee delegates in their deception, according to Welles, that the friends of Van Buren "had no conception of the duplicity in that quarter" until all was over, and then they were forced to support the party nominee. The "reserve" of Wright and the "indignant resentment" of Benton were caused by the discovery of this "treachery." The New York Democrats worked loyally for the ticket, and "few knew what doubt & repugnance their strongest men entertained for the candidate"[!]

The New Yorkers were chagrined by the defeat of their favorite, and not knowing all the facts, it was natural for them to suspect the motives of those who had profited by their defeat.

---

[80] Welles admits that for two years the Tennesseans had been loyal to Van Buren while others were intriguing against him. He states that New Yorkers desired to associate Polk on the ticket with the ex-President, instead of R. M. Johnson. This is extremely improbable.

It was rumored at Baltimore that Polk's nomination had been agreed upon at the Hermitage, and Whig papers made assertions to this effect.[81]   In stating to Polk his reasons for declining the Vice-Presidential nomination, Wright said that the people of New York believed that there had been intrigue against Van Buren in the convention and that votes for Polk could be procured in the state only by asserting that the candidate had had nothing to do with the intrigue.[82]   Doubtless Wright shared the belief of his associates; but even if all of the charges against the insurgent element had been true, Van Buren's rejection had been brought about not so much by *intrigue* as by the application of the Democratic doctrine of majority rule. To be sure, he received the votes of a majority of the convention, but the delegates had been selected before his views on Texas had become known; and although there is no means of ascertaining with certainty the desire of Democratic voters as a whole, there is ample reason for believing that a large majority of them did not prefer Van Buren after the publication of his anti-Texas letter. From the first, Calhoun Democrats had been openly hostile, and those led by Walker, whom Welles had called the "chief engine" of the convention, made no attempt to conceal their unalterable opposition to Van Buren. It is not easy to see why their efforts to defeat his nomination should be termed an *intrigue* any more than the efforts of his supporters to procure it. Even "Old Hickory" did not hesitate to say that no anti-Texas man could possibly win, and surely he could not be accused of *plotting* against his old friend and protégé. Naturally Polk's immediate friends did not confide

---

[81] "There is one circumstance, and only one," said the Nashville *Union* (June 11, 1844) in denying these charges, "which could impress any honest mind with the belief that General Jackson controlled the nomination—that circumstance is this: *the work is so well done, that to an honest mind, it looks reasonable that, it might have been done by old Hickory!*"

[82] Wright to Polk, June 2, 1844, *Polk Papers*. It has been said, continued Wright, that Van Buren was set aside because of his anti-Texas letter. Better leave it so. Had he (Wright), who held the same views, accepted the nomination on an annexation ticket, the people would have concluded that Van Buren had been dropped for some other reason.

their secret hopes to Wright or to Benton, and the realization of
these hopes was contingent on the defeat of Van Buren's nomination; but if this amounted to deception, it should be remembered that the ex-President's doom was sealed by the vote of 148
to 118 in favor of the two-thirds rule, and even if the Tennessee
delegates had joined with the minority, such action would not
have altered the result. Van Buren had always been indifferent
when Polk stood in need of assistance, consequently there was no
valid reason why the Tennesseans should continue to follow the
ex-President in his pursuit of a forlorn hope. On the first seven
ballots they voted for Cass, after which they transferred to Polk.

Irrespective of intrigues in his behalf, the selection of Polk
as the compromise candidate was quite natural, if not inevitable.
Apparently, a majority at least had come to Baltimore prepared
to support him for the second place. He was the only aspirant
who was not also a candidate for the Presidency, and for that
reason, objectionable to the different factions. The Van Burenites
would not support any of their hero's rivals, with the possible
exception of Colonel Johnson; and the other factions would never
consent to make Johnson the Presidential candidate. Some new
man must be selected; and of these, who had a better claim than
Polk's? As a member of Congress he had done valiant party
service, and had proved himself to be a man of ability and discretion. The statements made by Welles[83] that he "was destitute of
personal popularity" and especially that he had "no qualities to
recommend him" are gross exaggerations. Welles himself had
expressed a different opinion in 1844.[84] Even Horace Greely,
although he spoke disparagingly of Polk during the campaign,
had, in 1839, called him "one of the ablest men and most powerful

---

[83] Welles, *loc. cit.*

[84] In a letter written to Van Buren, Nov. 13, 1844, he asked whether
Polk would have sufficient energy and discernment to make the administration his own, and added that "my own belief is, that he will prove
himself worthy of being the choice of the democracy, after it could not
have its first choice" (*Van Buren Papers*).

speakers in the south west.''[85] General Jackson aptly summarized Polk's qualifications for office when he wrote that

his capacity for business [is] great—and to extraordinary powers of labor, both mental and physical, he unites that tact and judgment which are requisite to the successful direction of such an office as that of Chief Magistrate of a free people.[86]

Joseph Storey was ''thunderstruck'' by the selection made at Baltimore; Governor Letcher exclaimed ''Polk! Great God, what a nomination!'';[87] and the Whig journals predicted an easy victory. But the Democrats, in the public press and in private correspondence, gave abundant evidence of both satisfaction and relief because a party crisis had been averted. Of course, due allowance must be made for partisan zeal, and for a self-seeking desire to stand well with the nominee. No doubt many professed a friendship which they did not feel, and, in the hope of reward, claimed to have been influential in procuring the nomination.[88] Still, he was scarcely less *popular* than any of the other aspirants, and as the campaign proceeded it came to be recognized generally that the convention had chosen the leader who would be most likely to win.

The *Spectator,* which was supposed to voice the sentiments of Calhoun, while expressing surprise that Polk had been selected, nevertheless approved the choice which had been made.[89] Its

---

[85] *Biographical Annual*, 1841, p. 52. When quoting this the Washington *Globe*, July 12, 1844, called attention to the fact that Clay lived in the southwest.

[86] Letter dated June 24. Quoted by Nashville *Union*, Aug. 13, 1844.

[87] Story to McLean, Aug. 16, 1844, *McLean Papers*. Letcher to Buchanan, July 7, 1844, *Buchanan Papers*.

[88] ''If you were here,'' wrote Pillow, ''you would imagine yourself the most popular man in the world, and you would be sure you *never had* an enemy in the convention. You cannot know how much pains they take to give in to me *their adhesion* to you, and to impress me with the *great merit* of their *conduct*.'' ''Never,'' said Benton, ''was such a multitude seen claiming the merit of Polk's nomination, and demanding the reward, for having done what had been done before they heard of it'' (Pillow to Polk, May 30 (29?), 1844, *Polk Papers;* Benton, *Thirty Years' View*, II, 594).

[89] *Spectator*, May 29, 1844.

editor, John Heart, announced his intention to publish a weekly journal, to be called "Young Hickory" in honor of Polk. Tyler was nominated by a convention of his own, but his letter of acceptance intimated that he might cease to be a candidate if Texas should be annexed by treaty or otherwise.[90] Polk entered the canvass, therefore, supported by an apparently united Democracy, and with some prospect of eventual assistance from those who had recently unfurled to the breeze the banner of "Tyler and Texas."

---

[90] *Nat. Intell.*, May 31, 1844. Several years later he hinted that his main object had been to force the Democrats to stand firmly for Texas (Tyler to Wise, Tyler, *Letters and Times of the Tylers*, II, 317).

CHAPTER XIII

CAMPAIGN OF 1844

"Who is James K. Polk?" Such was the derisive query raised by the Whigs as soon as the result of the Democratic convention had been announced.[1] It was an effective campaign cry. More than argument could have done it attached to Polk the stigma of mediocrity and obscurity, and, to some extent at least, it appears to have influenced the opinion of later generations. But as it turned out this very cry recoiled as a boomerang upon those who hurled it, for this "obscure" person was soon to be known as the vanquisher of their own renowned "Prince Hal."

Justly or unjustly, both in 1844 and since that time, Clay has enjoyed the reputation of being a great man. On the other hand, Polk's opponents have rated him as a man possessed of scarcely second-class ability—a man whom accident alone had placed in an exalted position. Even his friends have usually been rather apologetic—not insisting that he was really a great man, but that he was more able than he has been represented to be by his adversaries.

The Whigs entered the campaign full of confidence in their standard bearer and delighted that the Democratic party had made the "blunder" of passing over a man of ability like Van Buren, and had as the *National Intelligencer* put it, "*let itself down*" to Polk. The Demcrats, on the contrary, while they rallied loyally to the ticket, were manifestly full of misgivings because one of the *prominent* men of the party had not been selected to

---

[1] Writing from Columbia, S. C., to Crittenden, Wm. C. Preston said: "The democrats here cry hurra for Polk in the street and come round to ask me who the devil he is" (undated letter in the *Crittenden Papers*, vol. 9).

enter the contest with Clay. Some of the newspapers, while admitting that Polk was not of the first rank, argued that great men and democracy were incompatible.

And yet, what is a great man, and by what standard is he measured? In his long career in the political field, Clay had been an opportunist, and, to a considerable degree, an adventurer. He had mounted one hobby after another in the hope of political advancement. There was little consistency in his record, for the panacea which he advocated on any particular occasion might differ radically in principle from the one offered only a year or two before. Many of the policies championed by Clay were visionary and impracticable, and few of them would now be considered sound. Furthermore, if greatness is to be rated by success, Clay's claim to it was not very well founded; for although he frequently succeeded in upsetting the plans of others, he was seldom successful in inaugurating his own most cherished policies. His greatest strength lay in his power of persuasion, and his greatest achievements were in compromising the divergent views of others and in procuring the adoption of measures after the compromise had been agreed upon.

Polk early adopted the fundamentals of the Jeffersonian creed. A conservative by nature, he was wary of experiments and shaped his course in accordance with the principles of the party which had been founded by his patron. His record, therefore, was consistent, and he could seldom be accused of trimming his sails to catch the varying winds of popular opinion. He was not a creator of issues, but his judgment on those which were presented was far sounder, as a rule, than that of his great opponent. With no pretense to oratory, he was an effective and convincing debater, while his thorough knowledge on public questions was conceded even by his foes. When he was nominated for the Presidency, he could point to a career of almost uniform successes, and as President few have had a more definite program to carry out or have succeeded so well in accomplishing their purposes. But in spite of all this Clay was conceded a place in the first rank of statesmen, while many, even of Polk's supporters, did not claim for their candidate more than second-rate ability. The *Democratic Review*,[2] although it denounced the methods by which Clay had achieved his fame, did not deny that in the popular mind Clay was rated higher than Polk, so it made the best of the situation by saying that "our opponents are welcome to all their pride in their chief as a 'great man'—we are content with ours as a good one, and great enough for all practical purposes."

At the time that the two men were nominated, it was natural enough that Clay should be heralded as the superior of his rival. It was a period that was dominated by great personalities, and spectacular qualities were regarded as essential attributes of greatness. The influence wielded by Clay, Webster, and Calhoun, resulted more from the eloquence of their delivery than from the soundness of their arguments. Even the tempestuous and generally illogical conduct of President Jackson was easily mistaken for statesmanship.

Polk was not possessed of spectacular qualities, and he never tried to cultivate them. He was by nature secretive, even sly,[3] and the degree of his influence in shaping public policies was known only to his intimate friends. In all of those qualities which are thought to make men *illustrious,* Polk suffered by comparison with his rival; but, as the *Review* pointed out, a Democratic candidate might succeed without possessing them, however essential they might be for the Whig.

In no other campaign has Democracy and Whiggery so definitely contested for victory; in no other campaign have the

---

[2] Article on "First and Second Rate Men," August, 1844.

[3] For example, he made a practice of sending his Nashville correspondence under an extra cover, addressed to General Armstrong, so that his opponents, through the Whig postmaster, might not learn its final destination.

candidates so clearly represented the principles and policies of their respective parties.[4]

Polk was the first "dark horse" ever nominated for President by a political party, but while his name had not been previously associated with that office, it is not true that he was *unknown* or that his nomination was entirely accidental. The Baltimore convention did not simply make a grab in the dark, with the hope that either Providence or Fate would save the party from disaster. The man who, as chairman of the Committee of Ways and Means, had borne the brunt of the war against the Bank was unknown to neither party; a Speaker who was so thoroughly hated that his opponents had wished to deny him the customary vote of thanks could not have been so soon forgotten—least of all by the Whigs. He had never filled any of the great executive offices, but he had been intrusted by his party, during a most critical period, with the two most responsible positions in the lower house of Congress. No faction of his party doubted his ability, but like John Quincy Adams, his personal following was small. For personal reasons, many in the party may have preferred another candidate, but, if a certain newspaper story is to be credited, Clay, at least, recognized that the wisest choice had been made.[5]

---

[4] "The two candidates indeed, with a felicity of adaptation and correspondence, which is no mere accident, may be said in a remarkable manner to represent, respectively, the spirit and character of the two great parties by whom they have been chosen. . . . Mr. Clay is truly the living embodiment and incarnation of his party. Eloquent, showy, versatile, adroit, imperious, . . . the first Whig in America. A second-rate man in point of eloquence, intellectual force, and eminence of rank, would never have answered—could never have been adopted—as the head of such a party. We concede them this credit. They are naturally fond of splendor and strength—large and sweeping action—bold and brilliant energy and enterprise. Such is precisely the character their instinct has ever tended and striven to impress upon the government." Thus abbreviated, this characterization of Clay and his party is by no means an inaccurate description, and it is quite as true that Polk would "have been perfectly satisfactory to us for the presidency, even if he possessed in a far less degree than he has already amply proved, the further addition of the latter qualification [intellectual eminence], for the high office to which he is about to be called" (*Dem. Rev.*, August, 1844).

[5] "When the news of the democratic nomination reached Ashland, young Clay, who was impatiently waiting its announcement at the office,

Apparently the Democrats of all sections received the news of the nominations with genuine satisfaction—only in the Van Buren camp were there signs of resentment and reluctant support. They had not looked with favor on Polk's claim to the Vice-Presidency, and now he had beaten their patron in the race for first place. One of Catron's letters throws some interesting light on the attitude of political leaders toward Polk. It indicates also that, aside from the Texas question, Polk had profited by a desire on the part of the younger Democrats to get rid of the older leaders, by whom they had "been treated as boys." Together with others to be cited presently, this letter seems to make it plain that Polk's desire for a new party organ did not result from any bargain with Calhoun, but from a real distrust of the *Globe,* which of course was the organ of Van Buren.[6]

Polk's nomination was a victory for the annexationists, and it was also a victory for the younger element of the party. All factions were in duty bound to support the ticket, but it was evident from the first that "old fogies" must give way to those

---

hastened with the news to his father, who remained at home. 'Well, my son, who is nominated?' 'Guess, father.' 'Why Matty, of course.' 'No, father; guess again.' 'Cass?' 'No.' 'Buchanan?' 'No.' 'Then who the devil have they nominated?' 'James K. Polk,' said the son. The old man started from his seat, and rushing across the room, with disappointed hopes painted on his countenance, exclaimed, 'Beat again, by G-d' " (N. Y. *Plebeian,* copied in the Washington *Globe,* Oct. 29, 1844).

6 "Mr. Van B.," said Catron, "was out of luck—we again have it. Had the Dem. Con. met a month sooner, we w'd have been ruined in the west & South for ten years. Clay is out fully—many of the undermen are out, on annexation—and we have the strength added of a *rejection* of our V. P. on the precise ground, drawing in all the Calhoun strength— a vast, & controlling power, in the South. Among the leaders, you have many jealousies to quiet; they feared to see you on any ticket as vice, for fear you would set up for chief, after the first success. My position has let me into the deepest recesses of these things. I traversed the city night after night, last winter, encountering and *pledging* myself to the contrary of this opinion: But, sir, I made no converts, as I then believed. Buchanan was for Johnson—Benton for King; the Van B. men for either, sooner than yourself" [Both Calhoun and Tyler friendly to Polk]. "The coarse brutality of the Globe, was loathed last winter, by a large majority of our party." . . . "Your strength lies mainly as I think in this; you are of the present generation—the old leaders are thrown off; to do this has been an ardent wish by nineteen in twenty of our party in the House

who were abreast of the times. Old in years, but young in spirit, Jackson gave his enthusiastic support to both platform and candidates;[7] nevertheless, even his wishes went unheeded in cases where he desired to restore any of the "old guard" to power.

Within a few days after Polk's nomination, his Tennessee friends in Washington began to formulate plans, not only for the campaign, but for his course as President of the United States. The most active—not to say presumptuous—of all was A. V. Brown, who did not hesitate to draft a list of instructions for the guidance of the candidate. First of all Polk was told that he *must*, in his letter of acceptance, commit himself to a one-term policy.[8] The Democratic platform had said nothing on this point, but it was evidently thought necessary to checkmate the Whigs, whose platform had limited their candidate to a single term. Besides, as Brown seems very clearly to intimate, other "deserving Democrats"[9] with high aspirations might be expected to support the campaign with more enthusiasm if they could be assured that the way would be open for them at the end of four

---

R. for two sessions—but they would not do it, as they believed—not as I believed. They are now gone" (Catron to Polk, June 8, [1844], *Polk Papers*).

[7] "Although I regret losing Mr. V. B. and the cause, yet I rejoice that the Convention have made choice of those worthy Democrats, Polk and Dallas. They are the strongest and best selection that could have been made" (Jackson to Gen. Planché, June 14, 1844, *Polk Papers*. Same to W. G. Reeves *et al.*, June 5, 1844, Wash. *Globe*, June 28, 1844). Polk doubted that the Planché (often spelled Plauche) letter was intended for publication, and thought it imprudent in Planché to publish it. He feared the cry of "dictation" (Polk to Donelson, July 11, 1844, "Polk-Donelson Letters").

[8] "In your acceptance you must some way or other express yourself in favor of the one term system. This is important—I might say all important—you will know exactly *how* it will be highly useful. The thing is right *per se* & under all the circumstances I think you ought not to *hesitate* to do it" (Brown to Polk, May 30, 1844, *Polk Papers*).

[9] Laughlin, although not without some doubt as to the wisdom of such a declaration, thought that "perhaps all in all it may be best—and will be making assurance doubly sure, and put us on an equality with the Whigs on that question" (Laughlin to Polk, May 31, 1844, *Polk Papers*).

years. Although Brown's suggestion may have been entirely superfluous, the one-term pledge found a place in Polk's letter of acceptance.[10]

The next instruction was for Polk to prepare data on his life and career for Brown to turn over to Bancroft, Kendall, or some other person who would incorporate it into a biography.[11] Another thing to be considered, said Brown, was whether the *Globe* was to be continued as "the Polk organ"; and while he was not yet certain that it should not be so continued, it is apparent that the discarding of that paper was already being discussed.[12]

Cave Johnson, as well as Brown and Catron, distrusted the *Globe*,[13] but he by no means believed in courting the favor of or permitting the domination by the southern wing of the party. On June 1 he wrote to Polk that the party was more united than at any time since the election of Jackson, but he pointed out that danger might result from the fact that the South had been zealous in procuring Polk's nomination. The *Globe*, he said, is noncommittal, and is already expressing doubts of Democratic success— a new paper of unquestioned loyalty is very much needed. Two weeks later he wrote that matters are growing worse and must soon come to a head. "The struggle now is by a few Southern men to appropriate *you* & the nomination to their exclusive benefit whilst the northern Democrats are determined to yield no such

---

[10] In 1835 Polk had, on the floor of the House, advocated a single term for all Presidents (*Cong. Globe*, 23 Cong., 2 sess., part 2, 292).

[11] Brown had asked Laughlin to write the biography and it was he in turn who had suggested Bancroft (Laughlin to Polk, May 31, 1844, *Polk Papers*).

[12] "Much is said here by *some* as to continuing the Globe as the Polk organ—this we will manage with sound discretion. The Globe will change its tone & perhaps take back much that it has said & go in *warmly* if not heartily—if so—well. But we will not commit ourselves to it *after* the election."

[13] "Benton & the Globe falls in but not with so good a grace as we expected" (Johnson to Polk, May 31, 1844, *Polk Papers*). He referred to an editorial of the 29th in which Blair had said that the nomination of Polk would at first be received with disappointment by those who had stood for favorites, but that a little reflection would convince all that it was for the best.

thing.'' Johnson had called a caucus in the hope of compromising differences, but the northern men became alarmed for fear the Calhoun members would get control; and Johnson decided that the best thing he could do was to prevent *anything* from being done.

I have been to see S. W. Jr. [Silas Wright] hoping to have it controled in some way & ended—he is furious and I think determined to push C[alhoun] and his clique to the wall or finish—in this battle.   The object *of both* will be to make us take sides—the Northern know, that you have always been with them, whilst the South think that the question & the position of Genl J[ackson] will take you with them—how both are to be kept I cannot see—already we have much secret talk of upsetting the Globe—turning Benton overboard &c.   I was disgusted to day, even Reuben Whitney talked of turning Benton out of the Democratic church.   I am sick of this state of things & see no means of avoiding the explosion & most anxious to leave here.[14]

Johnson's fears increased rather than abated, for a few days later he expressed a belief that the combined obstinacy of Benton and the South Carolinians would lead to a southern movement that might imperil not only the Democratic party but the Union itself.[15]   It seems very evident that Johnson had entered into no

---

[14] Johnson to Polk, June 13, 1844, *Polk Papers.*

[15] He has seen, he said, many prominent Democrats and all are pleased with the nominations, but ''the only difficulty I fear arises from the course of T. H. Benton, when connected with the movements of S. C.   The latter uses *immediate annexation* for the purpose of uniting the South and killing T. H. B. & will if practicable *identify you* & Genl J. with all their future movements—fears are entertained in the North, that this *may be so*—& if any incident takes place to confirm the suspicion, our cause is jeoparded. I have given every assurance to S. W. Jr. & a few others that you could not be induced to separate yourself from the Northern Democracy—instanced your former course, in the case of White &c &c and also thought it impossible that Genl J. should lend himself to any such purpose.   The only danger of the latter taking any step to favor the Southern movement they think will arise, from some letter from him, that will seem to favor the movement without sufficiently weighing the consequences.

''Can not you see him & have a free conversation as to the Southern movement & put him on his guard?''   Johnson fears that there will be a southern convention called to meet at Nashville, and advises that this should be forestalled by an earlier meeting to which Wright and other northern men should be invited.   ''I have the most serious apprehensions from the Southern movement not only to our cause but the country. Mason & Dickson's line now divides the Methodist church & will soon

agreement with southern delegates to procure Polk's nomination, and it is equally clear that he had no desire to see the party brought under southern domination. He desired harmony, to be sure, and support from all factions, but harmony that would leave Polk indebted to neither section—free and unhampered in shaping his own course. Polk's replies show that he fully agreed with the views expressed by Johnson. He promptly warned General Jackson and took other steps to forestall a sectional convention; "no countenance must be given to any attempt should it be made."[16] A few days later he asked Donelson to prepare an article on this subject for the Nashville *Union*. "The idea," said he, "of a Southern convention or a sectional meeting at Nashville or elsewhere *must not for a moment be entertained.*" He did not believe it to be necessary to allude specifically to disunion sentiments in South Carolina, but

> Let the article strongly enforce the leading idea, that a meeting of the masses from all sections of the Union is what is intended, and let every thing giving it the appearance of a sectional or Southern affair be expressly negatived. This would have the effect of allaying the fears of the North, by satisfying them that we in Tennessee gave no countenance to the suggestion for a Southern Convention upon the Texas or any other subject.[17]

While Johnson was warning Polk against the southern wing of the party, Catron was exhorting him not to listen to those who insisted that the salvation of Democracy depended upon the restoration to office of the old guard that had been ousted by Harrison, "cabinet & all," leaving no place for the rank and file whose money and talents would be responsible for the victory. "You who fought in the very van," said Catron,

divide the other churches. This movement will tend to divide political parties by it. The Texas question brings into the contest the fanaticism of the North with increased fervor. Our only safety for the country & our cause depends upon the Southern Democracy maintaining the position we have hitherto occupied—firm & consistent friends of the Northern Democracy—yielding much for conciliation & harmony'' (Johnson to Polk, Louisville, June 21, 1844, *Polk Papers*).

[16] Polk to Johnson, June 21 [?], 1844, July 1, 1844, "Polk-Johnson Letters," *Tenn. Hist. Mag.*, Sept., 1915, 245–246).

[17] Polk to Donelson, June 26, 1844, "Polk-Donelson Letters."

and who the worthy old gentlemen thought last winter, had died in the *ditch,* have been brought out alive, not by their consent, nor help, but [by] those who look to chances for themselves. "Treason & Traitor," "rotten to the core,"—have been the gentle epithets that have greeted every move tending to wrench the power, as a party, from the old clique. Mr. Van Buren thought this public opinion, if Col. Benton let him think at all, which I doubt.[18]

Like Johnson, Catron warned Polk against unnecessarily expressing his views, and, as he had "a soul to be *saved,*" he should avoid answering letters of the Sherrod Williams type.[19]

Benton had written a letter in which he had exonerated Polk and Dallas from any part in the "intrigue which had nullified the choice of the people,"[20] but on June 13 he openly accused A. V. Brown of having "vicariously" procured from Jackson the letter in favor of annexing Texas.[21] While General Jackson was charitable enough to attribute Benton's outbursts to insanity, caused by the Princeton disaster,[22] others knew that he was simply expressing what Van Burenites generally were thinking; and, although the appearance of harmony prevailed during the campaign, mutual distrust was manifest in private correspondence,[23] and a break was almost inevitable as soon as the election had been held.

In general, the Democratic press of all sections and factions rallied to the support of the candidates without reservation or

[18] Catron to Polk, June 10, [1844], *Polk Papers.*

[19] In 1836 Williams had catechised Van Buren, Harrison, and White as to their opinions on certain campaign isues. See Shepard, *Martin Van Buren,* 264.

[20] Dated June 3. *Nat. Intell.,* July 1, 1844; Benton, *Thirty Years' View,* II, 595.

[21] "A card," printed in the Wash. *Globe,* June 13, 1844.

[22] "Gen. Jackson was a good deal excited at Benton's course—said 'he shall hear from *me* soon'; and asserts that ever since the explosion of the big gun Benton has not been in his right mind. I think so too" (J. Geo. Harris to Bancroft, June 25, 1844, *Polk Papers*).

[23] For example, Sacfield Maclin, of Tennessee, wrote from Little Rock, Arkansas, to Polk, on June 14, that "Colo Benton and the Globe for the last eighteen months have done our party more damage than all the Whig papers in the Union. I have no doubt, and our friends here believe with me, that if Colo Benton thought he could hold his place in the affections of the Democratic party, and go against you, he would do so with all his energy" (*Polk Papers*).

qualification. Most enthusiastic and influential of all, perhaps, was the Richmond *Enquirer*,[24] but Calhoun's Washington organ was hardly less effusive in its praise.[25]

Cass bore his defeat with better grace than any of the other aspirants. At a ratification meeting held in Detroit he commended the action of the Baltimore convention and promised his support. He spoke of Polk as a man who would follow in the footsteps of Washington, Jefferson, Madison, and Jackson, a statement which caused the Charleston *Courier* to remark that Polk, in order to do this, would have to "walk all sorts of ways."[26] He took an active part in the campaign[27] and spent his energies freely in preaching the Texas gospel in a northern latitude.

Polk's letter accepting the nomination bore the date of June 12, 1844. In it the most significant phrase, aside from approval of the Baltimore platform, was that

I deem the present to be a proper occasion to declare, that if the nomination made by the convention shall be confirmed by the people, I shall enter upon the discharge of the high and solemn duties of the office with the settled purpose of not being a candidate for reëlection.

This self-denying declaration resulted evidently, as we have noted, from an effort to checkmate the Whigs and a desire to

---

[24] "Mr. Polk's nomination has been received at Baltimore, at Washington, and at Richmond, with enthusiasm. It heals all divisions, unites our party with bands of iron. It thwarts every hope the Whigs had indulged of discord and divisions. It blasts the election of Mr. Clay, and saves our country from the sceptre of the dictator. Mr. Polk is true to all our republican principles, and he is the friend of Texas." Quoted by Nashville *Union*, June 11, 1844.

[25] "The great mass of the people wantd a man pure in morals, sound in political principles, *and in favor of the immediate annexation of Texas*, and such they have in James K. Polk. He is a consistent and sound politician, of the Jeffersonian Democratic school; talented, firm and discreet" (Washington *Spectator*, May 29, 1844).

[26] Quoted in *Nat. Intell.*, June 24, 1844.

[27] Geo. N. Sanders to Polk, July 12; Austin E. Wing to Polk, Aug. 2, 1844, *Polk Papers*.

harmonize factional discords in Democratic ranks. "I said nothing to commit the party upon the *one term* principle," he told Cave Johnson, "but expressed simply my own determination."[28]

The pro-Texas Democrats may be said to have included three fairly well defined groups. The first was made up of the followers of Calhoun whose interest centered mainly in promoting his advancement. The second comprised those who were not friends of Calhoun, but who were interested primarily in wresting the control of the party from the hands of the older leaders. They saw in the Texas question a possible means of accomplishing this purpose; and, in addition, annexation would enlist southern sympathies and place the party reins in southern hands. Some of them were accused, and perhaps not unjustly, of being influenced by prospective profits from Texas land scrip. The third group was composed of men like Cave Johnson, and apparently Polk, who favored annexation but who, at the same time, did not desire southern domination. They wished above all things to harmonize differences which were threatening to disrupt the party, if not the Union itself. The second group was most active in the nominating convention, and Robert J. Walker, of Mississippi, was its reputed head. Catron and A. V. Brown were close friends of Polk but, unlike Cave Johnson, they had strong leanings toward the southern groups. Walker had long been interested in Texas. During Jackson's administration he had worked hard for the recognition of the new republic. In February, 1844, he had written a long letter in which many reasons were assigned why Texas should be annexed.[29] It was alleged by his opponents that he was influenced by the hope of profit from land speculations, but undoubtedly this personal motive was greatly exaggerated.

---

[28] Polk to Johnson, June 21 [?], 1844, "Polk-Johnson Letters," *Tenn. Hist. Mag.*, Sept., 1915, 245.

[29] For an excellent summary, see Smith, *Annexation of Texas*, 140–144.

The annexation of Texas was not the only question on which
the Democrats of 1844 were unable to agree. For a time considerable anxiety was felt for fear that Polk's well-known views
on tariff might cost him votes in northern states, particularly
in Pennsylvania. The discussion of Polk's views on this subject
was precipitated by the so-called Irvin-Hardin correspondence.
Shortly after Polk's nomination James Irvin, of Pennsylvania,
had addressed a letter to John J. Hardin, of Illinois,[30] asking
about the candidate's opinions on tariff. Hardin replied that
Polk was a believer in free trade. As soon as Polk read the
letters in the papers, he asserted that, although the second letter
had been signed by Hardin, it must have been written by Milton
Brown, a member of Congress from Tennessee. He asked that
the "trick" be exposed.[31]

Walker undertook to instruct the nominee as to the stand he
should take on this perplexing subject, and also as to the proper
treatment of Democrats who had left the party in 1840. He
suggested that Polk should make it known that he would welcome
"all Jacksonian Democrats." On the tariff he was to declare
for a revenue basis, adjusted in such a manner as to give "incidental aid" and a "reasonable profit" to every branch of domestic industries. He urged especially that the word *aid* should
be used instead of *protection*.[32] But before Walker's letter had
left Washington, Polk had already announced his views on the
tariff in a letter to J. K. Kane, of Philadelphia. When he penned
his "Kane letter," Polk had not of course read Walker's suggestions, but their ideas were practically identical and even
the phraseology of their letters was very much the same. More
straightforward than Walker, however, and less southern in his
leanings, Polk did not sugar-coat incidental protection by calling

---

30 Both men were members of Congress. Their letters, dated May 30,
1844, are printed in *Niles' Reg.*, LXVI, 234.

31 Polk to Johnson, June 8, 1844, "Polk-Johnson Letters."

32 Walker to Polk, June 18, 1844, *Polk Papers*.

it an "aid."[33] It was said at the time that Polk in drafting his letter made a definite attempt to face both ways—that his emphasis on incidental protection was for the North, while the substance was for the South. But if the tariff Democrats were in any sense deluded it must have resulted from a meaning which they had read into the letter, for, as Polk had pointed out in the letter itself, his present views were to be found in his own record, the record of his party, and the declarations that had been adopted at the Baltimore convention. In such a statement there was nothing equivocal—nothing to which a protectionist had reason to pin his hopes. "On all great questions," wrote General Jackson in a letter commending Polk, "from the Panama mission to the present day, he has been consistent, orthodox, and true to the standards of old-fashioned Jeffersonian democracy";[34] and the Kane letter promised no departure from such a course. To an intimate friend Polk wrote that his letter had been sent to Kane

with a request that he would show it to *Mr. Dallas* and *Mr. Horn,* and if in their judgment, it was absolutely necessary, they were at liberty to publish it, but not otherwise. It was but a re-declaration of the opinions upon which I have acted on that subject; it was carefully prepared and upon its doctrines I am ready to stand.[35]

---

[33] "I am," said Polk, "in favor of a tariff for revenue, such a one as will yield a sufficient amount to the Treasury to defray the expenses of the Government economically administered. In adjusting the details of a revenue tariff, I have heretofore sanctioned such moderate discriminating duties, as would produce the amount of revenue needed, and at the same time afford reasonable incidental protection to our home industries. I am opposed to a tariff for protection *merely,* and not for revenue." [Cites his votes on tariff bills.] "In my judgment, it is the duty of the Government, to extend as far as it may be practicable to do so, by its revenue laws & all other means within its power, fair and just protection to all the great interests of the whole Union, embracing agriculture, commerce and navigation" (Polk to Hon. J. K. Kane, June 19, 1844; copy of original in *Polk Papers;* printed copies in newspapers).

[34] Jackson to M. M. Jones, Utica, N. Y., June 25, 1844, Wash. *Globe,* July 20, 1844.

[35] Polk to Johnson, June 21 [?], 1844, "Polk-Johnson Letters."

Shortly after the adjournment of the Democratic convention the Senate took a vote on Tyler's treaty of annexation. Instead of the two-thirds in its favor which the President had promised the Texan diplomats, more than two-thirds (35 to 16) voted to reject it. Many who were not averse to annexation voted against the treaty, for they resented the manner of its negotiation and despised the renegade President and his Secretary of State. Tyler's friends tried to cast the blame for ill feeling on Calhoun and his Pakenham correspondence, while Calhoun regretted that the question had been brought forward under such a weak administration.[36] In the Senate, Benton now introduced a bill of his own for annexing Texas whenever Mexico should be ready to acquiesce, while McDuffie presented a joint resolution which would require simply a majority vote of both houses of Congress. Both failed, and without taking further action Congress adjourned on June 17, to await the result of the pending campaign.

When, on May 1, Clay was nominated at Baltimore, all signs seemed to augur success for the Whigs. The party was united and the choice of the candidate was unanimous. Tyler's annexation treaty had caused some annoyance to be sure, but by his "masterly" Raleigh letter Clay was thought to have made his own position unassailable. Besides, it did not appear that Texas would be an important issue, for Van Buren, whose nomination by the Democrats seemed a foregone conclusion, had also taken a stand against immediate annexation. Although Van Buren's nomination was fully expected, it was known that many Democrats had set their hearts on procuring Texas, consequently division and weakness appeared to be the inevitable result.

At first it did not seem that Polk's nomination had solved the difficulties which had confronted the Democrats, for despite the professions of harmony it was well known that Benton, Van

---

[36] Schouler, *Hist. of the U. S.*, IV, 470.

Buren, and their followers were dissatisfied with, if not indeed hostile to, their party. Tyler had been nominated on an annexation ticket, barring any accessions from Democrats who with him had deserted to the Whigs in 1840. His official organ even insisted that Polk should decline the nomination in favor of the man who had been responsible for bringing the Texas question forward.[37]

The Democrats had trouble in plenty, but the Whig program was likewise going awry. Van Buren had not been nominated as they had expected, and Clay's Raleigh letter, instead of settling the Texas question, bid fair to cost him many northern votes. In August, 1843, the Liberty party had nominated James G. Birney, of Michigan, on an anti-slavery ticket, and, after the publication of Clay's letter, many who under ordinary circumstances would have voted for him now announced their intention to support the Liberty candidate. Although Clay was a slaveholder and did not oppose the annexation of Texas with the consent of Mexico, still the Whigs had, originally, no reason to believe that the Liberty Party would be more hostile to him than to the Democratic candidate, who was likewise a slaveholder and, in addition, an advocate of immediate annexation. Nevertheless the unexpected happened, for on the stump Birney avowed a preference for Polk, arguing that Clay's superior ability, coupled with his equivocal attitude, made him the more dangerous and objectionable of the two.[38]

The Raleigh letter was denounced even more bitterly in the South, and, as will appear later, it was defection in this quarter which caused the candidate most alarm. No wonder that a leading Whig declared the Texas question to be "an enigma and

[37] "Mr. Polk is too wise a man to suffer the Blairs and Kendalls to set him up as a mark for the shafts of the Whigs . . . to enter the contest, with Mr. Tyler already in the field, and with the certainty of an overwhelming defeat awaiting him" (The Madisonian, June 1, 1844).

[38] Schouler, Hist. of the U. S., IV, 475; Smith, Annex. of Tex., 306, 308.

a puzzle to the most astute,''[39] for the most ardent advocates of annexation would lose, economically, by its consummation, while the opponents of annexation, for the sake of *principle*, were indirectly aiding Polk.

After Congress had adjourned, all parties were free to devote their energies to the campaign. The Democrats fully realized that the contest would be close, that defection must be prevented, and new recruits gained. Benton and the *Globe* must be whipped into line, and if possible, Tyler must be made to withdraw in favor of Polk. No one was in a better position than Old Hickory to perform this valuable service, and no one was more ready to undertake the difficult task. Jackson was much excited by Benton's heated reply to McDuffie while discussing his own annexation bill, and still more so by the report that his old friend had solicited the coöperation of John Quincy Adams.[40] His irritation was increased because Benton had not been convinced by a letter he had sent him stating that the Union could not be preserved except by annexing Texas and extending the laws of the United States over Oregon. He was certain that Benton had induced Van Buren to declare against annexation. He called Blair's attention to Polk's one-term pledge, and prophesied that Van Buren would succeed Polk if he should take the proper course. ''My dear friend,'' he pleaded with Blair, ''permit not Col. Benton to have controle over your

---

[39] Chas. A. Davis to Crittenden, New York, June 5, 1844, *Crittenden Papers*. It was a curious fact, said Davis, that on two important questions party considerations had made people in the South and West blind to their own interests; they had crushed the bank and thereby driven much needed capital back to the North and East, and were now clamoring for Texas, although the other sections would profit more by its annexation.

[40] Jackson to Blair (*confidential*), June 25, 1844, *Jackson Papers*. ''The last Washington papers give an account of the very irrated reply of Col. Benton to Mr. McDuffie on Benton's annexation Bill in the Senate after which Col. Benton seized J. Q. Adams by the hand & said 'we are both old men, we must now unite & save the constitution'—do my dear Mr. Blair inform me if this can be true—if it is, I want no better proof of his derangement, & it political[ly] prostrates him.''

editorial column, as he will ruin y^r paper. If he will, he must pursue his eratic course, which has, & will political[ly] destroy him if not already done.'' Blair assured Jackson that Benton was zealous in the cause of Polk and Dallas, but that he distrusted Calhoun and opposed his program of Texas with or without the Union. These views were shared by Blair himself. Jackson wrote again to Blair on July 12, criticizing Benton's attitude and urging Blair to attend the ratification meeting to be held at Nashville on the fifteenth of August.[41]

Before Jackson had received his reply from Blair he expressed his opinion of Benton in a letter to Polk.[42] Benton's hatred of Calhoun and his jealousy of the growing popularity of Tyler, said Jackson, had deranged him, but

> you will perceive I have estopped Benton or any others from believing that you or I could countenance nullification or disunion. Every letter I get gives us joyfull news—You will get 20 states at least & your one term [pledge] will get you 22.

He told Polk that, while it was quite unnecessary for Cave Johnson to put him on his guard lest he should inadvertently give aid to the nullifiers, still every Democrat should ''put his face against any meeting of *disunion,* or nullification—we must & will have Texas, with & in our *glorious Union.* The Federal Union must be preserved—A. J.''[43]

---

[41] Blair to Jackson, July 7; Jackson to Blair, July 12, 1844, *Jackson Papers.* The ''Texas, with or without the Union,'' program mentioned by Benton was an attempt made in South Carolina, while Tyler's treaty was before the Senate, to call a southern convention and annex Texas to the southern states if it should be rejected by the federal government. See Benton, *Thirty Years' View,* II, 616.

[42] Jackson to Polk, June 29, 1844, *Polk Papers.* ''In my reply to Col. Benton's first letter to me in which he adverted to my toast,—'The Federal Union must be preserved,' amongst other things, I said to him, *The Federal Union must be preserved,* and to do this effectually & permanently—Texas must be reunited to the United States—the laws of the Union extended forthwith over the Oragon, which would place this Federal Union on as permanent basses as the Rocky mountains, and preserve our glorious Union, & our Republican system as long as time lasted.''

[43] *Ibid.*

Johnson was still much concerned for fear that something might be said or done at the Nashville meeting which might be construed as an approval of the South Carolina program of "annexation or a dissolution of the Union." Doubtless he exaggerated both the strength and the determination of the disunion element. So far as the success of the campaign was concerned, much more was to be feared from the attitude of Benton, whose irascible temper could not be held in check. He did not hesitate to discuss, even with Whigs,[44] the "villany" of the Baltimore convention, and no plea for harmony could induce him to abate his attacks on those who had been responsible for reviving the Texas question. To be sure he had, in a public declaration exonerated Polk and Dallas from participation in the "intrigue," but in a speech made at St. Louis he said that the Texas question had been "exploded" only forty days before the Baltimore convention—"just time enough for candidates to be interrogated, and for the novices to amend their answers."[45] Polk was evidently the novice whom he had in mind.

As the campaign progressed Polk came more and more to distrust both Benton and Blair. "Since the nominations," he said in a letter to Donelson,

> none can fail to have observed the *coldness* or indifference of the Globe. After *Blair's* professions made confidentially to you, I had expected that he would come zealously into the support of the nominations, and not throw cold water upon them.

After quoting a letter in which Dallas spoke of this hostility, Polk suggested that Donelson and Jackson should urge Blair to alter the tone of his paper.[46]

---

[44] Letcher to Buchanan, July 19, 1844, *Buchanan Papers.*

[45] Speech printed in Wash. *Globe*, Nov. 6, 1844. Yoakum, of Tennessee, in calling Polk's attention to this speech says that he has "no doubt but Col. Benton has injured us 100,000 votes"! (Yoakum to Polk, Nov. 22, 1844, *Polk Papers*).

[46] Polk to Donelson, July 22, 1844, "Polk-Donelson Letters."

Toward the end of June certain overtures made by close friends of President Tyler gave hope that he might yet withdraw from the race. J. B. Jones, the editor of the *Madisonian*, approached A. V. Brown and others with a suggestion that J. George Harris should be brought to Washington to assist in editing that paper. Harris was an intimate friend of both Polk and Jackson, and had made the Nashville *Union* an effective party organ. Harris suggested to Polk that a new paper might be started with which the *Madisonian* (Tyler) and the *Spectator* (Calhoun) might soon be merged. A new paper, in his opinion, would be more likely to succeed because of prejudices against those already in existence. General Armstrong, like Harris, thought favorably of the plan to merge these papers, and believed that after the election even the *Globe* might be joined with the rest. Both Johnson and Brown, however, were opposed to this plan, and especially to putting Harris in charge of the *Madisonian*.[47]

Early in July R. J. Walker, who had from the first urged a friendly attitude toward the deserters of 1840, called on Tyler in order to ascertain his views. The President told Walker that he would withdraw at once were it not for the fact that his friends felt hurt by the abuse heaped upon them by the *Globe* and other papers. There were, he said, about 150,000 of his friends who had voted for Whigs in 1840; he would withdraw and his friends would support Polk and Dallas, provided that assurance be given that they would be welcomed by the Democratic party as brethren and equals. "Now I think," said Walker when reporting the conversation to Polk, "that the importance of this union & co-operation cannot be overrated"; therefore he suggested that Polk and Jackson might write letters to political friends, speaking kindly of Tyler and his followers.[48]

---

[47] Harris to Polk, June 27, 29; Johnson to Polk, June 28; Armstrong to Polk, June 30, 1844, *Polk Papers*.

[48] Walker to Polk, July 10, 1844, *ibid*.

After reading Walker's letter Polk sent it to the Hermitage by Gideon Pillow. In a letter of his own, sent by the same messenger, he told Jackson that, however desirable the object sought by Walker might be, he would not write any letter or make any promises. He would like of course to see a reunion of "all the old Jackson Democrats of '28 & '32," but he would neither write a letter to Tyler nor "make any pledges to any one—except as it regards my public principles, in advance of election." He suggested, however, that if the attacks of the *Globe* were responsible for Tyler's continuing in the race and thereby jeopardizing the result in certain states, something should be done to induce Blair to cease abusing the President. He told Jackson that he was the only one who could influence Blair, but as to the wisdom of exercising such influence Jackson must judge for himself.[49]

Jackson was disgusted with Walker's "want of common sense" in suggesting that he and Polk should write letters in commendation of the President. Such letters, he told Polk, would "damn you & destroy your election," for the Whigs would at once charge "bargain & intrigue."[50] Although not yet ready to ask favors from John Tyler, he was quite willing to remove, if possible, the cause of the President's injured feelings. On that very same day he dispatched a letter to Blair in which he condemned Benton's conduct, urged the importance of annexation, and ordered Blair to "support the cause of Polk & Dallas, & let Tiler alone—leave Calhoun to himself we in the South & West will attend to the Federal Union, it must be preserved."[51] Indeed, on the same day, he authorized Major Lewis to express to the President his (Jackson's) wish for the success of the

---

[49] Polk to Jackson, July 23, 1844, *Jackson Papers.* See also Polk to Donelson, same date, "Polk-Donelson Letters." In this he doubted the propriety of Jackson's writing a letter for publication; still, he seemed anxious that the general should write a private letter "which might reach the President's eye."

[50] Jackson to Polk, July 26, 1844, *Polk Papers.*

[51] Jackson to Blair, July 26, 1844, *Jackson Papers.*

administration and the assurance that Tyler's friends would be received as brethren into the Democratic fold.[52]

From various quarters pressure was brought to bear upon Tyler, and appeals to his vanity were not wanting. Ritchie, of the Richmond *Enquirer*, who was called the "king of the Democratic press," warmly urged the President to withdraw, while Democratic electors agreed to support Tyler in case it should develop that he was stronger than Polk. The Democratic general committee of New York, on August 6, drafted resolutions lauding the President and asking his support;[53] and on August 1 Jackson sent another letter to Major Lewis in which he argued that Tyler ought to withdraw, for if he did not, it would be said

---

[52] Jackson to Lewis, July 26, 1844 (Tyler, *Letters and Times of the Tylers*, III, 143–146). The letter read in part: "You know I have a great desire that Mr. Tyler should close his term with credit to himself. It is certain he can not now be elected, and he has now a fair field by withdrawing, to add great and lasting popularity to himself by the act, and free himself from the imputation that his exertions to re-annex Texas were to make himself President, and show that his energy in this case was from imperious public duty, to prevent a country so important to the defence, safety and great interest of our whole Union from falling into the hands of England, our most implacable enemy. On Mr. Tyler's withdrawal from the canvass every true American will say, Amen to his patriotism in the case of Texas.

"Several of Mr. Tyler's friends yesterday visited me, and wished me to cause it to be known to him their wishes, as his withdrawal at once would unite all the Democrats into one family without distinction. This would render our victory easy and certain by bringing Mr. Tyler's friends in to the support of Polk and Dallas, received as brethren by them and their friends, all former differences forgotten and cordially united once more in sustaining the Democratic candidate.

". . . It is impossible now that Mr. Tyler should be elected, and if he does not withdraw he will be charged with conniving with the Clay Whigs to defeat the Democratic nominees. *Although this would be untrue*, yet really it would have that affect and would do Mr. Tyler much injury. I told Mr. Tyler's friends I could not write to him on such a subject, but that I had such confidence in his good sense and patriotism, that I was sure he would withdraw in due time, as I believe him to be a good Democrat, and that he would do nothing to promote Clay or injure Democracy. If you think it prudent, you can make these suggestions to Mr. Tyler. I think he would receive them kindly, be his determination what it may. His proper dignified course is a magnanamous withdrawal, with such reasons as his good sense may suggest for the occasion. These hints flow from a real regard for Mr. Tyler and a sincere wish that he may retire with much credit."

[53] Tyler, *Letters and Times of the Tylers*, II, 337–339.

that he had adopted the annexation program merely to obtain a reëlection and that he was remaining in the field in order to defeat Polk. Tyler soon informed Jackson that this letter had determined him to retire,[54] and on August 20 his letter of withdrawal appeared in the *Madisonian*. His present action, he said, had resulted from changed conditions. The people had vindicated him by driving from power those who had tried to crush him; the Democrats had adopted his policies, and he no longer felt compelled to run. On the next day this paper stated that its sole object all the time had been to defeat Henry Clay, and, as the principles of Polk and Tyler were identical, it would henceforth support the Democratic candidates.[55] Two years later Tyler wrote that he had accepted the nomination "for the sole purpose of controlling events . . . . for the public good" and, having accomplished his purpose, he withdrew.[56]

The *Spectator*, also, gave Polk and Dallas its enthusiastic support, and Calhoun predicted that the results would "equal the defeat of 1828."[57] Doubtless he indulged hopes that he, in the event of Polk's election, would be the guiding spirit of the administration.

During the summer considerable anxiety was caused by the fear that British and French influence might induce Houston to agree to some arrangement with Mexico. Major Lewis was authorized by Calhoun to communicate "confidentially" to General Jackson that the State Department was in possession of reliable information that these nations had offered to acknowledge the independence of Texas without any pledge of abolition,

---

[54] Smith, *Annexation of Texas*, 310.

[55] The *Madisonian* (Aug. 24) even supplied an election pun: "Change—It is James *Knox* Polk now, it will be Polk knocks Clay, about election time."

[56] Tyler, *Letters and Times of the Tylers*, II, 341.

[57] Alex. Anderson to Polk, Aug. 22, 1844, *Polk Papers*. "We should have carried North Carolina," said Anderson, "but for the course and speeches of that arch Traitor Benton—so say our letters from North Carolina." Anderson was a strong adherent of Calhoun.

provided that Texas would agree to remain an independent
nation. Similar information was given to Polk by Calhoun's
friend, Alexander Anderson. Before he had seen these letters,
however, Jackson had written to Houston "as strong a letter
as he [I] could dictate," exhorting him not to yield to the wishes
of foreign nations.[58]

While politicians were emphasizing the foreign menace, the
Democratic Review was trying to win votes in northern states
by maintaining that the area of slavery would be restricted by
acquiring Texas, for slaves would be drawn to the new fields,
leaving the border states to the Yankees.[59] Some of the slavery
advocates, too, believed that such would be the result, and for
this reason violently opposed annexation.[60]

There was some defection from their own ranks and there
was fear that annexation might be defeated by an act of Texas
itself, but the Democrats as a party never wavered from
their position in favor of annexation. They had, therefore, the
advantage of a consistent program. Clay, on the other hand,
in order to retain his hold on both North and South, adopted a
shifty course and modified his views from time to time, as the
occasion seemed to demand. In his Raleigh letter of April 17
he had definitely opposed immediate annexation, but he soon
discovered that such a stand had made him unpopular in the
South and West. To retrieve his fortunes in those sections he
wrote to Stephen F. Miller, on July 1, his first "Alabama letter."
"Personally," said he, "I could have no objection to the annexation of Texas; but certainly I would be unwilling to see the
existing Union dissolved or seriously jeoparded for the sake of

[58] Lewis to Jackson, July 19, 1844, *Jackson Papers*. Jackson to Polk,
July 23, 1844, *Polk Papers*. See also, Polk to Donelson, July 22, 1844,
"Polk-Donelson Letters."

[59] *Dem. Rev.*, July, 1844.

[60] Letter of Waddy Thompson to editors of *National Intelligencer*,
printed in that paper, July 6, 1844.

[61] Printed in *Nat. Intell.*, Aug. 8, 1844.

acquiring Texas."[61] As this was not strong enough to win votes in the South, he wrote again on the twenty-seventh that if annexation might be accomplished "without national dishonor, without war, with the general consent of the States of the Union, and upon fair and reasonable terms, I should be glad to see it."[62] Both Democrats and Abolitionists seized upon the last phrase and widely advertised the fact that "Clay would be glad to see it." Other letters followed in an attempt to show that he had not changed his original views, but the more he explained the more he became the target of denunciation and ridicule. The papers made much sport of his "six manifestoes," while Jackson charged that Clay by his letters had made a "perfect devill" of himself.[63]

Although this was a campaign in which party principles were clearly defined and important questions involved, nevertheless the personal element was not wanting. The Whig ignorance even of Polk's identity was soon replaced by a minute knowledge not only of his own shortcomings but of those of his ancestors. It devolved, therefore, upon the candidate's friends in Tennessee to enlighten the public on his past record and to defend his reputation against the slanders of his opponents. As soon as the news of his nomination had reached Nashville a mass meeting was called to celebrate the event. Speeches were made by prominent Democrats, and A. O. P. Nicholson ridiculed the Whig cry of "Who is Polk?" Arrangements were made for another meeting in July to be composed of delegates from all parts of the state.[64] Biographical materials had already been forwarded to George Bancroft under the frank of General Jackson. But as Bancroft, according to Harris, was "somewhat sensitive on the

---

[62] Fourth Alabama letter, in which former letters are quoted (*Nat. Intell.*, Oct. 1, 1844). The letter of July 27 is printed in *Niles' Reg.*, LXVI, 439.

[63] Schouler, *Hist. of U. S.*, IV, 477. Smith, *Annex. of Texas*, 309.

[64] Nashville *Union*, June 8, 11, 1844.

point of *authorship*," and declined, it was decided that editorials in the *Union* would do quite as well as a biography.[65]

Some of the Whig papers charged Polk with being a duelist, while others said he was a cringing coward who had feared to fight Wise. The first allegation was refuted in letters written to the *Globe* by Cave Johnson and A. V. Brown, and the second, by the publication of an old letter of Jackson's in which he had expressed approval of Speaker Polk for having treated Wise with contempt.[66] For the purpose of injuring Polk in the North, the Whigs circulated widely the "Roorback" canard the gist of which was that a gang of slaves branded with the initials "J. K. P," had been seen on their way to southern markets.[67]

Polk was most annoyed by the revival of the story that his grandfather, Colonel Ezekiel Polk, had been a Tory during the Revolution. The Washington *Globe* and various northern papers repelled the charge, and the Nashville *Union* printed many letters and affidavits from persons who had certain knowledge that the elder Polk had been a Revolutionary officer; it published, also, a copy of his commission dated June 18, 1775. Under Polk's direction this material was printed in pamphlet form under the title of "A Vindication of Colonel Ezekiel Polk," and General Armstrong was instructed to send copies to prominent Democrats all over the United States.[68] To these Whig campaign stories the Democratic press retorted in kind. Clay's use of profane language was emphasized and he was called a drunkard, a duelist, a gambler, and a perjurer.[69]

---

[65] J. Geo. Harris to Polk, June 25, July 17, 19, 1844, *Polk Papers.* Doubtless Bancroft's sensitiveness on authorship resulted from his experience as campaign biographer of Van Buren.

[66] Wash. *Globe,* June 13, 19, 1844.

[67] See *Niles' Reg.,* LXVII, 73.

[68] *Union,* Sept. 11. Polk to Heiss, Sept. 13; Polk to Armstrong, Sept. 16, 1844, "Heiss Papers," *Tenn. Hist. Mag.,* June, 1916.

[69] The perjury consisted in the alleged violation of his oath of office by challenging John Randolph to fight a duel for words spoken in debate during the campaign. Henly, of Indiana, said on the floor of the House

Naturally Polk was especially desirous of carrying his own state, and his energy and skill as a machine politician are manifested in many ways. Realizing, as usual, the importance of a spirited party press, he induced Heiss to make J. George Harris joint editor with Laughlin of the Nashville *Union*. "The Union," he wrote, "should be made in Tennessee what Medary's Statesman is in Ohio, and what the Union itself was in 1839. It is looked to from all parts of the Union and must be a *great paper* during this canvass." In another letter he urged that "fire and spirit and power should be thrown into it" in order to counteract the Whig falsehoods and misrepresentations.[70]

On July 13 a dinner was given in Polk's home town, Columbia, in honor of delegates to the late nominating convention, Presidential electors, and members of Congress from Tennessee. To Cave Johnson was assigned the duty of inducing prominent Democrats to be present in order to counteract the effect of a Whig rally held at the same place.[71] Early in the campaign arrangements had been made for a great mass meeting to be held at Nashville on the fifteenth of August. Both Polk and Johnson were anxious that the northern states should be well represented at this meeting so that it could not be said that it was a gathering of disunionists. Once more it fell to Johnson to send the invitations and to urge the importance of a large and representative attendance.[72]

On the appointed day the multitudes assembled, and Nashville, according to the *Union*, "was from sunrise to sunset as

---

that "the standard of Henry Clay should consist of his armorial bearings, which ought to be a pistol, a pack of cards, and a brandy-bottle" (Adams, *Memoirs*, XII, 45).

[70] Polk to Heiss, July 31, Aug. 21, 1844; Heiss to Polk, Aug. 3, 1844, *Polk Papers*.

[71] Polk to Johnson, July 1, July 6, 1844, "Polk-Johnson Letters."

[72] Johnson to Polk, June 21, 1844, *Polk Papers*. Polk to Johnson, July 16, 1844, "Polk-Johnson Letters." Among those invited were Wright, Cass, Buchanan, Woodbury, Hubbard of New Hampshire, and Duncan and Medary, of Ohio.

a *Military* Camp.''[73] In the evening the Honorable Thomas F. Marshall, of Kentucky, addressed "thousands" in front of the courthouse on the annexation of Texas. On the second day, August 16, the throng gathered at Camp Hickory where by noon, "the great grove at the Camp, fifty acres in extent, was as full as it could hold," and there "were two miles of table on which the *Great Dinner* was served." Speaking followed the dinner, and Cave Johnson, as presiding officer, made the opening address. We have already noted his solicitude lest a disunion character might be attributed to this meeting, and he now embraced the opportunity

in the presence of this great assembly, to give a direct contradiction to the false charge of disunion, and a wish to dissolve the Union, which had been propagated by the whig press of this and other states, against those concerned in calling and getting up the present meeting.

The number in attendance was so great that speakers addressed crowds simultaneously in various parts of the grove; each speaker, following Johnson's lead, repelled the charge of disunion. General Case was the principal orator of the day; among the others were Gansevoort Melville;[74] Governor Clay, of Alabama; Colonel Terry, speaker of the house from the same state; and J. B. Bowlin, a member of Congress from Missouri. Letters were received from leading Democrats of both sections, regretting their inability to be present and expressing hearty coöperation.[75] Among these was Judge Douglas, but within a few days he was in Tennessee stumping the state for Polk and Dallas.[76]

[73] Nashville *Union*, Aug. 17, 1844. Also *Niles' Reg.*, LXVII, 3–4. "On every road to the city was to be seen approaching companies, battalions and regiments, mounted and on foot, with their bands of music, their banners and their mottoes, on their way to this great encampment of the sovereign people."

[74] A Tammany Hall leader.

[75] The same number of the *Union* contains copies of letters from Franklin Pierce, Silas Wright, Levi Woodbury, James Buchanan, Stephen A. Douglas, Geo. McDuffie, Robt. J. Walker, R. M. Johnson, *et al.*

[76] Polk to Johnson, Aug. 20, 22, 26, 1844, "Polk-Johnson Letters."

Despite the absence of so many of the party leaders the Democratic meeting was regarded as highly successful, but in glittering pageantry and boisterous enthusiasm it was far excelled by the "Great Whig Convention" which, on August 21, likewise essembled in the city of Nashville and was, to quote Phelan, "the finest of the kind ever held in the Southwest."[77] While the chief feature of the meeting was the display of gorgeous battalions and expensive campaign banners, there were soul-stirring addresses by prominent Whig orators. The great speech of the meeting was made by Sergeant S. Prentiss, of Mississippi, who was regarded by many as the peer of either Webster or Clay. On this occasion Prentiss surpassed even his own brilliant record, for to partisan considerations was added a personal hatred for the Democratic candidate whose casting vote had once deprived him of a seat in the House of Representatives.[78]

The enthusiasm caused by the Whig meeting spurred the Democrats to a still more vigorous effort to win the election in Tennessee. Custom did not permit Polk to mount the platform in his own behalf, but from his home at Columbia he directed the campaign, even to the minutest details. He planned itineraries, assigned speakers, and even arranged for barbecues.[79] Local orators were assisted by prominent politicians from other states. This list included Douglas, of Illinois, Pickens, of South Carolina, Melville, of New York, and Clay, Terry, and McClung, of Alabama. Of local men the most notable were the veteran campaigners, Nicholson, Brown, and Cave Johnson. Johnson was much broken in health, but so highly did Polk value his services that he goaded him to an active part in the campaign.[80]

---

[77] Phelan, *Hist. of Tenn.*, 419.

[78] See above, p. 120.

[79] Various letters of Polk to Johnson, Aug.-Oct., "Polk-Johnson Letters."

[80] *Ibid.* On Oct. 14 he told Johnson that "all our energies are necessary to keep the State safe, as I believe she now is. The least relaxation at the close of the canvass might loose her."

Near the close of the canvass Polk was confident of carrying the state by a "handsome majority," but, instead, he lost it by the small margin of one hundred and thirteen votes.

In southern states the Whigs had little hope of success in opposing the Democratic annexation program, nevertheless strenuous efforts were made to prevent defection from their own ranks because of this annoying issue. The indomitable Prentiss labored to show that Polk was not entitled to profit from the revival of this question,[81] and in a speech at Natchez he referred to Polk as a "blighted burr, that had fallen from the mane of the war-horse of the Hermitage." In an attempt to counteract the work of Prentiss and others, and to win Whig votes in the South, Senator Walker, of Mississippi, wrote a most inflammatory pamphlet entitled "The South in Danger"[82] in which he argued that as Whigs and Abolitionists had joined hands in the North, therefore all parties in the South should unite in the interest of annexation. The pamphlet probably did little good in the South, and many Democrats were fearful that it might do serious damage in the North.[93]

In Ohio the contest bid fair to be close, and, after Clay's repudiation of the utterances of his relative, Cassius M. Clay,[84] leading Democrats had hopes that many Whigs would desert him and vote for Birney.[85] But the result of the state elections made

---

[81] "If ever I join the Mormons," he wrote in August to the editor of the Vicksburg *Whig*, "I shall attach myself to Joe Smith, the founder of the sect, and not to one of his rival disciples, and should I ever turn Locofoco on the question of *the immediate annexation of Texas*, I will support *John Tyler, not James K. Polk*" (*Memoir of S. S. Prentiss*, II, 316).

[82] This pamphlet was issued by the Democratic Association of Washington, D. C., Sept. 25, 1844. Copy in Library of Congress.

[83] For example, William E. Cramer, editor of the Albany *Argus*, informed Polk that New York could never be won on the program outlined by Walker, while Ohio and other states would surely be lost (Cramer to Polk, Oct. 4, 1844, *Polk Papers*).

[84] C. M. Clay had represented Henry Clay as opposed to slavery. The latter in a letter contradicted the former's statements.

[85] Gansevoort Melville to Polk, Oct. 3; Cass to Polk, Oct. 4, 1844, *Polk Papers*. Both wrote from Cleveland and expressed the opinion that the Democrats would carry the state.

it evident that Clay's letter had not produced any defection,[86] while Walker's ill-advised pamphlet added strength to the Whigs.[87] The so-called "Garland forgery" transferred many votes from Birney to Clay, and may possibly have brought victory to Clay in Ohio.[88]

Pennsylvania was normally Democratic, yet there were misgivings lest the strong sentiment in favor of tariff might jeopardize Polk's success in that state. His "Kane letter" had been generally accepted as satisfactory, but the Whigs represented him to be an unqualified free-trader. The *Pennsylvanian* refuted this charge and, on October 15, published extracts from his speeches to prove that he had always favored incidental protection. As noted above, Polk, in his letter to Kane, did not pretend to favor tariff except that which might be necessary for revenue, but by means of construction Pennsylvanians were able to hold voters in line by representing him to be in favor of tariff. "We have succeeded," wrote the oily-tongued Simon Cameron, "in fixing the belief that you 'are as good a tariff man as Clay,'" and he added significantly that no man known to be opposed to protective tariff could possibly carry the state.[89] Polk did not of course take pains to undeceive his supporters in Pennsylvania; on the other hand, he did not, in any of his public utterances, commit himself to tariff for protective purposes. However, Cameron's ruse met with success, and Polk's strength in Pennsylvania greatly exasperated the Whigs.[90]

---

86 H. C. Williams wrote from Washington that "the letter repudiating C. M. Clay has had no effect in the northern states, while it satisfies the Southern Whigs. The Whig papers will not publish it." Democrats, he said, have to oppose all "fag end" parties, and Greely is now trying to stir up the Irish (Williams to Polk, Oct. 14, 1844, *Polk Papers*).

87 Armstrong to Polk, Nov. 5, [1844], *Polk Papers*.

88 See Birney, *James G. Birney and his Times*, 355.

89 Cameron to Polk, Oct. 18, 1844, *Polk Papers*.

90 Governor Letcher, of Kentucky, scoffed at the idea of Polk being in favor of tariff, and he tried to persuade Buchanan to refrain from advocating his election. "Polk," said Letcher, "has no more chance to be elected than if he were dead and *buried*, and d—nd, as he will be in due time" (Letcher to Buchanan, Aug. 3, 1844, *Buchanan Papers*).

"Native Americanism" was said to have cost the Democrats votes in Pennsylvania. Catholics, as a rule, affiliated with that party, and the Whigs made political capital out of the fact that Shunk, the Democratic candidate for governor, had been induced to march in a Catholic parade.[91]

It was alleged that the Whigs used money freely in Pennsylvania,[92] and that they were guilty of practicing frauds,[93] but it is unlikely that the Whigs were the sole transgressors in these respects.

New York was regarded as the pivotal state. There thirty-six electoral votes were to be won or lost, and the result seemed to be highly problematical. In this state various extraneous elements helped to complicate the political situation. Both "Native Americans" and Abolitionists commanded a considerable number of votes in the state, but it was by no means certain just how these votes would be cast. At the beginning of the campaign it was feared that the followers of Van Buren might not rally with enthusiasm to the party standard, and besides, there was lack of harmony in Democratic state politics with respect to policies and candidates. In order to carry the state it was necessary to hold the Van Burenites in line, and since the Baltimore convention many of them had been silently nursing their resentment. Governor William C. Bouck wrote that a number of Wright's friends had tried to get up a secret intrigue to procure Polk's defeat, but that Wright had been nominated for governor and his adherents brought into harmony.[94] Van Buren told Jackson that Wright had accepted the nomination reluctantly and not until

---

[91] J. Miller to Polk, Oct. 12; J. M. Porter to Polk, Oct. 12, 1844, *Polk Papers;* also, newspapers.

[92] For example, Kane informed Polk that $20,000 had been subscribed at the office of John Sergeant, of Philadelphia. Sergeant's nephew, Wm. B. Reed, had by mistake sent a letter regarding this money to some Democrat (Kane to Polk, Oct. 24, 1844, *Polk Papers*).

[93] Henry Horn, for example, wrote that desponding letters had been sent to his friends with his forged signature attached (Horn to Polk, Oct. 31, 1844, *Polk Papers*).

[94] Bouck to Polk, Sept. 7, 1844, *Polk Papers.*

he had been told that it was the only means of saving New York,[95] but the supporters of Bouck felt that he had been unceremoniously sacrificed to satisfy the ambitions of Wright and his friends.[96] Some of the extreme anti-Texas leaders in New York supported the candidates, but repudiated the annexation plank in the platform.[97] This was the policy of the New York *Evening Post*.

According to William E. Cramer, of the Albany *Argus*, the Democrats in New York "were on a volcano" until Clay repudiated the statements of Cassius M. Clay and changed his position on the Texan question. The Abolitionists, he said, held the balance of power and would poll from fifteen thousand to twenty thousand votes. "Before Mr. C's fatal letter they were hesitating whether they should not vote for him," but "this puts an impassable gulf between them."[98] On the other hand, in predicting victory for Polk and Dallas in New York, Wright reported that "Never have I witnessed an equal degree of enthusiasm among our democracy, not even in the days of Genl Jackson, nor have I, at any time, known greater harmony, activity or confidence."[99] Late in October another letter from Cramer stated that the Whigs were putting forth every effort to form coalitions with "Native Americans," Abolitionists, and Anti-renters, and that they were confident of winning the election. Prospect of success, he said, had brought them much campaign money from manufacturers who desired high tariff.[100]

---

95 Jackson to Polk, Sept. 26, 1844, *ibid*.

96 In a letter to Polk, Sept. 11, Marcy stated that Bouck had made a satisfactory governor, and that Wright had been nominated for political reasons; while an anonymous letter, Sept. 14, said that Bouck had been set aside without reason, and that the action might cause Polk to lose the state.

97 See the signed statement of Bryant and others in *Niles' Reg.*, LXVI, 371.

98 Cramer to Polk, Sept. 17, 1844, *Polk Papers*.

99 Wright to Buchanan, Sept. 23, 1844, *Buchanan Papers*.

100 "The report is that the Bostonians promised $100,000 provided they could receive ample assurance that it would secure New York for Mr. Clay!!" (Cramer to Polk, Oct. 22, 1844, *Polk Papers*).

Still other factors complicated the political situation in New York. The Abolitionists who had formerly voted the Whig ticket were appalled when Birney came out in favor of free trade and opposed to distributing among the states the proceeds derived from the sale of public lands, and it was feared in Tammany circles that his announcement might cause them to vote for Clay.[101] In order to win votes for their national ticket the Whigs withdrew some of their candidates for Congress and the state legislature in favor of the "Native American" candidates.[102] It availed them little, however, for Polk and Dallas carried the state.[103]

It appears that the Democrats, also, withdrew some of their candidates in favor of "Native Americans,"[104] and in the process of rapid naturalization they outrivaled their opponents. "Tammany Hall," wrote Melville, "is a perfect jam from 8 A. M. till after midnight. Naturalization going on among our friends to an immense extent. On Saturday 260—all Democrats—rec'd their papers."[105] Charges of wholesale frauds were made by both parties,[106] but it may be doubted that such frauds materially affected the election results.

The Texas question was of course the paramount issue of the campaign, although it was not, apparently, the chief factor in winning the election for Polk. Many contemporaries believed that Clay's defeat was not caused by the emergence of this question,

---

[101] Melville to Polk, Oct. 26, 1844, *Polk Papers.*

[102] Alex. Jones to Polk, New York City, Oct. 30, Nov. 6, 1844, *ibid.*

[103] Jones told Polk in a letter dated November 21, that some of the Whigs had been so confident of winning that they had bet all of their money, and even their homes. One had lost $38,000; another, $40,000. One Whig's wife lost her mind because of his losses (*Polk Papers*).

[104] John P. Heiss to Polk, Nov. 3, 1844, *Polk Papers.*

[105] Melville to Medary, Nov. 4, 1844, *ibid.*

[106] A correspondent from New London, Conn., informed Polk that in Connecticut, Massachusetts, and Rhode Island "the *lords of the spindle* compelled the degraded operators to vote their will, and thus obtained large majorities for your opponent" (Dr. Charles Douglas to Polk, Nov. 22, 1844, *Polk Papers*). For a useful summary of press opinions on frauds, see Smith, *Annexation of Texas,* 316 ff.

and this belief is held by Justin H. Smith,[107] who has recently made a thorough examination of conflicting opinions and carefully weighed their value. The *Democratic Review* evidently stated the truth when it said on the eve of the election that neither party had won or lost many votes on account of the Texas issue, and that "the issue is between the principles of the two parties more than ever before."[108] If Polk owed his success in the election to the Texas issue, it was due to the fact that it brought him the support of President Tyler and his followers. While we can not be sure that Tyler would have remained in the field if the Democrats had not espoused annexation, certainty that they would continue his Texas program at least furnished him with a plausible excuse for retiring from the canvass.[109]

Polk received 170 electoral votes; Clay only 105. In the North, Polk carried the great states of New York and Pennsylvania, while New Hampshire, also, contributed her six votes. Much to their delight the Whigs carried not only Polk's own state, Tennessee, but even the very precincts of both Jackson and Polk.[110] The Tennessee Democrats were keenly disappointed, of course, because they had failed to win the election in their candidate's own state; but their disappointment soon gave way to rejoicing over the general party victory. On receiving the news that New York had gone Democratic, Jackson sent the letter on to Polk with a marginal note, " 'who is J. K. polk,' will be no more asked by the coons—A. J."[111]

---

[107] Smith, *Annexation of Texas*, 317.

[108] "One Last Word before the Election" (*Dem. Rev.*, Oct., 1844). It thanked heaven that Polk was not a "military chieftain" and had never even killed an Indian; also, that "there is no peculiar eminent 'popularity' attaching to him, of a character personal to himself, and distinct from his simple position as the representative of the general principles and policy of the party whose candidate he is."

[109] See correspondence, including his letter of withdrawal, in Tyler, *Letters and Times of the Tylers*, II, 338 ff.

[110] Nashville *Banner*, Nov. 11, 1844. The *Union* on the 14th retorted that these precincts had been carried by non-resident Whigs who had gone there and voted illegally.

[111] Written on a letter from A. C. Flagg to Jackson, Nov. 7, 1844, *Polk Papers*. The "coons," of course, were the Whigs. The name had been attached to them during the "log-cabin" campaign of 1840.

Polk received the news of his election some hours before it was known to the people of either Columbia or Nashville. The New York mail arrived at Nashville at nine o'clock in the evening, and on the outside of the package the postmaster at Cincinnati had written a note stating that Polk had been elected. This attracted the attention of General Robert Armstrong, postmaster at Nashville and one of Polk's most intimate friends. Without giving out the news, Armstrong sent a messenger to Columbia with a note for Polk. At dawn he read the glad tidings which the note contained, but he said nothing about it to his neighbors and friends. For the next twenty-four hours he went about his work, and calmly received expressions of sympathy on his defeat.[112] Sphinx-like silence was a rôle that Polk dearly loved to play, and an opportunity to do so on this occasion no doubt added much to the gratification caused by the information contained in the note.

When the result of the election at last became known there was great rejoicing in Democratic ranks. On the other hand, desperado admirers of Clay, both in Tennessee and Kentucky, threatened Polk's life, and friends warned him to "take some thought of *where* you go & eat & drink."[113] No violence, however, was attempted, and apprehensions were forgotten in the din of exuberant celebrations. At Nashville Polk was given an elaborate reception. A. O. P. Nicholson made the principal address, and there was general rejoicing because the "Young Hickory" was soon to grasp the helm that had been so firmly guided by the "Old Hickory."[114]

Some of the Democratic factions had little love for Polk, but all could agree with the *Democratic Review* in thanking God for the defeat of Henry Clay. "Had he succeeded," said the *Review,* "it would have stamped him, his ideas and his character upon the future history of our government, with a fatal depth and extent of mischief never perhaps to be again effaced."[115]

---

[112] Nelson, *Memorials of Sarah Childress Polk,* 76–77.

[113] A. V. Brown to Polk, Nov. 13, 1844. Also Gen. John A. McCalla, Lexington, Ky., Nov. 22, 1844; both in *Polk Papers.*

[114] Nashville *Union,* Nov. 30, 1844.   [115] *Dem. Rev.,* Nov., 1844.

CHAPTER XIV

PRESIDENT-ELECT

Various individuals and factions claimed the credit for Polk's nomination and election, and as soon as the result of the balloting had become known their claims to recognition were presented. While in one sense it was true that the successful candidate owed his elevation to a number of discordant elements within the party, in another sense he was under no obligation to any of them. With the exception perhaps of the younger element the several groups within the party had united on Polk, not from choice but necessity, and not until each had found it impossible to procure the nomination of its particular favorite. The circumstances under which he had been nominated—the very fact that he had not been generally considered for the first place—relieved the President-elect from the necessity of making pledges to any one. Although Polk himself fully appreciated this fact and resolved to make the most of it, others did not and the "jockeying for position" at once began.

One of the first to congratulate Polk on his victory was James Buchanan. The Senator from Pennsylvania was usually numbered with the *old* leaders, but his plea, oddly enough, was for the recognition of young men in the distribution of offices. "The old office holders generally," said he, "have had their day & ought to be content. Had Mr. Van Buren been our candidate, worthy as he is, this feeling which everywhere pervaded the Democratic ranks, would have made his defeat as signal as it was in 1840." Even Polk, he added, would have run better in Philadelphia had it not been rumored that he would distribute the patronage among the "old hunkers."[1] Such a letter from Robert

---

[1] Buchanan to Polk, Nov. 4, 1844, *Polk Papers.*

J. Walker would not have been surprising, but Buchanan's solicitude for the younger men was significantly of recent origin.

Tyler's withdrawal from the canvass occasioned speculation as to the recognition which his friends would receive from the Democratic party, and during the campaign Polk received many letters which were designed to pledge him in advance. The candidate discreetly refrained from committing himself, although his supporters may have given assurance that the followers of the President would not be proscribed. Special importance was attached to a letter written by Jackson to Major Lewis[2] in which the General said that Tyler's friends would be received as brethren. Then, too, Walker, as chairman of the national Democratic committee, had made promises to influential adherents of the President. Nevertheless the Tylerites were apparently unwilling to run any risks, and soon after Polk's election they were charged by prominent Democrats with having concocted a scheme whereby they hoped to intrench themselves in office. One part of this scheme, according to H. C. Williams, was to procure the resignation of Whigs so that President Tyler might fill the offices with eleventh-hour Democrats whom it would be embarrassing for Polk to remove.[3] Probably such reports exaggerated the facts, especially as to Whig resignations, but it is certain that the Tyler faction believed themselves to be entitled to a share of Democratic patronage. In plaintive note, John Y. Mason, Tyler's Secretary of the Navy, expressed a willingness to remain in the cabinet. He had, he told Polk, from a sense of duty resigned a judgeship so that he might take charge of the Navy Department, and had felt "very unhappy" since Tyler had become a candidate. Jackson, whom he had consulted, had advised him to remain in the cabinet because Tyler would soon withdraw. He would resign of course on March 3 *unless Polk should*

---

[2] Dated July 6, 1844. See Tyler, *Life and Times of the Tylers*, III, 143 ff.

[3] H. C. Williams, Washington, Nov. 15; Henry Simpson, Philadelphia, Nov. 21, 1844, *Polk Papers.*

desire otherwise, therefore he desired a "frank statement" of Polk's intentions. Mason had been a college mate of Polk and they had since been warm personal friends, but with habitual caution the President-elect replied that he would leave all such matters to be settled after his arrival in Washington.[4]

Directly and indirectly Polk received much unsolicited advice on the subject of patronage, and especially on the selection of his cabinet. Through General Armstrong, H. C. Williams warned him that rival factions were already planning for the succession of their respective favorites, therefore he should discountenance all of them.[5] As usual, Judge Catron was free with his fatherly advice. He had been told by Governor Letcher, of Kentucky, that the Whigs confidently believed Polk to be under pledges to Calhoun; and that because Calhoun's friends and those of Van Buren and Benton could never work in harmony, discord and disaster would beset the new administration. Catron assured Letcher that Polk had made no pledges to any wing of the party, but despite the truth of his statement, the rumors regarding Calhoun continued to circulate. Since Polk had been elected without making promises, Catron's advice was that he should "go to Washington *entirely* unpledged, down to a post office." The cold shoulder, he said, might at first give offense; but no matter, for "you are under no pressure of obligation to your party, other than to administer the government through the agency of men of undoubted strength and worth of character, *from head to foot.*"[6] John Blair, of

---

[4] Mason to Polk, Nov. 16; Polk to Mason, Dec. 6, 1844, *ibid.*

[5] Williams to Armstrong, Nov. 26, 1844, *ibid.*

[6] Catron to Polk, Nov. 23, 1844, *Polk Papers.* Catron, like others, had his own individual preferences, but he continued to urge Polk to make his own selections. Both Johnson and Brown wrote on December 14 that Catron had suggested Buchanan, Wright, and Cass for the State, Treasury, and War Departments, respectively. "Of one thing I am absolutely certain," wrote Catron to Polk on February 4, "that you must begin as *absolute* master of your will, if this be possible, in framing your cabinet. Strength it must have, and men in it that will work in harmony: This done and you are perfectly safe, regardless of fretting for a brief space. The *old* dare not, as the young will overthrow them—and the young, set up no claim to such assumptions" (*Polk Papers*).

Tennessee, offered a happy solution for sectional discord—patronage in plenty for the North and principles for the South.[7]

Warnings and advice, however well meant, were entirely superfluous, for Polk felt himself to be fully capable of formulating his own plans. He could not prevent gossip and speculation, but he declared emphatically to Cave Johnson that he was "under no pledges or commitments to any of the cliques (if such exist) mentioned by the newspapers." The policy which he had chosen to follow relieved him in a great measure from consulting the wishes of discordant factions, and his success in executing it proved the wisdom of his choice. "My object," he told Cave Johnson,

will be to do my duty to the country, and I do not intend if I can avoid it, that my counsels shall be distracted by the supposed or not conflicting interests of those cliques. Another thing I will say—that I will if I can have a united and harmonious set of cabinet counsellors, who will have the existing administration and the good of the country more at heart than the question who shall succeed me, and that in any event I intend to be *myself* President of the U. S.[8]

No one can follow his career for the next four years without being convinced that he held the executive reins firmly in his own hands.

Selecting a cabinet from men of ability who would subordinate their own personal interests to those of the administration and of the country required an unusual degree of independence. The desired coöperation could not be obtained without the elimination of recognized leaders of factions; and such a course would inevitably subject the administration to attacks from all who had been disappointed.

The claims of the Tylerites might be ignored with impunity, but what to do with Calhoun was a more embarrassing question.

---

[7] "North of Mason & Dickson's line should be *plied* with patronage as principles more congenial to the South must of necessity be established & carried out whatever your personal predelections" may be (Blair to Polk, Dec. 2, 1844, *Polk Papers*).

[8] Polk to Johnson, Dec. 21, 1844, "Polk-Johnson Letters."

Although Calhoun denied emphatically that there had ever been any understanding between Polk and himself,[9] apparently he was not without hope that he would be invited to remain at the helm in the Department of State. Late in November one of his intimate friends, General James Hamilton, sounded Polk on the subject and dwelt on the desirability of having Calhoun continued in charge of the Texas and Oregon questions. For a southern member of the cabinet, said he, the entire South, from the Potomac to Louisiana, would prefer Calhoun.[10]

The difficulties which might result from any attempt to harmonize factions were set forth in a letter from Cave Johnson. He said that it was understood in Washington that Calhoun and other members of Tyler's cabinet desired to remain. It was also the general opinion that should Calhoun be retained Benton and his friends would oppose Polk's administration, while, on the other hand, the southern element would be hostile unless Calhoun should be continued in office. Calhoun, said Johnson, is the choice of southern men for Secretary of State, while many from the North want Silas Wright; and Benton is reported to have declared that should Polk retain any of the Tyler cabinet he would open fire on the "rotten eggs."[11] General Jackson's advice to Polk was the exclusion from his cabinet of "all aspirants to the presidency, or vice"; and the General was so confident that his advice would be followed that he assured Blair that neither Calhoun nor any other aspirant would be appointed. In another letter to Polk, Jackson urged that Calhoun must not be retained, because other members of the cabinet could not get along with him: "England is the place for him there to combat with my Lord Aberdeen, the abolition question." The entire cabinet,

---

[9] "Nothing has ever passed between Mr. Polk and myself, directly or indirectly, on the subject. I neither know his views nor he mine on the subject" (Calhoun to J. A. Stuart, Oct. 21, 1844, *Rep. of Am. Hist.*, 1899, II, 626).

[10] Hamilton to Polk, Nov. 29, 1844, *Polk Papers*.

[11] Johnson to Polk, Dec. 1, 6, 1844, *ibid.*

said he, ought to be composed of new men.[12] Writing late in December, Cave Johnson said that the friends of Benton and Calhoun feared each other's influence with Polk, consequently the breach between the wings of the party was widening. Especially did the northerners fear that Polk would be brought under the influence of Calhoun. In a similar strain A. V. Brown wrote that all elements were working to induce Polk not to retain Calhoun. There was, he said, scarcely less opposition to Cass; while Benton and Wright opposed Buchanan on account of the stand he had taken at Baltimore in favor of the two-thirds rule.[13]

While others were doing their utmost to prevent his retention, Calhoun himself was telling his friends that there was much speculation concerning the cabinet and not a little intriguing in various quarters. He reported himself to be ''perfectly passive'' and ''indifferent.'' Whether he would remain or not, if invited, would depend on the ''probable course of the administration.''[14] His supporters, however, were both active and hopeful. Some of them were sanguine enough to believe that Calhoun would be able to build up such a strong party following that Polk would not dare to remove him.[15] Hearing that Gideon Pillow had remarked that Polk's chief difficulty was ''how to get rid of Calhoun,'' even Duff Green felt constrained to warn the President-elect of the dangers which would result from sacrificing Calhoun in order to conciliate Benton and Wright. ''I make no pretense of friendship for you,'' he told Polk very frankly; but as a

---

[12] Jackson to Polk, Dec. 13, 16, *Polk Papers;* Jackson to Blair, Dec. 14, 1844, *Jackson Papers.*

[13] Johnson to Polk, Dec. 26; Brown to Polk, Dec. 29, 1844, *Polk Papers.*

[14] Calhoun to his son-in-law, Thos. G. Clemson, Dec. 13, 1844, *Rep. Am. Assn.*, 1899, II, 633. Dr. Gwin, who was supposed to be voicing Calhoun's views, suggested to A. V. Brown the following cabinet: Calhoun, Sec. of State; Walker, Sec. of Treasury; Woodbury, Sec. of War; Reed, of Pa., Atty. Gen.; Flagg, P-M Gen.; Mason, Sec. of Navy. Van Buren was suggested as minister to England (Brown to Polk, Jan. 5, 1845, *Polk Papers*).

[15] C. A. Davis, New York, to Crittenden, Dec. 17, 1844, *Crittenden Papers.*

friend of the South, he urged Calhoun's retention.[16] Calhoun himself continued to remain *passive* until February 26, when, in a personal interview, Polk informed him that there was to be an entirely new cabinet and offered to send him as minister to England. On the day following he sent Polk his resignation and assured him that there was neither dissatisfaction nor abatement of kind feelings on his own part.[17]

New England began at an early date to solicit a place in the cabinet. In New Hampshire, Hubbard and Woodbury were mentioned, but her congressional delegation preferred Pierce.[18] Bancroft was suggested as the New England member, but he informed Polk that he would prefer a foreign mission.[19] Maine was especially insistent in her claims for recognition, and Polk received numerous letters from politicians of that state. In several of them Governor Fairfield was suggested as Secretary of the Navy, and Nathan Weston as Attorney General.

The greatest rivalry, however, aside from the solicitation in Calhoun's behalf, was that between New York on the one side, and Pennsylvania and the West on the other. In Pennsylvania Buchanan and Dallas were the recognized heads of two rival factions, each of which was desirous of gaining a strategic position in the new administration. In order to accomplish his purpose, Dallas recommended that Robert J. Walker, of Mississippi, be made Secretary of State.[20] Dallas and Walker were connected by family ties as well as by political sympathies. In addition, Walker had the support of the aggressive forces in the southwestern states. Richard Rush urged the claims of Buchanan.

---

[16] Green to Polk, Jan. 20, 1845, *Polk Papers.* On January 1, Memucan Hunt wrote from Galveston that leading public men in Texas wished Calhoun to be retained and Donelson to be made Secretary of the Treasury.

[17] Calhoun to Polk, Feb. 27, 1845, *Polk Papers.* Same to Clemson, March 11, 1845, *Rep. Am. Hist. Assn.,* 1899, II, 647.

[18] John P. Hale to Pierce, Dec. 3, 1844, *Pierce Papers.*

[19] Lewis Josselyn, of Boston, to J. Geo. Harris, Dec. 4, 1844; Bancroft to Polk, Jan. 1, 1845, *Polk Papers.*

[20] Dallas to Polk, Dec. 15, 1844, *ibid.*

The latter had also received the formal endorsement of the Pennsylvania electoral college, but Dallas informed Polk that this action had been procured by the intrigue of a man who wished to be made collector of the port of Philadelphia. Dallas once more recommended Walker, dwelling on his command of foreign languages and upon the fact that he would be especially acceptable to the Texans.[21]

The rejection of Van Buren at Baltimore made it desirable that the powerful state of New York should be placated if possible. Polk very naturally, therefore, turned his thoughts in that direction, and his offer of the Treasury Department to Silas Wright was the first tender of a cabinet position to any one. Wright promptly declined the offer. The reason, as stated in his letter, was that he had pledged himself to serve as governor, if elected, and should he fail to do so it would be said that his nomination had been a trick to enable him to procure a cabinet position. When expressing regret because Wright had felt constrained to decline, Polk stated that while he had not yet decided upon a person for any of the cabinet positions, he intended to select either the Secretary of State or the Secretary of the Treasury from the state of New York. He asked Wright freely to suggest a man for either position.[22] In his reply Wright recommended Benjamin F. Butler for the State Department and Azariah C. Flagg for the Treasury. Lest Polk might think that he would have accepted the State portfolio, he assured the President-elect that he did not feel qualified to fill that office. Had he been at liberty to fill any such position he would have accepted the Treasury appointment.

In a letter dated January 4, 1845, Polk assured Van Buren that his nomination at Baltimore had been unsought and unexpected. He prevaricated to the degree of stating that: "Until

---

[21] Rush to Polk, Dec. 27, 1844; Dallas to Polk, Jan. 10, 1845, *ibid.*

[22] Polk to Wright, Dec. 7; Wright to Polk, Dec. 20, 1844; Polk to Wright, Jan. 4, 1845, *ibid.*

the moment it was made, it was very far from my thoughts, that any state of circumstances could arise, which could lead to such a result.'' He thanked the ex-President for his ''powerful support'' and requested his advice as to suitable members of the cabinet. Wright, he said, was the only selection he had made without consulting anyone, but as that offer had been declined, he would like to have Van Buren suggest persons for either the State or Treasury Departments.[23] In reply, Van Buren stated that Polk had acted just as he would have done in offering the Treasury portfolio to Wright, and that Wright's refusal to accept was due entirely to the political situation in New York. He knew of no one so well qualified to take charge of foreign affairs as Benjamin F. Butler, and he believed either Flagg or Cambreleng to be suitable for the Treasury Department. A month later he told Polk that Donelson would be a good man to have near him. He had desired to have Donelson in his own cabinet, but had feared that modesty would prevent him from accepting.[24] Jackson believed that Wright's refusal to accept a cabinet position had been due to the fear that Calhoun would be retained. He advised Polk to deliberate well and to make no final decisions until he had reached Washington. He believed Mason and Wilkins to be worthy men, but ''surely you will do well to select an entire cabinett fresh from the people as your own, & leave Mr. Tylers out to be provided for, if thought worthy otherwise.''[25]

Before making another tender of a cabinet office Polk prepared a form of invitation to be used in future cases. Its purpose was to make clear to those who might receive it that a cabinet position was not to be used, during the next four years, as a stepping-stone to the Presidency, and that each member

---

[23] Polk to Van Buren, Jan. 4, 1845, *Van Buren Papers*. Also, copy in *Polk Papers*.

[24] Van Buren to Polk, Jan. 18, 1845, *Polk Papers* and *Van B. Papers;* Van Buren to Polk, Feb. 21, *Polk Papers*.

[25] Jackson to Polk, Jan. 10, 1845, *Polk Papers*.

must devote his whole time to the duties of his office.[26] Although he was not a military man, Polk possessed at least one attribute of a true soldier. As a private in the ranks of his party he was ever ready to submit without complaint to the judgment of the leaders; and now, as party chieftain, he required from others a similar respect for authority. Jackson, who knew Polk thoroughly, assured Blair that ''He will have no caball about him, his heads of Departments must be a unit. *This is my opinion of the man,* and I think you will, when you know the men be pleased with his selection.''[27]

On January 28, 1845, Polk left his home at Columbia and set out for Washington. The fact that he was going to fill the highest office of his country did not for a moment overcome his habitual caution nor prevent him from giving thoughtful attention to minute details. He had written to Cave Johnson and other friends and asked them to procure rooms for him at Coleman's hotel, but the rates must be reasonable and the bargain made in advance.[28]

When he arrived in Washington in the middle of February the President-elect had not, with the exception of Buchanan, definitely decided upon any member of his cabinet.[29] Early in

[26] See *infra*, p. 325.

[27] Jackson to Blair, Jan. 21, 1845, *Jackson Papers.* There were, of course, those who held a radically different opinion. ''Polk,'' wrote Prentiss, ''was elected by a union of factions. He has neither honesty nor capacity to be the president even of his party—he will become at once the tool of those factions'' (Prentiss to Crittenden, Dec. 22, 1844, *Crittenden Papers*). J. K. Paulding, also, considered Polk weak and unable to cope with the situation, ''whether he selects a northern, a southern, or a mixed cabinet.'' ''He is by no means a great man—nor scarcely one of extraordinary mediocrity; and if the truth must be told, I admire Mrs. Polk much more than I do the colonel (Paulding to Van Buren, Jan. 19, 1845, *Van Buren Papers*).

[28] ''You know I have no money to spend unnecessarily,—and to avoid being subjected to an extravagant or enormous charge, it is necessary that a *distinct bargain* shall be made in advance'' (Polk to Johnson, Dec. 21, 1844, ''Polk-Johnson Letters'').

[29] According to Gideon Welles, he had also settled upon Bancroft for the Treasury and Walker for Attorney General, before leaving Tennessee (MS ''Rev. of Pol. Hist. of U. S. and Pres. Contests,'' *Welles Papers*).

the winter, at a meeting held at the Hermitage, Buchanan had
been discussed as a possible premier for the cabinet, but then
it was believed that his appointment would cause too much
jealously on the part of Benton, Calhoun, Cass, and Wright.[30]
However, on his arrival in Washington, Polk immediately invited
Buchanan to take charge of the State Department, and the tender
was promptly accepted.[31]

Having thus provided for Pennsylvania, Polk addressed another letter to Van Buren. When he last wrote, he said, he
intended to look to New York for either a Secretary of State or
a Secretary of War. Subsequently he had decided to call a
citizen of another state to the Department of State, but was still
desirous that a citizen of New York should take charge of the
Treasury. Such had been his intention when he came to Washington. On his arrival, however, he found that the South had
already united on a distinguished individual from that section
and that Indiana as well as other western states favored the same
person.

I was not satisfied that it was proper to appoint him to that Post—but became
convinced—that if I did not—great and extensive dissatisfaction would
prevail—unless I could find some individual in some part of the Union who
would be unexceptionable to them & also to the North.

Believing that Bancroft would fulfil these conditions, "my present determination therefore is to call him to that [Treasury]
Department." He was inclined, he said, to retain Mason in
charge of the Navy, and would be glad to have either Butler or
Marcy as his Secretary of War.[32] Evidently the distinguished
individual mentioned in the letter was Robert J. Walker, of
Mississippi. Writing early in January, A. V. Brown told Polk

---

[30] J. P. Brawles to Buchanan, Dec. 20, 1844, *Buchanan Papers*. Brawles
was told this by A. V. Brown, who had been present when Polk discussed
cabinet appointments with Jackson.

[31] Polk's letter was dated at Washington on Feb. 17 (*Buchanan Papers*)
and Buchanan replied on Feb. 18 (*Polk Papers*).

[32] Polk to Van Buren, Feb. 22, 1845, *Van Buren Papers*.

that Joseph A. Wright, Representative from Indiana, had reported that his own section as well as the Northwest wished Walker to be made Secretary of the Treasury so that he might have the appointment of land agents and other western officials. If, said he, Silas Wright should be given the office, he would use it to his own advantage and to the prejudice of Cass. From Cave Johnson, also, came the information that the "Cass men" all preferred Walker, and he gave the same reasons for their preference.[33]

Polk did not yield immediately to the importunities of Walker's friends; instead he held to his original plan of making Bancroft Secretary of the Treasury and Walker Attorney General. He even drafted a letter in which he invited Walker to accept the latter position, but probably it was never sent.[34] On February 25, without awaiting a reply from Van Buren, he offered the War portfolio to Benjamin F. Butler. Butler promptly declined because of "domestic and prudential considerations," although he would have made the *sacrifice* if he had been tendered either the State or the Treasury Department.[35]

Van Buren deliberated well before answering Polk's letter of February 22; but on March 1, he drafted a reply and sent it to Washington by his son, Smith Van Buren. In it he said that the "honest portion" of the New York Democracy were excited by a rumor that Woodbury was to be made Secretary of the Treasury, and that New York was to be passed over entirely. He did not say, but seemed to assume, that Butler would reconsider his refusal of the War portfolio.[36] Polk appears to have felt

---

33 Brown to Polk, Jan. 9; Johnson to Polk, Jan. 11, 1845, *Polk Papers*.

34 Copy, dated Feb. 19, 1845, *ibid.*

35 Butler to Polk, Feb. 27, 1845, *Polk Papers*. Mrs. Butler wrote to Van Buren that she was responsible for her husband's refusing the War portfolio; that she had promised that if he were offered the State Department she would not object, but this promise did not apply to other departments. Her reason was that she did not like to live in Washington (Mrs. Butler to Van Buren, Feb. 27, 1845, *Van Buren Papers*).

36 Van Buren to Polk, Albany, March 1, 1845, *Polk Papers*.

that Butler's prompt refusal and Van Buren's delay had absolved him from further obligation to that wing of the party, for, on March 1, he informed Van Buren that, as Flagg did not have a *national* reputation, he had decided to make Marcy Secretary of War. He hoped that this appointment would be satisfactory to New York. The rumor that Bancroft was to be made Secretary of the Treasury had "brought down upon me" the delegations from New Hampshire and Maine, and many—on account of the patronage he dispenses—were demanding the appointment of a southern man to that office.[37]

When Smith Van Buren arrived in Washington with the letter from his father he was chagrined to learn that Polk had already appointed Marcy. "Well," he reported to the ex-President,

the letter which you rec'd dated last night from the illustrious cabinet-maker of our day has advised you of the fate of my mission; and unless the excuses & explanations were more skilfully done in writing than in conversation, you will have seen through the flimsy pretexts—the contradictory & evasive & trimming character of the business, at least so far as New York is concerned.

Polk, he said, had declined to receive him for half an hour, in order to give himself and A. V. Brown time to "concoct" an answer. Polk wished that he might have seen Van Buren's letter a day earlier, but the matter had now been decided. "The Treasury arrangement [Walker's appointment] you perceive tells the whole story for New York. The only chance now is that your letter may upset the whole concern, & start anew the business to-morrow." In a letter written on the following day he said that when he read his father's letter to Polk, the latter, instead of feeling crestfallen, had the "impudence" to say that he felt relieved. "I denounced Marcy to him in good round terms" and

---

[37] Polk to Van Buren, March 1, 1845, *Van Buren Papers*. Evidently Marcy had been expecting an offer, for on Feb. 24 he wrote to Dickinson about "my appointment as a member of the cabinet." This must have been speculation, because on the day following (25th) Polk offered the War portfolio to Butler.

said that he was simply an office seeker in whom honest Democrats had no faith. Polk replied that he had never heard these things before and was "thunderstruck," although "Dix has told him the same thing over and over again."[38]

Instead of beginning anew with his cabinet making, Polk dispatched another letter to Van Buren. If he had committed an error, he said, it had been unintentional; and it pained him to think that Van Buren might think he had acted unkindly to him or his friends. He had acted, he said under no outside influence; he had followed his own judgment, and harbored no unkind feeling toward either Van Buren or Wright.[39] Nevertheless, Smith Van Buren had formed quite a different opinion. "The soundest judges here," he wrote, "think P. came here all right—but has been be-deviled since he arrived. To a large extent this is of course evident, but not wholly so."[40]

It is scarcely to be wondered at that Polk should have dissembled during the days just preceding his inauguration. He was beset on every hand by conflicting demands, all of which he was expected to satisfy. That he strove to harmonize factional discord so far as his own self-respect would permit, there is no reason to doubt. He tried to deal fairly with each faction, but to accept the dictation of none. If the Van Burenites suffered disappointment they had only themselves to blame, for Polk had given them more consideration than he had ever received from them. He had tendered cabinet positions to two of their number,

[38] Smith Van Buren to his father, March 2, 3, 1845, *Van Buren Papers.* Tilden and O'Sullivan, who bore letters from Butler to Polk, were, on the other hand, thoroughly captivated by the President-elect. The latter reported that Polk seemed like "one of us" and evinced great admiration for both Wright and Van Buren. "He certainly entirely won the hearts of both of us, and has effectually dissipated whatever slight degree of anxiety may have rested in our minds in regard to the Adm'n" (O'Sullivan to Van Buren, Washington, March 1, 1845, *Van Buren Papers*).

[39] Polk to Van Buren, March 3, 1845, *Polk Papers.*

[40] Smith Van Buren to his father, March 4, 1845, *Van Buren Papers.* "Armstrong," said he, "so far as I can observe, is the only honest man about him. He [Armstrong] is sick & very much affected by our affairs. He doubtless sees the approaching storm from Nashville."

and he had kept Van Buren fully informed regarding his plans. He had even told the ex-President of his intention to appoint Marcy unless Butler should accept the place offered to him. Van Buren had delayed in answering his letter, and it was unreasonable to expect Polk to wait indefinitely when inauguration day was already at hand. Surely Polk had the right to make his own choice for the office of Secretary of State, and it was cool effrontery on Butler's part to intimate that the position should have been bestowed upon himself.

Walker's assignment to the Treasury evidently was contrary to Polk's own wishes, yet he felt constrained to make this concession to the western element after his own choice, Bancroft, was found to be unpopular even in New England states. A new adjustment became necessary, therefore Mason was made Attorney General so that Bancroft might be assigned to the Navy. Mason's retention in the cabinet was due to personal friendship, and not to a desire to placate Tyler and his friends. Tyler had, in January, bestowed a diplomatic appointment upon William H. Polk, but the latter declined to accept it in order to free his brother from any obligation to the retiring President.[41] In fact, Tyler was much displeased by the ingratitude of his successor, and, in 1846, wrote that Polk seemed to be "avenging the supposed wrongs to Mr. Van Buren."[42] Marcy's acceptance of the War portfolio[43] completed the cabinet, for Cave Johnson had accepted the appointment as Postmaster General shortly after Polk's arrival in Washington.[44] Although many persons had suggested Donelson as the Tennessee member, Polk evidently preferred Johnson, and Jackson assured Polk that Donelson

---

[41] Cave Johnson to Polk, Jan. 8; J. L. O'Sullivan to Polk, Jan. 20, 1845, *Polk Papers*.

[42] Tyler to Alex. Gardner, July 11, 1846 (Tyler, *Letters and Times of the Tylers*, II, 342).

[43] Welles says that "Gen. [William O.] Butler of Kentucky accompanied the President-elect to the seat of government in expectation of the appointment [War Dept.] then tendered him" (MS "Rev. of Pol. Hist., etc."). I have seen nothing else to indicate that such an offer was made.

[44] Johnson to Polk, Feb. 26, 1845, *Polk Papers*.

would be satisfied with a foreign mission. Jackson had made it clear to Donelson, he said, that he was the one who had suggested a diplomatic appointment in preference to any other.[45] Johnson thoroughly deserved a place in Polk's cabinet, for no one had stood by him so loyally or had rendered more efficient service during his entire political career. Polk was by nature secretive and self-reliant, but to Johnson more than to any other person he disclosed his plans and his aspirations. Johnson had never failed him in the hour of need, and, both in Washington and in Tennessee, had done much to aid his political advancement. As a statesman, Johnson was conservative and rather narrow; but he was a crafty and capable politician, and a recognized leader in the House.

In selecting his cabinet, as in distributing the patronage, Polk had to steer between Scylla and Charybdis. When he tried to be fair to all wings of the party, he was charged with weakness; while independent actions were attributed to vanity and conceit, or characterized as downright treachery to his benefactors. It was freely predicted that leading cabinet members would dominate the President and reduce him to a mere figurehead, yet, from the beginning, Polk was master of the situation.

Scarcely less difficult than the selection of a cabinet was the choice of a party "organ" which would give ungrudging support to the new administration. Historians have indulged in no small amount of conjecture as to Polk's reasons for discarding Blair and the *Globe* despite General Jackson's vigorous protests. His action is usually said to have been the consummation of a preëlection bargain to obtain votes. Sometimes Tyler is made the other party to the contract, sometimes Calhoun; and in an attempt to make out a strong case, some have asserted that Blair's head on a platter had been offered to each of them in return for his political support. Usually their information has been derived

---

[45] Jackson to Polk, Jan. 10, Feb. 15, 1845, *ibid.* On account of Donelson's delicate health, Jackson asked that he might be sent as full minister to Spain, Brazil, or Mexico.

from Benton, and accepted without question. But even von
Holst, who had no difficulty in believing the Tyler story, balks at
the absurdity of a bargain between Polk and Calhoun.[46] For
very good reasons both Tyler and Calhoun despised the editor
of the *Globe,* and both supported the nominees of the Democratic
party, but such a coincidence does not imply any bargain between
them and the Democratic candidates. Calhoun's letter to Stuart
concerning the prospective cabinet[47] seems to indicate that he
had no knowledge of Polk's plans for the future, and Tyler has
specifically and emphatically denied that he and Polk had ever
entered into an agreement by which Tyler's withdrawal from
the canvass was made contingent on Polk's promise not to make
the *Globe* his official organ. As Tyler very aptly remarked,
"Blair was already dead," and it only remained for Mr. Polk to
chant his requiem.[48]

It is unnecessary to seek some mysterious intrigue or pre-
election pact in order to find Polk's motive for establishing a
new paper in Washington. The obvious reason for establishing
the *Union* was his desire to have an organ at the capital which
would give his administration its undivided and loyal support.
He had always believed Blair to be hostile or indifferent to his
political advancement when he had been a candidate for Speaker,
and when he had sought the Vice-Presidential nomination. Both
Polk and his friends believed that the *Globe* had supported the
nominees of the Baltimore convention with great reluctance and
that its editor was now, and would continue to be, under the
absolute domination of Senator Benton. This belief is the best
of reasons for Polk's refusal to make the *Globe* his official newspaper. Walker and others were hostile to Blair and undoubtedly

---

[46] von Holst, *History of the United States,* III, 7–8.

[47] See above, p. 288, note 9.

[48] Tyler to Ritchie, Jan. 9, 1851; same to John S. Cunningham, May 8,
1856 (Tyler, *Letters and Times of the Tylers,* II, 409 ff., 415). In the
second letter, Tyler said that the "conspiracy to supplant the *Globe,* by
substituting Mr. Ritchie or anybody else as the editorial mouth-piece of
Mr. Polk, is the sheerest invention that ever was conceived of."

desired his elimination. Their feelings may have strengthened
Polk's determination to look elsewhere for an editor, but there
is no reason for believing that they caused it. Polk's Tennessee
friends wrote freely concerning the advisability of establishing a
new paper, but in his correspondence there is no letter from
Walker on this subject.[49]

Polk's feelings toward Blair are manifested in a letter written
to Cave Johnson on January 21, 1844. "Amicus" had published
in the *Globe* an article which urged the claims of W. R. King to
the Vice-Presidency. In reply, S. H. Laughlin and H. L. Turney
prepared an article in Polk's behalf and sent it to Blair for publication. "Blair," said Polk, "surely cannot do me the injustice
to exclude it from his columns"; if so, he instructed Johnson to
have it published in pamphlet form. After alluding to his nomination by the Mississippi state convention, Polk wondered
whether Blair would suppress this news "or stick it in an obscure
corner as he did the Tennessee and Arkansas nominations?"[50]
Such remarks indicate that he did not, even at that time, regard
Blair as his friend.

Immediately after Polk had been nominated at Baltimore,
A. V. Brown reported from Washington that "much is said here
by *some* as to continuing the Globe as the Polk organ—this we
will manage with sound discretion. The Globe will change its
tone & perhaps take back much that it has said & go in *warmly*
if not heartily—if so—well—But we will not commit ourselves
to it *after* the election."[51] The last remark might seem to indicate
that Blair's fate *after election* had already been determined, but
this is disproved by letters written later in the campaign. Cave
Johnson, who was hostile to Calhoun and averse to the Tylerites,
wrote that the *Globe* was noncommittal and that a new paper was

[49] Although Ambler assigns to Walker the chief rôle in the overthrow
of Blair, he admits his inability to produce any tangible evidence (Ambler,
Thomas Ritchie, 252).

[50] Polk to Johnson, Jan. 21, 1844, "Polk-Johnson Letters."

[51] Brown to Polk, May 30, 1844, *Polk Papers*.

needed; but two weeks later, when he had come to believe that the southerners were trying to "appropriate" Polk, he spoke with disgust of the "secret talk of upsetting the Globe [and] turning Benton overboard."[52] Judge Catron vehemently denounced the *Globe* and declared that its "coarse brutality" was loathed by a large majority of the party.[53]

Late in June, J. B. Jones, editor of the *Madisonian*, invited J. George Harris to become joint editor of that paper. Harris and General Armstrong looked with favor upon the offer and believed that all three Washington papers—*Madisonian, Spectator* and *Globe*—might be merged into one. However, A. V. Brown, who had come from Washington recently, did not approve such an arrangement.[54] It was not yet a question of an *administration organ*, for there was no certainty that Polk would be elected, but many of Polk's friends felt that Blair's support of the ticket was merely perfunctory and that a more vigorous journal was needed. This feeling was not caused entirely by what appeared or did not appear in the columns of the *Globe*. The campaign leaders believed Blair to be under the thumb of Benton, and the latter was vociferously denouncing the "intrigue" which had deprived Van Buren of the nomination and, also, the annexation program. Despite the need of a reliable party organ there seemed to be no satisfactory solution of the difficulty, therefore the matter was dropped until after the election.

The correspondence does not disclose who it was that first suggested inviting Ritchie to come to Washington, but Brown rather than Walker seems to have been the prime mover. In a letter written to Polk, soon after the election, Brown said that Walker "entertains the same opinion with us" as to the importance of procuring Blair's half of the *Globe* for Ritchie. Blair would not be approached, he said, until Cave Johnson had gone

---

52 Johnson to Polk, June 1 [1844?, year not given], June 13, 1844, *Polk Papers.*

53 Catron to Polk, June 8, [1844], *ibid.*

54 Harris to Polk, June 27, 29; Armstrong to Polk, June 30, 1844, *ibid.*

to Richmond to sound Ritchie on the subject. "If that dont take—then B & Rives must sink into mere *proprietors,* with *an able & competent* Editor having *absolute* controul of the political character of the paper."[55] Cave Johnson, also, had become convinced that Blair must go. Some of the politicians, said he, fear that the *Globe* will be dominated by Benton and they will therefore oppose giving it the public printing; "I see no chance of a reconciliation with them if F. P. Blair is retained." A few days later he reported that "the Globe is regarded as Benton's organ by the friends of C[alhoun] & will oppose him to the uttermost & will in connection with the Whigs defeat him & therefore B[rown] & myself have been sounding, to learn the prospect of getting Ritchie . . . . T. H. B[enton] has a great dislike to Ritchie & I expect will be greatly provoked, if he learns any such movement."[56] This letter shows a desire to prevent opposition from the Calhoun faction, but it indicates, also, that there had been no preëlection understanding. Had there been any such understanding Johnson would have been one of the first to learn of it.

As soon as General Jackson heard of the scheme to supplant the *Globe* he took immediate steps to thwart it. Assuming that Polk knew nothing about the matter, Jackson warned him that an intrigue was being concocted in Washington which might divide the party and wreck his administration. Some, he said, wished to substitute the *Madisonian* for the *Globe;* others wanted to make Ritchie editor of the *Globe.* He urged Polk to discountenance such maneuvers for

the first would blow you sky high & destroy the Republican party— The second would be an insult to the Editor of the Globe & seperate him from you, whose administration he is determined to support— Keep Blairs Globe the administration paper, and William B. Lewis, to ferret out & make known to you all the plotts & intrigues Hatching against your administration and you are safe.

---

[55] Brown to Polk, Dec. 5, 1844, *ibid.*
[56] Johnson to Polk, Dec. 6, 12, 1844, *ibid.*

These men had been such a source of strength to Jackson himself that very naturally he desired his friend Polk to have the benefit of their services. But battling for Old Hickory was one thing, and loyal support of the man who had profited by the *intrigue* against Van Buren was quite another. Polk well knew that both men had always been ready to throw obstacles in his way, and he had no reason to believe that their feeling toward him had undergone any change.

Jackson may have been wrong in his belief that Blair and Lewis would labor for the glory of Polk's administration, but another part of his letter showed that he understood Ritchie's weaknesses better than did those who were so anxious to bring him to Washington. "Ritchie is a good Editor," he told Polk, "but a very unsafe one— He goes off at half bent, & does great injury before he can be set right."[57] Before many months had elapsed, Polk realized fully the accuracy of the General's statement.

On the following day, Jackson informed Blair of the scheme to merge the *Spectator* and the *Madisonian* into a Polk organ. He attributed this scheme to Calhoun. Believing that his word was still law, he told Blair that "I am sure polk when he hears of it will feel as indignant at the plott as I do."[58] In Washington the "plott" had already been discovered, and Cave Johnson (on account of his known intimacy with Polk) feared to go to Richmond for the purpose of negotiating with Ritchie. The premature discovery greatly annoyed Johnson, and he complained that "even old J. Q. A[dams] asked when we were going to Richmond."[59] Brown, who facetiously called himself "the President elect ad interim," was somewhat disconcerted by Johnson's timidity. He even suspected that his colleague did not desire to

---

57 Jackson to Polk, Dec. 13, 1844, *ibid*.

58 Jackson to Blair, Dec. 14, 1844, *Jackson Papers*.

59 Johnson to Polk, Dec. 14, 1844, *Polk Papers*.

get rid of Blair.[60] General Bayly, of the Virginia delegation, and a personal friend of Ritchie, now undertook to negotiate by letter with the veteran editor of the *Enquirer*. "If my road is blocked there," said Brown, "I shall then go for sinking Blair & Rives into *Proprietors* only & putting the political controul (absolute) into the hands of a new Editor & that man Burke would not be a bad one." Brown believed that Blair would not oppose the change "if he sees that Benton means to be antagonistic to your administration as many of his *Western* friends think likely enough. He shews no *mitigation* of his opposition & nothing but instructions plain & powerful can subdue him."[61] Here again is a statement of the main reason for wanting a new party organ— not pledges to Tyler or to Calhoun, but distrust of Blair and a fear that he would be controlled by Benton, who was considered to be an enemy of the incoming administration. Another indication that Polk had made no bargain with the Tylerites is the sentiment voiced in a letter written by J. B. Jones, editor of the *Madisonian*. The plan contemplated was, in his opinion, the only sensible one, for he believed that discord would surely result from the employment of any of the Washington editors. "When," said he, "Col. Polk shall convince all parties that he is in his own hands—that he will be the *President,* and not a partisan of any aspirant, there will be no door left open for the ingress of factious schemes."[62]

---

[60] "He feared some newspaper squibs at him & *I feared* he was rather indifferent about any matter that was against the Globe Benton & Co but perhaps I was wrong."

[61] Brown to Polk, Dec. 23, 1844, *Polk Papers*.

[62] Party factions can not "object to the [new] paper because its conductor entertains no special partiality for any one of the aspirants to the succession. But if *I* were to conduct the paper it would be said that Mr. Polk had thrown himself into the hands of the Tyler men—if the editor of the Globe, into the hands of Col. Benton—and if the Constitution [successor to the *Spectator*], into the hands of Mr. Calhoun" (Jones to ——, Dec. 23, 1844). Apparently this was written to J. Geo. Harris, for it was inclosed in his letter to Polk, Jan. 4, 1845, *Polk Papers*.

At first Ritchie did not take kindly to the plan which had been arranged for him, and, in a letter to Bayly, he declined the invitation. He was not able, he said, to purchase the *Globe,* and rival Democratic papers would do the party more harm than good.[63] After reading Ritchie's letter, Brown concluded that "If Benton goes right on Texas & Calhoun is not in the Cabinet there would be no insuperable difficulty with the Globe—but you would find it hard to keep in order."[64] Edmund Burke was once more considered, but his former affiliations with Calhoun were urged against his selection.[65] A few days of reflection seem to have convinced Brown that neither Benton nor Blair could be kept in order, for he presented for Polk's consideration an entirely new solution of the difficulty. He offered to purchase Blair's share of the *Globe* and to continue the paper under the firm name of Brown and Rives. Brown was to have exclusive control, and, with Kendall's help, to edit the journal in the interest of the administration.[66] His new scheme, like the others, came to naught, and no arrangement had been made when Polk reached Washington. Apparently the President-elect gave no encouragement to the editor of the *Globe,* for Smith Van Buren reported to his father that "Blair says—'Where am I to go?' "[67]

Polk's own opinions concerning a party journal were expressed in very definite terms before he left Tennessee. In a letter to Cave Johnson, he said:

As to the *press* which may be regarded as the Government organ, one thing is settled in my mind. It must have no connection with, nor be under the influence or control of any clique or portion of the party which is making war upon any other portion of the party—with a view to the succession and

---

[63] His letter, dated Dec. 28, is printed in full in Ambler, *Thomas Ritchie,* 247–249.

[64] Brown to Polk, Jan. 1, 1843 [1845], *Polk Papers.*

[65] Cave Johnson to Polk, Jan. 2, 1844, *ibid.*

[66] Brown to Polk, Jan. 5, 1845, *ibid.* He told Polk that if this plan did not work out he might consent to run for governor of Tennessee, although he would rather "rent a brick yard" than go through that campaign!

[67] March 2, 1845, *Van Buren Papers.*

not with a view to the success of my administration. I think the view you take of it proper and of the proposed arrangement the best that can be made. I hope it may be effected.[68]

Apparently Polk felt that he was regarded as a sort of *chargé d' affaires* who was to keep things running while the great men contended for the prize. He had no intention of playing such a rôle, and his determination to make the administration his own and to have a paper which would promote its interests was both characteristic of the man and an exhibition of sound sense.[69] Even von Holst, who has found little in Polk's career to commend, obsolves him from the charge of subserviency to factional leaders. He says,

Obedience to party commands, was certainly one of the principal articles of his political creed. But if politicians had expected that they were now going to have the mastery, because he was willing to play the part of a manikin, they were greatly mistaken in the man.[70]

As to patronage in general the President-elect maintained a discreet silence. There was much speculation concerning future rewards and punishments, but all had to wait until the new President had canvassed the situation and was ready to act. Although General Jackson made no exception to his rule of attempting to provide for his friends, he did not find Polk as accommodating as Van Buren had been. His solicitation for the welfare of Blair and Lewis has already been noted, and Polk had scarcely been elected before Jackson consulted Amos Kendall in order to ascertain the position which would be most acceptable to the star member of his "kitchen cabinet." Kendall selected the Spanish mission and his wishes were forthwith reported to

[68] Polk to Johnson, Dec. 21, 1844, "Polk-Johnson Letters." The "proposed arrangement" evidently refers to the attempt to procure Ritchie.

[69] A rumor that Laughlin was going to Washington to edit the *Madisonian* caused General Jackson much needless worry. He warned Polk to keep clear of Tyler influence, for, if he did not, he would be in as bad a position as Tyler himself (Jackson to Polk, Feb. 28, 1845, *Polk Papers*).

[70] von Holst, *History of the United States*, III, 21-22.

the President-elect. Jackson assured Polk that "there can be no delicacy in recalling Erwin [Washington Irving]—he is only fit to write a Book & scarcely that, and has become a good Whigg."[71]

Congress had already consented to annex Texas before Polk became President of the United States. Nevertheless, since one of the principal planks in the platform on which he had been elected related to this subject, and since he had been an indirect, if not a direct, participant in this important transaction, it is necessary to give a brief outline of the progress of events during the period between the rejection of Tyler's treaty and the passage of the joint resolution of annexation.

Tyler's annexation treaty was rejected by the Senate on June 8, 1844. Calhoun, we are told,[72] disheartened by this action, was ready to abandon all further attempts at annexation. His dejection was so great that Tyler thought of requesting his resignation, but he soon recovered his spirits and his old-time vigor. Since the treaty method had failed, nothing could be done without the coöperation of Congress. During the summer, a rumor to the effect that Tyler was about to convene Congress in extra session caused the Democratic candidate no little anxiety, and he appealed to Jackson as the only man who could dissuade the President from committing such a political error. A month later Jackson assured him that Congress would not be convened, although it is not clear whether Jackson was instrumental in preventing such a course.[73] At any rate no call for an extra session was issued, and no further action could be undertaken until winter; but the death of T. A. Howard, the American *chargé* in Texas, gave Tyler an opportunity to strengthen his position by assigning A. J. Donelson to the vacant post. When notifying

---

[71] Kendall to Jackson, Dec. 2; Jackson to Polk, Dec. 13, 1844, *Polk Papers.*

[72] Tyler, *Letters and Times of the Tylers,* II, 331.

[73] Polk to Donelson, Aug. 27, 1844, "Polk-Donelson Letters." Jackson to Polk, Sept. 26, 1844, *Polk Papers.*

Jackson of Donelson's appointment the President expressed the belief that the selection of "a member of your family . . . . will have a controuling influence with Gen¹ Houstin and incline him . . . . to pause ere he declares against annexation." He declared his determination to proceed with his Texas program, and to protect that country from the threatened aggressions of Mexico. Jackson informed Polk of the President's plans and remarked that "This is the true energetic course."[74]

On December 3, 1844, Tyler submitted to Congress his last annual message. In it he called attention to the threatening Mexican manifestoes that had resulted from the treaty which the United States had negotiated with Texas. Mexico, he said, had no cause for complaint; on the contrary, the measure "should have been regarded by her as highly beneficial." The treaty, said he, had been rejected by the American Senate on the ground that the question had not been submitted to the people, but popular approval had since been expressed at the recent election. Such being the case, he urged Congress to annex Texas by joint resolution.[75] He followed this up with another message on December 18, and along with it submitted a collection of correspondence. He called attention to the abusive character of this correspondence and to the barbarous measures which were threatened by Mexico. Especially did he resent Mexico's criticism of southern states, and he declared with emphasis that annexation was not a sectional question.[76] His statement that "the subject of annexation addresses itself, most fortunately, to every portion of the Union" was, to say the least, an exaggeration; still, since the election had been decided, there were many indications of a change in public opinion, and the question was becoming more *national* every day. Could the subject, when it was presented originally, have been divested of its factional and its sectional

[74] Tyler to Jackson, Sept. 17, 1844, *Jackson Papers*. Jackson to Polk, Sept. 26, 1844, *Polk Papers*.
[75] Richardson, *Messages*, IV, 341–345.
[76] *Ibid.*, 353–356.

concomitants, doubtless there would have been little opposition to annexation. Now that the election was over, those who had really wished to see Texas admitted into the Union no longer had the same incentive to oppose annexation for mere factional reasons. They might still cavil over ways and means, yet the prospect of eventual compromise was perceptibly brightening.[77] There was no certainty, however, that the friends of Texas would be able to effect annexation during the present session, for those who had been defeated at Baltimore still harbored a bitter resentment. Late in December, Calhoun believed that the House would take favorable action, but that annexation would be defeated in the Senate. "The real opposition is from the Benton V. Buren party" who would join with the Whigs against Texas; still he was not without hope that "publick opinion will force them to give up their opposition. Its effects are already apparent."[78] It was at this time that Calhoun was ready to make the "sacrifice" of accepting a place in Polk's cabinet, if the probable course of the administration should appear to be satisfactory.

While Calhoun denounced Benton and Van Buren for their obstructive tactics, others believed that the South Carolinian himself had sounded the knell of the Texas treaty. A long article on "Abolitionists" which· appeared in the January number of the *Democratic Review* held him responsible, in the main, for the widespread hostility to annexation. Although himself in favor of annexation, the writer flayed Calhoun for the position he had assumed regarding the slavery side of the question. In the writer's opinion, the fanatical demands of the Abolitionists and the "gag rule" of Congress were equally to be deplored; but the climax of absurdity had been reached when Calhoun, in his letters to Pakenham and King, had represented the United States as

---

[77] See press comments, Smith, *Annexation of Texas,* 323 ff.

[78] Calhoun to Clemson, Dec. 27; same to Hunter, Dec. 29, 1844, *Rep. Am. Hist. Assn.*, 1899, II, 634–636.

desiring Texas in order to protect slavery. In his effort to nation-
alize slavery, he had also nationalized abolition. Other critics
of Calhoun expressed similar sentiments. Since the opposition
had been aimed, for the most part, at the negotiators of the treaty
and their methods, acquiescence in annexation was made easier
when it became practically certain that Calhoun as well as Tyler
would soon depart from the scene of action.

Soon after Congress had convened in December various plans
of annexation were offered in each house, some to admit Texas as
a state, others to acquire it as a territory. In the House, after
several projects had met with serious objections, Milton Brown,
one of Polk's Whig antagonists from Tennessee, offered a resolution which, after certain alterations, was eventually adopted by
the House. Brown's resolution provided that the territory right-
fully belonging to Texas should be admitted as a state. The
federal government was to undertake the adjustment of the boundaries of the new state, but was not to assume her debt or take
over her public lands. Slavery was prohibted in all territory
north of 36° 30′; south of that line the people were to decide the
question for themselves.

In the early days of the session, McDuffie once more presented
the joint resolution of annexation which had failed to pass in the
spring. It voiced the sentiments of the Tyler administration
and was, in substance, a restatement of the rejected treaty. As
such, it was unacceptable to the Senator from Missouri, and Cave
Johnson reported to Polk that "the great battle between Mr.
T. H. B. [enton] & Mr. C. [alhoun] has commenced." Apparently the main reason for presenting the resolution in this particular form was the desire to embarrass the Van Burenites by
compelling them either to accept a measure which they had denounced or to incur the odium of opposing annexation after they
had endorsed the Baltimore platform. Such, at least, was the
opinion of Cave Johnson:

The friends of T. H. B.—— Silas Wright, who took general ground before
the people for annexation but against the Treaty are to be forced to take
that Treaty or appear before the people as hostile to Texas. Mr. C.
thinks that he has got the advantage of T. H. B. on this issue & intends
to drive him home upon it. The N. Y. democrats will go en-mass ag't the
treaty & I have no idea, that the friends of C—— will take any thing but
the Treaty.[79]

On the day following the appearance of McDuffie's resolution,
Benton met the issue by reintroducing his own bill which had
failed at the close of the last session, with a modification for
making the territory half slave and half free. Since this bill
could not by any possibility get but a few votes, Johnson considered Benton's conduct to be "outrageous." He asked the Senator
to coöperate in offering a joint resolution which would assert the
determination of the United States to defend Texas against all
assaults, leaving the question of annexation to Polk's administration. Benton declined to accept this resolution, and continued
to rage against his opponents.[80] Late in December Johnson
thought that the hostility between the two factions was increasing; each feared that the other would influence the incoming
President.[81] Benton blustered, of course, for, under the circumstances, he could hardly do otherwise. Since the election, however, he must have known that he was championing an unpopular
cause. There was also a future ahead, and his course had alienated a large majority of his party—even many of his lifelong
friends. In addition, the legislature of Missouri had, by resolution, requested members of Congress from that state to support
annexation.[82] This made it clear that his conduct did not meet
with approval at home; on the other hand, such a request made
it easier for him to modify his attitude on the subject. About
the same time a letter from Donelson told him "that his course
is injuring his friends and his country, and that I hoped he would

[79] Johnson to Polk, Dec. 12, 1844, *Polk Papers*.
[80] *Idem*, and Johnson to Polk, Dec. 14, *Polk Papers*.
[81] Johnson to Polk, Dec. 26, 1844, *Polk Papers*.
[82] Meigs, *Life of Thomas Hart Benton*, 351.

be willing to modify his position."[83] No doubt all of these manifestations of displeasure had their influence in determining Benton to retreat, provided he could do so in good order. His avenue of escape was by way of a new bill, and this he introduced on February 5, 1845. No mention was made in the new measure of obtaining the consent of Mexico. It provided for the admission of a state of suitable size and boundaries, said state to be formed out of the territory of the republic; the remainder of Texas was to be a territory of the United States. The measure was to become effective as soon as an agreement had been reached by the governments of the two nations concerned. His plan would delay, but not necessarily defeat, annexation, although defeat is evidently what its author desired. His bill and the House resolution seemed hopelessly irreconcilable until R. J. Walker, a few days later, offered as an amendment a combination of the two methods, and Haywood proposed to leave the choice between them to the President of the United States. To this modification Walker readily agreed.[84] Calhoun, according to a statement made later, believed that Benton's bill would have defeated annexation, and he was scarcely less opposed to the combination measure.[85] He used his "best efforts" to defeat both, but was unsuccessful in the second instance. Many counseled delay, but at the evening session of February 27, 1845, the Senate was ready to vote on Walker's combination amendment. Before the vote had been taken, however, Archer, of the Committee on Foreign Relations, offered a substitute bill. This proposed a transfer of the territory of Texas, with the assent of the people thereof, to the United States. The vote on the substitute resulted in a tie, and it looked for a time as if annexation were doomed. Nevertheless, relief was already at hand. When the vote on the Walker

---

[83] Donelson to Calhoun, New Orleans, Dec. 26, 1844, *Rep. Am. Hist. Assn.*, 1899, II, 1012.

[84] Smith, *Annexation of Texas*, 343. Smith gives an exhaustive account of the various proposals offered in each house (*idem*, chap. xvi).

[85] Calhoun to Donelson, May 23, 1845, *Rep. Am. Hist. Assn.*, 1899, II, 658.

amendment was taken in Committee of the Whole, Johnson, a Whig from Louisiana who had voted for the Archer bill, now swung to the Democrats and made the vote twenty-seven to twenty-five. According to Judge Catron, Johnson had difficulty in supporting the joint resolution on constitutional grounds, but, after consulting Catron, finally agreed to do so.[86] As soon as the committee had reported the measure to the Senate, Miller, of New Jersey, offered Benton's original bill as a substitute. Benton said from his seat that he would vote against this substitute, and when asked if he would destroy his own child, he replied, "I'll kill it stone dead." The substitute failed, and Walker's amendment passed the Senate by a vote of twenty-seven to twenty-five, Johnson again aligning himself with the Democrats.[87] The amended resolution was transmitted to the House for approval, and although it met with strenuous opposition there was never any doubt of its passage. This measure was given precedence over other matters; the Speaker, by his rulings, prevented filibustering; and, in Committee of the Whole, the debate was limited to five minutes. Milton Brown, the author of the House resolution, tried to "kill his own child," but the measure as amended by Walker passed by a vote of one hundred thirty-two to seventy-six.[88]

The President-elect had been in Washington since February 13, but whether and to what extent his influence was effective at this time is very difficult to determine. Before Polk had left Tennessee, Cave Johnson assured Calhoun that the incoming President and his friends desired to have Texas annexed during

---

[86] "The amendment offered by Mr. Senator Walker," continued Catron, "was rather sudden; it left the slave line at 36° 30' N. open. To this Gov. Johnson had most decided objections; it threw Mr. Senator Foster the other way, and endangered the measure." Johnson, said the judge, voted for the measure because he had confidence in Polk, and because he believed that 36° 30' would be definitely fixed as the northern boundary of slavery (Catron to Buchanan, March 15, 1845, *Buchanan Papers*).

[87] *Cong. Globe*, 28 Cong., 2 sess., 362; Smith, *Annexation of Texas*, 344-345.

[88] *Cong. Globe* (Feb. 28), 28 Cong., 2 sess., 372.

the present session, and Donelson informed Calhoun that both Jackson and himself hoped for immediate action by the existing Congress.[89] While at Coleman's hotel awaiting his inauguration the President-elect, according to his own account,[90] freely expressed the wish that annexation in some form might be effected before the adjournment of Congress. Should Congress fail to take definite action, he feared that Texas would be forever lost to the Union. He did not, he said, have time to examine the different measures proposed, but thought that any measure would be better than none. That he desired to have this vexed question settled before his inauguration, we may very well believe. Indeed, it was said that he offered rewards and threatened punishments for the purpose of influencing votes. Such charges rested on no tangible evidence and doubtless, for the most part, were unfounded, although it is quite probable that he may have let it be known that the disloyal need not look to him for favors. Always ready to "play the game" himself, he was a firm believer in party discipline.

Later, a more serious charge was brought against Polk in this connection—a charge of base deception instead of party discipline. In a letter printed in the New York *Evening Post,* July 28, 1848, Senator Tappan, of Ohio, asserted that, in February, 1845, Polk had personally assured Senator Haywood that, should the joint resolution pass, he would choose the Benton alternative and negotiate under it. In a letter to Tappan, F. P. Blair averred that he, also, had discussed the matter with Polk, and that the President-elect had promised to choose the Benton plan of negotiating a treaty with Texas. It was charged, therefore, that at least five Senators had voted for the joint resolution because they had been deceived by Polk.[91] Polk denied all recollection of any

---

[89] Johnson to Polk, Dec. 9, 1844, *Polk Papers.* Donelson to Calhoun, Dec. 26, 1844, *Rep. Am. Hist. Assn.,* 1899, II, 1012.

[90] Polk, *Diary,* IV, 41.

[91] The essential parts of both letters may be found in Benton, *Thirty Years' View,* II, 636–637.

conversation on the subject with either Blair or Haywood, and called attention to the fact that no complaint of violated pledges had been made at the time. In addition, he pointed out that in August, 1846, Blair had expressed to him a warm approval of the principal measures of his administration.[92] The members of Polk's cabinet disclaimed all knowledge of such a pledge, and even the fine-meshed dragnet of Justin H. Smith has failed to find any evidence to substantiate the charges made by Tappan and Blair. On the contrary, Smith offers some valuable suggestions as to why it is highly improbable that the President elect made pledges to any one.[93] Polk had committed himself to *immediate* annexation; and even if he had been as unprincipled as his enemies alleged, it seems incredible that so crafty a politician should have made so stupid a blunder. Besides, Polk was a man who seldom disclosed his intentions until he was ready to act, and, as Cave Johnson said in his letter, it was extremely unlikely that he would do so to Blair. It is significant, also, that, as soon as Texas had approved annexation, Polk wrote a letter to Haywood in which he commented on the wisdom of choosing the House resolution and expressed the belief that Texas would have been lost if the Benton alternative had been selected. "It was not," wrote the President, "until after I entered upon my duties that I had an opportunity—deliberately to consider the

---

[92] Polk, *Diary*, II, 84.

[93] Smith, *Annexation of Texas*, 347–350. In answer to Polk's request for a statement on the subject, Cave Johnson (Oct. 6, 1848) said that he conversed with the President-elect while the joint resolution was before Congress. Polk said that he hoped one of the alternatives would pass, but expressed no preference. After the measure had passed, he expressed no preference until the cabinet had met. Walker (Oct. 6) said that when the measures were before Congress, Blair came to him and, after saying that the House resolution could not pass, asked him to vote for the Benton bill. Walker refused. Blair stated that Texas would prefer Benton's bill. Walker then said that he would combine the two and let Texas take her choice. After consulting Benton, Blair said that they would support the combined resolution, if the choice were left to the President instead of Texas. Walker agreed, and so it passed. Polk expressed no preference—the cabinet was divided. Bancroft's letter of Oct. 13, Buchanan's of Nov. 9, Mason's of Nov. 12, and Marcy's of Nov. 20 all stated that Polk had not expressed any preference. All letters are in the *Polk Papers*.

two propositions—and select between them. I acted upon my own best judgment and the result has proved that I was right.''[94] It is inconceivable that he could write thus to a man to whom he had given a pledge to select the Benton method of annexation.

When the provision was added to the joint resolution which gave the choice of alternatives to the President, it was intended of course to give this selection to Polk. Nevertheless, it was suggested during the debate that Tyler and Calhoun might make the selection, but McDuffie, who was a close friend of both men, declared in the Senate that they would not have the ''audacity'' to do such a thing. When, therefore, the House passed the measure on February 28, it was fully understood that the choice would rest with President Polk. But the resolution gave this choice to the ''President of the United States,'' and for three days more that office was occupied by ''Captain'' Tyler. Despite McDuffie's assurances Tyler possessed the necessary *audacity,* for he immediately took steps both to make the selection and to carry it into effect. In 1848 he prepared a statement which gives his version of the transaction and explains his reasons for forestalling his successor. As soon as Tyler had approved the resolution, on March 1, Calhoun, the Secretary of State, remarked that the President now had the power to make his selection. Tyler replied that he had no doubt of his power, but that he had some doubt as to the propriety of exercising it. The danger of delay, urged Calhoun, was sufficient to overrule all feelings of delicacy regarding Polk. Next day, at a cabinet meeting, all agreed that Tyler ought to select the House resolution and act at once. He decided to do so and requested Calhoun to call upon Polk, after the meeting, ''and explain to him the reasons'' for immediate action. Calhoun complied with the request, and reported that ''Mr. Polk declined to express any opinion or to make any suggestion in reference to the subject.'' On the third instructions were dispatched to A. J. Donelson, whom Tyler had recently

---

[94] Polk to Haywood, Aug. 9, 1845, *Polk Papers.*

appointed to be *chargé d'affaires* at the capital of Texas.[95]   When
Polk became President he still had the option of reversing Tyler's
action[96] and recalling the messenger or of acquiescing in the choice
made by his predecessor.   Since he chose the latter alternative
there was little delay in carrying out the mandate of the Baltimore platform.   The progress of annexation under his administration will be considered in another chapter.

---

[95] See statement, Tyler, *Letters and Times of the Tylers*, II, 364–365.
At a later time Tyler was angered by Calhoun's assertion in the Senate
that *he* had selected the House resolution. *"If he selected*, then Texas is
not legitimately a State of the Union, for Congress gave the power *to the
President* to select, and not to *the Secretary of State."* He referred to
Calhoun as "the great 'I am,'" and to Benton as "the most raving
political maniac I ever knew" Tyler to Gardiner, March 11, 1847, *ibid.*,
420).

[96] There was a difference of opinion regarding this.   Walker, and perhaps other members of the cabinet, believed that Polk had no power to
reverse Tyler's action. See Polk, *Diary*, IV, 44.

CHAPTER XV

ADMINISTRATION AND PATRONAGE

On March 4, 1845, an unusually large "concourse of people" congregated in Washington to witness the inauguration of President Polk. The "arrangements were admirable"[1] and, in true American fashion, men who had bitterly assailed each other in the press and on the platform now joined in doing honor to the new chief executive. Climatic conditions proved to be the only disturbing element. Rain began to descend in torrents as the procession wended its way to the capitol where, according to the picturesque description given by John Quincy Adams, the new executive delivered his inaugural address to "a large assemblage of umbrellas." "At night," said the same writer, "there were two balls: one at Carusi's Hall, at ten dollars a ticket, of all parties; the other of pure Democrats, at five dollars a ticket, at the National Theatre. Mr. Polk attended both, but supped with the true-blue five-dollar Democracy."[2]

Not yet fifty years old, Polk enjoyed the distinction of reaching the highest executive office at an earlier age than any of his predecessors—a fact which he did not fail to note in his inaugural address. This address was in the main a reiteration of Jeffersonian principles and of his own oft-expressed opinions. Strong emphasis was laid on the value of the Union; "no treason to mankind since the organization of society would be equal in atrocity to that of him who would lift his hand to destroy it." On the other hand, he frowned upon the "schemes and agitations" which aimed at the "destruction of domestic institutions

---

[1] *Niles' Reg.*, LXVIII, 1.

[2] Adams, *Memoirs*, XII, 179. He added that "my family and myself received invitations to both, but attended neither."

existing in other sections,'' and urged the necessity of preserving
the compromises of the Constitution.

If the compromises of the Constitution be preserved, if sectional jealousies and heart-burnings be discountenanced, if our laws be just and the
Government be practically administered strictly within the limits of power
prescribed to it, we may discard all apprehensions for the safety of the
Union.

Having thus expressed his disapproval of both abolition and
disunion, he again declared himself to be in favor of a tariff for
revenue, but not for ''protection merely.'' He congratulated
the country on the passage of the joint resolution to annex Texas,
and he pronounced our title to Oregon to be ''clear and unquestionable.'' Experience, he said, had disproved the old belief that
a federal system could not operate over a large area, and like a
true expansionist expressed the opinion that as the system ''shall
be extended the bonds of our Union, so far from being weakened,
will become stronger.''

The reference to Texas must have been inserted shortly before the address was delivered, but certain letters written by
A. V. Brown indicate that the first draft of the inaugural was
written early in December and sent to Washington for criticism
and approval by Polk's political friends. The Brown letters
are too enigmatical to throw much light on the subject, but as
Polk had many times before expressed practically all of the views
contained in his address, there was no reason for believing that
it was not substantially his own product.[3]

---

[3] On December 14, 1844, Brown wrote from Washington to Polk: ''I
received yours of the 7th Inst. *our* friend called yesterday & informed
me that he would be ready in a few days & I shall loose no time after
examination to forward it to you.''

On December 23 he wrote: ''You must not be impatient—Our friend
has been sick a few days—has sent me for examination about *half* to be
returned with my comments & then the whole to be finished & polish'd—
say all by the first January or sooner. So far it is a happy conception
for instance in allusion to the Union.

'' 'If this be not enough, if that freedom of thought word and action
given by his Creator to fallen man & left by human institutions as free
as they were given, are not sufficient to lead him into the paths of liberty

Among the rejoicing Democrats none felt more sincere satisfaction in the defeat of Henry Clay or expressed a more ardent wish for the success of the new administration than did the "old hero" at the Hermitage. In a letter written two days after the inauguration he told Polk that

I have the pleasure to congratulate my country on your now being, really, president of the United States, and I put up my prayers to the great Jehova, that he may conduct you thro' your administration with honor to yourself, and benefit to our Glorious Union.

Success could be attained only by "continuing to take principle for your guide, and public good for your end, steering clear of the intrigues & machinations of political clickes."[4] If the General had any misgivings regarding Polk's independence, they must have been removed by the receipt of a letter from Judge Catron—a letter written before his own had reached Washington. "Our friend," wrote the judge, "is very prudent, and *eminently* firm, regardless of consequences. He came here to be—THE

& peace, whither shall he turn? Has the *sword* proved to be a safer and surer instrument of reform than enlightened reason? Does he expect to find among the ruins of this Union a happier abode for our swarming millions, than they now have under its lofty arch & among its beautiful columns? No, my countrymen never, until like the blind Israelite in the Temple of the Philistines, we find ourselves in chains and dispair, shall we be justified in thrusting those pillars from their base; for whenever we do, we shall like him be crushed by their fall.'

"It will be surely ready in time & finished with a polish suitable to the occasion. I shall enclose it to you under an envelope to our friend J. H. Thomas but securely sealed so that he shall [not] be aware of its contents." (Compare the part quoted by Brown with Polk's inaugural. See *Messages*, IV, 376. *Query:* Was Brown quoting from Polk's original draft, or was this paragraph written in Washington and remodeled by Polk?)

On December 26 Brown wrote: "In a few days now I shall hear from our friend K again & be ready to meet your wishes. The Major is here on yesterday we went up to see the President. He is acting very friendly but I shall encourage the idea of his remaining here but a short time or the letter writers will be speculating on the purpose of his visit &c." (*Polk Papers*).

Probably "K" means John Kane, of Philadelphia, but the identity of "our friend" and "the Major" is difficult to conjecture. Major Lewis was not a close friend of either Brown or Polk, and Major Donelson was then in New Orleans.

4 Jackson to Polk, March 6, 1845, *Polk Papers*.

PRESIDENT—which at this date is as undisputed as that you was THE GENL at N. Orleans.''[5]

On March 5 the new President submitted to the Senate his list of cabinet officials. James Buchanan, the Secretary of State, had long been a leader in Pennsylvania politics and for many years a Senator from that state. His selection was a concession to that wing of the party which believed in a moderate protective tariff, and his subsequent opposition to the tariff of 1846 caused the President no little annoyance. He was a man of more than average ability, but he possessed certain traits which made him the source of constant irritation to the President. With a timidity which caused him to quail before responsibility he combined an obstinacy and a petulance which manifested themselves in obstructive tactics and petty insolence. After four years of intimate association Polk concluded that ''Mr. Buchanan is an able man, but is in small matters without judgment and sometimes acts like an old maid.''[6] He was the only member of the cabinet whom the President found it necessary to discipline, and he was the only one whom Polk believed that he could not fully trust. Robert J. Walker, the Secretary of the Treasury, was a man of ability and industry. He was cordially hated by the Whigs and was disliked and distrusted by many Democrats. Originally selected for the office of Attorney General, he was called to the Treasury Department in order to placate the Cass-Dallas element of the party. He was the only member to whom General Jackson offered objections,[7] but Polk had full confidence in both his integrity and his ability. As Secretary of War, William L. Marcy

---

[5] Catron to Jackson, March [1845], *Jackson Papers.*

[6] Polk, *Diary,* IV, 355.

[7] ''*I say to you, in the most confidential manner,* that I regret that you put Mr. R. J. Walker over the Treasury. He has talents, I believe honest, but surrounded by so many broken speculators, and being greatly himself incumbered with debt, that any of the other Departments would have been better, & I fear, you will find my forebodings turn out too true, and added to this, under the rose, he is looking to the vice presidency'' (Jackson to Polk, May 2, 1845, *Polk Papers*).

displayed both ability and tact. He was a leader of that wing of the party in New York which opposed Van Buren, and his appointment greatly imbittered the friends of the ex-President; otherwise his appointment added strength to the administration. George Bancroft, the Secretary of the Navy, had had little experience in practical affairs. His appointment seems to have been a makeshift, and he was soon given a diplomatic position, for which he had originally expressed a preference. His most notable achievement as a cabinet officer was his success in procuring the establishment of the naval academy at Annapolis. John Y. Mason, a college mate of the President, was made Attorney General. He had served as Secretary of the Navy in Tyler's cabinet and was again put in charge of that department when Bancroft was made minister to England. Cave Johnson, the Postmaster General, had for many years been Polk's closest political friend. Although he was not considered to be a brilliant statesman, his good judgment and methodical habits well fitted him for the office assigned to him. He was a democrat *par excellence,* and when a member of Congress he was best known as an enemy of extravagant appropriations. His friends gave him the sobriquet of "watch-dog of the Treasury"; some called him the "scourge of private claimants," and Adams once referred to him as the "retrenchment monsoon."[8]

The appointment of an entirely new[9] cabinet caused general surprise and considerable press comment. None except his intimate friends realized that Polk was a man of unusual determination, and that he was resolved to be President in fact as well as in name. The belief that he would be a mere figurehead— a pliable instrument in the hands of able politicians—had become

---

[8] Adams, *Memoirs,* XI, 223.

[9] Mason, of course, had been a member of Tyler's cabinet, but not in the position assigned to him by Polk. "An entire new Cabinet, at the accession of a new President without a reverse of politics, is a novelty under the present constitution. Rumors of it have been in circulation for some weeks, which I did not believe" (*ibid.,* XII, 180).

so firmly fixed in the public mind that the most convincing evidence to the contrary had little weight. Although it is now well known that Polk dominated his cabinet to a greater degree than most chief executives, so keen an observer as Gideon Welles could at the time write:

In none of his [Polk's] Cabinet, I am sorry to say, have I any confidence. Yet this cabinet appears to me to have more influence and higher authority than any other I have ever known. The Cabinet is a sort of council of appointments, and the President is chairman of this council, instead of being President of the United States. It is, as I wrote our friend Niles, a sort of joint Stock Company in which the President is, by no means the principal partner. *Yet several of them have been at particular pains to tell me that the President has his own way—does as he has a mind to—makes his own appointments &c.* There is not, however, a man in the cabinet, except Johnson, who does not believe himself the superior of the President in abilities & qualifications as a statesman.[10]

Writing in 1860, Claiborne says that Polk's cabinet was "one of the ablest ever assembled around any executive," but that the President himself "can only be regarded as a man of mediocrity."[11] Both statements are exaggerations. Although each member of the cabinet performed well the duties of his office, none except Buchanan, Walker, and Marcy can be included among statesmen of the first rank. On the other hand, an executive who could formulate important and far-reaching policies, and successfully carry them out despite strenuous opposition, could not have been "a man of mediocrity." To say that the President ranked below the members of his cabinet is only to add praise to his executive ability, for, as a recent writer has well said: "In the Cabinet Council Polk was the unmistakable guide and master."[12] Welles had been correctly informed. Undoubtedly the President had "his own way."

---

10 Welles to Van Buren, April 29, 1845, *Van Buren Papers*. The italics are mine.

11 Claiborne, *Life and Correspondence of John A. Quitman*, I, 229–231.

12 Learned, *Some Aspects of the Cabinet Meeting*, 128.

Polk's control over his cabinet was not the result of accident or of incidental circumstances, for, with his usual forethought, he had planned to be "guide and master." Before leaving his home in Tennessee he prepared the draft of a letter a revised copy of which was sent to each prospective member of his cabinet. After calling attention to the "principles and policy" which he expected to carry out it was made very clear that he desired only such advisers as would "cordially co-operate" in effecting his purposes. Each member would be expected to give his time and ability in promoting the success of the present administration; whenever he should feel that he could no longer do so, he would be expected to retire. Should these restrictions prove acceptable, the person addressed was invited to become a member of the cabinet. The following is a copy of this interesting document:

Sir:

The principles and policy which will be observed and maintained during my administration, are embodied in the Resolutions adopted by the Democratic National Convention of Delegates, assembled at Baltimore in May last, and in my Inaugural address this day delivered to my Fellow Citizens.—

In making up my Cabinet I desire to select gentlemen who agree with me in opinion, and who will cordially co-operate with me in carrying out these principles and policy.

In my official action I will myself take no part,—between gentlemen of the Democratic party, who may become aspirants or candidates—to succeed me in the Presidential office, and shall desire that no member of my Cabinet shall do so. Individual preferences it is not expected or desired to limit or restrain.—It is official interference by the dispensation of public patronage or otherwise that I desire to guard against.—Should any member of my Cabinet become a candidate or an aspirant to the Presidency or Vice Presidency, of the United States,—it will be expected upon the happening of such an event, that he will retire from the Cabinet.—

I disapprove the practice which has sometimes prevailed of Cabinet officers absenting themselves for long periods of time from the seat of Government, and leaving the management of their Departments to Chief Clerks—or less responsible persons.—I expect myself to remain constantly at Washington—unless it may be an occasional necessary absence,—and then for a short time,—It is by conforming to this rule,—that the President and his Cabinet can have any assurances that abuses will be prevented—and that the subordinate executive officers connected with them respectively,—will faithfully perform their duty.—

If Sir: you concur with me in these opinions and views, I shall be pleased to have your assistance as a member of my Cabinet; and now tender you the office of   and invite you to take charge of the Department.—

I shall be pleased to receive your answer at your earliest convenience.

I am with great respect

Your Ob't S'v't.[13]

To every item of the program outlined in this letter the President rigidly adhered. He had "his own way" despite the incredulity of Gideon Welles. Catron's above-quoted remark, and not the opinion expressed by Welles, is a true statement of Polk's position as chief executive. Even Welles at a later date, although he continued to underrate the President's ability, was forced to admit that "he had courage and determination and shrank from no labor or responsibility."[14] Claiborne has called Polk a "political martinet":[15] he was likewise something of an executive martinet, but no member of his cabinet except Buchanan seems to have questioned his right to dictate the administrative policy of the government. Quite frequently the Secretary of State tried to substitute his own policies for those of the President, but invariably he was forced to submit to the will of his superior. On several occasions Polk was on the point of dismissing him from the cabinet for violating his pledge to put aside Presidential aspirations.

On questions of importance the President sought freely the advice of his cabinet, members of Congress and private individuals; very often the advice given led to modifications in matters of detail, but, except in very rare instances, the main essentials of his policies were carried into effect as originally planned by

---

[13] On the back is written: "Rough Draft of Letter. To be revised corrected. Jan. 15, 1845" (*Polk Papers*). The revised copy which was sent to Buchanan is printed in his *Works*, VI, 110.

[14] MS "Review of Pol. Hist. of U. S. etc.," *Welles Papers*.

[15] Claiborne, *op. cit.*, 228.

himself. His habit of considering carefully the problems involved before they were presented for discussion left little of importance for his advisers to suggest. He felt keenly the individual responsibility of his office; it followed, therefore, that his own, and not the opinions of others, should dictate the policies to be pursued.

The President yielded his convictions neither easily nor for petty reasons. Politics influenced him. But he seldom forgot principles even though he had to sacrifice the friendship and influence of men as powerful as Senator Benton of Missouri and to some extent the assistance of Buchanan.[16]

Polk was not indulging in idle flourish when he told prospective cabinet members that he would "remain constantly at Washington," for during his entire term he was absent from the capital not more than six weeks.[17] Being a strict sabbatarian he abstained from Sunday labor except in cases of absolute necessity. The other six days of each week were devoted to unremitting toil, and frequently his labors extended far into the night. Near the middle of his official term he noted in his diary:

It is two years ago this day since I left my residence at Columbia, Tennessee, to enter on my duties as President of the U. S. Since that time I have performed great labour and incurred vast responsibilities. In truth, though I occupy a very high position, I am the hardest working man in this country.

A few weeks later he wrote:

This afternoon I took a ride on horseback. It is the first time I have mounted a horse for over six months. I have an excellent saddle-horse, and have been much in the habit of taking exercise on horseback all my life, but have been so incessantly engaged in the onerous and responsible duties of my office for many months past that I have had no time to take such exercise.[18]

---

16 Learned, *op. cit.*, 124.

17 *Ibid.*, 120.

18 Polk, *Diary*, II, 360, 456. A year and a half later his story is the same: "Since my return early in July, 1847, from my Northern tour, I have not been more than two or three miles from my office, and during the whole period (13 months) my labours, responsibilities, and anxieties have been very great" (*ibid.*, IV, 85–86).

The office of President is never a sinecure, yet why, it may be asked, did Polk find it necessary to expend his energies more lavishly than other chief executives. The answer is that he felt under obligation to make himself familiar with all branches of executive government. He alone must bear the responsibility for efficient administration, consequently he alone must direct the affairs of the various departments. Supervision on so vast a scale meant a sacrifice of time and energy, but he had the satisfaction of believing that he had not sacrificed them in vain. We are not left in doubt regarding his feeling of self-reliance, for on September 23, 1848, he observed:

I have not had my full Cabinet together in council since the adjournment of Congress on the 14th of August last. I have conducted the Government without their aid. Indeed, I have become so familiar with the duties and workings of the Government, not only upon general principles, but in most of its intimate details, that I find but little difficulty in doing this. I have made myself acquainted with the duties of the subordinate officers, and have probably given more attention to details than any of my predecessors. It is only occasi[on]ally that a great measure or a new question arises, upon which I desire the aid and advice of my Cabinet. At each meeting of the Cabinet I learn from each member what is being done in his particular Department, and especially if any question of doubt or difficulty has arisen. I have never called for any written opinions from my Cabinet, preferring to take their opinions, after discussion, in Cabinet & in the presence of each other. In this way harmony of opinion is more likely to exist.[19]

Still another passage from his diary may be cited as indicative of his industry and of solicitude lest some duty might go unperformed:

No President who performs his duty faithfully and conscientiously can have any leisure. If he entrusts the details and small matters to subordinates constant errors will occur. I prefer to supervise the whole operations of the Government myself rather than entrust the public business to subordinates and this makes my duties very great.[20]

Although the excerpts just quoted were written during the last year of his administration, Polk's painstaking supervision

---

[19] Polk, *Diary*, IV, 130–131.
[20] *Ibid.*, 261.

of the "whole operations" of the government began as soon as he had entered upon the duties of his office. His searching examination of all documents presented for his signature and his ability to detect errors caused considerable newspaper comment.[21] His thorough knowledge of affairs enabled him to win a wager from the astute Buchanan in an argument concerning proper diplomatic usage.[22]

The introduction of systematic methods in the handling of department affairs added greatly to the efficiency of the administration. On questions of policy Polk preferred oral discussions to written opinions from his cabinet, but each member was required to report regularly on all matters relating to his department. In a circular dated April 11, 1845, he asked the head of each department to furnish him with a monthly report concerning the work of the various bureaus and clerks under his jurisdiction. The tendency of bureau chiefs to favor large expenditures made it necessary for each cabinet officer to "give vigilant attention" to all estimates, and to pare them down whenever possible.[23] Such reports, supplemented by discussions at regular meetings of the cabinet, enabled the President to understand thoroughly the operations of all departments.

As a rule the cabinet met regularly on Tuesdays and Saturdays of each week, and there were frequent special meetings on other days. Frequency of meeting afforded ample opportunity for the consideration of administrative policies. Apparently the President never attempted to interfere with a free expression of opinions, yet by adroitly directing the discussions he was able to

---

[21] For example: "The President is devoted to his official tasks. He signs nothing without the strictest examination, and has frequently, to the confusion of clerks, detected serious errors in the papers sent for his signature" (New York *Evening Post*, May 3, 1845; quoted by the Washington *Union*, May 8).

[22] Polk, *Diary*, III, 97–99. The bet was made in a jesting mood and the President declined to accept his basket of champagne. "I record this incident," said he, "for the purpose of showing how necessary it is for me to give my vigilant attention even to the forms & details of my [subordinates'] duties."

[23] Polk, *Diary*, I, 48, and *passim*.

"have his own way" without causing offense. That his method of dealing with his cabinet resulted in both harmony and unity of purpose is corroborated by the testimony of Buchanan, the most discordant member. "However various our views might have been and often were upon any particular subject when entering the cabinet council," he wrote, in advising Pierce to follow Polk's example, "after mutual consultation and free discussion we never failed to agree at last, except on a few questions, and on these the world never knew that we had differed." More surprising, perhaps, is his praise of the President for having personally directed diplomatic relations. "Mr. Polk," said he, "was a wise man, and after deliberation he had determined that all important questions with foreign nations should be settled in Washington, under his own immediate supervision."[24] Another proof of the President's ability to gain and to retain the good will of his cabinet is contained in a letter written by Bancroft in 1887 after he had made an exhaustive examination of the *Polk Papers:*

His character shines out in them just as the man he was, prudent, far-sighted, bold, excelling any democrat of his day in undeviatingly correct exposition of democratic principles; and, in short, as I think, judging of him as I knew him, and judging of him by the results of his administration, one of the very foremost of our public men and one of the very best and most honest and most successful Presidents the country ever had.[25]

In a letter written during the following year Bancroft again sounded the praises of his former chief and gave the reasons for the success of his administration:

His administration, viewed from the standpoint of results, was perhaps the greatest in our national history, certainly one of the greatest. He succeeded because he insisted on being its centre, and in overruling and guiding all his secretaries to act so as to produce unity and harmony. Those who study his administration will acknowledge how sincere and successful were his efforts, as did those who were contemporary with him.[26]

---

[24] Curtis, *Life of James Buchanan,* II, 72, 76.

[25] Bancroft to J. Geo. Harris, Aug. 30, 1887 (Howe, *Life and Letters of George Bancroft,* I, 294).

[26] Bancroft to J. G. Wilson, March 8, 1888 (Wilson, *The Presidents of the United States,* 230).

With a deep sense of personal integrity and a desire to avoid everything which might impair his absolute independence, Polk declined to accept presents of more than nominal value. Shortly after his inauguration Thomas Lloyd sent him a valuable saddle-horse, but he promptly gave orders that it should be returned to the donor. Another admirer who sent a consignment of wine and other delicacies for the President's table was instructed to send a bill or to take the articles away. It soon became known that he would accept nothing of greater value than a book or a cane. The same rule applied to presents for Mrs. Polk.[27] The same scrupulous regard for propriety is shown in his refusal to invest in government securities a certain sum of money belonging to his nephew and ward, Marshall T. Polk.[28] His public policies were denounced in unmeasured terms, and his political honesty was frequently impugned, but even his enemies credited him with personal integrity and purity of character. His own personal affairs were characterized by simplicity and frugality. This fact has already been noted in the care with which he guarded against exorbitant charges at the time of his inauguration.[29] On the other hand, his generosity is shown by loans and gifts to friends whenever he believed the recipients to be deserving.[30] The improvident beggar was unceremoniously dismissed, for Polk had no sympathy for the man who believes that the world owes him a living.

One of the first purely political questions which required the new President's attention was the establishment of a newspaper which would serve as the "organ" of the administration. We

---

[27] Letters among *Polk Papers;* also, Nelson, *Memorials of Sarah Childress Polk,* 89.

[28] Polk, *Diary,* III, 15–17.

[29] See above, p. 293, note 28. He was, according to a remark in the *Diary,* his "own barbour" (*Diary,* III, 9).

[30] For example, when the news came that Colonel Yell had fallen in the battle of Buena Vista the President wrote: "His eldest son, and perhaps his only son, is now at College at Georgetown, and as my impression is that Col. Yell died poor, I will in that event educate the boy, and shall take great interest in him" (*Diary,* II, 451–452).

have seen that the subject had already been discussed, but nothing definite had been accomplished when Polk entered upon the duties of his office. The refusal of Ritchie to leave Richmond determined the President to procure, if possible, the services of Donelson, for in no case would he consent to make Blair the administration editor. On March 17 he told Jackson in a ''confidential'' letter that

> There is at present no paper here which sustains my administration for its own sake. The Globe it is manifest does not look to the success or the glory of my administration so much as it does to the interests and views of certain prominent men of the party who are looking to succeed me in 1848. The arrangement which above all others I prefer would be that, the owners of the Globe would agree to place it in the hands of a new Editor,—still retaining the proprietorship of the paper if they choose. You may rely upon it, that without such an arrangement, the Democratic party who elected me cannot be kept united three months. If *Maj^r Donelson* would take charge of the Editorial Department—all the sections of the party would be at once reunited and satisfied.

Donelson and Ritchie, he said, were the only ones whom he would permit to edit his government organ.[31]

Within the next two weeks the President ''had full and free conversation with Mr. Blair and in good feeling frankly told him, that it was impossible for the whole party ever to be united in support of the administration whilst the Globe was regarded as the official organ,'' and that he must have a new paper. In sending this information to Donelson on March 28 Polk said that within the last forty-eight hours the whole matter had ''been brought almost to a head.'' Ritchie had been in Washington and Blair had agreed to sell the *Globe* and retire, leaving Ritchie and Donelson to take charge as joint editors. Blair had made but one stipulation, that the arrangement should be delayed until he could consult Van Buren and Jackson; ''he says positively that if *Genl Jackson* assents, he will at once sell and retire.'' After repeating the reasons, already given to Jackson, why he

---

[31] Polk to Jackson, March 17, 1845, *Jackson Papers*.

could not employ the *Globe* and expressing the hope that the arrangement then pending might be effected, he added that "if it should fail I am still deeply convinced that it will be indispensable to have a new paper and I have so informed *Mr. Blair*."[32]

After some further negotiation Blair and Rives consented to dispose of the *Globe* and retire. The purchasers were Thomas Ritchie, of the Richmond *Enquirer*, and John P. Heiss, of Tennessee, formerly editor of the Nashville *Union*. A new paper called the Washington *Union* succeeded the *Globe* with Ritchie as its chief editor and Heiss as its business manager. The daily edition of the new "Polk organ" made its début on May 1, 1845, and a semi-weekly followed four days later. Among the noteworthy features of the initial numbers were a eulogy on the late editors of the *Globe,* and the first installment of "Mrs. Caudle's Curtain Lectures," copied from the London *Punch.* The humor of the lectures may have been the more apparent to ingenuous readers.

General Jackson was quite as unsuccessful in his attempt to make Major William B. Lewis the "ferret" of the Polk administration as in his effort to have Blair retained as editor of the "organ." Lewis had for some time held the office of second auditor of the treasury, and, as he was considered to be a still more treacherous politician than Blair, the new President summarily dismissed him. In a letter to Polk, Lewis stated that he had learned from a private source that

you have intimated that my removal from office was rendered necessary, because the position I occupied was dangerous to the Government, in as much as it would enable me to impart information to a foreign power to the disadvantage of my own country.

He hoped that the report was unfounded but desired to know whether Polk had made such a remark. As the President made no reply to this or to other letters on the same subject, Lewis

---

[32] Polk to Donelson, March 28, 1845, "Polk-Donelson Letters."

left for his home in Tennessee and published the correspondence in a Nashville paper.[33]   Polk's reasons for declining to make explanations are given in a letter to a friend in Tennessee:

As to Maj. Lewis I shall of course enter into no controversy with him. What he desires most is to make himself conspicuous by such a controversy. His course since his removal from office proves his unworthiness of which I had full & ample proof before I dismissed him. . . . [Had Jackson known the reasons he would have approved.][34]

The enforced retirement of Blair and the dismissal of Lewis have been given special notice because many have cited them as evidence to convict Polk of ingratitude and disloyalty to General Jackson—the man to whom, it was said, he owed his own political advancement.   There is little consistency in some of the criticisms relating to this matter.   The man whom the critics denounced for being bold enough to ignore the wishes of "Old Hickory" was, by the same men, said to be weak and temporizing.   Such critics commended Jackson for discarding his old friend Van Buren on account of the Texan question; but they condemned Polk for dismissing his own detractors and obstacles to party success because these detractors happened to be friends of the General.[35]   Jackson himself, when replying to Lewis's complaints, pointed out that the President had the right to fill offices with men in whom *he,* and not others, had confidence.[36]

Although General Jackson was undoubtedly disappointed because his two most intimate friends had been dismissed, their removal does not seem to have impaired his friendship for the President or his desire for the success of the administration. The last letter which the General ever penned was written to

---

[33] The originals are among the *Polk Papers.*   Printed copies may be found in *Niles' Reg.,* LXVIII, 277.

[34] Polk to A. O. P. Nicholson, July 28, 1845, *Polk Papers.*   In a letter to Polk, July 19, J. Geo. Harris expressed the belief that both Blair and Lewis had plotted against Polk.

[35] Claiborne, for example, reflects these contrary opinions of Polk.   See *Life and Correspondence of John A. Quitman,* I, 228–229.

[36] Jackson to Lewis, April 10, 1845 (*Niles' Reg.,* LXVIII, 277).

Polk on June 6, 1845. It expressed not only personal friendship for the President, but warned him that certain rumored acts of Secretary Walker and land speculators might "blow you & your administration sky high." The letter was characteristic of the writer and exhibited his well-known traits—solicitude for his friend and protégé, a wish to supervise public affairs, and a patriotic desire to serve his country, even though his methods were not always of the best. "Here, my son," he said, as he handed it to Andrew Jackson Jr., "read this letter, I want you to be a witness to the fact that I have warned the government against the disaster with which it is threatened—and have done my duty." The letter was mislaid under some papers and not found until October and it was feared it had been stolen. The high value set upon it by the President, as well as his feeling toward the writer, is stated in a letter in which Polk asked that a search be made to recover it:

I shall prize the letter as above all price as being the last ever written by the greatest man of the age in which he lived—a man whose confidence and friendship I was so happy as to have enjoyed from my youth to the latest.[37]

On the question of ousting Whigs from office in order to make room for Democrats, Polk's own views accorded with those of his party,[38] and when making appointments, except a few military positions, political orthodoxy was a *sine qua non*. Despite the importunities of Buchanan, he refused to appoint John

---

[37] Jackson to Polk, June 6; J. Geo. Harris to Polk, June 28; Polk to Nicholson, June 28, 1845, *Polk Papers*. Andrew Jackson, Jr., approved what the President had done and when writing, on October 10, to explain how Jackson's last letter had been mislaid said: *"Our old friend Majr Lewis* has completely killed himself here & I expect else where by his imprudent publications—he is now very sick of it, and well he may be" (*Polk Papers*).

[38] In 1846 an officer who had been notified that he would be removed protested that, although he had once been a Federalist, he had been a Democrat for many years. "Although not the only reason for making the change proper," the President observed, "I have no doubt he is a Whig in all his feelings, and that his patronage is bestowed exclusively on members of that party, as far as he thinks he can do so with safety to himself" (*Diary*, II, 113–114).

M. Read to a place on the Supreme Bench, because that distinguished jurist had once been a Federalist. His remarks in this
connection on the perdurance of original ideas showed his political
sagacity, for Read later deserted the party and became a Republican:

> Mr. Read, I learned, was until within 10 or 12 years ago a leading
> Federalist, and a Representative of that party in the Legislature. Al-
> though he has since that time acted with the Democratic party, I have no
> confidence in the orthodoxy of his political opinions or constitutional
> doctrines, and was therefore unwilling to appoint him to a station for life,
> where he would almost certainly [have] relapsed into his old Federal
> Doctrines & been latitudinarian in his doctrines. I have never known an
> instance of a Federalist who had after arriving at the age of 30 professed
> to change his opinions, who was to be relied on in his constitutional opin-
> ions. All of them who have been appointed to the Supreme Court Bench,
> after having secured a place for life became very soon broadly Federal
> and latitudinarian in all their decisions involving questions of Constitu-
> tional power. Gen'l Jackson had been most unfortunate in his appoint-
> ments to that Bench in this respect. I resolved to appoint no man who
> was not an original Democrat & strict constructionist, and who would be
> less likely to relapse into the Broad Federal doctrines of Judge Marshall
> & Judge Story.[39]

Even Benton's son-in-law, William Carey Jones, was denied an
office because he had once edited a Federalist paper in New
Orleans. Like Jackson, Polk seemed to take it for granted that
honesty, except in very rare cases, was not to be found among
the Whigs, and his naïve remarks about the exceptions which he
discovered are very amusing. Senator Mangrum, for example,
"though a Whig, is a gentleman, and fair & manly in his opposition to my administration." Senator Crittenden, also, "though
differing with me in politics is an honorable gentleman."[40] He
does not, however, seem to have found a Whig honorable enough
to hold an appointive office. Still, though he declined to place
Whigs in appointive offices, he did not, on the other hand, dismiss them for partisan considerations merely. In his diary he

---

39 Polk, *Diary*, I, 137–138.
40 *Ibid.*, III, 381, II, 349.

has noted the gratitude of those whom he had retained in office, despite their political opinions:

Many Whigs whom I retained in office were among those who called. Though many removals & new appointments to fill vacancies have been made by me, my administration has not been proscriptive, and the Whigs who were faithful & good officers, whom I have retained in their places, seem to appreciate my liberality towards them and many of them have called to express their gratitude & to take leave of me.[41]

The independence displayed in dropping Blair and Lewis was characteristic of the policy which Polk endeavored to employ in all matters of patronage. He was soon to discover, however, that the dispenser of offices is by no means a free agent, and that "political considerations" must be taken into account.

Although many at the time alleged that the President had made preëlection pledges to the Tyler and Calhoun factions, there is now no reason for doubting Polk's oft-repeated assertions that he was "under no pledges or commitments"[42] to any of the political cliques. Even so, their wishes could not be wholly disregarded with impunity. Hostile elements within the party had united for the purpose of winning the election, and each was ready to claim its share of the "spoils." Having no assured "administration majority" in Congress, the success of his own program must depend upon his ability to enlist the support of several discordant factions. His effort to deal fairly with all of them resulted in general criticism, for each laid claim to all important offices and resented all favors accorded to its rivals. To have allied himself with any one of these factions would have resulted in disaster; the refusal to do so was attributed to timidity and a temporizing disposition.

It has been noted in the preceding chapter that there were three rather well-defined groups within the Democratic party. The first comprised the followers of Van Buren and Benton; the

---

[41] Polk, *Diary*, March 2, 1849, IV, 360.

[42] For example, Polk to Cave Johnson, Dec. 21, 1844, "Polk-Johnson Letters."

second, the adherents of Calhoun; and the third, that element in the South and West which accepted the leadership of Walker and Cass.[43] Until the appearance of Van Buren's anti-Texas letter nothing had occurred to disturb the harmony which long existed between the Van Burenites and Jackson's followers in Tennessee, consequently Polk had been identified with the first group even though his claim to the Vice-Presidency had met with no cordial response.

Due, no doubt, to this affiliation and to a desire to assuage the disappointment caused by the dropping of Van Buren by the Baltimore convention, Polk turned first to New York when making up his list of cabinet appointments. Wright, as we have already seen, was invited to take charge of the Treasury Department; and when this invitation was declined, Butler, on the advice of Van Buren, was tendered the War portfolio. Rebuffed a second time, Polk ceased his efforts to placate the Van Burenites, and appointed their rival, Marcy, to be Secretary of War. For the sake of harmony within the party he had done all that any self-respecting man in his position could have been expected to do, and if the friends of the ex-President did not receive their proper share of the "loaves and fishes," the blame rested entirely upon their own shoulders. The President's offer, a few months later, to send Van Buren as minister to England was likewise declined, and the attitude of the ex-President and his adherents continued to be one either of sullen reserve or of secret opposition to the administration. When Polk reached New York on his northern tour in July, 1847, Van Buren sent him a verbal invitation to call. Believing the invitation to be a mere "formal courtesy" impelled by public opinion, the President promptly declined to accept it. "The truth is," is the comment in his diary, "Mr. Van Buren became offended with me at the beginning of my administration because I chose to exercise my own judgment in the

---

[43] With characteristic pungency J. Q. Adams divided Democracy into two parts: "Southern Democracy, which is slavery, and Western Democracy, which is knavery" (*Memoirs*, XII, 11).

selection of my own Cabinet, and would not be controlled by him and suffer him to select it for me.''[44]

Although the President could not consent to retain Calhoun in his cabinet, he was prepared at the outset to deal fairly with that wing of the party. The British mission was offered first to Calhoun himself, and after his refusal, to his friends, Elmore and Pickins. But this faction, like the Van Burenites, declined to accept anything because their chief had not been permitted to control the administration.

The Treasury Department with the patronage incident to the office was assigned to Walker as a clear concession to the South and West. The selection of Greer, a friend of Dallas, for the Supreme Bench was likewise a recognition of the claims of this wing of the party. Apparently Cass did not seek an appointive office, but preferred to remain in the Senate.

When selecting federal officers the President did not, of course, overlook his own personal friends. First of all, Cave Johnson was made Postmaster General, and Donelson, after being considered as possible editor of the *Union*, was, on his return from Texas, sent as minister to Berlin. J. George Harris, whose vitriolic pen and exasperating "buzzard" had made the Nashville *Union* so effective a party journal, was made purser in the navy. The loyal but dissolute Laughlin was appointed to be recorder of the general land office as a reward for his services as editor of the Nashville *Union* and for his support of Polk in the Baltimore convention. The President's old friend and former law

---

[44] Polk, *Diary*, III, 74. Polk had received information from many sources concerning the hostility of the Albany regency. For example, Buchanan, who visited Albany in the fall of 1846, reported that, while Governor Wright himself was friendly, Cambreleng and others avoided him. A month later George Bancroft, who had always been a warm friend of Van Buren, after a similar visit informed Polk that New York politicians were hostile to the administration and that Van Buren evinced no desire to renew friendly relations with the President. Although Bancroft had originally suggested the tender to Van Buren of the British mission, he now advised that no further attempt be made to placate the ex-President (Buchanan to Polk, Sept. 5, 1846; Bancroft to Polk, Oct. 4, 1846, *Polk Papers*. Van Buren's correspondents freely criticized the President, *Van Buren Papers, passim*).

partner, Gideon Pillow, who claimed to be mainly responsible for Polk's nomination at Baltimore, was, when the war broke out, made a brigadier-general of volunteers. Even John O. Bradford, whom a Whig bishop had excommunicated for editing the Nashville *Union,* was now rewarded by a pursership in the navy. Most questionable of all, however, in point of propriety, was the appointment of the President's own brother, William H. Polk, to be *chargé d'affaires* at Naples.

Having pointed out that the President, in an effort to promote harmony, assigned to the several factions some of the most desirable appointive positions, and that friendship rather than merit dictated the selection of certain minor officials, we may now consider his general policy in dealing with the public patronage. The patronage incident to the office of chief executive is a source of great power, and for this reason the popular belief seems to be that it is also a source of great pleasure. The corollary is doubtful in any case and certainly is erroneous when applied to Polk, for his administration had not proceeded far before he came to regard patronage and office-seekers as a veritable nightmare.

Polk was a man of very positive ideas, and one of those ideas was that public office is an opportunity for public service. Although in the finesse of practical politics he was no more scrupulous than his fellows, he never regarded any position held by himself as a sinecure and he believed that offices should not be so regarded by others. The keynote of his policy was foreshadowed in the circular letter, already quoted, that was sent to prospective members of his cabinet. He would aid no aspirant for the Presidential nomination in 1848 and he would not permit his subordinates to use their offices for such a purpose; his and their energies must be devoted to the ''principles and policy'' of the existing administration. Determined to devote his whole time to the public service, he required that cabinet members should do likewise; intrusting of important business to chief clerks was not to be tolerated.

In theory, therefore, the President believed office to be an opportunity for present service and not a reward for acts already performed. And if we except the few instances already noted where appointments were made either for personal reasons or in an effort to promote harmony it may be said that Polk, at the beginning of his administration, sincerely endeavored to carry his theory into practice. The more important appointments received his own personal attention, and, in order that he might conserve his time for affairs of state, the selection of minor officials was turned over to his cabinet.[45] The *Union,* soon after its establishment, repelled in an editorial assertions made by politicians that Polk would have to dispense patronage in accordance with the wishes of the various candidates for the Presidency. On the contrary, said the editor, the President, in making his appointments, will take no thought of whether the person is a Van Buren man, a Calhoun man, a Cass man or a Buchanan man. His thought will be simply : ''Is the man honest and capable?'' Two months later the following editorial appeared :

Mr. Polk has avowed and acted, and will continue to act, upon the settled determination not to permit the course of his administration to interfere with, or influence, the selection of a candidate of the democratic party to succeed him. That important duty he will leave to be performed by the people, unbiased and uninfluenced by his official action. Can any portion of the democracy object to this course?[46]

---

[45] Commenting on this policy, *Niles' Register* said: ''The course adopted by President Polk, on taking hold of the helm of state, in relation to the importunities for office which had grown out of an erroneous course admitted by some of his immediate predecessors, seems to have given satisfaction to every body except those who were in full cry for office. We allude to his having announced semi-officially that personal attendance at the seat of government, and personal importunities for office would operate *against* the applicant;—that the papers designed to urge claims for appointment, must be submitted in the first place to the presiding officer of the department to which the office belonged, and must be by him deliberated upon and presented in due form, together with those of all other applicants for the same office, by the chief of the department to the president, for *his* deliberate judgment—with the whole subject before him.

This announcement occasioned a general *scatterfication.* Washington city immediately lost a large proportion of its transient crowd. It is to be hoped the position will be adhered to in its genuine spirit, and with due decision'' (*Niles' Reg.,* LXVIII, 51, March 29, 1845).

[46] Washington *Union,* May 13, July 14, 1845.

Despite the soundness of the President's position, it was already apparent that not only "any portion" but *every* portion of the party was displeased. A few days before the appearance of the latter editorial he had told Silas Wright that dispensing of patronage was his greatest source of annoyance. Concerning the general policy of the administration, said he, there seems to be no complaint, but much dissatisfaction about offices; "I sincerely wish I had no office to bestow."[47] Could he have seen contemporary private correspondence his wish undoubtedly would have been still more emphatic. For example, old line Democrats complained because room had not been made for them by the ousting of all "Federalists," and because Polk and Walker were too busy to see their fellow-citizens. One of them in reporting to Van Buren this sad state of affairs remarked that one "never had to call twice" to obtain an interview with either Jackson or Van Buren.[48] Enraged because he had not fared so well as certain other Tennesseans, Andrew Johnson pronounced Polk's appointments to be the "most *damnable*" ever made by any President,[49] and this fact he attributed to duplicity and the want of moral courage. Nevertheless, it required greater courage to resist importunities than to gratify them, and dissatisfaction from so many sources is but evidence that an attempt was being made to divorce patronage from factional politics, even though that attempt was destined to prove unsuccessful.

We are not left in doubt concerning the President's own opinions on the subject of patronage, for in making daily entries in his diary he seldom neglected to express his loathing for the

[47] Polk to Wright, July 8, 1845, *Polk Papers*.

[48] John P. Sheldon to Van Buren, Oct. 30, 1845, *Van Buren Papers*.

[49] "Take Polk's appointments all and all and they are the most *damnable* set that were ever made by any president since the government was organized, out of Tennessee as well as in it. He has a set of interested *parasites* about him who flatter him till he does not know himself. He seems to be acting on the principle of hanging one old friend for the purpose of making two new ones" (Johnson to ——? [someone in Tennessee], July 22, 1846, *Johnson Papers*).

office-seeker. He had the utmost contempt for those whose "patriotism" consisted solely of a willingness to draw a salary from the government; he regarded them not merely as an incubus but as a serious public menace. The personal boredom caused by listening to their tales became almost intolerable, but Polk was even more exasperated because they prevented him from devoting his time to important governmental affairs.

At the beginning of his administration Polk tried to follow the program announced in the *Union* of making his appointments on the basis of honesty and merit. He attempted also, as we have seen, to conserve his own time by delegating to his cabinet the lesser appointments. But for "practical" reasons he was constrained to modify this salutary program. In the first place his predecessors had made themselves accessible to the public and it was difficult for any President, particularly a Democratic President, suddenly to reverse the precedent. In the second place he had several important measures which could be carried into effect only by the coöperation of Congress, and he soon discovered that such coöperation could not be procured by ignoring the claim of members to their "share" of the patronage. Regardless of his own wishes, therefore, he was forced to give audience to individual office-seekers, and to make many appointments on the recommendation of members of Congress. In order to give a complete history of his patronage tribulations it would be necessary to reproduce his entire diary; some selected passages may serve to illustrate the annoyance experienced not only by Polk but by every chief executive.

Once the horde had been admitted to his presence the President, being a very courteous man, found it difficult to get rid of them. A few months' experience, however, taught him that "the only way to treat them is to be decided & stern." In February, 1846, Washington was infested with an unusually large number of persons "who are so patriotic as to desire to serve their country

by getting into fat offices.''[50] On the anniversary of his inauguration he wrote in his diary:

> I am ready to exclaim will the pressure for office never cease! It is
> one year to-day since I entered on the duties of my office, and still the
> pressure for office has not abated. I most sincerely wish that I had no
> offices to bestow. If I had not it would add much to the happiness and
> comfort of my position. As it is, I have no offices to bestow without
> turning out better men than a large majority of those who seek their
> places.[51]

The inconvenience of possessing a courteous disposition is illustrated by an entry made on June 4, 1846:

> When there are no vacancies it is exceedingly distressing to be com-
> pelled to hear an office [seeker] for an hour tell his story and set forth his
> merits and claims. It is a great and useless consumption of my time, and
> yet I do not see how I am to avoid it without being rude or insulting,
> which it is not in my nature to be.[52]

There were times, however, when politeness ceased to be a
virtue, especially after the same individual had called repeatedly
''on the patriotic business of seeking office.'' After a trying
experience with ''old customers,'' he observed on August 17,
1846:

> I concluded that it was useless to be annoyed by them any longer, and
> I was more than usually stern and summary with them. I said no! this
> morning with a free will and a good grace. The truth is that the persons
> who called to-day, with but few exceptions, were a set of loafers without
> merit. They had been frequently here before, and I find as long as I treat
> them civilly I shall never get clear of them.[53]

If, as the Whigs would have it, Polk needlessly precipitated
the war with Mexico, he suffered ample punishment in the form
of renewed scramble for office. Congressmen now not only sought
places for their constituents, but many of them desired military
positions for themselves. For the sake of harmony the President

---

50 Polk, *Diary,* I, 158 (Jan. 9, 1846); *ibid.,* 255.

51 *Ibid.,* 261.

52 *Ibid.,* 446–447.

53 Polk, *Diary,* II, 85. See also *ibid.,* 105–106.

was ready to suffer much inconvenience, but when it came to a matter of principle he was unyielding. The *Diary* for June 22, 1846, notes that

> The passion for office among members of Congress is very great, if not absolutely disreputable, and greatly embarrasses the operations of the Government. They create offices by their own votes and then seek to fill them themselves. I shall refuse to appoint them, though it be at the almost certain hazard of incurring their displeasure. I shall do so because their appointment would be most corrupting in its tendency. I am aware that by refusing their applications I may reduce my administration to a minority in both Houses of Congress, but if such be the result I shall have the high satisfaction of having discharged my duty in resisting the selfishness of members of Congress, who are willing to abandon their duty to their constituents and provide places for themselves. I will not countenance such selfishness, but will do my duty, and rely on the country for an honest support of my administration.

By December 16, 1846, the unscrupulous methods resorted to by members of Congress in their efforts to procure offices for their clients had become so appalling that Polk began "to distrust the disinterestedness and honesty of all mankind." Complaints and disaffection over petty offices gave him more trouble than did great national policies. "There is," he confided to his diary, "more selfishness and less principle among members of Congress, as well as others, than I had any conception [of] before I became President of the U. S."[54] Every day added new evidence of congressional depravity, and he was "disgusted with the trickery and treachery" exhibited in recommendations for office.[55] The way in which patronage had become a menace to both political parties and to the country is set forth in the entry for January 7, 1847:

> The passion for office and the number of unworthy persons who seek to live on the public is increasing beyond former example, and I now predict that no President of the U. S. of either party will ever again be re-elected. The reason is that the patronage of the Government will destroy the popularity of any President, however well he may administer

---

[54] *Ibid.*, 278–279.
[55] *Ibid.*, 296.

the Government. The office seekers have become so numerous that they hold the balance of power between the two great parties of the country. In every appointment which the President makes he disappoints half a dozen or more applicants and their friends, who actuated by selfish and sordid motives, will prefer any other candidate in the next election, while the person appointed attributes the appointment to his own superior merit and does not even feel obliged by it. The number of office seekers has become so large that they probably hold the balance of power between the two great parties in the country, and if disappointed in getting place under one administration they will readily unite themselves with the party and candidate of the opposite politics, so as to increase their chances for place. Another great difficulty in making appointments which the President encounters is that he cannot tell upon what recommendations to rely. Members of Congress and men of high station in the country sign papers of recommendation, either from interested personal motives or without meaning what they say, and thus the President is often imposed on, and induced to make bad appointments. When he does so the whole responsibility falls on himself, while those who have signed papers of recommendation and misled him, take special care never to avow the agency they have had in the matter, or to assume any part of the responsibility. I have had some remarkable instances of this during my administration. One or two of them I think worthy to be recalled as illustrations of many others. In the recess of Congress shortly after the commencement of my administration I made an appointment upon the letter of recommendation of a senator. I sent the nomination to the Senate at the last session & it was rejected, and, as I learned, at the instance of the same Senator who had made the recommendation. A few days afterwards the Senator called to recommend another person for the same office. I said to him, well, you rejected the man I nominated; O yes, he replied, he was without character & wholly unqualified. I then asked him if he knew upon whose recommendation I had appointed him, to which he replied that he did not. I then handed him his own letter & told him that that was the recommendation upon which I had appointed him. He appeared confused and replied, Well, we are obliged to recommend our constituents when they apply to us. The Senator was Mr. Atcheson of Missouri, and the person appointed & rejected was Mr. Hedges as Surveyor of the port of St. Louis.[56]

A week after the above had been written the begging for office had become "not only disgusting, but almost beyond endurance."

---

[56] *Ibid.*, 313–315. Polk crossed out the last sentence, but undoubtedly Atchison was the Senator in question. Members of Congress frequently signed enthusiastic recommendations for applicants and then sent private letters which requested Polk to pay no heed to the recommendation. The applicant of course blamed Polk when the appointment was not made. See *ibid.*, 278, note.

"I keep my temper," wrote the President, "or rather suppress the indignation which I feel at the sordid and selfish views of the people who continually annoy me about place." The rule which he had adopted under which no member of Congress was to be appointed to office, except diplomatic and high military positions, had already caused twenty disappointed applicants to oppose the measures of the administration; nevertheless he was determined to persist in applying the rule, regardless of consequences. "If God grants me length of days and health," he wrote in desperation, "I will, after the expiration of my term, give a history of the selfish and corrupt considerations which influence the course of public men, as a legacy to posterity. I shall never be profited by it, but those who come after me may be."[57] More than a year later he again expressed his determination to write an exposé of office-seeking,[58] and it is very probable that he would have done so had his death not occurred a few months after his retirement. It would have been an interesting volume, for he possessed both the data and the disposition to do the subject full justice.

The phrenologist who examined Polk in 1839 stated, among other things, that "when he suffers, he suffers most intently." No one who has followed the President's almost daily denunciations of place-hunters will be inclined to deny the truth of this statement. "I was doomed this morning," is the diary entry for February 18, 1847, "to pass through another pressure of importunate office seekers. I am ready to exclaim God deliver me from dispensing the patronage of the Government."[59] His suffering was made the more intense by his efforts to conceal it. His habit

---

[57] Polk, *Diary*, II, 328–330.

[58] Polk, *Diary*, III, 419. "If a kind Providence permits me length of days and health, I will, after I retire from the Presidential office, write the secret and hitherto unknown history of the Government in this respect. It requires great patience & self command to repress the loathing I feel towards a hungry crowd of unworthy office-hunters who often crowd my office."

[59] Polk, *Diary*, II, 382.

of reticence and a desire to preserve his dignity led him, for the most part, to endure the agony in silence; to his diary alone did he communicate his real opinions. "It is enough," he wrote on one occasion, "to exhaust the patience and destroy the good temper of any man on earth, to bear the daily boring which I have to endure. I keep, however, in a good humor as far as it is possible to do so."[60]   It was this same passive exterior which led many to believe that he did not have positive opinions on other subjects.

The severest of weather was no deterrent to the procession of the office-seeking "patriots," for "neither ice nor fire" could stop them. Polk "pushed them off and fought them with both hands like a man fighting fire," but "it has all been in vain."[61] He felt the need of "one of Colt's revolving pistols" to enable him to clear the office so that he might attend to his public duties.[62] Most disgusting of all were those who, on hearing a report of an officer's illness, rushed to the President with an application for the sick man's position, "if he should die." Nearly all of them were "mere loafers who are too lazy to work and wish to be supported by the public"—in a word, "the most contemptible race on earth."[63]   So far as members of Congress were concerned, Senator Breeze, of Illinois, enjoyed the distinction of being the champion pest. "He has," said the President, "no sooner procured an appointment than he sets to work to procure another," and his recommendations were governed by his political interests and not by the public good.[64]

Although Polk fully realized at the time of his inauguration that he was entering upon four years of incessant toil, he undoubtedly, like all who have not held the office, believed the Presidency to be a position of dignity as well as power. The political intrigues and factional jealousies with which he was beset soon

60 Polk, *Diary*, III, 250.

61 Polk, *Diary*, II, 360–361, 383.

62 Polk, *Diary*, IV, 246.

63 Polk, *Diary*, III, 331, IV, 79.

64 Polk, *Diary*, II, 426.

divested the office of much of its glamour; the political necessity of enduring the importunities of the office-seeking horde made it even contemptible. On this subject we may quote his own words:

> The office of President is generally esteemed a very high dignified position, but really I think the public would not so regard it if they could look in occasionally and observe the kind of people by whom I am often annoyed. I cannot seclude myself but must be accessible to my fellow-citizens, and this gives an opportunity to all classes and descriptions of people to obtrude themselves upon me about matters in which the public has not the slightest interest. There is no class of our population by whom I am annoyed so much, or for whom I entertain a more sovereign contempt, than for the professional office-seekers who have besieged me ever since I have been in the Presidential office.[65]

Scarcely less obnoxious than the office-seeker was the casual visitor who had no business to transact but who nevertheless wasted the President's valuable time. Even though he begrudged the time spent in pointless conversation he realized that a refusal to meet callers would cause adverse criticism and weaken his administration. "I feel," said he, "that I am compelled to yield to it, and to deprive myself of the ordinary rest, in order to attend to the indispensable duties which devolve upon me."[66]

Ceremonious notifications of royal births and deaths added their share of irritation to the busy and democratic President. "I confess," he noted on one occasion, "the practice of announcing officially the birth of Foreign Princes to the President of the United States, has always appeared to me to be supremely ridiculous."[67] When his attention was called by Buchanan to a grave

---

[65] Polk, *Piary*, IV, 160–161 (Oct. 19, 1848).

[66] Polk, *Diary*, II, 280–281.

[67] Polk, *Diary*, I, 237. When not too much absorbed in affairs of state, he sometimes saw the funny side as well. E.g. "These ceremonies seem to be regarded as of Great importance by the Ministers of the Foreign Monarchies, though to me they are amusing & ridiculous" (*ibid.*, II, 215–216). The solemn notification of the death in the royal family of Russia struck him as being so ridiculous that he could "scarcely preserve his gravity." "I simply remarked [to the Russian minister] that such occurrences would take place, and at once entered into familiar conversation" (*ibid.*, 374).

communication from the French Minister of Foreign Affairs relating to a dispute between American and French consuls over their claims to precedence, Polk related with approval a story of Jefferson's "pell mell" etiquette, and told Buchanan that "I was not a man of ceremonies, that he and Mr. Guizot might settle the dispute between the consuls in any way they pleased."[68]

Although Polk was not, as is generally believed, devoid of all sense of humor, the austerity of his bearing when President of the United States very naturally gave rise to this belief. His habitual gravity was caused in part by ill health, but still more by the weight of responsibilities. Official cares so filled his mind that no room was left for amusement. This fact is well illustrated by an incident which he has noted in his diary. One day a magician gave an exhibition before a select company at the executive mansion and the President was persuaded by Bancroft and Mrs. Catron to attend. The rest of the company derived much enjoyment from the entertainment, but Polk felt that his time had been unprofitably spent. "I was thinking," he wrote, "more about the Oregon & other public questions which bear on my mind that [than] the tricks of the juggler, and perhaps on that account the majority of the company might think my opinions entitled to but little weight." He could not, like Lincoln, find relaxation in a homely anecdote or in a chapter from some humorous writer. Official cares were constantly on his mind and he had no time for amusements.

The cares of office added much to the gravity of the President's naturally serious disposition. Indeed, he had become, as Claiborne has said, "grave almost to sadness."[69] While he willingly spent his energies in the public service, he longed for the day to arrive when he might relinquish the helm of state; it needed no one-term pledge to prevent him from standing for reëlection. "I have now," he wrote on his fifty-second birthday,

---

[68] Polk, *Diary*, II, 175.

[69] Claiborne, *Life and Correspondence of John A. Quitman*, I, 228.

''passed through two-thirds of my Presidential term, & most heartily wish the remaining third was over, for I am sincerely desirous to have the enjoyment of retirement in private life.''[70]

Polk's success as an executive and as a constructive statesman will, we believe, be made manifest in the chapters which follow. The topics to be considered cover the fields of war, diplomacy, finance, industrial development, and constitutional law. In all of these fields, the President formulated his own policies and, in the main, succeeded in putting them in operation. Soon after his inauguration he announced to George Bancroft that the ''four great measures'' of his administration would be: reduction of the tariff, establishment of an independent treasury, settlement of the Oregon question, and the acquisition of California.[71] He carried out this program in spite of vigorous opposition. And if we except the coercion of Mexico, upon which there is still a difference of opinion, it is the verdict of history that his policies were both praiseworthy and sound.

---

[70] Polk, *Diary*, III, 210.
[71] Schouler, *History of the United States*, IV, 498.

CHAPTER XVI

COMPLETION OF ANNEXATION

As we have noted in a preceding chapter, the joint resolution adopted by Congress on February 28, 1845, authorized the annexation of Texas by either of two methods. Under the first—the House resolution—Congress consented to admit Texas as a state as soon as the government and people of that republic had agreed to annexation and had conformed to certain requirements specified in the resolution. The second method—the so-called Benton plan—provided:

That if the President of the United States shall in his judgment and discretion deem it most advisable, instead of proceeding to submit the foregoing resolution to the Republic of Texas, as an overture on the part of the United States for admission, to negotiate with that Republic.

Three days before Polk's inauguration Tyler, as we have seen, approved the joint resolution and selected the first method —the one specified in the House resolution. On March 3 President Tyler dispatched a messenger with instructions to Donelson, the American *chargé d' affaires,* who was residing temporarily in New Orleans.

The action taken by Tyler did not, of course, effect the annexation of the lone-star republic. There was a possibility,[1] at least, that the new President might recall the messenger and select the Benton alternative of negotiating with Texas. Besides, annexation in any case was contingent on the acceptance of the proposed terms by the government and people of the Texan republic.

---

[1] See p. 318 and note 96.

When Calhoun called upon Polk to inform him that Tyler had decided to select the House resolution, the President-elect declined, as we have seen, to express an opinion. And, if we except the seemingly incredible statements made by Tappan and Blair, he did not reveal his opinions concerning the method of annexation up to the time of his inauguration. He says in his diary[2] that his mind was not fully made up as to the choice of method until he met his cabinet on March 10, 1845; he then decided to select the House resolution, or in other words, to acquiesce in the choice made by Tyler. Additional evidence that he arrived at no decision until he had consulted the cabinet is contained in a private letter written to Donelson on the seventh of March. He said:

A despatch was transmitted to you by the late administration on the 3rd Ins. In two or three days another will be forwarded to you on the same subject by a special messenger. But five members of my Cabinet have been confirmed by the Senate; the remaining members I hope will be confirmed at the next meeting of the Senate. I write now to say that I desire you, not to take any definite action in pursuance of the instructions given in the despatch of the 3rd Inst. until after you receive the one which will be forwarded in two or three days, and by which the instructions will probably be modified. I write you this informal note for the reason that *Mr. Buchanan* the Secretary of State has not entered the duties of his office, and because I desire to have the Cabinet complete before definite action is had on my part.[3]

Just what the President meant by saying that Tyler's instructions would probably be modified we can only conjecture. *Possibly* he may have been contemplating a reversal of Tyler's action, although his statement does not seem to warrant such an inference. More likely he was thinking of the reasoning contained in the instructions sent by his predecessor, for this, as we shall see, was criticized in the official dispatch which soon followed.

---

[2] Polk, *Diary*, IV, 44.

[3] Polk to Donelson, March 7, 1845, "Polk-Donelson Letters." The endorsement on the letter reads: "The President March 7. Recd. from Mr. Pickett on the 19th at New Orleans."

As soon as the decision to proceed under the House resolution had been reached Buchanan, by the President's order, delivered to Almonte, the Mexican minister, an answer to the protest against annexation which that official had addressed to Calhoun. In his letter Almonte characterized annexation as "an act of aggression the most unjust which can be found recorded in the annals of modern history—namely, that of despoiling a friendly nation like Mexico, of a considerable portion of her territory." After asserting that Mexico would exert all of her power in recovering her province of Texas, he concluded by demanding his passports. In reply Buchanan informed Almonte that while President Polk desired to continue friendly relations with Mexico, annexation was "irrevocably decided" so far as the United States was concerned, and that it was too late to raise the question of Texan independence.[4]

On the same day, March 10, Polk sent out another messenger, Governor Archibald Yell, with new instructions for Donelson. The instructions from both Presidents reached the *chargé d' affaires* at New Orleans on March 24, and he set out immediately for Texas.[5]

In the new instructions, Buchanan informed Donelson that Polk did not concur with Tyler in the belief that procedure under the Benton alternative would necessitate the conclusion of a treaty which must be ratified by the Senate, "yet he is sensible that many of the sincere friends of Texas may entertain this opinion." Should this prove to be the case, dissension and delay must be the inevitable result. From all points of view, said Buchanan, the House resolution was to be preferred, therefore he urged Texas to accept it without modification and to trust to sister states for desired adjustments. He desired especially that the public lands of Texas should be transferred to the United

[4] Almonte to Calhoun, March 6; Buchanan to Almonte, March 10, 1845 (Buchanan, *Works*, VI, 118–120).

[5] Donelson to Buchanan, March 24, 1845 (*Sen. Ex. Doc. 1*, 29 Cong., 1 sess., 45, 46).

States so that the federal government might extend its laws over the Indian tribes.[6]

Donelson reached Galveston on March 27 only to find that a British vessel had arrived there a short time before and that the British and French ministers had gone to Washington, Texas, to confer with the government of that republic. As it was rumored that these diplomats carried with them the promise of Mexico's recognition of Texan independence and an offer from England of a favorable commercial treaty, Donelson "put off in a hurry after them." When reporting this information to Polk, Yell said that should General Houston espouse the cause of annexation, President Jones would also support it. Yell had conversed with many Texan leaders, including Memucan Hunt. They talked, he said, of getting the people to demand that congress should be called for the purpose of considering annexation.[7]

Not all of the leaders, however, were pleased with the terms of annexation offered by the United States. Donelson did not believe that the people would acquiesce in annexation unless the proposition were presented to them by their own government, and he thought that President Jones was not in favor of the measure. He was not encouraged by the apparent attitude at the capital when he first reached there, but within a month he was able to report that he considered the question as settled, so far as Texas was concerned.[8]

The people proved to be in favor of annexation, and the leaders could not ignore their wishes;[9] nevertheless, the Texan government could not afford to disregard the wishes of General Houston, and he, at first, assumed a hostile attitude. On his arrival, Donelson found the Texan government disposed to offer objections to the American terms of annexation, and he had

---

[6] Buchanan to Donelson, March 10, 1845, *ibid.*, 35–38.

[7] Yell to Polk, Galveston, March 26, 1845, *Polk Papers.*

[8] Donelson to Buchanan, April 1, 3, May 6, 1845 (*Sen. Doc. 1*, 29 Cong., 1 sess., 47, 51, 56).

[9] Smith, *Annexation of Texas*, 434–435.

reason to believe that, in no small degree, this attitude was due to the hostility of Houston. The ex-President was sojourning at some distance from the seat of government. Donelson paid him a visit in the hope that he might overcome his objections to immediate annexation.

In a letter to Donelson, Houston had said that in the House resolution "the terms are dictated and conditions absolute." Believing that Texas should have something to say about the terms of union, he therefore preferred the Benton alternative of negotiation. The proposed method, in his opinion, left too many things uncertain. He opposed, especially, the cession of Texan property to the United States and the ambiguous character of the northwestern boundary.[10] Donelson reminded Houston that the specifications in the House resolution regarding property, debts, and public lands, were substantially those which had been suggested by Houston himself only a few months before, still the ex-President gave no intimation that he would withdraw his opposition.[11]

However sincere Houston's objections may have been, forces were at work which were likely to modify them. Donelson had brought to Houston a letter from General Jackson which praised the work he had already done and assumed that he would aid in its completion.[12] The immediate effect of this letter was not apparent, but Houston, like Benton, always wished to stand well with "the chief." In addition, he could never quite overcome a lingering desire to be once more under the folds of "old Glory." Then, too, the Washington *Globe* and other newspapers intimated that he might be chosen President of the United States in the

---

[10] Houston to Donelson, April 9, 1845 (*Tex. State Hist. Assn. Quar.*, Oct., 1897, 79 ff). Donelson to Buchanan, April 12, 1845 (*Sen. Doc.* I, 29 Cong., 1 sess., 52).

[11] Donelson to Calhoun, April 24, 1845 (*Rep. Am. Hist. Assn.*, 1899, II, 1029). Houston's memorandum of suggestions is given in Jones, *Republic of Texas*, 414–415.

[12] Jackson to Houston, March 12, 1845 (Yoakum, *History of Texas*, II, 441). See also, Duff Green to Calhoun, Dec. 8, 1844 (*Rep. Am. Hist. Assn.*, 1899, II, 1007).

event of annexation.[13] For the present, however, Houston was obdurate, and Donelson returned to the seat of government to continue the struggle with President Jones and his cabinet.

Although Jones was noncommittal and spoke of offers from Mexico, already there were indications that popular pressure would be brought to bear upon the government.[14] Some, it is said, even threatened to lynch Jones if he should attempt to prevent annexation.[15]

On the first of April Donelson transmitted the proposals of his government to Allen, the Texan Secretary of State, and with them a letter explaining why the House resolution had been selected. President Jones complained about the terms offered in the resolution, but on April 15 he issued a proclamation summoning the Texan congress to convene on the sixteenth of June.[16]

As public opinion in favor of annexation rose to a high pitch, Houston's attitude experienced a noticeable change, and early in May he set out for the Hermitage to visit General Jackson. After conversing with him at Galveston, Yell reported to Polk that the ex-President was now friendly and not the least opposed to annexation—that *"he is now safe."* He is, said Yell, the "Power behind the Throne, greater than the Throne itself." Donelson, in Yell's opinion, deserved much credit for the "heroic work" he had been doing; his relationship to the "old hero" had greatly assisted him in dealing with the Texans.[17] Whatever the reason may have been, Houston's conversion to annexation seems to have been complete, and late in May Jackson wrote with enthusiasm that "Texas comes into the union with a united voice, and Genl

---

13 Smith, *Annexation of Texas,* 439.

14 Letters to Jones from Underwood, Norton, Lubbock, Ashbel Smith, *et al.* (Jones, *Republic of Texas,* 442, 444, 446–449). Jones's endorsements on these letters claim that instead of being opposed to annexation, he was ''its chief author.'' This may be doubted.

15 Smith, *op. cit.,* 441.

16 Donelson to Allen, March 31; same to Buchanan, April 12; Proclamation of April 15, 1845 (*Sen. Doc. 1,* 29 Cong., 1 sess., 48, 52, 54).

17 Yell to Polk, May 5, 1845, *Polk Papers.*

Houston, as I know, puts his shoulders to the wheels to roll it in speedily. I knew British gold could not buy Sam Houston *all* safe & Donelson will have the honor of this important Deed.''[18]

Houston's conversion did not settle the matter. Another difficulty now presented itself. The House resolution required that a convention should be assembled in Texas for the purpose of framing a new state government, but the Texan constitution had, of course, made no provision for such proceeding. President Jones could block annexation by declining to exercise extra-legal authority, and for a time it was feared that he might do so. On May 5, however, Jones issued another proclamation. Admitting his want of authority, he nevertheless *recommended* that delegates be chosen to meet at Austin on July 4 for the purpose of considering the offer made by the United States.[19]

Allen now pointed out to Donelson that acceptance of the American proposal of annexation would very likely result in an invasion from Mexico. He therefore requested that an American army should be brought to Texas so that it might be ready to repel such an invasion.[20] Donelson submitted Allen's request to his government; but Polk and Buchanan had already antici-pated the wishes of Texas, and a promise of protection had been forwarded to Donelson. Buchanan was instructed by the President to say that as soon as Texas shall have accepted the American proposal, ''he will then conceive it to be both his right and his duty to employ the army in defending that State against the attacks of any foreign power.'' A force of three

---

[18] Jackson to Polk, May 26, 1845, *ibid.* Smith thinks it likely that Houston was influenced to some extent by the belief that the United States might seize Texas as it had seized West Florida (Smith, *op. cit.,* 443).

[19] *Sen. Ex. Doc. 1,* 29 Cong., 1 sess., 63–64.

[20] President Jones maintained later that Donelson, by a ''trick,'' had induced Allen to make the request for troops. This may be a misrepre-sentation, yet it is interesting to note that Polk and Buchanan made an offer of troops before they had received Allen's request (Jones, *Republic of Texas,* 53, 457–458). As to misrepresentation, see Smith, *Annexation,* 445, note 21.

thousand men, he said, would immediately be placed on the border, prepared to enter Texas and to act without a moment's delay.[21]

Shortly after this promise to protect Texas had been sent to Donelson a significant article appeared in the Washington *Union*. It may not, of course, have been inspired by the President; but the coupling of the American claims against Mexico and the desire for California with the question of annexing Texas accords so well with Polk's previously announced policy that one is tempted to assume that Ritchie voiced faithfully the views of the administration. Polk and his cabinet, said the article, are fully capable of handling the Texas and Oregon questions. It is uncertain what course Mexico will pursue, but

Her true interest will be found in peace. Let the great measure of annexation be accomplished, and with it the questions of boundary and of claims. But if she madly rushes on to the alternative of war, who shall pretend to set bounds to the consequences?

We infinitely prefer the friendly settlement of the great question now pending. It will secure the peace and welfare of the Mexican nation. It can now be done, and it should now be accomplished. For who can arrest the torrent that will pour onward to the West? The road to California will open to us. Who will stay the march of our western people? Our northern brethren also are looking towards that inviting region with much more interest than those of the South. They, too, will raise the cry of "Westward, ho!" However strongly many of them may now oppose annexation, yet let California be thrown open to their ambition and the torrent even of their population will roll on westwardly to the Pacific.[22]

The preliminary treaty between Texas and Mexico, which had been arranged by Captain Charles Elliot, the British *chargé*, was signed by the executive officers of the former country on the twenty-ninth of March. Under pretext of making a visit to South Carolina, Elliot had, in April, set out for the Mexican capital.[23] His artifice, for the time being, was successful.

---

[21] Donelson to Buchanan, May 6; Buchanan to Donelson, May 23 (*Sen. Ex. Doc. 1*, 29 Cong., 1 sess., 40, 56, 69, ff.).

[22] *Union*, June 2, 1845.

[23] "I shall go out in the 'Electra,'" Elliot wrote to President Jones on April 5, "but *change ships out of sight of land*, and go down in the

Having sent (May 6) to Buchanan the letter in which he stated that Texas desired military protection, Donelson left for New Orleans—partly to get news of conditions in Mexico, and partly to keep track of Elliot. At New Orleans he heard it rumored that a British fleet was coming to aid Mexico. He notified Buchanan immediately and urged that the United States should take steps to protect Texas. "Of course," said he, "if war should be declared against us, Texas will be its theatre, and the earlier we are in possession of the commanding points on the Rio Grande the sooner we shall be able to bring it to a close."[24]

While at Iberville, Donelson read in a New Orleans paper that Captain Elliot had induced Mexico to recognize the independence of Texas if she would agree to remain a separate nation. He returned immediately to Texas. Before starting, however, he dispatched another letter to Secretary Buchanan in which he prophesied that

Texas will be sure to call the proposal recognizing her independence as nothing but a *ruse* on the part of the British government, by which it is hoped that the people of Texas will be led to reject annexation; and the effect will be, still greater unanimity in favor of the United States, and against all interference on the part of Great Britain in a question *truly* American.

He believed that the United States should be prepared for "an immediate blow upon Mexico" in case that country should declare war, and that "Texas will be as ready as we are to defend the 'star spangled banner,' and denounce British dictation."[25]

On his arrival at Galveston, Donelson learned that Elliot was about to leave for Washington, Texas, for the purpose of submitting to the Texan government the plan of recognition to which Mexico had consented. The two men discussed the plan freely,

---

'Eurydice.' By this means I shall be reported as gone to 'Charleston' in the 'Electra,' and so hope to arrive unobserved'' (Jones, *Republic of Texas*, 443). The preliminary treaty is printed on pp. 473–475 of the same volume.

24 Donelson to Buchanan, May 11, 1845 (*Sen. Doc. 1*, 29 Cong., 1 sess., 56).
25 Donelson to Buchanan, May 22, 1845 (*ibid.*, 58–59).

and Donelson was disgusted by the hypocrisy displayed in the representation that the overture for an agreement had come from Texas. "Stripped of diplomatic phrase," he wrote, "this recognition is nothing more nor less than a contrivance of Great Britain to defeat the measure of annexation, or involve Mexico in a war with the United States." Since Mexico was reported to be concentrating troops on the Rio Grande "where Texas has, as yet, established no posts," Texas would probably send a force to remove these intruders and Captain Stockton would be ready to coöperate after the acceptance of annexation. In "addition to the suggestions before made on this subject, I would remark that the route for the infantry or artillery in our service which may be thought requisite on the Rio Grande, should be by *water* and not by *land*." Two days later he wrote again to the Secretary of State. He had just received Buchanan's letter of May 23 which promised protection, but it did not cover the whole ground. If Mexico should invade Texas to the Nueces or farther *before* the convention has had an opportunity to accept the American proposal, "are the United States," he asked, "to stand still and see the country thus invaded, without interposing protection?"[26]

In the same mail with Donelson's dispatches went a letter from Charles A. Wickliffe, Polk's confidential agent in Texas. It informed the President that Captain Elliot was boldly asserting that annexation would be followed immediately by a declaration of war by Mexico. Mexico, said Elliot, would declare war instantly; the United States would blockade the Mexican ports; but Great Britain would not submit to this, and, consequently, there would be war for twenty years. Nevertheless, said the agent, Elliot was fully aware that a majority of the Texans were in favor of annexation. Wickliffe urged that any attempt on the part of Mexico to invade Texas while negotiations for annexation were pending should be repelled with vigor by the United States.[27]

---

[26] Donelson to Buchanan, June 2, 4, 1845, *ibid.*, 64–66.
[27] Wickliffe to Polk, June 4, 1845, *Polk Papers.*

The letter just received from Buchanan authorized Donelson to guarantee protection *after* the American proposal had been accepted, and on June 11, he gave this qualified promise to the Texan Secretary of State. Elliot's bluster thoroughly aroused his indignation, and in his letter to Allen he said that

if Texas cannot be allowed to enjoy the blessings of peace and independence, as one of the sovereign members of the American Union, without asking permission of Mexico or of the monarchies of Europe, the fact is worth volumes of argument in explaining the duty of those who are struggling to maintain a system of government founded on the will and controlled by the authority of the people.[28]

The tone of this letter had a reassuring effect upon the Texans and lessened the hazard of an exercise of independent judgment.

The letters which Donelson and Wickliffe had written on the second and fourth of June procured prompt action on the part of their government. These communications reached Washington on the evening of June 14, and on the following day Polk wrote an interesting and important letter to Donelson. The threatened invasion, said the President,

increases our solicitude concerning the final action by the Congress and Convention of Texas upon our proposition of annexation. In view of the facts disclosed by you, not only as regards the approach of an invading Mexican army—but of the open intermeddling of the British Charge d' affaires with the question of annexation, I have lost no time in causing the most prompt & energetic measures to be adopted here. I am resolved to defend and protect Texas, as far as I possess the power to do so.

This statement makes it clear that Polk did not doubt the genuineness of the British menace, and that he was prepared to meet it at all hazards. He informed Donelson that General Besancon, the bearer of this letter, would be dispatched that night with instructions and that another messenger would be sent at the same time to Fort Jessup, bearing orders for the troops to march at once to the mouth of the Sabine. These

---

28 Donelson to Allen, June 11, 1845 (*Sen. Ex. Doc. 1*, 29 Cong., 1 sess., 71).

troops were to act as Donelson might direct, under his instructions from the Department of State. The *chargé* was told that the steamer *Spencer* had been ordered to leave New York to report to him at Galveston, and that an additional naval force would be sent immediately to the Gulf of Mexico. Polk urged that the Texan convention should, on the day of meeting, pass a general resolution accepting the offer made by the United States. "The moment they do this," said the President,

I shall regard Texas as a part of the Union; all questions of Constitutional power to defend & protect her by driving an invading Mexican Army out of her Territory will be at an end and our land and naval forces will be under orders to do so.

The convention could then proceed with its deliberations in safety, without fear of Mexican invasion or of "British intrigue" . . . . "The assent of the Convention is all we want." The question of employing the army and navy of the United States to repel a Mexican invasion during the interval between the acceptance of annexation by the Texan congress and the meeting of the convention, Polk left to the discretion of Donelson. He expressed the hope that there might be no necessity for exercising such discretion, nevertheless, should anything occur which was calculated to overawe or interfere with the peaceful deliberations of the convention—

then in my judgment the public necessity for our interposition will be such that we should not stand quietly by & permit an invading foreign enemy to occupy or devastate any portion of Texan Territory. Of course I would maintain the Texan title to the extent which she claims it to be & not permit an invading enemy to occupy a foot of the soil East of the *Rio Grande*.[29]

The troops stationed at Fort Jessup could not, as the letter pointed out, reach Texas in time to afford immediate protection to the convention which would assemble on July 4; nevertheless, as a definite statement of Polk's plans and purposes, this letter

[29] Polk to Donelson, June 15, 1845, "Polk-Donelson Letters." Also, a copy in *Polk Papers*.

is extremely interesting. Writing to Donelson on the same day, Buchanan said that Captain Elliot, by obtaining Mexico's consent to annexation, had "deprived that power of the only miserable pretext which it had for a war against the United States."[30]

The troops to be sent from Fort Jessup were commanded by General Zachary Taylor. By a confidential dispatch dated May 28, Marcy had given instructions for the general's guidance, should annexation be accepted by Texas. Taylor sent a messenger to consult with Donelson concerning the necessity of sending troops into Texas and to investigate the resources for their subsistence. Donelson reported to him that all branches of the existing Texan government had assented to annexation, and that the convention would do so on the fourth of July. If any reliance, said he, is to be placed upon the threats made by Mexico and the advice which it may be presumed will be given to her by the British and French governments, "an invasion of Texas may be confidently anticipated"; at all events, the General would be justified in moving to the western frontier in order to give the protection authorized by President Polk. He advised Taylor to transfer the troops from New Orleans directly to Corpus Christi, which is a healthy place and convenient for supplies, "and is the most western point now occupied by Texas." In the same letter Donelson remarked that the "occupation of the country between the Nueces and Rio Grande, you are aware, is a disputed question. Texas holds Corpus Christi; Mexico, Santiago, near the mouth of the Rio Grande."[31]

Von Holst has made much of the phrases just quoted. Isolating them from their context and giving to them an erroneous, or at least an ambiguous, translation, he has used them to substantiate his assertion that Donelson, in this letter which was forwarded by Taylor to Washington, "emphasized the fact that

---

[30] Buchanan to Donelson, June 15, 1845 (Buchanan, *Works*, VI, 174).
[31] Taylor to Adj. Gen., June 18; Donelson to Taylor, June 28, 1845 (*H. Ex. Doc. 60*, 30 Cong., 1 sess., 800, 805).

it was an open question to whom the land between the Nueces and the Rio Grande belonged."[32] His purpose is to show that Polk provoked a war by claiming unjustly a strip of land the ownership of which even his own subordinates had questioned. Whatever may have provoked the war, Donelson's letter conveys no such meaning. As a matter of fact his chief emphasis was placed on the healthful conditions at the places designated and his desire to avoid taking "an offensive attitude in regard to Mexico, without further orders from the government of the United States." Taylor was advised to limit his activities to the defense of Texas unless attacked, in which case he was to drive the Mexicans beyond the Rio Grande. Donelson spoke of *occupation*, not of *ownership*; but even if he had meant the latter, it is clear enough that it was not a "disputed question" so far as he was concerned. The paragraph which contained these phrases was followed by another which said that "the threatened invasion of Texas, however, is founded upon the assumption that Texas has no territory independent of Mexico." Von Holst found it convenient to omit this paragraph, for it did not harmonize with the thesis which he had set out to prove.[33] Donelson's views on the subject had already been expressed very clearly in his letters of May 11 and June 2, above quoted, in which he advised an early occupation of posts on the Rio Grande.

In this same connection, von Holst represents Taylor to have spoken of San Antonio as being situated on the *western boundary* ("redete gar von San Antonio als an der westlichen Grenze gelegen"); whereas the General simply spoke of the immediate occupation of "the western *frontier* (italics mine) of Texas,

---

[32] von Holst, *History of the United States*, German ed., II, 72, Eng. trans., III, 90.

[33] His remark concerning Polk's suppression of facts might well be applied to his own writings: "That his silence about them was deliberately designed is made clearer than day by the false coloring by means of which he manages, without exciting distrust by bold misrepresentations, to give to things which supported his assertion a weight which they did not remotely deserve" (*ibid.*, Eng. trans., III, 89).

from the coast to San Antonio, and ultimately further north."[34] On the same page we are told that the Texan Secretary of War asked Taylor to protect Austin, on the Colorado "da es an der Grenze ist," which the translators have made to read "because it is on the boundary." But the Secretary had written that

The town of Austin where the convention will assemble, and the most of the archives of our government are now deposited, being on the frontier, and exposed to Indian depredations and Mexican invasion, would require protection, as would also San Antonio de Bexar and Corpus Christi.[35]

In justice to von Holst it may be said that *Grenze* is the German equivalent of *boundary,* and that he may have been ignorant of the distinction drawn by Americans between the words *boundary* and *frontier;* and yet, it seems incredible that he could have so misunderstood the letters as a whole as not to have known that the American officials were speaking of a general region, and were not attempting to fix a boundary line. That von Holst himself meant *boundary* when he used the term *Grenze* is shown by the context, and his translators in converting his writings into English have invariably written *boundary* instead of *frontier,* which had been used in the original documents. Were it not for the fact that this writer's version of Polk's policy has influenced both writers and teachers of history, it would hardly be worth while to dwell on his misuse of official documents.

Donelson's belief that Captain Elliot and his government were striving to prevent annexation was by no means unfounded. Great Britain was not willing to extend her interference to the point of risking a war with the United States, but she was determined to apply every possible pressure that stopped short of this limit which she had set for her activities.[36] However, the

---

[34] *Ibid.,* Ger. ed., II, 72. Taylor to Adj. Gen., July 8, 1845 (*H. Ex. Doc. 60,* 30 Cong., 1 sess., 802).

[35] von Holst, *op. cit.,* Ger. ed., II, 72, Eng. trans., III, 90. Cook to Taylor, June 27, 1845 (*H. Doc. 60,* 30 Cong., 1 sess., 804).

[36] E. D. Adams, *British Interests and Activities in Texas,* chap. ix. It has been considered unnecessary, in a biography of Polk, to discuss in detail the acts and the motives of England, France, and Mexico, except in their bearing on Polk's policy. The part played by England is well presented in the volume by Professor Adams just cited.

officious meddling of Captain Elliot and the Mexican threats of invasion caused anxiety in Texas, and fear of the latter led the government to solicit the protection of the United States. By instructing Taylor to send dragoons to San Antonio and infantry to Corpus Christi, Donnelson had inspired the people with a feeling of safety, even though Taylor could not reach these points before the meeting of the convention.[37]

The preliminary treaty which Elliot had arranged between Texas and Mexico[38] provided for the suspension of hostilities until the people of Texas had either accepted or rejected the terms of the agreement. Accordingly, on June 4, President Jones issued his proclamaation declaring a truce. The general effect of this proclamation and of the mystery and secrecy employed by Elliot in bringing the two governments together[39] led the people still more to distrust both men, and, consequently, aided the cause of annexation. Donelson handled the question most skilfully and did much to solidify the sentiment in favor of joining the United States. On the other hand, he very sensibly refrained from doing anything which might antagonize the Texan officials who were still trying to maintain a neutral position.[40] Then, too, the apparent insincerity of Mexico added strength to the annexationists. As soon as President Jones had proclaimed a truce, Bankhead, the British minister in Mexico, pressed that government to issue a similar proclamation. Instead of complying, Cuevas, the Minister of Foreign Affairs, made dire threats of war on Texas.[41] Even those in the lone-star republic who were inclined to oppose annexation could no longer contend that Mexico would peacefully concede independence.

---

[37] Allen to Donelson, June 26; Donelson to Allen, June 30, 1845 (*Sen. Ex. Doc. 1*, 29 Cong., 1 sess., 92, 94). Smith, *Annexation of Texas*, 451.

[38] For a copy of this document see Adams, *op. cit.*, 210–211, or Jones, *Republic of Texas*, 473–475.

[39] Elliot was later reproved by the British Foreign Secretary for the secrecy of his proceedings because they "laid Great Britain open to the charge of intriguing in Texas" (Aberdeen to Elliot, July 3, 1845; cited by Adams, *op. cit.*, 220).

[40] Smith, *Annexation of Texas*, 452–454.

[41] Adams, *British Interests and Activities in Texas*, 221–222.

On June 16 the Texan congress assembled, and President Jones submitted the American joint resolution; two days later he placed before this body the terms of the conditional recognition of independence which Elliot had negotiated with Mexico. On the congress now devolved the duty of choosing between the two proposals; but as Mexico was already threatening war, there was little probability that any arrangement made with that country would be selected. Without loss of time the congress by a unanimous vote agreed to accept the offer made by the United States, and by a similar vote it rejected the proposed treaty with Mexico.[42]

As the time for the meeting of the popular convention approached, it appeared that there might be greater difficulty in winning the approval of that body. In several respects the terms offered by the United States were unacceptable to the Texans. The American joint resolution had not specified a definite boundary, and there were uncertainties regarding public lands, Indian policy, and other details. Some suggested, also, that before it had entered the Union the republic ought to be divided into several states, in order to increase its political importance.[43] On the other hand, Donelson had been instructed by his government to urge upon Texas the wisdom of accepting the proposed terms without modification, and before the meeting of the convention he had spared no effort in shaping public opinion to sanction such a course. In this connection he pointed out that many of the unsatisfactory matters could be adjusted after annexation, while haggling over terms would result in discord and delay.

---

[42] Donelson to Buchanan, June 23, 1845 (*Sen. Ex. Doc. 1*, 29 Cong., 1 sess., 83).

[43] Smith, *Annexation of Texas*, 456–457. General Houston, as we have noted, had had misgivings regarding the boundary question, and although he had left the scene of action Polk deemed it worth while to reassure him on the subject. "You may have no apprehensions," wrote the President, "in regard to your boundary. Texas once a part of the Union & we will maintain all your rights of territory & will not suffer them to be sacrificed" (Polk to Houston (copy), June 6, 1845, *Polk Papers*).

An interesting account of the part played by Donelson and of the attitude of the Texan officials is given in a letter written to Buchanan from Washington, Texas, by John G. Tod. Tod had evidently just arrived in Texas from Washington (D. C.), and his letter is in the form of a daily journal of events from July 1 to July 11, 1845.[44] Donelson, according to Tod, had no doubt whatever that annexation would be consummated, and he could not understand why officials in Washington were so excited about the question. " 'There has,' said he, 'never been any difficulty about it at all. President Jones has always been open and candid upon this subject and there was no room to apprehend trouble and difficulty if it is not created by the management of the matter in Washington.' "[45] Under date of July 2, Tod recorded that Jones, Allen, and Raymond[46] had called on Donelson. "The President and the latter laughed and joked a good deal about the excitement on the Potomac." After this meeting Tod had a long conversation with Jones and told him that Polk and his cabinet had become suspicious because Ashbel Smith, on his way to England, had passed right by Washington without calling on the President. With a remark that he was not responsible for Smith's acts, Jones proceeded to say that there never had been any doubt of or opposition to annexation. With apparent contradiction, however, Tod reported Jones to have said that "Major Donelson had conducted the affair very ably, and if it had not been for his prudence and good management, the last Congress would have involved the measure with much greater obstacles and probably defeated it." After predicting that there would be no war if the United States would "only keep quiet and cool," Jones said that there were two very

[44] *Buchanan Papers.* Tod was a Texas army captain and served as bearer of dispatches. Later, he was employed by Polk as special messenger to carry to President Jones a copy of the joint resolution of Congress which admitted Texas into the Union (Polk, *Diary*, I, 148).

[45] This was written on July 1. Evidently Donelson's opinion of Jones had undergone a change.

[46] Recently the Texan *chargé* at Washington.

unaccountable things connected with annexation: first, that the United States should feel any uneasiness, when the government as well as every man, woman, and child in Texas desired annexation; and second, that Elliot should have entertained any hope that the offer of independence or anything else would prevent Texas from joining the United States. He had, he said, told Elliot that he would lay his offer before the congress and the convention, but that he did not doubt that Texas would be annexed. " 'His object in obtaining the offer which he did from Mexico, was to strengthen the cause of Annexation, and place us on higher grounds with the world. It was truly a great advantage to our cause, that it disarmed Mexico entirely in the estimation of other Nations, and Mexico was fully aware of it.' "[47] Jones's statement that no attempt had been made to deceive Elliot accords with the reports which the British diplomat made to his own government.[48] Houston, also, testified that President Jones had not been guilty of double dealing and denied that European governments had been intriguing in Texas.[49] This denial does not, of course, mean that the ministers of England and France had not done all in their power to prevent annexation; but whether or not their activities amounted to *intrigue* depends upon the definition of the term. "At no time, in no manner," said Ashbel Smith long afterwards,

did the British government attempt to exercise or even hint the remotest wish to exercise any political influence in the affairs of Texas, or to possess any advantage, obtain any facility, enjoy any privilege that was not equally and as fully accorded to every other power in amity with Texas.[50]

On the day preceding that set for the assembling of the convention, some of the delegates, at an informal meeting,

[47] Under date of July 9, Tod said that the people of Texas were surprised because articles in American newspapers—even the Washington *Union*—expressed doubts that Texans sincerely desired annexation.

[48] Adams, *British Interests, etc.*, 216.

[49] J. Geo. Harris to Polk, June 12, 1845, *Polk Papers*. Harris had just seen Houston in Nashville.

[50] Smith, *Reminiscences of the Texas Republic*, 38.

drafted an ordinance expressing assent to the American joint resolution. Thus prepared, the convention, which formally organized on July 4, promptly voted to enter the Union, and by another vote agreed to wear crape for a month in memory of General Jackson. On the tenth, Allen, the Secretary of State, notified Elliot of the action taken by both the congress and the convention. When doing so, he pointed out that "these manifestations hardly admit of a doubt that the incorporation of Texas with the Federal Union is destined to an early consummation."[51] By the end of August the convention had finished drafting a constitution for the new state, and the second Monday in October was fixed as the day on which this constitution as well as the question of accepting the American offer of annexation should be submitted to a vote of the people. By November 10 President Jones was able to announce that the people had approved both annexation and the state constitution.[52]

Since both the government and the people of Texas had accepted the American offer, nothing remained to consummate annexation except formal admission into the Union by the Congress of the United States. When, therefore, Congress met in December, 1845, Polk announced that Texas had agreed to annexation and had submitted her new state constitution. Since this had been done, "the public faith of both parties is solemnly pledged to the compact of their union," and "strong reasons exist" why the new state should be admitted without delay.[53]

On December 10 Douglas reported from the House Committee on Territories a joint resolution which declared Texas to be a

---

[51] Allen to Elliot, July 10, 1845 (*Texas Diplomatic Correspondence*, III, 120). No further action was taken by Great Britain or her representatives, and Mexico was made clearly to understand that England would not support her in the event of trouble with the United States (Adams, *op. cit.*, 224–225).

[52] Smith, *Annexation of Texas*, 459–460. As late as September, W. D. Lee presented credentials as *chargé d' affaires* from the government of Texas, but Polk declined to recognize him in that capacity. Instead, he instructed Buchanan to deal with Lee as the agent of a state (Polk, *Diary*, I, 17–20).

[53] Richardson, *Messages*, IV, 386.

member of the Union on an equal footing with the original states. Although this resolution met with vigorous opposition, it was adopted eventually by a majority of nearly two-thirds. It was transmitted to the Senate where it encountered still further opposition, although there was small prospect that the dissenters would succeed in defeating it. Some of the Senators who had originally opposed annexation now agreed with the President that the national faith had been pledged, and the measure was adopted by a vote of thirty-one to fourteen. Within a short time the laws of the Union were extended over the new state, and the Republic of Texas ceased to exist. One important question, however, remained to be answered: What will Mexico do about it?

CHAPTER XVII

PRELUDE TO THE MEXICAN WAR

Under the promises made by President Polk, Texas, after the action taken by her convention on July 4, was entitled to the protection of the American army and navy. The query was raised at the time—and pressed vigorously by the Whigs afterwards—as to what constituted Texas and, consequently, what the United States was bound to protect. The joint resolution of the American Congress which Texas had just accepted had specified no definite boundary, but had consented to annexation "subject to the adjustment by this government of all questions of boundary that may arise with other governments." By an act passed on December 19, 1836, however, the Texan congress had declared the Rio Grande to be her boundary, although her territory as a department of Mexico had extended only to the Nueces; and early in his administration Polk expressed his determination to maintain the claim set up by Texas. Mexico herself made such a position easier by claiming all of Texas and by making no discrimination, at this time at least, between the land lying west of the Nueces and the rest of Texas. As above noted, however, Donelson did not believe that it would be either wise or necessary to provoke a war with Mexico by at once expelling the Mexican settlers on the east bank of the Rio Grande, or by stationing the military forces beyond the actual settlements made by Texas. But at the same time he made it clear that he did not intend by such a policy to abandon the claim to the Rio Grande as the boundary. On July 11, after his instruction to protect Texas had been made obligatory by the

acceptance of annexation by the convention, he again reverted
to the wisdom of such a policy. He told Buchanan that in his
correspondence with Texas he had avoided any discussion of the
boundary between Texas and Mexico, because the joint resolution
had left the question open, and the preliminary treaty of recognition arranged by Elliot had left the question in the same state.
Jones, in his truce proclamation, had in effect agreed to leave
matters as they were—with Texas in possession of part of this
territory, and Mexico in possession of another part. "What
the Executive of Texas," wrote Donelson, "had determined not
to fight for, but to settle by negotiation, to say the least of it,
could as well be left to the United States on the same conditions."
He added, however, that although he had not deemed it expedient
to discuss the boundary question,

> I have been far from advocating that the claim of Texas to the Rio
> Grande ought not to be maintained. This was not the question. It was
> whether, under the circumstances, we should take a position to make war
> for this claim, in the face of an acknowledgment on the part of this gov-
> ernment that it could be settled by negotiation.

In other words, he did not believe that the promise to protect
Texas made it incumbent upon the United States to expel immediately all Mexicans from the territory. What the United
States would decide to do on her own account was of course
another matter. Far from questioning the validity of the claim
to the Rio Grande as the boundary, Donelson, in the same letter,
suggested the grounds upon which this claim might be based.
They were the revolutionary rights of Texas, the agreement made
by Texas with Santa Anna in 1836, rights under the Louisiana
Purchase, and the capacity of Texas to maintain her claim by
force. The last, he said, Mexico herself had admitted but a short
time ago when she agreed to recognize the independence of
Texas.[1]

---

[1] Donelson to Buchanan, July 11, 1845 (*Sen. Doc. 1*, 29 Cong., 1 sess.,
101–103.)

In his letters to Donelson and Houston, Polk had made it clear that he would insist upon the Rio Grande as the boundary of Texas. The method by which he proposed to deal with the boundary question may be deduced from the instructions sent to the military and naval forces of the United States. It was in effect the same as that proposed by Donelson. On June 15, George Bancroft, temporarily in charge of the War Department, informed Taylor that the Texan convention would, in all probability, accept annexation on July 4, and that Texas would then be a part of the United States. Taylor was ordered to move his troops to the western frontier of Texas, with the Rio Grande as his ultimate destination. On July 8, Taylor was informed by Marcy that Mexico had some military posts on the east side of the Rio Grande, and that these were not to be molested "unless an actual state of war should exist." Similar instructions were sent to Commodore Conner on July 11, and in these Bancroft stated still more explicitly the policy of the administration. As soon as the Texan convention had approved annexation, Conner was to protect Texas like any other part of the United States, but it was the President's desire to avoid aggression and bloodshed.

That you may precisely understand what is meant by the aggression you are instructed to avoid, I will add, that while the annexation of Texas extends our boundary to the Del Norte, the President reserves the vindication of our boundary, if possible, to methods of peace.

For this reason, the Mexicans already on the east side of the river were not to be molested while peace continued. Positions were to be selected with regard to the health of the officers and men, and in "such a manner as will be most likely to disincline Mexico to acts of hostility." Should Mexico declare war, Conner was to dislodge all Mexican troops stationed east of the mouth of the Rio Grande, and *"if your force is sufficient,* [you] will take the castle of San Juan d'Ulla, it being the determination of the President to preserve peace, if possible; and, if war

comes, to recover peace by adopting the most prompt and energetic measures.''[2] A few days later the Washington *Union* said
that it would be ''difficult to estimate'' the importance of Polk's
energetic policy in deterring Mexico from hostile movements,
and in giving confidence to the Texans.[3] On the other hand,
the *National Intelligencer* asserted that Polk had, in order to
induce Texas to accept annexation, made promises which
exceeded his authority under the joint resolution.[4]

A private letter written by Polk late in July to a friend in
Tennessee indicates that the demonstrations, at this time, of
the military and naval forces on the Texas frontier were intended
purely for defensive purposes. After speaking of the Texan
convention and of sending the American forces to protect the
new state, he said: ''I do not however anticipate that Mexico
will be mad enough to declare war. I think she would have done
so but for the appearance of a strong naval force in the Gulf
and our army moving in the direction of her frontier on land.''[5]
The fact that Polk saw such beneficial results from sending the
troops toward the Mexican border doubtless explains why Marcy,
two days later, wrote to Taylor that the President wished him
to station a part of his army, at least, west of the Nueces.[6]   His

---

[2] Bancroft to Conner, July 11, 1845 (*H. Ex. Doc. 60*, 30 Cong., 1 sess.,
232–233. The ''methods of peace'' which the President wished to employ
meant, no doubt, the vigorous pressing of American claims.

[3] ''It was most fortunate that President Polk, and our minister, Mr.
Donelson, were known in Texas to have held, during their whole lives the
most intimate relations with the sage and patriot of the Hermitage, who
had manifested so much solicitude for the re-union of Texas with the
parent country,'' and they knew that ''Young Hickory'' would repel
any interference (*Union*, July 14, 1845).

[4] But, it added, ''why should any thing else be expected than that the
Executive should pay just as little regard to the Joint Resolution as
did they who passed it to the Constitution of the United States'' (*Nat.
Intell.*, July 19, 1845).

[5] Polk to A. O. P. Nicholson, July 28, 1845, *Polk Papers*.

[6] Taylor is still ordered to avoid aggressive measures toward Mexico
as long as peace exists. ''The Rio Grande is claimed to be the boundary
between the two countries, and up to this boundary you are to extend
your protection, only excepting any posts on the eastern side thereof,
which are in the actual occupancy of Mexican settlements over which

object seems to have been to prevent a hostile act on the part of Mexico by showing her at once that the United States would protect Texas to the Rio Grande at all hazards; but at the same time, he wished to avoid acts that might unnecessarily precipitate a war.

On August 6, Taylor was notified by the Adjutant General that although war might not take place he was authorized to call upon Texas for additional troops. Such troops were to be "received into the service of the United States when actually required in the field to repel invasion, actual or menaced, and not before."[7]

On the day after this order was issued, but apparently without knowledge of it, the *National Intelligencer* expressed a fear that the President was about to make war upon Mexico. It admitted that *necessity* might justify Polk in defending Texas, but

the President is quite indefensible, if, in exceeding the measure of the necessity, he keep not strictly on the defensive and within the *settled limits* of the land, whose proper *population* merely, and not its territorial pretensions, it is now necessary to defend. But it is apparent that Texas claimed, and we fear it is equally apparent that the Executive has granted, the occupation of everything up to the Rio Grande; which occupation is nothing short (as everybody knows) of an invasion of Mexico. It is *offensive war*, and *not* the necessary defense of Texas. And should it prove, as we think it will, that the President has gone this additional length, then the President will be MAKING WAR, in the full sense of the word, on his own authority and beyond all plea of need, and even without any thought of asking legislative leave.[8]

This is a succinct statement of the "disputed territory" argument which was arrayed against the President by the Whigs

---

the Republic of Texas did not exercise jurisdiction at the period of annexation or shortly before that event. It is expected that, in selecting the establishment for your troops, you will approach as near the boundary line, the Rio Grande, as prudence will dictate. With this view, the President desires that your position, for a part of your forces at least, should be west of the river Nueces" (*H. Ex. Doc. 60*, 30 Cong., 1 sess., 82–83).

[7] *Ibid.*, 83–84.

[8] *Nat. Intell.*, Aug. 7, 1845.

throughout the war period, and which has found its way into many histories and textbooks. The truth of the Whig assertion will be discussed later in this chapter; at this point it is sufficient to note that Americans, not Mexicans, first raised the cry of "disputed territory" as applied to the land lying between the Nueces and the Rio Grande. Mexico, at this time, laid no greater claim to this land than to the rest of Texas. In her eyes, the crossing of the Sabine was an invasion of Mexico and an act of war. To the assertions made by the *National Intelligencer* the *Union* answered that "Texas assumed by law" all territory to the Rio del Norte, including Santa Fé, to which the *National Intelligencer* retorted that their fears as to the President's position were now fully admitted. In reply to the charge made that going to the Rio Grande would be an offensive and not a defensive act, the *Union*, a few days later, cited a letter written by Robert J. Walker which "proves" that Texas as a part of the Louisiana Purchase had extended to the Rio Grande. It cited also a speech made by Walker in the Senate wherein he had quoted the organic law of Texas which essayed to fix the boundary line. Just how Walker's letters and speeches could *prove* anything it is not easy to see, but the *Union* accepted them as proof and from it argued that Polk was bound to enforce the law to the Rio Grande.[9] The President was far more disturbed by the annoyances of dispensing patronage than by the criticisms of the Whigs, and the success of annexation convinced him more than ever of the wisdom of the method that had been selected.[10]

The officials in Washington were rather in the dark regarding the plans and purposes of Mexico, yet on August 23, Marcy informed Taylor that there "is reason to believe" that Mexico is preparing to invade Texas. Upon what this belief was based

---

[9] *Nat. Intell.*, Aug. 9. *Union*, Aug. 11, 1845. For a discussion of the Spanish boundaries of Texas, see Garrison, *Westward Extension*, chap. vii.

[10] Polk to Senator Haywood, Aug. 9, 1845, *Polk Papers*. He expressed the opinion that Texas would have been lost to the Union had the Benton alternative been selected.

the letter does not state, but it was probably based on information given to the Department of State by Baron Gerolt, the Prussian minister at Washington. In a conversation with George Bancroft, Gerolt said that he had received authentic information from Mexico, under date of June 28, to the effect that Mexico was making preparations to invade Texas. Gerolt's informant stated that General Arista with three thousand men, chiefly cavalry, had been ordered to move toward the Del Norte, while Paredes, the commander-in-chief, and General Felisola, were ready to follow with a force of ten thousand men. Gerolt himself believed that the United States must expect protracted guerrilla warfare. Bancroft at once addressed a letter to Buchanan imparting the above information. Buchanan was away at the time, but Mason, who was acting in his stead, showed the letter to the President. Polk accepted the information as reliable. He thought it likely that the Mexicans would cross the Rio Grande, for the American forces already on the ground would be unable to prevent it. He took steps immediately to send additional forces to Texas, and in a letter to Buchanan he urged the Secretary of State to return as soon as possible to take up his duties, and especially, to hasten the settlement of the Oregon question.[11] Taylor was authorized by Marcy to accept volunteers from certain designated states, and, "should Mexico declare war, or commence hostilities by crossing the Rio Grande with a considerable force," he was to lose no time in letting these states know the number of troops needed.[12] This order was followed a week later by another which was more aggressive in tone. Marcy complained of lack of information regarding the activities of

---

[11] Bancroft to Buchanan, Aug. 7; Polk to Buchanan, Aug. 7, 1845 (Buchanan, *Works*, 223–224). Copy of the latter in *Polk Papers*. Buchanan did not share the President's apprehensions caused by Gerolt's information and views. In reply to Polk's letter he stated his belief that the American forces on the Rio Grande should be strengthened, but that the movement of the Mexican troops was mainly a demonstration to insure Herrera's election (Buchanan to Polk, Aug. 11, 1845, *Polk Papers*).

[12] Marcy to Taylor, Aug. 23, 1845 (*H. Ex. Doc. 60*, 30 Cong., 1 sess., 84–85).

Mexico and urged Taylor to write frequently to the War Department. "You have been advised," said Marcy,

that the assembling of a large Mexican army on the borders of Texas, and crossing the Rio Grande with a considerable force, will be regarded by the Executive here as an invasion of the United States, and the commencement of hostilities. An *attempt* to cross that river with such a force will also be considered in the same light.

In case of war, "either declared or made manifest by hostile acts," Taylor's main object was to be the protection of Texas, but in pursuit of this object he was authorized to cross the Rio Grande and take Matamoras and other places.[13] Polk at this time considered the propriety of convening Congress in the event of a declaration of war or an invasion of Texas by Mexico, but Senator Bagby, of Alabama, and perhaps others, advised against such a course.[14] The new order to Taylor was decided upon at a cabinet meeting held on the twenty-ninth of August.[15] It did not, however, result from any sudden panic in administration circles,[16] and Polk has been condemned for holding that even an attempt to cross the river would be an act of war. He has been condemned also for asserting that the crossing of that river by a Mexican army would be "an invasion of the United States."[17] But if it be conceded that Texas extended to the Rio Grande, then the ground taken in the new order was no more aggressive than that taken in the former. It was certainly the duty of the President to defend Texas, and if Texas did extend to the Rio Grande, an attempt to cross the river would indicate the disposition of Mexico to invade the United States quite as well as the actual crossing. Nations do not wait until a hostile fleet is within the three-mile jurisdiction limit before steps are

---

[13] Marcy to Taylor, Aug. 30, 1845, *ibid.*, 88–89.

[14] Polk, *Diary*, I, 12–13.

[15] *Ibid.*, 8–10.

[16] The Adjutant General had written only three days before, August 26, that the country was filled with rumors of movements of Mexican troops, but that they were believed to be exaggerated or untrue (*H. Ex. Doc. 60*, 30 Cong., 1 sess., 87).

[17] E. g., von Holst, *History of the United States* (Eng. ed.), III, 98–103.

taken to repel it. Why should they take greater chances when an invasion by land is threatened?

Whether the land on the east bank of the Rio Grande *was* legally a part of the United States is open to more serious question. From the first, Polk had claimed it to be a part of Texas and consequently of the United States. His right to do so involves points of constitutional law which the writer will not attempt to determine, although some phases of annexation may be recalled in order to indicate the questions upon which such a determination must be based. The joint resolution under which Texas had been annexed did not specify any territorial limits, but left that matter "subject to the adjustment by this government of all questions of boundary that may arise with other governments." The Texan claim to the Rio Grande rested mainly on the agreement made with Santa Anna after his defeat at San Jacinto in which he agreed to withdraw beyond the Rio Grande,[18] and on the act passed by the Texan Congress on December 19, 1836, which had declared that river to be the boundary of the republic. Whatever claim these transactions may have established passed, of course, to the United States. Without attempting to determine the effect of these events on the legal right of Texas to all land east of the Rio Grande, it may be noted that Santa Anna made his agreement under duress and perhaps without authority; and it is by no means certain that Texas could lawfully enlarge her territory by an ordinary legislative enactment. The United States government claimed, also, that Texas as a part of the Louisiana Purchase had extended to the Rio Grande; but, as Abraham Lincoln exclaimed in Congress, "what, under heaven, had that to do with the present boundary between us and Mexico?"[19] All claim to this region had been transferred to Spain by the Florida treaty of 1819. Congress, when passing the joint resolution, had left the boundary for future settlement;

---

[18] This agreement is printed in *Niles' Register*, L, 336.
[19] Lincoln, *Works* (Tandy ed.), I, 322.

and both Texas and Mexico, in the project of a treaty had, in March, 1845, agreed to settle the question by negotiation. By declaring all land east of the Rio Grande to be a part of the United States Polk may, indeed, have exceeded his authority, but it does not follow necessarily from this, so long as Texas asserted ownership, that the President was under no obligation to prevent a hostile army from entering the territory until the question of title could be determined. General Jackson and his loyal adherents had always held that the United States could never be adequately protected until it extended to the Rio Grande, and Polk had promised the Texans to maintain this boundary. Apparently the President attached more importance to these considerations than to an analysis of his constitutional powers.

Various letters written by General Taylor after his arrival in Texas in July, 1845, informed the Adjutant General of rumors that Mexico was preparing to invade Texas. As time passed, however, he came to regard these rumors as groundless, and by September he reported that reliable agents had ascertained that the Mexican government was not mobilizing its forces on the border. Taylor believed that the assembling of the American army along the Nueces had had a deterrent effect upon the Mexicans, but in October he advised a forward movement to the Rio Grande. "It is with great deference," he wrote to the Adjutant General,

that I make any suggestions on topics which may become matter of delicate negotiation; but if our government, in settling the question of boundary, makes the line of the Rio Grande an ultimatum, I cannot doubt that the settlement will be greatly facilitated and hastened by our taking possession at once of one or two points on or quite near that river. Our strength and state of preparation should be displayed in a manner not to be mistaken.

As Mexico had not yet either declared war or committed any overt act of hostility, he did not feel authorized to take this step without further orders from the War Department.[20] In a letter

---

[20] Taylor to Jones, Oct. 4, 1845 (*H. Ex. Doc. 60*, 30 Cong., 1 sess., 108).

dated October 16 Marcy suggested to Taylor the expediency of putting his army into winter huts, but in this as in other military matters the general was given wide discretion. By the first of November Taylor had received this letter, and on the fifth a letter from Commodore Conner informed him that W. S. Parrott had set out for Washington bearing a message that Mexico was willing to negotiate the questions in dispute between the two countries. Taylor deemed it unnecessary to build winter huts for his troops, but, with negotiations about to begin, he did not believe himself authorized to move to the Rio Grande. He nevertheless urged the occupation of posts on the boundary line at the earliest possible date.[21] Parrott was Polk's confidential agent in Mexico. He had been selected for this position soon after Almonte, the Mexican minister at Washington, had demanded his passports, and, on April 3, 1845, had taken passage on the same steamer that carried Almonte from New York to Mexico. He had at one time practiced dentistry in Mexico, and, later, had engaged in business there. He held a much inflated claim against the Mexican government, but of this Polk was probably not aware.[22] His selection was due no doubt to his knowledge of the Spanish language, for otherwise he was ill fitted for such a mission. Parrott's instructions bore the date of March 28, 1845, and at that time the President seems to have believed an immediate declaration of war by Mexico to be highly probable. On his arrival at Vera Cruz, if he should find that Mexico had actually commenced open hostilities against the United States, Parrott was to return immediately. In that case the administration was determined to "act promptly and vigorously in maintaining the rights and honor of the country." Should hostilities not have begun, the main object of his mission was to ascertain whether Mexico would renew diplomatic relations, and to do everything that could discreetly be done to

[21] Marcy to Taylor, Oct. 16; Conner to Taylor, Oct. 24; Taylor to Jones, Nov. 7, 1845 (*ibid.*, 89, 111, 112).
[22] Reeves, *American Diplomacy under Tyler and Polk*, 268–269.

bring this about. He was to get in touch with the high officials, if possible, and to let them know that, while Texas under no circumstances could be abandoned, the United States was prepared to settle other questions "in a liberal and friendly spirit." He was not to disclose his official character until it had been clearly ascertained that Mexico was ready to renew diplomatic relations, but the nature of his mission was soon discovered by the Mexican government.[23] The "liberal and friendly spirit" included, no doubt, the purchase of Cailfornia and New Mexico, although there seems to be no direct evidence that plans for such a purchase had been definitely formulated at this early date. In his correspondence with Buchanan, however, Parrott emphasized the danger of the seizure of Upper California by Great Britain. He did not believe that Mexico would go to war with the United States on account of Texas, but he nevertheless recommended a chastisement of that country. On August 26, he reported that Herrera and his new cabinet would not go to war, and that there was a desire, even publicly manifested, to receive a "commissioner" from the United States. He believed that an "Envoy possessing suitable qualifications for this Court might with comparative ease settle *over a breakfast* the most important national question."[24] Parrott's dispatch and others sent by John Black, United States consul at Mexico, and by F. M. Dimond, United States consul at Vera Cruz, of similar import, were discussed at a cabinet meeting held on September 16. It should be noted that Parrott used both terms, *commissioner* and *envoy*, for it is possible that this may have misled President Polk as to the desire of the Mexican government. At any rate Polk chose to regard Parrott's statement as assurance that Mexico would receive a "minister," and he determined at once to send an official of that character. It would be interesting to know

[23] Buchanan to Parrott, March 28, 1845 (Buchanan *Works*, VI, 132–134); Reeves, *op. cit.*, 269–270.

[24] Parrott to Buchanan, Aug. 26, 1845; quoted by Reeves, *op. cit.*, 271.

whether Polk had really been misled by Parrott's letter or whether he deliberately determined to send a regular minister regardless of the wishes of Mexico, for the nature of the credentials given to the American diplomat was later given by Mexico as the reason for declining to receive him. At the cabinet meeting just mentioned, it was decided that the mission should be offered to John Slidell, of New Orleans. The President recorded in his diary that one great object of the mission would be

> to adjust a permanent boundary between Mexico and the U. States, and in doing this the Minister would be instructed to purchase for a pecuniary consideration Upper California and New Mexico. He [the President] said that a better boundary would be the Del Norte from its mouth to the Passo [El Paso], in latitude 32° North, and thence West to the Pacific Ocean, Mexico ceding to the U. S. all the country East and North of these lines.

He believed that such a boundary might be procured for fifteen or twenty millions of dollars, but he was willing to pay as high as forty millions.[25] Here is an explicit statement of Polk's determination to purchase California, if possible. He probably had this method in mind when, shortly after his inauguration, he declared to Bancroft[26] that one of the great measures of his administration would be the acquisition of that country.

News of recent threats of war by the Mexican government, published in the New Orleans papers, led Polk to believe that Parrott had been mistaken, and he decided that it would be inexpedient to send Slidell until the facts could be ascertained. However, he wrote a confidential letter to Slidell asking him to accept the appointment and to be ready to leave for Mexico on a day's notice.[27]

About a month later the President sent for Benton, and sought his advice concerning both Oregon and California, although there had been no intercourse between the two men since the Missouri Senator had so bitterly denounced the rejection

---

[25] Polk, *Diary*, I, 33–35. [27] Polk, *Diary*, I, 35–36.
[26] See page 351.

of Van Buren by the Baltimore Convention. He told Benton that he thought of reasserting the Monroe doctrine against the planting of any foreign colony on the North American continent. His immediate object was to forestall any contemplated British colony in California. Benton approved such a course, generally, but doubted that the doctrine could be applied to the Frazer River valley in which the British had made discoveries and settlements.[28] Polk's anxiety about California had been increased by a dispatch received from Thomas O. Larkin, American consul at Monterey, California, which bore the date of July 10, 1845.[29] This dispatch stated that the agent of the Hudson's Bay Company had formerly furnished the Californians with arms and money to enable them to expel the Mexicans from that country, but that now Great Britain was instigating a Mexican invasion of California. He stated, also, that England maintained a vice-consul and France a consul in California, although they apparently transacted no commercial business. It was inferred from this that the two governments had designs on that province.

While he awaited developments in Mexico before sending instructions and a commission to Slidell, and influenced probably by the news received from the consul at Monterey, the President caused Buchanan to write a letter to Larkin, under date of October 17, 1845. Larkin was already consul at Monterey, and he was now, in addition, made a confidential agent in California. Polk's desire for California and the method by which he hoped to acquire it are made very clear in this letter. It is made equally clear that whether or not he should be able to acquire it for the United States, he was determined to resist its transfer to either Great Britain or France. "The future destiny" of California, wrote Buchanan, "is a subject of anxious solicitude for the Government and people of the United States." For this

---

28 *Ibid.*, 70–71.

29 Mentioned in Buchanan's letter to Larkin, Oct. 17, 1845, *infra.*

reason the President "could not view with indifference the transfer of California to Great Britain or any other Power. The system of colonization by foreign Monarchies on the North American continent must and will be resisted by the United States." Larkin was told that "this Government had no ambitious aspirations to gratify and no desire to extend our federal system over more territory than we already possess, unless by the free and spontaneous wish of the independent people of adjoining territories." After reiterating that the United States would "vigorously interpose" to prevent California from becoming a British or a French colony, Buchanan continued:

Whilst the President will make no effort and use no influence to induce California to become one of the free and independent States of this Union, yet if the people should desire to unite their destiny with ours, they would be received as brethren, whenever this can be done without affording Mexico just cause of complaint. Their true policy for the present in regard to this question, is to let events take their course, unless an attempt should be made to transfer them without their consent either to Great Britain or France. This they ought to resist by all the means in their power, as ruinous to their best interests and destructive of their freedom and independence.

Larkin was asked to assure the Californians of the friendship of the United States and to ascertain their feelings toward this and other countries. He was instructed further to gather various statistics and to inform his government generally regarding affairs in California.[30] Clearly Polk had hopes that the Texas program might be reënacted in California. Apparently, no conquest of this region was contemplated, unless, perhaps Great Britain or France should attempt to seize or colonize it. He was willing, of course, to purchase both California and New Mexico and thereby settle the whole question both peaceably and speedily. His constitutional authority to declare the so-called "disputed territory" to be a part of the United States has been

---

[30] Buchanan to Larkin, Oct. 17, 1845, brought to California by Commodore Stockton (MS in *Larkin Papers*, Bancroft Library, Univ. of Calif.) There is a printed copy in Buchanan, *Works*, VI, 275–278.

seriously questioned; it may be questioned, also, whether his promise to "receive as brethren" the Californians was not a stretching of executive powers.

The President appointed Lieutenant Archibald H. Gillespie, of the marine corps, confidential agent and assigned to him the duty of repairing to California to coöperate with Larkin. He was given a copy of the written instructions to Larkin, and was made the bearer of verbal instructions to both Larkin and Fremont. Just what these verbal instructions were no one has been able to ascertain with any degree of certainty. Buchanan's letter to Larkin bore the date October 17, but Gillespie was still in Washington as late as October 30. On that date Polk recorded in his diary that he had just held a confidential conversation with Gillespie concerning his secret mission, and added that "his secret instructions & the letter to Mr. Larkin,—will explain the object of his mission."[31] The letter to Larkin tells its own story, but the "secret instructions" to Gillespie have been the subject of considerable speculation. The latter will be considered in connection with the operations of Fremont.

The President did not confine his activities with respect to California to the sending of Gillespie with instructions for the consul at Monterey. While Buchanan was preparing these instructions, Bancroft, by the President's order, was inditing secret orders for Commodores Stockton and Sloat. These, too, were given the official date of October 17, 1845.

Commodore John D. Sloat had been for some time in command of the naval forces on the Pacific, and as early as June 24 Bancroft had sent him "secret and confidential" orders to seize San Francisco and blockade other ports, if he should "ascertain with certainty" that Mexico had declared war against the United States.[32] By the order of October 17 he was told that "in the event of actual hostilities" he was to dispose of his entire force

---

[31] Polk, *Diary*, I, 83–84.
[32] *H. Ex. Doc. 60*, 30 Cong., 1 sess., 231.

"so as to carry out most effectually the objects specified in the instructions forwarded to you from the Department in view of such a contingency."[33]

Commodore Robert F. Stockton was given command of the frigate *Congress* which had been equipped at Norfolk for duty in the Pacific. His sealed orders, which were not to be opened until he had passed beyond "the Capes of Virginia," directed him to proceed to the Sandwich Islands, and, eventually, to join the squadron of Commodore Sloat. To Stockton were intrusted the originals of the instructions to Sloat and Larkin, duplicates of which, as we have seen, were sent overland in care of Lieutenant Gillespie.

On November 9, 1845, Parrott reached Washington bearing a note from the Mexican Secretary of Foreign Affairs which expressed the willingness of his government to receive a commissioner from the United States.[34] Three days before Parrott's letter arrived, however, Bancroft had received a dispatch from Commodore Conner which stated that Mexico was willing to negotiate, and the President had directed Buchanan immediately to prepare instructions for Slidell. Slidell's commission was signed on the tenth, and this with his instructions was conveyed to him by Lieutenant Lanier of the navy. Parrott was selected as his secretary of legation.[35]

Slidell's instructions were an elaboration of the plans for territorial expansion which the President had laid before his cabinet on the sixteenth of September.[36] To Larkin had been assigned the task of winning the good will of the Californians, and of letting them know that they would be welcomed into the

---

[33] See Rives, *United States and Mexico*, II, 168.

[34] Polk, *Diary*, I, 93. Polk says that Mexico agreed to receive a *minister*. This, however, is an error, for the Secretary clearly said a "commissioner" . . . "to settle the present dispute" (Peña y Peña to Black, Oct. 15, 1845, in *H. Ex. Doc. 60*, 30 Cong., 1 sess., 16).

[35] Polk, *Diary*, I, 91–94.

[36] See above, p. 385.

Union should they see fit to declare their independence; to
Slidell authority was given to adjust the boundary question, and
to purchase New Mexico and California, if possible. Taken
together these documents indicate the ardent desire of the President to extend the United States to the Pacific, as well as the
methods by which he hoped to accomplish his purpose.

The instructions to Slidell first of all reiterated the substance
of the Monroe Doctrine and insisted that the United States could
not permit the establishment of European colonies in North
America. He was instructed to notify Mexico that the United
States had waited long and patiently for Mexico to pay the just
claims of American citizens, but that "these claims must now
speedily be adjusted in a satisfactory manner." It was well
known, Buchanan pointed out, that Mexico could not pay in
money, but "fortunately" the provision in the joint resolution
of annexation relating to the adjustment of boundaries presented
a means of satisfying these claims, "in perfect consistency with
the interests as well as the honor of both Republics." The means
was the assumption of the claims by the government of the United
States, and the cession of territory by Mexico as a compensation
therefor. With this introduction Buchanan proceeded to discuss
boundaries and the lands that might be claimed or purchased.
The independence and the annexation of Texas must be considered
as settled facts. The United States based her claim to the Rio
Grande as the boundary of Texas on the act passed by the Texan
Congress on December 19, 1836, and on the fact that that river
had been the boundary of the Louisiana Purchase; although
Buchanan himself admitted that all rights under the latter had
been transferred to Spain in 1819 by the Florida treaty. He did
not claim that New Mexico had belonged to Texas or had come
with that republic into the possession of the United States. To
"obviate the danger of future collisions," however, the American government would, in exchange for it, assume all claims of
her citizens against Mexico and pay in addition five millions of

dollars. In case Mexico should be unwilling to cede any lands west of the Rio Grande, then the claims would be assumed but the five millions would not be paid. If either of these objects could be attained, Slidell was authorized to conclude a treaty with Mexico.

Reeves, in his *American Diplomacy under Tyler and Polk,* makes the over-confident assertion that

Parrott's mission and Slidell's instructions taken together prove two things: (1) that the Mexican War was *not* the result of the annexation of Texas, and (2) that the reopening of diplomatic relations with Mexico was for the purpose of securing California by purchase.[37]

That one of the motives for seeking to reopen diplomatic relations was the desire to purchase California may be granted at once. But precisely how Parrott's mission and Slidell's instructions *prove* that the acquisition of this region was the main purpose of the administration, or that war did not result from the annexation of Texas the present writer is unable to see. Other evidence, which will be offered presently, indicates that Polk decided to wage war because Mexico had failed to satisfy the American claims; but instead of proving that the Mexican war was waged "for the fulfillment of Polk's designs upon California,"[38] Slidell's instructions indicate that the President, at the time these instructions were drafted, was ready to release Mexico from further obligation if she would cede only a part of New Mexico. Should he find it impossible to make better terms, Slidell was specifically authorized to conclude a treaty by which the United States would assume all claims if Mexico in return would cede that part of New Mexico lying east of the Rio Grande. Had Slidell been able to conclude such a treaty, Polk would have been deprived of all means of bringing pressure to bear on Mexico, except unprovoked military conquest. To be sure, the President was eager to acquire California. Larkin had been

---

37 Reeves, 275. He is speaking here of Slidell's original instructions.
38 *Ibid.,* 288.

instructed to assure the Californians that they would be welcomed into the Union should they see fit to separate from Mexico, and now Slidell was instructed to purchase that territory, and was told that "money would be no object when compared with the value of the acquisition." He was told, also, that his mission was "one of the most delicate and important which has ever been confided to a citizen of the United States," nevertheless there was not the slightest hint that the President had any intention of resorting to force in the event that Mexico should refuse her consent to the sale. On the contrary, as above noted, Slidell was to conclude a treaty which would assume all claims even though Mexico should confine her cession to territory on the east side of the Rio Grande. It would seem that, at this time, Polk's plan to acquire California was limited to purchase or to "manifest destiny" of the type that had succeeded so well in Texas. The outbreak of war was soon followed by the conquest of California, but this fact alone does not prove that the war "was waged for the purpose of conquest, for the fulfillment of Polk's designs upon California." Polk may have welcomed the war—possibly he may have provoked it—but his offer to cancel the claims for so small a tract of land seems to show that forcible conquest was not his intention at the time that Slidell was sent to Mexico.

Slidell was sent to Mexico in the capacity of envoy extraordinary and minister plenipotentiary, not simply as a commissioner to settle disputes incident to the annexation of Texas. The reception of a minister would have the effect of fully restoring diplomatic relations and of paving the way for the discussion of all questions concerning which that minister might bear instructions—unpaid claims, for example. For this reason Mexico declined to receive Slidell. According to a statement made long afterwards by Bejamin E. Green,[39] secretary of legation

---

[39] The statement is dated Aug. 8, 1889 (Tyler, *Letters and Times of the Tylers*, III, 176).

at Mexico in 1844, President Polk had been informed, before sending Slidell, that President Herrera would receive a commissioner, and that he was ready to settle all disputes and to cede New Mexico and California to the United States. He was told, on the other hand, according to the same statement, that the Herrera government doubted its ability to sustain itself against the power of Santa Anna if it should receive an ordinary minister as though nothing had happened. If this be true, then Polk must have known that, in all probability, Slidell would not be received, and his sincerity in sending the envoy may be seriously questioned. But it seems incredible that the President would deliberately jeopardize the success of a mission which promised to procure everything he could desire, even California, simply to gratify a whim of sending to Mexico the particular kind of a diplomatic agent which she did not want. Some allowance should be made for the fact that Green's statement was made many years after the event and that he was the son of Duff Green, the champion of Calhoun and the uncompromising opponent of Polk.[40]

On December 2, 1845, before the American envoy had reached his destination, Polk submitted to Congress his first annual message. In it he officially informed that body of the annexation of Texas, despite "British and French interference"; of the severance of diplomatic relations by Mexico; and of Slidell's mission. While expressing a "sincere desire for a peaceful adjustment of all difficulties," the message hinted at drastic measures in the event that negotiations should fail:

---

[40] It is true, of course, that Polk had before him the letter of Peña y Peña, which agreed to receive a commissioner and said nothing about a minister. See p. 389, note 34. It is true, also, that Joel R. Poinsett wrote soon after war was declared that "I took the liberty of remonstrating to one in the confidence of the government that the Mexican govt would not and dared not receive our Minister Plenipotentiary but could and would receive a Commissioner and that any movement of our troops from the Nueces would lead to hostilities. The reply was not to be uneasy. The Mexicans would not cross the Rio Grande to attack our troops & Genl Taylor had orders to remain on this side of the river, that a war with Mexico depended altogether upon the state of our relations with England" (Poinsett to Van Buren, May 26, 1846, *Van Buren Papers*).

The minister appointed has set out on his mission and is probably by this time near the Mexican capital. He has been instructed to bring the negotiation with which he is charged to a conclusion at the earliest practicable period, which it is expected will be in time to enable me to communicate the result to Congress during the present session. Until that result is known I forbear to recommend to Congress such ulterior measures of redress for the wrongs and injuries we have long borne as it would have been proper to make had no such negotiation been instituted.

This passage indicates that, even at this early date, the President believed that the United States had ample ground for war and that he would not hesitate to recommend it if Slidell's mission should end in failure.

Polk's reference to British and French interference in Texan affairs and his allusions to the Monroe Doctrine in connection with the Oregon question were not relished in British official circles. When reporting this fact to the President, McLane wrote that "a favorate scheme of the leading powers of Europe is to compose the Mexican troubles by giving her a settled monarchical form of Government, and supplying the monarch from one of their own families."[41] Doubtless McLane greatly exaggerated the desire for a Mexican monarchy, but his report harmonized so well with the suspicions already held by the administration that his opinions were probably accepted at face value.

Slidell arrived at the Mexican capital on December 6, 1845. His secretary of legation, Parrott, soon followed, accompanied

---

[41] McLane to Polk, Jan. 17, 1846, *Polk Papers*. Before the receipt of the message in England, the British press had spoken in praise of Polk's success in acquiring Texas. For example, the morning *Chronicle* said: "That immense question, the annexation of Texas, which seemed so difficult to solve that it affrighted the boldest men and parties, has been achieved by Mr. Polk in a thrice. The activity of English envoys, the suppleness of the French, the efforts of the most able and most eloquent partisans at home, all pointed at and making against annexation! All obstacles have been overcome. European interference has given color of reason to the act of annexation which it wanted before, since the measure was one which defeated and annulled European intervention. Then the great objection was that it would produce war. Annexation, however desirable, argued the Whigs, is not worth a drop of blood; but lo! it has not cost a drop of blood—the Mexicans are paralyzed.'' Quoted by the Washington *Union*, Jan. 2, 1846.

by Gillespie, who was on his way to California as bearer of dispatches to Larkin and Fremont. Black, the American consul at Mexico, had met Slidell at Puebla and informed him that the Mexican government was much perturbed by his early arrival, as he had not been expected until January. President Herrera seems to have feared that the arrival of the American envoy would be used by his enemies to undermine his power. There was foundation for this belief. Broadsides appeared warning the people that Slidell had come to acquire from the Herrera government not only Texas but New Mexico and the Californias, consequently to receive him would be treasonable. Peña y Peña, the Secretary of Foreign Affairs, promptly refused to receive Parrott as secretary of legation, because of his former activities in Mexico; but as to Slidell, he adopted a temporizing policy. His first objection, as already stated, was the early date of the envoy's arrival. After the receipt of Slidell's credentials, the Secretary had a more tangible ground for objection. He pointed out to Black that Mexico had agreed to receive a commissioner to negotiate the Texas dispute, but that Slidell's credentials represented him to be a minister resident. On this ground the Mexican government declined to receive the American diplomat.[42] Slidell did not, however, regard this as a final rejection, for on December 31, Herrera was forced to relinquish the government of Mexico, and on January 2, 1846, General Paredes became President, *ad interim*. It now remained for Slidell to seek recognition from the new government, and he repaired to Jalapa to await developments.

On January 28, 1846, after he had received Slidell's letter of December 17 which reported that the Mexican government had declined to receive him until it had given the matter further consideration, Buchanan wrote again to Slidell, approving his

---

[42] Black to Slidell, Dec. 15; Slidell to Buchanan, Dec. 17; Peña y Peña to Slidell, Dec. 20, 1845 (*H. Ex. Doc. 60*, 30 Cong., 1 sess., 23–27, 28–30, 37).

conduct and giving him further directions. As it was morally certain, said Buchanan, that Paredes would gain control of the government, Slidell was directed to apply again for recognition. The President, he was told, desired to preserve peace, because both inclination and policy dictated this course.

Should the Mexican Government, however, finally refuse to receive you, the cup of forbearance will then have been exhausted. Nothing can remain but to take the redress of the injuries to our citizens and the insults to our Government into our hands. In view of this serious alternative, every honorable effort should be made before a final rupture.

Slidell was therefore to wait a reasonable time for Mexico to decide on his reception, unless he should discover that she was inclined to trifle with "this Government." The length of time and the evidence of trifling were left to the envoy's discretion to determine. It will be noted that the President regarded a refusal to receive Slidell and a failure to pay the claims immediately as ample grounds for taking redress into his own hands— in other words, for making war on Mexico. Protection of Texas from threatened invasion had nothing to do with the question then under discussion. To make still more clear the President's intentions, Slidell was told in another paragraph that in case Mexico should finally decline to receive him he was to demand his passports and return to the United States. "It will then become the duty of the President to submit the whole case to Congress and call upon the nation to assert its just rights and avenge its injured honor." Additional naval forces had been sent to the Mexican coast and "should war become inevitable, the President will be prepared to conduct it with vigor."[43]

While Slidell was seeking an audience in Mexico an agent of Santa Anna (then in exile in Cuba) appeared in Washington and obtained an interview with President Polk. This agent was Colonel Alexander J. Atocha, a Spaniard by birth but a naturalized citizen of the United States. As a friend of Santa Anna he

---

[43] Buchanan, *Works*, VI, 363–365.

had been arrested when that wily ruler's government was overthrown, but on proving his American citizenship he was released and banished. He had called on Polk in June, 1845, for the purpose of urging the United States government to press certain claims which he held against Mexico. He had now returned from a visit to Santa Anna in Havana, prepared to lay before Polk the views of the ex-dictator. In his diary under date of February 13, 1846, Polk stated that Atocha called on that day, and the substance of the conversation was recorded. Atocha represented Santa Anna to be in constant communication with the Mexican leaders.

He said that Santa Anna approved the revolution headed by Paredes and that Santa Anna was in favour of a Treaty with the U. S., and that in adjusting a boundary between the two countries the Del Norte should be the Western Texas line, and the Colorado of the West down through the Bay of San Francisco to the Sea should be the Mexican line on the North, and that Mexico should cede all East and North of these natural boundaries to the U. S. for a pecuniary consideration, and mentioned thirty millions of Dollars as the sum.

This amount, Santa Anna believed, would pay the most pressing debts of Mexico and support the army until conditions had improved.

Col. Atocha said that Santa Anna was surprised that the U. S. Naval force had been withdrawn from Vera Cruz last fall, and that Gen'l Taylor's army was kept at Corpus Christi instead of being stationed on the Del Norte; and that the U. S. would never be able to treat with Mexico, without the presence of an imposing force by land and sea, and this, Col. Atocha added, was his own opinion. Col. Atocha did not say that he was sent by Santa Anna to hold this conversation with me; but I think it probable he was so.

Atocha requested that the conversation should be considered confidential, and said that he had more to communicate.[44]

Polk was evidently much interested in the views expressed by Atocha, and at a regular cabinet meeting held on the following day he related to the members the substance of the

---

[44] Polk, *Diary*, I, 222–225.

conversation. The idea of sending a confidential agent to confer with Santa Anna was mentioned. Walker was inclined to favor such a course, but Buchanan was decidedly opposed to it. The President said that although he did not propose to send such an agent, if one should be sent, C. P. Van Ness, former minister to Spain, would be the best man that could be selected.[45] Atocha called again to see the President on the sixteenth of February. After discussing relations with Mexico for nearly an hour the conversation was adjourned until afternoon when it was continued for more than an hour. Atocha repeated what he had said on February 13. Polk told him that Mexico must satisfy the claims of American citizens and that if her government had any proposition to make, such as he had suggested, the United States would consider it after it had been made. Atocha then pointed out that no government of Mexico would dare to make such an offer and that it "must appear to be forced to agree to such a proposition." It was the opinion of Atocha himself and of Santa Anna that

our [United States] army should be marched at once from Corpus Christi to the Del Norte, and a strong Naval force assembled at Vera Cruz, that Mr. Slidell, the U. S. Minister, should withdraw from Jalappa, and go on board one of our ships of War at Vera Cruz, and in that position should demand the payment of [the] amount due our citizens; that it was well known the Mexican Government was unable to pay in money, and that when they saw a strong force ready to strike on their coasts and border, they would, he had no doubt, feel their danger and agree to the boundary suggested. He said that Paredes, Almonte, & Gen'l Santa Anna were all willing for such an arrangement, but that they dare not make it until it was made apparent to the Archbishop of Mexico & the people generally that it was necessary to save their country from a war with the U. States. He said the last words which Gen'l Santa Anna said to him when he was leaving Havanna a month ago was, "when you see the President, tell him to take strong measures, and such a Treaty can be made & I will sustain it."

Atocha said that Mexico owed half a million dollars to the archbishop, and that he could be reconciled by assurance that he would be paid as soon as Mexico had obtained the money from

---

[45] *Ibid.*, 226.

the United States. He reported Santa Anna as having said that he could be in Mexico in April or May and would probably "go into power again," but that he and Paredes must have money to sustain themselves. With half a million in hand, they could make the treaty and retain control until the balance had been paid. Arista, he said, was friendly to the United States and in favor of ceding the northern departments to that country —in fact, he was anxious to do so, as he owned a large plantation near Monterey. Atocha intimated an intention to return to Havana and seemed desirous of getting Polk's views to carry to Santa Anna, but the President remained silent. Polk thought him to be a man of talents, but one who could not be trusted; "I therefore heard all he said but communicated nothing to him."[46] We may well believe the President's statement that he listened attentively but offered no hint of his own intentions, for this habit was one of his best known characteristics. Although he believed Atocha to be a person who could not be relied upon, events which followed make it evident that he looked with favor upon the suggestions which had been offered. Some of them were followed, as we shall soon have occasion to note, in the new instructions given to Slidell and in the request made to Congress for money to be used in conducting negotiations.

That Polk was influenced by Atocha's suggestions there can be no doubt, and that his first impulse was to follow these suggestions very closely is made evident by the discussion which took place in the cabinet meeting on the following day, February 17. In giving an account of this meeting Polk says in his diary that, after relating the conversation held with Atocha,

I expressed the opinion that it would be necessary to take strong measures towards Mexico before our difficulties with that Government could be settled; and I proposed that in addition to Mr. Slidell's present instructions, he should be further instructed to demand an early decision of the Mexican Government, whether they would receive him as Minister or not; and, if they received him, whether they would without unnecessary delay pay the

---

[46] *Ibid.*, 228–230.

amount due to American claimants; and that if that Government refused to do one or both, that he should leave the country, but instead of returning immediately to the U. States as he had beeen instructed to do, he should go on board one of our Vessels of War at Vera Cruz, and there remain until he had further instructions from his Government.

I stated that in that event I would send a strong message to Congress calling on that body to authorize me to cause another demand to be made by Mr. Slidell, from on board the vessel of war, on the Mexican Government to pay our demands, and if this was refused by Mexico, to confer authority on the Executive to take redress into our hands by aggressive measures.

Walker, Marcy, and Bancroft favored the plan suggested by the President. Johnson was inclined to hold a different opinion, but was willing to acquiesce. Buchanan objected, because—as Polk thought—he was peeved over certain appointments and because he could not control the administration. However, it was decided that Buchanan should prepare new instructions for Slidell, in accordance with the wishes of the President. But within an hour after the meeting had adjourned Buchanan, who was in no amiable mood, sent to the President by messenger a draft of instructions, commencing with "I am directed by President" etc. He requested Polk to make corrections in pencil and return it in time for the mail. Polk was dissatisfied with the draft and replied that he would attend to it on the following day. Buchanan immediately sent the messenger back with a note stating his reasons for dissenting from the decision of the President. On receiving no reply Buchanan sent another note on the same subject, but again he received no response. Polk did not see Buchanan on the following day, but decided, on account of the Secretary's hostility, to postpone instructing Slidell for the present.[47]

The Mexican question was allowed to slumber for about three weeks, and during that time Oregon claimed the attention of both the President and Congress. On March 9 dispatches from

---

[47] *Ibid.*, 233–236, 238. Polk considered the conduct of his Secretary to be decidedly reprehensible, and he closed the entry for the day with the remark: "The draft of the despatch and the two notes, Numbered 1 & 2, I will preserve."

Slidell, for which Polk had been waiting, arrived, and were discussed in cabinet meeting on the day following. The essential features of new instructions to Slidell were agreed upon, and Buchanan was directed to draft them.[48] While the new instructions, which bore the date of March 12, reflected in some degree the suggestions offered by Atocha, their tone was somewhat less bellicose than the declaration made by the President to his cabinet on February 17. The change was probably due to the opposition of Buchanan. Slidell was directed to make a formal demand to be received by the new government. Apparently the administration had slight hopes that Paredes would comply but Buchanan pointed out that the demand should be made in order to satisfy the American people that everything had been done to avoid the necessity of resorting to war. "On your return to the United States, energetic measures against Mexico would at once be recommended by the President, and these might fail to obtain the support of Congress, if it could be asserted that the existing Government had not refused to receive our Minister." Slidell was to make it known to Paredes "in some discreet manner" that the United States was both able and willing to relieve him from pecuniary embarrassment the moment that a treaty had been signed and ratified by Mexico.[49] A rumor was afloat, said Buchanan, of a design of European powers to establish a monarchy in Mexico and to place Prince Henry of Spain on the throne. He thought that these rumors were probably idle speculations, but "should Great Britain and France attempt to place a Spanish or any other European Prince on the throne of Mexico, this would be resisted by all the power of the United States." Whether he should be received or not Slidell was advised to delay his return to the United States, for the Oregon question was rapidly approaching a crisis and his return might influence its settlement by creating public alarm.[50] Nothing

---

[48] *Ibid.*, 282, 287.

[49] This is evidently an echo of the suggestion made by Atocha.

[50] Buchanan to Slidell, March 12, 1846 (Buchanan, *Works*, VI, 402–406).

was said about Slidell's repairing to a war vessel for the purpose of making another demand, as Atocha had advised and Polk had recommended to the cabinet. Apprehension concerning the Oregon question as well as the opposition of Buchanan may have been responsible for the President's change of mind.

Polk seems to have been confident that Slidell would be received by Paredes. At a cabinet meeting held on March 28, he expressed the belief that Slidell's dispatches indicated his reception to be probable. He apprehended that the greatest obstacle to the conclusion of a boundary treaty, such as Slidell had been instructed to procure, would be the want of authority to make a prompt payment of money at the time of signing it. Paredes was in great need of money to pay his troops and keep them loyal, and Polk was of opinion that if Slidell could be authorized to pay a half million or a million dollars as soon as the treaty had been signed, it "might induce him [Paredes] to make a Treaty, which he would not otherwise venture to make." Some of the cabinet members raised the question of how this money could be obtained from Congress without exposing to the public and to foreign nations the object in voting it. "That object," said the President,

as may be seen from Mr. Slidell's instructions, would be in adjusting a boundary to procure a cession of New Mexico & California, & if possible all North of latitude 32° from the Passo [El Paso] on the Del Norte & West to the Pacific ocean; or if that precise boundary cannot be obtained, then the next best boundary which might be practicable so as at all events to include all the country East of the Del Norte and the Bay of San Francisco. For the boundary desired, see Mr. Slidell's instructions.

The cabinet, except the Secretary of State, agreed. Buchanan thought the plan of asking for an advance appropriation to be impracticable. Polk called attention to the act passed in 1806 to enable Jefferson to purchase the Floridas, and suggested that members of Congress might be consulted informally for the purpose of ascertaining the probability of obtaining the appropriation. He had already broached the subject to Ingersoll, of

Pennsylvania, and Cullom, of Tennessee. After the meeting had adjourned Polk summoned Benton and asked his opinion concerning the feasibility of the plan. Benton concurred in the views of the President and promised his coöperation.[51] On examining the laws Polk found another precedent for his proposed appropriation—the two millions voted in 1803 to enable Jefferson to purchase Louisiana. He conversed with Allen, chairman of the Senate Committee on Foreign Relations, and with Senator Cass. Both approved his plan. On the advice of Allen and Benton the President sent for Calhoun and asked his opinion on the proposed appropriation and on the purpose for which it was to be used. Calhoun was in favor of procuring a boundary which would include California, and said that he had contemplated trying to procure such a boundary when he was Secretary of State. He did not, however, like the boundary suggested by the President. Neither did he approve the plan to ask for an appropriation, for fear it might interfere with the settlement of the Oregon question.[52]

While the President was exerting his influence to obtain from Congress an appropriation to facilitate negotiations, a dispatch arrived, on April 6, from the American consul at Vera Cruz stating that Slidell would probably not be received. The dispatch was read in cabinet meeting next day, and Polk recorded in his diary:

I stated that in the event Mr. Slidell was not accredited, and returned to the U. S., my opinion was that I should make a communication to Congress recommending that Legislative measures be adopted, to take the remedy for the injuries and wrongs we had suffered into our own hands.

On the evening of the seventh dispatches from Slidell arrived, informing the President that he had not been received and that he had demanded his passports.[53]

---

[51] Polk, *Diary*, I, 303, 305–308.
[52] *Ibid.*, 309–313.
[53] *Ibid.*, 319, 322.

On March 12, the day on which Buchanan penned his final instructions to Slidell, the Mexican Minister of Foreign Relations notified the American envoy that he could not be received. He was told that the annexation of Texas had always been and was still regarded by Mexico as a *casus belli*. In spite of this fact she had agreed to receive a commissioner to discuss this question, but the United States had sent instead a minister resident. Should the United States persist in its present course the Mexican government would "call upon all her citizens to fulfill the sacred duty of defending their country," and if war should result, the entire blame would rest upon the United States. As soon as he received this letter Slidell asked for his passports, and they were sent to him by Castillo on the twenty-first of March.[54] He had left, therefore, for the United States before the arrival of Buchanan's instructions of March 12. With one government maintaining that aggressive measures must follow the refusal to receive the American envoy, and the other asserting that an insistence upon his reception must be met by an appeal to arms, it will be seen that Slidell's mission played an important part in bringing about a collision between the two nations. To be sure, Mexico still regarded the annexation of Texas as a *casus belli* and Castillo did not expressly state that she was prepared to acquiesce in its incorporation into the American Union, but at least he still intimated a willingness to negotiate on this limited question.

On receipt of Slidell's dispatch which announced that he had been rejected and had demanded his passports, the President consulted Benton concerning "the steps proper to be taken and especially if the principal Powers of Europe should attempt to force a Foreign Prince on the throne of Mexico." He consulted Houston, of Texas, and Allen, of Ohio, also, and it was agreed that nothing should be done until it had been ascertained that passports had actually been given to Slidell.[55] About a week later

---

[54] Castillo y Lanzas to Slidell, March 12 and March 21; Slidell to Castillo, March 17, 1846 (*H. Ex. Doc. 60*, 30 Cong., 1 sess., 67–72, 79).

[55] Polk, *Diary*, I, 325–327.

(April 18) the President told Calhoun that he "saw no alternative but strong measures towards Mexico." Calhoun deprecated war and expressed the opinion that if the Oregon question could be settled first there would be no difficulty in adjusting the difficulties with Mexico, for he believed that Great Britain desired to prevent a war between the United States and Mexico. Polk, on the contrary, believed that the British minister in Mexico had exerted his influence to prevent Slidell's reception. Calhoun urged against sending a message to Congress on Mexican affairs until the Oregon question had been settled. "I told him," said Polk,

> that I would delay a reasonable time, but that whatever the settlement of the Oregon question might be, I would feel it my duty to lay the Mexican question before Congress, with my opinion on the subject, in time for their action at the present Session.[56]

Three days later Polk told his cabinet that "our relations with Mexico could not be permitted to remain *in statu quo*"; that he contemplated asking Congress to adopt strong measures, but thought it prudent to await news from England before taking this step. He did not have long to wait, for on the following day (April 22) a dispatch from McLane was received. McLane was of opinion that Great Britain would take no step on the Oregon question until the Senate had come to some decision on the bill to terminate joint occupation of Oregon. On the twenty-third, the conference committee of the two houses came to an agreement on the bill to give England the required twelve months' notice; and on the twenty-fifth, Polk informed his cabinet that he deemed it to be his duty to make a communication to Congress without delay. "I expressed my opinion," the President recorded,

> that we must take redress for the injuries done us into our own hands, that we had attempted to conciliate Mexico in vain, and had forborne until forbearance was no longer either a virtue or patriotic . . . and that we should take a bold and firm course towards Mexico.

---

[56] *Ibid.*, 337–338.

Buchanan, whose opinion was first requested, thought that the President should recommend a declaration of war, while the other members suggested that a message be prepared and submitted to them within the course of a week. After considerable discussion Buchanan was requested to collect materials and prepare the draft of a message for the President's consideration.[57] While Buchanan was preparing "a succinct history" of wrongs on which to base a message to Congress the President once more consulted Benton. The Missouri Senator had not yet made up his mind, but he expressed a decided aversion to a war with Mexico, if it could be avoided. He advised delay until the Oregon question had been either settled or brought to a crisis. "I told him," said Polk, "we had ample cause of War, but that I was anxious to avoid it if it could be done honourably & consistently with the interests of our injured citizens." He would delay, he said, until the arrival of Slidell in Washington, but he could not permit Congress to adjourn without laying the subject before them.[58]

It should be noted that up to this point the President dwelt entirely on the refusal to receive Slidell and the failure to adjust the claims of American citizens. These furnished, in his opinion, ample grounds for war. This fact is significant, for Mexico was in such dire financial straits that she could not pay the claims except by a cession of territory. In other words, the President was ready to wage war to procure a territorial compensation for claims against Mexico. He does not, up to this time, mention any military aggressions on the part of Mexico. But on May 5 Polk received a dispatch from Taylor, dated April 15, stating that he had been ordered by Ampudia to fall back across the Nueces, and the President noted in his diary that "the probabilities are that hostilities might take place soon."[59] On May 8,

---

[57] *Ibid.*, 343, 344, 347, 354.

[58] *Ibid.*, 375–376.

[59] Taylor to Adj. Gen., April 15, 1846 (*H. Ex. Doc. 60*, 30 Cong., 1 sess., 138). Polk, *Diary*, I, 380.

Slidell, who had just returned from Mexico, called on the President and told him that there was only one course left—for the United States to take the redress of its injuries into its own hands. "In this I agreed with him," said Polk, "and told him it was only a matter of time when I would make a communication to Congress on the subject, and that I had made up my mind to do so very soon."[60] The cabinet met on the following day and the President informed them that, although no open act of aggression by the Mexican army had been reported, it was imminent that such would be committed. All agreed that if Taylor's forces should be molested the President ought to recommend a declaration of war. Polk then asked each member whether, in his opinion, a message should be sent to Congress on the following Tuesday,[61] and whether it should recommend a declaration of war. All answered in the affirmative except Bancroft, who, however, favored immediate war should Mexico commit any hostile act. It was agreed that a message should be prepared and considered at the next meeting.[62] On that same evening a dispatch from Taylor arrived, giving an account of the killing of American dragoons on the east bank of the Rio Grande. Polk summoned the cabinet to a special meeting, and it was agreed unanimously that the President should lay the matter before Congress and urge prompt measures to enable the Executive to prosecute the war. At noon on Monday, May 11, the war mesasge was ready and on its way to the capitol. Mexico herself had removed the obstacle which had worried both Bancroft and Buchanan. In addition, she rendered the President a distinct service by enabling him to base his war message on more tangible grounds— grounds which all friends of the administration could endorse with enthusiasm, and those which the opponents, for patriotic reasons, found it difficult to assail. Before the message was sent

---

60 Polk, *Diary*, I, 382.

61 This was on Saturday, May 9.

62 Polk, *Diary*, I, 384–385. Buchanan said that he would feel better if Mexico had committed some hostile act, but as matters stood, there was ample cause for war, so he gave his assent.

to Congress, Benton called, by appointment, and criticized some parts of it. He was, he said, in favor of defending our territory, but was not prepared to make aggressive war on Mexico. Although he had remained silent, he had not favored marching the army from Corpus Christi to the Rio Grande, and he doubted that the territory of the United States extended west of the Nueces river.[63]

The departure of Slidell from Mexico ended all attempt to adjust the international dispute by negotiation. Both nations now agreed on one point at least—that arms alone could settle the controversy. But which nation was the aggressor? Which committed the first overt act of war; and to what extent, if any, was the American occupation of that strip of territory lying between the Nueces and the Rio Grande the real cause of the war? We have already seen that Polk was ready to recommend war because Mexico would not pay the American claims by a cession of territory. Let us now consider the effect of Taylor's march to the Rio Grande upon Mexico's decision to attack the enemy.

As a department of Mexico Texas had extended to the Nueces only; the land lying west of that river belonged to the department of Tamaulipas. Except Santa Anna's agreement of 1836 and the Elliot treaty of 1845, Mexico never recognized the independence of Texas, much less the extension of her boundary. Texas of course claimed everything to the Rio Grande, but throughout her career as a republic the territory between the two rivers remained unoccupied by either country except that Mexico held a few posts on the east bank of the Rio Grande. The legitimate extent and boundaries of Texas, therefore, were not determined when that republic joined the American Union, and the joint resolution of annexation left them as vague as before. "What, then, is Texas?" was the embarrassing question asked by the Whigs, as soon as the administration took steps to protect the new state from invasion. Texas, they said, was bounded by the Nueces, not by the Rio Grande; and they denied the President's authority to send an army into the "disputed territory" between the two rivers.[64] The occupation of this territory was later used by Mexico as an excuse for attacking the American army; but at the time that diplomatic relations were severed, the question of boundary was not a definite issue. Almonte demanded his passports and left Washington soon after the joint resolution had passed, without waiting to see what boundary would be claimed. His conduct was approved by his government, and Mexico continued to assert her determination to reconquer Texas—not simply the "disputed territory," but all of it. There was no intimation of an intention on her part to acquiesce in the annexation of Texas until she agreed to receive a commissioner to negotiate that question, and she declined to receive Slidell because his credentials were unacceptable.

Although Polk had, before annexation was completed, announced his intention to claim the Rio Grande as the boundary of Texas, the western frontier was not occupied immediately. On July 30, 1845, Taylor was instructed to station part of his forces west of the Nueces, but it was not until January 13, 1846, that he was ordered to move his army to the east bank of the Rio Grande. On receipt of this order, early in February, Taylor at once made preparations to carry it into effect, and he reported that he did not anticipate that his advance would be resisted. Before leaving Corpus Christi, Taylor prepared and had translated into Spanish an "order" which he caused to be circulated among the inhabitants dwelling along the Rio Grande. This order stated that the advance to the Rio Grande was not a hostile move, and that both the personal and the property rights of the inhabitants on either side of that river would be respected.[65]

---

[64] On September 13, 1845, the *National Intelligencer* said that if the Army of Observation should be sent beyond the Nueces it would not be in Texas and not defending Texas. "Is the *disputed* territory, then, a part of Texas? No. It was not within Texas, as a part of Mexico. It has not been since acquired by arms or treaty."

[65] Taylor to Adj. Gen., Feb. 4 and Feb. 16, 1846 (*H. Ex. Doc. 60*, 30 Cong., 1 sess., 116–117). "Order No. 30," dated March 8, 1846 (*ibid.*, 119–120).

The march of Taylor toward the Rio Grande was undisputed by the Mexicans until he reached the Arroyo Colorado on March 19. Here a party of cavalry was encountered, and their commander warned Taylor that he was under orders to fire on the Americans should they attempt to pass that river. The warning was unheeded by Taylor and the Mexicans retreated without interposing armed resistance, but during the parley one of the officers placed in Taylor's hands a bellicose proclamation which had been issued on March 18 by General Francisco Mejia. This document is of interest, not only as being the first specific challenge to the advance of the American army, but because it draws a sharp distinction between Texas and land lying between the Nueces and Rio Grande. The "degenerate sons of Washington," said Mejia, not satisfied with annexing Texas, were now advancing to take possession of a large part of Tamaulipas. This they had begun "whilst endeavoring to lull us into security, by opening diplomatic relations." "The limits of Texas," he continued, "are certain and recognized; never have they extended beyond the river Nueces; notwithstanding which, the American army has crossed the line separating Tamaulipas from that department." Even though Mexico might acquiesce in the annexation of Texas,

nevertheless the territory of Tamaulipas would still remain beyond the law of annexation, sanctioned by the American Congress; because that law comprises independent Texas, the ground occupied by the rebellious colony, and in no wise includes other departments, in which the Mexican government has uninter[r]uptedly exercised its legitimate authority.

All Mexicans were therefore exhorted to defend their country.[66] While Taylor was on the march from the Arroyo Colorado to Point Isabel he was met by a civil deputation from Matamoras bearing a protest from the prefect of the northern district of Tamaulipas. It stated that Taylor's march was regarded as an invasion of Mexico, and the prefect pointed out that "nothing has been said officially by the cabinet of the Union to the Mexican

---

[66] *Ibid.*, 125–129.

government, respecting the extension of the limits of Texas to the left bank of the Rio Bravo.'' The citizens of the district, he said, would never consent to separate themselves from Mexico and join the United States.[67] To this protest Taylor paid no heed, but moved on to take a position opposite Matamoras. His batteries bore directly on the public square of that town, and "their object," reported Taylor, "cannot be mistaken by the enemy." A parley was held on the Mexican side of the river by General Worth and General Vega in which Worth demanded an interview with the American consul at Matamoras. The demand was refused, and Worth informed the Mexican commander that he regarded this refusal as a belligerent act. Worth stated also that Taylor would regard the crossing of the Rio Grande by Mexican forces as an act of war.[68] On March 31, General Mejia addressed a note to Taylor stating that all Mexicans looked upon the occupation of the east bank of the Rio Grande as a "positive declaration of war on the Part of the United States." Taylor's march could not be viewed as pacific, "inasmuch as a question of limits is depending between our respective governments." It could not be so viewed, "because it is not easy to conceive the reason or justice of taking forcible possession of the very territory in dispute, pending the negotiation."[69] Had such a communication been addressed to President Polk he might have had difficulty in explaining the *peaceful* nature of the advance of the American army, but it was Taylor's duty to obey orders and not to justify his movements. He very wisely declined to assume the rôle of a diplomat.

On April 11, General Ampudia arrived at Matamoras and took command of the Mexican forces. By "explicit and definite orders of his [my] government," he at once summoned Taylor

[67] Cardenes to Taylor, March 23, 1846 (*ibid.*, 130–132).

[68] Taylor to Adj. Gen., April 6, 1846; Minutes of the parley held on March 28 (*ibid.*, 133–138).

[69] *Ibid.*, 1204.

to retire beyond the Nueces within twenty-four hours, there to remain until the limits of Texas should be determined by the two governments. "If you insist in remaining upon the soil of the department of Tamaulipas," he was told, "it will clearly result that arms, and arms alone, must decide the question." Taylor replied on the same day that he would remain where he was, "leaving the responsibility with those who rashly commence hostilities." As a result of Ampudia's note, Taylor immediately ordered a blockade of the Rio Grande, which cut off supplies from Matamoras.[70] On April 24, Ampudia was superseded by General Arista, who at once notified Taylor that Mexico could not submit to the indignities heaped upon her by the United States, and that hostilities had commenced. Taylor replied on the following day that he had carefully refrained from committing

any act which could possibly be interpreted into hostility, until the peremptory summons of General Ampudia to vacate my position within twenty-four hours, rendered it necessary to take some action, and I then chose a measure not in itself hostile, but a simple defensive precaution, viz: a blockade of the Rio Bravo.[71]

Although this definition of a blockade may have relieved the conscience of the man who made it, such a bottling-up of the opponent is usually regarded as an act of war. Ampudia protested vigorously and demanded the free use of the river, but Taylor refused to raise the blockade "unless indeed you desire an armistice pending the settlement of the question between the two governments."[72]

The Mexican President likewise considered Taylor's blockade to be an act of war. On April 23, Paredes issued a proclamation directing a "defensive war" to begin. After a recital of the injuries which, since 1836, the United States had inflicted upon the people of Mexico; the sending of Slidell as minister resident

---

[70] Ampudia to Taylor, April 12; Taylor to Ampudia, April 12; Taylor to Adj. Gen., April 15, 1846 (*ibid.*, 138–140).

[71] *Ibid.*, 1204–1206.

[72] Taylor to Ampudia, April 22, 1846 (*ibid.*, 144–147).

at the very moment when the American troops were occupying Mexican territory; and the blockade of the Rio Grande by war vessels: Paredes asserted that

hostilities therefore have been begun by the United States of America, who have undertaken new conquests in the territory lying within the line of the Departments of Tamaulipas and Nueva León while the troops of the United States are threatening Monterey in Upper California.

He had therefore directed the commanding general to "attack the army which is attacking us; to answer with war the enemy who makes war upon us." Like Taylor, Paredes invented a definition to suit his purposes, for he declared the proposed hostilities to be not a war against the government of the United States, but simply a defense of Mexican territory which had been invaded.[73]

Arista, who assumed command of the Mexican forces on the day after Paredes had issued his proclamation, took immediate steps to cross the Rio Grande. General Torrejon, with all of the cavalry and a small body of infantry, was sent across the river above Matamoras, while the main body of infantry and artillery was to cross below Matamoras and cut Taylor off from his base of supplies at Point Isabel.[74] On April 25, Torrejon encountered a scouting party of sixty-three American dragoons, under Captain Thornton. An engagement followed in which sixteen Americans were killed or wounded and the remainder forced to surrender. The prisoners were taken to Matamoras and treated kindly by the Mexicans.[75] The long-threatened war with Mexico

---

[73] "I solemnly announce that I do not decree war against the government of the United States of America, because it belongs to the august Congress of the nation, and not to the Executive, to decide definitely what reparation must be exacted for such injuries. But the defense of Mexican territory which the troops of the United States are invading is an urgent necessity, and my responsibility before the nation would be immense if I did not order the repulse of forces which are acting as enemies; and I have so ordered. From this day defensive war begins, and every point of our territory which may be invaded or attacked shall be defended by force" (*México á través de los Siglos*, IV, 559). Rives, *The United States and Mexico*, II, 141–142.

[74] Rives, *op. cit.*, 143.

[75] Taylor to Adj. Gen., April 26, 1846; Reports of Captains Thornton and Hardee (*ibid.*, 288, 290–292).

was at last a reality. The killing of Thornton's dragoons by the
Mexican forces under Torrejon was soon described by President
Polk as an unprovoked act of war. In a message sent to Congress
on May 11, 1846, the President asserted that

> after reiterated menaces, Mexico has passed the boundary of the United
> States, has invaded our territory, and shed American blood upon the
> American soil. She has proclaimed that hostilities have commenced, and
> that the two nations are now at war.
>
> As war exists, and, notwithstanding all our efforts to avoid it, exists
> by the act of Mexico herself, we are called upon by every consideration
> of duty and patriotism to vindicate with decision and honor, the rights,
> and the interests of our country.

He therefore recommended prompt and energetic measures for
bringing the war to a speedy and successful termination.[76]

Whether or not Taylor's advance into the "disputed territory" was the actual cause of Mexico's refusal to renew diplomatic relations and of her determination to resort to arms, it at
least served as an excuse for such a course on her part. Although
she had from the first claimed the occupation of any part of Texas
to be an invasion of Mexico and a *casus belli*, she had, on various
occasions, intimated that she might acquiesce in the annexation
of Texas and discuss its limits. It was not until Taylor had
crossed the Nueces that she actually took steps to attack the
American forces. Polk may or may not have acted within his
rights in assuming the boundary claimed by Texas, but at least
there was some justification in the contention of the Whigs that
he precipitated the war by ordering Taylor to the Rio Grande.

---

[76] Richardson, *Messages and Papers of the Presidents*, IV, 442–443.

CHAPTER XVIII

WAR IN NORTHERN MEXICO

President Polk's war message was sent to Congress on May 11, 1846. After a brief debate of two hours the House, by a vote of one hundred and seventy-four to fourteen, passed a bill which authorized the President to prosecute the war that exists ''by the act of the Republic of Mexico.''[1] Garrett Davis, of Kentucky, denied the truth of the statement just quoted and asserted that: ''It is our own President who began this war'' by sending General Taylor beyond the Nueces river. In defense of the administration, the Washington *Union* answered this contention by calling attention to the fact that Mexico had always claimed Texas to the Sabine, and that there was no reason for believing that her invading army would stop at the Nueces.[2]

Greater opposition was encountered in the Senate, and for a time the President feared that Benton and Calhoun would join the Whigs and thereby defeat the House bill. However, after a day's debate, the Senate, having added a few amendments, passed the measure by a vote of forty-two to two. Benton voted for the bill and Calhoun, having opposed a declaration of war, declined to vote either way.[3] Some of the members based their objections

---

[1] *Cong. Globe*, 29 Cong., 1 sess., 795. Polk, *Diary*, I, 392.

[2] ''No man has yet alleged, so far as we know, that a Mexican invasion of Texas, if permitted by us, *would have stopped at the Nueces;* or would have thought of stopping there. . . . The claim of Mexico is, in terms, that she owns Texas up to the Sabine. She makes not the slightest difference in any one of her state papers between her ownership up to the Nueces and her ownership up to the Sabine. In a great multitude of state papers of old date, and of most recent date, Mexico says that Texas—*all Texas*— is her soil. This claim to *the whole of Texas* is the claim on which she refused negotiation. On this claim, and none other, Almonte threw up his passports. On this claim Mr. Shannon was sent home'' (*Union*, May 15, 1846).

[3] *Cong. Globe, loc. cit.*, 804. Polk, *Diary*, I, 394.

on the lack of information as to what had happened on the Rio Grande; others denounced the President for having invaded territory which did not belong to the United States. In general, the Van Burenites of both houses supported the administration with their votes, but in private their criticisms were quite as severe as those of the Whigs. Although Cambreleng was not a member of Congress at the time, a letter which he wrote to the ex-President well expresses the feelings of this faction. The letter is especially interesting, for when Polk occupied the Speaker's chair, Cambreleng was his most loyal supporter. Having pronounced Polk to be worse than John Tyler and invoked divine pardon for having aided in his election, Cambreleng said:

With regard to Mexico, they make inquiry through a consul—Mexico proposes to receive a Commissioner to treat about Texas if we will withdraw our naval forces—then we send in hot haste, and most secretly, a Minister Plenipotentiary, at a moment too when a revolutionary movement was going on and when it was obvious, that our minister could do nothing whatever but help Paredes to overthrow Herera, which he did very effectively and returned home with his credentials. [Taylor marched across Tamaulipas and blockaded the Mexicans] as if he had instructions [to make war, and Mexico had no choice but to fight].[4]

The bill which decreed war against Mexico was signed by the President on May 13, and General Scott was given command of the army for which it provided, although Polk did not consider him to be "in all respects suited" for the position.

At a cabinet meeting held on the same evening the President and his Secretary of State had a sharp disagreement concerning the scope and the objects of the war. Buchanan had brought to the meeting the draft of a dispatch which was to be sent to American ministers at foreign courts. Its purpose was to notify those governments of the declaration of war, and to announce the intentions of the American government. In his draft Buchanan disavowed any intention of dismembering Mexico, and of making conquests. He stated specifically that the war had

---

[4] Cambreleng to Van Buren, Washington, May 16, 1846, *Van Buren Papers.*

not been undertaken "with a view to acquire either California or New Mexico or any other portion of Mexican territory." Polk "thought such a declaration to Foreign Governments unnecessary and improper," and believed the causes for war set forth in his message to be entirely adequate. He told his Secretary that while the United States had not gone to war for the purpose of conquest,

yet it was clear that in making peace we would if practicable obtain California and such other portion of the Mexican territory as would be sufficient to indemnify our claimants on Mexico, and to defray the expenses of the war which that power by her long continued wrongs and injuries had forced us to wage. I told him it was well known that the Mexican Government had no other means of indemnifying us.

Buchanan expressed the fear that Lord Aberdeen would demand from McLane, United States minister in London, a statement as to whether his government intended to acquire Mexican territory, especially California. Should a satisfactory answer be withheld, he feared that both England and France would join Mexico in the war against us. Polk replied that the present war did not concern any European power, a demand such as Buchanan had mentioned would be an insult, and "if made I would not answer it, even if the consequence should be a war with all of them." He would give no pledges as to the terms on which he would ultimately make peace with Mexico. Buchanan insisted that if assurances were not given we would surely have war with England, and probably with France, for neither would permit California to be annexed to the United States. "I told him," wrote the President, "that before I would make the pledge which he proposed, I would meet the war which either England or France or all the Powers of Christendom might wage," and that "neither as a citizen nor as President would I permit or tolerate any intermeddling of any European Power on this Continent." Although Buchanan still maintained that unless some pledge were given the Oregon question could not be adjusted and that England would declare war, the President was immovable and said that he would take the responsibility of a war rather than give a pledge which would prevent him from "fairly and honourably" acquiring California. The other members of the cabinet supported this position, and Polk was "much astonished at the views expressed by Mr. Buchanan on the subject." The President himself drafted a paragraph to be substituted for the one which Buchanan had submitted.[5]

Scarcely had the President reduced his Secretary of State to proper subordination when difficulties with his Whig generals presented themselves.[6] He had planned first of all to seize the northern provinces of Mexico and to hold them until the enemy had been forced to make peace. Without hesitation Congress voted the necessary troops and supplies, but the question of selecting suitable commanders to lead the troops to victory caused the President no little anxiety and annoyance. As Scott was the ranking general, Polk tendered him the command and consulted him concerning military arrangements, but he regarded the general as "visionary" and his advice as of no great value.[7]

From the beginning of his administration Polk seems to have looked upon the conquest of Mexico as an easy matter. Like most civilian executives he did not fully appreciate the time required to equip an army for active service. On the other hand, General Scott took both himself and his position very seriously, and was desirous of making his descent upon Mexico as imposing as possible. He was a competent officer, and doubtless his intentions were good, but his vanity and tactless utterances soon involved him in difficulties.

---

[5] Polk, *Diary*, I, 396–399. For the dispatch as finally sent to the American ministers abroad, see Buchanan, *Works*, VI, 484.

[6] Polk was told that not only Scott but General Wool and Adjutant General Jones were using their influence with members of Congress to prevent the passage of a bill to authorize the appointment of two new major generals and four brigadier generals (Polk, *Diary*, I, 418).

[7] "I did not think that so many as 20,000 [the number which Scott had requested for immediate service] volunteers besides the regular army was necessary, but I did not express this opinion, not being willing to take the responsibility of any failure of the campaign by refusing to grant to Gen'l Scott all he asked" (Polk, *Diary*, I, 400–401).

Without consulting the War Department, Scott announced that he probably would not be ready to set out for the seat of war until the first of September. Through the Secretary of War, the President notified him that unless he should proceed to the Rio Grande very soon he would be superseded by another commander.

Polk undoubtedly bore a prejudice against the general from the beginning and may have been too impatient with his delay; on the other hand, Scott's amazing indiscretions soon gave the President no alternative but to deprive him of his command. Not satisfied with telling applicants for military positions that these places had been created "to give Commissions or rather pay to western democrats," he responded to Marcy's notice that the President desired greater promptness, by returning a most insulting and vainglorious letter. Although Polk had verbally tendered Scott the command of the Mexican expedition, the general now complained because he had not received a written order assigning him to the command; he had, nevertheless, been incessantly employed in making preliminary arrangements. "In the midst of these multitudinous and indispensable occupations," wrote the irate general,

I have learned from you that much impatience is already felt, perhaps in high quarters, that I have not already put myself in route for the Rio Grande; and now, with fourteen hours a day of preliminary work remaining on my hands for many days, I find myself compelled to stop that necessary work to guard myself against, perhaps, utter condemnation in the quarters alluded to. I am too old a soldier, and have had too much special experience, not to feel the infinite importance of securing myself against danger, (ill will or pre-condemnation,) in my rear, before advancing upon the public enemy.

He had no fear of the enemy ahead, but unless he could feel confident of support in Washington the selection of another commander was advised. For fear that Marcy and Polk might not have sufficient mental capacity to grasp his meaning, the general added: "My explicit meaning is, that I do not desire to place

myself in the most perilous of all positions—*a fire upon my rear
from Washington, and the fire in front from the Mexicans.*" So
clear was his explanation that both men saw at once the injustice
of placing the gallant and overworked general in such a dangerous predicament. In a very able and dignified—but, at the same
time, withering—letter, Marcy notified Scott that, instead of
leading the Mexican expedition, he was to remain in Washington.[8]
In itself Marcy's letter was galling enough to the pompous general's pride, but, as if to add insult to injury, it was handed to
him just "as he [I] sat down to a hasty plate of soup." In
another letter he made a lame attempt to explain that his allusions to "high quarters" meant members of Congress instead of
the President, but he could not refrain from sneering at Polk's
"magnanimity" in not having him court-martialed.[9] The effrontery exhibited in his letters indicates that the general was still
deluded by the campaign cry, "Who is James K. Polk?" Marcy
enlightened him, for the time being at least. Indeed the President felt himself to be fully competent to discharge the duties
which the Constitution had assigned to the chief executive. To
one of his many volunteer advisers he remarked that: "I hoped
my friends in Congress and elsewhere would suffer me to conduct
the war with Mexico as I thought proper, and not plan the campaign for me."[10]

As already noted, Polk did not anticipate great difficulty in
defeating the Mexican armies. Apparently, he feared most of
all the influence of the Mexican priests. He thought that designing persons in Mexico had led the priests to believe that the

---

[8] After calling attention to the importance of the position to which
Scott had been assigned by the President, Marcy said: "How could you,
under these circumstances, arrest your labors of preparation, and suffer
your energies to be crippled, for the purpose of indulging in illiberal imputations against the man who has just bestowed upon you the highest
mark of his confidence?"

[9] Polk, *Diary*, I, 395, 400, 413–415, 419–421. The correspondence is
printed in *Niles' Reg.*, LXX, 231–233.

[10] Polk, *Diary*, I, 427.

United States had planned to pillage their churches and to overthrow their religion. So long as the priests harbored such fears
they would do much to incite the people stubbornly to resist the
advance of the American army. Being desirous of weakening
the power of the Mexican government by winning the good will
of the people, especially in the northern provinces, Polk attached
great importance to disabusing the minds of the priests. "If the
Catholic Priests in Mexico," he told Benton,

can be satisfied that their churches and religion would be secure the conquests of the Northern Provinces of Mexico will be easy and the probability is that the war would be of short duration; but if a contrary opinion
prevails the resistance to our forces will be desperate.

He therefore sought interviews with Bishop Hughes, of New
York, and the Bishop of Missouri and asked them to select priests
who might accompany the army as chaplains and assure the Mexican clergy that their fear of Americans was groundless. A proclamation in the Spanish language which promised religious freedom and kind treatment was prepared and sent to General Taylor
with instructions that it should be distributed among the inhabitants.[11]

In planning the campaign against Mexico the President attached great importance to getting possession of California. As
early as May 26 he proposed, and his cabinet unanimously agreed,
that an "expedition be immediately fitted out against Upper
California" if it should be found that the mounted regiments
assembled at Independence, Missouri, could reach the Sacramento
region before winter. On May 30 he again impressed upon the
cabinet the importance of having military possession of California
when the time for making peace should have arrived. "I declared," said he, "my purpose to be to acquire for the U. S.
California, New Mexico, and perhaps some others of the Northern

---

[11] *Ibid.*, 408–411. For the proclamation see *H. Ex. Doc. 60*, 30 Cong.,
1 sess., 284–287. In it the Mexicans were told that their government was
in the hands of "tyrants and usurpers," and that the United States was
doing the people a real kindness by invading their country.

Provinces of Mexico whenever peace was made.'' Colonel Stephen
W. Kearny, who had already been transferred from Fort Leavenworth to Santa Fé for the purpose of affording protection to
American traders, was now selected to lead the expedition to
California. By a new commission which accompanied his instructions he was made a brevet brigadier-general. A requisition
was sent to the governor of Missouri for one thousand mounted
men to supplement the force of dragoons under Kearny's command. It was agreed that Kearny should be authorized to take
into his service any American citizens whom he might find in
California. He was to be given authority, also, to enlist a few
hundred of the Mormons who were now on their way to California,
''with a view to conciliate them, attach them to our country, &
prevent them from taking part against us.'' The President directed that arms and provisions should be sent immediately from
New York to the Pacific for the use of Kearny's army.[12] About
two weeks later he consulted his cabinet on the propriety of sending from New York by sea a regiment of volunteers to join
Kearny's forces in California. Benton, whose advice was sought
by the President, favored sending such a regiment, but he believed that the men should go as emigrants and be discharged in
California at the end of their service.[13] This policy was subsequently adopted.

Although Polk was interested primarily in the acquisition of
California and New Mexico he desired to procure, if possible, a
much larger area; and the amicable settlement of the Oregon

---

[12] Polk, *Diary*, I, 429, 437–439, 443–444. On June 3, J. C. Little, a
Mormon from Petersborough, N. H., called on Polk for the purpose of
ascertaining the policy of the government towards this sect. He was told
that they would be treated like any other American citizens and that they
would be invited to enlist in the army. Polk did not mention the projected
expedition under Kearny. Little offered to overtake the Mormons and to
muster 500 of them into the United States army; but fearing that they
might reach California before Kearny and not wishing that the province
should be at the mercy of Mormon soldiers, the President declined the offer.
He decided, also, that Kearny should not enlist any of that sect until after
they had arrived in California (*ibid.*, 445–446, 449–450).

[13] *Ibid.*, 473, 481.

question by the treaty signed on June 15 made interference by Great Britain less probable. The extent of territory which he wished to acquire is stated very definitely in his record of a cabinet meeting held on June 30, 1846. At this meeting an animated discussion arose between Buchanan and Walker regarding the objects to be attained as a result of the war. Buchanan expressed himself as being in favor of making the Rio Grande the boundary up to El Paso, in latitude about 32°; from this point a line was to be drawn due west to the Pacific ocean. He opposed the acquisition of any land south of 32° because the North would be unwilling to acquire a tract that was likely to become slaveholding territory. Walker held very different opinions. He proposed that the boundary should begin at the mouth of the Rio Grande, in latitude about 26°, and extend directly westward to the Pacific. The other members of the cabinet took no part in the discussion, but Polk agreed with Walker. "I remarked," wrote the President,

that I preferred the 26° to any boundary North of it, but that if it was found that that boundary could not be obtained I was willing to take 32°, but that in any event we must obtain Upper California and New Mexico in any Treaty of Peace we would make.[14]

At this point we may leave the President to develop his program of conquest while we consider a parenthetical episode which affected his policy of territorial expansion but which was not, apparently, a part of it.

Long before General Kearny could reach California, John C. Fremont had, by his indiscretions, come into collision with the Mexican officials of that province, and the famous "Bear Flag" republic had been proclaimed. These events, however interesting in themselves, call for small space in a biography of Polk, for, so far as any known evidence exists, they formed no part of the President's California program and were in no degree inspired by him. The only possible link which might connect these events

---

[14] *Ibid.*, 495–496.

with the plans of the administration is the "secret instructions" carried by Gillespie, and Fremont had already resisted Mexican authority before the arrival of Gillespie in California. Thomas O. Larkin, American consul at Monterey, who doubtless was cognizant of all instructions brought by Gillespie, continued to use his influence for peace until after the "Bear Flag" insurrection. Another reason for believing that Fremont and his adherents acted without authority from Washington is the fact that the President, in all of his known instructions to naval and military officers, laid special stress on winning over the inhabitants by kind treatment. Fremont adopted the opposite course, and even went out of his way to antagonize them.

During Tyler's administration Fremont had made two expeditions into the western country, and in the summer of 1845 had undertaken a third. Early in 1846 he reached California, and, after making brief stops at Sutter's Fort and San Francisco, he paid a visit to Larkin at Monterey. He explained to the Mexican authorities at Monterey that he was bound for Oregon on a scientific expedition, and his statement was accepted as satisfactory.

Instead of proceeding to Oregon, Fremont, having gone as far north as San José, retraced his steps until he had reached a point not far from Monterey. The excuse for his return southward, long afterward given by Fremont himself,[15] was the desire to find a seaside home for his mother!

His original entry into the province without passports was a violation of Mexican law, and when, contrary to agreement, he returned to the vicinity of Monterey, he was ordered by José Castro, the *comandante general,* to retire from the department. After sending a verbal refusal to obey this order, Fremont repaired to Gavilan Peak, erected a log fort, and hoisted the flag of the United States. Here he was warned by Larkin of the danger of such a proceeding, and, after much vain blustering, he set out for Sutter's Fort, which he reached late in March.

---

[15] Fremont, *Memoirs*, I, 457.

Breaking camp on March 24, Fremont and his party proceeded northward until they had reached Klamath Lake, where they were overtaken, on May 8, by messengers who announced that Lieutenant Gillespie was close behind bearing dispatches from the government of the United States. The dispatches turned out to be a letter of introduction from Buchanan, a letter from Senator Benton, and whatever verbal communications Gillespie may have conveyed. Despite Fremont's assertions that it was made known to him "that to obtain possession of California was the chief object of the President," he has admitted that he learned nothing from Buchanan's letter and that Benton's epistle was equally harmless except when "read by the light of many conversations and discussions with himself and others at Washington."[16] Concerning the verbal instructions related by Gillespie, we are told by Fremont himself that they "had for their principal objects to ascertain the disposition of the California people, to conciliate their feelings in favor of the United States."

As Fremont's subsequent relations with the Californians were anything but conciliatory, and as he received no communications from Washington other than those just mentioned, and finally, as his belligerent attitude toward the California government was so out of harmony with Polk's general policy of conciliation, we must conclude that Fremont's later activities were undertaken without authority from the President.

After Gillespie's arrival at his camp, Fremont returned to the Sacramento Valley in California. If further evidence were necessary to prove that the messenger had brought no orders to precipitate a revolution, it is furnished in letters written by both men under date of May 24, 1846. To Benton, Fremont wrote

---

[16] "The letter from Senator Benton, while apparently of friendship and family details, contained passages and suggestions which, read in the light of many conversations and discussions with himself and others at Washington, clearly indicated to me that I was required by the Government to find out any foreign schemes in relation to California and so far as might be in my power, to counteract them" (*ibid.*, 489).

that "I shall now proceed directly homewards, by the Colorado, but I cannot arrive at the frontier until late in September." "He now goes home from here [Peter Lassen's]," said Gillespie when speaking of Fremont in a letter to Larkin of the same date.[17]

While Fremont was encamped at the "Buttes of Sacramento," General Castro at Santa Clara was collecting a body of troops for the purpose of going to Los Angeles to attack Governor Pio Pico, with whom he had had a disagreement. With this object in view he had sent a man named Francisco Arce to Sonoma to purchase mules for his troops. American settlers, having concluded that Castro was planning to attack them, reported the purchase to Fremont. A party led by Ezekiel Merritt set out from Fremont's camp and, on June 10, captured and brought back the mules. On the following day Merritt set out for Sonoma and captured the town on the fourteenth. After a lively debate California was declared an independent republic and the "bear flag" chosen as its emblem. Fremont did not participate personally in these acts, but they were performed with his knowledge and consent.

Captain John B. Montgomery, commander of the United States ship *Portsmouth* in San Francisco Bay, declined to identify himself with the "bear flag" episode. The revolutionists therefore received no assistance from the navy until the arrival of Commodore Sloat, on July 2, at the port of Monterey. While off the Mexican coast Sloat had heard of Taylor's victories and of the blockade of Vera Cruz, and, on June 7, had set out for Monterey. On July 7, Sloat, after five days of hesitation which was due probably to Larkin's desire to win California by conciliatory methods,[18] caused the United States flag to be raised at Monterey. On the following day Montgomery, acting under

---

[17] Letter to Benton, Fremont, *Memoirs*, I, 499. Gillespie to Larkin, *Larkin Papers*, Bancroft Library.

[18] Bancroft, *California*, V, 228, note 6.

orders from Sloat, took possession of the posts on San Francisco Bay. The party at Sonoma now abandoned their "bear flag" republic and hoisted the stars and stripes.

After a circuitous voyage via the Sandwich Islands, Commodore Stockton, on board the *Congress,* reached Monterey on the fourteenth of July. About two weeks later he succeeded Sloat as commander of the Pacific squadron. More arrogant than his predecessor, Stockton rejected peace overtures sent from Governor Pio Pico and General José Castro, then at Los Angeles, and demanded their unconditional surrender. Seeing that resistance was futile, these officials fled to Mexico, and Stockton, with the coöperation of Fremont and Gillespie, took possession of southern California. Having thus completed the "first conquest" of California, Stockton, acting on his own responsibility, undertook to establish a government over the inhabitants.[19]

In antagonizing the Californians and in attempting to establish a civil government Stockton, as we have already noted, acted on his own responsibility, for nothing in instructions which had been received by himself or his predecessor authorized his arbitrary procedure. Instructions prepared by Secretary Bancroft under the direction of the President—some prior and some subsequent to Stockton's arrival in California, but of course not received at the time—expressed very definitely the desires of the administration with respect to California. One addressed to Sloat on June 8, 1846, ordered him to "endeavor to establish the supremacy of the American flag without any strife with the people of California." If California should be inclined to separate from Mexico and establish "a government of its own under the auspices of the American flag," he was to encourage such action, but no authority to make a conquest was given. The United States, said Bancroft, desired to make California a friend and not an enemy, "to hold possession of it, at least during the war; and

---

[19] Except where noted, this summary of the first conquest has been drawn principally from Rives, II, chap. 34, and Bancroft, *California,* V.

to hold that possession, if possible, with the consent of the inhabitants.'' On July 12 he stated explicitly why possession was so much desired by the administration. ''The object of the United States,'' Sloat was told,

has reference to ultimate peace with Mexico; and if, at that peace, the basis of the *uti possidetis* shall be established the government expects, through your forces, to be found in actual possession of Upper California.

A month later, August 13, Bancroft stated that ''if the treaty of peace shall be made on the basis of *uti possidetis,* it may leave California to the United States.'' Possession at the date of peace negotiations, and not a revolution as had been effected by Fremont and Stockton, was all that the President had contemplated. To be sure, Bancroft, in his letter of July 12, spoke of the necessity of establishing some sort of civil government under the protection of Sloat, and a copy of Kearny's instructions was inclosed; but he urged that ''in selecting persons to hold office, due respect should be had to the wishes of the people of California, as well as to the actual possessors of authority in that province.''[20] Necessarily the officers in California did not know the contents of these letters, for two of them were written after they had taken possession of California; still, the instructions show clearly that Stockton and Fremont did not, in the course they pursued, correctly divine the wishes of the President.

A discussion of the uprising of the Californians under General Flores, the second conquest by the United States forces, and the establishment of a government by General Kearny, acting under instructions from President Polk, must be postponed while we follow the advance of the main army into Mexico. While the President was making plans for acquiring new territory, and while subordinates without his sanction were making conquests on the Pacific coast, General Taylor was winning battles for his government, and laurels for himself, on the banks of the Rio Grande.

---

[20] Instructions of Bancroft to Sloat, Stockton and Biddle, June 8, July 12 and Aug. 13, 1846 (*H. Ex. Doc. 60,* 30 Cong., 1 sess., 237–241).

The first bloodshed, as we have seen, occurred on April 25 when Captain Thornton's dragoons, after a loss of sixteen men, were surrounded and forced to surrender. As a result Taylor, by authority already vested in him by the President, called upon the governors of Texas and Louisiana for eight regiments of volunteers. Before these could be available, however, he was obliged to meet the invading Mexican army with his small force of regulars. First of all he constructed and garrisoned a fort opposite Matamoras and with his main army returned to his base of supplies at Point Isabel, which was threatened by Arista.

After strengthening the position at Point Isabel, Taylor set out on his return to the fort opposite Matamoras, upon which an attack had been made and the commander, Major Brown, killed. On the way back to this fort, which now took the name of Fort Brown, Taylor, on May 8, met and defeated Arista at Palo Alto. At daybreak on the following morning the Mexican commander retreated to Resaca de la Palma, where Taylor overtook him in the afternoon and won another victory. The Mexican army was completely disorganized, and scattered groups, after a precipitate flight across the Rio Grande, reassembled at Matamoras. This place was abandoned without resistance as soon as Taylor began to cross the river on the eighteenth of May. "The battles of Palo Alto and Resaca de la Palma," wrote General Grant long afterwards, "seemed to us engaged, as pretty important affairs; but we had only a faint conception of their magnitude until they were fought over in the North by the Press and the reports came back to us."[21]

In these battles the Mexican forces outnumbered their adversaries more than two to one, but the American army was better equipped and led by a more capable commander. Fearless and unassuming, Taylor enjoyed the confidence of his soldiers. They were always eager to respond to the call of "Old Rough and Ready." Ever prepared to do his duty, Taylor had no thirst for military glory. In a private letter written on the day after

---

[21] Grant, *Personal Memoirs*, I, 99–100. Grant was then a lieutenant.

his occupation of Matamoras he said that "I heartily wish the war was at an end."[22]

News of Taylor's victories reached Washington on May 23, the day on which Polk read to his cabinet Scott's letter about being fired upon in front and rear. When he received this news the President made no comment in his diary, except to record the fact that the news had arrived, but three days later he sent a message to the Senate nominating Taylor as major-general by brevet.[23] On May 30, just one week after the receipt of Taylor's official dispatch, the new commission was ready and Marcy forwarded it to the general along with an assignment to the chief command. On the same day the President in a letter to Taylor praised the general's "gallant conduct and distinguished services," and stated that the "battles of Palo Alto and Resaca de la Palma rank among our most brilliant victories."[24]

There is no reason for believing that, at the time of Taylor's promotion, Polk harbored other than the most kindly feelings toward the victorious general. The delay in preparing the cordial letter just quoted was due to the pressure of executive business such as planning the California expedition and reducing Scott and Gains[25] to proper subordination. Not knowing the reason why the President's expression of approval had been delayed, Taylor felt slighted, and his distrust of the administration was aroused. "It is strange passing strange," he wrote to his son-in-law, "that I have heard nothing from Washing[ton] since my official report of the battles of the 8th & 9th reached there, which I have seen published in the National Intelligencer & Union." He hinted at politics in high quarters, and mentioned a rumor that members of Congress from the South and West had protested to the President against his being superseded by Scott.

---

22 Taylor to his son-in-law, Dr. R. C. Wood, May 19, 1846, *Taylor Letters*, 4.

23 Polk, *Diary*, I, 422, 425, 428. Until this promotion Taylor had been a colonel in actual rank, but brigadier-general by brevet.

24 *H. Ex. Doc. 60*, 30 Cong., 1 sess., 282–283.

25 Gains had, without authority, been enlisting troops for the Rio Grande campaign.

He hoped that the report was untrue, for "I consider this command properly his, & I have no wish to prevent his exercising it."[26]

When another week brought no word from Washington Taylor became convinced that the administration was more interested in playing politics than in defeating the Mexicans. Merit and long service, in his opinion, were disregarded at the national capital; "the more one does the more they expect of him, and his services or standing is estimated by political considerations." He was "perfectly disgusted" with the inefficiency in Washington, for small boats and wagons could be brought "from Liverpool" in less time than it had taken the government to supply them. "Was I a prominent or ambitious aspirant for civil distinction or honors," he wrote, "I might very readily suppose there was an intention somewhere among the high functionaries to break me down"; and he feared that such would be the result of the government's policy, "whether from design or not." He regarded as "ridiculous" a report which had just reached camp to the effect that Scott had declined to take command of the army for fear of injuring his Presidential prospects, and that a quarrel with Polk had resulted from his refusal. "They need have no apprehensions," he added, "of being interfered with by me for that high office, which I would decline if proffered & I could reach it without opposition."[27] As late as August 4 he expressed the hope that Scott would be the Whig candidate in 1848, but he put away the crown from his own head with a far less resolute hand.[28]

---

[26] Taylor to R. C. Wood, June 12, 1846, *Taylor Letters*, 9–10. Scott had already notified Taylor that he [Scott] had been assigned to the command, but would not go to Mexico immediately.

[27] Taylor to R. C. Wood, June 21, 1846, *ibid.*, 12–14. When more definite news of Scott's quarrel with the President arrived, Taylor expressed regret, for it would keep him in Mexico "which I by no means desire" (Taylor to R. C. Wood, June 24).

[28] "So far as I am concerned I wish to have nothing to do with that high office; & if I had, this is not the proper time to discuss the subject; let this war at any rate be first brought to a close" (Taylor to R. C. Wood, *ibid.*, 35).

His attitude toward the administration was based on groundless suspicions, for at this early date there was surely no desire to "break him down." Even the receipt of Marcy's letter which assigned him to the chief command and inclosed his new commission did not change his antipathy toward his superiors. The honor of his promotion, in his opinion, was more than overbalanced by his assignment to command an expedition which "must be a failure owing to the ignorance of some in regard to some matters, & the imbecility of others, for all of which I shall be made the scape goat." He must have received Polk's laudatory letter in the same mail, but of this he made no mention. He pronounced Scott "crazy" because of his letters to Marcy, and he was certain that "Gen'l S. will never hear the last of a fire from his rear, or a hasty plate of soup."[29]

While in this mood, Taylor questioned the good faith of the government in its dealings with Mexico. He was confident that "our ambitious views of conquest & agrandisement at the expense of a weak power will only be restrained & circumscribed by our inability to carry out our view." He did not rate that ability very high, for he predicted that if the Mexicans should hold out for six or eight months "we will be fully as anxious to make peace as they are." Three weeks later he hoped that peace negotiations would soon begin, but he feared that the United States would claim a vast amount of territory as a war indemnity and for "real & pretended roberies committed on our commerce; which will no doubt be double & treble award to certain claimants over & above what they ever lost." No land grabbing act of the British government had been "more outrageous" than Polk's plan to take permanent possession of California.[30]

---

[29] Taylor to R. C. Wood, June 30 and July 7, 1846, *ibid.*, 18–25.

[30] Taylor to R. C. Wood, July 14, Aug. 4, and Aug. 23, 1846, *ibid.*, 28, 37, 49. Undoubtedly Taylor's distrust was increased by letters from Whig friends in the United States. See letters from Scott and Crittenden, in Coleman, *Life of John J. Crittenden*, 256, 278.

Taylor had reason enough to complain of the want of transportation facilities,[31] although the cause was to be sought, not in any desire to ''break him down,'' but in the lack of preparation usually experienced at the outbreak of a war, and more especially in the ignorance of the Washington officials concerning everything in Mexico.

The President and his cabinet knew little of the topography of the country, or of its seasons, fertility, and accessibility. Even the geography was something of a mystery. As a result, considerable confusion and frequent misunderstandings were only to be expected. For the necessary information the executive departments had to depend largely on the reports of General Taylor; and the general, fearing that the main object of the administration was to make a ''scape goat'' of him, did not feel free to offer advice or to act without explicit orders.

In a letter addressed to Taylor on June 8, 1846, Marcy stated that nothing had been heard from him since his brief dispatch announcing the victories of Palo Alto and Resaca de la Palma, but it was assumed that Matamoras had been occupied. He expressed the hope that Taylor would get possession of all places on the Rio Grande as far up as Laredo, and that he would be able to capture Monterey. The measures to be pursued, however, were left to the general's ''own discretion and judgment.'' The President very much desired, said Marcy, to have Taylor's ''views and suggestions in relation to the fall campaign.'' Being desirous of prosecuting the war with vigor, the President wished to know whether, in the general's opinion, the present expedition should be conducted with a view of striking at the City of Mexico, or of operating in the northern provinces only. ''Your views on this point,'' said Marcy, ''will doubtless have an important influence upon the determination of the government here.'' Information was requested, also, on overland transportation facilities and

---

[31] ''I consider there is an entire break down in the Qr M [quartermaster's] department every where'' (Taylor to R. C. Wood, June 21, 1846, *ibid.*, 13).

on the probability of obtaining adequate provisions, and the general's opinion was asked concerning the number and character of troops to be employed. Four days later Scott impressed upon Taylor the importance of obtaining information regarding movements and designs of the enemy, and authorized him to pay *"employes"* liberally for procuring such information. Kearny's expedition to New Mexico and California, said Scott, would necessarily be independent of Taylor's command, but that of General Wool against the city of Chihuahua would be under Taylor's general directions. The general was authorized to agree to an armistice with a view to peace negotiations, provided he was convinced of the enemy's good faith.[32]

In his reply to these letters, Taylor stated that he had little definite information to impart. He gave, however, his opinions regarding the probabilities of obtaining supplies in the interior. Should the inhabitants prove friendly, he thought that his army might obtain provisions sufficient to enable it to penetrate as far as Saltillo; still, in his opinion, the army under his command should confine its operations to the northern provinces and should not attempt to reach the City of Mexico. He "purposely" abstained "from any reference to movements against Tampico or Vera Cruz." He complained that he was greatly embarrassed by the lack of transportation facilities and closed his letter with the remark that:

I am waiting with the utmost impatience the arrival of steamboats suited to the navigation of this river to establish a depot at Camargo, and throw the troops gradually forward to that point.[33]

Although General Taylor may have been overcautious in offering suggestions, he seems to have reported all the information in his possession. But officials in Washington, especially Quartermaster General Jesup, were inclined to excuse their own shortcomings by pleading lack of information from Taylor, and the

---

[32] *H. Ex. Doc. 60*, 30 Cong., 1 sess., 323–327.

[33] Taylor to Adj. Gen., July 2, 1846, *ibid.*, 329–332.

President came to feel that the general did not possess the initiative and the vigor necessary for the command which had been intrusted to him. Polk admitted that he had no knowledge of military affairs, but he had "a strong conviction" that necessary equipments had been too long delayed. He told the quartermaster general that some of his subordinates had become gentlemen of leisure who "required to have a coal of fire put on their backs to make them move promptly." He feared, also, that Taylor was not the man for the general command:

> He is brave but does not seem to have resources or grasp of mind enough to conduct such a campaign. In his communications to the War Department he seems ready to obey orders, but appears to be unwilling to express any opinion or to take any responsibility on himself. Though he is in the country with means of knowledge which cannot be possessed at Washington, he makes no suggestion as to the plan of the campaign, but simply obeys orders and gives no information to aid the administration in directing his movement. He is, I have no doubt, a good subordinate officer, but from all the evidence before me I think him unfit for the chief command. Though this is so, I know of no one whom I can substitute in his place.[34]

These remarks greatly exaggerated Taylor's taciturnity, yet the President was sorely in need of information to aid him in directing the campaign. When in October an expedition to Tampico and Vera Cruz was being considered, so little was known of the character of the coast that Polk found it necessary to send to Rhode Island for F. M. Dimond, former consul at Vera Cruz, "believing that from him reliable information could be obtained." Nearly a month later the quartermaster general just awoke to the fact that: "Had we foreseen the nature of the Rio Del Norte, and built suitable steamboats several months ago, a million of dollars might have been saved by this time."[35]

---

[34] Polk, *Diary*, II, 117–119.

[35] *Ibid.*, 180, 196. Jesup to Marcy, Nov. 7, 1846 (*H. Ex. Doc. 60*, 30 Cong., 1 sess., 564). So vigorously had Taylor complained of inefficiency in the quartermaster's department, in a letter dated September 1, that Jesup was sent to New Orleans so that he might personally supervise the equipping of Taylor's army (Corresp. of Taylor, Marcy and Jesup, in same *Doc.*, 557 ff.).

Although the President was lacking in military experience, and although, according to his own testimony, he found it to be "impossible to give much attention to the details in conducting the war," his brain was most fertile when it came to concocting schemes for undermining the control of the Mexican government over its own citizens. Ample proof of this is furnished in a confidential letter sent to Taylor under date of July 9, 1846. The letter was signed by Marcy, but was drafted by Polk, with some assistance from Benton. The President approved Taylor's conciliatory conduct toward the Mexicans and urged him to continue friendly intercourse with the inhabitants. The general was instructed to

take occasions to send officers to the headquarters of the enemy for military purposes, real or ostensible . . . . in which opportunity may be taken to speak of the war itself as only carried on to obtain justice, and that we had much rather procure that by negotiation than by fighting.

Racial and social discords, he was told, made it possible to induce a large portion of the people to wish success to invaders who had no desire to injure them:

In all this field of division—in all these elements of social, political, personal, and local discord—there must be openings to reach the interests, passions, or principles of some of the parties, and thereby to conciliate their good will, and make them co-operate with us in bringing about an honorable and a speedy peace . . . . . Policy and force are to be combined; and the fruits of the former will be prized as highly as those of the latter.

Another paragraph, which was penned by the President alone and which he considered to be the most important, was still more specific in outlining the policy of the administration:

Availing yourself of divisions which you may find among the Mexican people . . . . it will be your policy to encourage the separate departments or States, and especially those which you may invade and occupy, to declare their independence of the central government of Mexico, and either to become our allies, or to assume, as it is understood Yucatan has done, a neutral attitude in the existing war between the United States and Mexico.

After peace had been concluded such departments were to "decide for themselves their own form of government." As to temporary governments Taylor was authorized to follow the course laid down in the instructions to Kearny, a copy of which was inclosed. He was informed that an expedition against Mexico City would probably be sent from Tampico or Vera Cruz, and not from the Rio Grande. Information was requested, and Taylor was instructed to send his answer "directly to the *President of the United States.*"[36] Only two days before this Houston, of Texas, had introduced in the Senate a resolution which extended the thanks of Congress to Taylor for his victories on the Rio Grande, and requested the President to present the general with a gold medal "as a tribute to his good conduct, and generosity, to the vanquished."[37]

As usual, Buchanan was ready with a dash of cold water for the President's scheme of benevolent assimilation of Mexican territory. He was in favor of taking and holding California as far as Monterey but no farther. "He was opposed, too," said the President, "to giving the inhabitants of Tamaulipas or of any of the Provinces South of New Mexico any encouragement to annex themselves to the U. S." Both Walker and Polk preferred to extend the boundary farther south, and the President was sorry to find his Secretary of State "entertaining opinions so contracted & sectional."[38]

About the same time, members of Congress gave the President no little annoyance by introducing resolutions of inquiry concerning the purposes of the war and the manner of conducting it. On June 29 the Senate had passed a resolution, introduced by Johnson, of Maryland, which called on the President for all

---

[36] Marcy to Taylor, July 9, 1846 (*H. Ex. Doc. 60*, 30 Cong., 1 sess., 333–336). Polk, *Diary*, II, 16–17. "I will preserve the original draft for future reference," Polk recorded in his diary, "should it become proper. I do this because it is a document of more than ordinary importance."

[37] *Cong. Globe*, 29 Cong., 1 sess., 1064.

[38] Polk, *Diary*, II, 15–16.

correspondence incident to the raising of volunteer troops. Polk sent for Johnson, on July 6, and by showing him the correspondence convinced him that it would be unwise to comply, for the projected conquest of California would be revealed, and this would "excite the jealousy of England and France, who might interfere to prevent the accomplishing of our objects."[39] For the purpose of ascertaining why nothing had been done by Taylor's army since the occupation of Matamoras, Hannegan, on July 8, introduced a resolution which purposed to ask the President for information concerning all orders sent to the general since the ninth of May. By his renewal of friendship with Benton the President had procured an able defender, and the Missouri Senator was successful in sending this resolution to the table by asserting that if an officer should furnish the information sought he would be court-martialed and shot.[40]

In truth, the executive departments had little information to impart. On August 1, Taylor answered the letter of July 9, which Benton and Polk had so carefully prepared, by saying that he had little to add to his dispatch of July second. He still declined to venture an opinion on the practicability of an expedition against Vera Cruz, for the "Department of War must be much better informed than I am on that point." He told the President that he would obey his order to seek friendly intercourse with Mexican generals, and to induce the people to declare their independence, but he stated very frankly that he did not anticipate much success.[41]

President Polk's subterranean diplomacy was not confined to an attempt to undermine the loyalty of Mexican generals and people. Since his conversations with Atocha, he had never quite abandoned the hope of making use of Santa Anna, and he now decided to assist the ex-dictator in regaining power in Mexico.

[39] *Ibid.*, 13–14.

[40] *Cong. Globe*, 29 Cong., 1 sess., 1068.

[41] Taylor to Polk, Aug. 1, 1846 (*H. Ex. Doc. 60*, 30 Cong., 1 sess., 336–338).

On May 13, 1846, two days after the President had sent his war message to Congress, Secretary Bancroft instructed Commodore Conner to blockade the Gulf ports of Mexico. At the same time, he inclosed a "private and confidential" order which read: "If Santa Anna endeavors to enter the Mexican ports, you will allow him to pass freely." Atocha, it will be remembered, had told Polk that Santa Anna would probably return to Mexico in April or May, and that he was in favor of ceding territory to the United States. Apparently the President had this conversation in mind when he caused Bancroft to issue the order to Conner.[42]

Early in June Polk decided to send a special messenger to Havana for the purpose of learning the plans of Santa Anna. The messenger selected was Alexander Slidell Mackenzie, a naval officer and a nephew of John Slidell, the minister whom Mexico had rejected. He was furnished with a letter from Buchanan to Campbell, the United States consul at Havana, a copy of Bancroft's confidential order to Conner, and verbal instructions from the President. Mackenzie gave the purport of these instructions when reporting to Buchanan the result of his interview with Santa Anna.[43] He arrived in Havana on July 5 and, by Campbell, was introduced to Santa Anna. From Polk's verbal instructions he had prepared a memorandum, and this he read to the ex-President of Mexico. In substance it stated that the United States had taken up arms to redress its grievances and was determined to prosecute the war with vigor, but that the President was desirous of ending the conflict speedily if an honorable peace could be made. Believing Santa Anna to be able and willing to make such a peace, "the President of the United States would see with pleasure his restoration to power in Mexico." It was made clear that Polk would insist on the Rio Grande as the boundary of Texas and that he must at least have enough of California to

---

[42] *Ibid.*, 744. Polk, *Diary*, I, 229.

[43] Mackenzie to Buchanan, June [July] 7, 1846 (duplicate in *Polk Papers*). This letter is printed in full in Reeves, *Diplomacy under Tyler and Polk*, 299–307.

include the port of San Francisco. For the latter concession he would pay liberally, and his present intention was to demand no indemnity for the expenses of the war. Although, according to Mackenzie's account, Santa Anna aserted that the Nueces was the real boundary of Texas, he finally agreed to make all necessary concessions rather than see Mexico delivered into the hands of a foreign prince or continue under the monarchistic government of Paredes. He even suggested plans under which Taylor could most easily defeat the Mexican armies, and advised the occupation of Tampico. Mackenzie considered these suggestions of such importance that he exceeded his instructions and carried them directly to General Taylor. He had an interview with Taylor late in July,[44] but it is not likely that the general was influenced by Santa Anna's recommendations.

Mackenzie's report of his interview with Santa Anna, according to a note appended by Buchanan, reached Washington on the third of August. The President did not mention the subject in his diary either at the time of sending the messenger or when the report was received. In January, 1848, however, after he and his cabinet had decided not to include this report with other documents submitted in response to a call from the House, the President recorded his version of the mission. In this account Polk stated that he had given Mackenzie no written instructions, and that he had sent "no message" to Santa Anna. In reducing the conversation with the President to writing and in reading it to Santa Anna, the messenger had acted wholly without authority. As to whether Mackenzie's memorandum correctly reported his conversation with Polk, the record in the diary is somewhat ambiguous. "It is fortunate," is the President's comment, "that what he puts into my mouth could do me no injury, if it was genuine & was published; but it would exhibit me in a ridiculous attitude." For this reason, he decided to withhold it from the House.[45]

---

[44] Meade, *Life and Letters*, I, 116.   [45] Polk, *Diary*, III, 290–292.

The President was eager to settle all differences with Mexico by diplomacy instead of war, provided he could obtain the territory he most coveted. Without waiting to learn the results of Mackenzie's mission, he made one more attempt to make a satisfactory treaty with the government of Paredes. On Sunday, July 20, he sent for Benton and read to him a dispatch which had been prepared by Buchanan. It was addressed to the Mexican Minister of Foreign Relations. Benton approved the dispatch and advised that it should be sent. A week later a revised copy was forwarded to Commodore Conner with instructions that it should be delivered to the Mexican government. The document stated that the President was no less anxious to terminate the war than he had been to avoid it in the beginning. To accomplish this purpose he was ready to send an envoy who would be clothed with power to make "a peace just and honorable for both parties." Should Mexico prefer to negotiate in Washington, her envoy would be treated with kindness. "In the present communication," said Buchanan, "it is deemed useless and might prove injurious, to discuss the causes of the existing war."[46]

Having decided to seek a settlement with Mexico through diplomatic channels, Polk revived the plan of asking Congress for money to be used in negotiating a treaty. When discussing with Benton the dispatch just mentioned, the President expressed the belief that he could procure both California and New Mexico if Congress would furnish him with two million dollars which might be paid to Mexico as soon as a treaty had been signed. Benton favored such an appropriation and advised Polk to consult with members of the Committee on Foreign Affairs. The President sent for McDuffie, Cass, and other members of the committee. He cited the appropriation which had enabled Jefferson to purchase Louisiana and urged the expediency of making a similar appropriation now. Archer, the Whig member, agreed to take

---

[46] Buchanan to Min. of For. Rel., July 27, 1846; Buchanan to Conner, same date (*Sen. Ex. Doc. 107*, 29 Cong., 2 sess., 2–3). The former is also in Buchanan, *Works*, VII, 40.

the matter up with Senators of his party. Having thus paved the way, Polk sent a confidential message to the Senate on August 4, 1846, and along with it, a copy of the dispatch already forwarded to the Mexican Minister of Foreign Relations. Believing that "the best mode of securing perpetual peace and good neighborhood between the two Republics" would be the acquision of Mexican territory, he asked for an advance appropriation of two million dollars as a means of facilitating such an acquisition.[47] After the Senate had given its approval, the message was transmitted to the House so that a bill might be drafted.

As soon as the message had been read in the House, McKay, of North Carolina, presented a bill which provided that two million dollars be appropriated "for the purpose of defraying any extraordinary expenses which may be incurred in the intercourse between the United States and foreign nations," said money to be applied under the direction of the President. While Polk's plans for acquiring California were not, of course, generally known at the time, the Whigs at once charged that the money was to be used for this purpose, either by direct purchase or indirectly by bribing Mexican officials. The necessarily indefinite wording of the bill gave ample room for partisan interpretations. White, of New York, was the most uncompromising critic of the President. He asserted that Polk himself had, in his war message, furnished abundant evidence that this war had been "projected, planned, and provoked" long before Congress had been consulted in the matter. He intimated, also, that the purpose of the bill was to extend slaveholding territory, and he challenged any Democrat to propose an amendment which would exclude slavery from the territory to be acquired. During the evening session of the same day Wilmot accepted this challenge by offering his famous "proviso" that slavery should not be permitted in any teritory to be obtained from Mexico.

---

47 Polk, *Diary*, II, 50–66. Richardson, *Messages*, IV, 456.

The position taken by John Quincy Adams is interesting. A violent opponent of the administration on nearly every occasion, he had supported Polk's claim to 54° 40′ as the Oregon boundary, and he now warmly advocated the appropriation of the two million dollars for which the President had asked. For the sake of clearness, he asked McKay to substitute "Mexico" for "foreign nations," but, despite his sympathy with Wilmot's amendment, he was ready to "vote for the bill in any form." He did not believe an anti-slavery amendment to be necessary, for the institution had been abolished by Mexico and would not be reëstablished.[48] Based on the past, this was sound argument, but he could not forsee what the future would bring forth.

The McKay bill, supplemented by the Wilmot amendment, passed the House by a vote of eighty-seven to sixty-four. On the day following, the last of the session, it was considered by the Senate, but Davis, of Massachusetts, prevented a vote on the measure by holding the floor until the session had expired. Whether the Senate would have pased the bill as amended we are, of course, unable to say, but the President believed that it would have struck out Wilmot's "mischievous & foolish amendment" and that the House would have concurred. "What connection slavery had with making peace with Mexico," said he, "it is difficult to conceive." In order to preclude all doubt concerning his motives, he confided to his diary an explicit statement of his reasons for requesting the advance appropriation.[49]

---

[48] "There are no slaves in California—slavery is abolished there; and if we were to make peace, and in that peace to acquire California, there could be no law of slavery established there, unless it was made an article of the treaty itself."

[49] "My object in asking this appropriation has not been fully stated in this diary. It was this. Mexico is indebted to the U. S. in a large sum, which she is unable to pay. There is also a disputed question of boundary. The two countries are now engaged in War. When peace is made the only indemnity which the U. S. can have will be a cession of territory. The U. S. desires to acquire Upper California, New Mexico, and perhaps some territory South of these Provinces. For a suitable cession of territory we are willing to assure the debts to our own citizens & to pay an additional consideration. My information induces the belief that Mexico would be willing to settle the

The disappointment which resulted from the defeat of the appropriation bill was somewhat assuaged by news of the conquest of California which reached Washington on the last day of August. The welcome information and a copy of Sloat's proclamation were brought by a messenger who had just come from Mexico City bearing dispatches for the British minister. The diplomat reported the news to Buchanan immediately, and the President noted in his diary: "This important intelligence comes to us through no other channel."[50] The conquest, however, was of little immediate value, for Polk was soon to learn that Mexico had declined to accept his proffered "honorable peace."

Santa Anna, and not Paredes, dictated the answer to Buchanan's letter of July 27 in which Mexico was invited to open peace negotiations. Relying on Polk's assurances that he would not be molested, Santa Anna left Havana on August 8, 1846, on

---

difficulty in this manner. No Government, however, it is believed, is strong enough to make a treaty ceding territory and long maintain power unless they could receive, at the time of making the treaty, money enough to support the army. Whatever party can keep the army in its support can hold the power. The present Government is without any regular revenue, & without a prompt payment as a part of the consideration would not venture to make a Treaty. Having no doubt that I could effect an adjustment of the pending war if I had the command of $2,000,000, I felt it to be my duty to ask such an appropriation. This I did in the first instance by a confidential communication made to the Senate in Executive Session on the 4th Instant. The Senate on the 6th Inst. passed resolutions approving my views and declaring that it was proper to make the appropriation asked. The Resolution approving my views passed the Senate by a vote of ayes 43 to nays 2, and the Resolution approving the appropriation by yeas 33 to nays 19 (. . .). With a full knowledge of all this Senator Davis had recourse to the desperate resort of speaking against time, to defeat a measure which he had been unable to defeat by his vote. Had the appropriation been passed I am confident I should have made an honorable peace by which we should have acquired California, & such other territory as we desired, before the end of October. Should the war be now protracted, the responsibility will fall more heavily upon the head of Senator Davis than upon any other man, and he will deserve the execrations of the country. I desired when I made the communication to the Senate in Executive Session, to consult that body in secret Session, to the end that the appropriation, if approved, should have been passed quietly and without attracting public attention, or exciting the jealousy of the Powers of Europe; but contrary to my wishes great publicity has been given to it by Congress" (*Dairy*, II, 75–78).

50 *Ibid.*, 108.

board the British ship *Arab,* and eight days later he landed in Vera Cruz. With him came Almonte, former minister to the United States, and Rejón and Basadre who had been members of his cabinet at the time he was forced to leave Mexico. The way had been prepared for his return by *pronouncement* of the troops, and General Salas, the commander-in-chief, stood ready to do the bidding of the returned exile.

On the day of his arrival, August 16, Santa Anna issued an address which was filled with specious promises and high sounding phrases.[51] If these were to be accepted at face value, the ex-dictator had returned a sincere patriot and a champion of the Constitution of 1824, ready to subject himself "entirely to the decisions of the constitutent assembly, the organ of the sovereign will of the nation." For a time, Salas continued to act as chief executive while Santa Anna, the general-in-chief, sojourned at a country residence. But the late exile selected the cabinet and controlled the affairs of the nation.

By the last of August internal affairs were adjusted sufficiently to enable the new government to consider the offer made by the United States. In reply to. Buchanan's note Rejón, the new Secretary of Foreign Relations, said that the general-in-chief could not but "fix his attention strongly" on the passage in that note which suggested the omission of all discussion concerning the causes of the war. He felt himself unable to negotiate on such terms; and besides, he was obliged to postpone a definite answer until the Mexican congress had met on the sixth of December.[52] This aggravating snub was Polk's reward for helping to reinstate Santa Anna in Mexico. Before many months had passed he had still greater reasons for regretting that he had listened to the advice of Atocha.

Rejón's letter reached Washington on September 19 and was considered by the President as a virtual refusal to negotiate. He

---

[51] A copy in translation, *H. Ex. Doc. 60,* 30 Cong., 1 sess., 777–785.

[52] Rejón to Buchanan, Aug. 31, 1846 (*H. Ex. Doc. 4,* 29 Cong., 2 sess., 43.)

at once decided that the character of the war should be changed
so that the Mexican people might be made to feel the consequences of their government's refusal to make peace. The conciliatory policy of paying liberally for supplies was now to be
changed for one of forcible seizures. The President directed
that the towns in Tamaulipas should be occupied and that a
descent should be made upon the coast at Tampico. Contrary
to his usual custom of refraining from all labor on the Sabbath,
Polk held cabinet meetings on September 20 in order to hasten
aggressive movements against the enemy. Colonel Stevenson,
who had been put in command of the New York regiment destined
for service in California, was reprimanded by the President because his departure had been so long delayed, and Polk ''intimated plainly to Col. S. that if further delay occurred he [I]
would cause the officers who produced it to be arrested & tried.''
During the next few days much energy was devoted to war and
naval preparations. Major-General Patterson was selected to
command the Tampico expedition, and Pillow and Shields were
chosen as his assistants. Polk gave personal attention to the
quartermaster's department so that there might be no delay.
The failure of his diplomatic overtures and the lax conduct of
subordinates put the President in a petulant mood. He charged
Whig officials with indifference regarding military operations,
while General Scott, instead of being an aide to the War Department, was a constant embarrassment. ''I will observe his course,''
wrote the President in his diary, ''and if necessary will order
him to some other post.''[53]

While making preparations for war, Polk still left the way
open for negotiations with Mexico. Under his direction, Buchanan, on September 26, prepared and sent a reply to Rejón's
note of August 31. He charged the Mexican government with
having distorted the meaning of his former letter. He told
Rejón that ''the President will now await with patience and

---

[53] Polk, *Diary*, II, 143–151.

with hope the final decision of the Mexican Government.'' He informed the minister, however, that in the meantime the war would be prosecuted vigorously, and there was a veiled threat that Mexico would be required to pay the costs. Buchanan's original draft had stated explicitly that Mexico must indemnify the United States for the expenses of the war, but Polk and Marcy deemed it politic to reserve this blunt demand until negotiations had opened.[54] Commodore Conner was instructed to notify Slidell at New Orleans immediately in the event that the Mexican government should at any time show a disposition to negotiate.[55]

From the middle of May, when he occupied Matamoras, until the first of September, General Taylor spent the time in training and equipping an army for an advance upon Monterey. Due to General Gaines's unauthorized call for volunteers, Taylor was overwhelmed with troops, but the quartermaster had failed to furnish him with adequate supplies or means of transportation. Commenting on the impatience felt by people in the United States, and even by volunteer troops, because the army did not advance into Mexico, Lieutenant Meade said in a letter:

These wise people forget that soldiers cannot march or fight unless they have something to eat, and when in a country totally devoid of resources, they must carry with them the means of sustaining physical nature, and in consequence must have the means of carrying their provisions and other supplies.

He thought that Scott was right in not wishing to go immediately to the Rio Grande, there to idle away his time ''waiting for wagons and pork''; but ''unfortunately, he [Scott] chose to ascribe political reasons to what, I believe, was simply military ignorance on the part of Mr. Polk.''[56]

---

[54] Polk, *Diary*, II, 156–158. Buchanan to Min. of For. Rel., Sept. 26, 1846 (*H. Ex. Doc. 4*, 29 Cong., 2 sess., 44–45).

[55] Buchanan to Conner, Oct. 1, 1846 (*Works*, VII, 90).

[56] Meade, *Life and Letters*, I, 101–111. ''This, with his 'hasty plate of soup,' '' continued Meade, ''has ruined him forever, for it is much better in this country for a man to commit a gross crime than to make himself ridiculous; the former he may get over, the latter, never.''

By the last of August Taylor had collected his invading force at Camargo, and within a few days his army was advancing on Monterey. The march was tedious, and on arriving at that place he found it to be well fortified. The attack upon the city began on September 20, and on the twenty-fourth Ampudia, the Mexican commander, offered to evacuate the city if Taylor would permit the troops to retain their arms and other movable property. Taylor at first demanded "a complete surrender of the town and garrison, the latter as prisoners of war"; but he finally consented to allow the Mexicans to march out with all of their arms and accoutrements. He also agreed to a truce of eight weeks, or until further orders had been received from their respective governments.[57] The period of inactivity was destined to be longer than that agreed upon in the truce, for the President soon determinted to modify his plan of reducing Mexico to submission.

The special messenger whom Taylor had dispatched with a report of the battle of Monterey reached Washington on Sunday, October 11, and the President was much displeased because the general had agreed to the armistice.[58] At a cabinet meeting held on the following day all agreed that the general had committed a "great error." After the meeting, Polk noted in his diary:

But two reasons could have justified the terms granted to the enemy in the capitulation. The first is, if he believed that he could not capture them; & the 2nd. is, that Gen'l Ampudia may have induced him to believe that in consequence of the recent change of rulers in Mexico that Government was disposed to make peace. If the first reason existed Gen'l Taylor has not stated it in his despatches, and we have no information to justify

---

[57] Taylor's reports (*H. Ex. Doc. 4*, 29 Cong., 2 sess., 83–102). A good account of this battle is given in Rives, *United States and Mexico*, II, chap. 37.

[58] "In agreeing to this armistice Gen'l Taylor violated his express orders & I regret that I cannot approve his course. He had the enemy in his power & should have taken them prisoners, depriving them of their arms, discharge them on their parole of honour, and preserved the advantage which he had obtained by pushing on without delay further into the country, if the force at his command justified it. . . . It was a great mistake in Gen'l Taylor to agree to an armistice. It will only enable the Mexican army to reorganize and recruit so as to make another stand" (*Diary*, II, 181).

the existence of this reason, though it may have existed.   If the second
reason was the one upon which he acted, then Gen'l Ampudia has over-
reached & deceived him . . . . .   The Cabinet were united in the opinion
that if Gen'l Taylor had captured the Mexican army, deprived them of their
arms, and discharged them upon their parole of honour not to bear arms
during the war or until they were regularly exchanged, that it would have
probably ended the war with Mexico. . . . .   It was agreed unanimously
that orders should be forthwith sent to Gen'l Taylor to terminate the
armistice to which he had agreed, and to prosecute the war with energy
and vigor.[59]

Taylor's agreement had, in fact, placed his government in a
most awkward position, but the difficulty was due more to the
slow means of communication than to bad judgment on the part
of the general or the administration.   On receipt of Rejón's letter
Polk decided immediately, as we have already noted, to strike a
blow at both northern Tamaulipas and Tampico, and Marcy,[60]
on September 22, notified Taylor of the change in the President's
plans.   General Patterson was at the same time ordered by the
President to invade Tamaulipas.   To be sure Taylor had no knowledge of this arrangement when he made the agreement with
Ampudia, but his armistice, if permitted to remain in force, would
paralyze in a great measure the aggressive movement which had
been assigned to Patterson.

The letter in which Marcy instructed Taylor to terminate the
armistice was not so drastic as the comments in Polk's diary
would lead one to expect.   In fact, it contained no phrase that
should have given offense to the victorious general.   The President, he said, regretted that "it was not deemed advisable to
insist upon the terms which you had first proposed," but he
added that the "circumstances which dictated doubtless justified the change."   After explaining the new plan of campaign
and the necessity of beginning operations at once, he instructed
Taylor to give the notice necessary for ending the truce.[61]

---

[59] Polk, *Diary*, II, 183–184.
[60] *H. Ex. Doc. 60*, 30 Cong., 1 sess., 341–343.
[61] Marcy to Taylor, Oct. 13, 1846 (*ibid.*, 355–357).

Although nothing in Marcy's communication could reasonably be construed as a reflection upon Taylor, the ever-suspicious general drew from it evidence of a conspiracy to discredit him and to deprive him of his command. While admitting that Marcy's letter praised him, he detected in it a very cold tone. He believed that the administration was hostile to him simply because his friends had been indiscreet enough to connect his name with the Presidency.[62] In his reply to the War Department, he stated that with his limited force he could not have prevented the escape of the enemy from Monterey, and that his equipment did not warrant the pursuit of Ampudia into a country devoid of supplies. He admitted that he had been influenced, also, by Ampudia's statement that Santa Anna was in favor of making peace, and with a thrust at the President, he added: "It is not unknown to the government that I had the very best reason for believing the statement of General Ampudia to be true."[63] This pointed reference to Polk's part in the reinstatement of Santa Anna must have been read at the White House with anything but pleasure, yet Taylor could not be blamed for believing that the President desired, most of all, a peaceable adjustment with Mexico. All of his instructions had emphasized this point. He was aware of Polk's overtures to Santa Anna and of his recent offer to the Paredes government. Since he had not received Marcy's instructions of September 22 his agreement with Ampudia accorded very well with the policy of his government, so far as he knew it at the time. Still, he had no reason to complain because he had been instructed to end the truce, and the political motives which dictated these instructions existed only in his own very active imagination. The main difficulty, as already stated, was the slow means of communication which made it impossible for either the general or the administration to know the conditions

---

62 Taylor to Wood, Nov. 10, 1846, *Taylor Letters,* 67.

63 Taylor to Adj. Gen., Nov. 8, 1846 (*H. Ex. Doc. 60*, 30 Cong., 1 sess., 359–360).

which governed the actions of the other. Even before the armistice had been disapproved, Taylor felt abused because the President had tried to facilitate the advance upon Tamaulipas by sending orders directly to General Patterson,[64] but in this case, also, Polk's action was governed by military rather than political considerations.

Santa Anna's declaration in favor of restoring the constitution of 1824 led President Polk to abandon the hope of inducing the northern provinces of Mexico to declare their independence of the central government. Since the main purpose of Taylor's advance into Nueva León and Coahuila, and that of Wool into Chihuahua, had been to effect this separation, the President decided that both of these expeditions, especially the latter, had now become "comparatively unimportant." Accordingly he suggested at a cabinet meeting that Taylor should be authorized to remain at Monterey, and, if he saw fit, to order Wool to the same place. He suggested, also, that the most effective means of bringing Mexico to terms would be an invasion from Vera Cruz. Marcy embodied these views in a letter to Taylor and his letter was carefully discussed at a special cabinet meeting. In the meantime Marcy's draft had been shown to Scott whereupon the general expressed a desire to command the Vera Cruz expedition, and recommended an army of twenty-five or thirty thousand men. But Polk had not forgotten Scott's indiscreet letters, consequently the request was not granted. After a discussion of more than two hours instructions were agreed upon and delivered to Robert M. McLane who had been selected as special messenger. They covered the points already noted, and the choice between remaining at Monterey or advancing into the interior was left entirely to Taylor's discretion. He was informed that General

---

64 "I conceive that this mode of regulating details and ordering detachments direct from the Department of War is a violation of the integrity of the chief command in the field, pregnant with the worst of evils, and against which I deem it my duty respectfully but earnestly to protest" (Taylor to Adj. Gen., Oct. 15, 1846, *ibid.*, 354).

Patterson would probably command the Vera Cruz expedition, and he was asked to send about two thousand of his regulars to this commander, if, in his judgment, they could be spared. On the other hand, he was forbidden to send them if, in his opinion, his own position would be endangered.[65]

---

[65] Polk, *Diary*, II, 198–205. Marcy to Taylor, Oct. 22, 1846 (*H. Ex. Doc. 60*, 30 Cong., 1 sess., 363–367).

CHAPTER XIX

CAMPAIGN AGAINST THE CITY OF MEXICO

For some time after instructing Taylor to remain at Monterey the President remained undecided as to what policy he would pursue. He had difficulty in making up his mind whether, after the capture of Vera Cruz, the army should simply hold the territory in possession and wait for Mexico to treat, or whether an advance to Mexico City should be undertaken. Before any decision had been reached, Colonel Richard B. Mason was sent to California via Panama, and instructed to command the troops in that region until the arrival of General Kearny.[1]

Financial as well as military considerations impeded the formation of a definite war policy. Department estimates caused so much apprehension concerning the cost of the war that the number of volunteers asked for by Marcy was cut down from 25,000 to 10,000 men. No decision had been reached as to whether the government should simply preserve the *status quo,* or "prosecute the war into the heart of Mexico." Buchanan advocated the former policy and, apparently, Polk did not wish to decide the question either way until he had consulted the Senator from Missouri. Benton called by appointment on the same evening (November 7) and expressed himself as strongly in favor of taking Vera Cruz and of following this up with a crushing movement against Mexico City. To confine the military operations simply to holding the territory then in possession would, in his opinion, prolong the war and ruin the Democratic party; for "ours were a go-ahead people and . . . . our only policy either

---

[1] This action resulted from Polk's want of confidence in Colonel Stevenson who had been sent round the Horn with the New York volunteers (Polk, *Diary,* II, 209, 215).

to obtain a peace or save ourselves was to press the war boldly.''
He believed that commissioners vested with authority to offer
peace, ''before a battle, during the battle, & after it was over,''
should accompany the army headquarters, and he offered to be
one of the number. Three days later the Senator suggested that
some man of ''talents and resources'' and of military training
ought to be made lieutenant-general, and he modestly offered to
accept the position if it should be created by Congress. After
alluding to his original preference for Van Buren he declared
that he was now ready to give Polk his unqualified support. To
make his declaration more emphatic, he reminded the President
that he [Benton] had quarreled with General Jackson and had
subsequently defended him ''in the gloomy period of the Bank
panic.''[2] The would-be commissioner continued to urge the
necessity of an advance upon the Mexican capital, but the President was reluctant to undertake such an expedition if it could
be avoided. By November 17, however, Polk had decided to
attack Vera Cruz, although he still ''considered it to be an open
question, to be determined according to circumstances hereafter,
whether a column should be sent from Vera Cruz against the
City of Mexico.'' If, by that time, Mexico should decline to make
peace, he would be ''decidedly in favour'' of taking the capital
city.[3]

The selection of a commander for the Vera Cruz expedition
caused the President great anxiety. He would gladly have chosen
Benton; but the Missouri Senator would not accept a rank lower
than that of lieutenant-general, and there was no reason for believing that Congress would create such an office. Polk had lost
faith in Taylor's ability as a commanding officer. He had also
come to regard him as the partisan dupe of Bailie Peyton and
George W. Kendall, ''who were cunning & shrewd men of more
talents than himself, and had controlled him for political purposes.'' ''His constant effort has been to throw the responsibility

---

2 Polk, *Diary*, II, 221–223, 227–228.　　　3 *Ibid.*, 241.

of any disaster which might happen on the administration. In this he had been most ungrateful for the kindness which he has received at my hands.'' These impressions had been derived, in part, from Taylor's dispatches. In addition, Polk's mind had been poisoned by adverse criticisms contained in private letters written to him by his friend and benefactor, General Pillow.[4] Taylor had quite a different story to tell about *responsibility*. He told Crittenden in a letter that:

When it was supposed I was in great peril from which, had I not succeeded in extricating myself, the administration & its friends were prepared to throw the whole responsibility on me—[by saying that he had no authority to take a position on the Rio Grande].[5]

For some time Polk's aversion for Scott precluded all thought of assigning him to the chief command. Scott had, in September, requested that he might be sent to Mexico, and at that time his request was denied.[6] When, however, a majority of the cabinet, at a meeting held on November 17, reluctantly came to the conclusion that Scott ought to be appointed in spite of his faults, Polk consented to ''think further on the subject,'' although ''after his very exceptional letter in May last nothing but stern necessity and sense of public duty could induce me to place him at the head of so important [an] expedition.'' Benton was consulted, and when he, too, advised that, under present circumstances, Scott should be appointed, the President at last felt ''constrained to assign him to this command.'' When notified of his appointment Scott was, according to Polk's account, so grateful ''that he almost shed tears.''[7] If so, his gratitude proved to be ephemeral.

---

4 *Ibid.*, 227, 229, 236, 241. Peyton, it will be recalled, had been one of Polk's most hated political opponents in Tennessee. At this time he was a member of General Worth's staff. Kendall was editor of the New Orleans *Picayune* and accompanied Taylor's army in the capacity of war correspondent.

5 Taylor to Crittenden, Sept. 15, 1846, *Crittenden Papers.*

6 Scott to Marcy, Sept. 12; Marcy to Scott, Sept. 14, 1846 (*H. Ex. Doc. 60*, 30 Cong., 1 sess., 372–373).

7 Polk, *Diary*, II, 241–245.

Meanwhile the President was busily engaged in preparing his annual message to Congress. The original draft was shown to Benton, and the Senator suggested certain alterations.

In his *Thirty Years' View,* Benton stated that the draft contained a ''recommendation to Congress to cease the active prosecution of the war, to occupy the conquered part of the country (. . . .) with troops in forts and stations, and to pass an act establishing a temporary government in the occupied part; and to retain the possession until the peace was made.'' He stated further that he persuaded the President to give up the ''sedentary project.'' Apparently these statements grossly exaggerated the facts, for they agree neither with the President's general war policy, nor with his own description of his original drafts. His diary for December 1 reads:

> I had proposed in my draft to submit to Congress the propriety, *at the same time that the war should be vigorously prosecuted* [italics mine] to establish a line of boundary securing to the U. S. a sufficient territory to afford indemnity for the expenses of the war, and to our citizens who hold pecuniary demands against Mexico. I proposed, also, that a more permanent Government should be provided by Congress over the conquered provinces than the temporary Governments which had been established by our own Military and Naval commanders according to the laws of war. Col. Benton thought these passages should be omitted, and submitted to me in writing the reasons for this opinion.

Whether wise or unwise, these recommendations certainly did not advise a ''sedentary'' policy. The fact that Walker, who wanted all of Mexico, preferred Polk's draft to that of Benton is another indication that the President had no intention of terminating ''the active prosecution of the war.'' Although no suggestion to this effect seems to have been included in Polk's draft, certain modifications were made in order to please the Missouri Senator, for otherwise it was feared that he would oppose, and probably could defeat, everything which the President was about to recommend.[8]

---

[8] Benton, *Thirty Years' View,* II, 693. Polk, *Diary,* II, 258–260.

On December 7, 1846, the twenty-ninth Congress began its second session and, on the next day, received the President's annual message. In it Polk repelled the charge made by some of his opponents that the war with Mexico was unjust and unnecessary. "A more effectual means," said he, "could not have been devised to encourage the enemy and protract the war than to advocate and adhere to their cause, and thus give them 'aid and comfort.'" The intended application of this quotation from the constitutional definition of treason could not be misunderstood, and Polk at once became the object of violent denunciation. In order to disprove the charges that had been made, he gave a history of events leading up to the war, laying emphasis on the fact that Mexico had violated two treaties in which she had agreed to pay American claimants damages awarded to them by a joint commission. The first of these treaties was negotiated in 1839. The second, which postponed the dates of payment, declared upon its face, said the President, that " 'this new arrangement is entered' into for the accommodation of Mexico.'" "Notwithstanding this new convention was entered into at the request of Mexico[9] and for the purpose of relieving her from embarrassment, the claimants have only received the interest due on the 30th of April, 1843, and three of the twenty installments."

---

[9] In this connection a letter of Waddy Thompson, who negotiated these treaties, is of interest: "In the unquestionable vindication of the Mexican war by the President I see that much prominence is given to two points both of which I claim exclusive credit of as they were both not only without instructions but in violations of the orders of the state department. By the Treaty of 1839 the Mexican government had the option to pay the awards in cash or in Treasury notes. These latter were worth then not more than 20 cents in the dollar and now are worth even less. But the whole debt could have been paid with less than one fifth of its nominal amount. The brevity of a letter will not allow me to state to you the various means by which I managed to close the eyes of Mexico to the advantages which they possessed. But I did so and on my *own responsibility* made a provisional arrangement subject to the ratification of my government. It was approved with certain alterations. Mr. Webster sent me the draft of a Treaty. The preamble stated that this new arrangement was made at the instance and desire of the American claimants. I took the responsibility of changing this and stated in my despatch accompanying the Treaty that if Mexico failed to comply with the terms of the Treaty it would give us a much stronger justification for inforcing payment than if it had been stated in

The President maintained that the United States had had ample grounds for war long before the Mexican army crossed the Rio Grande. He asserted, also, that hostilities had not been precipitated by Taylor's advance to the western frontier, for "Mexico herself had never placed the war which she has waged upon the ground that our army occupied the intermediate territory between the Nueces and the Rio Grande." After an elaborate argument which proved, to his own satisfaction at least, the Rio Grande to be the rightful boundary of Texas, he said that it would be "difficult to justify the Executive, whose duty it is to see that the laws be faithfully executed if . . . . he had assumed the responsibility of yielding up the territory west of the Nueces."

One passage in the message relating to conquered territories was subsequently attacked in the Senate. Having urged a vigorous prosecution of the war the President went on to say that:

In the Provinces of New Mexico and of the Californias little, if any, further resistance is apprehended from the inhabitants to the temporary governments which have thus, from the necessity of the case and according to the laws of war, been established. It may be proper to provide for the security of these important conquests by making adequate appropriation for the purpose of erecting fortifications and defraying the expenses necessary incident to the maintenance of our possession and authority over them.

---

the Treaty that the change in the Treaty had been made at the instance of the claimants. I see that it is so regarded by the President in his message."

Concerning article six of the treaty of 1843, which Polk had also mentioned, Thompson said: "The sixth clause of the Treaty which provides for a new convention for claims not then adjusted was inserted by me not only without instructions, but it was disapproved by Mr. Webster but nevertheless retained" (Thompson to Buchanan, Dec. 13, 1846, *Buchanan Papers*). In this same letter, Thompson spoke of letters which he and Webster had written to Bocanegra, Mexican Secretary of Foreign Relations, in 1842. These are printed in the appendix of his book, *Recollections of Mexico*. There Thompson agrees that Webster had written his letter before having seen his [Thompson's], but in the letter to Buchanan he accuses Webster of plagiarism: "Mr. Webster stole my reply to Mr. Bocanegra's letter to him and to the diplomatic corps and published it as his own—in a letter to me. He says in his letter to me endorsing his reply to Mr. Bocanegra that he had not received mine when he wrote his. In this he lied. That is the word and no other word will express the idea. He had received it & stole it, and then lied about it. Telling a falsehood to conceal a larceny—a petty larceny if you please—of this I have the proof." But cf. *Recollections*, 284–304.

As will be seen later, some members of Congress interpreted this as a recommendation to provide for permanent possession, before any treaty had been made.

So far as it related to the war, the message concluded with a renewal of the request for an appropriation of two million dollars to be used at the discretion of the President for diplomatic purposes. The reasons which had induced him to ask for that amount at the preceding session, said he, "still exist," and he believed that it would have been granted then if a vote had been taken.[10]

When the message came up for discussion in the Senate, Westcott, of Florida, moved that the part relating to conquered territories, above quoted, be referred to the Committee on Territories. Benton objected, and a discussion ensued as to whether the President's recommendation had contemplated the establishment of permanent governments. Westcott contended that no other meaning could be drawn from it, while Benton insisted that it meant nothing of the kind. No decision was reached, for, on motion made by Crittenden, the question was sent to the table.[11]

In the House, Garrett Davis, of Kentucky, caused a heated debate by introducing a resolution which requested the President to submit for examination all orders to military and naval officers relating to the establishment of civil governments in the conquered provinces. He had in mind, of course, the governments set up in New Mexico and California by General Kearny and Commodore Stockton, and he wished to know whether the acts of those officers had been authorized by the President; if so, he demanded to know "by what imperial or regal authority his majesty undertook to act in the premises." If Polk, said Davis, had authorized the organization of civil governments in foreign provinces, he was guilty of usurpation; and if the Santa Fé region was a part of Texas, as the message seemed to assert, then, the President had no right to set up a government over a portion

10 Richardson, *Messages*, IV, 472–495.
11 *Cong. Globe*, 29 Cong., 2 sess., 42–44.

of a sovereign state. Similar arguments were made by Schenck,
of Ohio, and by other opponents of the administration. The
defense of the President was led by Douglas, although many
other Democrats rallied loyally to his support. After a week's
debate, the resolution was passed on the fifteenth of December.[12]

The establishment of a government in California by Stockton
and Fremont has already been discussed. A brief summary will
indicate the objectionable features of Kearny's conquest of New
Mexico which led the House to call upon the President for
information.

Leaving Fort Leavenworth late June, 1846, in command of a
small force made up of United States dragoons and Missouri
volunteers, Kearny reached Santa Fé on August 18 and, without
resistance, took possession of the capital of New Mexico. Four
days later a proclamation was issued in which Kearny announced
that he would hold the department "as a part of the United
States, and under the name of the 'territory of New Mexico.' "
After promising a representative government at an early date,
the proclamation added that

> The United States hereby absolves all persons residing within the boundaries
> of New Mexico from any further allegiance to the republic of Mexico,
> and hereby claims them as citizens of the United States.

Before the end of September he had framed and put into operation an elaborate civil government under the title of the "Organic
law for the territory of New Mexico. . . ."[13]

Kearny's authority for thus assuming the rôle of lawgiver
was based on the following confidential instructions sent to him
by the Secretary of War on June 3, 1846:

> Should you conquer and take possession of New Mexico and Upper
> California, or considerable places in either, you will establish temporary
> civil governments therein. . . . . You may assure the people of those
> provinces that it is the wish and design of the United States to provide
> for them a free government, with the least possible delay, similar to that

---

12 *Ibid.*, 12–33.

13 For the proclamation, "organic law," and other documents, see *H.
Ex. Doc. 60*, 30 Cong., 1 sess., 169ff.

which exists in our territories. They will then be called upon to exercise the rights of freemen in electing their own representatives to the territorial legislature. It is foreseen that what relates to the civil government will be a difficult part of your duty, and much must necessarily be left to your own discretion.[14]

The explicit directions given in this letter, supplemented as they were by wide discretionary powers, seem to give ample authority for the action taken by General Kearny. Furthermore, when Polk received the news, on October 2, that Kearny had proclaimed New Mexico to be "a part of the United States," he noted in his diary that "Gen'l Kearny has thus far performed his duty well."[15] Whether, had no objections been raised, he would have given similar approval to the "organic law," we have no means of knowing. This document did not reach Washington until November 23, and, according to their own statements, it was not examined by either Marcy or Polk until after information regarding it had been requested by the House.[16]

Whatever he might have done with respect to Kearny's territorial governments had Congress interposed no objections, Polk now realized that part, at least, of Kearny's work could not be justified. At a cabinet meeting held on December 19, Buchanan expressed the opinion that the House resolution ought not to be answered, but the President decided to transmit the desired documents. In the evening he made the following comment:

Among them was a document from Brigadier Gen'l Kearney, containing a form of Government over the conquered territory of New Mexico, which among other things declared that territory to be a part of the U. S. and provided for the election of a Delegate to the Congress of the U. S. In these and some other respects he exceeded the power of a military commander over a conquered territory. It was agreed that in my message to Congress I must disapprove this part of the Document, though, without censuring the Gen'l, who had misconceived the extent of his authority, but who had, no doubt, acted from patriotic motives.

---

[14] Marcy to Kearny, June 3, 1846 (*ibid.*, 244).

[15] Polk, *Diary*, II, 169–170.

[16] Marcy's report to the President, Dec. 21, 1846 (*H. Ex. Doc. 60*, 30 Cong., 1 sess., 151). Polk's Message of Dec. 22, 1846. Nothing is said in the *Diary* about this document until the matter had been brought up in the House.

A message to this effect, with an additional statement that "such excess has resulted in no practical injury," was sent to the House a few days later. And yet, not two months before this, the President had expressed satisfaction because Kearny had proclaimed New Mexico to be a part of the United States![17]

While awaiting information respecting territorial governments, the House engaged in an acrimonious debate on the President's annual message and the causes of the war. Polk was assailed for having stated in his message that his opponents had, by their attacks upon the administration, been giving "aid and comfort" to the enemy. In turn, he was charged with having given "aid and comfort" to Santa Anna, the most powerful and unscrupulous of the enemies. Whigs averred that the President had wantonly plunged the country into a war of aggression in order to show the world "who James K. Polk was." Even those who had voted for the declaration of war now asserted that the executive was conducting "an unconstitutional war." Most abusive of all was Gentry, of Tennessee. Polk, he said, was a "petty usurper" who "had come into power without the will of the people of these States, and almost without the wish or knowledge even of his own party"; and his message was "nothing but a low demagogical attempt to deceive the nation—to tell just enough of the truth to cause the people to believe a lie." On the other hand the President was ably defended by his Democratic supporters[18] who maintained, not only that his message had given a true history of relations with Mexico, but that Polk's remark about giving "aid and comfort" to the enemy had been amply vindicated by utterances which were being made on the floor of the House. The receipt of the special message, accompanied by the orders issued to military and naval officers, produced no change in the character of the discussion. The Whigs

---

[17] Polk, *Diary*, II, 170, 281–282. Richardson, *Messages*, IV, 506–507.

[18] In defending the President, Bayly, of Virginia, arraigned the arguments and the attitude of Garret Davis in such scathing terms that a challenge followed. The arrest of Bayly by the municipal authorities prevented a duel (Polk, *Diary*, II, 297).

still continued to fulminate against the "President's war," and to characterize the establishment of civil governments in the conquered provinces as an unwarranted assumption of unconstitutional powers.

The man thus portrayed as a usurper whose imperial ambitions neither Congress nor the Constitution had been able to check believed himself to be hampered by want of adequate authority. Upon his shoulders rested the responsibility of military victory, yet the officers at his disposal were, in his opinion, disloyal to the administration and interested solely in their own political advancement. However erroneous this opinion may have been, there is no reason for doubting that Polk believed both Scott and Taylor to be incompetent and unreliable. Having arrived at the conclusion that Taylor was a "narrow minded, bigotted partisan" who had been "made giddy with the idea of the Presidency," the chief executive felt the need of a commander more in sympathy with the administration. He had selected Scott to lead the attack on Vera Cruz, not because he had great confidence in the general's ability or his loyalty, but for the reason that Scott was the only man in the army "who by his rank could command Taylor."[19] The admixture of war and politics had created a dilemma from which the President saw but one avenue of escape, namely, to follow the advice of Benton, and ask Congress to authorize the appointment of a lieutenant-general.

Before Scott had had time to reach the seat of war Polk began to sound members of Congress for the purpose of ascertaining whether a bill to create such an office could be passed. He even sent for Calhoun and asked his assistance, explaining that Benton would be appointed should Congress see fit to create the position. Calhoun, however, was "decidedly opposed to having such an officer,"[20] and Polk's best friends doubted that Congress could

---

[19] Polk, *Diary*, II, 249, 277.

[20] *Ibid.*, 282. Calhoun believed that the President was governed by political motives—by a desire to deal a blow at Taylor and Scott (Calhoun to Duff Green, April 17, 1847, *Rep. Am. Hist. Assn.*, 1899, II, 727).

be induced to take favorable action. Indeed, the President himself did not believe that the necessary law could be procured, but Benton urged him to make the recommendation, "and if Congress rejected it the responsibility would be theirs." Influenced partly by his own desire to have a Democratic commander and partly by the dread of Benton's opposition, Polk drafted a message on Christmas day in which he asked Congress for authority to appoint a lieutenant-general.[21]

Although a bill for creating the coveted office was tabled by the Senate on January 15, the President by his action succeeded in retaining, for a time at least, the good will of the Missouri Senator. This in itself was of no small importance, for the defection of Calhoun and his coterie of adherents had converted the normal Democratic majority into a minority, and Benton wielded a far greater influence than did Calhoun. On the day that the Senate tabled the bill, Polk noted in his diary:

> With a large nominal majority in both Houses, I am practically in a minority. The several cliques & sections of the Democratic party are manifestly more engaged in managing for their respective favourites in the next Presidential election, than they are in supporting the Government in prosecuting the war, or carrying out any of its great measures. The only corrective is in the hands of the people. I will do my duty to the country and rejoice that with my own voluntary free will & consent I am not to be a candidate. This determination is irrevocable.[22]

He was greatly discouraged because Congress delayed legislation on war measures which he had recommended, among them provision for ten additional regiments of regular troops. "Instead," said he, "of acting upon the great measures of the country, they are spending day after day and week after week in a worse than useless discussion about slavery."[23] His discomfort was increased

---

[21] "I found Col. B. fixed upon this point," said the *Diary*. "If I do not propose it, it is manifest from my interview with him that both he and his friends will be greatly dissatisfied" (Polk, *Diary*, II, 275, 286, 293). The message was sent to Congress on December 29.

[22] *Ibid.*, 328.

[23] *Ibid.*, 334. He referred to the debate on King's slavery restriction resolution introduced in the House on Jan. 4, 1847.

by cabinet opposition to the advance upon the Mexican capital and to the acquisition of any territory except New Mexico and California, although the members believed that other northern provinces should be encouraged to declare their independence. Even Walker, who up to this time had advocated expansion on a large scale, now gave his approval to a restrictive policy. Donelson, also, from his post at Berlin, entered a protest against unrestricted expansion. Since war had come, he believed the Rio Grande boundary to be necessary and Upper California to be desirable; but he was decidedly averse to holding central Mexico. Even California, in his opinion, was not indispensable, for it would eventually become an independent nation any way. He hoped that Polk would not listen to those who desired to incorporate Mexico into the Union.[24]

On January 13, 1847, when the President was downcast because of obstacles which impeded a vigorous prosecution of the war, a harbinger of peace appeared in the person of Colonel Atocha. He came not as an avowed agent of Santa Anna, but as one who professed to have intimate, though unofficial, knowledge of the plans and purposes of his crafty patron. He showed to Benton personal letters received from Santa Anna, Almonte, and Rejón, all of which expressed a desire for peace with the United States. With Atocha's permission, Benton showed the letters to Polk and Buchanan. All agreed that he had been sent by Santa Anna as a confidential agent charged with the duty of ascertaining the terms on which Polk would make peace. When asked about the terms which would be agreeable to Santa Anna, Atocha said that Mexico would consent to the Rio Grande as the boundary of Texas, but "reserving a space of territory between that River & the Nueces as a barrior between the two

---

[24] *Ibid.*, 301. Donelson to Buchanan, Dec. 22, 1846 (rec'd Jan. 27, '47), *Buchanan Papers*. In a letter written two weeks later, he said that Europeans did not like Polk's message and were opposed to his war policy. They feared, he said, that Mexico, when defeated, would desire admission into the Union and would be admitted (Donelson to Buchanan, Jan. 8, 1847, *Buchanan Papers*).

countries." He said, also, that Mexico would cede California for a consideration of fifteen or twenty million dollars, but on the subject of New Mexico he seemed to have no authority to speak. He advised that commissioners should meet in Havana and that. pending negotiations, the blockade at Vera Cruz should be raised. As a concession to Mexican pride, he urged that the invitation to negotiate should come from the United States.

For several days the President held consultations with Benton and with members of the cabinet. Although willing to open peace negotiations, he rejected some of the suggestions which had been made by Atocha. New Mexico as well as California must be ceded to the United States, and the proposal to create a neutral zone between the Nueces and the Rio Grande must not be entertained. The blockade of Vera Cruz would not be raised until a treaty had been made, for if it were raised and no treaty resulted, the administration would be subjected to ridicule. At a cabinet meeting held on January 16 Buchanan was directed to prepare a letter to the Mexican Minister of Foreign Relations. In it the Mexican government was invited to appoint peace commissioners who were to meet similar representatives from the United States at either Havana or Jalapa. On seeing the letter, Atocha objected to the passage which said that the war would be prosecuted vigorously until a treaty had been signed. On his suggestion, the President consented to vest the commissioners with authority, "in their discretion after meeting the Mexican commissioners," to raise the blockade and to suspend hostilities. The letter was so modified and delivered to Atocha, and Secretary Walker arranged to have a revenue cutter convey him from New Orleans to Vera Cruz. He was not regarded as an official bearer of dispatches but as "an individual to whom a sealed letter was entrusted to be delivered."[25]

---

[25] Polk, *Diary*, II, 323, 325–327, 331–334, 335–336, 339. The letter to the Mexican Minister is printed in Buchanan, *Works*, VII, 198–199, also in *Sen. Ex. Doc. 1*, 30 Cong., 1 sess., 36.

Polk's desire for a diplomatic victory was strengthened by obstacles which seemed to preclude military success. Congress appeared to be more interested in practical politics than in "strengthening the Executive arm," and the President had no faith in either the competency or the loyalty of his commanders in the field. Coincident with Scott's arrival in New Orleans on his way to the seat of war the newspapers of that city published a full account of the administration's plan of campaign. No one except the general could have imparted the information, and the President at once attributed this violation of secrecy to Scott's "inordinate vanity."[26] To cap the climax a New York newspaper published a letter, written by Taylor to Gaines, in which the administration was denounced and its military plans completely exposed.[27] Apparently the "Whig generals" were determined to prevent the Mexican army from being taken by surprise. In his private letters, Taylor said that keeping him "in the dark" seemed to be the "great object" of the administration,[28] and generosity may have led him to protect his Mexican adversaries from similar annoyance!

The President decided that the administration could be vindicated most effectively by the publication of all correspondence which had passed between Taylor and the War Department, and, evidently by his request, a resolution calling for these documents was introduced in the House by Thompson, of Mississippi.[29] Ashmun, of Massachusetts, offered an amendment which solicited information concerning the secret agent who had been sent to confer with Santa Anna at Havana. This amendment and the

---

[26] Ibid., 327–328. "I have no doubt," Polk wrote a few weeks later, "the Mexican Government and Military commanders are as well apprised of the secret instructions which were given to Gen'l Scott when he left Washington as he is himself. His vanity is such that he could not keep the most important secrets of the Government which were given to him" (ibid., 393–394).

[27] Ibid., 393–394.

[28] Taylor to Wood, Jan. 26, 1847, Taylor Letters, 82.

[29] Polk, Diary, II, 362. Cong. Globe, 22 Cong., 2 sess., 296. Taylor was reminded by Marcy (Jan. 27) that his offense had made him liable to dismissal (H. Ex. Doc. 60, 30 Cong., 1 sess., 391).

appointment of the returned exile to the position of "lieutenant general for Mexico" gave an opportunity for a new assault upon the President, although the speakers were unable to add many items to the catalog of iniquities which they had been compiling since the opening of the session.

The Thompson resolution was passed by the House and the correspondence was published, yet Congress seemed unwilling to coöperate with the President by enacting the laws which he had recommended. "I am in the unenviable position," he wrote on February 5, "of being held responsible for the conduct of the Mexican War, when I have no support either from Congress or from the two officers (Scott & Taylor) highest in command in the field. How long this state of things will continue I cannot forsee." For this state of affairs he blamed factious members of his own party who were more interested in the next Presidential election than in the welfare of the country. Said he:

> In truth faction rules the hour, while principles & patriotism is forgotten. While the Democratic party are thus distracted and divided and are playing this foolish and suicidal game, the Federal Party are united and never fail to unite with the minority of the Democratic party, or any faction of it who may break off from the body of their party, and thus postpone and defeat all my measures.[30]

This statement was verified within the next few days when Calhoun and his friends united with Whigs in temporarily blocking the passage of a bill for raising ten additional regiments of troops. As a result Polk now regarded Calhoun as the "most mischievous man in the Senate," and he attributed the South Carolinian's hostility to the fact that he had not been retained in the cabinet.[31] Senator Turney, a friend of the President, charged Calhoun with impeding necessary legislation by depriving his party of a majority in the Senate. He proclaimed this fact to the people so that they might "place the responsibility exactly in the proper quarter."[32] However, the rejection of the

---

30 Polk, *Diary*, II, 368.
31 *Ibid.*, 371–372.   32 *Cong. Globe*, 29 Cong., 2 sess., 395.

ten-regiment bill, as reported from the conference committee, proved not to be final; after a reconsideration, it was passed by the Senate on the tenth of February. Congress had already authorized the emission of twenty-three million dollars in treasury notes, for war purposes. The satisfaction which Polk experienced as a result of this new turn of events was counterbalanced by his disgust because members of Congress demanded for their personal friends all offices which had been created by the military bill. "Take the day altogether," he wrote on February 15, "I am sure I have never been so wearied and annoyed in my life."[33]

When the Senate voted, in the first instance, to reject the ten-regiment bill, the Washington *Union* characterized this action as "Another Mexican Victory":

> If Santa Anna, Ampudia, or any other Mexican general could snatch from our soldiers a corresponding victory, we should place them upon the same elevation where their compatriots, friends, and fellow-soldiers in the Senate of the United States now stand.

By a resolution passed on February 13 the editors, Ritchie and Heiss, were denied admission to the floor of the Senate—an action concerning which the President wrote:

> It is a second Duane case, & strikes a blow at the liberty of the press. The foul deed was perpetrated by the votes of the undivided Federal Senators, and Senators Calhoun & Butler of S. C. & Yulee & Wescott of Florida.[34]

On March 3, 1847, the twenty-ninth Congress ended its labors. Although Polk's opponents had filled pages of the *Congressional Globe* in charging him with miscellaneous crimes and misdemeanors, he had nevertheless been provided with men and money so that he might continue his "unholy war" against Mexico. The bill for granting him three million dollars to be used in negotiating a peace was also enacted into law, but not until the "Wilmot proviso," which sought to exclude slavery from all territory to be acquired, had been rejected by both houses.

---

[33] Polk, *Diary*, II, 380.

[34] *Cong. Globe*, 29 Cong., 2 sess., 392, 417. Polk, *Diary*, II, 378.

During the last evening of the session, while the President was at the capitol for the purpose of signing bills, an incident occurred which tested not only his patience but his courage as well. Among the bills which were expected to pass was one authorizing the appointment of two major-generals and three brigadier-generals. His original intention had been to ignore New York, when filling these positions, for he knew that he could not satisfy both Democratic factions in that state—one led by Marcy and the other by Senator Dix, the close friend of Van Buren. However, Marcy insisted that one of the lesser positions should be given to his friend, General Clark, while Dix emphatically opposed the appointment. As a compromise, Polk decided to appoint Enos D. Hopping, who, although affiliated with the Marcy faction, had been recommended for a colonelcy by both wings of the party. Although both Marcy and Senator Dickenson threatened to resign if Clark were not appointed, Polk defied their attempt to "bully" him, and appointed Hopping as soon as the bill had been signed. "I had become perfectly indifferent," was his comment, "whether Mr. Dickinson and Mr. Marcy resigned or not. I knew that neither of them could be sustained in such a course for such a cause."[35]

Among the appointments made and confirmed during the closing hours of the session was that of Benton as major-general. He had solicited the appointment, and had, at the time, attached no conditions to his acceptance, but it soon developed that he had no intention of serving unless the President would assign him to the chief command of the army and invest him with "plenary Diplomatic powers to conclude a Treaty of peace." The cabinet objected to clothing Benton with diplomatic powers, and, besides, Polk himself had planned to send Buchanan as commissioner, should Mexico consent to negotiate. He would gladly have put Benton at the head of the army if he could have done so without recalling the four major-generals already in the field. According

[35] Polk, *Diary*, II, 399–405

to his own statement, he would "have no hesitation" so far as Scott and Taylor were concerned, but he thought it would be unjust to recall Butler and Patterson. When informed of the President's decision, Benton declined to accept the appointment.[36]

Polk was ready to go a long way to avoid offending the Missouri Senator, for Benton was the only man in public life for whom he seemed to harbor a feeling of awe.[37] He was influenced still more, however, by his aversion for the Whig generals and by his desire to transfer the chief command to a member of his own party. At the time that Benton was appointed, Polk was especially hostile to General Scott on account of alleged discrimination against Democratic officers.[38]

Since the congressional batteries had ceased their "fire upon his rear," the President could devote more attention to the enemy across the Rio Grande. After consultation with Benton and the cabinet he decided to raise the blockade of the Mexican ports and to substitute a tariff, the proceeds of which were to be used for war purposes. He took steps to hasten the recruiting and equipping of the new regiments which Congress had voted, and to eliminate the "extravagance & stupidity" of the quartermaster's department.[39]

---

[36] *Ibid.*, 406–413.

[37] But there were limits to his concessions. It was about this time that he refused to appoint Benton's son-in-law (Jones) to office, because he "was a short time ago the editor of a Federal paper in New Orleans" (*ibid.*, 455).

[38] He had, said the President, "arbitrarily & without cause" degraded Colonel Harney, of Tennessee. "Gen'l Taylor had acted with the same proscriptive spirit, not only towards Col. Harney, but other gallant Democratic officers." Against the advice of his cabinet, Polk directed that Harney should be restored: "I told the Secretary of War that if he was unwilling to write the letter . . . I would do it myself. . . . I am resolved that Col. Harney shall not be sacrificed to propitiate the personal or political malice of Gen'l Scott" (*ibid.*, 384–386).

[39] "The truth is," he wrote, "that the old army officers have become so in the habit of enjoying their ease, sitting in parlours and on carpeted floors, that most of them have no energy, and are content to jog on in a regular routine without knowing whether they are taking care of the public interest or not" (*ibid.*, 431).

While the President's mind was thus engrossed with details concerning military contracts and pack-mules, Atocha returned to Washington, on March 20, bearing Mexico's reply to his offer to negotiate a peace. "The question of Texas," said the Minister of Foreign Relations, "was a cover to ulterior designs, which now stand disclosed"; nevertheless his government would "accede cheerfully" to the invitation to appoint commissioners, but such appointment would not be made "unless the raising of the blockade of our ports and the complete evacuation of the territory of the Republic by the invading forces shall be previously accepted as a preliminary condition."[40]

For the present this communication put an end to all hope of a peaceable adjustment, for Polk at once declared the conditions to be "wholly inadmissible," leaving no alternative but a "crushing movement" against Mexico. Buchanan interposed objections to an advance upon the Mexican capital, but

I [Polk] replied that I differed with him in opinion, & that I would not only march to the City of Mexico, but that I would pursue Santa Anna's army wherever it was, and capture or destroy it. I expressed the opinion that if I had a proper commander of the army, who would lay aside the technical rules of war to be found in books, which required a long train of baggage wagons; one who would go light & move rapidly, I had no doubt Santa Anna & his whole army could be destroyed or captured in a short time.

On the same evening rumors reached Washington that Taylor's army was in great danger, consequently the President was still more determined to deal Santa Anna a speedy and crushing blow.[41]

It is necessary at this point to turn aside from the administrative side of the war in order to give a brief sketch of the military operations of Kearny in California, and of Scott in his campaign from Vera Cruz to Mexico City.

---

[40] Monasterio to Buchanan, Feb. 22, 1847 (*Sen. Ex. Doc. 1*, 30 Cong., 1 sess., 37–38). Also, Buchanan, *Works*, VII, 223–224.

[41] Polk, *Diary*, II, 432–434.

On September 25, 1846, having put his "organic law" in operation in New Mexico, Kearny, with a force of three hundred dragoons, set out for California. At Socorro, on October 6, he met the scout, Kit Carson, who was on his way to Washington with dispatches from Stockton and Fremont announcing the conquest of California and the subjugation of its inhabitants.[42] As this news seemed to indicate that no further trouble was to be expected, Kearny sent back two hundred of his dragoons, and retained but one hundred as a personal escort. He forwarded the dispatches by another messenger, and Carson (much against his will) was required to guide the way to California.

Reaching the junction of the Colorado and Gila rivers on November 23, Kearny's army intercepted a messenger bearing mail from California to Sonora, and from the letters examined, Kearny received his first intelligence of the uprising of the Californians under General Flores.[43] On December 2 he reached Warner's rancho, the most eastern settlement in California. Here he was visited by an Englishman named Stokes, who volunteered to carry a letter to Commodore Stockton, at San Diego. On receipt of this letter (December 3) Stockton sent a small force of thirty-nine men, under Captain Gillespie, to coöperate with Kearny. At San Pascual, on December 6, Kearny's army fought a battle with a Mexican force under Captain Andrés Pico. A greater number of Americans than Mexicans were killed, but as Pico retreated, leaving Kearny in possession of the field, it was called a victory.[44] As soon as the troops had recovered sufficiently, Kearny proceeded on his way to the coast. At several

---

[42] Porter, *General Stephen W. Kearny and the Conquest of California,* 11. This interesting pamphlet is a strong defense of Kearny's conduct in California.

[43] Emory, *Notes of a Military Reconnoissance; H. Ex. Doc. 41,* 30 Cong., 1 sess., 96. This document gives a detailed account of Kearny's march from Ft. Leavenworth to San Diego.

[44] Bancroft, *Hist. of California,* V, 341 ff. See also Porter, *op. cit.,* who criticizes Bancroft and defends Kearny.

points Pico harassed his little army; but on the evening of December 10 he was met by a body of marines sent by Stockton, and two days later he reached San Diego in safety.[45]

Kearny's instructions, as we have seen, authorized him to take possession of California and to establish a temporary civil government. All orders relating to that country which were issued by the War Department clearly indicated that the President desired Kearny to have the chief command as soon as he had reached California. Despite this fact Stockton, who had constituted himself "commander-in-chief and governor," declined to surrender the command, even after Kearny had exhibited his instructions, and until the arrival of other land forces, the general was not in a position to assert his rights. He declined to accept a subordinate command under Stockton, yet in the "second conquest" of California, which soon followed his arrival, he loyally coöperated with the commodore.

When Kearny reached San Diego he found the country, except a few of the seaports, in possession of the Flores revolutionists, whose headquarters were at Los Angeles. It had already been planned that Fremont should attack Los Angeles from the north. After consulting with Kearny, Stockton decided to move north from San Diego for the purpose of striking Los Angeles from the south. Having made the necessary preparations the army left San Diego on December 29 under the nominal command of Stockton, although Kearny seems actually to have directed the operations. An engagement occurred on January 8 at San Gabriel River, and another on the following day near Los Angeles. Flores and Pico now abandoned that city; the former fled to Mexico, while the latter moved northward and surrendered to Fremont on favorable terms. Although Stockton and Kearny were displeased with Fremont's assumption of authority in granting these terms to the enemy, they decided to avoid further

---

[45] Emory, *Notes, etc.*, 112–113.

trouble by ratifying the agreement.[46] The "second conquest" of California was now complete, and no further resistance was offered to the authority of the United States.

Stockton and Fremont, still ignoring General Kearny's authority, proceeded once more to set up a civil government. Kearny returned to San Diego, and soon after repaired to Monterey, where he found Commodore Shubrick, the successor of Stockton. Shubrick promptly recognized Kearny's authority, and the general took steps to organize a civil government. Monterey was made the capital city and on March 1, 1847, Kearny assumed the office of governor. Having put the government in operation, he turned it over to Colonel Richard B. Mason, on May 31, and set out for Washington. By his order, Fremont accompanied him, under separate escort, and at Fort Leavenworth the pathfinder was put under arrest and ordered to report to the adjutant-general in Washington.[47] Both arrived at the capital city about the middle of September and laid their respective complaints before the Government. President Polk was very favorably impressed with Kearny. He regarded the general as "a good officer & an intelligent gentleman" and one who had "performed valuable and important services in his late expedition to New Mexico & California."[48]

After Kearny had filed charges against Fremont, Polk discussed with the cabinet the propriety of constituting a court of inquiry instead of a court-martial. The latter tribunal was selected. Benton and his son-in-law, William Carey Jones, endeavored to have the scope of investigation broadened so that Fremont might bring counter charges against his opponents, but Polk would grant no favors even though he expected that his refusal would subject him to the wrath of the whole Benton

---

[46] Porter, *op. cit.*, 25–29.

[47] Bancroft, *Hist. of Cal.*, V, 451–452. Porter, *op. cit.*, 32–33.

[48] Polk, *Diary*, III, 168, 175.

clan.[49] Fremont was convicted and sentenced to dismissal from the army. The President approved the sentence of the court, except on the charge of mutiny, but remitted the penalty and ordered Fremont to report for duty. The pathfinder, however, declined to accept this clemency, and sent in his resignation. As the President had anticipated, approval of the court's verdict caused an immediate break with Benton. All intercourse between the two men ceased as soon as Polk's decision was announced. About a year later a member of the Blair family told Secretary Mason that Benton was about to publish one of Polk's letters which would injure him in the eyes of the public. Unterrified by the threat, the President noted in his diary:

> I told Judge Mason that he had no such letter. I do not know what this means. I am, however, at the defiance of both Blair & Benton. The former has proved himself to be unprincipled and the latter, I fear, is no better. From the day I approved the sentence of the Court martial in Col. Fremont's case, Col. Benton, for no other cause than that I dared to do my duty, has been exceedingly hostile to me. He has not called on me, nor have I spoken to him for more than twelve months. [Also, February 10, 1849.] There is every indication now that he [Benton] will join the Whigs in the support of Gen'l Taylor, at all events until he can get offices for his three sons-in-law. If I had failed to do my duty in Col. Fremont's case, and given an office which he sought for his Whig son-in-law (Jones) he would never have quarreled with me. His course towards me and my administration for more than a year past has been selfish and wholly unprincipled.[50]

It was mainly on Benton's recommendation that Kearny had been selected to lead the expedition to California, yet, after the

---

[49] "I have always been upon good terms with Col. Benton," Polk noted in his diary, "but he is a man of violent passions and I should not be surprised if he became my enemy because all his wishes in reference to his family" are not gratified. . . . "I am resolved that Col. Fremont shall be tried as all other officers are tried. I will grant him no favours or privileges which I would not grant to any other officer, even though I should incur his displeasure & that of his friends by refusing to do so" (*ibid.*, 177, 198, 204). See also page 203 where John Randolph Benton, the Senator's son, threatened Polk for declining to give him an office.

[50] Polk, *Diary*, IV, 227, 330. For Benton's account of the court-martial, see his *Thirty Years' View*, II, 715–719.

court-martial, the Senator embraced every opportunity to deal a blow at his former friend. When, in August, 1848, Polk nominated Kearny to be brevet major-general, Benton declared that he would "speak out the balance of the Session, and defeat all public measures before Congress, rather than suffer the vote on Gen'l Kearny's nomination to be taken." In fulfillment of this threat he harangued the Senate for thirteen days with execration of Kearny and laudation of Fremont, at the end of which he announced that he would "break off," although he had not finished a third of what he had intended to say.[51] His effort failed to produce the desired result, for Kearny's appointment was confirmed and he repaired to Mexico for service under Scott.

As already noted, Scott was chosen to supersede Taylor after Congress refused to create the position of lieutenant-general. He received notice of his appointment on November 18, 1846, and within a few days he was on his way to Mexico. From New York he sent an effusive letter to Taylor—praising that general's gallantry and achievements but notifying him that he would be deprived of a large part of his army. He realized that his action would be "infinitely painful" to Taylor, but he relied upon the general's "patriotism to submit to the temporary sacrifice with cheerfulness."[52] According to the plans of operation decided upon in Washington before Scott's departure, Taylor's duties were to be confined to holding the territory already conquered, yet, as will soon appear, Scott greatly misjudged the *cheerfulness* with which Taylor would leave himself exposed to attacks of the enemy.

On November 12, nearly two weeks before Scott had written from New York, Taylor informed the War Department that he

---

[51] "I mean to show," he said, "that this brevet nomination of General Kearny ought to be rejected; that the affair of San Pasqual was a disastrous defeat, through his mismanagement; that his conduct in New Mexico was unfortunate, and in California criminal; and that infamy, not honor, settles upon his name" (Polk, *Diary*, IV, 59. *Cong. Globe*, 30 Cong., 1 sess., App., 977–1040).

[52] Scott to Taylor, Nov. 25, 1846 (*H. Ex. Doc. 60*, 30 Cong., 1 sess., 373).

was about to press forward into the enemy's country. As late as January 7, 1847, he was only "unofficially advised" of Scott's presence in Mexico. By that time he had driven the Mexicans from Saltillo, Parras, and Victoria, while Commodore Perry had captured the port of Tampico.[53]

Although Scott arrived in New Orleans on December 19, it was not until the middle of January that his several communications reached Taylor, and that the victorious general learned that he was to be deprived of a large part of his army. With his usual indiscretion, Scott had not only disclosed his plans to the newspapers while at New Orleans, but when giving orders to his subordinates, he intimated that Taylor was purposely keeping at a distance so that he might avoid the orders of his superior. In a letter written to Scott, Taylor indignantly repelled this insinuation and complained of being left to face an enemy twenty thousand strong with only a thousand regulars and a few volunteers. "I cannot," he wrote,

misunderstand the object of the arrangements indicated in your letters. I feel that I have lost the confidence of the government, or it would not have suffered me to remain, up to this time, ignorant of its intentions, with so vitally affecting interests committed to my charge.

He felt "personally mortified and outraged" by such treatment, yet he promised to obey the orders of his government so long as he remained in Mexico. Soon after this, in a letter to the adjutant-general, he gave vent to his resentment because he had not been notified by special messenger of the government's determination to supersede him. He had been assigned to the command by the President, and had he "chosen to be punctilious," he would have declined to part with his troops without direct orders from the same authority. However, he had decided not to follow this course, and his only regret was that the "President did not think proper . . . to relieve me from a position where I can no longer serve the country with that assurance of confidence and

---

53 Letters of Taylor to Adj. Gen. (*ibid.*, 374–388).

support so indispensable to success." He requested that this letter might be submitted to the President.[54] By this time Taylor was thinking of *serving the country* in another capacity. Nearly two months earlier he had decided to accept the nomination for the Presidency, should it be tendered to him.[55]

Scott's answer to Taylor's letter was conciliatory in tone. He passed over the caustic remarks which it contained by expressing a "wish to forget them." After explaining that conditions had made it necessary to deal directly with Taylor's subordinates without previously consulting him, he asked the general to abandon Saltillo and to make no detachments, except for *reconnoissance* beyond Monterey.[56]

A few days after Scott had sent this letter, and before it had reached its destination, Taylor received word that a reconnoitering party which he had sent out on the road to San Luis Potosí had been captured. He considered this disaster to be a direct result of the "intrigue" of Marcy and Scott to discredit him, and he resolved to fight Santa Anna, "be the consequences what they may."[57] His determination to hold Saltillo at all hazards was not altered by the receipt of Scott's letter asking him to withdraw to Monterey. It reached him while he was at Agua Nueva, eighteen miles beyond Saltillo, and he notified Scott that he would remain there unless "positively ordered to fall back by the government at Washington."[58] In a private letter he alluded to the correspondence with Scott and said that "he & myself now understand each other perfectly, & there can for the future be none other than official intercourse between us." His

---

[54] Taylor to Scott, Jan. 15; Taylor to Adj. Gen., Jan. 27, 1847 (*ibid.*, 863, 1101).

[55] Taylor to Wood, Dec. 10, 1846, *Taylor Letters*, 76.

[56] Scott to Taylor, Jan. 26, 1847 (*H. Ex. Doc. 60*, 30 Cong., 1 sess., 864).

[57] "We now begin to see the fruits of the arrangements recently made in Washington, by an intrigue of Marcy, Scott & Worth to take from me nearly the whole of the regular forces under my command, while in the immediate front of the enemy if not in their presence" (Taylor to Wood, Jan. 30, 1847, *Taylor Letters*, 84).

[58] Taylor to Scott, Feb. 7, 1847 (*H. Ex. Doc. 60*, 30 Cong., 1 sess., 1162).

enemies, in his opinion, believed that he would leave Mexico in disgust and that they might use such action to his disadvantage, "but in this I shall disappoint them."[59]

The main Mexican army, commanded by Santa Anna, was stationed at San Luis Potosí. Taylor's perversity in refusing to take Scott's advice about falling back to Monterey left his army in danger of being annihilated by a greatly superior force. However, he took a gambler's chance and won the battle of Buena Vista. He had planned originally to meet the enemy at Agua Nueva, but, on Santa Anna's approach, he fell back to Buena Vista, within seven miles of Saltillo. The battle opened on the afternoon of February 22 and lasted until dark on the following day, when Santa Anna retreated toward San Luis with his thoroughly demoralized army. According to his own report, Taylor's force numbered 4500 men, while Santa Anna commanded 20,000.[60]

Taylor's first reward for defeating the enemy at Buena Vista was the receipt of a reprimand from the President and the Secretary of War. Marcy's letter, dated January 27, rebuked him for having, in his letter to Gaines, criticized the administration and exposed the plans of campaign. Ignoring his own indiscretion which had called forth the rebuke, Taylor was now "satisfied," according to his own statement, that "Scott, Marcy & Co. have been more anxious to break me down" than to defeat Santa Anna. Marcy had supposed him to be powerless since his troops had been taken away, and consequently afraid to defend himself; "but he will find himself somewhat mistaken, & I have no doubt when he gets my reply to his abusive & contemptable letter, he will regret the course he has pursued." Believing Marcy to be "entirely incompetent," he thought that friends of soldiers who had fallen at Buena Vista should hold meetings and memorialize the President to remove him and to recall Scott to Washington.[61]

---

[59] Taylor to Wood, Feb. 9, 1847, *Taylor Letters*, 85, 87.

[60] Taylor to Scott, March 1, 1847 (*H. Ex. Doc. 60*, 30 Cong., 1 sess., 1168).

[61] Taylor to Wood, March 20, 1847, *Taylor Letters*, 90–91.

Two weeks later he received a letter from Marcy[62] which expressed the President's "high appreciation" of his "distinguished services," but this did not in the least remove his distrust of the administration. It will be seen, however, that the distrust on both sides resulted for the most part from misunderstandings due to the slow means of communication.

Although General Scott, as we have seen, arrived at New Orleans on December 19, 1846, it took until the middle of February to assemble troops and make other preparations for his attack upon Vera Cruz. On February 15 he set out from the Brazos de Santiago, and, after stopping at Tampico and Lobos Island, his fleet of transports appeared off the coral island of Vera Cruz harbor on the fifth of March. Not knowing that Santa Anna had gone to attack Taylor, Scott expected that his landing would be vigorously opposed; but instead, he was able to land his troops on the sandy beach in front of the city without resistance from the enemy. For about four days American land batteries and the warships of Commodore Conner kept up a continuous bombardment, and on March 29 the Mexican commander offered to capitulate. Scott took possession of both the city of Vera Cruz and the castle of San Juan de Ulúa.[63]

After the battle of Buena Vista, Santa Anna set out for Mexico City, where he took the oath of office as President and adjusted a revolt of the clerical party.[64] Leaving the government in charge of a substitute President, he left the city on April 2, 1847, and prepared to meet Scott at the pass of Cerro Gordo, about twenty miles east of Jalapa. He occupied a position very difficult to approach, but in the battle of Cerro Gordo, which occurred on the seventeenth and eighteenth, the forces of General Scott won a comparatively easy victory. Within a few days Jalapa and Perote were occupied without resistance, and on the

---

[62] Marcy to Taylor, April 3, 1847 (*H. Ex. Doc. 60*, 30 Cong., 1 sess., 1133).

[63] *Sen. Ex. Doc. 1*, 30 Cong., 1 sess., 216–230.

[64] See Rives, *United States and Mexico*, II, 391 ff.

fifteenth Worth took possession of Puebla. While Scott was at Jalapa, Trist arrived on the scene bearing a commission to negotiate a treaty, but a discussion of the controversy which followed his arrival is reserved for another place.

Late in May Scott left Jalapa and established his headquarters at Puebla. Here he remained for several weeks, impatiently awaiting reinforcements. His time, however, was fully, if not profitably, occupied in quarreling and making friends with Trist, in bombarding the War Department with complaints and denunciations, and in a futile attempt to procure a peace treaty by bribing the Mexican officials.

During the same period Santa Anna was in Mexico City making preparations to defend the capital. By an act passed on April 20, two days after the battle of Cerro Gordo, the Mexican congress had authorized him to "adopt all necessary measures to carry on the war," but had deprived him of the power of making peace except with the consent of the congress.[65] While engaged in his military preparations he received Polk's offer to negotiate a treaty, which Trist had transmitted by the aid of the British minister. The action taken by Santa Anna and his congress will be discussed in the next chapter; it may be said here, however, that nothing resulted at this time from Trist's attempt to negotiate. After he had received for his own use ten thousand dollars from Scott's secret service fund, the Mexican President decided that the time for peace had not yet arrived.

While encamped at Puebla, Scott's army had been augmented by troops which had arrived during the summer. The health of his soldiers was much improved, and they had been made efficient by constant drill. By the seventh of August, nearly four months after the battle of Cerro Gordo, all of the reinforcements had arrived and the army began its march on the City of Mexico. The first engagement occurred at Contreras, where on the nineteenth and twentieth of August Scott's army won a signal victory

---

[65] *Ibid.*, 434.

over its adversaries.[66]   On the following day the Mexicans were again defeated, and this time thoroughly demoralized, in the battle of Churubusco. It is quite probable that if Scott had chosen to pursue the enemy he could have entered the capital and ended the war.[67]

Scott, however, did not follow up the advantage gained at Churubusco. Instead, he agreed to an armistice in order to afford an opportunity for Trist to enter into negotiations with commissioners appointed by Santa Anna. In his report to the Secretary of War he admitted that he might have occupied the capital "with but little additional loss," but Trist and himself had "been admonished by the best friends of peace—intelligent neutrals and some American residents—against precipitation." This admonition and the fear that by "driving away the government" peace would be delayed were the reasons assigned for consenting to an armistice.[68] The "intelligent neutrals" were members of the British legation, and their opinions seem to have carried more weight than did the wishes of his own government. As will appear in the next chapter, Santa Anna's commissioners declined to accept the terms offered by Trist, and the armistice resulted simply in giving the Mexican army a chance to recuperate.

The commissioners held their last meeting on September 6, and on the same day Scott addressed a note to Santa Anna. In it he stated that the armistice had been violated and that it would be terminated at noon on the following day, unless by that time he should receive "complete satisfaction" for the offenses which had been committed. Santa Anna's reply was anything but *satisfactory,* for he not only contradicted Scott's assertions but,

---

[66] In reporting this battle to the Secretary of War, Scott wrote: "I doubt whether a more brilliant or decisive victory . . . is to be found on record" (*Sen. Ex. Doc. 1,* 30 Cong., 1 sess., 308).

[67] Ripley, *War with Mexico,* II, 283. Ripley served on General Pillow's staff.

[68] *Sen. Ex. Doc. 1,* 30 Cong., 1 sess., 314.

in turn, charged the American commander with violating the principles of civilized warfare.[69] Such an exchange of courtesies meant, of course, that hostilities would be renewed.

Unofficial news of Scott's victories and subsequent armistice reached Washington on the fourteenth of September. As the President had recently decided to force a peace by ordering Scott to prosecute the war relentlessly and to defray his expenses by levying contributions, he was not well pleased when he learned of the truce. He noted in his diary:

> Judging at this distance, I would think he should have improved his victories by pressing the Mexican Government to an immediate decision upon the terms of peace which Mr. Trist was authorized to offer to them, and if they refused these terms I think he should have taken immediate possession of the City, and levied contributions upon it for the support of his army. I fear the armistice was agreed to by the Mexican Commander only to gain time to re-organize his defeated army for further resistance.[70]

On October 4, although he had already heard of the capture of Mexico City, the President decided to recall Trist. "Mexico," he wrote, "must now first sue for peace, & when she does we will hear her propositions."[71] Apparently, he had little hope that the fall of the capital would induce the enemy to make peace, for two days later Marcy, under his instructions, sent to Scott new orders for continuing the war. He was told that reënforcements were on the way. It was hoped that they would enable him to "carry on further aggressive operations; to achieve new conquests; to disperse the remaining army of the enemy in your vicinity, and prevent the organization of another." It was expected that he would conduct operations in the most effective way to "induce the rulers and people of Mexico to desire and consent to such terms of peace as we have a right to ask and expect." One means of effecting this result was the levying of

---

[69] Scott to Santa Anna, Sept. 6; Santa Anna to Scott, Sept. 7, 1847 (*Sen. Ex. Doc. 52*, 30 Cong., 1 sess., 346–348).

[70] Polk, *Diary*, III, 156, 170–172.

[71] *Ibid.*, 185–186.

military contributions.[72] These instructions did not reach Mexico City until the middle of November, and at that time Scott did not feel disposed to follow them.

On September 8, the day following the termination of the armistice, Scott ordered Worth to make an attack on the Molino del Rey (king's mill), which was erroneously reported to be used as a cannon foundry.[73] Worth succeeded in capturing the mill, but not without severe loss. A few days later General Pillow made a "successful, but bloody" attack upon the fortifications at Chapultepec.[74] Scott's army now began its advance on the capital city. Santa Anna offered further resistance at Belén and San Cosmé, but, on the night of September 13, he evacuated the capital and withdrew to Guadalupe Hidalgo.

Although defeated and driven from the capital, Santa Anna was not ready to lay down his arms. Being now thoroughly discredited, there was but one hope of maintaining his authority, namely, by achieving some unexpected military victory. He therefore determined to fall upon the small garrison which Scott had left to hold possession of Puebla. Having issued a decree in which he resigned the Presidency and assigned the duties of this office to Peña y Peña and two associates, he set out for Puebla, where he arrived on the twenty-first of September. His attempt to overwhelm the garrison ended in failure, as did, also, an attempt to capture a force under General Joseph Lane which was on its way from Vera Cruz to Mexico City. While near Huamantla, Santa Anna received an order from Querétaro, dated October 7, which directed him to turn over his command to a subordinate and to appear before a court of inquiry. He complied with the first part of the order, but not with the second.

---

[72] Marcy to Scott, Oct. 6, 1847 (*Sen. Ex. Doc. 52,* 30 Cong., 1 sess., 138–140).

[73] Hitchcock, *Fifty Years in Camp and Field,* 296.

[74] "In later years," was Grant's comment, "if not at the time, the battles of Molino del Rey and Chapultepec have seemed to me to have been wholly unnecessary" (Grant, *Memoirs,* I, 152–154).

After keeping under cover in Mexico until the following spring, he set out for Jamaica, there to await a favorable opportunity to regain his lost power.

The order which came from Querétaro, and which deprived Santa Anna of his command, was dictated by Peña y Peña, who claimed the right to exercise the office of President, not by virtue of Santa Anna's decree, but by the constitution and the laws of the republic. We are not here interested in the validity of this claim. For our present purpose we are interested simply in the fact that Peña's action removed Santa Anna from control and opened the way for a resumption of negotiations. These and earlier negotiations will be discussed in the following chapter.

CHAPTER XX

TREATY OF GUADALUPE HIDALGO

In January, 1847, as we have noted in the preceding chapter, President Polk, in response to overtures made by Atocha, invited the Mexican government to send commissioners to Havana or to Jalapa for the purpose of negotiating a treaty with diplomatic representatives of the United States. In March, Atocha, who had carried the invitation to Mexico, returned to Washington with the reply that Mexico would not consent to appoint commissioners unless the raising of the blockade and the evacuation of Mexican territory "shall be previously accepted as a preliminary condition." Polk at once pronounced such terms to be "wholly inadmissible" and decided to deal a crushing blow at Mexico City.

Before Atocha had set out on his journey to Mexico, and while the personnel of the proposed commission was under discussion, Buchanan expressed a desire to be chosen as one of the number. I told him," wrote the President, "it struck me favourably, but that if he went he must do so in his character of Secretary of State, & go alone & without being associated with others."[1] When the conditons demanded by Mexico became known there was, of course, no immediate necessity for making an appointment.

The idea of creating a commission which might accompany the army and take advantage of the first opportunity to negotiate peace appears to have originated in the fertile brain of Senator Benton. He suggested such a commission in December, 1846,

[1] "I told him," Polk continued, "that would be due to his position, & that the administration, if he went alone, would be entitled to the whole credit of the arrangement. It seemed to strike him favourably. Indeed I had no doubt he was highly delighted with the idea" (Polk, *Diary*, II, 388).

when the President had under consideration the appointment o
Benton to the position of lieutenant-general. His plan provides
for three commissioners who were to accompany the main army
and who were to be clothed with full diplomatic powers. Polk
approved the suggestion and mentioned Slidell as one of the
number. To this Benton interposed vigorous objections and, in
turn, proposed the names of John J. Crittenden, Silas Wright
and himself. The President was willing to nominate any of the
men named, but he did not wish to slight Slidell, who had already
performed valuable services in Mexico. Benton would not yield
his objections to Slidell's appointment, and the matter was
dropped.[2] The Senator's next attempt to procure a diplomatic
appointment was his request, during the following March, that
the President should make him commander-in-chief of the army
and invest him with power to negotiate a treaty.[3]

When, on March 20, 1847, Atocha returned to Washington
bearing an unsatisfactory reply to the American offer, the President announced to the cabinet his intention to "lay aside the
technical rules of war to be found in books" and to crush Santa
Anna at all hazards.[4] His belligerent mood, however, did not
preclude a desire for peace at the earliest possible moment.

Nothing occurred which led the President to believe that
Mexico might of necessity be ready to accept his peace terms
until April 10, when news of the fall of Vera Cruz reached Washington. The effect of this news upon Polk's determination to
appoint an ambulatory commissioner and his reasons for selecting
Nicholas P. Trist to fill the position are recorded in his own
memorandum of a cabinet meeting held on that day:

The subject of consideration today was the Mexican War. I ha
several times mentioned to Mr. Buchanan the importance of having
commissioner vested with Plenipotentiary powers, who should attend th
headquarters of the army ready to take advantage of circumstances a
they might arise to negotiate for peace. I stated to the Cabinet to-da

2 *Ibid.*, 262–270.   3 *Ibid.*, 412.

4 *Ibid.*, 432. On this same day the mails brought the news of the battl
of Buena Vista.

that such was my opinion, and that I thought it more important since the news of the recent victories, and especially since the information received this morning of the fall of Vera Cruz & the Castle of San juan D'Ulloa. All the members of the Cabinet present concurred in this opinion. The embarrassment in carrying it out consisted in the selection of a suitable commissioner or commissioners who would be satisfactory to the country. This was a great difficulty. Such is the jealousy of the different factions of the Democratic party in reference to the next Presidential Election towards each other that it is impossible to appoint any prominent man or men without giving extensive dissatisfaction to others, and thus jeopardizing the ratification of any Treaty they might make. In this also the Cabinet were agreed. I stated that I preferred that the Secretary of State should be the sole commissioner to negotiate the Treaty, & that I would have no hesitation in deputing him on that special service if the Mexican authorities had agreed to appoint commissioners on their part, but as they had refused to do this he could not attend the head-quarters of the army for an indefinite period of time and with no assurance whether the Mexican authorities would agree to negotiate. Mr. Buchanan expressed his entire concurrence in this view. He said he would be willing to go in person if there was any assurance that negotiations would be speedily opened, but under the circumstances & with our present information he could not, of course, think of going. Mr. Buchanan then suggested that Mr. N. P. Trist, the chief clerk of the Department of State, might be deputed secretly with Plenipotentiary powers to the head-quarters of the army, and that it might be made known that such a person was with the army ready to negotiate. Mr. Trist, he said, was an able man, perfectly familiar with the Spanish character and language, & might go with special as well as defined instructions. The suggestion struck me favourably. After much conversation on the subject it was unanimously agreed by the Cabinet that it would be proper to send Mr. Trist, and that he should take with him a Treaty drawn up by the Secretary of State approved by the Cabinet, which he should be authorized to tender to the Mexican Government, and to conclude [a treaty] with them if they would accept it; but that if they would not accept it, but would agree to appoint commissioners to negotiate, that Mr. Trist should in that event report the fact to his Government, when Mr. Buchanan could go out as the commissioner.

After the entire cabinet had approved such a mission, Trist was sent for and the nature of the mission explained. He accepted the appointment. He and all others cognizant of the President's diplomatic venture were pledged to profound secrecy.[5]

---

[5] *Ibid.*, 465–468. Of the necessity for secrecy Polk wrote: ''To give publicity to such a movement before it was commenced, and to have the federal papers giving their own version of it, and, as their habit is, to have

Although Trist, as we have just noted, was selected on the recommendation of Buchanan, his past career and his qualifications were not entirely unknown to the President. He had studied law under Jefferson, whose granddaughter he had married, and after a brief term of service as clerk in the Treasury Department President Jackson had made him his private secretary. In 1833 he was appointed consul at Havana by Jackson, and, after eight years of service in that capacity, he was recalled by Tyler because he had been charged by Great Britain with having aided the slave trade in Cuba. Similar charges had been made during Van Buren's administration, and even his brother-in-law, Thomas Jefferson Randolph, advised Van Buren to remove him unless they were disproved. "Mr. Trist is disinterested and honorable," said Randolph, "his judgment I have never confided in; whatever his errors may have been they have been doubtless of his judgment, but indiscretions may be carried too far."[6] This characterization seems apposite to his entire career. Bad judgment and inordinate conceit were his besetting sins.

Shortly after Polk's inauguration, Trist began to importune the new President for office and to enlist the influence of the Donelson family in his behalf.[7] Unsuccessful at first, he was, on August 28, 1845, given a commission as chief clerk in the Department of State.[8]

In appointing Trist to conduct the negotiations with Mexico the President, as it turned out, made a most unfortunate selection; yet in passing judgment upon the President's act, the

---

them by every means in their power thwarting the objects of the Government by discouraging the enemy to accede to the measure, would in all probability be to defeat it, hence the necessity of secrecy.'' Trist's appointment was not, of course, ratified by the Senate.

[6] Randolph to Van Buren, Dec. 16, 1839, *Van Buren Papers.*

[7] Trist to Polk, March 14 and April 2, *Trist Papers.* Polk's name does not appear on the latter, but it speaks of "your Inaugural." With customary indiscretion he lectured the President on the meaning of sovereignty.

[8] Buchanan to Trist on that date "hereby appointing" him to that position (*Trist Papers*).

special task which was assigned to the commissioner should be taken into consideration. He was given a definite project of a treaty for submission to the Mexican government, with but little discretion to alter its terms. In case Mexico should prove unwilling to accept the essential parts of the project, but nevertheless willing to negotiate, it was Polk's intention to appoint Buchanan or some other qualified person, or persons, to conduct the negotiations. A task so definitely limited did not require a diplomat of the first rank.

Having decided to send Trist to Mexico, Polk directed Buchanan to prepare a project of a treaty and, also, a reply to the Mexican communication which had been brought back by Atocha.

Buchanan's draft of a treaty was submitted and fully discussed at a cabinet meeting held on the thirteenth of April. It fixed the boundary of Texas at the Rio Grande, and provided that New Mexico and both Upper and Lower California should be ceded to the United States. Another article stipulated that the United States should have the right of transit across the isthmus of Tehuantepec. In addition to the assumption of the claims of its citizens against Mexico, the United States was to pay the sum of fifteen million dollars. In the President's opinion, the sum named was too large, but, if necessary, he was willing to go as high as thirty millions. The Secretary of State still opposed increasing the amount. Walker attached greater importance to the free passage across the isthmus than to the cession of both New Mexico and the Californias. If this could be procured he was willing to pay thirty millions, otherwise not. He wished it to be made a *sine qua non*. "To this," said Polk, "I objected & stated that it constituted no part of the object for which we had entered the War"—an indirect admission that he had entered the war to acquire territory. Finally, all agreed to accept the President's terms. Nothing was made a *sine qua non* except the acquisition of Upper California and New Mexico—the Rio

Grande boundary being considered as already settled.[9] The project in its final form provided for cession to the United States of both Californias and New Mexico, while the United States agreed to assume the claims and to pay fifteen million dollars; but Trist's instructions stipulated the modifications which he might make.

The instructions covered the points agreed upon at the cabinet meeting of April 13 (see note 9) and, in addition, authorized Trist to incorporate, if necessary, an article guaranteeing rights to the inhabitants similar to those stipulated in the treaty by which Louisiana had been acquired. Should such an article be included he was to insist upon a provision which would invalidate all recent land grants. Should he fail to make a treaty, he was authorized to arrange for a peace commission, provided that "a reasonable prospect shall exist" that Mexican commissioners would agree to the ultimata already specified by the United States.

Under the same date (April 15) as the instructions to Trist, Buchanan prepared a letter to the Mexican Minister of Foreign Relations. It was a reply to the minister's note of February 22 which Atocha had brought back and in which Santa Anna had declined to treat unless the blockade were raised and Mexican territory evacuated. It also informed the Mexican government of the purpose of Trist's mission. In this letter Buchanan said that a demand such as Mexico had made was both unprecedented and unreasonable—that "the war can never end whilst Mexico refuses even to hear the proposals" which the United States has always been ready to make. "The President," he continued,

---

[9] Polk, *Diary*, II, 468, 471–475. The maximum amounts to be paid were to be governed by the cessions procured—$30,000,000 for all desired; $25,000,000, without passage across the isthmus; $20,000,000 if only Upper California and New Mexico could be obtained. Trist was to reduce these amounts, if possible. Polk's views on territorial expansion are expressed very clearly in his diary entry for January 5, 1847: "New Mexico and California is all that can ever probably be acquired by Treaty, and indeed all that I think it important to acquire" (*ibid.*, 308).

"will not again renew the offer to negotiate, at least until he shall have reason to believe that it would be accepted by the Mexican Government."[10]

On April 16, 1847, Trist set out for Mexico bearing his instructions and the project of a treaty and, also, Buchanan's letter to the Mexican minister. Marcy instructed Scott to deliver the last mentioned document to the Mexican commander with a request that it should be laid before the government.[11] The secrecy with which the President tried to envelop the mission[12] was of short duration. On April 21 he was chagrined by discovering in the New York *Herald* a letter which gave a very accurate account of Trist's mission and its purposes.[13] William S. Derrick, a Whig clerk in the State Department, who had assisted in copying the documents, at once became the object of suspicion, but the source of the leakage could not be ascertained.

Arriving at Vera Cruz on May 6, 1847, Trist hastened to tell Buchanan "the results of his [my] reflections" since his departure from Washington as well as his opinions on affairs in Mexico.[14] With characteristic egotism he immediately assumed responsibilities which were never intended for him. A military detachment, selected by himself, was sent on ahead as bearer to General Scott of Buchanan's letter to the Mexican government,

---

10 Project and instructions, *Sen. Ex. Doc. 52*, 30 Cong., 1 sess., 81–89. Buchanan to Min. of For. Rel., April 15, 1847 (*Sen. Ex. Doc. 1*, 30 Cong., 1 sess., 38–40). All are printed in Buchanan, *Works*, VII, 267–279. Trist's commission and a copy of his authority from Walker to draw on the U. S. treasury for $3,000,000 (both dated April 15) are among Trist's papers.

11 Marcy to Scott, April 14, 1847 (*Sen. Ex. Doc. 52*, 30 Cong., 1 sess., 118–119).

12 On the day of Trist's departure Polk wrote in his diary: "Had his mission and the object of it been proclaimed in advance at Washington I have no doubt there are persons in Washington, and among them Editors of the *National Intelligencer*, who would have been ready and willing to have despatched a courrier to Mexico to discourage the Government of that weak and distracted country from entering upon negotiations for peace" (*Diary*, II, 479).

13 *Ibid.*, 482–483. "I have not been more vexed or excited," noted the President, "since I have been President than at this occurrence."

14 *Sen. Ex. Doc. 52*, 30 Cong., 1 sess., 153–156.

the confidential instructions from Marcy, as well as a letter from Trist himself. His failure to deliver these documents directly was the main cause of the misunderstanding which followed.

Marcy's letter to Scott[15] explained that Trist had been invested with authority to arrange for a suspension of hostilities, and

Should he make known to you, in writing, that the contingency has occurred in consequence of which the President is willing that further military operations should cease, you will regard such notice as a direction from the President to suspend them until further orders from the department, unless continued or recommended by the enemy.

In addition, Scott was informed that Trist bore a communication from Buchanan to the Minister of Foreign Relations, and he was instructed to "transmit that despatch to the commander of the Mexican forces, with a request that it may be laid before his government."

The communication which Scott was thus ordered to transmit to the Mexican general had been sealed, but Trist carried a copy which the Washington officials expected him to show to Scott at the time of delivering the original. As already noted, however, Trist did not personally deliver the communication to General Scott. He forwarded it from Vera Cruz, without inclosing a copy; besides, his own letter, which accompanied it, did not explain fully the nature of his mission.

When the documents reached Scott at Jalapa on May 7 other things besides the absence of Trist's copy of Buchanan's letter tended to make the general both suspicious and irritable. While at New Orleans he had learned of the President's attempt to make Benton a lieutenant-general, and, as a result, he regarded Polk as "an enemy more to be dreaded than Santa Anna and all his hosts."[16] Although "very slightly" acquainted in Washington, Trist and Scott had, according to the general's account,

---

[15] Dated April 14 (*ibid.*, 118–119).
[16] Scott, *Autobiography*, II, 400, 403.

developed "feelings of mutual dislike." Indeed, Scott foolishly thought that Trist's "well-known prejudice against him [me] had had much weight in his appointment." Then, too, the general had concluded from a conversation held in Washington that Polk had originally intended to invest him with diplomatic powers—a fact which made him all the more resent Trist's appearance in Mexico.[17]

Nettled by what he considered to be encroachments upon his authority, and without waiting to learn all of the facts, Scott entered into an indiscreet and insolent correspondence with both Trist and Marcy. "I have just received your note of yesterday," he wrote to Trist, "accompanied by communications to me from the Secretary of War, and one (sealed!) from the Department of State to the minister of foreign affairs of the republic of Mexico." After complaining that the army had been weakened by sending the detachment to carry the dispatches from Vera Cruz, and declining to "commit the honor" of his government by having any direct agency in "forwarding the sealed despatch you have sent me from the Secretary of State," the general indignantly continued:

I see that the Secretary of War proposes to degrade me, by requiring that I, the commander of this army, shall defer to you, the chief clerk of the Department of State, the question of continuing or discontinuing hostilities.

I beg to say to him and to you, that here, in the heart of a hostile country, from which, after a few weeks, it would be impossible to withdraw this army without a loss, probably, of half its numbers . . . . this army must take *military* security for its own safety. Hence, the question of an armistice or no armistice is, most peculiarly, a *military* question, appertaining, of necessity, if not of universal right, in the absence of direct instructions, to the commander of the invading forces; consequently,

---

[17] *Ibid.*, 576. There is no reason for believing that Polk ever intended to give Scott such an appointment. The entries in his diary concerning possible commissioners do not mention Scott's name, and from the first, he had a very poor opinion of the General's discretion and judgment. Scott's own account admits that Polk merely left him "half at liberty to believe" that he might be associated with Wright or some other eminent statesman, for "What could have been more natural?"(!)

if you are not clothed with military rank over me, as well as with diplomatic functions, I shall demand, under the peculiar circumstances, that,
in your negotiations, if the enemy should entertain your overtures, you
refer that question to me, and all the securities belonging to it.[18]

We need not. wonder that Trist was provoked by the tone of
Scott's letter; still, there was no good reason why he should
commit the folly of following the example set by his adversary.
A little common sense on his part might, no doubt, have smoothed
the ruffled feathers of the irate general. Common sense, however, was a quality of which Trist seldom availed himself. Instead of awaiting a personal interview, at which he might have
shown his own instructions and a copy of Buchanan's "sealed"
letter, thereby removing the general's misapprehensions, he chose
to answer Scott not only in writing but in language still more
abusive than that used by the general himself.

A man possessed of Trist's peculiar characteristics very naturally preferred written replies to oral explanations. Quite as
vain as Scott himself, proud of his rhetoric and insinuating invective, he was so facile a writer that he could cover folio pages
more easily than most persons can write sentences. The fatigue
experienced by any one who peruses his tedious and rambling
discourses was equaled, apparently, by the pleasure which their
author had in penning them. It would have been unreasonable,
therefore, to expect him to forego the pleasure of writing, even
though a commonplace interview might more effectively have
answered the purpose for which he had been sent to Mexico.

While camped at San Juan del Rio, on May 9, he began his
reply, and installments were added whenever the army halted
on its march to Jalapa. It was finished after that place had been
reached and sent to Scott, along with another letter, on the
twenty-first of May.

---

[18] Scott to Trist, May 7, 1847 (*Sen. Doc. 52*, 30 Cong., 1 sess., 120–121).
A copy of this letter, accompanied by a very crisp note, was sent to Marcy
on the same day (*ibid.*, 119).

Some of his remarks were sensible and to the point. When he had sent his brief note from Vera Cruz, he told Scott, he did not anticipate that a correspondence between them would arise, "or that any communication whatever would be made on your part until I should have the pleasure of congratulating you in person upon the brilliant success which has attended your movements." He pointed out, also, that his instructions, which he had intended to show on his arrival, would have made clear to the general that hostilities were to be suspended only after the conclusion of a treaty, and not at the caprice of the chief clerk of the State Department. He reminded Scott that the order to transmit the diplomatic note to the Mexican commander had come directly from the President—an officer who surely had a right to issue it. Commodore Perry, he said, had not caviled at a similar order sent to him—due perhaps to the want of "discernment" or to "his not having equal reason for believing his own personal consequence to be so excessive."

Having made clear to Scott that the purposes of the government had been misapprehended, Trist might well have rested his case. He chose, however, to show the general that these misapprehensions had resulted from Scott's own density of intellect, jealousy and self-esteem. After stating that there had been no intention to interfere with the general's proper military functions, he continued:

In a word, sir, the course determined upon by our government, respecting the suspension of hostilities, is what any man of plain, unsophisticated common sense would take for granted that it must be; and it is not what your exuberant fancy and overcultivated imagination would make it.

Marcy's letter, however, was rather ambiguous on this point,[19] whatever might have been taken for granted. In a sarcastic vein Trist accused Scott of being piqued because the President had not selected him to negotiate with Mexico. Admitting that Polk might not have been "duly sensible" of Scott's superior

---

[19] See above, p. 494.

qualifications for performing such a service, yet, he did not see
that the blame should rest upon the one who had been selected
to perform it. In any case, said he, it was the general's duty to
obey orders from Washington, whether documents were sealed
or unsealed.

This reply to the "tirade against our government," as Trist
called Scott's letter, was inclosed in another letter dated May
20, 1847. After informing the general that more important
business would "compel me to decline the honor of maintaining
a correspondence with you," he ordered Scott to transmit
Buchanan's note to its intended destination.[20] Happy in the
belief that he had "finished" the "greatest imbecile" that he had
ever encountered, Trist thought, apparently, that his fulmina-
tions would be approved by the President.[21]

On May 20—the day before he had been *finished* by receiving
Trist's letters—Scott wrote from Jalapa an insolent letter to
Secretary Marcy. He had, of course, received Marcy's somewhat
ambiguous instructions, but he had made no attempt to learn
from Trist the real intentions of his government. In it he said:

Mr. Trist arrived here on the 14th instant. He has not done me the
honor to call upon me. Possibly he has thought the compliment of a
first visit was due to him! I learn that he is writing a reply to my
answer to him dated the 7th instant. . . . It is not probable that I shall
find leisure to read his reply, much less to give a rejoinder.

20 *Sen. Ex. Doc. 52*, 30 Cong., 1 sess., 159– 168.

21 On May 15, while the letter to Scott was being prepared, he said in a
letter to Mrs. Trist: "There is a most extraordinary state of things here
between myself & General Scott—decidedly the greatest imbecile (and rendered so by his utter selfishness & egregious vanity) that I ever had any thing
to do with. If I don't finish him I will give any body leave to say that
all the time I have passed in study has been passed in vain. Show this to Mr.
B[uchanan] who can show it to the President." His egotism and his desire
for notoriety is still further exhibited in a letter written to Mrs. Trist on
May 21. She was instructed to tell Buchanan that he had made his letter
to Scott long "in order that he [Scott] should not have a hair's breadth of
ground left to support him, and because I knew that this correspondence
will make much noise & produce such excitement that what is said in my
letter will be read by 100 persons to *one* who would read the same thing
better said in editorials of the Union or any other paper. This is my
conviction, & this is what supports me through the task. If I have not
demolished him, then I give up" (*Trist Papers*).

It should be noted that when this was written Scott had received no communication from Trist except a brief announcement of his arrival at Vera Cruz. The fact that Trist subsequently proved himself to be quite as devoid of judgment as was Scott himself can be no excuse for the general's attitude at this time. Besides, no matter what Trist's qualifications may have been, he was, nevertheless, the diplomatic representative of the President, and it was no part of Scott's proper military functions to abuse or to ignore him. As superior in authority to both of them the President had a right to command their services.

In another paragraph, Scott expressed resentment because Polk had thought of investing both Benton and Taylor with diplomatic powers, while the same had been withheld from himself. It was quite natural, perhaps, that he should have felt hurt because of this discrimination, but surely he had no right to *claim* functions not purely military.

His complaint regarding Marcy's instructions was based on more valid grounds, although he had wholly misinterpreted the wishes of the administration. "I understand your letter," he told Marcy, "as not only taking from me . . . . all voice or advice in agreeing to a truce with the enemy, but as an attempt to place me under the military command of Mr. Trist." After quoting a passage from the Secretary's letter, he added: "That is, I am required to respect the judgment of Mr. Trist here on passing events, purely military, as the judgment of the President, who is some two thousand miles off!" There was, he said, one other instance like it in American history—when Bancroft in 1845 instructed Taylor to obey the orders of Donelson—and "I wrote to General Taylor, with the permission of both Mr. Bancroft and yourself, to correct that blunder." He closed by stating that he would cheerfully obey direct orders of the President, but not those of the "chief clerk of the State Department."[22]

---

[22] Scott to Marcy, May 20, 1847 (*Sen. Ex. Doc. 52*, 30 Cong., 1 sess., 124–127).

Scott was neither "finished" nor "demolished" by Trist's rhetorical effusions, which were handed to him as he was about to leave Jalapa. On May 29, having reached Puebla, he acknowledged their receipt and informed their author that he had taken the precaution to have them opened in the presence of staff officers. Said he:

My first impulse was to return the farrago of insolence, conceit and arrogance to the author; but on reflection, I have determined to preserve the letters as a choice specimen of diplomatic literature and manners. The Jacobin convention of France never sent to one of its armies in the field a more amiable and accomplished instrument. If you were armed with an ambulatory guillotine, you would be the personification of Danton, Marat, and St. Just, all in one.

After expressing gratitude to the President for not having degraded him by associating him with Trist on a peace commission, Scott asked the diplomat to make his future communications purely official, for

If you dare to use the style of orders or instructions again, or to indulge yourself in a single discourteous phrase, I shall throw back the communication with the contempt and scorn which you merit at my hands.[23]

While the President was absent from Washington, attending Commencement exercises at the University of North Carolina, Marcy received and answered Scott's note of May 7, in which the general's first letter to Trist (same date) had been inclosed. In a statesman-like manner—and a style in pleasing contrast with the extravagant language employed by the general and the diplomat—the Secretary of War pointed out that Scott's "distressing apprehensions of being degraded" had resulted entirely from his not having waited to ascertain the nature of Trist's mission. He had no doubt that "more reflection and better information" would remove the general's fears. Trist, said Marcy, had been instructed to submit all documents to Scott for

---

[23] Scott to Trist, May 29, 1847 (*ibid.*, 172–173). Original in *Trist Papers.*

examination; and had the general, instead of declining to see Trist, read the documents, he would have seen that nothing unusual had been asked of him.[24]

Apparently, the Washington officials believed that the teapot tempest raging at Jalapa would be quelled by the information contained in Marcy's letter, for Polk made no mention of the incident in his diary until the arrival, on June 12, of Scott's insulting letter of May 20th. This, of course, was written before Scott had received Marcy's letter; but it showed that the general had made no effort to ascertain the facts, although Trist had been at his camp for nearly a week. In another respect this communication was more offensive than the note of May 7, which had been received during the President's absence. That had been addressed to Trist and simply inclosed in a brief note to the Secretary of War; the letter just received was addressed to Marcy himself, and, as noted above, was both impudent and defiant. Little wonder that Polk pronounced it "highly exceptionable in character." He wrote in his diary:

It appears that Gen'l Scott has taken offense because Mr. Trist was sent to his Head Quarters as a Commissioner invested with Diplomatic Powers & full authority to conclude a Treaty of peace. He desired to be invested with this power himself, and although Mr. Trist had been at his camp for six days at the date of his despatch, he states he had not seen him. It is clear from his despatch, as well as one of previous date enclosing a letter from Gen'l Scott to Mr. Trist, that he would not co-operate with Mr. Trist in accomplishing the object of his mission, the conclusion of an honourable peace. His two last despatches are not only insubordinate, but insulting to Mr. Trist and the Government. I gave my views on the subject, in which the Cabinet unanimously concurred. In accordance with them I directed the Secretary of War to prepare a despatch to General Scott rebuking him for his insubordinate course, and repeating the order in a peremptory manner to him to carry the despatch borne to him by Mr. Trist addressed to the Mexican Government to that Government, and requiring an immediate answer, to be returned by the bearer of the despatch, whether he had obeyed or intended to obey the former order of the Secretary of War. He deserves for his conduct in

---

[24] Marcy to Scott, May 31, 1847 (*Sen. Ex. Doc. 52*, 30 Cong., 1 sess., 121–124).

this matter to be removed from the command. I conclude[d], however, to
delay acting on his conduct until his answer to the communication which
I this day ordered to be addressed to him shall be received. . . . . Gen'l
Scott arrogates to himself the right to be the only proper channel through
whom the U. S. Government can properly communicate with the Government of Mexico on any subject; which is an assumption wholly unwar-
rantable & which I will not tolerate. The truth is that I have been compelled from the beginning to conduct the war against Mexico through the
agency of two Gen'ls highest in rank who have not only no sympathies
with the Government, but are hostile to my administration. Both of
them have assumed to control the Government. To this I will not submit
& will as certainly remove Gen'l Scott from the chief command, as she
[he] shall refuse or delay to obey the order borne to him by Mr. Trist.
My doubt is whether I shall delay to remove him until I can hear further
from him.[25]

A few days later the President declared that should Scott
persist in disobeying orders he would have the general arrested
and tried by court-martial. But his caution was stronger than
his resentment. He took no step until he had consulted the
cabinet, and although fearful that Scott's "arrogance & inordinate vanity" might have jeopardized peace by causing delay,
he decided to await further news from Mexico. Marcy and
Buchanan were instructed to inform the commander and the
diplomat that their conduct had been highly displeasing to the
President. Surely he had ample cause for being displeased, for
seldom, if ever, has any President had to cope with such folly
and such insolence on the part of his agents.

Elated by the thought that he had "finished" General Scott,
won the approval of the President, and achieved fame by newspaper commendation, Trist must have been shocked when informed by Buchanan that his *orders* to Scott were both superfluous and unwarranted. He was told that when he had placed
the communication to the Mexican government in the hands of
Scott his "whole duty respecting it was then performed"; and
if the general did not obey orders he was answerable neither to
the Department of State nor to the commissioner, but to the

---

25 Polk, *Diary*, III, 57–59.

military branch of the government. He was directed by the President, said Buchanan, to avoid personal altercations, and to submit to Scott his instructions and the project of a treaty.[26]

Marcy's letter to Scott once more expressed surprise that the general could have so misconceived his instructions. There had, said the Secretary, been no intention to put him under the command of Trist in any particular. The President had ordered him [Scott] to transmit a document to the Mexican commander and

he [Polk] is wholly unable to conceive how you can reconcile with duty and subordination the making of it a topic of remark, I may say of incidental reproof of your common superior, in an official communication to a subordinate officer in another branch of the public service.[27]

While Marcy was writing the above letter another note from Scott was on its way to Washington. Unlike its predecessor this note did not breathe defiance, but with childlike petulance the general asked to be recalled. He inclosed a copy of his rejoinder to Trist's last epistle which, with his usual facility at phrase coining, he called a ''flank battery'' planted against him amidst critical military operations. ''Considering,'' said he, ''the many cruel disappointments and mortifications I have been made to feel since I left Washington, or the total want of support and sympathy on the part of the War Department which I have so long experienced, I beg to be recalled.''[28]

The President was absent on a tour of the northeastern states when Scott's letter reached Washington. After his return, this letter as well as a communication from Trist, dated June 3, was considered at a cabinet meeting held on the ninth of June. Polk had good reason for thinking that these dispatches disclosed a ''wretched state of things'' in Mexico. He writes:

---

[26] Buchanan to Trist, June 14, 1847 (*Sen. Ex. Doc. 52*, 30 Cong., 1 sess., 112–113).

[27] Marcy to Scott, June 15, 1847 (*ibid.*, 127–129).

[28] Scott to Marcy, June 4, 1847 (*ibid.*, 130–131).

Gen'l Scott has written foolish & bitter letters to Mr. Trist & Mr. Trist has written as foolish a letter to him. Between them the orders of the Secretary of War & the Secretary of State have been disregarded; the danger has become imminent that because of the personal controversy between these self important personages, the golden moment for concluding a peace with Mexico may have passed. Gen'l Scott's last despatch to the Secretary of War is full of passion & vanity & is highly insubordinate. In view of the whole case & of the present critical condition of affairs in Mexico, I submitted to the Cabinet for their advice whether they should not both be recalled.

The cabinet agreed in condemning the conduct of both men, but it was not deemed expedient to recall them. Consenting to await further developments, the President directed Buchanan and Marcy to command their respective subordinates to "cease their correspondence and personal controversy and to act in harmony, each in his respective sphere, in obeying the orders, and carrying out the views of the government." He suggested sending some one to act with Trist, and mentioned Pierre Soulé in this connection; but no appointment was made.[29]

On July 14 Colonel Wilson set out for Mexico, bearing the new instructions which had been prepared by the two cabinet officers and revised by the President. In his letter to Trist, Buchanan once more emphasized the fact that so far as the communication to the Mexican government was concerned Trist was simply the bearer of the dispatch for delivery into the hands of General Scott. In all other respects his functions were purely diplomatic, and it was no part of his duty to discipline or supervise the commander-in-chief. Having repeated the President's order to confine his activities to the diplomatic field, Buchanan authorized Trist to make certain modifications in the boundary which had been proposed in the original treaty project.[30]

---

29 Polk, *Diary*, III, 76–77.

30 Buchanan to Trist, July 13, 1847 (rec'd by Trist on Sept. 6) (*Sen. Ex. Doc. 52*, 30 Cong., 1 sess., 113–117). Original in *Trist Papers*. In a private letter written to Trist on the same date Buchanan said: "I most deeply regret your quarrel with General Scott. It has been made the text for much Whig abuse & misrepresentation. Still we must bear it as we can. Governor Marcy has written a powerful letter to General Scott by

Marcy's letter to Scott was a very clear-cut and admirable document. With commendable patience he again pointed out that in no way had the government given Scott cause for offense. He assured the general that anything done by Trist, except the mere delivery of the dispatch addressed to the Mexican government, had been wholly unwarranted. In answer to Scott's request to be recalled, Marcy, by the President's order, denied the request and indignantly repelled the charges upon which it had been based.[31]

The new instructions did not reach their destination until September 6, and by that time there was no need of urging co-operation on the part of the commissioner and the commander-in-chief. They had become fast friends; indeed, before the instructions had been drafted they had already taken steps to negotiate a treaty.

On April 20, 1847, soon after the battle of Cerro Gordo, the Mexican congress had passed a law by which Santa Anna had been deprived of the power to negotiate with the United States. Nevertheless, within ten days, overtures were made to General Scott, through the British minister, but nothing resulted from

---

the messenger which will bear you this. The President's apprehensions are great lest the misunderstandings may defeat or delay the conclusion of a Treaty. Still he is well disposed to do you justice'' (*Trist Papers*). In a letter dated June 3, 1847, Trist had inclosed a communication from an unnamed person regarding a boundary line. The main point of it was that the line should be modified so as to include El Paso within the United States. Trist recommended this alteration. See *Doc. 52*, 168–172.

[31] ''Of 'the many cruel disappointments and mortifications I (you) have been made to feel since I (you) left Washington,' you have omitted to specify a single one, and whether they are real or imaginary is left in great uncertainty. The sending of Mr. Trist to Mexico as a commissioner of peace, and the suspicion you cherished that you had been degraded by his being clothed with military authority to interfere with your rightful command, are probably prominent among these 'cruel disappointments and mortifications.' The exposition which has been made of that case, shows the lamentable extent to which error may prevail in personal matters when prejudice and suspicion pre-occupy the mind. Should your other undisclosed 'cruel disappointments and mortifications' be of a like unsubstantiated character, as it is presumed they are, you may well conclude that they constitute no sufficient motive with the President to grant the indulgence you ask'' (Marcy to Scott, July 12, 1847; *Sen. Ex. Doc. 52, loc. cit.*).

them.[32] Late in May Santa Anna abandoned Puebla and repaired to Mexico City where he resumed the Presidency and prepared to defend the capital. Scott reached Puebla on May 28 where he remained several weeks awaiting reënforcements. Trist followed Scott to Puebla and established himself at the headquarters of General Persifer F. Smith, but for some time there was no intercourse between him and the commander-in-chief.

Scott, as we have seen, had refused to deliver Buchanan's dispatch to the Mexican government and, on June 6, Trist addressed a note to Charles Bankhead, the British minister at Mexico City, asking if he would deliver Buchanan's note and make known verbally to the Mexican government that Trist had arrived at army headquarters.[33] Bankhead immediately sent Edward Thornton, Secretary of Legation, to receive the dispatch and to consult with both Scott and Trist. Thornton, who reached Puebla on June 10, told Trist that Señor Baranda, the Minister of Foreign Relations, had frequently expressed a desire to discover some way of opening negotiations with the United States, but that he lacked the courage to avow it openly and had resigned. The voting of three million dollars for diplomatic purposes by the United States Congress had, said Thornton, made a bad impression in Mexico, for many believed that the money was to be used in bribing certain Mexican officials.[34] Trist inclosed copies of his notes to Bankhead in a letter to Buchanan, dated June 13, in which he complained because Scott would give him no information concerning affairs in Mexico.[35]

As soon as Thornton had returned to the capital Bankhead delivered Buchanan's dispatch (of April 15) to Domingo Ibarra who had recently succeeded Baranda as Minister of Foreign

---

[32] Rives, *United States and Mexico*, II, 432–435.

[33] Trist to Bankhead, June 6, 1847 (*Sen. Ex. Doc. 52*, 30 Cong., 1 sess., 181–183). Copy also in *Trist Papers*.

[34] Thornton's report to Bankhead, quoted in Rives, *United States and Mexico*, II, 440–441.

[35] *Sen. Ex. Doc. 52*, 30 Cong., 1 sess., 178–181.

Relations. In a brief note, dated June 22, Ibarra informed Buchanan that the "decision on the affair" would rest with the Mexican congress.[36] Two days later Thornton arrived at Puebla with Ibarra's note, and notified both Scott and Trist that Santa Anna had called a special session of the congress so that it might consider the question of peace negotiations.

Since the Mexican government had thus taken a step in the direction of arranging for peace, the question of meeting possible overtures now presented itself to the American representatives. They were not as yet on speaking terms, and since Trist was the one who had been assigned the duty of conducting negotiations, he was forced to make the first move. Consequently, on June 25, the day after Thornton's return from Puebla, he addressed a note to General Scott. In it he stated that since the information given to himself and to Scott, by Thornton, seemed to indicate that Mexico was inclined to treat, he wished to notify the general that he was ready to negotiate a treaty. He inclosed a copy of his commission.[37] Scott acknowledged the receipt of his note, and "this," wrote Trist to Buchanan, "constituted the commencement of our official intercourse with reference to the duties with which I am charged."[38] It was not, however, the beginning of their friendship.

The next step in the "official intercourse" seems to have been a note written to Trist by General Worth, which stated that Don Emanuel Ibarra, a brother of the Minister of Foreign Relations, lived near by. He was, said Worth, an intelligent man, and in favor of peace. On the same day some one replied, stating that Trist wished to thank Worth for the information, but was too ill

---

[36] Ibarra to Buchanan, June 22, 1847 (*Sen. Ex. Doc. 1*, 30 Cong., 1 sess., 40–41).

[37] Trist to Scott, June 25, 1847, *Trist Papers*. This seems to be the only copy of the letter available. Rives (II, 442) says that no copy has been preserved. Trist inclosed a copy of this, as well as one of Scott's reply to it, in his dispatch No. 8, July 7, 1847, but neither the dispatch nor the letters reached the Department of State (see *H. Ex. Doc. 60*, 30 Cong., 1 sess., 830, and note).

[38] Trist to Buchanan, July 23, 1847 (*H. Ex. Doc. 60*, as cited above, 831).

to write.[39] At the same time, Scott sent to Trist a letter written by Thornton which seems to contain the first suggestion about bribing Mexican officials. On July 3, Trist wrote to Thornton as follows:

Your note to Mr. Hargous, in which you refer to the impossibility that I frankly told you existed to my adopting your suggestion upon a certain point, has been sent to me for perusal by Gen'l Scott, who moreover offers at once to make every arrangement which may be necessary for immediately carrying that suggestion into the fullest effect, which circumstances may admit.

This being the present state of the case, I shall, of course, be thankful for any information pertinent to the subject. If there be any person, who, in your opinion, could be safely intrusted with the whole affair, I should very gladly put it into his hands.[40]

Evidently the following copy of a letter is the one referred to, although the date appended is somewhat confusing:

(Copy)

My dear Sir:

Mr. Trist does not seem to think there is the smallest possibility of making use of money in Mexico for what I mentioned to you; however I told him how he might do it *por si acaso*. Should it be in your way, pray use your influence with Gen'l Scott to allow a *reasonable* time for taking the note into consideration before advancing.

Yours very truly,

L. Hargous Esq.,

&c &c &c

Nemo the name of the writer of the above letter is omitted out of National delicacy. The writer was at the time on a vist to Mr. Trist, at Puebla—about June 24, 1847.

Winfield Scott,

Puebla, July 19, 1847.[41]

---

[39] Worth to Trist, July 2, 1847; copy of unsigned letter to Worth of same date (*Trist Papers*).

[40] Trist (the copy is unsigned, but is in Trist's hand) to Thornton, July 3, 1847, *Trist Papers*. A pencil note on the margin says that a copy was "enclosed in my No. 8" to Buchanan. No. 8, as already noted, did not reach its destination. Louis Hargous was an American merchant in Mexico City.

[41] On the side margin is written: "(the writer of this was Edw. Thornton)." Since Trist mentioned what seems to be this note in his letter of July 3 to Thornton, apparently a copy (the above) was made for him on the date appended, i.e. on July 19. This is in the *Trist Papers*.

Officially, both Scott and Trist had evinced a disposition to coöperate; but, as yet, there was no indication that a personal reconciliation was near at hand. Nevertheless, a reconciliation came within a few days, and the incident which seems to have effected it was quite as trivial as was the cause of their bitter feelings toward each other. Scott's sensitive nature frequently led him to make dire threats, yet he was an extremely kind-hearted man, even when dealing with his adversaries. The following brief note and the act of kindness mentioned in it, seems to have won Trist's heart completely, and to have been the first step in the amicable adjustment of their differences:

My dear Sir:

Looking over my stores, I find a box of Guava marmalade which, perhaps, the physician may not consider improper to make part of the diet of your sick companion.

Yrs very truly
Winfield Scott,

Genl. P. F. Smith,   July 6, 1847.[42]
    &c &c &c

The marmalade seems to have had an immediate effect upon Trist's health and his disposition, for on the following day he told Buchanan in a letter that his health had improved and that

With Gen'l Scott's reply to my letter, I received a message from him evincing so much good feeling that it afforded me the sincerest pleasure to meet it as I did, in a way which should at once preclude all constraint & embarrassment between us.[43]

Indeed, their mutual "good feeling" and admiration soon became so pronounced that they rated each other's judgment higher than that of their respective chiefs in the cabinet, or even the judgment and the authority of the President of the United States.

---

[42] The "sick companion" was Trist, who was staying at Smith's headquarters. On the back of the note Trist wrote: "Brought to my bed side by Genl Smith, and left there with the box of guava, as I lay ill at Puebla."

[43] Trist to Buchanan, July 7, 1847, *Trist Papers*. This is a copy of the dispatch "No. 8" which never reached Washington.

The first fruit of the reconciliation between the two men was the consideration of bribing the Mexican government to consent to peace negotiations. It is evident from the above correspondence that Thornton had discussed the subject with Trist, but whether he or some one else named the definite amount of money asked by the Mexicans is not clear. Trist himself mentioned ''specific information obtained from various sources,'' and Hitchcock wrote that English merchants in Mexico ''say a peace can be had for a little money.'' In another place he said that ''our agents in this business are Englishmen.''[44] It is probable that Thornton himself gave Trist the information, and that he had received the demand for money from one close to the Mexican President.

On July 15 Trist and Scott held a conference, and on the following day the former addressed a rambling letter to the latter, fully committing himself to the plan of paying a bribe. ''We are both convinced,'' said he, ''beyond a shadow of a doubt, *that the only way in which the indefinite protraction of this war can possibly be prevented . . . . is by the secret expenditure of money at the city of Mexico.''* The amounts named as ''necessary & sufficient'' were ten thousand dollars in advance and one million dollars on the ratification of a treaty. He admitted that nothing of the kind had been contemplated by his government and that he had no authority to take such action, but this fact he deemed it his ''duty to disregard.'' Concurring in Scott's view that a part of the war fund might be used most advantageously in buying peace—the real object of the war—he requested the general[45] to join with him in giving the requisite pledge that the money would be paid. Trist believed that such a pledge would ''entirely supersede the necessity for the occupation of the capital.''[46]

---

[44] Hitchcock, *Fifty Years in Camp and Field*, 266, 268.

[45] Scott was, of course, more eager than Trist to give the pledge. It had, however, been arranged beforehand that the request should come from Trist, as commissioner. See Hitchcock, *op. cit.*, 267.

[46] Trist to Scott, July 16, 1847, *Trist Papers*, both the original draft and a ''fair copy.''

Scott was already fully committed to the plan of purchasing a treaty, but in a transaction so irregular he naturally desired the approval of his generals, especially that of General Pillow who was a close personal and political friend of the President. On receipt of Trist's note, therefore, he called together his chief officers—including Pillow, Quitman, Twiggs, Shields, and Cadwalader—in order that he might "post them up" and win their approval. According to Colonel Hitchcock, who was present at the meeting, Pillow "fully and eloquently" supported the scheme after Scott had explained that it was customary to use money when dealing with such people as the Mexicans. Quitman approved the "motives" which had inspired the plan, but was not in favor of paying bribe money. Twiggs "approved the whole scheme." Shields had misgivings, but was willing to leave the whole matter to Trist. Cadwalader expressed no opinion.[47] As a result of the conference Scott "very cheerfully" responded to Trist's letter on the following day. He said:

I fully concur with you, with several of the general officers of this army & with many foreigners of high standing, here & at the capital, who have volunteered their opinions, that the occupation by the U. States' forces of twenty of the principal places in this Republic, in addition to those in our hands, would not, probably, in a year or more, force the Mexican authorities to sue for, or accept a peace on any terms honorable or just to our country—*without the administration, or pledge in advance, of doucers to some of the principal authorities in this miserably governed country.* We have both learned, thro' the most unquestionable channels, that this is invited & expected as an indispensable condition precedent to any negotiation. Indeed the minimums have been specifically indicated:—ten thousand dollars, in hand, to one high functionary, & a million (to be divided, probably among many) on the ratification of a definite treaty of peace.

He had, he said, already sent the ten thousand dollars, and he agreed to unite with Trist, at the proper time, in giving a pledge to pay the million dollars. This amount was to be paid by means of a draft on the War Department under the head of "army

---

[47] Hitchcock, *Fifty Years in Camp and Field*, 266–268. Some of the men concerned later gave a very different version of their respective attitudes.

contingencies,'' and Trist was asked to send a note of explanation to the Secretary of War. Concerning the ethics of the contemplated action, he wrote:

In regard to the morality of the transaction in question, I have, like yourself, not the slightest doubt. We have tempted the integrity of no one. The overtures we propose to meet, if corrupt, come from parties previously corrupted, & we only profit by that corruption to obtain an end (peace) highly advantageous to both the U. States & Mexico. Such transactions have always been considered allowable in war.[48]

The Mexican congress, to which Santa Anna had referred Buchanan's note of April 15, declined to take any part in diplomatic affairs. A committee of that body held that the *Acta de Reformas* of May 18, 1847, had, by readopting the Constitution of 1824, rendered inoperative the law of April 20 which had deprived Santa Anna of his power to conduct negotiations. Although the congress might easily have solved the difficulty and prevented ambiguity by specifically repealing the law of April 20, it laid the matter on the table without deciding the question of the President's authority.[49]

It is probable that Santa Anna never intended to make peace, and that he made overtures merely for the purpose of procuring money from the American officials. But in view of the fact that he had been promised a much larger sum, on the conclusion of a treaty, it is more likely that his refusal to carry out his understanding with Trist and Scott was due to the attitude of his congress. At any rate he gave this as an excuse. On July 24 a note from Thornton reached the camp at Puebla. It stated that while Santa Anna was in favor of peace he could not induce his congress to repeal the resolutions which had made it treason for him to negotiate with the United States. The American army must, said Thornton, advance on the capital, and it will be met by a flag of truce before Peñon has been reached. ''So,'' wrote Hitchcock, who recorded in his diary the substance of

---

[48] Scott to Trist, July 17, 1847, original, in *Trist Papers.*
[49] See Rives, *United States and Mexico,* II, 444–446.

Thornton's letter, "the idea of peace is all knocked into a cocked hat."[50] As a result, doubtless, of Thornton's advice, Scott, according to a letter written by Hitchcock some months later, prepared a memorandum and sent a copy to Santa Anna. In it the Mexican President was informed that Scott was about to advance upon the capital, and that he would either "defeat the enemy in view of the city," should resistance be offered; or he would halt and give the government an opportunity to make peace.[51] As it turned out, the program outlined in this memorandum was quite closely followed, but apparently the general did not, at the time it was prepared, have much hope of a peaceable adjustment.[52]

Trist and Scott were now fast friends, and each expressed to his chief in the cabinet a desire that the acrimonious letters which both had sent to Washington might be suppressed. Trist now believed that the general's whole conduct had been characterized by the "purest public spirit," while Scott now found the commissioner to be "able, discreet, courteous, and amiable." At this time Scott had not received Marcy's most severe criticism of his conduct, but he resented the rebuke contained in the Secretary's letter of May 31st. Although he had this letter in his possession for nearly three weeks, he told Marcy that the reason "I do not here triumphantly vindicate myself is not from want of will, means, or ability, but *time*."[53] Neither he nor the commissioner mentioned the fact that his time had been occupied in

---

[50] Hitchcock, *Fifty Years in Camp and Field*, 269. He states that "T" wrote the letter, which undoubtedly means Thornton.

[51] *Sen. Ex. Doc. 65*, 30 Cong., 1 sess., 521–532.

[52] Under date of July 30 Hitchcock speaks in his diary of a dinner given by Pillow to the other generals and Trist. He adds: "Everything now shows that the Mexicans intended to carry on the war to the utmost of their ability, and the probability now is that our attempt to enter the capital will be met with most determined opposition" (Hitchcock, *op. cit.*, 269).

[53] Trist to Buchanan, July 23; Scott to Marcy, July 25, 1847 (*H. Ex. Doc. 60*, 30 Cong., 1 sess., 831, 1011–1012). In another insolent passage Scott said: "You will perceive that I am aware (as I have long been) of the dangers which hang over me at home; but I, too, am a citizen of the United States, and well know the obligations imposed under all

trying to purchase a treaty from Santa Anna, and before the news of that questionable transaction reached Washington many interesting events had occurred.

The first division of the American army left Puebla on August 7, 1847, followed on the next day by Trist and Scott, one bearing the olive branch, the other the sword.[54] The latter was first to be used, for, not until the battles of Contreras and Churubusco had been fought was the Mexican President ready for the olive branch. On the evening of August 20, after his defeat at Churubusco, he sought, through the British legation, to arrange for a suspension of hostilities. A deputation from the legation—including Thornton, the secretary, and Mackintosh, the consul-general—met Scott at San Augustin, "ostensibly to ask for a safe-guard for the English Minister and British subjects, but really to prepare the way for peace."[55]

Near midnight of the same day Pacheco, the Mexican Minister of Foreign Relations, called on Bankhead and asked him to use his influence in inducing Scott to save the city from being sacked. The British minister, according to his own account, would not interfere further than to transmit a letter from Pacheco to Trist. It was decided, however, that the letter should be addressed to Buchanan (as a reply to his note of the previous April) instead of Trist. Bankhead himself wrote to Trist, and expressed the hope that peace might be concluded at an early date. Both letters were sent to the commissioner.[56]

The note addressed to Buchanan stated that Santa Anna had continued the fight until the American army had reached the

circumstances by an enlightened patriotism." Due to negligence on the part of the messenger, this letter did not reach Washington until December, 1848.

[54] From Ayotla Trist wrote: "It is, indeed, a *noble* army, full of confidence in itself, and full of confidence in its commander. . . . . To appreciate the man, to *know* him at all, one must see him in this sphere." To Buchanan, Aug. 14, 1847 (*Sen. Ex. Doc. 52*, 30 Cong., 1 sess., 187).

[55] Hitchcock, *Fifty Years in Camp and Field*, 280.

[56] Pacheco to Buchanan, Aug. 20, 1847 (*Sen. Ex. Doc. 52*, 30 Cong., 1 sess., 189). Bankhead to Trist, same date, *Trist Papers*. For Bankhead's report to his government, see Rives, II, 496–497.

gates of the capital, and that he had now resolved to hear the proposals which the American commissioner had been instructed to make. In doing so, said Pacheco, the President was acting under the powers conferred upon him by the constitution. This meant, of course, that Santa Anna was ready to ignore the law of April 20, which made it treason for him to negotiate with the United States. This law may, indeed, have been rendered void by the subsequent readoption of the constitution, but since the law in question had not been specifically repealed, some doubt remained as to the legality of any treaty he might make.

On the morning of August 21, while Scott and Trist were on their way from San Angel to Tacubaya, they were met by a "fine carriage" containing General Mara y Villamil, bearer of the letters written by Pacheco and Bankhead to the American officials. Trist read the letters, and a conference was held.[57] The letter addressed to Trist did not expressly ask for an armistice, but apparently Mara verbally made it known that such was the wish of the Mexican President. With more magnanimity than judgment Scott, instead of demanding that the request for a cessation of hostilities should come from the defeated commander, proposed an armistice in a note addressed to Santa Anna. The proposal was accepted, and two days later an armistice was arranged.[58] The agreement made at Puebla probably was Scott's real reason for taking the initiative; the reasons which he gave to the Secretary of War were a desire to leave Mexico "something on which to rest her pride," and the fear that a more drastic course would "scatter the elements of government" and make the negotiation of a treaty impossible.[59]

After some delay commissioners were appointed by Santa Anna, and with them Trist held his first meeting on August 27,

---

[57] Hitchcock, *op. cit.*, 279.

[58] The correspondence and armistice are printed in *Sen. Ex. Doc. 52*, 30 Cong., 1 sess., 308–312.

[59] Scott to Marcy, Aug. 28, 1847 (*Sen. Ex. Doc. 1*, 30 Cong., 1 sess., 314).

1847.[60] He soon discovered that the powers of the Mexicans simply permitted them to receive his propositions for transmission to Santa Anna. He told them that he had been authorized to treat only with commissioners provided with full powers; nevertheless, he delivered to them a statement of the propositions which he was ready to make.[61]

As soon as the American project had been received, Pacheco drafted instructions to the commissioners and furnished them with full powers, but the instructions required them to make such extravagant demands that the commissioners immediately offered their resignations. As a result, Santa Anna, through Pacheco, authorized the commissioners to make such modifications as the "circumstances of the country may exact."[62]

The Mexican diplomats met Trist on September 1, and for two days the questions at issue were discussed. The terms of settlement now suggested by the Mexicans were much like those mentioned by Atocha in the preceding January. He had spoken of the Rio Grande as a boundary, with a neutral strip on the American side; they asked for the Nueces as a boundary, with all territory between that river and the Rio Grande as neutral

---

[60] The Mexican commissioners were ex-President Herrera, Bernardo Couto, Ignacio Mara y Villamil, Miguel Atristain, and José Arroyo.

[61] Trist to Buchanan, Aug. 27, 1847 (Sen. Ex. Doc. 52, 30 Cong., 1 sess., 191–192). On the morning of August 27 an attack made by a Mexican mob on American supply wagons threatened to prevent negotiations, but an apology temporarily smoothed over this difficulty. For details, see Rives, II, 510–511.

[62] For the instructions (in translation) and the correspondence relating to them, see Sen. Ex. Doc. 52, as cited above, 330–335. By their instructions the commissioners were to demand: Mexico would relinquish Texas—not as a result of annexation, but of negotiation. Its boundary must be the Nueces, and the United States must pay for the land one half of the price fixed by Texas laws. All debt claims against Mexico must be cancelled, as "an equivalent for entering into negotiation"(!) and ten leagues on either side of the boundary was to be neutral territory. Cession of New Mexico and California must be refused, but, as a last resort, a factory port at San Francisco might be granted to the United States. A passage over the Isthmus of Tehuantepec was to be refused. Duties on American goods brought into Mexico must be paid. The United States must restore Mexican forts to the condition in which they were found. Lastly, the commissioners were to insist on indemnity for all damages done by the American army.

ground in which no settlement might be made by either party. He had claimed no authority to discuss a cession of New Mexico; they said that their instructions forbade a cession of this territory. He had stated that Mexico was willing to cede Upper California for a money consideration; they were ready to cede the upper part of this territory, but insisted that Mexico must retain all of Lower California and a land connection with it. They declined to grant a transit across the Isthmus of Tehuantepec. Trist offered to withdraw the claim for Lower California and the transit across the isthmus, if Mexico would cede Upper California and New Mexico for a money payment. He agreed, also, to submit the Nueces boundary question to his government for consideration; they, in turn, agreed to submit to their government the terms which he had proposed.[63] Four days later, and before Trist had taken steps to refer the matter to President Polk, another meeting was held, and the Mexican commissioners presented a counter-project and an explanatory note. The cession of New Mexico was refused, an offer to cede Upper California north of 37° was made, and it was suggested that England should be asked to guarantee the proposed treaty. Trist, of course, declined to accept these terms and, for the time being, negotiations were abandoned. This in itself automatically abrogated the armistice, but General Scott chose to terminate it on the ground that its terms had been violated by the interference of Mexicans with American supply wagons.[64]

At the very moment, almost, when Santa Anna was rejecting the project of a treaty offered by the United States, President Polk was announcing his intention to demand additional territory from Mexico. On September 4 he told his cabinet that, unless the next dispatch from Trist should announce that a treaty had been signed, the commissioner ought to be instructed to

---

[63] Trist to Buchanan, Sept. 4, 1847, and inclosures (*Doc. 52*, as cited above, 195–201).

[64] Commissioners to Trist, Sept. 6, 1847; Trist's reply, Sept. 7; Scott to Santa Anna, Sept. 6 (*ibid.*, 375–380, 214–222, 346).

demand more territory. Three days later he expressed himself as in favor of acquiring Tamaulipas. The question of modifying Trist's instructions was discussed, but when, on the ninth, a rumor reached Washington that the Mexican congress had been called for the purpose of considering the American proposals, Polk noted in his diary: "I sincerely hope that a Treaty of peace may have been concluded and signed."[65]

The mail of September 14 brought the President both encouragement and disappointment. By it he learned of the victories at Contreras and Churubusco, but, also, of the armistice which followed them. The same mail contained Trist's brief dispatch of August 29, in which the government was informed that negotiations had begun. Polk was not pleased with the armistice. He believed that Scott should have demanded an immediate decision on the terms offered by the United States, and in the event of their rejection by Mexico, he should have entered the capital and levied a contribution for the support of his army. "I fear," noted the President, "that the armistice was agreed to by the Mexican Commander only to re-organize his defeated army for further resistance. . . . . I shall wait very anxiously for further information from the army." He waited until October 4, and, as no favorable news arrived, he decided that Trist should be recalled and that Scott should be directed to levy contributions on the enemy.[66]

Letters embodying these views were prepared by Buchanan and Marcy and forwarded to their respective representatives in Mexico. The Mexican counter-project Buchanan pronounced "a most extraordinary document," and the proposal of such terms "a mere mockery." The commissioners must have known,

---

[65] *Diary*, III, 161, 164, 167.

[66] "Mr. Trist is recalled," said he, "because his remaining longer with the army could not, probably, accomplish the objects of his mission, and because his remaining longer might, & probably would, impress the Mexican Government with the belief that the U. S. were so anxious for peace that they would ultimate[ly] conclude one upon the Mexican terms. Mexico must now first sue for peace, & when she does we will hear her propositions" (*ibid.*, 170–172, 185–186).

he said, that the United States would never relinquish New Mexico, Upper California, or the territory between the Nueces and the Rio Grande. The assertion made by the Mexicans that Trist had agreed to refer to his government the surrender of the last mentioned territory was not believed in Washington. If, at the time of receiving Buchanan's letter, a treaty had been signed, Trist was to bring it home with him; otherwise he was to suspend all negotiations and return home ''by the first safe opportunity.'' The letter to Scott instructed him to support his army by contributions levied on the enemy. Any proposals from Mexico to reopen negotiations were to be forwarded by him to the President.[67]

Polk has been criticized for ordering the employment of measures which might destroy all organized government in Mexico, and for demanding that future peace offers must come from the enemy. His reason for adopting this policy, whether valid or not, was his belief that Mexico would never come to terms so long as she held the erroneous opinion that the government at Washington was over-anxious for peace, or too weak to continue hostilities.[68] In a private letter the Secretary of State said that ''the spirit of the Country is now thoroughly aroused & the war will be prosecuted with the utmost vigor. This is the character of the American people. They find that peace cannot be made with Mexico upon honorable terms & they are determined to see it out.''[69] Owing to the fact that there was, for some time, no communication between Vera Cruz and the interior,

---

[67] Marcy to Scott, Oct. 6, 1847; Buchanan to Trist, same date (*Sen. Ex. Doc. 52*, 30 Cong., 1 sess., 91–93, 138–140). The original of the latter, as well as a duplicate and triplicate are in the *Trist Papers*. Some one (undoubtedly Trist) has underlined in red the part which says that the United States will never surrender Upper California or the land between the rivers Nueces and Rio Grande. The dates of receipt are noted.

[68] In the letter to Trist, just cited, Buchanan said: ''They [the Mexicans] must attribute our liberality to fear, or they must take courage from our supposed political divisions. Some such cause is necessary to account for their strange infatuation.'' For criticism of Polk's change of policy, see Rives, II, 523–525.

[69] Buchanan to Trist, Oct. 7, 1847, *Trist Papers*.

these letters did not reach Trist until November 16 and the same mail contained another dispatch from Buchanan, dated October 25th. When this dispatch was written the Secretary of State had received the letter from Trist which submitted the Mexican proposal regarding a neutral territory between the Nueces and the Rio Grande. The Secretary had, he said, been instructed by the President to say that he "could not for a single moment entertain the question of surrendering a portion of Texas." Surprise and regret were expressed because the commissioner had "gone so far beyond the carefully considered ultimatum" as to refer it to his government. "The President," he added, "has directed me to reiterate your recall." In a private note Buchanan said that he was "extremely sorry" to be obliged to write such a dispatch, but

to propose to consult the Gov't whether they would abandon that portion of the country where Mexico attacked our forces & on our right to which the Whigs have raised such an unfounded clamor, will be a fruitful cause of assault against us in the next Congress. I hope, however, there may never be a necessity for sending this dispatch to either House of Congress.[70]

Notice of his recall and of the adoption of a more drastic military policy were destined to have small influence upon Trist's diplomatic activities, for soon after the dispatches had arrived an opportunity was presented for reopening negotiations. He and General Scott were now boon companions,[71] and while setting a high value on their own combined judgment, each deemed an order from the President and his cabinet to be a nuisance which, in important cases, should be disregarded. If, therefore, the commissioner and the general believed that a treaty ought to be made, why should the President interfere!

---

[70] Buchanan to Trist, Oct. 25, 1847, *Trist Papers*. Rec'd Nov. 16. The official dispatch is printed in *Doc. 52*, as cited above, 94–95.

[71] On October 18 Trist wrote to his wife: "I am General Scott's friend for life. I know him *thoroughly*: he is the soul of honor & probity, and full of the most sterling qualities of heart & head: affectionate, generous, forgiving, and a lover of justice. . . . . Tell *all* my intimate friends of the entire revolution, from the conception I had formed of Gen S. *in my ignorance* of his character, to what I now *know* of him" (*Trist Papers*).

After the interruption of negotiations and the renewal of hostilities Scott's army had won the battles of Molino del Rey and Chapultepec and had captured Mexico City. On September 16 Santa Anna, then at Guadalupe, resigned the Presidency and directed that the office should be held by Peña y Peña, president of the supreme court, until the Mexican congress should otherwise direct. He then set out on an unsuccessful expedition against a small force of Americans stationed at Puebla. Peña assumed the office, not however by virtue of the retiring President's decree, but in accordance with the constitutional provision that the head of the supreme court should succeed to the Presidency in the event of a vacancy. After removing Santa Anna from his military command, the new President succeeded in establishing a government—one of doubtful legality in certain respects—but one which prevented anarchy until the congress could provide another. On November 11 that body selected General Anaya to be President ad interim, and the new executive at once made Peña y Peña his Minister of Foreign Relations.[72]

Nearly a month before he had received notice of his recall Trist had taken steps to renew peace negotiations. On October 20, during the brief administration of President Peña y Peña, he sent a letter, through the British legation, to Luis de la Rosa, the then Minister of Foreign Relations. This letter was dated September 7, 1847, for the reason that it purported to be a reply to the commissioners with whom he had negotiated before the armistice had been terminated.[73] Rosa notified Trist[74] that

---

[72] Technically, Peña was not president of the court—that office being vacant—but as senior member, he acted as president. Hence his right to assume the Presidency was somewhat doubtful. Trist to Buchanan, Jan. 26, 1848 (*Sen. Ex. Doc. 52*, 30 Cong., 1 sess., 281). For other details, see Rives, II, 584–589.

[73] Trist to Buchanan, Oct. 31, 1847 (copy in *Trist Papers*). Printed in part in *Sen. Ex. Doc. 52*, as above cited, 212–213. The part omitted tells of Thornton's endeavor to induce the Mexicans to negotiate. The letter to the commissioners may be found in *Doc. 52*, 214 ff. In a letter dated Oct. 25 Trist told Buchanan that there was a general desire on the part of both Mexicans and foreigners for the annexation of all of Mexico to the United States (copy in *Trist Papers*). This part is omitted from the same letter printed in *Doc. 52*, 205–212.

[74] Rosa to Trist, Oct. 31, 1847 (*Doc. 52*, as above cited, 227–228).

commissioners would be appointed, but this promise was not fulfilled until after Anaya had become President.

On November 22 the new minister, Peña, notified Trist that President Anaya had appointed peace commissioners. Two of the men selected, Bernardo Couto and Miguel Atristain, had been members of the commission which had declined, in September, to accept the American project. The others were Manual Rincon and Gonzago Cuevas. The former declined to serve and his place was not filled. Peña's note was transmitted to Thornton, who accompanied it by a letter of his own. In this, Thornton stated that he had informed Peña of Trist's recall, and that the minister was "thunderstruck" and disappointed. Thornton expressed the hope that Trist might go on with the negotiations, since the Mexican government had been induced to appoint commissioners by the prospect of a speedy peace. Peace could be had now, he said, but delay might jeopardize the prospect of a peaceful settlement.[75] This argument seems eventually to have appealed with great force to Trist's shallow intellect. He did not, however, immediately follow the advice offered, for, two days later, he formally notified Peña of his recall and stated that any communications regarding peace should be handed to General Scott for transmission to Washington.[76]

In thus declining, in the first instance, to proceed with the negotiations after he had received notice of his recall, Trist was not actuated by respect for superior authority; he was influenced solely by the belief that any other course would be futile. On the same day that he formally notified Peña of his recall he told Thornton in a letter that no dread of "the displeasure of those entrusted with the power of dispensing office" would deter him

---

[75] Peña to Trist, Nov. 22, 1847; Thornton to Trist (formal letter of same date) (*Doc. 52*, as above cited, 98–99, 231). Thornton to Trist (confidential), same date, *Trist Papers*. Thornton's confidential letter was written at Peña's urgent request. See Thornton to Palmerston, Nov. 29, 1847, quoted by Rives, II, 595.

[76] Trist to Peña, Nov. 24, 1847 (*Doc. 52*, as above cited, 99–100). Original, recalled by Trist, in *Trist Papers*.

from "disobeying positive & peremptory instructions,"[77] if the President had not deprived him of "all shadow of authority to do anything whatever." However, when Peña y Peña argued that the offer made prior to the receipt of his recall had committed his government, when the British diplomats urged prompt action, and when General Scott "encouraged him, nevertheless, to finish the good work he had begun" and expressed the belief that such action would be "duly ratified at Washington," a man of small mental caliber and excessive vanity, like Trist, could hardly fail to be influenced.[78]

Despite all this pressure he did not decide immediately to disregard his instructions. On November 27 he drafted another dispatch to Buchanan. In it he petulantly resented the President's criticism of his course in offering to refer to Washington the question relating to the boundary of Texas. After pointing out the futility of demanding that Mexican peace proposals must be sent to Washington, he urged that a new commission should be chosen to negotiate with the one already appointed by Mexico. He then expected to leave Mexico in about twelve days.[79] That he had at this time no intention of making a treaty is made clear by a letter written to Mrs. Trist on the following day. "I have," said he, "bid adieu *for ever* to official life. This decision is irrevocable." She was asked to tell Buchanan, with kindest regards, that Trist would not resume his place in the State Department, for he [Buchanan] "will soon

---

[77] But, he added, "not only am I divested entirely of the official character which I lately held, and with it of all shadow of authority to do anything whatever; but I deem it certain, that, in the actual state of things at Washington, the cause of Peace could not fail to be seriously prejudiced, were I to pursue any other course than that of the most absolute & unqualified acquiescence in the Executive will, as announced to me." He will go to Washington, he says, and do what he can for peace: "In a word, the signing of a Treaty of Peace is reserved for another hand than mine" (Trist to Thornton, Nov. 24, 1847 [copy], *Trist Papers*).

[78] Peña to Couto, Nov. 24, 1847, quoted by Rives II, 596. Scott, *Autobiography*, II, 576.

[79] Trist to Buchanan, Nov. 27, 1847 (*Sen. Ex. Doc. 52*, 30 Cong., 1 sess., 228–230). Complete copy in *Trist Papers*.

see the impossibility of this, or my having *anything* to do with Mr. Polk." Apparently the last remark was induced by the belief that the President had been unduly influenced by General Pillow.[80]

We are not left in doubt concerning the date of Trist's decision to reopen negotiations, for, with characteristic egotism, he announced with loud trumpet the very hour on which he decided to play Caesar and cross the Rubicon. In a letter to his wife, he said:

Procure the key to this cipher (. . .) and decipher the following, to be read to him [Buchanan] most secretly. This determination, I came to, this day, at 12 o'clock. It is *altogether* my OWN.

Knowing it to be the very last chance, and impressed with the dreadful consequences to our country which cannot fail to attend the loss of that chance. [Here follows cipher which was interpretd to mean] I will make a treaty, if it can be done, on the basis of the Bravo, by 32°; giving 15 millions besides the 3 millions cash.[81]

In spite, however, of this precision as to the time of making his decision, Trist seems to have told the Mexican commissioners at least a day earlier that he probably would take the responsibility of disobeying his instructions.[82] He had become obsessed

---

[80] Say to Buchanan, he wrote, "that a baser villain, and dirtier scoundrel does not exist out of the Penitentiary, nor in it, than Genl Pillow. This is, not an *opinion*, but a matter of fact, which will be proved to the world." He told Mrs. Trist that he expected to leave for the United States about December 6. Instead, he wrote his famous letter on that date. In a letter written to John A. Dix (copy in *Trist Papers*) on October 31 he had expressed his opinion of Polk's political generals. In it he urged Dix to beware of precipitancy in the confirmation of generals, lest the Senate should become involved in "a deep, damning, irretrievable disgrace—which no earthly power, nor all earthly powers combined, can avert."

[81] Trist to Mrs. Trist, Dec. 4, 1847, *Trist Papers*. In a similar strain he told Edward Thornton that "this letter will occasion you great surprise, but no greater than I should myself have experienced a few hours ago, had a seer, in whose prophetic powers I put faith, foretold to me that I was to write it" (Trist to Thornton, Dec. 4, 1847, *Trist Papers*). This letter with blanks for Thornton's name is printed in *Doc. 52*, as cited above, 266–268. Thornton's reply, dated Dec. 11, is in the *Trist Papers*. He commends Trist's proposed action and feels certain that the United States "will highly applaud your decision." He, too, expressed the belief that peace could be had "*now* or *never*."

[82] Couto to Peña, Dec. 3, 1847, quoted by Rives, II, 597.

with the belief that "if the present opportunity be not seized *at once,* all chance for making a treaty *at all* will be lost for an indefinite period—probably forever" (letter to Thornton, just cited); and a desire for fame doubtless helped to reënforce this belief.

Having decided to make a treaty, if possible, Trist informed Buchanan of the fact in a very extraordinary letter, the manuscript of which covered sixty-five large pages. It is not only prolix and extremely tiresome, but, in addition, is one of the most gratuitously insulting documents in our diplomatic annals. He assigned, as reasons for resuming negotiations in spite of his recall, a conviction that his government still desired peace; a belief that a treaty could be made then, but not later; certainty that Mexico would not and could not consent to yield more than his instructions had demanded; and the belief that his recall had been based on "a supposed state of things in this country *entirely the reverse of that which actually exists.*" Had he limited himself to these general statements the letter might not merit severe criticism, whatever might be thought of his assumption of authority. But Trist never knew when he had said enough; his pen rambled on where his brain declined to follow. Consequently, each topic was amplified—but not illuminated—by a seemingly endless profusion of words.

Under the first heading he gave a dissertation on the President's responsibilities, and then proceeded to philosophize upon Polk's mental operations. Having reached the conclusion that the President must still desire peace, he pointed out that the executive indignation mentioned in Buchanan's recent letter was entirely wasted on a weak power like Mexico. Despite his certainty that the President must still desire peace, he hinted very pointedly that Polk wished to convert a defensive war into one of conquest, and for such a wish he should be ashamed of himself. Later in the letter he again recurred to the subject of annexing all of Mexico. He believed ultimate absorption to be desirable;

but a dissolution of the Union would be preferable to the calamity of immediate annexation.[83]

As if disregarding his instructions and questioning Polk's motives were not enough, Trist had the bad taste and the audacity to volunteer opinions which could have no other effect than to wound and to exasperate the President. Well knowing, of course, that the Washington *Union* reflected the President's views, he declared its criticism of Scott's armistice to be "balderdash," "stuff," and "nonsense," which no one outside of Washington, "however low in understanding," would believe. Again, a tactful subordinate would not have told the President that his close friend, General Pillow, was an "intriguer" of "incomprehensible baseness of character." Trist did this. He asserted, also, that because the President had relied on "supposition" and "private representations" from this intriguer, "everything was seen upside down." Having referred to Pillow and Santa Anna as "twin phenomena" in "moral obliquity," he did not hesitate to speak of the former as "an individual who gives himself out as the *maker* of the President (by having procured his nomination at the Baltimore convention), and as the President's *other self*— a pretension which I have reason to believe but too well founded." Even the "justice" done the President in charitably excusing his shortcomings by attributing them to "a blind confidence" in Pillow did not help matters very much. It could not have given Polk extreme pleasure to read that "infallibility of judgment . . . . is not among the attributes of the President of the United States," or to be told that Scott's armistice, instead of being a blunder, had rescued the administration and the Democratic party from a "perilous position."[84] While reading his

<hr />

[83] In this very letter Trist told Buchanan how easily annexation could be accomplished; and, according to Lionel Davidson, agent of the Rothschilds in Mexico, he had, late in November, been in favor of permanent occupation (Davidson to Thornton, Nov. 23, 1847, *Trist Papers*). And yet he condemned Polk for his supposed desire to acquire the republic.

[84] Trist to Buchanan, Dec. 6, 1847 (*Sen. Ex. Doc. 52*, 30 Cong., 1 sess., 231–266). Complete copy also in *Trist Papers*.

tedious letters one is tempted, at times, to give Trist credit for sincerity—to think that he really believed himself to be performing deeds of heroism; albeit such charity for his motives must be at the expense of his intelligence. On the other hand, certain letters written to his wife show a want of sincerity, and brand him as a man who craved notoriety.

The American diplomat's decision to cut the Gordian knot in order to save both Mexico and his country from impending disaster did not result in an immediate reopening of negotiations. The Mexican officials who had been so anxious for him to remain now pleaded want of authority, and interposed various pretexts for delay. Since the impediments to formal discussions on the part of the diplomats were not removed until the latter part of December, we may turn our attention to Washington for the purpose of ascertaining the views of the administration.

On Ocober 6, as we have seen, the President ordered Trist's recall, not on account of the commissioner's misconduct, but because it was thought that he would be unable to make a treaty. When, however, Polk learned that the commissioner had agreed to consult his government regarding a neutral zone between the two rivers, he remarked that "Mr. Trist has managed the negotiation very bunglingly and with no ability."[85] The recall was repeated in still more emphatic terms.

Having no reason, of course, for believing that Trist would disobey his instructions, Polk gave his attention to the war policy which he purposed to recommend when Congress should have assembled in December. It was necessary that his message should be drafted with extreme care because the control of the House had now passed to his opponents. At a cabinet meeting held on November 9, Buchanan, whose Presidential aspirations had revived, told Polk that his message must advise one of two courses —to designate the part of Mexico which the United States would hold as indemnity, or to occupy all of that country by a greatly

---

[85] Polk, *Diary*, III, 199.

increased miltiary force. He did not recommend either course, but the President thought that he favored the latter. As Buchanan had up to this time wished to confine the acquisition of territory within very narrow limits, Polk believed that the change was due to political considerations. Since there seemed to be some uncertainty as to the policy of the administration, the President read a paragraph which he intended to include in his message.

My views as thus reduced to writing [said he] were in substance that we would continue the prosecution of the war with an increased force, hold all the country we had conquered or might conquer, and levy contributions upon the enemy to support the war, until a just peace was obtained; that we must have indemnity in territory, and that as a part indemnity the Californias & New Mexico should under no circumstances be restored to Mexico; but that they should henceforth be considered a part of the U. S., & permanent territorial Governments be established over them; and that if Mexico protracted the war, additional territory must be required as further indemnity.[86]

During the next two weeks the President revised what he had written, and, at his request, Buchanan drafted a paragraph which embodied the Secretary's opinions on a proper Mexican policy. Both drafts were presented for discussion at a cabinet meeting held on the twenty-third of November. Avowing a wish to take all of Mexico, Walker preferred Buchanan's draft, for he believed that its construction would make such acquisition possible. "I replied," wrote Polk, "that I was not prepared to go to that extent; and furthermore that I did not desire that anything I said in the message should be so obscure as to give rise to doubt or discussions as to what my true meaning was."[87] This remark indicates that Trist's fears regarding the President's change of policy were wholly unwarranted.

On December 7 Polk submitted to Congress his third annual message. He told of Trist's mission and of his failure to conclude a treaty. The commissioner had, he said, been instructed to demand a cession of territory as indemnity, for in no other way could Mexico satisfy the claims of the United States.

---

[86] *Ibid.*, 216–218. [87] *Ibid.*, 229.

The doctrine of no territory is the doctrine of no indemnity, and if sanctioned would be a public acknowledgment that our country was wrong and that the war declared by Congress with extraordinary unanimity was unjust and should be abandoned—an admission unfounded in fact and degrading to the national character.

He recited the substance of Trist's instructions and urged the necessity of acquiring New Mexico and the Californias. The war had abrogated the treaties regarding claims, making it necessary for the United States to pay American claimants and to reimburse itself by taking territory. California, he said, should be acquired in order to forestall the attempt by any other nation to infringe upon the Monroe Doctrine. He disagreed with those who advocated the policy of retiring to a fixed line and confining the war to defensive operations. Instead, he recommended the establishment of governments in New Mexico and California, and a vigorous prosecution of the war. Having outlined his policy, he added: "It has never been contemplated by me, as an object of the war, to make a permanent conquest of the Republic of Mexico or to annihilate her separate existence as an independent nation," but a peace "must bring with it indemnity for the past and security for the future."[88]

---

[88] Richardson *Messages*, IV, 533–546. Walker still favored the absorption of all of Mexico. A paragraph in the first draft of his financial report to Congress practically advocated such a policy, but on the President's advice this paragraph was omitted (Polk, *Diary*, III, 241–242). Among the *Trist Papers* is an interesting letter written by a young Mexican to his father. It was written in Washington and bears neither date nor signature, but an accompanying newspaper shows the writer to have been Carlos Landa, and a comparison with events mentioned in Polk's diary shows that the letter was written in December, 1847. Landa visited the Secretary of the Treasury on December 13 and reported that "Walker is entirely in favour of the annexation of the whole of Mexico to the United States; he told me so frankly & also spoke of the manner of governing it during the first years by a suitable form of government which should not be in opposition to the institutions of this country." Regarding Walker as the most important member, he concluded that Polk and the rest of the cabinet likewise desired annexation. He visited Van Buren, Corcoran, Calhoun, and other prominent politicians. He says that Walker was stricken with epilepsy on December 9; Polk in his diary for that day notes that Walker "had been taken suddenly ill & had fallen down in the Treasury building."

The message was vehemently assailed in both houses of Congress. As in the preceding session, the history of the outbreak of the war was discussed in all its details. These recitals shed no new light on the subject, for already nearly every argument had been pressed into service to show that Polk had wantonly usurped authority so that he might rob a sister republic of her territory. On January 3, 1848, by a vote of eighty-five to eighty-one, the House formally declared that the war had been "unnecessarily and unconstitutionally begun by the President of the United States." Among the new Whig members who had the pleasure of adding their votes to the denunciation of the President was Abraham Lincoln. With that consummate skill in debate which was later to expose the sophistry of the "Little Giant," he averred that Polk had falsified the history of our difficulties with Mexico by telling a half truth. The statements in the message reminded him of instances he had known of a lawyer's "struggling for his client's neck in a desperate case, employing every artifice to work round, befog, and cover up with many words some point arising in the case which he dare not admit and yet could not deny."[89]

Resolutions, too, there were in plenty. Dickinson presented one on December 14 which asserted that the "true policy" of the government required the annexation of contiguous territory. In the Senate, on the following day, Calhoun offered a counter resolution to the effect that a conquest of Mexico would be disastrous to the United States, and that "no line of policy in further prosecution of the war should be adopted." On the twenty-second, Lincoln made his début as a legislator by calling upon the President to designate the exact "spot" on which the war had begun, and for proof as to the ownership of that spot.[90]

---

[89] *Cong. Globe*, 30 Cong., 1 sess., 95, 155. The quotation is taken from Lincoln, *Works* (Tandy ed.), 337, which differs slightly from that reported in the *Globe*.

[90] *Cong. Globe*, *loc. cit.*, 64.

Three days after his message had been sent to Congress the President received a letter from General Pillow which told of the attempt made by Scott and Trist to procure a treaty by the use of bribe money. At a meeting held on December 11 he told the cabinet of the news he had received, and expressed "in the strongest terms" his condemnation of their conduct. Scott's immediate recall was discussed, but it was thought prudent to seek further definite information from Generals Shields and Quitman, who were expected to arrive in Washington within a few days.[91] Although he must have known better,[92] Shields, when consulted, asserted that bribery had not been considered, and that the discussion had related simply to paying part of the money for the territory in advance of the ratification of the treaty. Polk did not accept this version of the matter, and resolved that those implicated in the scheme must be punished, even though his friend Pillow might be one of the number. For the present, however, he was obliged to await further information concerning the "infamous transaction."[93]

Before news of the bribery episode had reached Washington, Polk and his cabinet had discussed the feasibility of promising protection to the peace party in Mexico, if they would form a government and agree to make a treaty. Incensed on account of the bribery scandal and because Scott had arrested Pillow and Worth, the President, against the advice of members of the cabinet, determined to recall both Scott and Trist. The question of their successors had now to be considered. Marcy and Walker felt that Taylor should be put in command of the army, but Polk fixed upon General W. O. Butler. His intention to invest Butler

---

[91] Polk, *Diary*, III, 245–246.

[92] See Hitchcock, *Fifty Years in camp and Field*, 267–268.

[93] Polk, *Diary*, III, 253, 262–3, 340, 383–4. In a letter to Marcy, Scott stated that he had used secret service money simply "to purchase valuable information" (*H. Ex. Doc. 60*, 30 Cong., 1 sess., 1085)—a statement which Polk pronounced "evasive, and leaves the irresistible inference that such a transaction took place and that it will not bear the light" (*Diary*, III, 346). Of course the transaction did take place. See above, pp. 510–512.

with diplomatic powers was opposed by Buchanan, who insisted that the commissioner should be a civilian. A choice was made unnecessary by the arrival of news that Trist had already reopened negotiations.[94] The President's belief that Taylor was wholly out of sympathy with himself and his administration was by no means erroneous. On one point only did the two men agree—they both distrusted and detested General Scott. "Between ourselves," wrote Taylor to his son-in-law on hearing of the victories near Mexico City,

Gen'l Scott would stoop to anything however low & contemptable as any man in the nation, to obtain power or place, & be as arbitrary in using it when in possession; between him, Trist & the powers that be, old Harry may take the hindmost, they are all of a piece.

When, about a month later, a false report of Polk's death reached camp, the hero of Buena Vista remarked: "While I regret to hear of the death of any one, I would as soon have heard of his death if true, as that of any other individual in the whole Union."[95] Perhaps his own brief term in the White House caused him to realize more clearly the perplexities which confront the chief executive of the nation.

On January 4, 1848, Polk was much surprised to read in a letter sent from Vera Cruz by Colonel Wilson that Trist was negotiating with the Mexican commissioners.

Mr. Trist [was his comment] has acknowledged the receipt of his letter of recal[l], and he possesses no diplomatic powers. He is acting, no doubt, upon Gen'l Scott's advice. He has become a perfect tool of Scott. He is, [in] this measure, defying the authority of his Government. . . . He seems to have entered into all Scott's hatred of the administration, and to be lending himself to all Scott's evil purposes. He may, I fear, greatly embarrass the Government.

Next day Mrs. Trist showed to Buchanan the letter of December 4 in which her husband announced, in cipher, that he would make a treaty in accordance with his original instructions.[96]

---

94 Polk, *Diary*, III, 251, 266, 280–281.

95 Taylor to Wood, Sept. 27, Nov. 2, 1847, *Taylor Letters*, 136, 148.

96 Polk, *Diary*, III, 283, 286. For Trist's cipher letter, see above, p. 524.

Before the President had recovered from the amazement caused by Trist's open defiance of authority, his vexation was increased by a call from the House for a copy of Slidell's instructions and for information regarding the return of Santa Anna and Paredes to Mexico. With the concurrence of the cabinet Polk decided to furnish the House with Conner's instructions regarding Santa Anna, but Slidell's instructions and all relating to McKenzie's mission were withheld on the ground that their publication would be prejudicial to public interest.[97]

Truly the new year had brought anything but pleasure to the chief executive. One annoyance succeeded another in such rapid succession that his patience was taxed to the utmost. Three days after he had declined to give the House full information on diplomatic affairs, the mail brought Trist's celebrated sixty-five page letter (of December 6) in which the President was told that the commissioner had decided to save the administration and the party from a "perilous position," and the country from disaster, by making a treaty with Mexico. No wonder that he pronounced this epistle to be the "most extraordinary document" he had ever read.

His despatch is arrogant, impudent, and very insulting to his Government and even personally offensive to the President. He admits he is acting without authority and in violation of the positive order recalling him. It is manifest to me that he has become the tool of Gen'l Scott and his menial instrument, and that the paper was written at Scott's instance and dictation. I have never in my life felt so indignant, and the whole Cabinet expressed themselves as I felt. I told Mr. Buchanan that the paper was so insulting and contemptably base that it require[d] no lengthy answer, but that it did require a short, but stern and decided rebuke, and directed him to prepare such a reply. I directed the Secretary of War to write at once to Maj'r Gen'l Butler, directing him, if Mr. Trist was still with the Head Quarters of the army, to order him off, and to inform the authorities of Mexico that he had no authority to treat. If there was any legal provision for his punishment he ought to be severely handled. He has acted worse than any man in the public employ whom

---

[97] *Ibid.*, 287–291. Richardson, *Messages*, IV, 565–567. For McKenzie's mission, see p. 439.

I have ever known. His despatch proves that he is destitute of honour or principle, and that he has proved himself to be a very base man. I was deceived in him. I had little personal knowledge of him, but could not have believed [it] possible that any man would have acted so basely as he would have [has] done.[98]

Preparation of letters to Trist and Butler (who had superseded Scott) was delayed for several days while Polk and the cabinet discussed the propriety of submitting Trist's treaty to the Senate, if it should turn out that he had already signed one. Some of the members urged that unless the President had determined to reject such a treaty the suggested notice to the Mexican government might prove embarrassing. Polk was now unwilling to restrict his demands to those embodied in Trist's instructions, and yet he declined to say that he would not accept a treaty made in accordance with those instructions. Consequently General Butler was told that if Trist had actually concluded a treaty he was to send it to Washington, where it would be disposed of as the President should deem best; if none had been concluded, he was to inform the Mexican government that the United States would not recognize a treaty made by the former commissioner.[99]

Polk waited for additional information regarding his insubordinate diplomat. The Mexican mail arrived on February 7, but contained no dispatches from either Trist or Scott. It brought, however, a letter from the irrepressible Atocha, and as usual he was ready to engage in underground diplomacy. "Atocha is a great scoundrel," was the President's comment,

and his letter contained the infamous suggestion that he should be furnished with money to bribe the Mexican Congress to induce them to ratify a Treaty of peace, though he does not state whether a Treaty had been signed by Mr. Trist or not.

---

[98] Polk, *Diary*, III, 300–301.

[99] *Ibid.*, 313–317. Marcy to Butler, Jan. 26, 1848 (*Sen. Ex. Doc. 52*, 30 Cong., 1 sess., 146). On February 2 the President, in response to a call, sent to the Senate correspondence relating to Trist's negotiations with the Mexican commissioners at the time of Scott's armistice (Richardson, *Messages*, IV, 569).

He said that Trist claimed to possess a bribe fund, and Polk thought it likely that the commissioner was base enough to make such an assertion. Silence, in Polk's opinion, indicated a conspiracy on the part of Trist and Scott, and he had little doubt that a treaty would be made: "a few days more will, I trust, develop what they have been doing."[100]

While he awaited developments, troubles nearer home fully occupied the time and taxed the patience of the overworked executive. The hoards of office seekers multiplied. The Whigs, not satisfied with aiding the enemy by "unpatriotic sentiments" and annoying resolutions, were now, in the President's opinion, "insidiously attempting to produce a panic in the money market and thereby, if possible, to break down the Treasury, and thus compel the inglorious withdrawal of our army from Mexico." There were dissensions within the Democratic party among the supporters of rival aspirants for the Presidency, and Polk suspected Buchanan of using his position in the cabinet as a means of injuring General Cass. Members of the party urged the President to cease reiterating his determination not to accept another nomination, for they said that he might be nominated regardless of his own wishes. "To all of them," says the *Diary,* "I have given the same answer, & repeated my sincere desire to retire & my fixed purpose to do so." At this same time he was called upon to perform a duty which was personally disagreeable, and one which would bring additional opposition to his administration. He approved the conviction of Colonel Fremont for disobedience to the orders of General Kearny, and, although the sentence of dismissal was remitted, he fully expected to incur the powerful opposition of Senator Benton.[101] The suspense regarding Trist's activities was broken on February 19 by the arrival of a messenger bearing the treaty of peace. Before discussing

---

[100] Polk, *Diary,* III, 328–330.

[101] *Ibid.,* 319–322, 327. After the approval of the court's decision, Benton, as noted elsewhere, ceased speaking to the President.

its reception, however, we may turn our attention to the negotiations by which it had been concluded.

As noted above, negotiations did not begin as soon as Trist
had announced his intention to remain in Mexico. Peña y Peña,
the Minister of Foreign Relations, said that the appointment of
commissioners must be confirmed by the senate and that the new
congress would not meet until January. Both Edward Thornton
and Percy W. Doyle, who had recently returned to his post as
secretary of the British legation, urged the Mexican government
to waive formalities, but, for a time, their arguments produced
no effect. Although Trist held informal interviews with the commissioners, not until late in December did Peña consent to take
the responsibility of instructing the commissioners to treat with
the American diplomat. Even then, in true Mexican fashion,
he required them to ask for impossible concessions; and before
an agreement had been reached, President Anaya's term of office
had expired. As a quorum of the congress had not yet assembled,
his successor could not be elected, therefore Peña, as head of the
supreme court, again assumed the office of President. Once
more, also, Luis de la Rosa was made Minister of Foreign Relations.

Negotiations were resumed, but the new government at first
seemed less disposed than the old to make the necessary concessions. The commissioners sat in Mexico City, while the seat of
government was at Querétaro, consequently much time was lost
in transmitting messages between the two places.

Before the change of government Trist had made it clear
that the Rio Grande boundary and the inclusion of San Diego
within Upper California would be insisted upon by the United
States. He said, also, that his government would not pay Mexico
more than fifteen million dollars. On assuming office Rosa objected to the boundary mentioned by Trist, and insisted that the
sum to be paid must be at least thirty millions. Doubtless he
would have interposed obstacles indefinitely had it not been for

threatened uprisings in some of the Mexican states, and had Scott not taken steps to renew military operations. When arguments had failed, Trist threatened to break off negotiations unless a treaty could be signed by the first of February, while Doyle urged both Rosa and the commissioners to avert the calamity of a renewal of hostilities. Such pressure could not be withstood. On January 31 a messenger left Querétaro for Mexico City bearing documents which authorized the commissioners to sign the treaty as agreed upon with Trist. Not until the afternoon of February 2 were all details arranged and copies in both languages completed. In accordance with the wishes of the Mexican commissioners, the treaty was not signed in the capital where the meetings had been held. For affixing the signatures they repaired to the near-by town of Guadalupe Hidalgo, and from that place the treaty took its name.[102]

In the treaty the United States procured the things which had been made ultimata in Trist's instructions. The Rio Grande was recognized as the boundary of Texas; Upper California and New Mexico, but not Lower California, were ceded to the United States. In return, Mexico was to be paid fifteen million dollars; and in addition, the United States agreed to pay all liquidated claims of American citizens against Mexico, and to assume unadjusted claims to the extent of three and a quarter million dollars. Mexico was specifically relieved from the payment of claims not covered by the treaty. The privilege of transit across the Isthmus of Tehauntepec, desired by the American government, was not granted. In a word, Trist contented himself with the minimum which the administration had, in April, 1847, authorized him to accept. As soon as the signatures had been affixed the treaty was borne to Washington by James D. Freanor, a war correspondent of the New Orleans *Delta,* better known

---

[102] For further details concerning the last stage of negotiations, see Rives, *United States and Mexico,* II, 602–613. Some of the Mexican projects in the *Trist Papers* were, according to a note appended by Trist, translated by Thornton and the copies are in his handwriting. Evidently he was familiar with all of the proceedings.

by his pen name, "Mustang." Trist had already asked Scott to disregard his positive orders and to "pledge his word" that he would suspend hostilities.[103]

Freanor arrived in Washington on February 19, 1848, and Buchanan placed the treaty in the President's hands at nine o'clock of the same evening. As Trist had announced his intention to resume negotiations, no surprise was expressed when the document arrived. After a hasty reading of the treaty, Polk confided to his diary:

> Mr. Trist was recalled in October last, but chose to remain in Mexico and continue the negotiations. The terms of the Treaty are within his instructions which he took out in April last, upon the important question of boundary and limits. There are many provisions in it which will require more careful examination than a single reading will afford. Mr. Trist has acted very badly, as I have heretofore noted in this diary, but notwithstanding this, if on further examination the Treaty is one that can be accepted, it should not be rejected on account of his bad conduct.[104]

To this sensible attitude of not permitting personal pique to warp his judgment on matters of state the President steadily adhered. Although Trist's arrogance and unwarranted insolence had greatly exasperated him, the simple fact of negotiating without instructions probably did not worry Polk very much. In April, 1847, while Trist's instructions were being prepared, Buchanan received a letter from Moses Y. Beach, of the New York *Sun*, whom the President had appointed as secret agent in Mexico, and the agent intimated that he might make a treaty. He had not, of course, been clothed with diplomatic powers, yet after reading Beach's letter Polk noted in his diary:

> It is clearly to be inferred from his letter that he will make a Treaty with them if he can. Should he do so, and it is a good one, I will waive his authority to make it, and submit it to the Senate for ratification. It will be a good joke if he should assume the authority and take the whole country by surprise & make a Treaty.[105]

---

103 Trist to Scott, Jan. 28, 1848, *Trist Papers*.

104 Polk, *Diary*, III, 345.

105 Polk, Diary, II, 477. Beach's commission is printed in Buchanan, *Works*, VII, 119.

Probably Trist may have heard the President make similar remarks, and, if so, they may have had some influence on his own
conduct in Mexico. However this may have been, Polk, in the
present instance, failed to see the humorous side of the transaction.

So important did the President regard an early disposal of
the treaty that he waived his scruples against Sunday labor and
summoned the cabinet to a special meeting on the evening of the
twentieth of February. Of this meeting we have two accounts,
one in Polk's diary for the day, another by his nephew and
private secretary, J. Knox Walker. After a general discussion
Polk asked the opinion of each member concerning the advisability of submitting the document to the Senate for ratification.
All agreed that the tenth article relating to land grants in Texas
should be stricken out. On the question of accepting the treaty,
thus amended, the cabinet was divided—Buchanan and Walker
advised a rejection of the whole treaty, while Marcy, Mason,
Johnson, and Clifford were in favor of accepting all but the tenth
article. After Buchanan's opposition to extensive annexation
his present attitude so nettled the President that he asked the
pointed question: ''Will you take the responsibility of its rejection?'' Buchanan's reply, that he would ''take all the responsibility which properly pertains to me as Sec'y of State
giving such advice,'' led Polk to believe that the Secretary was
playing politics at the expense of his chief. He reminded Buchanan that at the beginning of the war the Secretary had drafted
instructions to American ministers at foreign courts which asserted that the government had no intention of taking territory
from Mexico—an assertion which the President had required him
to omit. He reminded him, also, of his persistent opposition to
the acquisition of any land except Upper California and New
Mexico—now he objected to the treaty because it did not procure
a large enough area. Buchanan admitted this. He told the
President that he might go further and mention his (Buchanan's)

opposition to Scott's march from Vera Cruz to Mexico City. But, he added, his advice was not taken, and "I am not now willing to acquire for indemnity what I would then have been very willing to take. The line of the Sierra Madre will give us 'indemnity for the past & security for the future.'" No agreement was reached at this meeting.[106]

Another meeting was held on the following day, and the President announced that he had decided to submit the treaty to the Senate for ratification, with a recommendation that the tenth article be stricken out. The reasons assigned for this decision are recorded in his diary:

They were, briefly, that the treaty conformed on the main question of limits & boundary to the instructions given to Mr. Trist in April last; and that though, if the treaty was now to be made, I should demand more territory, perhaps to make the Sierra Madra the line, yet it was doubtful whether this could be ever obtained by the consent of Mexico. I looked, too, to the consequences of its rejection. A majority of one branch of Congress is opposed to my administration; they have falsely charged that the war was brought on and is continued by me with a view to the conquest of Mexico; and if I were now to reject a Treaty made upon my own terms, as authorized in April last, with the unanimous approbation of the Cabinet, the probability is that Congress would not grant either men or money to prosecute the war. Should this be the result, the army now in Mexico would be constantly wasting and diminishing in numbers, and I might at last be compelled to withdraw them, and thus loose the two Provinces of New Mexico & Upper California, which were ceded to the U. S., by this Treaty. Should the opponents of my administration succeed in carrying the next Presidential election, the great probability is that the country would loose all the advantages secured by this Treaty. I adverted to the immense value of Upper California; and concluded by saying that if I were now to reject my own terms, as offered in April last, I did not see how it was possible for my administration to be sustained.[107]

On the next day, February 22, he sent the treaty to the Senate, accompanied by a message which recommended that all except

---

[106] Polk, *Diary*, III, 345–346. Walker's account is in the *Polk Papers*. In a note he says that he prepared it February 22, two days after the meeting. He does not say whether he had been present at the meeting, but comment in Polk's *Diary*, III, 351, indicates that he had been.

[107] Polk, *Diary*, III, 347–348.

the tenth article should be ratified. With it he transmitted copies of the instructions given to both Slidell and Trist, which up to this time had been withheld.[108]

Truly, the President had been placed in an awkward position by his officious diplomat. The war had been unpopular even while Mexico had refused to treat, and Polk had good reasons for believing that he could not hope for means with which to continue it, if he should reject his own terms. During his entire career he had shown excellent judgment as to what was and what was not attainable, and besides, the treaty gave him all that he had set his heart upon. Tamaulipas or part of Sonora might be desirable, if it could be obtained without difficulty; but Polk was not the man to risk losing the objects which he had set out to procure, when the prospect of better terms was by no means certain. Despite all that his opponents might say it seems clear that the President never welcomed a war, and he neglected no opportunity which gave prospect of ending it. He was determined to have Upper California and New Mexico at any cost, for these formed a part of his original program. His interest in further acquisition was never very great. Buchanan's sudden desire for more territory confirmed rather than altered Polk's decision, for he believed that the Secretary was inspired by purely selfish motives.

He wished [wrote the President] to throw the whole responsibility on me of sending the Treaty to the Senate. If it was received well by the country, being a member of my administration, he would not be injured by it in his Presidential aspirations, for these govern all his opinions & acts lately; but if, on the other hand, it should not be received well, he could say, ''I advised against it.''[109]

Doubtless Polk was justified in attributing to political motives Buchanan's recent change of front on the territorial question. At any rate he had lost faith in the Secretary's loyalty to the

---

[108] Richardson, *Messages,* IV, 573–574.
[109] Polk, *Diary,* III, 350.

administration. He had not concealed his resentment when discussing the treaty, and a few days later he had occasion to speak still more pointedly. Buchanan told him that it was rumored in the streets that he was to be removed from the cabinet because a friend of his named Nugent, a correspondent for the New York *Herald,* had criticized the administration. Polk told him that the rumor was untrue, but that the vile effusions signed by Nugent had been attributed to the Secretary of State. He remarked ''in a stern manner'' that Buchanan himself must judge of the propriety of having a member of the cabinet holding familiar intercourse with an unprincipled person who ''was in daily habit of calumniating'' the President. ''Their object,'' said Polk, ''seems to be to abuse Gen'l Cass, Mr. Woodbury, and myself, and to praise Mr. Buchanan. The[y] falsely represent that I am intriguing to obtain the nomination for a re-election to the Presidency.'' He did not doubt that Buchanan had encouraged these attacks, for his own purposes; but he did not wish to act on suspicion alone. ''If,'' said he, ''I obtain any reliable proof that Mr. Buchanan has given countenance to Galvienses [Nugent] he shall not remain in the Cabinet. He denies that he has done so, and I am bound to believe him.'' When informed by Clifford that both Walker and Buchanan had spoken of resigning on account of the controversy over the treaty, he declared that he would follow his own course, regardless of consequences. Although surprised to hear that Walker had made such remarks, he was neither surprised nor perturbed by the hostility of the Secretary of State. ''I expressed to Mr. Clifford,'' says the *Diary,* ''an indifference as to the course which Mr. Buchanan might think proper to pursue, but told him there was not the slightest danger of his resigning.''[110]

---

[110] *Ibid.,* 353–355, 359. Galvienses was Nugent's pen name. ''Mr. Buchanan's real trouble,'' was another comment in the *Diary,* ''is that he cannot use my administration and shape his [its] course according to his own ever varying whims, in order to promote his aspirations to the Presidency. He cares not for the success or glory of my administration further than he can make it subservient to his own political aspirations.''

When he had received the treaty and submitted it to the Senate the President no doubt believed that he had received the last of Trist's abusive epistles. If so, he was greatly mistaken. Indeed, Freanor had brought two more along with the treaty, but by an oversight they had not been delivered to Polk until two days after that document had been sent to the Senate. The first bore the date of December 29, and the main point developed was that Polk's annual message had jeopardized peace negotiations by aiding the *puros,* the party which desired to annex all of Mexico to the United States. The particular part of the message criticized was that which suggested that necessity might force the United States to establish a government with which it could make a treaty. By preventing the *moderados,* now in control, from making peace, the *puros* hoped, by continuing hostilities, to force the United States to take all of Mexico, or at least to establish some form of protectorate over it. The second letter, of January 12, 1848, dealt with the difficulty of suspending hostilities, and was still more offensive than the other. At the time of Trist's recall, Polk had required the commander-in-chief to transmit all peace proposals to Washington; at the same time, Scott was instructed to pursue the war with renewed vigor. Such an arrangement, said Trist, prevented any suspension of hostilities while peace proposals were under consideration—except by disobedience of orders—and was "a wanton sporting with the lives of men," a course which, if followed, would cause the whole civilized world to "burst forth with one universal cry of horror."[111]

The arrogant character of these letters completely exhausted the patience of the President, and their author was characterized as "an impudent and unqualified scoundrel." Through Marcy, Polk instructed General Butler to prevent Trist from exercising any official authority in Mexico and to drive him away from the army headquarters. When Marcy hesitated to issue so drastic

---

[111] Trist to Buchanan (*Sen. Ex. Doc. 52,* 30 Cong., 1 sess., 274–280).

an order, the President not only dictated its terms but prepared a note for the files of the War Department to show that Polk himself had assumed the entire responsibility.[112]

Had Polk received at this time another long letter written by Trist, he would, if possible, have been still more exasperated. It bears a date earlier than Freanor's departure for Washington, but apparently it was not sent until later. Besides giving a detailed account of the negotiations, Trist made some really sensible remarks concerning the obligation of the United States to protect its adventurous citizens who had engaged in hazardous enterprises in Mexico. As usual, however, he could not refrain from saying disagreeable things. In his discussion of the boundary he committed the unpardonable sin of asserting that the land between the Nueces and the Rio Grande was as much a part of Tamaulipas (and not of Texas) as the counties of Accomac and Northampton were a part of Virginia.[113] If so, the President was justly entitled to the sobriquet "Polk the mendacious," for his war message had been premised on a falsehood and hostilities had been wantonly provoked.

Private letters written at this time show that Trist derived real pleasure from playing *enfant terrible*. He had developed an inveterate hatred for both Polk and Buchanan, and he seemed to believe that he possessed information which, when disclosed, would make the throne totter. He presumed that the arrival of his treaty had caused a commotion, but it could have been "*nothing* to the *uproar* that is to come."

> Until I shall be ready to speak, [he continued with a solemnity born of conceit], let them remain in the doubt and the hopes, as to my future course, inspired by the falseness & baseness of their own ignoble hearts. Let them go on hoping that I am, or may be made, like themselves; capable of being *bought,* if not to active villany, at least to passive; to silence, if to nothing else.

---

[112] Polk, *Diary,* III, 357–358. Marcy to Butler, Feb. 25, 1848 (*Sen. Ex. Doc. 52,* as above cited, 148–150).

[113] Trist to Buchanan, Jan. 25, 1848 (*Sen. Ex. Doc. 52,* 30 Cong., 1 sess., 290).

These remarks are interesting as coming from one of the two men who alone had been guilty of *buying* others. The disclosures which he expected to cause the "uproar" were Polk's confidential correspondence with Pillow, whom Trist, in his letter, was pleased to call a reptile.

As to whether he was entitled to payment for the extra time put in since his recall, Trist's mind was not quite clear; but he would accept nothing which might depend upon even the "official decision" of the President.

His official mind is too corrupt or too imbecile. Nothing proceeding from it—in the way of *advantage*, at least—shall touch me. I say the same of every man capable of retaining a seat in his cabinet during the last 3, 4 or 5 months.

The court of inquiry selected to investigate the charges made against Pillow and other accused military officers was, in Trist's opinion, a "pitiable device of the pitiable being in the Presidential chair." When notified by General Butler that he must leave Mexico, Trist once more paid his compliments to the President and denied his authority to order a private citizen out of a foreign country. He was probably right in holding that

I deem it my duty to deny the lawfulness of any requirement from the President of the United States, pretending to impose upon me the obligation, either to leave the *Republic of Mexico* or to *return to the United States*. I recognize no authority in that functionary competent to create any such obligation. The pretension to create it, & the use of the armed power confided to him, for the purpose of enforcing it, are, to my mind, alike usurpations; usurpations differing but slightly in the shades of enormity.[114]

The President, as we have seen, sent Trist's treaty to the Senate on February 22, but on account of the illness and death of John Quincy Adams its consideration was delayed several days.

---

[114] Trist to Mrs. Trist, March 2, 1848; Trist to Butler, March 17, 1848, *Trist Papers*. In a letter dated March 18 he told Butler that he would not embarrass him by resisting the order. He had, on February 1, written to his wife that he would go to West Chester and keep a boarding school. "For my own part, I will live on bread & water before I ever again hold office of any kind." Also in *Trist Papers*.

Immediately, however, unofficial reports predicted that the treaty would probably be rejected. Cave Johnson shared this belief, and he told the President of a rumor that both Buchanan and Walker had been exerting their influence against ratification. Polk was still more perturbed by another "astounding" rumor—also reported by Johnson—which charged Walker with giving aid to the Presidential candidacy of General Taylor. "If I ascertain this to be true," was the comment in his diary, "it will be inconsistent with the success of my measures for Mr. Walker to remain in my Cabinet. I will require strong proof however before I can believe it to be true."[115]

The Whigs and a small group of Democrats who had been devising means of compelling the President to end the war, now that a treaty had been made, did their utmost to cause its rejection. The prospect for ratification was not encouraging. On February 28 Senator Sevier, chairman of the Committee of Foreign Affairs, reported to Polk that all of the committee except himself had resolved to recommend that the treaty should be rejected and that the President be advised to send to Mexico a new commission, invested with power to make a new treaty. They did not, said Sevier, object to the treaty itself but to the fact that Trist had no authority to make it. The absurd suggestion offered by the committee did not appeal to Polk's practical mind:

I told him [Sevier] I condemned the insubordination & insolent conduct of Mr. Trist, but that the Treaty itself was the subject for consideration and not his conduct, and that if the provisions of the Treaty were such as could be accepted, it would be worse than idle ceremony to send out a grand commission to re-negotiate the same Treaty. I told him, also, that if the Senate advised me to send out such a commission, I hoped they would advise me also what they would accept. . . . Extremes sometimes meet. . . . They have done so in this instance. Mr. Webster is for *no* territory and Mr. Hannegan is for *all* Mexico, and for opposite reasons both will oppose the Treaty. It is difficult, upon any rational principle, to assign a satisfactory reason for anything Col. Benton may do, especially in his present temper of mind, wholly engrossed as he seems to have been for some months past with the case of his son-in-law, Col. Fremont.

---

[115] Polk, *Diary*, III, 361.

His suspicion that Walker and Buchanan would use their influence against ratification seems to have been removed by their volunteering to urge Senators to vote against the plan for creating a new commission.[116]

While the President was conversing with Sevier, the Senate was passing resolutions which requested him to submit all correspondence that had passed between Trist and the State Department. Without consulting the cabinet, he decided to send it all, despite its exceptionable character. On the next day he was told that the fate of the treaty was extremely doubtful and that about a dozen Democrats would vote against it because of their desire for more territory. Not for this reason, but from personal motives, Polk feared most of all the opposition of Benton:

He has heretofore maintained that the true boundary of Texas was the Nueces instead of the Rio Grande, & he is apt to think that nothing is done properly that he is not consulted about.[117]

If some Democrats declined to uphold the administration by supporting the treaty, so, also, were certain Whigs unwilling to put ratification on a purely party basis. Polk was especially pleased when on March 1 he was told by the banker, W. W. Corcoran, that Joseph Gales, of the *National Intelligencer,* had refused to prepare an article against ratification, when requested to do so by Whig Senators. For several days after this the fate of the treaty hung in the balance, its chief opponents being Webster and Benton. Polk blamed the insurgent Democrats most of all, for as he said, "if the Democratic party were united in favour of the Treaty, I doubt whether a single Whig would vote against it." Both parties, in his opinion, were interested primarily in the approaching Presidential election, and he did not believe that Whigs would care to incur the odium of casting a strictly party vote.[118]

After much heated discussion and many calls upon the President for information (among other things for "information in

---

[116] *Ibid.*, 363–367.   [117] *Ibid.*, 367.   [118] *Ibid.*, 368–371.

regard to any disposition or overtures on the part of any considerable portion of the Mexican people to be annexed to the U. States''), the Senate, by a vote of thirty-eight to fourteen, ratified the treaty on the tenth of March. The tenth article and the secret article relating to an extension of time for ratification were eliminated as the President had recommended. Other modifications made by the Senate, on its own account, caused Polk to fear that Mexico might decline to ratify the treaty. He greatly appreciated the assistance given by Senator Mangum, of the Committee of Foreign Affrirs, who ''though a Whig, is a gentleman''— apparently a rare combination, in the President's opinion.[119]

As soon as there was any indication that the treaty would be ratified, Polk began to cast about for a suitable commissioner whom he might send to Mexico to urge its acceptance. He fixed upon Louis McLane, of Maryland, and when he declined to serve, Senator Sevier, of Arkansas, was appointed. Scarcely, however, had Sevier's appointment been ratified by the Senate when he was taken ill and, in order to save time, Attorney-General Clifford was chosen to be his associate. Clifford set out for Mexico at once, while Sevier's health was sufficiently improved within the next few days to enable him to follow his colleague.

Ratification of the treaty by the Senate did not entirely relieve Polk's anxiety, for he feared that his opponents might yet defeat it by indirect methods. Evidence of a disposition to employ such methods was seen in a motion, offered in executive session on March 14, to remove the injunction of secrecy from the Senate proceedings. Its adoption would expose to the Mexicans the

---

119 *Ibid.*, 369, 377, 381. When the records of the executive session were finally made public on May 31 it was discovered that several rather drastic resolutions had been offered. Webster, for example, moved that all discussion of the treaty be postponed and that the President be asked to appoint a new commission. Houston held that since Trist had no authority to negotiate, his treaty was ''utterly void,'' and ought to be rejected. Both Houston and Jefferson Davis wanted more territory, while Baldwin, of Connecticut, tried to incorporate into the treaty a provision for excluding slavery from all territory to be acquired. The proceedings are printed in *Sen. Ex. Doc. 52*, 30 Cong., 1 sess., 4 ff.

confidential instructions which had been given to Slidell and Trist and, also, the division of opinion in the Senate. They might as a result be induced to reject the modified treaty in the hope of obtaining better terms. No action was taken on this resolution until the last of May, but in the meantime the New York *Herald* began to publish Polk's message which had accompanied Trist's treaty to the Senate and, also, Slidell's instructions and parts of the diplomatic correspondence. As Nugent, the Washington correspondent for that paper, was known to be on intimate terms with Buchanan, the Secretary of State at once became the object of suspicion. Polk was loth to believe that Buchanan could be guilty of such treachery; still, he advised Senators to make a thorough investigation, and he was prepared to dismiss the Secretary if it should be found that he had in any way been connected with giving out the documents. When summoned before a Senate committee, Nugent refused to disclose the name of the person who had furnished him with copies of the documents, but he stated in writing that it was not Buchanan. Polk believed the Secretary of State to be both weak and self-seeking, yet he was very much gratified to have Buchanan "relieved from so injurious an imputation."[120]

Ratification of the treaty by the Senate did not terminate discussion on military affairs. It was not certain, of course, that Mexico would accept the alterations which had been made, consequently the administration forces urged that the pending ten-regiment bill should be enacted into law. Polk's whole war policy was assailed and defended, as before, while opposition members kept annoying the President with requests for additional information. Among other items called for by the Senate was a copy of the letter which, in 1845, Gillespie had carried to Thomas O. Larkin, United States consul at Monterey, California. Our chief interest in this resolution is that when commenting upon it in his diary Polk distinctly implied that Fremont had

---

[120] Polk, *Diary*, III, 396–409.

not been authorized to foment a revolution in California. He transmitted a copy of the letter to the Senate in executive session, so that if it were made public, and trouble should result, the responsibility would rest upon the Senate and not upon himself.[121]

Clifford arrived in Mexico City with the modified treaty on April 11, 1848, Sevier four days later. Under the President's supervision Buchanan had prepared instructions which were to guide them in their discussions with the Mexican officials. Among other things they were to avoid diplomatic notes whenever possible and to hold personal conferences, which would be more conducive to a speedy adjustment of differences of opinion. In a letter to the Minister of Foreign Relations, written at the same time, Buchanan explained in detail the changes which had been made by the Senate. While his letter was very friendly in tone, a pointed reference to the fact that ''four votes, taken from the majority, and added to the minority, would have defeated the treaty'' was intended to impress upon the Mexican government the futility of asking for better terms.[122]

During the period of more than two months between the signature of the treaty and the arrival of Clifford and Sevier in Mexico the several factions in that country had had time to discuss the question of making peace with the United States, although the details of the treaty were not known to the public. The *puros,* or radicals, being anxious for annexation to the United States, naturally were hostile to ratification. For an entirely different reason the propertied class looked forward with dismay to the withdrawal of the American army, because they feared that adequate protection of their property would be gone. According to his own account, ''certain leaders'' desired Scott to proclaim himself dictator for six years, with the eventual purpose of joining the United States. The general ''ultimately declined''

---

121 *Ibid.,* 395, 399. Richardson, *Messages,* IV, 578.

122 Buchanan to Min. of For. Rel., March 18, 1848 (*H. Ex. Doc. 60,* 30 Cong,. 1 sess., 67).

the invitation. One of his reasons was that he had already suggested annexation and "President Polk's Government carefully withheld its wishes from him thereon."[123]

The work of the American commissioners was delayed by the fact that the Mexican congress, which alone could ratify the treaty, had not convened at the time of their arrival. Although the members had been elected in March, not until the first week in May did a quorum assemble in Querétaro. The apparent reluctance of the Mexican government to meet the issue led Polk to believe that ratification "may be regarded as doubtful."[124]

After meeting, however, the congress acted with unusual promptitude. President Peña y Peña in his message, although regretting that the treaty had been modified, nevertheless advised its ratification. In addition, his ministers of war and finance showed by verbal reports that Mexico was too weak to continue hostilities if the treaty should be rejected. On May 19 the chamber of deputies gave its assent and the Minister of Foreign Relations invited Clifford and Sevier to visit Querétaro and present their credentials to the President. They arrived on May 25, just after the senate had ratified the treaty. Ratifications were exchanged on the thirtieth and the commissioners returned to Mexico City and arranged for the fulfillment of the financial obligations of the treaty.[125]

"At 6 o'clock this morning," wrote Clifford on June 12,

the flag of the United States was taken down from the national palace in this city and that of the Mexican republic was hoisted. The customary honors were paid to both, and the ceremony passed off in perfect quiet, although the great square was thronged.[126]

With this formality the two years' war with Mexico had been brought to a successful termination. President Polk had not

---

[123] Scott, *Autobiography*, II, 581–582. Doyle to Palmerston, Feb. 13, 1848, quoted by Rives, II, 643–644.

[124] Polk, *Diary*, III, 447.

[125] Sevier and Clifford to Buchanan, May 25 and 30, 1848 (*H. Ex. Doc. 60*, 30 Cong., 1 sess., 72–73). See also Rives, II, 651–653.

[126] *H. Ex. Doc. 60*, as cited above, 74.

only "conquered a peace," but in all essential details he had effected his program of national expansion. Determined from the beginning to add California and New Mexico to our national domain, he pursued this object with a dogged persistence which neither opposition nor denunciation could weaken. Whatever may be thought of his motives or his methods, to him is due the credit (or censure, if you please) of extending to the Pacific the boundaries of the United States.

The letter in which Sevier and Clifford had announced that the treaty had been ratified by the Mexican congress reached the President on the fifteenth of June. Comment in his diary is limited to a statement that the letter had been received, for he was ill at the time and his mind was occupied with the contemplated purchase of Cuba. His pleasure at being relieved from the burdens of war may be judged by a remark made on the second anniversary of its beginning: "It is two years ago this day since War was declared by Congress against Mexico. They have been two years of unceasing labour and anxiety with me."[127]

On July 4, just as the President had returned from the ceremonies connected with laying the corner stone of the Washington monument, a messenger arrived with the treaty of Guadalupe Hidalgo. He at once directed Buchanan to prepare a proclamation so that it might be signed on "the anniversary of Independence." His private secretaries were set to work at copying a message which had already been prepared, and two days later this and the treaty were submitted to both houses of Congress. Among the documents sent with the treaty was a copy of the instructions given to Slidell in 1845. When the House had asked for these instructions earlier in the session, their request had been denied, but now, as the President noted, "the reasons for withholding them at that time no longer exist."

As a true expansionist the President fully appreciated the importance of his achievements. "The results of the war with

---

[127] Polk, *Diary*, III, 448, 492.

Mexico,'' said his message, ''have given the United States a national character which our country never before enjoyed.'' New Mexico and California ''constitute of themselves a country large enough for a great empire, and their acquisition is second only in importance to that of Louisiana in 1803.'' He saw, on the other hand, that evil as well as good might follow in the wake of the war, and he took advantage of the occasion to warn Congress against unwise legislation. In organizing governments for the new territories, he invoked a spirit of concession and conciliation, so that sectional discords might be avoided and the Union be preserved. The army should be reduced to its ante-bellum footing, for ''our standing army is to be found in the bosom of society.'' A true disciple of Jefferson, he urged that

Upon the restoration of peace we should adopt the policy suited to a state of peace. In doing this the earliest practicable payment of the public debt should be a cardinal principle of action. Profiting by the experiences of the past, we should avoid the errors into which the country was betrayed shortly after the close of the war with Great Britain in 1815. In a few years after that period a broad and latitudinous construction of the powers of the Federal Government unfortunately received but too much countenance. Though the country was burdened with a heavy public debt, large, and in some instances unnecessary and extravagant, expenditures were authorized by Congress. The consequence was that the payment of the debt was postponed for more than twenty years, and even then it was only accomplished by the stern will and unbending policy of President Jackson, who made its payment a leading measure of his Administration.[128]

Some of Polk's friends, including Houston and Davis, of the Senate Committee on Military Affairs, did not share his views concerning a reduction of the army. Not satisfied with his recommendation, the House, also, asked him for additional information. On August 1 he submitted a report from the Secretary of War, and along with it, a message saying that he had ''seen no reason to change the opinion'' expressed in the preceding

---

[128] Richardson, *Messages*, IV, 587–593. The original draft of this message contained a paragraph on the ''misnamed & exploded 'American system,' but by the advice of the cabinet it was omitted (Polk, *Diary*, III, 496).

July. He was "decidedly opposed" to an increase in the army,
and he attributed the anxiety for more adequate defense to self-
seeking military men and extravagant Whigs. Concerning the
latter he said in his diary:

> Some Whig members of Congress favour the measure because it is in
> harmony with their general policy. They favour, as a party, large ex-
> penditures, high tariffs, & Banks, and in addition to this they would be
> pleased to have a large increase of the standing army fastened on the
> country, which they would for political effect charge to be a consequence
> of the Mexican War.[129]

The forebodings of the President regarding the sectional bitterness which might result from attempts to establish governments for the new territories were not without foundation. The
Wilmot Proviso had not been forgotten, and already, indeed, the
debate on the Oregon bill foreshadowed the breakers ahead.
Renewed agitation of the slavery question resulted from the
Mexican war, but was not a part of it; its consideration as a
domestic question is reserved for another chapter.

---

[129] Richardson, *Messages*, IV, 603. Polk, *Diary*, IV, 48.

CHAPTER XXI

OREGON

The treaty of peace which terminated the Revolution fixed the boundary between the United States and Canada east of the Mississippi River. By the purchase of Louisiana with its indefinite boundaries, in 1803, the United States acquired whatever claims France might have to territory lying west of the Mississippi; and by the Florida treaty of 1819 Spain ceded to the United States all her claims to territory lying west of Louisiana and north of the forty-second parallel of north latitude. In general terms, all this was clear enough, but the difficult problem was: What, precisely, are the proper limits of these claims?

The British claim to the Pacific coast region was based mainly on the explorations made by Captain Cook in 1776; the interior of the Oregon region was claimed as a result of the discovery of the Frazer River valley by Alexander MacKenzie in 1793. In 1789, however, the Spaniards, who laid claim to all of this region, sent out from Mexico an exploring expedition. At Nootka Sound they seized two British ships and nearly precipitated a war between the two countries. The matter was adjusted by a convention signed in 1790 which admitted the right of British subjects to establish trading posts for the purpose of carrying on commerce with the natives. The question which came to be disputed later was whether, in this convention, Spain had transferred to England the ownership of the land, or simply the temporary use of it. Russia, also, had laid claim to this region, but by treaties—one with the United States in 1824, and another with England in 1825—had relinquished everything south of 54° 40′ north latitude.

In addition to claims derived from Spain and France, the United States based her title to Oregon upon discoveries and settlements made by her own citizens. In 1792, Captain Robert Gray, of Boston, had explored the Columbia River and named it after his ship; and in 1811, John Jacob Astor had founded the trading post of Astoria. This place had been taken by the British during the War of 1812, but under the terms of the Treaty of Ghent it was restored in 1818.

After 1825, when Russia limited her claims, the Oregon question was reduced to this: Does either Great Britain or the United States have a valid title to all of the territory west of the Rocky Mountains and included between 42°, the northern boundary of California, and 54° 40′, the southern boundary of Alaska; if not, how should it be divided? The United States claimed this region by right of discovery—both direct and acquired; on similar grounds Great Britain claimed it, at least as far south as the Columbia River.

Prior to Polk's administration several attempts had been made to establish a definite boundary line between the United States and Canada. In the treaty of 1818 the forty-ninth parallel was agreed upon as the boundary from the Lake of the Woods to the Rocky Mountains. The country west of the mountains was left open to what was commonly called joint occupation; that is, each nation might make use of it without prejudice to the claims of the other. In 1827 "joint occupation" was continued indefinitely, but either nation might terminate the agreement by giving twelve months' notice to the other.

At an early date members of Congress began to take an interest in Oregon. In December, 1820, the House appointed a committee and assigned it the duty of considering the propriety of taking possession of the territory. A month later the committee's report was submitted by Floyd, of Virginia. In substance it recommended that the government should take steps to safeguard the interests of the United States on the Pacific coast.

No action resulted from this recommendation, but two years later after England had (1821) extended her laws over the territory, another committee was appointed to consider the subject. Their report was similar to that made in 1820, but again no action resulted.

A bill to authorize the occupation of the Oregon River valley was introduced in the House in December, 1828. Its most active sponsor, Floyd, of Virginia, urged the necessity of extending over this region the laws of the United States, and of constructing military forts to insure the protection of Americans. Gurley, of Louisiana, proposed an amendment under which lands might be granted to colonists from the United States. Polk opposed both the bill and the amendment on the ground that they would violate the treaty of "joint occupation" with Great Britain. He pointed out that those who participated in the debate had "confined themselves to the expediency of the measure, and have had no reference to the present state of our negotiations in reference to the preliminary question of title to the country." After quoting the terms of the treaty of 1818, he remarked that "The question is not now whether it was wise to make this treaty, but, having made it, what is its spirit and meaning?" Until the treaty has been abrogated, he said, it is the "supreme law of the land," and it can not be abrogated until twelve months' notice has been given. He moved that the Committee of the Whole be discharged from further consideration of the bill and that the subject be referred to the Committee on Territories. He moved further that this committee be instructed to report in favor of extending over the American citizens in that region the jurisdiction of the courts of Michigan Territory, and of providing for the exploration and survey of the Northwest coast. Neither this nor solutions offered by other members were accepted by the House. On January 9, 1829, Polk voted with the majority in rejecting the entire bill.[1]

---

[1] *Reg. of Deb.*, 20 Cong., 2 sess., 125–153. Also, *Abridg. of Deb.*, X, 273–315.

In 1833 the Missionary Board of the Methodist church selected a number of missionaries and sent them forth to found a settlement in Willamette Valley.[2] Two years later President Jackson sent William A. Slacum to investigate conditions in that region, and in December, 1837, Slacum's favorable report was laid before Congress.[3] On February 7, 1838, Linn, of Missouri, introduced in the Senate a bill to organize Oregon as a territory and to establish on the Columbia River both a port of entry and a custom house.[4] As early as December 29, 1829, Linn had offered a resolution which purposed to give the twelve months' notice necessary for terminating the conventions of 1818 and 1827.[5] In both cases Congress declined to take any action, but interest in Oregon continued to increase. Every year added to the number who exhorted Congress to do something for the protection of American citizens in that country. Great Britain, it was urged, had extended her laws throughout Oregon as early as 1821; why should the United States continue to disregard the rights of its citizens?

The arrival in Washington of Lord Ashburton, in April, 1842, gave rise to the hope that the whole vexed question of boundary might be adjusted, for the northwest as well as the northeast boundary was included in the scope of the British diplomat's instructions.[6] But, as Tyler informed Congress in his second annual message, "it became manifest at an early hour in the late negotiations" that any attempt to settle the Oregon question "would lead to a protracted discussion, which might embrace in its failure other more pressing matters."[7]

Eager to succeed where others had failed, Tyler proposed a tripartite treaty whereby he hoped to settle not only the Oregon question, but, also, the diplomatic difficulties with Mexico which

---

2 Gray, *History of Oregon*, 106 ff.   4 *Cong. Globe*, 25 Cong., 2 sess., 168.

3 *Sen. Doc. 24*, 25 Cong., 2 sess.   5 *Abridg. of Deb.*, XIV, 18.

6 Aberdeen to H. S. Fox, Oct. 18, 1842 (*Sen. Doc. 1*, 29 Cong., 1 sess., 139).

7 Richardson, *Messages*, IV, 196.

had resulted from the revolt of Texas and the non-payment by Mexico of American damage claims. He was willing to let England have Oregon down to the Columbia River if she in turn would induce Mexico to recognize the independence of Texas and to make territorial concessions to the United States. England was to cancel certain claims against Mexico and to induce her to cede to the United States that part of California lying north of the thirty-sixth parallel, and as a compensation for this service the United States was to relinquish her claim to that part of Oregon lying north of the Columbia River. At the time that he formulated this plan, Tyler apparently had little doubt that England would readily agree, or that the combination which he had suggested would reconcile opposing interests in the United States. ''Texas might not stand alone,'' he told Webster, ''nor would the line proposed for Oregon. Texas would reconcile all to the line, while California would reconcile or pacify all to Oregon.''[8] Despite this hopeful language, however, he endeavored, after he had retired from office, to represent this whole matter as a passing fancy to which little importance should be attached. ''I never dreamed,'' he wrote,

of ceding this country [between 49° and the Columbia] unless for the greater equivalent of California which I fancied G. Britain might be able to obtain for us through her influence in Mexico—and this was but a dream of policy which was never embodied.[9]

Nothing, of course, came of Tyler's ingenious scheme for killing so many birds with one stone. Ashburton expressed, unofficially, the belief that Great Britain would not oppose a cession of territory by Mexico to the United States, but that she could take no part in the transaction.[10] While there was never any prospect that Tyler's plan would succeed, had it been

---

[8] Tyler, *Letters and Times of the Tylers*, II, 260–261. See also Webster to Everett, Jan. 29, 1843 (Curtis, *Life of Webster*, II, 175).

[9] Tyler to his son, Dec. 11, 1845, MS in Library of Congress. Also printed copy in *Tyler, op. cit,.* 447.

[10] Schafer, ''British Attitude toward the Oregon Question,'' *Am. Hist. Rev.*, XVI, no. 2, p. 293.

accepted by the other governments concerned the Mexican war might possibly have been averted. Webster soon left the cabinet and the President turned his attention to the annexation of Texas. The Oregon question remained unsettled and became one of the leading issues of the campaign of 1844.

A bill introduced in the Senate on December 19, 1842, by Linn, of Missouri, gave opportunity for debate on the Oregon question and prepared the way for the approaching Presidential campaign. Among other things the bill provided for the building of forts along the route to Oregon and at the mouth of the Columbia River, and for the granting of land to American settlers. It can hardly be said that the discussion was sectional in character, although westerners were more insistent than others that the government should take some action. Webster attributed the agitation entirely to politics,[11] but it is evident that many were sincerely interested in westward expansion.

The chief opponents of Linn's bill were Senators Calhoun and McDuffie, of South Carolina. The former declared that the passage of the land-grant section would violate the treaty with Great Britain. Besides, he opposed the whole bill on the ground that precipitate action might result in the loss of the entire territory. England, he said, could transfer troops by sea in a very short time, while it would take months for our army to reach Oregon by overland routes. Consequently the sound policy for the United States to pursue was that of "wise and masterly inactivity." McDuffie was averse to the bill, not because he feared that its passage might result in the loss of Oregon, but because he regarded the territory as an incubus which ought to be discarded. He would not give "a pinch of snuff for the whole territory," because it was totally unsuited as a home for civilized beings.[12] Benton and Linn made strong arguments in favor of the bill, and refuted in detail the positions taken by the Senators from

---

11 Webster to Everett, Jan. 29, 1843, as cited above.

12 *Cong. Globe*, 27 Cong., 3 sess., 198–200; *idem*, App., 138–141. Benton, *Thirty Years' View*, II, 471–472.

South Carolina. Sevier, of Arkansas, resisted an attempt to strike out the section for granting land to settlers, for he justly regarded this provision to be "the very life and soul of the bill."[13] After passing the Senate by a vote of twenty-four to twenty-two, the bill was sent to the House where it remained to the end of the session without being voted upon.

The importance of the Linn bill can not be measured by its failure to reach a vote in the House, for it elicited a debate in Congress and an agitation in the press which focused the attention of the people on Oregon and made it an important campaign issue. Then, too, its introduction caused British statesmen to give the subject more serious attention. Palmerston went so far as to declare in the House of Commons that should the bill be passed and put in operation "it would be a declaration of war."[14]

Dissatisfied because Webster had not procured, in the Ashburton treaty, all that the United States had claimed on the Maine border, and fearful that Everett, in London, might, under Tyler's directions, compromise the Oregon question, opposition members took steps to prevent such action on the part of the executive. On December 28, 1843, Senator Allen, of Ohio, moved a call upon the President for the instructions given to our minister in London as well as the correspondence that had passed between the two governments. On January 8, 1844, Semple, of Illinois, moved that the President be requested to give the notice necessary for terminating the convention of 1827.[15] It was soon ascertained that no negotiations were in progress in London and consequently Semple's resolution was defeated, but the debate helped to agitate public opinion. Extremists objected to any negotiation whatever on the ground that it would be an admission that Great Britain might have some claim to the territory.

Negotiations were soon renewed, however, but in Washington instead of at the court of Saint James. The man selected

---

[13] *Cong. Globe,* 27 Cong., 3 sess., 153.
[14] Hansard, *Parliamentary Debates,* LXVII, 1217.
[15] *Cong. Globe,* 28 Cong., 1 sess., 77, 116.

by Lord Aberdeen for the American mission was Richard Pakenham (later Sir Richard), and early in 1844 he arrived in Washington. If his official instructions were to be followed there was small prospect of an adjustment, for they required him to insist upon the Columbia River as the southern boundary of Oregon. It is evident, however, that Aberdeen himself did not expect the United States to accept this proposal, and that he was prepared to concede better terms if he could obtain the sanction of Parliament and of public sentiment in England. In a private letter dated March 4, 1844, Pakenham was instructed to

endeavor, without committing yourself or your gov't, to draw from the American negotiator a proposal to make the 49th degree of latitude the boundary, with the proviso that the ports to the south of that parallel to the Columbia inclusive, shall be free ports to G. Britain.[16]

The tone of this letter augured well for the future.

Upshur's tragic death interrupted negotiations before they had fairly begun, and the task of discussing the Oregon boundary with Pakenham devolved upon John C. Calhoun to whom Tyler now intrusted the State Department. According to statements made later, Tyler and Calhoun were reluctant to resume negotiations, consequently the Secretary of State decided that the *"true* policy" was *"to do nothing to excite attention, and leave time to operate."*[17] Nevertheless both Calhoun and Pakenham presented and advocated the claims of their respective governments—including an offer from Great Britain to submit the whole subject to arbitration—but as neither side would yield the essential points, the Oregon question remained unsettled at the close of Tyler's administration.

"Reannexation of Texas" and "reoccupation of Oregon" were twin planks in the platform adopted by the Democratic

---

[16] Quoted by Schafer, "The British Attitude toward the Oregon Question, 1815-1846," *Am. Hist. Rev.*, XVI, 296 (Jan., 1911).

[17] Calhoun to Mason, May 30, 1845 (*Report Am. Hist. Assn.*, 1899, II, 660). Tyler to Calhoun, Oct. 7, 1845 (*ibid.*, 1059).

convention of 1844. Although the former was the main topic of discussion during the campaign, the party was nevertheless committed to the claim that "all of Oregon" was the property of the United States. The candidates accepted the platform without reservation, while the rank and file voiced their approval by lusty shouts of "54° 40′ or fight." Did the platform and the campaign cry mean what they said, or were they intended simply to arouse enthusiasm and to win votes for the party? In either case the victorious candidate was placed in an awkward position; to accept less than "all of Oregon" would repudiate the party pledge, while insistence upon the demand made in the platform would almost certainly result in war with Great Britain.

In his inaugural address President Polk bluntly asserted that "our title to the country of the Oregon is 'clear and unquestionable!'" He did not say "all of Oregon," but left it to be inferred that this was what he meant. In addition, he recommended that the laws of the United States should be extended over the people who had established their homes in that distant region. If the propriety of his recommendations may be questioned,[18] the fault lay with the party which had framed the platform rather than with the President who was pledged to carry it out.[19]

The new President's inaugural reached England late in March and his remarks on the American title to Oregon were by no means relished in London. In Parliament and in the press they elicited expressions of surprise and denunciation. Opposition members were especially resentful. On the contrary, Lord Aberdeen was disposed to treat the matter lightly and to regard the address as a declamation rather than an official document.[20]

---

[18] See Benton, *Thirty Years' View*, II, 649, and von Holst, *Hist. of the U. S.*, III, 159.

[19] It is interesting, however, to note that Polk reversed the position which he had taken in 1828. See above, p. 557.

[20] "I wish to observe that this speech is not an address made to Congress—it is a speech made to the public, the Congress not being sitting. Undoubtedly, no speech of such a nature could be made by the President of the United States without drawing towards it the most serious attention. Nevertheless, it does not possess the importance of an official message, forming a part of legislative proceedings."

He believed that a peaceful settlement was still possible; if not, he could only say that "we possess rights which, in our opinion, are clear and unquestionable; and, by the blessing of God, and with your support, those rights we are fully prepared to maintain." In the House of Commons, Sir Robert Peel expressed a desire for an amicable adjustment, but he severely criticized President Polk for referring to "other contingencies than a friendly termination" of pending negotiations.[21] The London *Times* held that the interests of both countries would be served best by a compromise adjustment like that which settled the dispute over the northeast boundary; nevertheless it thought that Americans should be warned that their pretensions, if persisted in, must surely result in war. The editor was not disposed to aggravate "the very serious difficulties with which the indiscreet language of Mr. Polk has already surrounded the Oregon question," still, the extravagant claims of the President could never be admitted.[22]

During April and May the British newspapers discussed the diplomatic situation in all its bearings, and speculated as to what policy Polk really meant to pursue. Only one, the London *Colonial Magazine,* believed that a war with the United States would be "productive of good"; the others cared little about Oregon itself, but they resented the "blustering attitude" of the American President and people. For example, the *Times,* on May 9, said:

As long as we saw in these grotesque exhibitions of national vanity nothing but the expedients of presidential candidates, or the squibs of electioneering rivals, the foreign policy of the United States had nothing very serious or very formidable in its vacant thunders. But the election being over, and the new president installed by the voices of the democratic party for the next four years, foreign nations acquire something more than an indirect interest in his character and position. If President Polk intends to sustain the heroic line in which he passed through his electioneering probation and entered upon his high office, he may rely on having before

---

21 Hansard, *Parl. Deb.,* LXXIX, 121, 123, 199.
22 London *Times,* April 5, 1845, quoted by *Niles' Reg.,* LXVIII, 114–115.

him a career of no ordinary toil, agitation, and peril. But if he purposes to subside into a positive business-like president, more like the foreman of a thriving business in the city than the champion of an empire, the sooner he descends from the high horse the better; and he would have done well to throw aside the embroidered vestments of the candidate before he delivered the inaugural address of the president. Nobody supposes that in using the very exaggerated and unbecoming language in which Mr. Polk spoke of the American claims to Oregon, he intended deliberately to breathe defiance to the Queen of Great Britain, or to threaten the rights of Her Majesty's subjects with instant violence. He intended simply to flatter a delusion common in all democratic states, but especially amongst the democratic party in the United States, which forces the statesman whom they have chosen to govern their country to gratify their own popular vanity by affecting a temerity and an overbearing recklessness towards foreign nations which, as individuals, neither the president, nor any of his vociferous supporters, can be supposed to feel.

Rulers of democracies, said the London *Standard,* on May 15, are apt to be inclined to war for the purpose of increasing their power and their patronage. To this fact it attributed the claims set forth by President Polk, and therefore it did not believe that the people would support him, except verbally. Americans could not possibly gain anything by precipitating hostilities, "therefore we hold a war to be extremely improbable, if not an absolute impossibility, let Mr. Polk do all that he can." The *Examiner* (April 25) considered Oregon "really valueless to England and to America." It therefore congratulated Lord Aberdeen on his conciliatory attitude, and advocated arbitration or a partition of the territory.[23]

The utterances of British statesmen greatly exasperated the "old hero" of the Hermitage who, in characteristic style, urged the President to combat British pretensions by a vigorous and uncompromising policy:

Weak and debilitated as I am I could not resist endeavoring to wade through the debate in the English parliament—comments on your inaugural as it relates to oragon. This is the rattling of British drums to alarm us, and to give life to their friends in the United States, such as the Hartford convention men—the blue light federalists & abolitionists, and to prevent

[23] Extracts from these papers quoted in *Niles' Reg.,* LXVIII, 236–239.

if Britain can, the reannexation of Texas, by shadowing forth war &
rumors of war, to alarm the timid, & give strength to the traitors in our
country against our best interests & growing prosperity. This bold avowal
by peel & Russell of perfect claim to oragon must be met as boldly, by our
denial of their right, and confidence in our own—that we view it too plain
a case, *of right,* on our side to hesitate one moment upon the subject of
extending our laws over it & populating with our people—permit me to
remind you that during the canvass, I gave a thousand pledges for your
cour[a]ge & firmness, both in war & in peace, to carry on the administration
of our government. This subject is intended to try your energy—dash
from your lips the council of the times on this question, base your acts
upon the firm basis, of asking nothing but what is *right* & permitting
nothing that is wrong—war is a blessing compared with national degredation. The bold manner of peels & Russells annunciation of the British
right to oragogon, the time & manner require a firm rebuke by you in
your annual message, and has opened a fair field to compare their claim
to oragon with their right to the Territory claimed by Britain on our north
East boundary, & which we were swindled out of, there being on file in
archives of England the maps on which was laid down our boundary agreeable to the treaty of 1783, which Lord Browman said in eulogy of Lord
Ashburton shewed that England in her claim to that territory *had not* a
leg of right to stand upon—Just so with oragon, & peel & Russell both
well know it—*still, now,* a perfect right to oragon is claimed—make a note
of this, & in your annual message expose England's perfidy to the whole
civilized wor[l]d. To prevent war with England a bold & undaunted
front must be exposed. England with all her Boast dare not go to war.
You will pardon these my friendly suggestions. The Whiggs have held
you forth to England as feeble & inenergetic, & would shrink at the threat
of war—I am sure you will meet this with that energy & promptness that
is due to yourself, & our national character.[24]

As will be seen presently, Polk did not, in the first instance
at least, follow this fatherly advice. But ere the President had
decided to renew the compromise offer which his predecessors
had made, General Jackson had passed to a land where "peel &
Russell" no longer disturbed his repose. Even if he had lived
it is highly improbable that his views would have influenced the
President's foreign policy. Polk was ever ready to pay homage
to Jackson on matters of no vital importance. But when the
occasion demanded independent action—as in the discarding of

---

[24] Jackson to Polk, May 2, 1845, *Polk Papers.*

Blair and Lewis—he did not hesitate to follow his own judgment, even at the risk of incurring the General's displeasure.

In the selection of a minister to represent the United States at London Polk was hampered by political considerations. However, his embarrassment was somewhat lessened by the fact that negotiations were already pending in Washington and by the slight probability that they would be transferred to London. Since Calhoun had not been retained in the cabinet, many Democrats thought that he should be given the British mission; even Jackson considered England to be the proper place for him, "there to combat with my Lord Aberdeen the abolition question."[25] But Calhoun made it known that he would not accept the position; so, also, did his friends, Pickens and Elmore, decline the appointment.[26] Having failed in his overtures to the Calhoun wing of the party, the President, through Bancroft, sounded Van Buren on the subject. In reply Van Buren stated his belief that an ex-President should not accept a foreign mission unless there was a crisis to meet. He did not believe a crisis to exist, but if the President thought otherwise, he would, of course, regard it as his duty to go.[27] Levi Woodbury declined the appointment for "domestic reasons," and Louis McLane, of Baltimore, was finally chosen.[28]

About the middle of May, while Bancroft was in correspondence with Van Buren and before any official communications had passed between Buchanan and Pakenham, the recently established Washington *Union* announced what it believed to be Polk's Oregon policy:

Some say we want war—some that we "cannot be kicked into war." Several predict that there will be war. Now, without undertaking to say positively that *there will be war*, or that *there will not be war*, we venture

---

25 Jackson to Polk, Dec. 16, 1844, *ibid*.

26 After declining the mission himself Calhoun spoke favorably of Elmore, but he thought General Hamilton to be best qualified for the position (A. V. Brown (undated) to Polk, *ibid*.).

27 Van Buren to Bancroft, May 12, 1845, *Van Buren Papers*.

28 Correspondence with Woodbury and McLane, *Polk Papers*.

to predict that it is not Mr. Polk's wish to plunge his country into war, and still less to sacrifice her rights and her honor. He will never abandon either; and without meaning to bluster or to brave the British ministers, we undertake to say that this is the general and enthusiastic sentiment of the American nation. The President will carry out the wishes of the people. It will not be his fault if our differences about Oregon should terminate in hostilities; but it will be his fault, and a fault which we are sure he would never encounter, to sacrifice our "clear and unquestionable claims" and our sacred honor to any visionary danger, or to any apprehensions of danger." "Young Hickory," it added, will make good his title.[29]

Although this article purported to give merely the views of the editor, Ritchie, no doubt it had the previous endorsement of the President. Apparently its purpose was to prepare the people for a compromise adjustment of the Oregon question, but, also, to inform the British minister that the administration would not be intimidated by the prospect of a war.

When the Tyler administration declined to accept the terms offered by Great Britain, Pakenham, in a note dated September 12, 1844, asked Calhoun to specify what arrangement he was "prepared to propose for an equitable adjustment of the question." Calhoun did not see fit to comply with this request, and four months after Polk's inauguration no formal reply to Pakenham's note had been made. On July 12, 1845, however, in a communication to the minister, Buchanan set forth the American claims and offered to accept the forty-ninth parallel as a compromise boundary. Whatever Polk's private reasons for thus suddenly reversing the policy announced in his inaugural may have been, his official reasons were set forth in a letter which Buchanan, on the same day, addressed to Louis McLane, the American minister in London. In it he said:

The President, at a very early period of his administration, was called upon to decide whether he would break off or continue this negotiation. Placed in a responsible position, he first inquired whether the national honor required that he should abruptly terminate it by demanding the whole territory in dispute. War before dishonor is a maxim deeply engraven upon the hearts of the American People; and this maxim ever shall regulate

29 *Union* (semiweekly), May 12, 1845.

his conduct towards foreign nations. But it was impossible for him to conceive that there could be dishonor in pursuing the course which had been adopted by Mr. Monroe, his patriot Revolutionary predecessor, more than a quarter of a century ago, and had been either expressly sanctioned or acquiesced in by all succeeding administrations.[30]

In his note to Pakenham, Buchanan gave a comprehensive statement of the American claims to Oregon—both direct and indirect.[31] "The title of the United States," he said, "to that portion of the Oregon territory between the valley of the Columbia and the Russian line in 54° 40' North Latitude, is recorded in the Florida Treaty," which transferred to the United States all of the claims of Spain. He refuted the claims which Great Britain based on the Nootka Sound convention, for, as he said, no title to land had been acquired by this convention. The valley of the Columbia, said he, belonged to the United States by virtue of the discoveries of Captain Gray, the explorations of Lewis and Clark, and the settlements made by Astor and other American citizens.

"Such being the opinion of the President in regard to the title of the United States," Buchanan told Pakenham, "he would not have consented to yield any portion of the Oregon territory, had he not found himself embarrassed, if not committed, by the acts of his predecessors." But as they had uniformly proceeded upon "the principle of compromise," Polk felt constrained to do likewise. He had therefore instructed Buchanan again to propose that the Oregon country be divided by the forty-ninth parallel from the Rocky Mountains to the Pacific Ocean, with free ports for Great Britain on the portion of Vancouver's Island lying south of that parallel.

---

[30] Buchanan to McLane, July 12, 1845 (Buchanan, *Works*, VI, 190). He emphasized the fact that even General Jackson had been satisfied with joint occupation. But he passed over the other important fact that none of Polk's predecessors had barred themselves from compromise by emphatically claiming title to *all* of the territory.

[31] In a letter written to John G. Palfrey, June 24, 1848, Buchanan said that it was from Greenhow's *Oregon and California* "that my information as to the facts in support of our claim was principally derived" (*Works*, VIII, 106).

The line proposed will carry out the principle of continuity equally for both parties, by extending the limits both of ancient Louisiana and Canada to the Pacific along the same parallel of latitude which divide them east of the Rocky Mountains; and it will secure to each a sufficient number of commodious harbors on the northwest coast of America.[32]

Pakenham replied on the twenty-ninth of July. He controverted every argument which Buchanan had made, and in addition, he endeavored to place the American Secretary of State in a somewhat awkward position. If, said he, Spain had had exclusive title to Oregon down to the Florida treaty of 1819, then Gray as well as Lewis and Clark had been interlopers on Spanish territory and their discoveries could not give the United States a valid title to the Columbia River valley. On what grounds, he asked,

unless it be upon the principle which forms the foundation of the Nootka convention, could the United States have acquired a title to any part of the Oregon territory previously to the treaty of 1819, and independently of its provisions?

The Nootka convention, he continued, was not the ''main reliance'' of Great Britain in this discussion, but it barred the United States from acquiring ''exclusive dominion'' from Spain by the Florida treaty. He argued at length to show that the Nootka convention was still in force, and that none of the American explorations had given the United States exclusive title to any part of Oregon. Although he had not referred Buchanan's letter to his own government, Pakenham concluded his reply by declining the offer made by the President, and by expressing the hope that

the American plenipotentiary will be prepared to offer some further proposal for the settlement of the Oregon question more consistent with fairness and equity, and with the reasonable expectations of the British government.[33]

The British minister's categorical rejection of Polk's offer came as a shock to the administration and aroused the fighting

---

[32] Buchanan to Pakenham, July 12, 1845 (Buchanan, *Works*, VI, 194 ff.).
[33] Pakenham to Buchanan, July 29, 1845 (*ibid.*, 212–220).

blood of the President. Regarding Pakenham's note as insolent, Polk decided to withdraw his offer of compromise and to reassert claim to the whole territory. In the belief that the relations with England had become critical in the extreme, he personally dictated the main features of the reply to the British minister. In order to prevent misunderstandings concerning his directions to Buchanan, or discussions in cabinet, he began keeping a diary in which the events of each day were recorded. This daily record is of great historical importance, for it not only gives information nowhere else available, but it displays the motives which inspired the President's policies—at least the motives which he desired posterity to accept as the key to his official acts.[34]

The diary opens on August 26, 1845, and the day's record is concerned principally with cabinet discussion of the Oregon question. As early as August 7, after the Prussian minister had informed Bancroft of a threatened invasion of Texas by Mexico, Polk urged Buchanan, who was on a visit to his home, to return to Washington as soon as possible. "I must confess," he said, after explaining the Mexican situation, "that the developments which are taking place, as well as my daily reflections, make it, in my opinion, more and more important that we should progress without delay in the Oregon negotiation."[35] By August 26, the date of the cabinet meeting just mentioned, the President had become impatient because of Buchanan's delay in drafting a reply to Pakenham's note of July 29. He asked the Secretary when the reply would be ready for consideration by the cabinet; but, without waiting to learn what Buchanan had prepared, he proceeded to tell the cabinet "the settled decision to which his mind had come." In his reply to Pakenham, Buchanan was directed to "assert and enforce our right to the whole of the Oregon territory from 42° to 54° 40′ North Latitude." He was to state that the President had offered to agree

[34] For his own version of his reasons for keeping a diary, see *Diary*, II, 100–101.

[35] Polk to Buchanan, Aug. 7, 1845, *Buchanan Papers.*

upon the forty-ninth parallel solely in deference to his predecessors and because of his desire to preserve peace between the
two nations. Since the British minister had, without referring
the matter to his government, rejected the compromise "in
language, to say the least of it, scarcely courteous or respectful"
the offer was now to be withdrawn. "Let the argument of our
title to the whole country be full," said the President, "let the
proposition to compromise at latitude 49° be withdrawn, and
then let the matter rest, unless the British Minister chose to
continue the negotiation."

Buchanan agreed with the President so far as the assertion
of title and the withdrawal of the compromise offer were concerned, but he believed that a paragraph should be added to the
effect that Polk would consider any proposition which Pakenham
might submit. To such an implied invitation for further negotiation the President objected. "Let our proposition be absolutely withdrawn & then let the British Minister take his own
course." With his usual timidity, Buchanan urged that should
Polk's views be carried out, war would result, but the President
replied that "if we do have war it will not be our fault."
Buchanan expressed the opinion that the answer to Pakenham
ought to be postponed until it could be ascertained whether there
would be a war with Mexico, but Polk, after asserting that there
was no connection between the two questions, insisted upon an
immediate reply to Pakenham's note. To his remark that the
United States would do its duty towards both nations and leave
the rest to God and the Country, Buchanan retorted that "God
would not have much to do in justifying us in a war for the
country North of 49°." Secretary Walker concurred in the
President's views, and the other members expressed no opinions.
Undeterred by the opposition of his Secretary of State, Polk
called a special cabinet meeting for the following day and directed
Buchanan to have a draft of his answer to Pakenham ready for
consideration. The draft presented by Buchanan at the special

meeting was considered satisfactory—even admirable—so far as the historical array of facts relating to the title was concerned, but the President ordered changes to be made in the part relating to the withdrawal of the compromise offer. Although the Secretary of State argued that the answer ought to be postponed, Polk ordered him to deliver it as soon as it could be copied. At the close of the discussion the other members of the cabinet gave their hearty support to the policy adopted by the President. Having thus declined to make further overtures to John Bull, Polk, on the following day, directed that orders be sent to General Taylor that in case Mexico should declare war or begin hostilities he was to drive her army across the Rio Grande and invade Mexico.[36]

The note to Pakenham, in its completed form, was an able document. The historical part, prepared by Buchanan, presented the claims of the United States to the whole territory with precision and clearness. The Nootka Sound convention, he asserted, had not procured for Great Britain any territorial rights, and all privileges acquired by that agreement had been cancelled by a subsequent war with Spain. To Pakenham's contention that the admission of Spain's title to Oregon before 1819 would invalidate all claims based by the United States on discovery, Buchanan retorted that "this is a most ingenious method of making two distinct and independent titles held by the same nation worse than one—of arraying them against each other, and thus destroying the validity of both." The United States, said he, now possessed both its own and the Spanish titles; either was better than that of England, and certainly the two, combined, could not be weaker than one.

The compromise offer was officially withdrawn, but Polk's original intention of making no allusion to further negotiations was not carried out. Presumably in deference to the wishes of Buchanan, it was stated that "the President still cherishes the

---

[36] Polk, *Diary*, I, 1–9.

hope that this long-pending controversy may yet be finally adjusted in such manner as not to disturb the peace or interrupt the harmony now so happily subsisting between the two nations.''[37]

In taking such a firm stand the President may have been influenced, to some extent at least, by the knowledge that Pakenham's prompt rejection of the compromise offer had not been authorized by his government. On August 19, Polk had received a private letter from McLane which stated that

The result of all I have learned is that this Government is earnestly desirous of adjusting the Oregon question, & willing to do so upon liberal terms. *Their chief difficulty arises from the opposition & influence of the Hudson's Bay Company.*

His information, he said, had not come directly from Lord Aberdeen, but he felt certain that England would agree to the forty-ninth parallel to the Straits of Fuca, leaving Vancouver's Island to Great Britain.[38] At the same time Robert Armstrong, the American consul at Liverpool and an intimate friend of the President, wrote that it was generally understood that England held a mortgage on California. Great Britain, he urged, must never possess California; Oregon should be made the bone of contention to prevent it.[39]

Several weeks passed during which neither party attempted to break the diplomatic deadlock. At a cabinet meeting held on October 21, however, a dispatch sent by McLane on the third was read and discussed. In an interview with McLane, Lord Aberdeen had expressed regret because Pakenham had rejected the American offer. After condemning Pakenham's act, he intimated

---

[37] Buchanan to Pakenham, Aug. 30, 1845 (Buchanan, *Works*, VI, 231-254). On the same day that Buchanan delivered his official note, Calhoun wrote from his home in South Carolina deploring the possibility of a rupture with England. ''It is beyond the power of man,'' said he, ''to trace the consequences of a war between us and England on the subject of Oregon. All that is certain is, that she can take it & hold it against us, as long as she has the supremacy on the ocean & retains her Eastern dominions. The rest is rapt in mystery'' (Calhoun to Buchanan, Aug. 30, 1845, *ibid.*, 230).

[38] Copy of McLane to Polk, Aug. 4, 1845, *Buchanan Papers*.

[39] Armstrong to Polk, Aug. 4, 1845, *Polk Papers*.

a willingness to agree upon a modified proposition, and asked whether President Polk would negotiate further on the subject. Anticipating that Pakenham had received new instructions by the same mail and would make new overtures, Buchanan asked the President what answer he should make. Polk promptly replied that

all that could be said to him was, that if he had any further proposition to make on his part, it would be received and considered. . . . . No intimation should be given to him of what the views or intentions of the administration were, & [but] leave him to take his own course.

He declared, also, that should Pakenham propose to agree upon the adjustment recently offered by the United States he would not accept the proposal. Should the minister make some other offer, this would either be rejected or submitted to the Senate for its advice. To Buchanan's question whether he might inform the British diplomat that a proposition made by him would be submitted to the Senate, the President answered that such a course "would be improper; the British Minister had no right to know our councils or intentions." Although the Secretary of State prophesied war, Polk was obdurate and refused to modify his views. He told the cabinet that in his first message to Congress he "would maintain all our rights, would reaffirm Mr. Monroe's ground against permitting any European power to plant or establish any new colony on the North American Continent."[40]

The conjecture that Pakenham had received new instructions from Lord Aberdeen seems to have been well founded, for two days after the cabinet meeting he called at the State Department and expressed regret because the American offer had been withdrawn. He suggested that negotiations might be reopened by the signing of a protocol, but as he was not prepared to make a definite offer of terms, Buchanan was not at liberty to accept the proposal. When the conversation was reported to the President,

[40] Polk, *Diary,* I, 62–65.

he insisted that "the British Government must move first," and he doubted that any offer would be made which the United States could accept.[41]

Up to this time there had been an estrangement between the President and Senator Benton, as a result of the latter's violent criticism of the course pursued by the Baltimore convention. Due, however, to a common interest in Oregon and, also, to the influence of Buchanan, a reconciliation was effected. With Polk's consent, Buchanan showed Benton the correspondence that had passed between himself and the British minister; he intimated, also, that the Senator would be kindly received if he should feel inclined to call upon the President. Benton approved the action that had been taken and expressed a desire to converse with the President, therefore a meeting was arranged for the twenty-fourth of October. Polk was already preparing his message to Congress, and it is evident that he was anxious to win Benton's support for the policy which he was about to recommend. The Missourian's judgment was not always sound, but he wielded an influence which could not be disregarded.

During the interview the two men agreed upon the following points: that the twelve months' notice for abrogating the convention of 1827 should be given; that the laws of the United States should be extended over Oregon in the same degree that British laws had been extended in 1821; that forts should be built on the route to Oregon; and that the Indian policy of the United States should be extended to the whole region. On some phases, however, Benton was not prepared to go so far as the President; he thought that Great Britain possessed a good title to the Frazer River valley, and he was willing to accept the forty-ninth parallel as a sastisfactory boundary. To Polk's suggestion of reasserting the Monroe Doctrine against all colonization on the North American continent, he replied that while foreign nations should be excluded from California and the Columbia River

[41] *Ibid.*, 66–67.

valley, the Frazer River valley was already occupied by the British.[42] From the date of this interview until the court-martial of Fremont the Senator gave his support to the administration. And his support was of no small importance, although his arrogance and dictatorial manner often taxed the patience of the President.

Three days after his conversation with Benton (*i.e.*, October 27), the President received a call from T. W. Ward, Boston agent for the Baring Brothers. After speaking of the absurdity of a war between the two nations and of the unsettled business conditions which had resulted from war rumors, Ward intimated a desire to know whether Polk would persist in claiming title to the whole of Oregon. His visit did not elicit the desired information, for the President told him that "no one but myself & my Cabinet could know what had occurred or what was likely to occur." Two hours later Buchanan sent to the President a diplomatic note which he had just received from the British minister, and as it bore the date of October 25, Polk concluded that it had been held back until Pakenham had learned the result of Ward's interview with the President.[43]

When presenting the note to Buchanan, Pakenham remarked that he would regard it as official or unofficial as he might deem best after he had ascertained the answer which it would receive. A reply was prepared by Buchanan and carefully edited by the President after its contents had been discussed at two cabinet meetings. Against the wishes of the Secretary of State, who desired to leave the way open for further negotiation, Polk directed him not to submit his answer or to reveal its contents unless Pakenham would decide, in advance, to regard his note as official. He was unwilling, he said, to do anything "which would have the appearance of inviting Great Brittain to make another proposition." When told that no answer would be made except to an official communication, Pakenham, after some

---

[42] *Ibid.*, 55, 70–71.   [43] *Ibid.*, 73–75.

anxious hesitation, withdrew the note. During the conversation he denied that he had rejected the American offer, but had merely refused to accept it—a distinction which he held to be of great importance. Copies of the note and the reply which had been prepared were sent to McLane so that he might know precisely what had transpired.[44] The President, at this same time, was holding conversations with Lieutenant Gillespie, preparing him for his mission to California with secret instructions for Larkin, the consul at Monterey, and two weeks later Slidell was sent to negotiate with Mexico.

During the latter half of November Polk was busily engaged in drafting his first annual message to Congress. He discussed the proposed recommendations with Ritchie and with several members of Congress, and all parts of his original draft were read and considered at cabinet meetings. In general all members of the cabinet, except Buchanan, concurred in the President's views; the Secretary of State dissented from his Oregon policy and seriously considered leaving the cabinet to accept the position of Justice of the Supreme Court. He made various suggestions which were intended to soften the tone of the message, and when they were not adopted the President noted that ''Mr. Buchanan seemed to be depressed in spirits, and, as I thought, greatly concerned lest the controversy about Oregon might lead to War.''[45] When his own protests had failed he tried to influence the President by saying that many members of Congress were in favor of accepting parallel forty-nine as the boundary, but Polk replied that he, too, had conversed with congressmen, nine-tenths of whom were in favor of ''going the whole length.'' The diary states further that:

Mr. B. expressed the opinion with some earnestness that the country would not justify a war for the country North of 49°, and that my greatest danger would be that I would be attacked for holding a warlike tone. I

---

44 *Ibid.*, 75–82. Buchanan to McLane, Oct. 28 and Nov. 5, 1845 (Buchanan, *Works*, VI, 285–286, 289).

45 Polk, *Diary*, I, 102.

told him that my greatest danger was that I would be attacked for having yielded to what had been done by my predecessors and in deference alone, as he knew, to their acts and commitments, [and for having] agreed to offer the compromise of 49°. I told him that if that proposition had been accepted by the Brittish Minister my course would have met with great opposition, and in my opinion would have gone far to overthrow the administration; that, had it been accepted, as we came in on Texas the probability was we would have gone out on Oregon. I told him we had done our duty by offering 49°, and that I did not regret that it had been rejected by the Brittish Minister. . . . . The truth is Mr. Buchanan has from thhe beginning been, as I think, too timid and too fearful of War on the Oregon question, and has been most anxious to settle the question by yielding and making greater concessions than I am willing to make.[46]

The twenty-ninth Congress convened on the first of December, and on the following day Polk submitted his first annual message. While he congratulated Congress on "the continued prosperity" of the country, he nevertheless felt called upon to make many important recommendations. Foreign relations were given first attention, and on the topics of Texas and Oregon the views expressed by the President were uncompromising, if not menacing, in tone.

After giving a brief history of the attempts made by his predecessors to settle the Oregon boundary question, the President informed Congress of the offer which he had made and which Great Britain had rejected. He had become convinced that England would not agree to any adjustment which the United States ought to accept, consequently "the proposition of compromise which had been made and rejected was by my direction subsequently withdrawn and our title to the whole of Oregon Territory asserted, and, as is believed, maintained by irrefragable facts and arguments." Since England by her rejection of the compromise offer had relieved the President from being further influenced by the acts of his predecessors and had left him free to assert the full rights of the United States, two things were recommended: first, notice should be given that the convention

---

[46] *Ibid.*, 107–108.

of "joint occupancy" made in 1827 will be terminated at the end of twelve months; and second, "it will become proper for Congress to determine what legislation they can in the meantime adopt without violating this convention."

While thus fully admitting the right of Congress to determine the degree of protection which might be given to American citizens in Oregon before the termination of joint occupancy, Polk nevertheless freely suggested the laws which he considered to be proper and necessary. "Beyond all question," said he, "the protection of our laws and our jurisdiction, civil and criminal, ought to be immediately extended over our citizens in Oregon." They should be extended to the same extent that England had extended her laws in 1821. Forts should be built along the route to Oregon to facilitate emigration to that region. He doubted that land grants could be made until the convention had expired, but emigrants might rest assured that they would be given land as soon as "joint occupancy" had ended.

So far as Great Britain was concerned, the most objectionable part of the message was that which outlined the policy to be followed by the United States after the convention of 1827 had expired. "At the end of a year's notice," said the President,

should Congress think it proper to make provision for giving that notice, we shall have reached a period when the national rights in Oregon must either be abandoned or firmly maintained. That they can not be abandoned without a sacrifice of both national honor and interest is too clear to admit of doubt.

The claim of Great Britain to the Columbia as a boundary "can never for a moment be entertained by the United States without an abandonment of their just and clear territorial rights, their own self-respect, and the national honor." Evidently with California as well as Oregon in mind, he reasserted the Monroe Doctrine against European colonization on the North American continent.[47]

---

[47] Richardson, *Messages*, IV, 392–399.

According to the account recorded in Polk's diary, Democrats generally—even many of Calhoun's friends—expressed enthusiastic approval of his message.[48] Archer, a Whig member from Virginia, was especially pleased with the part relating to Oregon, and remarked that "he believed he was half a Polkman." "Well!" said Benton, "you have sent us the message," and "I think we can all go it as we understand it," to which Polk replied (alluding to Jackson's famous remark) that the Senator had very high authority for saying "as we understand it." The real meaning of Benton's remark, as further conversation developed, was that England's title to the region drained by Frazer's River was quite as good as that of the United States to the valley of the Columbia.[49]

The President was not moved to modify his uncompromising policy by the opinions expressed by so influential a person as Senator Benton; neither did the continued opposition of Buchanan disturb his equanimity. At a cabinet meeting held on December 9, the Secretary of State, after stating that he anticipated a call from Pakenham, asked the President what reply he ought to make if the British minister should interrogate him on the Oregon question. "Suppose," said he, "Mr. Pakenham inquires whether any further proposition which the British Government might make would be received, what shall I say to him?" Polk replied that Pakenham had no right to ask such a question. The minister, he said, knew the contents of the annual message and of the diplomatic correspondence he had received; let him take his own course without any intimation as to how any future offer would be received. "Mr. B. repeated his anxiety to settle the question at 49° & avoid war. I told him that I did not desire war, but that at all hazards we must maintain our just rights." Pakenham called two days later, and, after expressing an earnest desire for peace, desired to know what the United States proposed

---

[48] Among those mentioned were Cass, McDuffie, Holmes, Seddon, Hunter, and Wilmot.

[49] Polk, *Diary*, I, 116–117.

to do at the end of the year's notice, but Buchanan was, of course, unable to give him a satisfactory reply.[50] In spite of his "high tone," Polk seems to have been rather uneasy because England was reported to be engaged in "warlike preparations," and McLane was instructed to ascertain whether they had been induced by possible hostilities over Oregon.[51]

On December 23 "a grave discussion" took place in the cabinet regarding the probabilities of a war with Great Britain. Buchanan expressed himself as decidedly in favor of vigorous preparations for defense, and in such a policy the President heartily concurred. The Secretaries of War and Navy were directed to communicate the views of the administration to the military and naval committees of Congress and to aid them in drafting suitable bills. Still in fear of war, Buchanan inquired whether, in case Pakenham should offer to compromise on the forty-ninth parallel, leaving Vancouver's Island to England, Polk would submit the offer to the Senate for its advice. "I told him," wrote the President,

if an equivalent, by granting to the U. S. free ports North of 49° on the sea & the Straits of Fuca should also be offered, I would consult confidentially three or four Senators from different parts of the Union, and might submit it to the Senate for their previous advice.

As this was the first intimation, since the withdrawal of the American offer, that Polk might modify his claims, in deference to the Senate, Buchanan regarded the commitment so important that he reduced to writing what the President had said.[52]

Pakenham called at the State Department on December 27, and, after an unsuccessful attempt to induce Buchanan to recall his withdrawal of the American offer, proposed to refer "the whole question of an equitable division of that territory [Oregon] to the arbitration of some friendly sovereign or State." In

---

[50] *Ibid.*, 119–121.

[51] Buchanan to McLane, Dec. 13, 1845 (Buchanan, *Works*, VI, 341–342).

[52] He appended the memorandum: "I took down the foregoing from the lips of the President in the presence of the Cabinet" (Polk, *Diary*, I. 133–136).

anticipation of such an offer Polk and his cabinet had, on that very same day, decided to reject it, if it should be made. Buchanan could not, of course, reject the offer without referring it to the President, but he frankly told the British diplomat that he did not believe it would be accepted. Pakenham regretted that there seemed to be no way of reopening negotiations and intimated that the American government did not desire an amicable settlement. He said, on the other hand, that "the British government would be glad to get clear of the question on almost any terms; that they did not care if the arbitrator should award the whole territory to us."[53] This frank remark indicated that England cared little about Oregon—except that she did not wish to be coerced—and the prospects of an amicable adjustment seemed very much brighter.[54]

In his answer to Pakenham, which had been carefully edited by the President, Buchanan explained why the offer of arbitration could not be accepted. The offer to refer to an arbitrator the "equitable division" of Oregon, said he, "assumes the fact that the title of Great Britain to a portion of the territory is valid, and thus takes for granted the very question in dispute"; the President could not admit such an implication, for he believed that England had no claim to any part of the land. Pakenham now asked if the United States would agree to submit to arbitration the question as to whether either nation possessed a valid title to the whole territory, and his query was answered in the negative, because the President did not "believe the territorial rights of this nation to be a proper subject for arbitration."[55]

[53] Pakenham to Buchanan, Dec. 27, 1845; memorandum of the interview in Buchanan, *Works*, VI, 349–353.

[54] Pakenham's report of his government's attitude agrees with a statement made by Ashbell Smith: "In the conversation Lord Aberdeen remarked that the British government did not care a pin, comparatively, about Oregon and the Puget sound country; but that the universal conviction in England was that the country to the Columbia river belonged of right to Great Britain and that the United States was attempting to bully England out of it" (Smith, *Reminiscences of the Texas Republic*, 41).

[55] Buchanan to Pakenham, Jan. 3 and Feb. 4; Pakenham to Buchanan, Jan. 16, 1846 (Buchanan, *Works*, VI, 355, 357, 370).

Polk's unyielding attitude did not necessarily mean that he either expected or desired a rupture with England. Apparently, he believed that he would yet be offered a proposition to which he could agree. When, on January 4, Black, of South Carolina, asked him to use his influence with Congress to induce that body to postpone the date for abrogating the convention of 1827, he declined with the remark that "the only way to treat John Bull was to look him straight in the eye; that he [I] considered a bold & firm course on our part the pacific one."[56] Despite, therefore, the blunt answers to Pakenham, McLane was authorized to let Lord Aberdeen know, "cautiously and informally," that, while the President himself would accept nothing less than the whole of Oregon, he would, should Great Britain offer the forty-ninth parallel as a boundary, refer the proposition to the Senate for its advice. Anything less advantageous to the United States would be rejected by the President without such a reference; "it is manifest, therefore, that the British Government should at once present their ultimatum."[57] A few days before these instructions had been sent Polk had suggested to his cabinet that a settlement might possibly be made on the basis of a mutual reduction of tariffs and the payment to England of a sum of money for the surrender of her Oregon claims. This sum was to enable her to indemnify the Hudson's Bay Company. The subject was postponed for further discussion and seems never to have been seriously considered.[58]

Before he had received the above-mentioned instructions Mc-Lane, in a private letter to Buchanan, said that although the Oregon question was becoming more critical every day, yet he believed that the President had it in his power to adjust the matter "upon a basis of a reasonable compromise," should he feel inclined to do so. He believed, also, *"that it may be made to appear* in the end that his [Polk's] mode of conducting the

---

[56] Polk, *Diary*, I, 155.
[57] Buchanan to McLane, Jan. 29, 1846 (Buchanan, *Works*, VI, 366–368).
[58] Polk, *Diary*, I, 191.

negotiation had enabled *him* to do what his predecessors had been unable to accomplish.''[59] The latter suggestion was entirely superfluous, for the President was already endeavoring to create such an impression by his method of conducting the negotiations. His judgment proved to be sounder than that of his critics. His uncompromising attitude did not result in the war which they so confidently predicted, but, eventually, in another and better offer from the British government.

In the meantime Congress was engaged in a spirited debate upon the President's message and the validity of the American title to Oregon. In the Senate, on December 8, Benton presented a memorial from the people of Oregon which stated that they had set up a temporary government and asked its approval by Congress. They requested Congress to create for them a territorial government, or at least to give them civil and military protection.[60] Next day Cass introduced resolutions which instructed the military and naval committees to inquire into the defensive needs of the country.

When first presented, Cass's resolutions elicited no comments, but when, on December 15, he came to urge their adoption the character of his speech caused no little consternation. Negotiations, he said, had failed to settle the dispute, and Great Britain was assuming a menacing attitude; adequate military preparation was the best means of avoiding war. The President, in his opinion, could never recede from the position he had taken, and it was better ''to fight for the first inch of national territory than for the last.'' Allen, the chairman of the Committee on Foreign Affairs, agreed that the best method of averting war was to prepare for it, ''but the only, or rather the most effectual, preparation which could be made in the United States for this state of things, was the preparation of the hearts of the people.'' Webster, Crittenden, and Niles deplored warlike talk, and thought that

---

[59] McLane to Buchanan, Feb. 3, 1846, *Buchanan Papers*.

[60] Unless otherwise stated, the opinions and remarks of congressmen have been derived from the *Congressional Globe* under dates given.

Cass's remarks were most unfortunate. Webster did not believe that Polk expected war, and, in his opinion, the message had been intended as an ultimatum to induce England to make a better offer. Sevier, on the other hand, would not accept this interpretation. There would certainly be war, he said, for the United States could not recede, and Great Britain would not; the only recourse for the United States was to drive the British out of the territory. There was little opposition to the resolutions themselves—the criticism was aimed at the remarks which they called forth—and they passed near the close of the day (December 16) by a unanimous vote.

The Senate having taken the first step in "preparing the hearts of the people" for war, Allen, on the eighteenth, presented a joint resolution which advised the President "to give, forthwith," the necessary notice for terminating the convention of 1827 with Great Britain. On the same day Atchison, of Missouri, moved to instruct the Committee on Territories to inquire into the expediency of organizing a government for Oregon. During the next two weeks Texas rather than Oregon claimed the attention of the Senate, but on December 29 Hannegan, of Indiana, offered a resolution which declared all of Oregon to be "part and parcel" of the United States, and that "there exists no power in this Government to transfer its soil, and the allegiance of its citizens, to the dominion, authority, control, and subjugation of any foreign prince, state, or sovereignty."

The Oregon question was introduced in the House on the second day of the session when Ingersoll read a petition from the citizens of that region asking for a territorial government. It was read and laid on the table, but on December 15 Douglas succeeded in having it referred to the Committee on Territories, of which he was chairman. On the nineteenth, Douglas reported from his committee a bill which provided for the protection of the rights of American citizens until the termination of joint occupation. It was read twice and referred to the Committee of the Whole, there to be made a special order for the first Tuesday in January, and to continue such from day to day until it had been adopted or rejected. Scarcely had the reference been made when Winthrop, of Massachusetts, offered resolutions to the effect that the differences with England were still open to negotiation or arbitration, and that war would be highly discreditable to both nations. Douglas responded immediately with resolutions which asserted that the title to any part of the territory south of 54° 40′ was not open to compromise or arbitration. From the Committee on Military Affairs, Brinkerhoff, on December 31, reported a bill for constructing forts along the route to Oregon; this, also, was referred to the Committee of the Whole.

While the House had been discussing the proposed government for Oregon, its Committee on Foreign Affairs had been trying to agree upon a joint resolution for giving notice to England that the convention of 1827 would be terminated. As the members were unable to agree, Ingersoll, the chairman, on January 5, reported a resolution for the majority of his committee. It directed that the President ''forthwith cause notice to be given'' that the convention would be abrogated twelve months after the notice had been served. Garrett Davis, of Kentucky, then reported that the minority of the committee—himself and two colleagues—believed that the convention could be abrogated by the treaty-making power only. The House, he said, had nothing to do with it; Congress neither made the convention nor could unmake it, except by a declaration of war. The contention of the minority was well founded, even though the objectors were governed more by partisan feelings than by constitutional scruples. Although the convention of 1827 did not specify by whom the notice should be given, the natural inference was that it meant the treaty-making power.

As soon as the reports had been read, the House proceeded at once to consider the resolution. Giddings, who opened the debate, stated that heretofore he had opposed expansion, but since the South had succeeded in annexing Texas he now wanted all of Oregon. The South, he said, was not interested in Oregon, and he believed that Polk would surrender all north of the forty-ninth parallel. Rhett repelled the charge that southern men who opposed giving notice to England were governed by sectional motives. His own reason for opposing the notice was that John Quincy Adams favored it; he would be "blackballed" in South Carolina if he should vote on the same side as the member from Massachusetts. Cobb, of Georgia (January 9), regretted that southern men should question the title to all of Oregon; if Congress should fail to back up Polk's message, Great Britain would be still less inclined to settle the question. In his opinion, it would be very unfair for Congress to shirk the responsibility by leaving the discretion to the President. The Washington *Union* in urging abrogation of the convention pointed out that so long as joint occupation continued England had no interest in the settlement of the question, for *"she has now all that she asks for."*[61]

As the debate proceeded, many arguments—some of them most unique—were offered in support of the notice and for the claim to the whole territory. Levin, of Pennsylvania (January 9), based the claim to all of Oregon upon the "genius of American institutions" and the "laws of God"; Kennedy, of Indiana, upon the "American multiplication table," the operation of which made it necessary for the people to have more room.[62] Brinkerhoff, of Ohio, was captivated by the convincing logic of Buchanan's defense of the American title as was "the Queen of Sheba, when gazing on the architectural wonders of Jerusalem."

---

[61] *Union*, Jan. 12, 1846. "If we are to govern Oregon peaceably," said the *Union* on January 16, "we must first get rid of 'joint occupation.' If we are to govern *any part* of Oregon peaceably, we must first get rid of 'joint occupation' in that part."

[62] "Our people are spreading out with the aid of the American multiplication table. Go to the West and see a young man with his mate of eighteen; after the lapse of thirty years, visit him again and instead of two, you will find twenty-two. That is what I call the American multiplication table" (*Cong. Globe*, Jan. 10, 1846).

Sawtelle, of Maine, praised Polk for his firm stand, for he wanted no compromise like the Ashburton treaty; "we want no more half-English half-American secretaries to barter away any other portion of our territory." Douglas would not be satisfied so long as Great Britain held an inch of territory on the northwest coast, and he commended the President for reasserting the Monroe Doctrine. He seems clearly to have believed that Polk would not conclude a treaty of any kind with Great Britain. Had he believed otherwise he would hardly have uttered the remark about to be quoted, for his language would brand the President as unworthy of confidence as soon as the treaty had been signed. After citing the passage in Polk's message which stated that in future no European colony might be planted in North America with the consent of the United States, he asserted that the conclusion of any treaty with England—whether the line esablished were 49° or 54° 40′—would be giving such consent. "But the President," said he,

Has announced distinctly to the world, as our settled policy, that that consent cannot be given. Sir, he who knows the character of the man—he who knows the stern integrity of his political character—he who knows the consistency of his whole political life—he who knows his fidelity to his principles, must know that, during his four years, this "settled policy" will not be unsettled by him. Sir, he is not the man to put the distinct declaration forth to the world in the name of his Government of a settled policy, and then to sneak back from it, to violate it, to disgrace himself and his nation during that very presidential term in which he gave the notice. Then, I say, that during these four years, it is a settled, irrevocably settled question, that no treaty fixing a boundary for the northern part of Oregon can be made. Sir, the making of any treaty fixing a boundary, would be a palpable violation of the very principle the President has put forth in his message.[63]

Great difference of opinion existed as to who possessed the power and whose duty it was to notify England that the convention would be abrogated. Could the President alone do so, or must he have the advice and consent of the Senate; could

---

[63] Jan. 27, 1846 (*Cong. Globe,* 29 Cong., 1 sess., 259–260).

Congress alone, or with the approval of the President, serve the notice; if Congress alone lacked power to give the notice, could it direct, or simply advise, the President, to do so? The Whigs, generally, favored leaving the question of serving the notice to the discretion of the President so that he might bear the responsibility, although many of them professed to be certain that notice would be followed by war. On January 7, Hilliard, of Alabama, moved an amendment which empowered the President to give or to withhold notice; Democrats opposed the amendment and declared it to be both partisan and cowardly. "But a few months ago," said Thurman, of Ohio,

Many of them [the Whigs] professed to be unacquainted as to who Mr. Polk was. But so rapid had been their progress, that they had not only found out who he was, but they had ascertained that he was entitled to such confidence that they proposed to confer upon him what they argued was the war-making power.[64]

Andrew Johnson condemned southern men who had accepted the Baltimore platform and supported the candidate and who now refused to sustain the President; Strong, of New York, quoted the London *Examiner* as proof that England hoped to profit by a division in the Democratic party.

Had John Randolph been living at this time he would have beheld another alliance quite as strange as that between "puritan and blackleg,"[65] for the "puritan," Adams, now sided with the Oregon Democrats. He did not, he said, expect to add much to the argument, for in no debate had the subject been "more thoroughly and completely exhausted." He wished to have the convention of 1827 abrogated so that the United States might get *actual possession,* for "that is the only thing we now want, to have a perfect, clear, indisputable, and undoubted right to the

---

[64] When Polk was nominated, said Cathcart, of Indiana, the Whigs cried, "Who is James K. Polk?"; "and yet these immaculate apostles of consistency are willing to vote this tremendous power [the war power] into the hands of this very same James K. Polk!"

[65] On the alliance of Adams and Clay in 1824, see Schouler, *Hist. of the U. S.,* III, 367.

territory of Oregon.'' The government should therefore give notice to England, and occupy the territory. In his *Memoirs,* Adams makes the interesting statement that neither Monroe nor he, when President, really intended to divide the territory with Great Britain:

This offer was formerly made under the impression that it would not be accepted, but that its effect would be to preserve the peace between the two countries, and postpone the issue of the controversy until the time should come when we should be able to maintain our claims by an appeal, if necessary, to arms.[66]

His independence and his want of sympathy with the attitude of his political associates is manifested in his remarks concerning a conversation held with Representative Moseley, of New York:

He is a member of the Whig party, the policy of which among the people appears to be concentrating itself upon a system of opposition to the present Administration on the ground of its propensity to war with Great Britain. Dangers of war, and a very contemptuous estimate of the object for which they suppose the President is provoking it, are the only theme upon which they dwell, without sufficiently considering that their terrors and prognostics may furnish to Mr. Polk motives and pretexts for yielding to the pretensions of our adversary, and sacrificing our own just claims to the territory in dispute, of which I think there is much greater danger than of a war for the maintenance of them.[67]

The President's adversaries were unable to agree concerning the most effective method of opposing his Oregon policy. Insurgent Democrats, as a rule, argued against abrogating the British convention because, as they said, war would result. Some of the Whigs offered similar arguments; others, as we have seen, were willing to invest Polk with power to abrogate the convention, and to make him responsible for the consequences. Tooms, of Georgia, Campbell, of New York, Ewing, of Tennessee, as well as others, did not regard the American title to be ''unquestionable'' except to the Columbia River valley; they were ready,

---

[66] Adams, *Memoirs*, XII, 221.
[67] *Ibid.*, 226.

therefore, to agree upon the forty-ninth parallel. King, of Georgia, wished to settle the question by arbitration, while Davis, of Mississippi, like Calhoun, advocated "masterly inactivity." He thought that Polk was in need of being saved from his friends; if the title to Oregon was as "perfect" as the President claimed, it was dishonorable for him and his predecessors to have offered to compromise with Great Britain.

On February 9, 1846, the Committee of the Whole ceased debating and prepared to vote on the bill as reported from the Committee of Foreign Affairs. Numerous amendments were offered,[68] but few modifications were permitted. After much wrangling the House resolved by a vote of one hundred sixty-three to fifty-four that the President "cause notice to be given" to Great Britain that the convention of 1827 would be abrogated at the end of twelve months. A second paragraph explained that such action was not intended to preclude further "negotiations for an amicable settlement." In this form the resolution was sent to the Senate for its approval.

The House resolution reached the Senate on the tenth but instead of giving it immediate consideration, that body continued to debate various joint resolutions which had been proposed by its own members. Among these was one that had been offered by Crittenden, on January 26, and this, with slight modifications, was the one finally adopted as an amendment to the House resolution. Before its adoption, however, the Senate indulged in a prolonged and acrimonious debate.

The question of abrogating the convention of 1827 was discussed from every possible angle, and yet very little new light was contributed by either the friends or the opponents of the administration. Although not a political supporter of the President, Clayton, of Delaware, was willing to trust Polk's judgment

---

[68] For example, as to whether Polk should be requested, required, or left to his discretion, with respect to giving notice to England. Some wanted a long preamble, others, provision for further negotiation (*Cong. Globe,* 29 Cong., 1 sess., 345–350).

in the matter of giving notice. He expressed the belief that war would not result from abrogation of the convention, and quoted the Manchester *Guardian* to show that the British were in favor of such action.[69] Relying with the utmost confidence on Polk's "honesty, integrity, and firmness," Colquitt, of Georgia, was ready to follow the recommendations made in the President's message, for

It has been very properly said that no message that ever emanated from a President of the United States has met with more general approbation on the part of the people than the one to which I now allude. It is able, dignified, and peaceful. All that he has said and all that he has done, and all that he has offered to do, has met a favorable response from the public.

Colquitt did not believe, however, that the American title was so clear as to preclude further negotiation, and he was confident that Polk would not reject a reasonable offer to settle the dispute. In the course of his remarks Colquitt twitted Hannegan, of Indiana, with having been indifferent to the acquisition of Texas. "Both Texas and Oregon," replied Hannegan, "were united in the Baltimore convention. But I dreaded—if Texas went first— I dreaded Punic faith. Yes, Punic faith."[70] Others besides Hannegan accused southern members with having declined, for sectional reasons, to support the President's Oregon policy, but for the most part these accusations seem to have been groundless.

One of the most exhaustive speeches in support of Polk's policy was delivered by John A. Dix, of New York. He did not

---

[69] "With respect to the notice for terminating the joint occupation of Oregon," said the *Guardian*, "we are not sure that President Polk *may not receive it from the English Government before he can possibly be in a condition to give it himself.* But whether given by the one side or the other, we do not conceive that it will add materially, if at all, to the chance of a hostile collision."

[70] "Texas and Oregon," said Hannegan on December 30, 1845, "were born the same instant, nursed and cradled in the same cradle—the Baltimore convention—and they were at the same instant adopted by the democracy throughout the land. There was not a moment's hesitation, until Texas was admitted; but the moment she was admitted, the peculiar friends of Texas turned, and were doing what they could to strangle Oregon!"

agree with Allen's assertion that the time for discussing the title
"had gone by," nor with Clayton's contention that "it had not
yet arrived." His argument in support of the American claim
was so thorough and conclusive that Benton, who followed him,
declared that "He [Dix] has left nothing for me to say on the
point of title, familiar as I have been with that subject for thirty
years."[71] The exhaustive character of Dix's speech may have
been sufficient reason for Benton's eschewing the subject of title
himself, but a better reason, perhaps, was his own real belief,
as he had already informed the President, that England held a
valid title to Frazer's River valley. Dix had relieved him from
the necessity of dwelling on this subject, and had left him free
to employ more general terms in his defense of the administration. Whatever his mental reservations may have been, he supported Polk's Oregon policy with enthusiasm, the first fruit of the
recent reconciliation. "I concur with the President," said he,
"in what he has done—both in what he has offered—in what he
has rejected—and in what he has recommended to Congress to
do." In his opinion, the policy pursued had produced a good
effect both at home and abroad, had removed misapprehensions,
and created a feeling favorable to friendly negotiation. He had
no fear of war, for both governments were in good humor and
desirous of peace.

To Webster, Polk's Oregon policy was a riddle which baffled
solution. He desired to know what the President intended to do,
for he did not act like a man who expected a war:

There is nothing in his recommendations to the other House, nor to this,
indicative of such an expectation. There is nothing of preparation for
defense, indicating that the President expects war. Well, then, he can

---

71 "He has placed the American title to the Columbia," Benton continued, "and to the coast north of it, on ground from which it can never
be removed, and which must put an end to the argument wherever that
speech is read. A speech more perfect in its proofs—better sustained by
history—more crowded with material pertinent to the issue—more satisfactory to all lovers of truth and justice—more judiciously conceived and
victoriously executed, I have never heard delivered."

expect nothing but a continuance of this dispute, or its settlement by negotiation. I am bound to suppose that he expects its settlement by negotiation. What terms of negotiation? What basis of negotiation? What
grounds of negotiation? Everything that we hear from the Executive department is "the whole or none"; and yet negotiate! Sir, it is vain to
conceal from ourselves, from the country, or from the world, the gross inconsistency of this course of conduct. It is the spirit of that correspondence
[Buchanan's] to which my honorable friend has alluded, that the whole of
Oregon is ours, and that nothing can be done which admits the existence of
a doubt as to our right to the whole, or the possibility of a right existing
in another; and yet we are to negotiate! Pray, what is negotiation? Does
the Administration expect that, by negotiation, it can persuade the British
Government to surrender the whole territory to us? Is that its expectation? It may do that. I cannot say it will not. If that is the expectation
of our Government, why then, of course, it will try its hand at it. I wish
it success! That is to say, I wish the country could be rid of the dispute.
Take the whole of Oregon, if you can get it; but, at all events, settle the
question between the two countries fairly and reasonably. But I say I
do not understand the position in which the Executive government has
placed itself; in favor of negotiation all the time; but all the time refusing to take anything less than the whole! What consideration—what compromise—what basis—what grounds, therefore, for negotiation? If the
Government of the United States has made up its mind—I speak of the
Executive government—that, so far as it is concerned, it will not treat for
anything less than the whole of Oregon, then it should say so, and throw
itself on the two houses of Congress and on the country. It should say so.

He promised to support the administration in maintaining
the rights of the United States, but insisted upon knowing
whether the President intended to negotiate or to make war. In
his own opinion, the latter course would be very unwise—the
question should be adjusted by a compromise.[72]

---

[72] "The speech of Mr. Webster, Mr. Calhoun, and others in the Senate
advocating peace and the Brittish title to a large portion of the country,"
wrote the President some weeks later, "have made the Brittish Government & people more arrogant in their tone and more grasping in their
demands. If war should be the result, these peace gentlemen & advocates
of Brittish pretensions over those of their own country will have done
more to produce it than any others" (Polk, *Diary*, I, 345). Webster had
denounced the war spirit as early as November 7, 1845, in a speech in
Faneuil Hall: "The man who shall incautiously, or led on by false ambition or party pride, kindle those fires of war over the globe on this
[Oregon] question, must look out for it—must expect himself to be consumed in a burning conflagration of general reproach" (Curtis, *Life of
Webster*, II, 258).

Polk told Benton that he had endeavored to write his message "in plain English, & thought no part of it could be misunderstood."[73]   Nevertheless, members of Congress seemed to find it ambiguous, and Webster's remarks caused another attempt to fathom its meaning. Colquitt was certain that the President did not mean to insist absolutely on procuring the whole of Oregon. Allen was equally certain that Polk would accept nothing less, since Great Britain had rejected the offer he had made. When asked by Reverdy Johnson, however, whether his assertions had been authorized by the President, Allen had to admit that he possessed no information except that contained in the official message. When making his declaration, Allen knowingly misrepresented the President. In fact Allen himself had, on December 24, 1845, advised Polk, in case England should offer to compromise on the forty-ninth parallel, to submit the offer confidentially to the Senate before acting upon it. Polk "agreed in the propriety of the course he advised," but did not authorize Allen to speak for him.[74] Haywood, a Democrat from North Carolina, although willing to accept 49°, wished to intrust the whole question to Polk, for he would not

do the President so much wrong as to suppose that, if we passed the notice, and thus put into his hand a great moral weapon, that he could be guilty of so miserable a trick as to use it to the dishonor of his country on the one hand, or the reckless provocation of war on the other.[75]

Reverdy Johnson thought that the President was bound to accept the forty-ninth parallel, if offered by England. " 'Who is James K. Polk?' was a question once asked. We all know now who he is, though there are some who do not know what he is." He is President of the United States, said Johnson, and if he had felt bound by the offers made by his predecessors, certainly he could not reject an offer once made by himself. Atchison, of Missouri,

---

[73] Polk, *Diary*, I, 117.

[74] *Ibid.*, 139.

[75] Like Allen, Haywood had not been authorized to speak for the President (*ibid.*, 262).

was unable to see how his colleagues could discern *compromise* in the President's declarations. Polk had accepted the Baltimore platform, and both his inauguaral and his message had claimed all of the territory: ''The very moment he gave up any portion of Oregon, every honest man would condemn it.''[76]

The debate in the Senate on the question of giving notice to England continued until the middle of April. Many of the Whigs and a few of the Democrats opposed the joint resolution,[77] but Democrats, generally, rallied to its support. The advocates of the resolution still differed in opinion as to the result of abrogating the convention; some argued that such action would lead

---

[76] W. C. Rives, of Virginia, believed that Polk and his supporters in Congress were simply playing politics: ''Surely, such a spectacle was never exhibited before in any country as is now presented in ours. Every conciliatory advance of the British government unceremoniously repelled—the most extreme claims urged on our side—a tone of menace & disdain freely indulged by the chosen champions of the administration in both Houses—everything done which could apparently provoke a *war*—and yet I learn a settled purpose to accept any compromise that can be obtained! The minds of the whole nation kept in constant & painful anxiety & all its business operations deranged, to enable a knot of small politicians to play brag for the retention of public office, & to acquire credit, with a people whom they hope thus to delude, for superior patriotism, spirit & valour! It is impossible to speak with patience, of such low & despicable manoevering, even if it can be carried on without committing the peace of the country. But the game is a most *hazardous* one, & Mr. Polk may yet find he has not the skill to play it out'' (Rives to McLean, Feb. 18, 1846, *McLean Papers*). Tooms, of Georgia, likewise charged the President with insincerity: ''I do not think a war in the least probable. Mr. Polk never dreamed of any other war than a war upon the Whigs. He is playing a low grog-shop politician's trick, nothing more. He would be as much surprised and astonished and frightened at getting into war with England as if the Devil were to rise up before him at his bidding. . . . His party were already committed to him to 54° 40', they would stand by him, and he expected finally to be forced by the British Whigs and Southern Calhoun men to compromise; but he greatly hoped that he would not be forced even to this alternative until he had 'all Oregon' on every Democratic banner in the Union for his 'second heat.' I have not the least doubt but that he fully calculated that the 'notice' would be rejected by a combination between the Whigs and Calhoun men of this Congress, and then he could have kept it open for a new presidential campaign'' (Tooms to G. W. Crawford, Feb. 6, 1846, in *Rep. Am. Hist. Assn.*, 1911, II, 73–74).

[77] ''Most of the Whigs in the Senate incline to remain rather quiet, and to follow the lead of Mr. Calhoun. He is at the head of a party of six or seven, and as he professes still to be an administration man, it is best to leave the work in his hands, at least for the present'' (Webster to Sears, Jan. 17, 1846, in Webster, *Private Corr.*, II, 215).

to compromise and settlement, others, that the sequel would be occupation of the entire territory. No agreement could be reached as to what the President would do if the resolution should pass, and nothing came from the "Executive Mansion" to aid in solving the mystery. "Was there ever such a case known," exclaimed Mangum, of North Carolina, "as an Executive without an organ of his views and opinions in either House of Congress?"—the *Union* had definitely stated that no one could speak for him; "that no man, beyond his Cabinet, knew his views." It had not been so in Jackson's time, said Mangum, and it would not be so now if Clay, Benton, or Calhoun were at the head of the government. "The present Administration," he continued, was "remarkable chiefly for one thing in the management of this question, and that was, its secretiveness."[78] In answer to Mangum, Cass so far lifted the veil as to disclose that both Polk and Buchanan had given their approval, in advance, to his [Cass's] resolutions which called upon the army and navy departments for information regarding the defensive strength of the country. As to Polk's intentions for the future, however, Cass had nothing to impart. In the opinion of the President himself the debate had

taken a strange direction; that instead of examining and discussing my views as communicated in these documents [message and correspondence], Senators had been guessing and conjecturing what I might do hereafter, and were approving or condemning what they supposed I might or might not do.[79]

---

[78] A few days before, March 30, Barrow, of Louisiana, said: "There never before had been a period when some one in the Senate was not authorized to speak for the Executive, acquainted with his views, and ready to put those right who misconstrued his language or his views."

[79] Polk, *Diary*, I, 285–286. In a letter written a little later Crittenden said: "Bitter dissensions are already manifested among our opponents; they are about equally divided in the Senate. They quarrel about what the President's sentiments and purposes are in relation to Oregon,—each interprets the 'oracle' to suit himself, and each pretends to speak for him, while all are suspicious and jealous of him and of each other. They know that one side or the other is cheated and to be cheated, but they can't yet exactly tell which. In the mean time they curse Polk hypothetically. If he don't settle and make peace at forty-nine or some other parallel of compromise, the one side curses him; and if he yields an inch or stops a

After the Senate had discussed its own resolution for more than two months, Allen who had originally reported it from his committee moved, on April 16, that it be sent to the table and that the Senate proceed to consider the resolution which had been passed by the House on the ninth of February. The motion was carried, and Reverdy Johnson at once offered an amendment to the House resolution. It was almost an exact replica of the Crittenden proposal which, along with other amendments to the Allen resolution, had just been laid on the table. After some discussion, and attempts to alter it, the Johnson amendment was passed by a vote of 30 to 24. The resolution as passed by the House had directed the President to notify England that the convention would be abrogated; as amended by the Senate, Polk was "authorized, at his discretion" to give such notice. After the amendment had been passed, but before the whole resolution, as amended, had reached a vote, Allen bitterly assailed the modification made by the Senate and announced his intention to vote against the measure. The preamble, he said, advised negotiation, while the main clause left the question of notice to the discretion of the President: "they throw the whole subject back to the President, to be managed in future according to his discretion, after having condemned him for a want of discretion in his past management." The measure was passed by a vote of 40 to 14. The effect of attaching this amendment to the House resolution may not, as Allen asserted, have been to array each house against the other, and both against the President; but the affirmative vote on the preamble must have made it clear to Polk that the Senate would ratify a compromise treaty and that, in all probability, it would not coöperate with him in an aggressive Oregon policy. Undoubtedly this action of the Senate had some influence in modifying his diplomatic program.

---

hair's breadth short of fifty-four degrees forty miuntes, the other side damns him without redemption. Was ever a gentleman in such a fix? 'He might almost say like Satan, that 'hell was around him' '' (Crittenden to Letcher, March 9, 1846, in Coleman, *Life of John J. Crittenden*, 235).

On April 18 the House proceeded to consider the joint resolution as amended by the Senate. After adopting an amendment offered by Owen, of Indiana, by which the President was "authorized and requested" to serve notice upon Great Britain, the measure was passed by a vote of 144 to 40. Two days later the House received notice that the Senate had rejected the Owen amendment and had adhered to its own. A conference was then arranged. Slight modifications were made in the Senate preamble, but the main part of the resolution was left unchanged. In the final form the President was "authorized, at his discretion" to give the notice, and, by a vote of 142 to 46, the resolution was passed by the House on the twenty-third of April.[80] The President regretted that action had been so long delayed and that the preamble had been prefixed by the Senate; but "after all," he added philosophically, "Congress by authorizing the notice, have sustained the first great measure of my administration, though not in a form that is altogether satisfactory or one that was preferred."[81] He decided at once to transmit the notice directly to the British government instead of giving it to Pakenham.

---

[80] The Van Buren Democrats supported the administration by their votes, although some of them did so reluctantly. Undoubtedly C. C. Cambreleng voiced the sentiments of many of them when he wrote: "Heaven forgive me for having had any hand in laying the foundation of this blundering administration. Tyler was bad enough but he had this advantage—there was no mock-mystery nor genuine duplicity in his conduct—if he betrayed his friends he was an honest knave, without any hypocritical cant about the sabbath &c &c. But apart from that I am utterly astonished at the little judgment and less integrity which has distinguished the course of this administration. First as it regards England—when some three or four months ago she was making war-like preparations—McLane was instructed to inquire of Aberdeen whether these preparations were intended for us—and now it appears that before that enquiry was made, Bancroft was 'confidentially' recommending ten war steamers—the Bureaus forty war steamers and Marcy fifty thousand volunteers with the knowledge and approbation of the President! . . . How uncandid and dishonorable must the conduct of the President and his prime minister appear in the eyes of all honest men" (Cambreleng to Van Buren, May 16, 1846, *Van Buren Papers*).

[81] Polk, *Diary*, I, 348.

While the resolution for giving notice to England was under discussion attempts were made by both friends and opponents of the measure to induce the President to alter or to supplement the views expressed in his annual message. Opponents of the resolution wished him to commit himself to compromise; its friends, on the contrary, desired additional pledges that he would insist upon the whole of Oregon.

The first to approach him was James A. Black, a South Carolina member of the House and a personal friend of Calhoun. Calhoun was much opposed to the resolution, and his friends had endeavored to effect a compromise with certain western Senators who were its chief advocates. Black visited Polk on January 4, 1846, and told him that he had just held a conversation with Senators Semple, of Illinois, and Atchison, of Missouri. He thought they would agree not to press the notice resolution if the South would unite with the West in supporting the other measures recommended in Polk's message, including that for granting lands to Oregon settlers. He therefore asked the President to induce his western friends to postpone action on the resolution. Polk declined to follow Black's suggestion, for, as he said, his mind had not changed since he had recommended that notice should be given. "I remarked to him," he noted in his diary,

that the only way to treat John Bull was to look him straight in the eye; that I considered a bold & firm course on our part the pacific one; that if Congress faultered or hesitated in their course, John Bull would immediately become arrogant and more grasping in his demands.[82]

The advocates of notice and 54° 40′ were quite as unsuccessful in their efforts to commit the President to a definite future policy. As representatives of a caucus of Senate Democrats, Hannegan and Atchison interviewed Polk on the seventh of March and put the direct question whether he would insist upon 54° 40′, or, if necessary, compromise on 49°. "I answered him [Hannegan]," Polk recorded,

[82] *Ibid.*, 154–155.

that I would answer no man what I would do in the future; that for what
I might do I would be responsible to God and my country and if I should
hereafter do anything which should be disapproved by himself or others,
it would be time enough to condemn me. . . . . . I said, I am charged
with the Foreign relations of the country, and it was unheard of that
the President should declare in advance to any one out of his Cabinet
his intentions in reference to them.[83]

Although the President declined, at all times, to commit himself as to his future course, he was careful, on the other hand, to
leave the way open for possible concessions. On several occasions
he informed both extremists and compromisers that if England
should offer the forty-ninth parallel as a boundary he might,
before acting, submit the question to the Senate. He was careful,
also, to let both factions know that no member of Congress had
been authorized to speak for him, and that the policy outlined
in his annual message would remain unchanged unless modified
by a future official communication.[84]

The want of harmony among Democrats in the Senate was
highly displeasing to the President, and the more so because he
attributed it to personal ambition rather than to honest difference
of opinion. ''The truth is,'' he wrote, on April 22, 1846,

that in all this Oregon discussion in the Senate, too many Democratic
Senators have been more concerned about the Presidential election in '48
than they have been about settling Oregon either at 49° or 54° 40'.
''Forty-eight'' has been with them the Great question, and hence the
division in the Democratic party. I cannot but observe the fact, and for
the sake of the country I deplore it. I will however do my duty whatever may happen. I will rise above the interested factions in Congress,
and appeal confidently to the people for support.[85]

---

[84] *Ibid.*, 262–263 and *passim.*

[83] *Ibid.*, 273.

[85] Polk, *Diary*, I, 345. On March 9 he had observed: ''This whole
excitement in the Senate has grown out of the aspirations of Senators and
their friends for the Presidency. Mr. Allen has such aspirations himself.
Mr. Haywood probably prefers Gov. Wright of N. York. Gen'l Cass has
aspirations but is more prudent than some others. Mr. Calhoun has aspirations. My fear is that these factions looking to the election of my
successor in 1848, will so divide and weaken the Democratic party by their
feuds as to defeat my measures and render my administration unsuccessful
and useless. Each one of the factions doubtless desire[s] to use the

Although the joint resolution in its final form was not, as we have seen, entirely satisfactory to the President, he accepted it as preferable to no action at all.[86] He had two reasons for desiring some action on the part of Congress, even though details might be unsatisfactory. He suspected that a majority in the Senate would gladly see notice in any form defeated and would therefore effect their purpose if the House would decline to yield. He believed, also, that Great Britain would not make another offer until Congress had taken final action, and evidently he was confident that the serving of notice would induce such an offer. Consequently when the fate of the joint resolution was hanging in the balance, he and members of the cabinet sought interviews with their friends in the House, and apparently it was due to their influence that that body consented to accept the Senate amendment.[87]

While the question was still undecided, no one perused the published correspondence with more care nor followed the debates with more interest than the veteran diplomat, Albert Gallatin. Having negotiated the conventions of "joint occupation," he naturally took an interest in their abrogation, and he now prepared a series of articles in which he considered both the validity of the respective titles and the expediency of abrogating the conventions. He was not in favor of giving immediate notice to Great Britain, for, "in the present state of excitement, an immediate amicable arrangement is almost hopeless." In his opinion,

---

administration for their own advancement, and out of this circumstance has grown the excitement & unfortunate collision in the Senate. They will all be disappointed. I am not a candidate for re-election myself and will lend myself to none of them. I will not be identified with any of them. I will do my duty to the country & if my measures fail the responsibility shall rest where it belongs." He also attributed Buchanan's recent war-like attitude to a desire to supplant Cass in the good graces of the extremists (*ibid.*, 280, 297).

[86] While the Senate amendment was before the House, he told Cullom, of Tennessee, that: "I would have preferred a naked notice; that next to that I preferred the House Resolutions; but it being now ascertained by repeated votes in the Senate that neither could be had, I decidedly preferred the Senate form of notice to no notice at all" (*Diary*, I, 341).

[87] Polk, *Diary*, I, 334–337.

the first and indispensable step towards an amicable arrangement consists in the investigation, not so much of the superiority of one claim over the other, as of the question whether there be sufficient grounds to sustain the exclusive pretensions of either Governmnet.

This was substantially the policy advocated by Lord Aberdeen.

Unlike J. Q. Adams, Gallatin did not believe that either nation possessed an exclusive title to the Oregon territory; therefore, both might recede from their extreme pretensions "without impairing national honor and dignity." Clear title for the United States must, in his opinion, be based on the claims derived from Spain, and he did not regard the Spanish title as unquestionably complete. He did not, however, accept Pakenham's contention that the claim which the United States based on the Spanish title and that based on settlements made by American citizens were mutually exclusive. Believing that the President, in view of the policy outlined in his message, would be bound to assert title to the whole of Oregon, should the convention be abrogated, he was in favor of withholding the notice and of dividing the territory by negotiation.[88]

On April 13, when it seemed probable that the resolution for giving notice to England would pass, the House, in Committee of the Whole, gave its attention to the bill, which Douglas had reported in December, for extending judicial and military protection to American citizens in Oregon. Among other things this measure proposed to extend to Oregon the jurisdiction of the Iowa supreme court, to build forts, to make grants of land to settlers, and to establish a mail route between Saint Joseph, Missouri, and the mouth of the Columbia River. The debate was not prolonged, and the alignment of advocates and opponents was much the same as it had been when the resolution concerning notice was under discussion. There was difference of opinion among those who favored the bill as to whether jurisdiction should be extended to the whole territory or to the southern

---

[88] Gallatin, *The Oregon Question*, 1–33, *passim*.

part only. Adams once more championed the American title to the whole of Oregon and, in defense of his consistency, called attention to the fact that he, in the Florida treaty, had procured the Spanish claims to that region. When asked if the relinquishment of Texas by the United States had not been "a consideration" in procuring these Spanish claims, he replied emphatically that "it was no consideration at all"—that the two territories had in no way been associated in the Florida negotiations. Douglas, the chief spokesman for the bill, advocated extending jurisdiction without designating boundary limits as the better way of procuring the desired effect with the least annoyance to Great Britain. He desired to have it understood, however, that he was not in favor of yielding an inch of territory south of 54° 40', for any administration, present or future, which would consent to relinquish any portion of Oregon would be guilty of "perfidy." As already noted, such comments from Douglas and other ardent supporters of the administration seem to indicate that Polk's most intimate friends did not believe that he would consent to a compromise. Surely they could not have intended to brand him in advance as a man about to commit an act of "perfidy" and "treachery."

After certain amendments had been added, one of which extended the jurisdiction of the Iowa courts to "all that portion of the territory of the United States which lies west of the Rocky Mountains," without defining limits, the House, on April 18, passed the bill and sent it to the Senate for its concurrence.

The Senate Committee on Territories disapproved the House bill. On May 21 its chairman reported that, since a majority deemed immediate legislation on the subject to be inexpedient the committee desired to be discharged from further consideration of the bill.

During the debate which followed the presentation of this report Benton expressed his real views on the American title to Oregon, a subject which he had avoided when discussing the resolution for giving notice to Great Britain. Oregon, he said, included three main divisions: the islands, Frazer's River valley, and the Columbia River valley. To the last only did the United States possess a clear title. He therefore moved to recommit the House bill to the committee and that it should be instructed to offer the following amendments: (1) to extend the laws of the United States over the territory to the same extent that England had extended hers; (2) the bill to become effective at the termination of the convention; (3) certain provisions for the administration of justice and for fortifications; (4) the boundaries to be settled by treaty, but until this had been done the line of 49° should be regarded as the northern limit of American territory. Cass assailed Benton's arguments and his proposed instructions, and, on Crittenden's suggestion, the latter were withdrawn. Within two weeks further action by Congress was made unnecessary by the conclusion of the Oregon treaty which divided the territory between the two nations.

As the President had anticipated, the passage of the joint resolution for abrogating the convention of 1827 was soon followed by a new overture from the British government. A dispatch from McLane arrived on June 3, 1846, and gave the substance of a proposition which Lord Aberdeen had said would soon be made to the United States by Pakenham. The proposition, as outlined by McLane, was so unsatisfactory that Polk was "certain" that it must be rejected.[89] However, when the subject was brought before the cabinet on the following day, all members present were inclined to think that the project ought to be submitted to the Senate for advice. The most objectionable feature of the British proposal was a stipulation which guaranteed free navigation of the Columbia River to the Hudson's Bay Company. Buchanan suggested that this privilege might

---

[89] "If I reject it absolutely and make no other proposition the probable result will be war. If I submit it to the Senate and they should advise its acceptance I should be bound by their advice yet I should do so reluctantly" (*Diary*, I, 444–445).

be limited to the duration of the company's existing charter, which would expire in 1859.[90]

When the cabinet met again, on June 6, Buchanan laid before it the formal proposition of the British government, which had arrived in the meantime and been delivered to him by Pakenham. It proposed to divide Oregon by the forty-ninth parallel from the Rocky Mountains to the Straits of Fuca, thence through the main channel to the sea. Two reservations were stipulated: first, the Hudson's Bay Company and actual British occupants were to retain title to their lands lying south of 49°, but subject to the jurisdiction of the United States; second, free use of the Columbia was retained for the Hudson's Bay Company and for British subjects when trading with that company. The question was raised as to whether, according to the proposal submitted, the privilege of navigation to be accorded to the Hudson's Bay Company would cease at the expiration of its existing charter in 1859. Without waiting to decide this question, the President asked the cabinet whether he should submit the offer, as received, to the Senate with a request for its advice. Walker, Marcy, Bancroft, and Johnson advised him to submit the offer to the Senate. Buchanan, who had recently assumed a belligerent attitude, said that his opinion would depend upon the character of the message which would accompany the document. "He said the 54° 40' men were the true friends of the administration and he wished no backing out on the subject." Although nettled by this poniard-thrust about "backing out" the President suppressed his feelings and even prevented Walker from openly resenting the insinuation. He told the cabinet that in case he should decide to submit the British offer to the Senate, he would reiterate the views already expressed in his annual message. Should the Senate advise its acceptance, with or without modifications, he would follow the advice; "but if they declined to express an opinion, or by the constitutional majority to give their advice, I

---

[90] Polk, *Diary*, I, 447–448.

should reject the proposition.'' After hearing this, Buchanan advised that the proposal be submitted to the Senate, but he declined to prepare a message embodying the President's views.[91]

The ill feeling caused by Buchanan's attitude continued for several days. Other members of the cabinet freely criticized his conduct and recalled that he had repeatedly advocated the renewal of the compromise offer. After a conversation on the subject with Marcy and Bancroft, the President wrote:

> My impression is that Mr. Buchanan intends now to shun all responsibility for the submission of the Brittish proposition to the Senate, but still he may wish it to be done without his agency, so that if the 54° 40' men complain, he may be able to say that my message submitting it did not receive his sanction. I shall be disappointed if any message which can be drawn will receive his assent. He will choose to dissent and if it is condemned he will escape all responsibility. In his despatches to Mr. McLane I have more than once, & in the presence of the Cabinet, caused paragraphs to be struck out yielding as I thought too much to Great Brittain, and now it is most strange that he should take suddenly, and without the assignment of any reason, the opposite extreme, and talk as he did yesterday of ''backing out from 54° 40'.'' His course is one which I cannot approve. Mr. Marcy and Mr. Bancroft both condemned it in decided terms.[92]

Buchanan called on the following day and expressed doubts concerning the wisdom of submitting to the Senate the correspondence which passed between McLane and himself on the Oregon question. Although he surmised that these doubts had been prompted by the Secretary's fear that his inconsistency might be exposed, Polk permitted him ''to select what portions of the correspondence, if any, should be sent.'' His indulgence was rewarded by renewed insolence, for Buchanan not only refused once more to draft a message for the President, but he had the

---

[91] *Ibid.*, 451–454. Polk attributed Buchanan's change of front to a desire to curry favor with the extremists. ''It was not until within a short time since that he gave indications of a change of position. The first indication I had of it was a remark which fell from him incidentally when speaking of the subject, to the purport that Gen'l Cass had made character by his course in the Senate on the subject. Gen'l C. was a 54° 40' man.''

[92] *Ibid.*, 456.

audacity to remark that "when you have done your message I will then prepare such a one as I think ought to be sent in." At last thoroughly aroused by the insolence of his Secretary, the President indignantly asked:

For what purpose will you prepare a message? You have twice refused, though it is a subject relating to your Department, to give me any aid in preparing my message; do you wish, after I have done, to draw up a paper of your own in order to make an issue with me?

Buchanan at once resumed his normal state of timidity and explained that his remark had been entirely misunderstood. Nevertheless, when Polk submitted his message to the cabinet for discussion, the Secretary of State raised so many objections that some of the passages were eliminated.[93]

On June 10 the President transmitted the British proposal to the Senate and, in an accompanying message, requested advice as to whether it should be accepted. He made it clear that his own opinions, as expressed in his annual message, remained unchanged, and that he would reject the offer unless the Senate by a "constitutional majority" should recommend its acceptance. After two days of deliberation the Senate, by a vote of 38 to 12, advised him to accept the proposal, and on the fifteenth Buchanan and Pakenham signed the treaty which terminated the long-debated Oregon question.[94] As shown by the vote, not many of the extremists were ready to risk a war by rejecting the British overture. Most uncompromising of all was Allen, chairman of the Committee on Foreign Affairs. On the day that the treaty was signed, after a free expression of his feelings, he resigned from the committee.

---

[93] *Ibid.*, 459–462.

[94] Richardson, *Messages*, IV, 449–450. Polk, *Diary*, I, 467, 470. The treaty may be found in Malloy, *Treaties and Conventions*, I, 656. It fixed the boundary at 49°, from the Rocky Mountains to the Straits of Fuca, leaving all of Vancouver's Island to England; the Hudson's Bay Company retained the use of the Columbia River on the same footing as citizens of the United States; that company and British occupants retained title to land already possessed south of 49°.

The adjustment of the Oregon question by an extension of the existing boundary between the United States and Canada was eminently fair to both nations. Indeed it was the only sensible solution of the long-standing dispute. The more one examines the respective claims the more apparent it becomes that neither party possessed a "clear and unquestionable" title to the entire territory. Was, therefore, President Polk justified in asserting claim to "all of Oregon," and if so, must be he condemned for accepting less? Neither query can be answered by an unqualified yes or no. Whether wise or unwise, whether designed or controlled by circumstances, Polk's Oregon policy was not so inconsistent as his opponents represented it to be. He offered to divide the territory, and when this offer was declined he steadfastly refused to make another offer of any kind. While he continued to assert that the American title to the whole territory was "clear and unquestionable," at no time did he say that he would decline a compromise, if offered by England. On the contrary, he told both supporters and opponents in Congress that if England should offer 49°, or anything approaching it, he would seek the advice of the Senate before rejecting the proposal. As Webster said in the Senate, Polk did not at any time act like a man who expected war, and the President told Black that he "considered a bold & firm course on our part the pacific one." He stated repeatedly that he did not look for an offer from England until Congress had passed the resolution terminating joint occupation, and, although he did not specifically say so, he inferred that its passage would undoubtedly be followed by an overture from that government. This opinion was well founded—the "bold and firm course" of abrogating the convention proved, indeed, to be the pacific one, for Great Britain very soon afterward made the offer to compromise.[95] Without loss of time, Polk did what he

[95] Commenting on the success of Polk's policy, Richard Rush wrote: "For one, I am unshaken in the belief, that it was the President's opening message to the first congress he met on the second of December last, that produced the settlement of the Oregon difficulty. It was like a great

had long promised to do; he submitted the proposal to the Senate, but with a warning that unless that body should advise its acceptance he would reject the offer and adhere to the party platform. It would have been unfair to expect the President to stand alone in demanding the full measure asked by that platform after the debates in Congress and the press had made it plain that neither Congress nor the people would approve his rejection of a reasonable offer. It was not cowardly to ascertain the wishes of the Senate on so important a question, and it would have been criminal to provoke a war for the sake of maintaining a campaign cry, when it was evident that neither Congress nor the people desired it to be maintained.

---

bomb-shell thrown into the British cabinet. It took them by surprise, and first roused them to the unavoidable necessity of a settlement. I thought when it appeared, that it would lead to war—so bold was it, though every word was just; whereas it led to peace'' (Rush to Trist, Sept. 21, 1846, *Trist Papers*).

CHAPTER XXII

SLAVERY AND TERRITORIAL GOVERNMENTS

Although a lawyer by profession, Polk owned slaves and employed them in cultivating his plantation in Mississippi. As a southern man he despised abolitionists, yet at no time during his career does he seem to have taken a deep interest in the slavery question—especially in the extension of the slaveholding area. Like Jackson, he desired to extend the boundaries of the United States and to increase its power and prestige, but neither man was interested in promoting the spread of slavery. In supporting the annexation of Texas and in planning the acquisition of other Mexican territory Polk acted as an expansionist, and not as a slaveholder.

As early as 1826, while a proposed amendment to the Constitution was being debated, remarks made in the House by members from New England led Polk to express his views on the slavery question:

I have regretted exceedingly, sir, that scarcely any subject of general concern can be agitated here, without having this unfortunate subject of slavery, either collaterally, or incidentally, brought into view, and made to mingle in our deliberations. . . . . When this country became free and independent, this species of population was found amongst us. It had been entailed upon us by our ancestors, and was viewed as a common evil; not confined to the locality where it was, but affecting the whole nation. Some of the States which then possessed it have since gotten clear of it: they were a species of property that differed from all other: they were rational; they were human beings.[1]

Fully admitting that the institution was an evil, he did not believe that this fact should affect the solution of great national questions.

---

[1] *Abridg. of Deb.*, IX, 16–17.

As Speaker of the House, Polk was called upon to decide many points in which the slavery question was involved. His task was simplified by the operation of the so-called gag rule under which nearly all petitions and memorials relating to the subject were referred automatically to the "committee of oblivion." As a party man, he rigorously enforced this rule, but in cases which did not clearly fall within its scope he did not seem disposed to support the extreme southern view. For example, when an attempt was made, on February 6, 1837, to prevent John Quincy Adams from presenting abolition petitions submitted by other states than Massachusetts, Speaker Polk decided that "every member had a right to present a petition, come from what quarter it might."[2] This decision ran counter to the well-known southern claim that while, under the Constitution, all citizens possessed the right to petition for a redress of their own grievances, they had no right to concern themselves about the grievances of others.

The Speaker's decision in favor of Adams was not induced by admiration for the ex-President or by approval of his conduct. In a manuscript to be found among his papers[3] Polk complained that Adams, by his petitions, "has consumed so much of the present session of Congress, to the delay of the public business, to the annoyance of the whole House, and the degredation of his own character." After asserting that it was necessary to have a general rule, since the House could not take time to consider each petition, he continued:

Mr. Adams was unwilling to submit to the decision of the majority. On every petition day, he made constant attempts to wreck that decision, to violate the rules, and defy the authority of the House. Upon the plainest propositions he would take appeals from the Speaker's decisions, and consume time in debating the appeal. . . . .

Mr. Adams knew . . . . that it was the duty of the Speaker to observe and execute the *rules* and *orders* adopted by the House for its government. . . . .

---

[2] *Cong. Globe*, 24 Cong., 2 sess., 164.

[3] "Notes on Mr. Adams' letter to the Quincy Patriot," undated, *Polk Papers*.

The Speaker carries out and enforces the decisions of the majority & therefore he represents in his letter that the ''Speaker and the majority of the House'' have undertaken to exercise ''arbitrary authority.'' If Mr. Adams is unwilling to submit to the decisions of the majority of the House, he is unfit to be a member of that body. He seems to have an utter aversion to decisions made by majorities. This principle lies at the foundation of all our institutions. Majorities must govern, and it cannot be helped if a few such refractory spirits as Mr. Adams are unwilling to submit to that Government.

The manuscript is of considerable value, for, as Polk was the presiding officer, his opinions on this important subject cannot be found in official records.

On one occasion during his term as governor of Tennessee, Polk was called upon to repel outside interference with the ''peculiar institution.'' In the summer of 1840 a ''World's Convention'' met in London to consider ways and means of abolishing slavery and the slave trade. Letters were addressed to officials in the United States, and, among others, to Governor Polk. In his last message to the legislature, October 7, 1841, the governor stated that he had received two such letters.

Viewing these communications [said he], as an impertinent and mischievous attempt on the part of foreigners to interfere with one of the domestic institutions of this State, and having received the countenance of a member of the Congress of the United States, under whose official frank one of the packages containing them came to me, I declined entering into a correspondence with a foreign convention, but addressed to the member of Congress alluded to the letter, a copy of which is herewith transmitted to you, accompanied by the communication.[4]

His answer asserted the right of a state to control its own affairs, but it was a vindication of state rights rather than a defense of slavery. In the words of a local editor, he

came boldly and manfully out before the country with a letter containing the sound doctrine of the Constitution of our Union, and rebuked the foreign interference with our State affairs in a spirit as becoming to the patriot and the man as it was honorable to the State over which he presided as Chief Magistrate.[5]

---

[4] *Tenn. Sen. Jour.*, 1841–42, 22–42.

[5] Nashville *Union*, April 15, 1841.

Agitation in favor of annexing Texas to the United States began as soon as that province had declared its independence in 1836. Although its principal supporters were southern men there is little evidence that they were moved by a desire to extend the institution of slavery.[6] When, however, Tyler turned his attention to the annexation of Texas, the question took on a more distinctly southern aspect; and Calhoun, in his correspondence as Secretary of State, brought slavery into prominence by distinctly asserting that the United States desired to annex Texas in order to protect that institution. When commenting on this correspondence, early in 1845, the *Democratic Review* declared that Calhoun, the apostle of state rights, had, in fact, *nationalized* the slavery question:

> What has become of this position [that the national government can not interfere with slavery in the District of Columbia] after a Southern President and a Southern Secretary of State—and that Secretary, John C. Calhoun, of all men living!—have so nationalized, so federalized, the question, as we have lately seen done? When that has been not only acted upon, but avowed, argued, vehemently urged—*that, and that almost exclusivley*—as the ground for a large and momentous measure of national policy![7]

In general, Calhoun's intimate friends were interested in Texas because they were interested in slavery. For example, Dixon H. Lewis deemed annexation to be "the greatest question of the Age" on account of the political power which it would bring to the South. "It will," he wrote, *"unite the hitherto divided South,* while it will make Abolition & Treason synonymous & thus destroy it in the North."[8] This feeling, however, was not shared by the Jackson Democrats.

When his views as a candidate for the Vice-Presidency were solicited, Polk declared himself to be unequivocally in favor of annexing Texas.[9] Neither his public utterances nor his private

---

[6] For a discussion of this whole subject, see Justin H. Smith, *Annexation of Texas.*

[7] *Dem. Rev.,* January, 1845, article on Abolitionists. The whole article is worth reading.

[8] Lewis to Crallé, March 19, 1844, *Crallé Papers.*

[9] Answer to S. P. Chase *et al.,* April 23, 1844, *Polk Papers.* Printed, also, in various newspapers.

letters indicate any interest in extending slavery; on the contrary, the correspondence with his most intimate friends shows a desire to avoid an affiliation with the southern wing of the party. It has been noted elsewhere that Polk's bosom friend, Cave Johnson, tried to induce Van Buren to declare himself in favor of annexation, and that Polk was anxious to coöperate with that wing of the party which was indifferent or hostile to slavery. After Polk's nomination, Johnson warned him repeatedly that the southern faction would try to claim and to control him. When issuing invitations to the Nashville ratification meeting, great care was taken to preclude any attempt to identify the candidate with the South Carolina radicals.[10]

Throughout the campaign of 1844 neither Polk nor his associates urged additional protection for the South, much less for slavery; nevertheless, both of these subjects, to a certain degree, became party issues. Some excitement was created by the appearance of a pamphlet entitled *"The South in Danger."* It was prepared by Robert J. Walker, chairman of the Democratic national committee, and its object was to show that Whigs and Abolitionists had united in the North and that all in the South should join in defeating them. It was published without Polk's knowledge and was deplored by his intimate friends.[11] Despite the fact that the candidate and his chief supporters were interested in territorial expansion rather than in slavery, his opponents undoubtedly believed with John Quincy Adams who, on hearing the result of the election, wrote: "It is the victory of the slavery element in the constitution of the United States."[12]

Having received notice that the Mexican government had agreed to renew diplomatic relations, President Polk, in August, 1846, asked Congress for an appropriation of two million dollars

---

[10] Johnson to Polk, June 21 and June 28, 1844, *Polk Papers*.

[11] W. E. Cramer to Polk, Oct. 4, 1844; Armstrong to Polk, Nov. 5, 1844, *ibid*. The Walker pamphlet was published by the "Democratic Association of Washington, D. C." and bore the date Sept. 25, 1844.

[12] Adams, *Memoirs*, XII, 103.

to be used in conducting negotiations. In making this request the President unwittingly precipitated an "irrepressible conflict" which ceased only with the end of the Civil War.

When he asked for this appropriation Polk had no thought of slavery. He desired to buy Mexican territory and he wished to be able to assure the Mexican government that he could pay an installment of the purchase price as soon as a treaty had been concluded. But when the subject came before the House the slavery question emerged, for Wilmot introduced his well-known "proviso" by which slavery would be excluded from all territory to be acquired by the use of the appropriation. After adopting what the President called Wilmot's "mischievous & foolish amendment," the House passed the bill by a vote of 87 to 64. The amended bill came before the Senate on the last day of the session, and, as Davis, of Massachusetts, obtained the floor and refused to yield it, no vote could be taken. Polk was astonished and chagrined by the unexpected turn of events. He blamed Wilmot for having introduced an irrelevant topic, but he blamed Davis still more for preventing the Senate from acting on the measure. "What connection slavery had with making peace with Mexico," is the remark in his diary, "it is difficult to conceive."[13] While this comment undoubtedly expressed the real attitude of the President, it has nevertheless been charged that his request for the money was "caused by the burning desire to acquire additional slave territory."[14]

On August 5, 1846, the day after the request for the two millions had been sent to the Senate, General Armstrong arrived from London bearing the ratified Oregon treaty. On the same day the President asked Congress to frame a territorial government and to adopt regulations for making land grants to settlers in that region. But the session was nearing its close, and Congress adjourned without having taken action on the subject.

---

[13] Polk, *Diary*, II, 75. He believed that, if permitted, the Senate would have eliminated the proviso and that the House would have acquiesced.

[14] Jay, *Review of the Mexican War*, 184.

When Congress reassembled in December, Polk renewed his request for a two million dollar appropriation. He renewed, also, his recommendation that Oregon should be provided with a territorial government.[15]

On December 23, in response to the latter recommendation, Douglas reported from the Committee on Territories a bill to establish a government in Oregon; it was read twice and referred to the Committee of the Whole. The twelfth section of this bill extended to Oregon both the privileges and the restrictions of the Ordinance of 1787, the most important *restriction*, of course, being the prohibition of slavery.

On the evening of the same day Wilmot called by appointment on the President, and the proviso which he had attached to the appropriation bill at the last session was the topic of conversation. Wilmot told the President that he would not again offer his proviso, but that he would have to vote for slavery restriction if it should be proposed by another member. In his record of this interview Polk thus stated his opinions on the slavery question:

> I told him I did not desire to extend slavery, that I would be satisfied to acquire by treaty from Mexico the Provinces of New Mexico & the Californias, and that in these Provinces slavery could probably never exist, and the great probability was that the question would never arise in the future organization of territorial or State Governments in these territories. I told him that slavery was purely a domestic question, and to restrict the appropriation which had been asked for, so as to require the President to insert it in a Treaty with a Foreign Power, was not only inappropriate and out of place, but if such a Treaty were made it must be opposed by every Senator from a slave-holding State, and as one third of the Senators could reject a Treaty, it could not be ratified, though it might be satisfactory in all other respects.

This argument, of course, overstated the effect of the Wilmot proviso, for no one had asked that it should be incorporated into the treaty. Wilmot answered that in any case he would be satisfied with a simple legislative declaration, and that he would not again take the initiative in asking for this.[16]

---

15 Richardson, *Messages*, IV, 495, 504.
16 Polk, *Diary*, II, 288–290.

In spite of Polk's effort to bury the slavery discussion by an agreement with Wilmot, the question of excluding the institution from territories was soon brought before the House. On January 4, 1847, Preston King, of New York, offered a bill to appropriate two million do'llars for diplomatic purposes the second section of which was virtually a restatement of the Wilmot proviso. King was not permitted to introduce this bill, and on February 1, when another bill for granting the President three million dollars came up for discussion in the House Wilmot, in spite of the promise made to Polk, moved to amend the bill by adding his anti-slavery proviso.[17] When informed of King's bill Polk noted in his diary:

> The slavvery question is assuming a fearful & most important aspect. The movement of Mr. King to-day, if persevered in, will be attended with terrible consequences to the country, and cannot fail to destroy the Democratic party, if it does not ultimately threaten the Union itself. [At the close of a cabinet meeting held on the following day, he again reverted to the subject.] Slavery has no possible connection with the Mexican War, and with making peace with that country. Should any territory be acquired by a Treaty with Mexico, Congress will have the full power to raise the question of slavery in it upon the organization of a territorial Government in it, or upon its admission as a state of the Union. Its introduction in connection with the Mexican War is not only mischievous but wicked. It is, moreover, practically an abstract question. There is no probability that any territory will ever be acquired from Mexico in which slavery could ever exist.

Buchanan expressed himself as willing to extend the Missouri Compromise line to the Pacific, and in this view all other members of the cabinet agreed. Polk declined to commit himself on this method of dealing with the subject, although urged to do so by both Buchanan and Walker. "Though willing myself," said he, "to assent to the proposition, I was not ready, until I saw further developments, to recommend it to Congress as the policy of the administration." On the same evening he presented the

---

[17] *Cong. Globe*, 29 Cong., 2 sess., 105, 303.

proposition to Benton in order to see if it would meet with his approval, but the Senator declined to give an immediate answer.[18]

While the President was not interested in the extension of slavery, he was, on the other hand, unable to appreciate the fact that there might be such a thing as honest opposition to the spread of that institution. Except as it affected party interests he seemed quite as indifferent toward the subject as Douglas was at a later date when he declared that he did not care whether slavery was "voted down or voted up." Polk attributed all agitation of the subject to the same cause that he attributed everything which thwarted his plans—a desire to promote the interests of candidates for the Presidency. Politicians of both parties and both sections were criticized for their unpatriotic conduct. Commenting on the delay in enacting war measures, he wrote in his diary:

Even the question of slavery is thrown into Congress and agitated in the midst of a Foreign War for political purposes. It is brought forward at the North by a few ultra Northern members to advance the prospects of their favourite. No sooner is it introduced than a few ultra Southern members are manifestly well satisfied that it has been brought forward, because by seizing upon it they hope to array a Southern party in favour of their favourite candidate for the Presidency. There is no patriotism on either side, it is a most wicked agitation that can end in no good and must produce infinite mischief.[19]

On the day after this was written he told Crittenden that

I deprecated the agitation of the slavery question in Congress, and though a South-Western man & from a slave-holding State as well as himself, I did not desire to acquire more Southern Territory than that which I had indicated [California and New Mexico], because I did not desire by doing so to give occasion for the agitation of a question which might sever and endanger the Union.[20]

King's appropriation bill, with the section prohibiting slavery in all territory to be acquired, not only raised the issue with respect to anticipated cessions from Mexico, but it affected also

---

[18] Polk, *Diary*, II, 304–309. At a meeting held on January 16 the cabinet again unanimously advised the extension of the 36° 30′ line to the Pacific.

[19] Polk, *Diary*, II, 348.   [20] *Ibid.*, 350.

the Oregon bill. It will be remembered that the twelfth section
of the measure proposed by Douglas extended to Oregon the
Ordinance of 1787. When the bill came up for discussion on
January 14, 1847, Burt, of South Carolina, moved to amend this
section by adding an explanatory statement to the effect that
the restrictions of the Ordinance were extended to Oregon "inasmuch as the whole of the said territory lies north of 36° 30' north
latitude."[21] While willing, apparently, to let slavery be excluded
from Oregon, Burt nevertheless denied categorically the power
of Congress to prohibit slavery in any state or territory. He
argued at some length to prove that neither the Ordinance of
1787 nor the Missouri Compromise was a constitutional law.
This denial of the federal government's power to exclude slavery
from *any* territory was soon echoed by other southern members;
consequently, an attempt was made to eliminate the prohibition
from the Douglas bill or else to defeat it altogether.

The President was embarrassed, and his opponents assisted,
by the hearty support given to his policy of territorial acquisition by southern enthusiasts, both in Congress and in the press.
For example, the *Charleston Patriot* trusted "that our southern
Representatives will remember that this is a southern war," and
the *Charleston Courier* asserted that the war would widen the
field of southern enterprise and power.[22]

In the House, Seddon, of Virginia, declared King's bill to be
grossly unconstitutional. "It more than violates a single specific
clause of that instrument. It outrages its whole scope and spirit,
and subverts the very basis of its being." Bedinger, of the same

---

[21] *Cong. Globe*, 29 Cong., 2 sess., 178.

[22] The former is quoted in Jay, *Review of the Mexican War*, 182. See also
other excerpts from southern papers there given. The latter is thus quoted
by Rathbun of New York: "Every battle fought in Mexico, and every
dollar spent there, but insures the acquisition of territory which must
widen the field of southern enterprise and power in the future. And the
first result will be to readjust the whole balance of power in the Confederacy *so as to give us control over the operations of the Government in all
time to come*. If the South be but true to themselves, the day of our depression and suffering is *gone, and gone forever*" (*Cong. Globe*, as cited
above, 364).

state, still loved the Union; but he would cease to love his wife
(if he had one), "if, like the farfamed Mrs. Caudle, she were
forever taunting me with what she chose to regard as a great
deformity and annoyance."[23] Should the North persist in its
purpose to restrict slavery, he saw no remedy short of a dissolution of the Union. During the debate on the Oregon bill Rhett,
also, denied absolutely the power of Congress to exclude slavery
from territories, for they belonged to the states and not to the
United States.

> For that [Oregon] territory [said he], we care but little, since it is
> not probable that a single planter would ever desire to set his foot within
> its limits. But the right is important, because it applies to future acqui-
> sitions of territory; and by refusing to acknowledge the obligations of
> the Missouri compromise, you force open the whole question of power.[24]

The question of the control of Congress over slavery in territories came before the Senate by a more indirect route. On
January 19, 1847, Sevier reported, from the Committee on Foreign Relations, a bill for granting the President three million
dollars with which to conduct negotiations with Mexico. When
it came up for discussion on February 1, Berrien, of Georgia,
a southern Whig, gave notice of his intention to offer an amendment. His amendment, among other things, declared that "the
war with Mexico ought not to be prosecuted by this Government
with any view to the dismemberment of that republic, or the
acquisition by conquest of any portion of her territory." A few
days later Cass offered a substitute which authorized the President to demand indemnity from Mexico. To those who desired
an extension of slavery Berrien's amendment was quite as offensive, except in principle, as the Wilmot proviso itself; for
no acquisition of territory meant no extension of political power.
During the debate, Berrien warned southerners that slavery

---

[23] "These northern Mrs. Caudles," he continued, "will not let us rest
by night or by day. We get no sleep for them! Their eternal din will
drive us to distraction. They interfere with our domestic matters; they
enter our very kitchens, and intrude upon our most sacred household
affairs!" (*Cong. Globe*, 29 Cong., 2 sess., App., 86). For Seddon's remarks,
see *ibid.*, 76.

[24] *Ibid.*, 346.

would surely be excluded from all land acquired; therefore both the interest and the safety of the South "demands that we should oppose ourselves to any and every acquisition of territory."

Berrien was not the only southern man who was averse to territorial acquisition. Whigs would naturally oppose any policy advocated by the administration, but there was a still more potent reason why certain Democrats, as well as Whigs, did not favor expansion. This reason was a conviction that slavery would be excluded; and that while their section could not hope to gain any advantage, further agitation of the subject might result in a dissolution of the Union. Why, asked Morehead, of Kentucky, should a policy (of expansion) be followed which would precipitate discord over slavery and probably destroy the institution? In the House, Alexander H. Stephens vigorously opposed the acquisition of territory and gave as one of his reasons his fear of the results of slavery agitation. He had faith in the strength of the Union, but he had "no disposition to test its strengh by running against that rock upon which Mr. Jefferson predicted we should be finally wrecked."

Calhoun joined the Whigs just mentioned in combating the President's expansion policy. He saw even more clearly than they did the approaching "irrepressible conflict." In a lugubrious speech made in the Senate on February 24 he declared that

Every Senator knows that I was opposed to the war; but none knows but myself the depth of that opposition. With my conception of its character and consequences, it was impossible for me to vote for it. . . . On the passage of the act recognizing the war, I said to many of my friends that a deed had been done from which the country would not be able to recover for a long time, if ever; and added, it has dropped a curtain between the present and the future, which to me is impenetrable; and for the first time since I have been in public life, I am unable to see the future. I also added, that it has closed the first volume of our political history under the Constitution, and opened the second, and that no mortal could tell what would be written in it. . . . Since then less than a year has elapsed; but in that short period enough has already been developed to make what was then said look like prophecy.[25]

[25] *Cong. Globe*, 29 Cong., 2 sess., 500. Also, Calhoun, *Works*, IV, 371.

The thing which had developed, of course, was the inclination of the North to resist the spread of slavery, and Calhoun fully realized that that section possessed the power if the people should decide to make use of it. His first remedy for the impending disaster was to prevent, if possible, the acquisition of more territory. Later, when he became convinced that this could not be done, he felt constrained to deny that Congress possessed the power to restrict the institution.

Already, indeed, Calhoun had been offered an opportunity for asserting the latter doctrine. On February 15 Douglas had attempted in the House to extend the Missouri Compromise line through the territory to be acquired, as an alternative to excluding slavery from all of it. His amendment for this purpose was rejected by a considerable majority. Four days after this action had been taken, Calhoun announced in the Senate that he was "against any compromise line." He had always, he said, considered the Missouri Compromise to have been a great error, although he had acquiesced in respecting it in order to preserve peace. But since its rejection as a solution of the new territorial question, he was now ready to insist upon the full rights of the South in all territories. An enumeration of these rights he embodied in a series of resolutions which Benton was unkind enough to call a "string of abstractions." In substance the resolutions declared territories to be the property of the several states, consequently Congress did not possess the constitutional power to prevent a citizen of a state from migrating with his slaves to any of the territories.[26]

The real reason why Calhoun and his supporters felt obliged to abandon the historic method of compromise and to deny the power of Congress over slavery in territories is obvious; they were confronted by a condition of affairs which had never before existed. In all land previously acquired slavery was already established, therefore the institution might continue unless

---

[26] *Cong. Globe, loc. cit.*, 453–455. Calhoun, *Works*, IV, 339–349.

specifically prohibited by Congress. In the proposed acquisition slavery had been abolished by Mexican law, and, according to international custom, this law would continue in force until supplanted by positive legislation on the subject by the United States. Now Congress had never specifically authorized slavery anywhere, and there could be no hope that it would do so in the present instance. Consequently a new doctrine must be promulgated; it must deny the power of Congress to exclude slave property from land which belonged to the *several states.* For the sake of consistency the doctrine must apply to Oregon as well as to the proposed Mexican cession.[27] The issue was now squarely joined. The advocates of the Wilmot proviso claimed full power to exclude slavery from all territories, while Calhoun and his adherents denied *in toto* the existence of such a power. After Congress had adjourned, Benton told his constituents that at last extremes had met—Calhoun and the abolitionists had joined hands in subverting the Union.[28]

Congress adjourned on March 3, 1847, without having provided a government for Oregon. A bill for this purpose had passed the House on January 16, but on the last day of the session it was laid on the table by the Senate. Under Polk's direction,

---

[27] The *Baltimore American,* Feb. 17, 1847, pointed out very clearly why southern members, after applauding the plan suggested by Cass, Buchanan, and Dickinson for letting the people of the territories decide the question, turned suddenly to oppose it. ''To leave to the territories themselves the absolute decision of the existence of slavery upon their soil, might do very well if slavery had been previously established there, as was the case when Louisiana was purchased, when Florida was acquired, and when Texas was annexed. But in the present case it would not do. The old formula must be changed. The long and fondly cherished doctrine of state sovereignty, so conveniently inchoate in a territory as the germ of a state—even this must be abandoned.'' Quoted in *Niles' Reg.,* Feb. 19, 1848, LXXIII, 392.

[28] The Calhoun resolutions, said he, ''go the precise length of the northern abolitionists, and with the same practical consequence, only in a reversed form. The abolition creed is, that the admission of slavery in any part of the Union is a violation of the constitution, and a dissolution of the Union; the new resolutions declare that the prohibition of slavery in any territory of the Union is a violation of the constitution and the rights of the states, and a subversion of the Union! So true it is, that extremes meet, and that all fanaticism, for or against any *dogma,* terminates at the same point of intolerance and defiance'' (speech at St. Louis (no date given), quoted in *Niles' Reg.,* June 5, 1847, 223).

Buchanan expressed to the people of Oregon the President's regret because they had been left by Congress without a government. Ignoring the real difficulty, Buchanan stated that the failure of Congress to act had not resulted from indifference to the interests of the territory, but to a pressure of business which did not allow time to perfect the details of the bill![29] Just before adjourning, however, Congress passed the "three million bill" which enabled the President to use this sum in conducting negotiations with Mexico. As we have seen, efforts were made to attach to this bill either the Wilmot proviso or an extension of the Missouri compromise line, but all such restrictions were rejected.

During the session which had just closed Calhoun felt that he had attained a commanding position. "My friends," he wrote, "think I never stood higher, or stronger than I now do"; and he was "now certain that there will be no more Baltimore nominations, or if there should be, the nominee will be assuredly defeated." Through Benton, he said, the administration was trying to build up the old Van Buren party, but their efforts would end in failure.[30] After Congress had adjourned, he went home to begin an active compaign for uniting the South in defense of slavery. He desired, first of all, to prevent the reëlection of Polk, or the election of any of his adherents; if Calhoun himself could not be elected, he was ready to support General Taylor.[31] It is interesting to note that while northern Whigs and "proviso" Democrats were denouncing the President as a slavery extensionist, Calhoun and his supporters were identifying him with Van Buren and other enemies of "southern institutions."

[29] Buchanan, *Works*, VII, 258.

[30] Calhoun to Thos. G. Clemson, Jan. 30, 1847, in *Rep. Am. Hist. Assn.*, 1899, II, 717.

[31] "The days of hunkerism is numbered. Mr. Polk is the last of the dynasty. It never can rise again to power. . . . As much as I am opposed to military chieftains for presidents, I shall, thus thinking, be content to see him [Taylor] elected against Mr. Polk, or any one, who contributed to make the war; and, let me add, against the nominee of a convention, either democrat, or Whig" (Calhoun to Clemson, May 6, 1847, *ibid.*, 728).

Early in April the President was informed by his Secretary of the Navy that Calhoun was soliciting signatures for an address to the people on the subject of slavery. "I remarked to Mr. Mason," says the *Diary,*

that Mr. Calhoun had become perfectly desperate in his aspirations to the Presidency, and had seized upon this sectional question as the only means of sustaining himself in his present fallen condition, and that such an agitation of the slavery question was not only unpatriotic and mischievous, but wicked.

He was as little pleased with a story told by Benton to the effect that the supporters of Silas Wright "would be rejoiced at the opportunity to take issue with Mr. Calhoun on such a question."

The truth is, [he continued], there is no patriotism in either faction of the party. Both desire to mount slavery as a hobby, and hope to secure the election of their favourite upon it. They will both fail and ought to. The people of the U. States, I hope, will cast off all such intrigues, and make their own selection for the Presidency, and this if they are wise they will do. I now entertain a worse opinion of Mr. Calhoun than I have ever done before. He is wholly selfish, I am satisfied has no patriotism. A few years ago he was the author of Nullification & threatened to dissolve the Union on account of the tariff. During my administration the reduction of duties which he desired has been obtained, and he can no longer complain. No sooner is this done than he selects slavery upon which to agitate the country, and blindly mounts that topic as a hobby. Gov. Wright's friends in Congress as unpatriotically have shown by their course that they desire to mount the same hobby in the North and hope to be successful by their opposition to slavery. They both forget that the Constitution settles [those] questions which were the subjects of mutual concession between the North and South. I am utterly disgusted at such intriguing men in high place, & hope they will be rebuked by the people.[32]

---

[32] Polk, *Diary,* II, 457–459. Although Polk was wrong in attributing the sectional discord wholly to President-making, it was true that the slavery question was being used on both sides of Mason and Dixon's line to break down party lines and to solidify public opinion either for or against the "peculiar institution." A few months later Holmes, of S. C., wrote: "I wish the Southern Representatives would consent to act together without regard to Whig or Democrat. The Wilmot Proviso is paramount to all Party. We are in great danger. The North is resolved to crush Slavery—are we equally in the South resolved at all hazards to defend it?" (Holmes to Cobb, Aug. 21, 1847, in *Rep. of Am. Hist. Assn.* 1911, II, 88).

What the President desired most of all was to eliminate the slavery question entirely and to have Congress confine its attention to the policies of his administration. However, since the slavery question had emerged, he could not maintain simply a negative attitude with respect to it. He was compelled, against his will, to adopt some positive program for dealing with slavery in the territories. As early as January 5, 1847, the cabinet suggested an extension of the Missouri Compromise line, but at that time Polk declined to commit himself.[33]

About a week after the cabinet had made this suggestion Atocha appeared in Washington and the prospect of an early acquisition of Mexican territory seemed brighter. Since Congress persisted in discussing slavery, some positive plan on the part of the administration seemed desirable. In his diary for January 16 Polk lamented that the session was nearly half over and that Congress, instead of enacting necessary military measures, was engaged in "a worse than useless discussion about slavery." He and the cabinet deprecated this discussion, but "all feared it would be impossible now to arrest it." Although every member of the cabinet advised an extension of the 36° 30' line through the territory to be acquired, Polk was not ready to commit himself to this solution.[34] In fact, the President does not seem to have decided upon any definite policy during the session, although he intimated to Crittenden that the Missouri Compromise line would be extended;[35] and as Congress voted the three million dollars without attaching the Wilmot restriction, slavery for the time being ceased to be a vital question.

In June, the President decided to made a tour of the northeastern states. Although we have no direct evidence that political considerations induced him to make this decision, it is quite

---

[33] See above, p. 619.

[34] Polk, *Diary*, II, 335.

[35] He told Crittenden that the slavery question in California and New Mexico would not be a practical one "because there would be but a narrow ribbon of territory South of the Missouri compromise line" (*Diary*, Jan. 23, II, 350).

probable that he hoped, by making the journey, to retain the
support of northern Democrats and to prevent further defections
on account of slavery agitation. Among those who accompanied
him was Edmund Burke, commissioner of patents and his close
personal friend. No doubt Burke voiced the President's views
when, on the eve of the journey, he told Franklin Pierce that
the signs of the times portended a coalition of the South and
West against the North. He attributed this state of affairs to
the "foolish course" pursued by the "proviso" Democrats; "it is
clear that the Northern and Southern Democracy are now divided,
a consummation which the federalists of the North have sought
for fifty years to accomplish."[36] Polk did not, during the summer, decide upon any definite policy with respect to slavery in
the territories, though his approval (somewhat reluctant, to be
sure) of Buchanan's open espousal of an extension of the 36° 30′
line indicated that he would not oppose this plan as a solution of
the question.[37]

When Congress convened in December, 1847, the President,
in his third annual message, informed that body of the failure
of Trist's mission. He recommended that California and New
Mexico should be retained permanently by the United States and
that Congress should at once provide each of these territories with
a civil government. In this connection he made no allusion to
slavery, but he concluded his message by quoting Washington's
admonition regarding the value of union and the calamity of
sectional controversies.

How unimportant [said Polk] are all our differences of opinion upon
minor questions of public policy compared with its preservation, and how
scrupulously should we avoid all agitating topics which may tend to dis-
tract and divide us into contending parties, separated by geographical
lines, whereby it may be weakened or endangered.

On December 8, two days after Congress had convened, the
Vice-President laid before the Senate a memorial from the Oregon

---

36 Burke to Pierce, June 21, 1847, *Pierce Papers*.

37 Polk, *Diary*, III, 142. Buchanan to Berks County Democrats (Buchanan, *Works*, VII, 385).

"Legislative Assembly" praying for the confirmation of their land titles and for the adoption of measures to promote education. This assembly had been created by the people of Oregon, without authority from the United States government. The movement to establish a temporary government began as early as 1843, and one section of the "Organic Laws" prohibited slavery.[38]

On December 14, before any consideration had been given to this memorial, Dickinson, of New York, submitted resolutions which attempted to define the policy of the government for both acquiring and governing territories. They asserted that "true policy" required the United States to strengthen its political and commercial relations on the continent by the acquisition of contiguous territory, and that in all such territories the people should be left free to settle "all questions concerning the domestic policy therein," without any restrictions imposed by the federal government. In other words, Dickinson advocated the "popular sovereignty" program which Douglas later mounted as a hobby in 1854. In his well-known "Nicholson letter" Cass made a bid for the Presidential nomination by casting doubt on the power of Congress over slavery in territories and by espousing the doctrine of "popular sovereignty."[39]

The Dickinson resolutions were followed by others in which individual Senators endeavored to commit the government to what each deemed to be the "true policy" respecting territories. One offered by Calhoun opposed holding Mexico as a province, or incorporating it into the Union. As a substitute for the Dickinson plan, Yulee, of Florida, offered a resolution which declared that territory owned or to be acquired by the United States "is the common property of the Union," and that neither the federal nor the territorial government can prevent any citizen from enjoying full rights therein. Hale, of New Hampshire, offered another substitute which purposed to exclude slavery entirely from lands

---

[38] Gray, *History of Oregon*, chaps. xiii–xiv.

[39] Cass to A. O. P. Nicholson, Dec. 24, 1847. Printed in *Niles' Reg.*, Jan. 8, 1848, LXXIII, 293.

that might be acquired. All of these proposals were defeated, yet they afforded an opportunity for airing divergent views and for illustrating the impossibility of arriving at any practical settlement of the slavery question.

On January 10, 1848, Senator Douglas presented a bill for establishing a territorial government in Oregon, and on February 9 Caleb Smith, of Indiana, reported from the House Committee on Territories a bill for the same purpose. Both measures were referred to committees, and for some time war legislation precluded their consideration.

The Douglas bill did not come before the Senate until May 31, and then Hale moved to amend by adding section twelve of the Senate bill of the last session—the section which extended to Oregon the Ordinance of 1787. Calhoun opposed the inclusion of a slavery restriction, while others like Hannegan and Benton thought such restriction to be unnecessary, since slaves would never be taken to Oregon. Benton was unwilling to have necessary legislation delayed by the introduction of this "pestiferous question." He was especially anxious that military protection should be extended immediately to the people of Oregon. But Hale was obdurate, and insisted upon a positive prohibition of slavery. "If this Union," said he, "with all its advantages, has no other cement than the blood of human slavery, let it perish!" When the discussion was resumed on June 5, Foote moved to amend by inserting in section twelve the words: "provided the same [the slavery restriction] be compatible with the laws and Constitution of the United States." In this way he undoubtedly hoped to obtain a "Dred Scott decision" at that early date. After Underwood, of Kentucky, had denied the authority of Congress to interfere with local institutions and Baldwin, of Connecticut, had declared that slaves were held solely by state laws and that when a slave left the confines of a slave state—even if accompanied by his master on a temporary sojourn—"his shackles fell off," Badger, of North Carolina, offered, as a substitute for

Foote's proposal, a proviso which would exempt the people of Oregon from the operation of the sixth article (the one prohibiting slavery) of the Ordinance of 1787. Foote accepted the modification. After considerable discussion this amendment was withdrawn by the mover on June 23, and Davis, of Mississippi, presented another which asserted that nothing in the bill should be so construed as to prohibit slavery in Oregon while it remained a territory.

After a long delay the House, on March 28, proceeded to consider Caleb Smith's Oregon bill. In a most ingenious speech Gayle, of Alabama, asserted that all laws by which Congress had excluded slavery from territories had been based on precedent merely and had not been authorized by the Constitution. He held that territories were legally states before entering the Union;[40] on the other hand, he denied that their government thereby possessed the power to exclude slavery. In reply, Smart, of Maine, declared that Congress not only had the power but was bound by the will of the majority to prevent slavery from entering all territories.

The President, as we have seen, was reluctant to announce a definite policy regarding slavery in territories, even though the Van Burenites believed this to be the issue nearest his heart.[41] Both he and his cabinet opposed the Wilmot proviso,[42] and, since a negative policy could not be pursued indefinitely, Polk at last decided to advocate an extension of the Missouri Compromise line.

---

[40] "Now, sir, how can a 'new State be admitted into the Union' unless it was a State before admission?"

[41] "The slavery question," wrote John M. Niles, "is evidently first & foremost with the administration; it overrides the Mexican war & any other question. The slave power rules as tyrannically here as it can in Louisiana; that, is made the test & tie of fealty to the administration" (Niles to Van Buren, Dec. 16, 1847, *Van Buren Papers*).

[42] After Clifford had been sent to Mexico the President announced his intention to select some northern man to fill his place. All members expressed an unwillingness to be associated with a Wilmot proviso man (Polk, *Diary*, III, 431).

As already noted, the President desired most of all to eliminate the subject of slavery, but forces beyond his control made
it apparent that this could not be done. Indeed, since the Treaty
of Guadalupe Hidalgo had been ratified by Mexico, the question
of governments for California and New Mexico had become more
urgent than ever. Congress persisted in discussing slavery and
there seemed to be no prospect of an agreemnt on the subject.
On May 26 a messenger arrived from Oregon and laid before
the President a memorial from the legislative assembly of that
territory, stating that the Indians were making war on the inhabitants. Polk transmitted the memorial to Congress along with
a message recommending the immediate creation of a government
for Oregon. He said nothing about slavery.[43] But on June 24,
in a conversation with Senator Hannegan concerning "the dis-
tracting subject of slavery, which is embarrassing the Bill to
establish a Territorial Government in Oregon," he advised the
Senator to "bring forward & press the adoption of the Missouri
compromise line & extend it to the Pacific." Hannegan, as well
as the entire cabinet, agreed with Polk that "the adoption of the
Missouri compromise was the only means of allaying the excitement & settling the question." The President sent for other
members of Congress and urged them to support this policy in
order to checkmate the action of the Barnburners:

The necessity for settling the question is the greater since the convention of Barnburners, held at Utica, New York, on the 22nd Instant,
have bolted from the regular Democratic nominations made at the Baltimore convention in May last, and have nominated Martin Van Buren for
President and Henry Dodge of Wisconsin for Vice President distinctly
upon the ground of the Wilmot Proviso. This is a most dangerous attempt
to organize Geographical parties upon the slavery question. It is more
threatening to the Union than anything which has occurred since the
meeting of the Hartford convention in 1814. Mr. Van Buren's course is
selfish, unpatriotic, and wholly inexcusable. The effect of this movement of
the seceding and discontented Democrats of New York will be effectually

---

[43] Polk, *Diary*, III, 463. Message dated May 29, 1849 (Richardson,
Messages, IV, 584).

co[u]nteracted if the slave question can be settled by adopting the Missouri compromise line as applied to Oregon, New Mexico, & Upper California at the Present Session of Congress. If the question can be thus settled harmony will be restored to the Union and the danger of forming geographical parties be avoided. For these reasons I am using my influence with members of Congress to have it adopted.[44]

He was quite indifferent regarding the extension of slavery, but he was vitally concerned over preserving the Union and insuring the success of his party. He did not believe that sound principles, or what he considered to be such, should be jeopardized by a sudden change in the popular viewpoint. After the Baltimore convention, Cass showed to Polk the first draft of his letter of acceptance, one sentence of which declared that the government should keep pace with public opinion. "I suggested to him," is the comment in the *Diary*, that the assertion

might be misconstrued to mean that constitutional principles might be changed, in order to accommodate themselves to what might seem from time to time to be public opinion, which I thought was an untenable & dangerous doctrine.[45]

A few days after his conversation with Hannegan the President discussed the Oregon bill with Senators Bright, of Indiana, and Foote, of Mississippi. He dictated an amendment which would extend the 36° 30′ line to the Pacific. When Bright introduced the amendment in the Senate, Calhoun again asserted that Congress could not, without violating the Constitution, prevent a slaveholder from carrying his *property* to any territory.[46]

During the first two weeks in July, Polk conversed with various southern members of both houses, nearly all of whom were ready to accept an extension of the 36° 30′ line. Judge Catron wrote from Nashville that the position taken by those who denied the power of Congress over slavery in acquired territory could not be maintained. He was in favor of excluding the institution

---

44 Polk, *Diary*, III, 501–503.
45 *Ibid.*, 471–472.
46 *Ibid.*, 504–505. *Cong. Globe*, 30 Cong., 1 sess., 875–876.

from Oregon and believed that it would be wise, politically, to do so.[47] The pleasure which Polk derived from the support of so many southern men was offset by the acerbity of Alexander H. Stephens. By a resolution introduced on July 10 Stephens called upon the President for information concerning the governments which had been set up in California and New Mexico. In a violent speech he scathingly denounced the President and General Pillow, and characterized the former as ''Polk the mendacious.''[48]

In the Senate, on July 12, after Jefferson Davis had upheld the right of a slaveowner to locate with his ''property'' in any territory, Clayton, of Delaware, moved that the question of slavery in territories be referred to a committee of eight to be selected by ballot—four from the North and four from the South. During the discussion of this proposal Westcott, of Florida, asserted that should the Wilmot proviso be attached to the bill, ''we have a Chief Magistrate at the other end of the avenue who would put his veto on it.'' However true this statement may have been, it must have been based upon pure conjecture, for Polk would hardly have given advance information to a man whom he detested as he did Westcott. The Senate passed the resolution and Clayton was made chairman of the select committee.[49]

Calhoun was made a member of the Clayton committee and, on July 14, Polk expressed to the Senator's friend, Elmore, a hope that he might recede from his extreme position and accept the 36° 30′ line as a compromise. He could not with propriety,

---

[47] ''Were I in Congress, not a moment's hestiation would be felt in voting for the exclusion of slavery from [in?] the Oregon bill; and if this is done, with the sanction of the Democratic party—as it must be in the Senate, the Barnburners may hang their harp on the willows, so far as capital is sought from this slavery question; not that I think so much will come of it as has been supposed, for Mr. V. Buren will have to carry his abolition brethren, who will be very apt to absorb his party, & to incorporate his good self, & Son John.'' Catron ''w'd feel much gratified to see this slavery question adjusted by a compromise on 36° 30′—the true division as I think'' (Catron to Polk, July 12, 1848, *Polk Papers*).

[48] Polk, *Diary*, IV, 14. *Cong. Globe*, 30 Cong., 1 sess., 912.

[49] *Cong. Globe*, 30 Cong., 1 sess., 927–928, 932.

he said, ask Calhoun to call and discuss the subject,[50] so Elmore, two days later, brought the Senator to call upon him. After Polk had expressed a "decided opinion" in favor of adjusting the slavery question by an extension of the compromise line, Calhoun said that the Clayton committee had as yet been unable to agree upon a solution. He stated that a suggestion had been made in committee which he was willing to accept: that the existing Oregon laws which prohibited slavery be allowed to operate until changed by the territorial legislature; and that the governments of California and New Mexico be prevented by Congress from legislating on the subject of slavery, leaving the question, should it arise, to be decided by the local judiciary. Polk was willing to accept this adjustment, although he preferred an extension of the compromise line. Calhoun now produced the *loaded dice* by which he hoped to win the game so far as the Mexican cessions were concerned:

He said that much would depend on me, in appointments to be made of Governor, Secretary, & Judges; that they might be Northern men in Oregon, but that they ought to be Southern men in California & New Mexico, who would maintain the southern views on the subject of slavery. The tone of his conversation on this point seemed to be designed to elicit a pledge from me to this effect. I at once felt the delicacy of my situation & promptly replied that that was a subject upon which I could not speak, that if the laws passed in the form suggested I would do my duty, and jocosely added that my friends, as Gen'l Harrison's Cincinnati Committee in 1844 [1840?] said for him, must have a "generous confidence" that I would do so.[51]

Calhoun returned on the following day and reported that the committee had agreed upon the general terms above mentioned, but that the northern members insisted upon a provision which would allow appeals from the territorial courts to the Supreme Court of the United States. He and two other members would

---

50 "I told him I could not invite Mr. Calhoun to call, 1st, because he was an older man than myself, had been longer in public life, and 2nd, because he might suppose that I desired to exercise some official influence over him."

51 Polk, *Diary*, IV, 19–21.

not admit this provision, and he now suggested that the whole subject might be postponed until the next session of Congress. Since Polk urged immediate action, the Senator, after another vain attempt to carry his point in committee, finally yielded on the subject of appeal. "There is now some prospect," wrote the President, "that the question may be settled at the present session of Congress, and I sincerely hope it may be." On July 18, Clayton reported a bill which left undisturbed the prohibition in Oregon. The status of slavery was left for the Supreme Court to determine, and until this had been done, the territorial governments were not to legislate on the subject.[52]

When the bill came up for discussion, on July 22, Niles, of Connecticut, asked Clayton whether his bill answered the important question whether Congress had or had not the power to interfere with slavery in territories. He replied that it "neither affirms nor denies the power, and herein consists the compromise." Northern members were unable to discern a compromise in a measure which left slave-owners free to enter California and New Mexico without hindrance, except an improbable decision of a pro-slavery court. The northern press was equally suspicious. Said the New York *Evening Post:*

Talk as we may of the impartiality of our courts, a judge from the Southern States, allied to the aristocracy of those States, would share their prejudices and decide according to their views. This compromise is, therefore, an ingenious method of giving Mr. Calhoun his own way in the controversy.

And the New York *Tribune:*

We protest against this juggle. We say it [slavery] has acquired no right to a single foot of the new territory; the South avers the contrary. We press Congress for a decision, and it is refused us. Instead of deciding Congress undertakes to run the matter through so many different crucibles, that slavery will finally be established and that inveterate old rascal, Nobody, be alone responsible for it. . . .

A governor and three Judges are to be the law makers and the law expounders in each Territory—said governor and judges being appointed

[52] *Ibid.*, 21–24. *Cong. Globe,* 30 Cong., 1 sess., 950.

by Polk, and of course chosen from among the most determined, wily and unscrupulous champions of slavery extension. Nobody can pretend to doubt how they will construe the constitution.[53]

The discussion in the Senate continued until the morning of July 27, when, after an all-night session during which numerous amendments were rejected, the measure as submitted by the select committee was passed. On the following day, after a brief debate, the House laid the Senate bill on the table and proceeded to consider its own Oregon government bill.

The President was sorely disappointed by this action on the part of the House. He was especially mortified because the defeat of the bill had been accomplished by the votes of New York Barnburners and Democrats "who are timid & afriad to risk their popularity at home." The result of leaving the slavery question unsettled, to be agitated by "ambitious aspirants & gamblers," would be to produce an organization of parties on geographical lines and to endanger the Union. He did not doubt that the bill would have passed if there had been no Presidential election pending. The Whigs were desirous of preventing any adjustment during the present session,

doubtless in the expectation that in the chapter of accidents growing out of the excitement & agitation which must follow, that they may stand some chance to elect a Whig President. I deplore as a national calamity the want of patriotism which seems to actuate the conduct of the leaders of the Whig party in Congress; and I exceedingly regret that any portion of the Northern Democrats from timidity or other causes have been induced to act with them.[54]

By the eighth of August he had become convinced that Congress would not, at the present session, create governments for New Mexico and California, yet he believed that the Oregon bill, with its clause excluding slavery, might be passed. He asked the cabinet whether, in case this bill should pass, he ought to sign it. Each member responded that, since the whole territory

---

[53] Both quoted in *Niles' Reg.*, LXXIV, 55–56.
[54] Polk, *Diary*, IV, 33–35.

lay north of 36° 30′, he ought to do so. He then asked whether he ought to accompany his approval with a message stating that he had signed the bill because the territory lay north of the Missouri Compromise line. Buchanan feared that such a statement might injure the campaign of General Cass; the others believed that it should be made, either in a message or in the Washington *Union*.[55]

The House passed its own bill on August 2 and sent it to the Senate for approval. The Senate attached certain amendments which the House promptly rejected, and it looked for a time as if no agreement could be reached. Polk was ready to approve slavery restriction for Oregon, but he told the cabinet that he did not wish it to be inferred that he would sanction a restriction south of 36° 30′.[56]

In taking his stand against the application of the Wilmot proviso to all territory it is evident that the President was animated not by a wish to extend slavery but by a desire to preserve the Union. He believed that the Union could be saved by an extension of the compromise line—and, perhaps, in no other way. He had set his heart on having the whole territorial question settled by the adoption of such a policy. The elimination of Oregon would make the adjustment more difficult, consequently he preferred to have the matter setled by a measure that would apply to all three territories. He believed that the South was entitled to the privilege of occupying with its "property" the southern part of the Mexican session; but, personally, he was most interested in allaying sectional discord. He was equally insistent—in defiance of southern pressure—upon prohibiting slavery north of 36° 30′, although he samewhat doubted the

[55] *Ibid.*, 61–62.

[56] "I expressed the opinion that if I approved and signed the Bill in the usual form without assigning my reasons, my opinion in regard to California & New Mexico would not be understood, and that it might be inferred that I had yielded the question in regard to the Territory South as well as North of the Missouri compromise line, which would not be true" (*ibid.*, 67–68).

constitutional power of Congress to apply such a restriction. In this, too, he was moved not by any feeling against the institution, but by the opinion that nothing else would satisfy the North and prevent further agitation. In a word, his attitude toward slavery was one of indifference.

When, on the morning of August 13, Polk learned that the Senate, at the close of all-night session, had passed the House Oregon bill, with its prohibition of slavery, he realized that he must decide the question of affixing or withholding his signature. Although disappointed because the compromise line had not, at the same time, been extended through the Mexican cession, he nevertheless decided to approve the Oregon bill and, in a message, to state his reasons for so doing. Buchanan did not wish Polk to state in the message that he would veto any bill which purposed to exclude slavery south of 36° 30′; Mason, Marcy, and Ritchie advised such an announcement. While the President was drafting his message to the House, Senator Turney, of Tennessee, called and urged him to veto the bill; and Hannegan, although he had voted for the bill, offered to sustain a veto. Calhoun and Burt, of South Carolina, importuned him to veto the measure, but he informed them that he would sign it, "although I would do so reluctantly";

> I told him [Calhoun] that if the question of imposing the restriction was an original one arising for the first time, I would have serious doubts of its constitutionality. I remarked that there might be questions arise effecting [affecting] the very existence of the Union, upon which we ought to yield individual opinions, in deference to what our predecessors had done, and I considered this one of them.

He reminded Calhoun that the Clayton committee of which the Senator was a member had been willing to exclude slavery from Oregon, and that many southern Senators had voted for the Clayton bill. He reminded him also that Burt, who was present, had proposed the amendment in the House for prohibiting slavery in Oregon, on the ground that the territory lay north of the compromise line. Calhoun pleaded for a veto, but

I repeated that I would sign it, and told him that if I were to veto it
after all that had occurred, and in the present excited state of Congress
& of the public mind, I should do more to inflame that excitement & to
array the country into geographical parties and to rend the Union, than
any act which had ever been done by any President or any man in the
country. He left me fully understanding my opinions & what I would do.[57]

Congress had agreed to adjourn on August 14, the day after
Polk had held the above-mentioned conversation with Calhoun.
The President rose early and carefully revised his message to
the House before the cabinet had assembled for the purpose of
accompanying him to the capital. To Buchanan's caustic remark
concerning Ritchie's assistance in the preparation of the message
Polk retorted indignantly that none of the editor's suggestions
had been followed. The Secretary then reiterated his opposition
to sending the message.

Shortly after Polk had reached the Vice-President's room at
the capitol he was informed that both houses were engaged in
a debate against suspending the joint rule under which bills
could not be submitted to the President for his signature on the
last day of the session. Unless it were suspended not only the
Oregon bill but the army appropriation bill would fail. The
President communicated to several members his determination to
call an extra session on the following day if this session should
terminate without passing the appropriation bill. The joint rule
was suspended and both bills presented for his approval. As
he was about to affix his signature, Calhoun asked him not to
assign his reasons in a message, but the request was denied. Nominations to fill the offices created by the Oregon bill were made and
confirmed. When the hour for ending the sessoin had arrived
the House was so pressed for time that it adjourned in confusion
without having read the President's message.[58]

In his message Polk told the House that he had signed the
territorial bill, even though New Mexico and California had been

---

[57] Polk, *Diary*, IV, 70–74.
[58] *Ibid.*, 74–77.

left without governments, because Oregon urgently needed legal organization and protection. Turning to the cause of sectional discord, he thus stated the position of the slaveholder:

> In the progress of all governments questions of such transcendent importance occasionally arise as to cast in the shade those of a mere party character. But one such question can now be agitated in this country, and this may endanger our glorious Union, the source of our greatness and all our political blessings. This question is slavery. With the slave-holding States this does not embrace merely the rights of property, however valuable, but it ascends far higher, and involves the domestic peace and security of every family.

After commending the "mutual concession" shown by the framers of the Constitution in dealing with the subject of slavery, as well as the compromise adjustments of the Missouri and Texas questions, he stated that he had not felt at liberty to withhold his approval of the Oregon bill, because all of the territory lay north of 36° 30'. "Had it embraced territories south of that compromise," he continued, "the question presented for my consideration would have been of a far different character, and my action upon it must have corresponded with my convictions." Since the extension of the Missouri Compromise line would leave but a small area in which the people might hold slaves, if they saw fit, "is this a question to be pushed to such extremities by excited partisans on the one side or the other, in regard to our newly acquired distant possessions on the Pacific, as to endanger the Union of thirty glorious States, which constitute our Confederacy?"[59]

Nowhere in his political career did Polk speak so emphatically as a southern man as he did in this message, and yet, as we have just noted, Calhoun tried to dissuade him from sending it to the House. It is unlikely, even at this time, that Polk was desirous of spreading slavery, but he feared that unless some concession were made to the South a dissolution of the Union would

---

[59] Richardson, *Messages,* IV, 606–609.

result. His desire for some immediate and permanent settlement of the slavery controversy was intensified by the defection of the Barnburners and the consequent weakening of the Democratic party. If the vexed question could not be settled during his administration there was, in his opinion, grave danger that no adjustment could be made which the South would accept.

Chagrined because the Van Buren Democrats had coöperated with the Whigs in defeating the California and New Mexico territorial bills, he resolved, as soon as Congress had adjourned, to punish leading Barnburners for inciting insurrection in Democratic ranks. His punitive measures must of necessity be confined to persons actually holding offices, and of these the most objectionable was Benjamin F. Butler, whom he had made United States Attorney for the southern district of New York. At the Barnburner convention, which had recently met at Buffalo to nominate Van Buren, Butler had made a speech in which he had denounced the administration and had practically defied the President to remove him. Polk accepted the challenge and summarily removed Butler from office. He would not have removed the attorney ''for his mere opinions upon abstract questions, nor for his free expression of them,'' but Butler's action in throwing obstacles in the way of successful administration of the government had forfeited his right to an office of honor and profit. In Polk's opinion, Butler was now ''one of the worst enemies of the Democratic party and its principles in the Union,'' and his newspaper organs in New York were more hostile to the administration than any of the Whig papers:

Indeed the whole party of Barn-burners in New York, of which Mr. Butler is a leading & controlling member, are not only abusive of me & my administration, but they seem to challenge and defy me to remove Mr. Butler, in the hope, no doubt, that they may enlist the public sympathy over him as a martyr for opinion's sake. By his removal to-day I have gratified [them], & they may make the most of it.[60]

---

[60] Polk, *Diary*, Sept. 1, 1848, IV, 114–115.

The harrowing question of slavery in the territories could not be disposed of so easily as could obnoxious office holders. As soon as Congress had adjourned, the redoubtable Missouri Senator gave the President new cause of annoyance by writing an officious letter to the people of California. Benton informed the Californians that since Congress had failed to legislate for them they were without a lawful government.[61] Therefore he exhorted them to meet in convention and frame a government under which they could take care of themselves until Congress should act. He sketched the type of government which would suit their purposes and suggested that a governor would be necessary to administer it. The Senate, he said, had voted seven million dollars to pay the people of California for miltiary services, but the bill for this purpose had been killed in the House committee by lies against Colonel Fremont.

Polk was much perturbed by this letter and sought advice from his cabinet as to the best means of counteracting its influence. Without admitting that the governments established in the new territories had "been void from the beginning" he was aware that the military governments had "ceased to exist" and that "the Executive had no authority to organize a civil Government over them." Benton's "extraordinary letter," he told the cabinet, had been sent to California

by Col. Fremont, the son-in-law of the writer, and the inference is plain enough that he means they shall make Col. Fremont the Governor of the Independent Government they shall form. Indeed I think it pretty clear that this was the main object.

He believed that the Secretary of State should inform the Californians, by letter, that the President would urge Congress to

---

[61] "The edicts promulgated by your temporary Governors (Kearny and Mason, each an ignoramus) so far as these edicts went to change the laws of the land, are null and void, and were so far the beginning. . . .

"Having no lawful government, nor lawful officers, you can have none that can have authority over you except by your own consent. Its sanction must be in the will of the majority" (Benton to the People of California, Aug. 27, 1848. Printed in *Niles' Reg.*, LXXIV, 244. Also in *Alta California*, Jan. 11, 1849).

frame a government for them, and that they "need not be deceived by the semi-official and officious proclamation of Senator Benton."[62] A few days later the matter was again brought before the cabinet, and the more the subject was discussed the greater number of legal difficulties did it present. Polk thought it probable that the military government in California was still "a Government *de facto*," yet he was not certain that the President could enforce obedience to it. Toucy, the Attorney General, thought that "the sovereignty of the territory rested in the people, and that they could, in the absence of the action of Congress, govern themselves as they chose." Mason and Walker believed that the sovereignty rested with the people of the United States and that Toucy's view would permit even the establishment of a monarchy. "I stated," wrote Polk,

that it was a subject which from its novelty was surrounded with many difficulties, but I thought instructions could be prepared which would avoid the decision of any abstract, doubtful question.

He instructed Buchanan to tell the people that they had no right, under the Constitution, to abrogate their *de facto* government and form one of their own. These views were embodied in a letter written by the Secretary of State and intrusted to William V. Voorhies, who was about to set out for California in the capacity of postal agent for that territory.[63]

The election of a Whig President made Polk more anxious than ever for an adjustment of the territorial question during his own term of office. His fourth annual message contained an urgent plea for the immediate establishment of civil governments in New Mexico and California. The reasons for the failure to do this at the last session, he said, "are well known and deeply to be regretted," and it would be irrational further to agitate a domestic question which is coeval with the existence of the government itself.

---

[62] Polk, *Diary*, IV, 135–138.

[63] *Ibid.*, 140–143. Buchanan to Voorhies (Buchanan, *Works*, VIII, 211-215).

In the eyes of the world and of posterity how trivial and insignificant will be all our internal divisions and struggles compared with the preservation of this Union of the States in all its vigor and with all its countless blessings! No patriot would foment and excite geographical and sectional divisions. No lover of his country would deliberately calculate the value of the Union.

Although a staunch Union man, the President's conception of the rights of a slaveholder in the territories was quite as southern as that of Calhoun himself. The people of every state, he told Congress, had helped to conduct the war, consequently "it would not be just for any one section to exclude another from all participation in the acquired territory." Whether slavery would enter these territories, even if left to the slaveholding states, was believed, he said, to be rather abstract than practical; but however that might me, "the quesion, involving, as it does a principle of equality of rights of the separate and several States as equal copartners in the Confederacy, should not be disregarded."

His views on the constitutional aspects of the question were quite as southern as those on the political side. The Constitution, he pointed out, had imposed upon Congress no duty to legislate on the subject of slavery in the territories, "while their power to do so is not only seriously questioned, but denied by many of the soundest expounders of that instrument."

Considering the several States and the citizens of the several States as equals and entitled to equal rights under the Constitution, if this were an original question it might well be insisted on that the principle of non-interference is the true doctrine and that Congress could not, in the absence of any express grant of power, interfere with their relative rights.

Since Congress, however, had, when dealing with previously acquired territory, divided the area between slavery and freedom, he was in favor of adjusting the present dispute in a similar manner, but if

Congress shall now reverse the decision by which the Missouri compromise was effected, and shall propose to extend the restriction over the whole territory, south as well as north of the parallel 36° 30', it will cease to be a compromise, and must be regarded as an original question.

After this implied threat to veto any bill for prohibiting slavery south of 36° 30', he expresesd a willingness to accept an extension of the compromise line, the policy of letting the people decide for themselves, or the submission of the whole subject to the decision of the courts.[64]

If the President had entertained hopes that his message would arouse Congress to take action, they seem to have vanished soon after his recommendations had been submitted. In less than a week he expressed to the cabinet a fear that Congress would do nothing and that California would establish an independent government and be lost to the Union. The rapid influx of population would make the demand for civil government imperative, and he believed that "the leading Federalists (alias Whigs) would be glad to avail themselves of the opportunity to give up the country for the purpose of relieving Gen'l Taylor of his embarrassments upon the Wilmot Proviso." This party, he said, had always opposed expansion, and had combated the purchase of Louisiana with as much vigor as they had opposed the present acquisition. Although the prospect seemed discouraging, he urged the members of the cabinet to use their influence with their friends in Congress. "It is," said he, "a question of rising above ordinary considerations. We have a country to serve as well as a party to obey."[65]

Even though the President was ready to go nearly as far as Calhoun in defending "southern rights," apparently his attitude was not prompted by an interest in slavery *per se*. He was willing—even anxious—to admit California immediately as a state, although there was every probability that slavery would be prohibited by its constitution.[66] On December 11, Douglas

---

[64] Richardson, *Messages*, IV, 640–642.

[65] Polk, *Diary*, IV, 231–233.

[66] Indeed, if newspapers may be taken as an index of public opinion, it was certain that slavery would be excluded, for the only two journals in California were emphatic on this point. The *California Star* of March 25, 1848, asserted that ninety-nine hundredths of the population opposed the imposition of "this blight" upon the territory, and the "simple recognition of slavery here" would be a greater misfortune than to remain in

had introduced in the Senate a bill for admitting both territories as one state, but Polk believed the area to be too large and the settlements too scattered for a single government. He summoned Douglas and advised the admission of California as a state, and the creation of a government for New Mexico by a separate bill. Douglas approved this policy, but Calhoun, when consulted, refused to commit himself. On that very day, however, the House by a considerable majority voted its approval of the Wilmot proviso, some of the Democrats reversing the votes which they had cast during the preceding session. Polk now saw no hope of an adjustment except, possibly, the admission of the whole territory as a state under the bill offered by Douglas.[67]

Not content with approving the Wilmot proviso the House, on December 21, instructed its committee to bring in a bill for abolishing the slave trade in the District of Columbia. Southern members were much excited and took immediate steps to arrange for a caucus. When informed of this fact, Polk declared slavery agitation to be "a mere political question on which demagogues & ambitious politicians hope to promote their own prospect for political promotion." About seventy members, both Democrats and Whigs, attended the caucus, and, after appointing a committee to prepare an address to be sent to southern states if the anti-slave-trade bill should be pressed, it adjourned to meet at a later date.[68]

In another effort to procure some positive action, the President sent for Senator Butler, of South Carolina, chairman of the Judiciary Committee to which the Douglas bill had been referred. He told Butler that no territorial bill which did not include the Wilmot proviso could pass the House, and that if such a bill

---

the present state of disaster. The *Californian* of October 11 was certain that the people preferred to remain as they were rather than have "this blighting curse" put upon them. On December 13 Benton presented in the Senate a petition from a New Mexico convention which asked Congress to protect the people there from the introduction of slavery (*Cong. Globe*, 30 Cong., 2 sess., 33).

[67] Polk, *Diary*, IV, 232–235.   [68] *Ibid.*, 248–253.

should pass both houses he would be compelled to veto it. The only way to save California was to admit her as a state; he therefore asked Butler's aid in bringing this about. Like Calhoun, Butler left the President in doubt as to what he would do. Polk then sent for Douglas who, after considerable persuasion, agreed to alter his bill so that California might be admitted and a territorial government be provided for New Mexico.[69]

The adjourned meeting of the southern caucus was scheduled for January 15, 1849, and on the fourtheenth Polk held a consultation with several of the southern leaders. They told him that the address to southern states, which Calhoun had prepared, was of such a nature that neither they nor their friends could sign it. The President approved their decision, for he thought that such an address would be mischievous. When nearly all of the Whigs and many of the Democrats who attended the caucus declined to sign Calhoun's address, it was returned to the committee for report at a future meeting. On the following day Calhoun called on the President and said that the South could no longer delay in resisting the aggressions of the North upon its rights. Polk advised the admission of California and spoke with approval of a plan suggested by Douglas for joining to Texas all of the remaining territory south of 36° 30'. When Calhoun opposed every suggestion and declined to offer a solution of his own Polk became convinced that the Senator did not desire an amicable adjustment. "I was firm and decided," said he, "in my conversation with him, intending to let him understand distinctly that I gave no countenance to any movement which tended to violence or the disunion of the States."[70]

The President had come to distrust Calhoun thoroughly and to believe that he compassed a dissolution of the Union. This opinion of the Senator is made very clear in the report of a conversation held with Representative Stanton, of Tennessee, who approved the address to southern states. After urging the

---

[69] *Ibid.*. 253–255, 257.   [70] *Ibid.*, 284–288.

admission of California, Polk told Stanton that meetings and addresses would weaken the South and add to the strength of the northern abolitionists. A gathering of members from any section quietly to discuss a political question was proper, but

I told him that I could not avoid the suspicion that there were two or three individuals, perhaps not more than *one* (but I named no one [Calhoun?]) who desired to have no set[t]lement of the question, but who preferred a sectional excitement in the South & a dissolution. I set my face against being involved in any such movement. I urged the necessity and importance of going to work in earnest *in Congress,* and not *in caucus,* to settle the question. I told him it was time enough to think of extreme measures when they became inevitable, and that that period had not come. I told him that the people everywhere were devoted to the Union, and that it would be a heavy responsibility if Southern members of Congress should prevent an adjustment of the slavery question by meeting *in caucus* & publishing addresses, instead of meeting *in Congress,* where their constituents had deputed them to act. He seemed surprised at these views. I told him I was a Southern man, and as much attached to Southern rights as any man in Congress, but I was in favor of vindicating and maintaining these rights by constitutional means; and that no such extreme case had arisen as would justify a resort to any other means; that when such a case should arise (if ever) it would be time enough to consider what should be done.[71]

Hopes and fears alternated in the President's mind as daily reports came to him of the debates in Congress on the admission of California. At a cabinet meeting held on January 20 letters received from Commodore Jones, Consul Larkin, and Paymaster Rich were read and discussed. Each reported that, on account of the gold rush, veritable anarchy prevailed and some form of government should be established at once. Polk directed that these letters be published in the *Union* in the hope that they might influence Congress to pass the California bill. He feared, however, that no bill could pass which did not include the Wilmot proviso; and he felt bound to veto any measure which prohibited

---

[71] *Ibid.,* 289–291. Polk was not alone in believing that Calhoun wished to disrupt the Union. ''It is thought here,'' wrote Horace Mann, ''by many of the most intelligent men, that Mr. Calhoun is resolved on a dissolution of the Union'' (Mann, *Life of Horace Mann,* 273).

slavery south of 36° 30'. He desired the immediate admission of California and thought that no southern man ought to object to its admission, but he feared that southern extremists led by Calhoun and northern extremists led by Hale and Giddings would prevent an amicable settlement of the question. "I stated" to the cabinet, was his comment, "that I put my face alike against southern agitators and Northern fanatics, & should do everything in my power to allay excitement by adjusting the question of slavery & preserving the Union." Once more he exhorted his cabinet advisors to use their influence with members of Congress. His efforts failed to prevent the caucus from adopting Calhoun's address to the southern states, and he apprehended further excitement as a result of this proceeding.[72]

The southern Whigs were not ready for extreme measures. This fact was shown by their support of an address presented by Berrien at the southern caucus as a substitute for the one drawn by Calhoun. On January 22 Tooms told Crittenden that California could never be a "slave country" and that it ought to be admitted as a state. "We have," he wrote, "only the point of honor to serve, and this will serve it and rescue that country from all danger of agitation."[73] Even some of the extreme advocates of the "peculiar institution" had little hope of installing it in the new domain. For example, the Mobile *Tribune* said that nothing could save the territories from becoming free states. If necessary, it was prepared to defend by extreme measures "our abstract right to a participation in them," yet it believed that "the victory would be barren."[74]

In order to facilitate matters and to avoid certain technical difficulties, the Senate referred the California question to a select committee of which Douglas was made chairman. On January 29 he reported a bill by which California was to be

---

[72] Polk, *Diary*, IV, 296–299, 306.

[73] Coleman, *Life of John J. Crittenden*, I, 335.

[74] Quoted in *Niles' Reg.*, LXXV, 75.

admitted as a state and New Mexico given a territorial government. In the evening he called to tell the President that he had
strong hopes of its passage. During the next few days Polk
conversed with various southern members and advised them to
support the bill, for, as he told them, this was the only way to
allay "geographical excitement" on the subject of slavery.[75]
However, northern members attacked certain paragraphs in the
bill which purposed to extend laws of the United States to the
proposed state and territory. They charged that the committee
was attempting to introduce slavery into these communities by
a jugglery of words.

The end of the session was approaching and those who did
not approve the Douglas bill endeavored to prevent debate upon
it by urging the necessity of considering the general appropriation bill. In this they were outgeneraled by Walker, a "dough
face" from Wisconsin, who, after consultation with Foote, of
Mississippi, offered an amendment which joined the territorial
government bill, as a rider, to the appropriation bill. By this
amendment the Constitution of the United States and certain
specified laws were extended to the territories, and the President
was given wide discretion in selecting the laws and regulations
to be enforced.[76] The introduction of the Walker amendment
gave rise to an animated debate on constitutional points, and
Webster and Calhoun took leading parts. It is unnecessary here
to follow this debate, yet it may be said that northern members
considered the amendment to be an instrument for smuggling
slavery into the territories through executive action and judicial
interpretation. Their charges to this effect had more real foundation than those of similar purport already brought against the
Douglas bill. There was a momentary excitement among Democrats due to a rumor that Free Soilers and Whigs had planned
to attach the Wilmot proviso to the Walker amendment and

---

[75] *Cong. Globe*, 30 Cong., 2 sess., 381. Polk, *Diary*, IV, 312–313, 316.
[76] *Cong. Globe*, 30 Cong., 2 sess., 561.

thereby to force the President either to accept the proviso or to veto the entire appropriation bill. When informed of this rumor by Venable, of North Carolina, Polk announced that he would veto an application of the proviso to territory south of 36° 30', no matter in what form it might be presented to him. In a slightly altered form, the Walker amendment was passed by a bare majority of the Senate on February 26; on the following day, by a vote of 126 to 87, the House passed its own bill by which slavery was excluded from the territories.

Only a few more days of the session remained and nothing short of a miracle seemed likely to break the deadlock of the two houses; and unless some adjustment could be made the government would be left without funds. On March 2 the House rejected the Walker amendment, and on the next day—the last of the session—a conference committee of the two houses reported its inability to agree upon any plan of settlement. The appropriation bill would now be lost unless the Senate should consent to eliminate the Walker amendment. Officially, the session expired at twelve o'clock on March 3, but the Senate indulged in a heated debate—even fist-fights[77]—until daybreak on March 4 without coming to an agreement. Hunter, of Virginia, was ready to let the government go without funds rather than sacrifice southern rights, while Douglas believed a government for California to be more important than either.

Polk had come to the capitol armed with a message with which he intended to veto the Wilmot proviso if it should be attached to the Walker amendment. Late at night he was told that the House had voted to amend the Walker amendment by a provision which declared the laws of Mexico to be in force until altered by Congress. The effect of this provision, as Polk at once saw, would be to sanction the law by which Mexico had abolished slavery. Buchanan, Walker, Marcy, and Toucy advised him to sign the bill if it should be presented in this

[77] Mann, *Life of Horace Mann*, 277.

form. "They drew a distinction, which I did not perceive," wrote the President, "between the amendment in this form and the Wilmot Proviso." Mason, on the contrary, advised him to veto the bill, while Johnson thought that he had no right to take any action, since his term of office had expired. Members of Congress came to the President in excitement and asked him to veto any bill containing the House provision. After telling them that he had already decided to do so he began to alter his veto message so as to meet the new situation. "It was a moment of high responsibility," says the *Diary*, "perhaps the highest of my official term. I felt the weight most sensibly, but resolved to pursue the dictates of my own best judgement and to do my duty." About four o'clock in the morning he retired to his hotel, and two hours later he was aroused by a committee from the two houses of Congress. Having reported that both the Walker amendment and the House provision had been eliminated, the committee presented for his signature a simple appropriation bill and another for extending federal revenue laws over California. He signed these, although he had some doubt that he was still President of the United States; the appropriations were saved, but California and New Mexico were still without governments.[78]

As a believer in territorial expansion, if for no other reason, Polk was sorely disappointed because Congress had not given governments to these territories, for apparently he fully believed that the Whigs would acquiesce in their separation from the United States. He had some reason for this belief, although it is evident that he attached too much importance to statements made by certain members of this party. For example, when he asked Senator Clarke, of Rhode Island, to save California to the Union by supporting the bill for admitting her as a state, the Senator replied with indifference: "Let her go." In the House, Alexander H. Stephens tried to block the payments to Mexico for

---

[78] Polk, *Diary*, IV, 362–369. *Cong. Globe*, 30 Cong., 2 sess., 682–698.

the territories, and when Buchanan remonstrated with him he answered that he was opposed to retaining those lands.[79] Polk was disposed to accept these utterances as indicative of the Whig policy because, as he said, the ''Federalists'' had always been averse to expansion. As if to cap the climax, Taylor, as the two men rode together in the inaugural procession, stated his belief that Oregon and Califonia were too far distant to become members of the Union and that it would be better for them to form an independent government of their own. Doubtless Polk was not surprised to hear these remarks from the Whig leader, nevertheless he thought that they were ''alarming opinions to be entertained by the President of the U. S.'' and he hoped that they had not been well considered.

Gen'l Taylor is, I have no doubt, a well meaning old man. He is, however, exceedingly ignorant of public affairs, and, I should judge, of very ordinary capacity. He will be in the hands of others, and must rely wholly upon his Cabinet to administer the Government.[80]

Such was his opinion of a successor whom he had never met until a few days before this. He did not foresee that Taylor would develop very decided views on the territorial question and that he would, in effect, adopt Polk's own latest policy of having both California and New Mexico admitted as states.

---

[79] Polk, *Diary*, IV, 294, 300.

[80] *Ibid.*, 375–376. Taylor's attitude toward California was not new. He had opposed the acquisition of this country while he was fighting in Mexico (Taylor to Wood, Aug. 23, 1846, *Taylor Letters*, 49).

CHAPTER XXIII

TARIFF, INTERNAL IMPROVEMENTS, AND THE INDEPENDENT TREASURY

Throughout his political career Polk had been a consistent opponent of protective tariff, and of internal improvements undertaken by the federal government. He believed the so-called "American System" to be decidedly un-American—a breeder of extravagance and a menace to the constitutional rights of the states. Entering Congress at the same time that John Quincy Adams became President, he took a vigorous stand against that administration, particularly against its advocacy of internal improvements. His views on this subject, as well as on others, accorded with those of General Jackson with whom he maintained an intimate correspondence.[1]

In his first annual message, Jackson stated his opinions concerning both tariff and internal improvements. He regretted that nations did not, by common consent, see fit to abolish all trade restrictions; as they did not, he was in favor of adjusting the tariff in a "manner best calculated to avoid serious injury and to harmonize the conflicting interests of our agriculture, our commerce, and our manufactures." He urged that the public debt be extinguished at the earliest possible date and that all revenue not otherwise needed be applied to this purpose. As there seemed likely to be a permanent surplus revenue after the national debt had been paid he was in favor of distributing this among the states, since internal improvements undertaken by

---

[1] In a letter to Polk, Jackson, after expressing friendship for and approval of Polk, stated that "I am sure the general government has no right to make internal improvements within a state, without its consent first had & obtained" (Jackson to Polk, Dec. 4, 1826, *Polk Papers*).

the federal government were considered to be both inexpedient and unconstitutional. All loyal adherents of the President accepted this announcement as the party program.

Polk's utterances in Congress at this time were in full accord with Jackson's message. On December 30, when the House was discussing the expediency of distributing among the states the proceeds from the sale of public lands, he opposed such a distribution as premature, since the public debt had not yet been paid. After it had been paid, he favored distributing the surplus among the states rather than have Congress spend it on public improvements.[2] When discussing the Maysville road bill, which Jackson vetoed later, Polk expressed himself as "opposed altogether to this system of appropriations for sectional purposes." He "conceived these applications to be most pernicious in their tendencies, and unconstitutional in principle." The country, he said, "looked to the present Executive for the adoption of a system of economy and retrenchment," a system entirely out of harmony with the purposes of this bill. During the same session a proposal to allow a drawback on rum made from imported molasses gave him a chance to assert that he was "upon principle opposed to the whole system of the protecting policy called tariff."[3]

Always an advocate of strict economy, Polk, while a member of congress, did not hesitate to apply this rule to small as well as to large expenditures. At the risk of being considered "ungracious" he opposed, in 1831, a resolution for giving thirty cords of wood to the suffering poor of Georgetown. The fact that Congress was the legislature of the District of Columbia did not, in his opinion, entitle it to give the national revenue to the inhabitants. Should it adopt such a practice "the poor of the other sections of the country had nothing to do but to come and sit down here, in this District, and apply to Congress for relief." The resolution was passed, but a year later he succeeded in

---

[2] *Abridg. of Deb.*, X, 594.   [3] *Ibid.*, 677–678, XI, 67.

defeating a semi-philanthropic project to pay forty thousand dollars to certain persons for giving instruction in silk culture. It was absurd, said he, to appropriate public money for such purposes.[4]

In 1832 Polk was made chairman of the Committee of Ways and Means. In this position his most difficult task was the management of Jackson's war on the bank, but he had also to supervise all questions of finance. His attempts to enforce economy very naturally led his opponents to charge him with arbitrary conduct. In 1834 Adams accused him of attempting to force the general appropriation bill through without adequate discussion, while Lincoln, of Massachusetts, charged him with trying to starve the opposition into submission.[5] Criticism did not deter him; he persisted in his opposition to unnecessary appropriations and in many cases was able to carry his point. For example, he advocated, and successfully carried, a reduction in the appropriation for the Cumberland road from $652,00 to $300,000.[6] This was a triumph for economy, and a damper on internal improvements as well.

As early as 1832 Clay became interested in a scheme to distribute among the states the proceeds from the sale of public lands. Successive bills to effect his purpose met with disaster—one by the President's veto—and during the session of 1835-1836 another distribution bill was introduced. It passed the Senate and was brought up in the House on June 7, 1836. A motion made to refer it to the Committee of the Whole for discussion received a vote of 97 to 96. Polk, who was then Speaker of the House, added his vote to the minority and prevented a

---

[4] *Ibid.*, XI, 306–307, 691–693.

[5] "The chairman of the Committee of Ways and Means," said Lincoln on April 25, 1834, "came into this House when we had got only to the 45th line of this bill, with the declaration that he was determined to press this bill through before the House adjourned. We were in consequence kept here eight or nine hours without refreshment, and exhausted by the fruitless efforts of the honorable chairman to accomplish his purpose."

[6] *Cong. Globe*, 23 Cong., 1 sess., 340, 347, 461.

reference to the committee.[7] This particular measure was laid on the table. Another bill was introduced in the House which, instead of giving the surplus to the states, proposed to "deposit" it with them subject to recall. It passed both houses in this form, and while everybody knew that in all probability the money would never be recalled, the modification satisfied Jackson's scruples sufficiently to enable him to affix his signature. The money was to be deposited in four installments, beginning on January 1, 1837.

The panic of 1837 which paralyzed all business activities soon after Van Buren's inauguration transformed the surplus into a deficit and created a demand for legislation to replenish and to safeguard the national treasury. The Whigs very naturally advocated a restoration of the Bank of the United States, but the Democrats, quite as naturally, could not think of rehabilitating the "monster" which they had so recently and so thoroughly crushed. Neither could the latter party rely any longer on "pet banks," for these too had gone down in the general crash.

On May 15 Van Buren issued his proclamation, summoning Congress to meet in extra session on the first Monday in September. It convened on the appointed day and, on the first ballot, Polk was reëlected Speaker over his Whig rival, John Bell. In the message which was submitted on September 5 the President, after calling attention to the financial distress of the nation, recommended legislation designed to separate government finances from all banks and to make the government the custodian of its own funds. The plan which he proposed was known officially as the "independent treasury," but it was more frequently called the "sub-treasury." Despite the vociferation against the continuance of the policy inaugurated by Jackson's "specie circular," the President boldly insisted that government finances

---

[7] This was a power of which a Speaker "rarely, if ever, avails himself," said the *National Intelligencer*, June 9, 1836, in criticizing his act.

should be conducted on a hard money basis. Nearly a month before this message was submitted to Congress, General Jackson learned of the recommendations which Van Buren intended to make, and his approval is thus expresesd in a letter written to Polk:

I have rec'd lately some very pleasant information from the city—all is harmony and the object of the Executive is, or will be, to separate the Government from all Banks—collect & disburse the revenues by its own agents,—receipts of all public dues in gold & silver coin, leaving the Banks & the commercial community to manage their transactions in their own way.[8]

Polk, like Jackson, approved the sub-treasury plan; on the other hand, it met with opposition even among Democrats in Tennessee.[9] Judge Catron believed that the government should be the custodian of its own money, for, "I care not what private Banks you put it into, it will convert the keepers into Federalists in principle & practice in a few years";[10] but his solution of the financial depression was a large emission of paper money. In the letter just quoted, he stated that a "Treasury circulation must be adopted," and, after reading Van Buren's message, he pronounced the President's recommendations "sound in principle, but hardly possible in practice." The people, said he, are governed by habit and want paper money. They would not be able to understand Van Buren's plan, and the "party will go down with it." A few weeks later he urged Polk to

---

[8] Jackson to Polk, Aug. 6, 1837, *Polk Papers*.

[9] In a letter, August 7, informing Polk of his overwhelming defeat in his race for Congress, W. C. Dunlap stated that every candidate for the state legislature favored some kind of a federal bank. James Walker in a letter to Polk, August 27, stated that should the administration adopt the sub-treasury plan it would find itself in a minority in Tennessee (both letters in *Polk Papers*).

[10] "The treasury," he continued, "dare not pass from the majority, without power passing with it—the Treasury is the arm of power, as much in this Gov't as in any on Earth; the placing it in private hands, is to raise up a rival power in the place of the popular will—of numbers, which will govern in fact, in Congress, & out of it, by sops."

Strike boldly—it is your habit, & the means of your elevation; it is expected of you. Go for 30 or 40 millions, to be circulated fast as may be by the Govt—go for 20ties & over in gradations of tens. Strike out the interest feature—boldly declare that the farmers will hoard the notes bearing 5 per cent.[11]

Polk did not adopt Catron's advice to strike out boldly for paper money. He agreed with Jackson and Van Buren in supporting a hard money policy, although his position as Speaker prevented him from taking an active part in the House debates. At its session of 1837–38 the Tennessee legislature instructed her United States Senators to vote against the sub-treasury bill; and Cave Johnson reported that although he was heartily in favor of the measure, the people did not understand the new financial plan and consequently were opposed to it.[12]

At the extra session of Congress a bill to create an independent treasury was introduced by Silas Wright, a close friend of the President; it passed that body by a small majority, despite the vigorous opposition of both Webster and Clay. In the House it was laid on the table by the combined votes of Whigs and conservatives. Nothing was done to relieve the financial situation except to postpone payment of the fourth installment under the distribution act and to authorize the emission of $10,000,000 in treasury notes to meet the present emergency. Van Buren renewed his recommendation, and at both regular sessions of the twenty-fifth Congress an independent treasury bill was introduced, but each time the plan was rejected. Not even a letter from "Old Hickory" in which he admitted the iniquity of the "pet banks" that he had selected as repositories and commended Van Buren's plan, had weight enough to influence the vote.[13]

With this Congress Polk closed his career as a legislator. He was fully in sympathy with the financial policy of the administration although, as he said in his farewell address, "a sense of

---

[11] Catron to Polk, Sept. 2, Sept. 10, Sept. 27, 1837, *Polk Papers.*

[12] James Walker to Polk, Jan. 25, 1838; Cave Johnson to Polk, March 25, 1838, *Polk Papers.*

[13] Jackson to Moses Dawson, Dec. 17, 1837 (*Niles' Reg.*, LIII, 314–315).

propriety'' had precluded him from taking part in the debates. The fact that he had once supported Jackson's state bank policy and now favored a divorce from all banks subjected him to severe criticism from opposition members of the House. Williams, of Tennessee, quoted a speech made by Polk during the session of 1834–35 as the best argument that could be made in favor of employing state banks and against such a fiscal agent as the independent treasury.[14] After Polk had left Congress to become governor of Tennessee the independent treasury bill (but not under that name) passed both houses of the twenty-sixth Congress, only to be repealed by the victorious Whigs at the first session of the Harrison-Tyler administration.

We have noted elsewhere that Polk's ''Address to the People'' by which he opened his canvass for the governorship of Tennessee dealt principally with national issues. It was an able state paper[15] and, among other things, expressed his views on the ''American System'' and the independent treasury. One result of protective tariff, he said,

was to take the property of one man and give it to another, without right or consideration. It was to depreciate the value of the productive industry of one section of the Union and transfer it to another—it was to make the rich richer and the poor poorer.

Another result of protection was the accumulation of unnecessary funds in the national treasury, and means had to be devised to get rid of the money without lowering the tariff. ''This plan was soon found in an unconstitutional and gigantic system of internal improvements,'' and these were parceled out among communities where the tariff politicians hoped to get votes.

---

14 ''But all must now be abandoned,'' said Williams, ''for the sub-Treasury scheme, even at the expense of a political somerset. What, Mr. Chairman, is this much-talked-of Sub-Treasury bill? It is simply to substitute individuals in the place of banks as the fiscal agents of the Government. I propose to adopt as my own Mr. Polk's speech, delivered at the session of 1834–5, against this change. It is an excellent argument; I cannot better it; let it speak for itself'' (*Cong. Globe* (Feb. 22, 1839), 25 Cong., 3 sess., App., 372).

15 See page 143 and note.

The assumption and exercise of the power, by Federal authority, to construct works of internal improvement within the States, constituted an essential branch of the system of which Mr. Clay was the reputed father and head, and to which the popular but false name of the ''American System'' was given. It was an essential branch of the falsely called ''American System,'' because it was the great absorbent, the sponge which was to suck in and consume the excessive, unequal, unjust and oppressive exactions upon the people, and especially upon the people of the planting States, levied by a high protective tariff. High, unnecessary and oppressive taxes, levied by a high protective tariff—lavish and wasteful expenditures of the surplus money, by a gigantic system of internal improvement, and high prices of public lands, that emigration to the west might be checked—the laboring poor retained in the manufacturing districts, in a state of dependence on their richer neighbors in whose employment they were, constituted Mr. Clay's far famed and miscalled ''American System.''

The United States Bank, said he, was closely allied to the American System. By use of it ''Federalism'' saw the means, under another party name, to accomplish the ''dangerous purposes'' of Alexander Hamilton—''extending the power and patronage of the General Government, [and] corrupting the sources of Legislation.'' Banks, both federal and state, had ''proved to be faithless fiscal agents,'' and therefore he now advocated the adoption by law of the independent treasury plan.[16]

With the bank controversy of the Tyler administration which followed the repeal of the independent treasury act, Polk had nothing to do. His friend Catron still retained his belief in the virtue of paper money and thought that the Democratic party could regain control if it would take a stand in favor of some sort of a bank—something like the one proposed by Tyler, which would issue paper currency. The party, said he, could not hope to win by simply ''offering nothing,'' and the sub-treasury had always been ''an absurd shadow''; in addition, ''the hard money plan is a theory—& deemed a feeble & exploded theory, by the people.''[17]   Uninfluenced by Catron's arguments, Polk held

[16] Copy in pamphlet form in *Polk Papers*.
[17] Catron to Polk, Jan. 2, 1842, *Polk Papers*.

fast to his orthodox opinions. This fact is evidenced by his reply
to a series of questions propounded by a group of persons in
Memphis during his campaign for governor in 1843. He was in
favor, he told them, of a sub-treasury and of metal money,
although he did not object to a limited amount of paper currency if issued by state banks. He was in favor, also, of a
"moderate tariff," but for revenue purposes only.[18]

The Democratic platform of 1844 said nothing about tariff,
except to reaffirm the very general plank in the platform of
1840; nevertheless this subject formed one of the issues of the
campaign. The compromise tariff arranged by Clay and Calhoun in 1833 as a settlement of the nullification trouble provided for biennial reductions until 1842, after which it was to
remain at a uniform rate of 20 per cent. In 1842, however, just
as this rate was about to go into operation, a new act was passed
which abandoned the Democratic revenue basis and fixed the
rates in accordance with the Whig policy of protection. In addition to protective tariff, the Whigs desired to enact Clay's pet
measure of distributing among the states the money derived
from the sale of public lands, but Tyler blocked this by insisting
upon retaining the so-called safety-valve proviso which had been
incorporated into the distribution law passed during the extra
session of 1841.[19] It was well known that a revival of the policy
of distribution and internal improvements would follow Whig
success in 1844, consequently the Democrats, in the Baltimore
platform, declared distribution to be both inexpedient and unconstitutional and reaffirmed the declaration of 1840 against internal
improvements.

Absence of any new tariff plank in the Democratic platform
made it desirable for the candidate, Polk, to declare his views
on the subject, and such a declaration was made in the "Kane
letter" of June 19, 1844. As noted elsewhere, he expressed his

---

18 Reply dated May 15, 1843. Printed in Nashville *Union,* June 2, 1843.
19 This safety-valve provided that distribution should cease whenever
the rate should be raised above 20 per cent.

belief in revenue tariff, sufficient "to defray the expenses of
the Government economically administered." In adjusting it,
he believed in shaping the revenue laws so as to afford just protection to the interests of the whole Union, "embracing agriculture, manufactures, the mechanic arts, commerce and navigation." In other words, he adhered to the historic doctrines
of his party—tariff for revenue, with incidental protection. To
be sure, Cameron and others may have tortured this letter into a
promise of protective tariff in order to delude Pennsylvanians
and other tariff Democrats, but nothing in the Kane letter itself
warranted such a construction.

In his inaugural address President Polk reiterated his well-
known views on the tariff. After quoting from his "Kane letter"
he stated that, when levying duties, revenue should be the object
and protection the incident:

> To reverse this principle and make *protection* the *object* and *revenue*
> the *incident* would be to inflict manifest injustice upon all other than
> protected interests. In levying duties for revenue it is doubtless proper to
> make such discriminations within the *revenue principle* as will afford
> incidental protection to our home interests. Within the revenue limit
> there is a discretion to discriminate; beyond that limit the rightful exercise
> of the power is not conceded.

Soon after he had taken the oath of office, he announced to
George Bancroft "the four great measures" of his administration: first on the list came the reduction of the tariff; and
second, the reëstablishment of the independent treasury.[20] Since
Congress does not convene until December, his attention was
first of all directed to foreign affairs; he did not, however, lose
interest in these party measures, even in the midst of foreign
complications.

As early as October the President began to draft the part
of his annual message relating to the tariff and the "Constitutional Treasury" as he preferred to designate what others called
the independent or sub-treasury. His draft when submitted to

---

[20] See Schouler, *History of the United States*, IV, 498.

the cabinet was approved by all except Buchanan. The Secretary of State approved the recommendation to abolish the "minimum principle" and, in general, that of substituting ad valorem for specific duties, but thought that specific duties should be retained on certain articles such as iron, coal, and sugar.[21] Polk agreed to consider Buchanan's suggestions, but eventually he decided not to follow them.

As submitted to Congress on December 2, 1845, the message invited the attention of that body to "the importance of making suitable modifications and reductions" in the existing tariff rates. All duties, he said, should be kept within a "revenue standard," consequently it was necessary to understand distinctly what was meant by that term. By specific illustrations he showed that revenue diminished or ceased after a certain rate had been reached, and the point at which it began to diminish was the maximum limit of the revenue standard. No rate should go beyond this point, and all duties within the revenue standard should be no higher than the expenses of the government should make necessary. Rates need not be uniform, for discrimination within the revenue standard was permissible, but such discrimination must be for the general welfare and not in favor of a particular industry or section.

The tariff of 1842, he told Congress, violated the cardinal principles which he had laid down, because its object had been "protection merely" and not revenue. Its use of "minimums, or assumed and false values" and the imposition of specific duties had benefitted the rich and worked injustice to the poor. Such abuses should be remedied, and

I recommend to Congress the abolition of the minimum principle, or assumed, arbitrary, and false values, and of specific duties, and the substitution in their place of *ad valorem* duties as the fairest and most equitable indirect tax which can be imposed. By the *ad valorem* principle all articles are taxed according to their cost or value, and those which are of inferior quality or of small cost bear only the just proportion of the

21 Polk, *Diary*, I, 85.

tax with those which are of superior quality or greater cost. The articles consumed by all are taxed at the same rate. A system of *ad valorem* revenue duties, with proper discriminations and proper guards against frauds in collecting them, it is not doubted will afford ample incidental advantages to the manufacturers and enable them to derive as great profits as can be derived from any other regular business. It is believed that such a system strictly within the revenue standard will place the manufacturing interests on a stable footing and inure to their permanent advantage, while it will as nearly as may be practicable extend to all the great interests of the country the incidental protection which can be afforded by our revenue laws. Such a system, when once firmly established, would be permanent, and not be subject to the constant complaints, agitations, and changes which must ever occur when duties are not laid for revenue, but for the "protection merely" of a favored interest.

Attention was next directed to safe-guarding the government funds after they had been collected. Banks, both national and state, had, in his opinion, proved to be unworthy custodians; besides the framers of the Constitution never intended that the funds of the nation should be turned over to private corporations to be used by them for profit and speculation. Believing that government moneys should be completely separated from banking institutions, he recommended that "provision be made by law for such separation, and that a constitutional treasury be created for the safe-keeping of the public money." The money of the people should be kept in the treasury of the people in the custody of agents directly responsible to the government:

To say that the people or their Government are incompetent or not to be trusted with the custody of their own money in their own Treasury, provided by themselves, but must rely on the presidents, cashiers, and stockholders of banking corporations, not appointed by them nor responsible to them, would be to concede that they are incapable of self-government.[22]

These two recommendations—for a revenue tariff and for a constitutional treasury—formed the keynote of Polk's domestic policy. He may have been less brilliant than his illustrious opponent, but few will now deny that he held sounder views on

[22] Richardson, *Messages*, IV, 406–408.

the industrial and the financial needs of the country. His policy was simple and economically sound; and because, under it, the business of the country was, so far as possible, to be left free to seek its natural channels, little positive legislation was required. Clay, on the other hand, like Hamilton, reveled in thaumaturgy and legerdemain. His system of a government bank, protective duties, and the collection of revenue to be distributed among the states, was highly artificial; and even if they were not unconstitutional, surely Polk was right in saying that they had never been contemplated by the framers of that document.

So far as his own party was concerned the message was well received. Cass told the President that in the part relating to tariff "You have struck out the true doctrine, you have cut the Gordian Knot." His tariff policy was, of course, highly acceptable to southern Democrats, and many of them called to express their approbation. "We Pennsylvanians," Cameron told him, "may scratch a little about the tariff but we will not quarrel about it"; Wilmot, on the other hand, remarked that "the doctrines on the tariff were the true doctrines & he would support them."[23] It was rumored that Secretary Walker had written the paragraphs relating to the tariff, but Polk asserted indignantly that "the tariff part of the message and every other part of it is my own."[24]

Without waiting to see whether the Van Buren independent treasury would prove to be a success or a failure the triumphant Whigs abolished it in 1841, but, much to their discomfiture, Tyler blocked the reëstablishment of the United States bank. After the election of 1844 the Democrats carried through the House a bill to revive the independent treasury, but as it failed in the Senate the whole financial question went over to the Polk administration. The new President, as we have seen, made it one of his leading measures and recommended the establishment

---

[23] Polk, *Diary*, I, 109–110. Cameron, despite his remark, opposed the tariff bill when it came before the Senate.
[24] *Ibid.*, 124.

of a "constitutional treasury" which was simply another name for the independent treasury. In following his advice it can not be said that Congress actually created anything; all that was asked and all that was done was to authorize the executive to collect the government revenues in gold and silver, and to deposit them in the treasury vaults until disbursed in the course of ordinary business transactions. Congress simply made the government the custodian of its own funds instead of having them deposited in banks.[25] When, therefore, on March 30, 1846, Dromgoole, of Virginia, presented the bill which had been prepared by the Committee of Ways and Means, the title merely authorized the building of fireproof vaults for the safekeeping of public money, which vaults were formally declared to be the "Treasury of the United States."[26] The requirement that metal money alone should be received by the government was added later in the form of an amendment.

Caleb Smith, of Indiana, at once opened the attack upon the bill and offered an amendment, the gist of which was to authorize the Secretary of the Treasury to deposit government funds in "any bank or banks which he may deem expedient, and also to receive the Government dues in the paper of specie-paying banks." As this amendment would nullify the main purpose of the proposed law there was, of course, no prospect that it would be adopted. It served, however, to make the issue definite, to align on the one side those who believed in a government treasury and hard money, and on the other, the friends of banks and bank currency.

---

[25] The same may be said of the Van Buren independent treasury.

[26] "*Be it enacted &c.*, That the rooms prepared and provided in the new treasury building at the seat of Government for the use of the Treasurer of the United States . . . and also the fireproof vaults and safes erected in said rooms for the keeping of the public moneys in the possession, and under the immediate control of said Treasurer of the United States; and the said Treasurer of the United States shall keep the public moneys which shall come into his hands in the Treasury of the United States as hereby constituted, until the same shall be drawn therefrom according to law" (*Cong. Globe*, 29 Cong., 1 sess., 574).

Smith's arguments in opposition to the independent treasury were not very convincing. He stated, erroneously, that the Democrats had not made the subject an issue in the recent election; that Polk and other Democrats had once favored state banks; and that the Van Buren measure was a "miserable humbug" which had never really been carried into effect. On the other hand, Grider, of Kentucky, asserted that the sole purpose of introducing the bill was to redeem party pledges, for he was certain that many Democrats did not approve of "reckless financial experiments." J. R. Ingersoll, of Pennsylvania, saw nothing in the measure "to commend it to respect"; besides, everything contained in the bill was already covered by the law of 1789 which had created the Treasury Department. In general the arguments against the bill were so lacking in force—and frequently in pertinence—that Daniel, of North Carolina, had good reason for concluding that the Whigs themselves had "the internal conviction" that much good would result from its passage.

The Democrats had small need for arguments, as they were certain that they could command the requisite number of votes. They maintained with justice that a fiscal agent was superfluous, and that the government was most competent to protect and disburse its own funds. They ridiculed the assertion that the measure was a device to draw all metal money into the coffers of the government, leaving the people with nothing but "rag money." Dromgoole, who made the principal argument for the bill, denied the charge of discriminating against banks, for, as he said, they had no legitimate claim to the use of public money. On April 2, after Dromgoole had added an amendment which required payments to the government to be made in gold and silver, the bill passed the House by an overwhelming majority.[27]

On the following day the bill was received by the Senate and referred to the Committee on Finance. Nothing more was

---

[27] 122 to 66 (*Cong. Globe*, 29 Cong., 1 sess., 595).

heard of it until the twenty-second of April. On that date Webster asked the chairman, Dixon H. Lewis, when it was likely to be reported to the Senate and whether the committee had settled upon any amendments. In response to this inquiry Lewis stated that it was the intention of the committee to give precedence to bills relating to warehousing and mints. This apparent indifference to immediate action on one of the "leading" administration measures did not escape the watchful eye of the President. He sent for Lewis and urged him to give precedence to this and the tariff bill, as postponement might endanger their passage.

> I then told him [said he] that I had great anxiety for the passage of the Constitutional Treasury Bill and the reduction of the Tariff, which I had recommended in my annual message. I told him that I considered them as administration measures and that I intended to urge them upon Congress as such, and that I considered the public good, as well as my own power and the glory of my administration, depended in a great degree upon my success in carrying them through Congress.

Lewis was an ardent supporter of Calhoun, and the President embraced the opportunity to read him a lecture on the way southern men were jeopardizing important measures by petty opposition to the confirmation of northern appointments. Northern Senators, he said, had ratified appointments of southern men, and there was no good reason why southern Senators should not reciprocate. To Lewis's complaint that Colhoun and his friends had been turned out of office, Polk replied that he had made his appointments without reference to any aspirant for the Presidency. Being "the first President who had taken bold ground and fully satisfied the South on the tariff," he thought men from that section ought "to cease their opposition upon these small matters in which no principle was involved, for the sake of enabling me to carry out the great measure which involved principle."[28]

---

[28] Polk, *Diary*, I, 367–371. Polk believed that northern men attached more importance to appointments than southern men did. "I reminded him that Mr. Jefferson's plan was to conciliate the North by the dispensation of his patronage, and to rely on the South to support his principles for the sake of these principles."

Despite the President's anxiety the bill was held by the committee until the eighth of June. Lewis then reported it to the Senate with sundry amendments, the most important of which postponed for six months the operation of the specie clause. After another period of slumber the measure was brought up for consideration, and, after three days of debate, it was passed by a small majority on August 1, the day after the President had signed the tariff bill. The House concurred in the Senate amendments, and the constitutional treasury bill became the law of the land.

As early as January 9, 1846, the erratic McConnell, of Alabama, asked leave to introduce a "bill to repeal the tariff of 1842, with all its iniquities," but not until April 14 did McKay, of North Carolina, chairman of the Committee of Ways and Means, report a revenue bill based on recommendations made by the President and the Secretary of the Treasury. Under it, all duties were to be ad valorem. Commodities were grouped in schedules; those in the first group were to pay 100 per cent, others 75, 30, 25, etc., until the free list was reached. It was by no means a free-trade measure, yet it was attacked as such by the advocates of protection. They seemed to regard the tariff of 1842 as something sacred, something which could not be altered without prostrating industry and ruining the country. "We are in one breath told," exclaimed Biggs, of North Carolina, "that if you do not protect the manufacturers they must be prostrated; and in the next you are informed that by your protection you diminish their profits.[29]

Opponents of the measure denounced the ad valorem principle and charged that it was an invitation to commit fraud in valuation. They ridiculed the claim of the administration that a lower tariff would produce more revenue. "We are called on now," said Senator Evans, of Maine,

---

[29] *Cong. Globe*, 29 Cong., 1 sess., 1022. He quoted from Clay (1833) to the effect that "In general it may be taken as a rule, that the duty upon an article forms a portion of its price."

to reduce the rates of duty, not because too much revenue is raised, but because there is too little, and because more can be obtained by a reduction of the rates. Well, sir, I commend the prudence of those who take this view of the subject. Whether they may be able to demonstrate it in a satisfactory manner, is another matter.[30]

Personal abuse of the President was not wanting. Gentry, from his own state, denounced, in the House, what he termed "the great, damnable, and infamous conspiracy" (Kane letter) by which the people of Pennsylvania had been defrauded out of their votes, and by which the men who had perpetrated it had reached the positions they now occupy: these men were "James K. Polk and James Buchanan."[31]

Seaborn Jones, of Georgia, was selected as chief spokesman for the House Committee of Ways and Means, and indirectly, for the administration. All sections of the Union, he contended, would be benefited by a revenue tariff; for it was based on justice and would insure stability for all lines of industry. "Protection," on the other hand, "operates as a hotbed in bringing forth exotics which the soil and climate would not naturally produce"; and the fostering of special industries was not a legitimate function of government.[32] Of northern Democrats, Wilmot, of Pennsylvania, was one of the most enthusiastic supporters of Polk's tariff policy. He branded the tariff of 1842 as the " 'bill of abominations,' in violation of the genius of our institutions, of the provisions of our Constitution, and fatally subversive of the rights and liberties of the people." He favored a "constitutional tariff" such as the one under consideration, one "which would grant equal protection to all, exclusive privileges to none."[33]

On July 3, after divers amendments had been rejected[34] and an attempt to lay the whole question on the table had been

---

[30] *Ibid.*, 1090.   [31] *Ibid.*, 1047.   [32] *Ibid.*, 990–991.   [33] *Ibid.*, 1045.

[34] While nearly all of the amendments related to adjustments in rates, a few were grotesque. For example, Schenck, of Ohio, wished to insert Polk's Kane letter in the bill, and Stewart, of Pennsylvania, moved to make the title read: "A bill to reduce the duties on the *luxuries* of the

defeated, the House passed the tariff bill and submitted it to the
Senate for approval. On learning the good news, Polk recorded
in his diary:

I was much gratified to hear the result, as this was one of the leading
and vital measures of my administration. It was in truth vastly the most
important domestic measure of my administration, and the vote of the
popular branch of Congress, which had fully endorsed my opinions and
recommendations on the subject of the tariff, could not be otherwise than
highly gratifying.[35]

The House bill was taken up by the Senate on July 6, and
after two readings by title, Sevier, of Arkansas, moved that it be
made a special order. Evans, of Maine, endeavored to have it
referred for consideration to the Committee on Finance, but
many Democrats contended that such reference would cause
unnecessary delay. During the debate Clayton, of Delaware, in
an attempt to outmanoeuver the administration forces, moved
certain amendments and instructions which would, if followed,
compel the committee to consider the whole bill. He was not
successful, however, for Dixon H. Lewis, of Alabama, whose
"twenty score of flesh"[36] was a host in itself, promptly reported
the measure back from the committee with a request to be excused
from its consideration.

As chairman of the Committee on Finance, it devolved upon
Lewis to lead the debate in favor of the bill. The belief so widely
held, said he, that ad valorem duties would fail to produce sufficient revenue was "one of those axiomatic errors which, upon
examination, will be found to be wholly fallacious"; even under
the tariff of 1842 such duties had produced more than half of
the revenue. Hannegan, Bagby, and many other Senators supported the measure; the main arguments urged in its favor were
the abolition of the minimum and specific duties, and the read-
justment of rates upon a revenue basis.

---

rich, and increase them on the *necessaries* of the poor; to bankrupt the
treasury; strike down American farmers, mechanics, and workingmen; to
make way for the products of foreign agriculture and foreign labor . . .
etc.'' [35] Polk, *Diary*, II, 11.

[36] Adams, *Memoirs*, XII, 25. Lewis weighed 430 pounds.

Opponents of the tariff bill consumed more time than did its friends. In replying to Lewis, Webster attacked the policy of relying upon ad valorem duties, and he hoped

to show to the Senate and to the country that this bill, so novel, so danger-ous, so vicious in its general principles; so ill considered, so rash, and I must say so intemperate in many of its provisions, cannot but produce in the country the most serious and permanent mischief if it should become a law.[37]

"As a friend of the Administration," Niles, of Connecticut, pro-foundly regretted the introduction of the bill, and "as a friend of the Administration he would vote against it."[38] Of the Demo-crats, Cameron, of Pennsylvania, was the most aggressive in com-bating the measure; but his charge that Pennsylvanians had been deceived by the Kane letter came with bad grace from his lips, for if deception had been employed, Cameron himself had been the chief offender. Benton did not approve all features of the bill, yet he declared himself ready to vote for any measure which would rid the country of the tariff of 1842.

The attitude of two members merits special notice, for the Senate was so evenly divided that the fate of the tariff bill rested in their hands. Like other Democrats, Haywood, of North Carolina, wished the tariff to be reduced, but he maintained that the House bill would effect too radical a change. After several attempts to amend the bill had failed, he broke with his party and resigned his seat in the Senate.[39] Although his act was severely condemned by the party press, the President believed him to be sincere and conscientious.[40]

---

[37] *Cong. Globe*, 29 Cong., 1 sess., 1089.   [38] *Ibid.*, 1117.

[39] The reasons which he assigned for his resignation are given in his "Address to the People of North Carolina" (*Cong. Globe*, 29 Cong., 1 sess., App., 1178 ff.).

[40] Polk, *Diary*, II, 48. He thought that the Senator might be piqued because he had not been given a part in framing the bill, yet "I believe him to be an honest and pure man, but a man of great vanity and possess-ing a good deal of self esteem. . . . I give not the slightest heed to the painful insinuations which I learn this evening are made by illiberal persons as to the motives & causes which have induced his course."

After Haywood's resignation attention centered on Senator Jarnagin, of Tennessee, for with him rested the power to pass or to defeat the "great domestic measure." Jarnagin was not only a Whig and a believer in protective tariff, but in his home state he had been a bitter personal and political opponent of the President. On the other hand, the legislature of Tennessee had instructed him to vote for the administration tariff bill, and it remained to be seen whether he would follow his instructions. On July 25 the President was much perturbed by a report that Jarnagin had threatened to resign; for "should he do so, and Mr. Haywood's successor reach here in time, the tariff bill will be lost by one vote." Polk sent for Senator Turney, who promised to ascertain the intentions of his colleague. Jarnagin agreed to remain in the Senate and to obey his instructions; but Polk was not wholly relieved from anxiety, for Turney informed him that manufacturing interests were attempting to win votes by the use of bribe money and that even he (Turney) had been offered a bribe.[41]

Jarnagin's position was a most unenviable one. Although he thoroughly disapproved the administration bill, his instructions required him to support it. On July 27 he denounced the measure but declared his intention to vote for it; he did not, however, believe that his instructions precluded him from voting for amendments which did not affect its main purpose—the abolishment of the minimum and specific duties. When, therefore, Clayton moved a reference to the Committee on Finance, with instructions to amend, Jarnagin voted with his party. Polk took this to mean that he would break both his pledges and his instructions. "Jarnegan," he observed in his diary, "holds the fate of the Bill in his hands and there [is] no reliance to be placed upon him," and he regretted the folly of Haywood in resigning at such a critical moment.[42] But the President was mistaken, for Jarnagin yielded the "pound of flesh" even though

[41] *Ibid.*, 49–50.   [42] *Ibid.*, 51.

he succeeded in making the operation annoying to his opponents. On July 28 he again announced his intention to vote for the administration tariff, but

I shall, when the question comes on the engrossment of the bill, transfer the whole responsibility, as far as I am concerned, to the keeping of the representative of the whole people, and then we will know whether it be a Democratic measure or not.

He meant of course that on incidental questions he would refrain from voting and compel the Vice-President to save the measure by his casting vote; this done, he would obey his instructions and help to pass the bill. He kept his promise,[43] and the bill was passed by a vote of twenty-eight to twenty-seven after an amendment proposed by Webster for guarding against under-valuation had been adopted. Before the final vote was taken Webster predicted that the measure would be repealed at the next session, for ''it is as impossible that the sun should go backward and set in the east, as that the people should suffer the principle contained in this bill to prevail.''

Even after the Senate had passed the tariff bill the President was pessimistic. He doubted that the House would concur in the Senate amendment. A report that certain Democrats from New York and Pennsylvania would join the Whigs in opposing the amendment gave him ''great uneasiness.'' They did vote with the Whigs on incidental questions, but, due to fear so the President thought, they joined with their own party on the final vote. Polk's gratification found expression in his diary:

This great measure of reform has been thus successful. It has given rise to an immense struggle between the two great political parties of the country. The capitalists & monopolists have not surrendered the immense advantages which they possessed, and the enormous profits which they derived under the tariff of 1842, until after a fierce and mighty struggle.

---

[43] Writing from his post at Naples to his brother, W. H. Polk said that he had trembled when he read that the fate of the tariff bill depended on ''the *doubtful honesty* of Spencer Jarnagin.'' He had up to this time believed that Jarnagin would sell out even if the price were labeled in plain sight; ''his rare honesty in this case, is to me wholly inexplicable!'' (W. H. Polk to J. K. Polk, Nov. 6, 1846, *Polk Papers*).

This City has swarmed with them for weeks. They have spared no effort within their power to sway and control Congress, but all has proved to be unavailing and they have been at length vanquished. Their effort will probably now be to raise a panic (such as they have already attempted) by means of their combined wealth, so as to induce a repeal of the act.[44]

The President had reason to be gratified with the passage of this important party measure. It not only dealt a severe blow to Clay's "American System," but it put in operation a tariff policy which Polk had advocated ever since he had been in public life. Much to the disappointment of his critics no industrial calamities resulted from it, and the act was not repealed as Webster had so confidently predicted. Despite the scoffing of Evans, reduction of the tariff rates was followed by an increase in the amount of revenue; it became redundant in 1857 and was still further reduced. While it would be absurd to attribute the prosperity of this decade to the operation of the "tariff of '46," no longer could it be said that an ad valorem revenue tariff would block the wheels of industry.

The reëstablishment of the independent treasury gave additional reason for gratification, and, like the tariff bill, it caused none of the disasters which its opponents had prophesied. With few modifications, the "constitutional treasury" has continued to the present day, and it has done much to extricate national revenue from the field of party politics. With the enactment of these two measures and the settlement of the Oregon question Polk had effected three of the four items of his administrative program. There was no longer need of anxiety for the "glory" of his administration, even though Davis had talked the diplomatic appropriation bill to death.

Having faithfully complied with the recommendations contained in the President's message, Congress believed, apparently, that the law of compensation entitled it to a free hand in "pork barrel" legislation. Despite the heavy drain on the treasury for military purposes, items were recklessly added to the river and

---

[44] Polk, *Diary*, II, 54–55.

harbor bill until it called for appropriations amounting to nearly a million and a half dollars. Clay himself could scarcely have asked for a more cordial endorsement of his internal improvement policy, and especially from a Congress controlled by Democrats.

Polk promptly vetoed this bill, and his message to the House is an able statement of the Jeffersonian doctrine of strict construction. In his opinion, the measure under consideration was both unconstitutional and inexpedient, and parts of it "a disreputable scramble for the public money." "It is not questioned," said he,

that the Federal Government is one of limited powers. Its powers are such, and such only, as are expressly granted in the Constitution or are properly incidental to the expressly granted powers and necessary to their execution.

After quoting Madison's rule for determining the scope of implied power, Polk maintained that:

It is not enough that it may be regarded by Congress as *convenient* or that its exercise would advance the public weal. It must be *necessary and proper* to the execution of the principal expressed power to which it is an incident, and without which such principal power can not be carried into effect. The whole frame of the Federal Constitution proves that the Government which it creates was intended to be one of limited and specified powers. A construction of the Constitution so broad as that by which the power in question is defended tends imperceptibly to a consolidation of power in a Government intended by the framers to be thus limited in its authority.

National appropriations, in his opinion, should be confined to national purposes, and Congress ought to refrain from exercising doubtful powers. He censured in particular the present attempt to include purely local items by a jugglery of words. "To call the mouth of a creek or a shallow inlet on our coast a harbor can not confer the authority to expend the public money in its improvement."[45] Although he did not consult the cabinet on the advisability of vetoing this bill, he believed that Buchanan, Marcy, Bancroft, and perhaps Walker, would, if consulted, have

[45] Richardson, *Messages*, IV, 460 ff.

advised him to sign it.[46] He declined, also, to sign a bill for
making improvements in the territory of Wisconsin, but his veto
message was not submitted until the following December.[47]

In the interest of economy and as a check upon political job-
bery the President put his veto on a bill to grant five million
dollars in land scrip to persons who claimed damages for French
spoliations prior to 1800. In his message he pointed out that
this question had often been discussed, yet no former Congress
had seen fit to pay these claims, even when there had been a
surplus in the treasury. Since the United States had never received anything from France for the injuries done he saw no
reason for the assumption that our government had become responsible to the claimants for aggressions committed by a foreign
power.[48]

As frequently happens at the halfway point of an administration, the autumn elections showed a decrease in Democratic
strength. Doubtless the main cause of defection was the unpopularity of the Mexican War; but the Whigs attributed much of
it to abhorrence of the "free trade" tariff, although that law
had not yet become operative. Among others, Governor Wright,
of New York, failed in his canvass for reëlection, and administration candidates were defeated in Pennsylvania. With his
usual delight in causing the President discomfort, Buchanan attributed these defeats to the reduction of the tariff. Probably
he hoped to get some concessions for his friends in Pennsylvania,
but instead, Polk told him that he would, in his next message,
recommend that no change whatever be made in the law until
it had been given a fair trial. Wright's defeat had, in Polk's
opinion, been caused by the treachery of the "Old Hunkers"
who no longer deserved to be called Democrats; "this faction
shall hereafter receive no favours at my hands if I know it."[49]

---

[46] Polk, *Diary*, II, 58.   [47] Richardson, *Messages*, IV, 610 ff.

[48] *Ibid.*, 466 ff.

[49] Polk, *Diary*, II, 217–218. In a letter to Henry D. Foster, of Pennsylvania, Nov. 19, 1846, Buchanan said that he had always disapproved

When, early in November, the President began the preparation of his second annual message, the war estimates of Marcy
were so large that doubts were expressed in the cabinet as to the
ability of the government to meet its financial obligations. In
accordance with Democratic tradition, financial ills were readily
traced to "the money power," and the difficulty in floating a loan
was attributed to the machinations of bankers in Boston and
New York who were endeavoring to force a repeal of the independent treasury law. The gloomy Secretary of State doubted
that the war could be conducted on a hard money basis; and
although he had advocated the independent treasury, he was now
satisfied that the government could not finance the war under its
operation.[50]

In his message the President dealt with financial questions in
very general terms. It was too early, he said, to estimate the
revenue to be derived from the new tariff law; but by the simul-
taneous abandonment of the protective policy by England and
the United States, commerce had received a "new impulse," while
labor and trade "have been released from the artificial trammels
which have so long fettered them." The present tariff law had
been framed in accordance with sound principles and consequently ought not to be disturbed. In order to meet the extraordinary expenses of the war a revenue duty might well be placed
on certain articles now on the free list, but it should be repealed
as soon as the needs of the treasury would permit. Walker, in
his report, recommended, for the war period, a special duty of
twenty-five per cent on tea and coffee, but like the President, he
was averse to making changes in the existing tariff law.[51]

---

the tariff of 1846, and he hoped that a modification "will be effected before the Manufacturers & Coal Dealers can be seriously injured" (Buchanan, *Works*, VII, 117).

[50] Polk, *Diary*, II, 221.

[51] Richardson, *Messages*, IV, 498–502. Walker's Report (*H. Ex. Doc. 7,
29 Cong., 2 sess.*). "All experience," said Walker, "is against the protective policy. . . . It is as unwise and unjust as it is repugnant to equal
rights and republican principles, to force, by legislation, any class of the
community to buy from or sell to another."

The tariff of 1846 remained the source of revenue for the remainder of the administration, for this Congress and its successor steadfastly refused to vote additional war duties. Nevertheless, Walker was able to say in his annual report of December, 1847, even while renewing his request for duties on tea and coffee, that

It is now proved that a tariff for revenue not only yields a larger income than the protective system, but also advances more rapidly, in a series of years, the prosperity of the manufacturers, by the augmentation of their foreign and domestic market.

In like manner he could truthfully assert that, instead of paralyzing industry as had been predicted, the independent treasury and hard money had benefited those who had so vigorously opposed them:

Domestic manufactures require for their permanent and successful operation the basis of specie, checking vibrations and inflations of the paper system. . . . If our manufacturers desire great advantages from the home market, it must be abundantly and permanently supplied with a large specie circulation, which alone can sustain that market for a number of years, and prevent those calamities which follow an inflated paper currency. A home market for our manufacturers, when based upon specie and low duties, is solid, permanent, and augmenting; but when founded upon paper credits, it is inflated one year, only to be depressed the next, or some succeeding year—thus depriving the manufacturer of any well-assured and permanent domestic market.[52]

The Whig Congress was not disposed to aid the administration by voting additional war revenue. On the contrary, the President was certain that attempts were being made to create a panic and paralyze public credit.

The truth is [he observed] that the Whig party and leading presses, having failed to defeat the Government in the prosecution of the war by the ''aid & comfort,'' they have given to Mexico by their unpatriotic sentiments, are now insidiously attempting to produce a panic in the money market and thereby, if possible, to break down the Treasury, and thus compel the inglorious withdrawal of our army from Mexico.[53]

---

[52] *H. Ex. Doc. 6*, 30 Cong., 1 sess. When he saw the original draft of this report Polk wrote that ''though in the main sound in its doctrines, I thought some parts of it speculative, and perhaps too highly wrought'' (*Diary*, III, 229).

[53] Polk, *Diary*, III, 322.

While this may have been an exaggerated portrayal of Whig machinations, the intemperate abuse of the President for having "deliberately plotted the war" naturally led him to believe that his opponents would resort to any means of crippling his administration.

If Congress could embarrass the President by declining to follow his recommendations, he was equally determined to thwart its attempt to force his hand on the question of internal improvements. Late in July, 1848, the House passed a civil and diplomatic bill which contained, in the form of a rider, an item for money to improve the Savannah River. Polk well knew that the object was to compel him to abandon the principles of his last veto message, or to incur the odium of defeating the entire appropriation. The Senate later eliminated the obnoxious item, but before this had been done Polk outlined in his diary the course which he intended to pursue:

My mind is made up. I will veto the Bill, if it comes to me with this item in it, whatever may be the consequences. I will do so, if it comes on the last night of the session, and if I am over-ruled by two thirds, & Congress should adjourn without passing the Civil Diplomatic [Bill], I will issue my Proclamation conv[en]ing an extra session of Congress for the next day.

He was much depressed by the "want of patriotism" displayed by Whigs and bolting Democrats, both in the matter of appropriations and in their refusal to create governments for the territories. "Whilst I deplore this state of things, all I can do during the remainder of my term is to adhere undeviatingly to my principles & to perform my whole duty. This I will do at any hazard." The present Congress, in his opinion, was as reckless and extravagant as any he had ever known; the success of its improvement schemes would bankrupt the treasury.[54]

The adjournment of Congress did not relieve the President from the schemes of improvement promoters, for the Secretary of State now presented a project for *external* improvement. He

<hr>

[54] Polk, *Diary*, IV, 35–36, 66.

called Polk's attention to the provision in the treaty recently negotiated with New Granada whereby American citizens had been given the right of passage across the Isthmus of Panama. It was of great importance, he said, that a railroad or canal should be constructed there, and he recommended that engineers should be ordered to make a survey. Without consulting other members of the cabinet the President promptly put a quietus on Buchanan's project. If the government could make the survey, said he, it could also construct the works, and he believed that it did not have the constitutional authority to do either.[55]

Polk's aversion to internal improvements had become almost an obsession, and during the month of October he spent his spare moments in formulating a more thorough exposé of the whole "American System." Originally it was his intention to incorporate his exposé in a veto message, for he fully expected that Congress would pass another internal improvement bill.

> Should another veto become necessary I desire to make it a strong paper, so that if I should be over-ruled, as I may be, by a united Whig vote and a part of the Democratic members, making a vote of two thirds, I may leave my full views on record to be judged of by my countrymen & by posterity. I can add to the strength of my veto message on the same subject of the 15th of December last. If I should not have occasion to use it, it will be left among my papers at my death. I am thoroughly convinced that I am right upon this subject, and therefore I have destowed much labour in preparing a paper which may contribute to convince others that I am so.

His purpose, as he recorded in another place, was to show that the "American System" consisted of several closely allied branches: a federal bank, protective tariff, distribution of the land fund, and internal improvements; that the system had been overthrown in all branches except the last; and if this should be

---

[55] "I told him furthermore that if any improvement Bill should during my time be presented to me, I should certainly veto it, and that if I were to yield my sanction to his proposition it would be argued by my opponents in Congress that while I denied the power to make internal improvements, I was exercising the power, and that too without an act of Congress, to make foreign surveys with a view to make foreign improvements" (*ibid.*, 139–140). How different from the attitude of a later President, who could boast that "I took the canal!"

permitted to survive, all the others would soon be revived.[56] One
may, or may not, agree with his views, yet there can be no doubt
of the President's own belief that, in demolishing this network
of special privilege which had been woven by Hamilton and Clay,
he was performing a most patriotic service. Those who have
charged him—and justly charged him—with being a strong party
man have failed to appreciate his conscientious belief in the
principles of his party. No former President—not even Jefferson himself—had succeeded so well in putting Jeffersonian theories into actual operation. He was grieved by the thought of
retiring without having crushed the last remnant of the system
so elaborately constructed by Hamilton and Clay. He could no
longer hope for reward or distinction from his party, yet he was
quite as willing as he had been in 1834 to ply the oar of the
"galley-slave"[57] in promoting the principles of his party, because
he regarded them as most beneficial to his country. Even if
laborious effort to indite a document so convincing that posterity
must heed it is but an exhibition of personal conceit, still there
can be no doubt that he was impelled by patriotic motives and by
a desire to save his country from what he considered to be a real
and serious menace.

On the advice of his cabinet, Polk decided not to leave the
promulgation of so important a document to the chance passage
of an internal revenue bill. Yielding to their judgment, he made
it a part of his last annual message. The message is well written
and shows a firm grasp of the entire subject. It deserves careful
reading, for it is distinctly the most able indictment of the
"American System" to be found among our public documents.
Although the historical, and perhaps the best, part of the message relating to this subject is too long to be quoted, a few
paragraphs will serve to indicate the conclusions which he had
reached:

---

[56] Polk, *Diary*, IV, 144, 157–158, 167–168.

[57] "Polk worked like a galley-slave to cram down his report" (Adams,
Memoirs, IX, 83).

The several branches of this system were so intimately blended together that in their operation each sustained and strengthened the others. Their joint operation was to add new burthens of taxation and to encourage a largely increased and wasteful expenditure of public money. It was the interest of the bank that the revenue collected and the disbursements made by the Government should be large, because, being the depository of the public money, the larger the amount the greater would be the bank profits by its use. It was the interest of the favored classes, who were enriched by the protective tariff, to have the rates of that protection as high as possible, for the higher those rates the greater would be their advantage. It was the interest of the people of all those sections and localities who expected to be benefited by expenditures for internal improvements that the amount collected should be as large as possible, to the end that the sum disbursed might also be the larger. The States, being the beneficiaries in the distribution of the land money, had an interest in having the rates of tax imposed by the protective tariff large enough to yield a sufficient revenue from that source to meet the wants of the Government without disturbing or taking from them the land fund; so that each of the branches constituting the system had a common interest in maintaining the public debt unpaid and increasing its amount, because this would produce an annual increased drain upon the Treasury to the amount of the interest and render augmented taxes necessary. The operation and necessary effect of the whole system were to encourage large and extravagant expenditures, and thereby to increase the public patronage, and maintain a rich and splendid government at the expense of a taxed and impoverished people.

*   *   *   *   *   *   *   *   *   *   *   *   *

Under the pernicious workings of this combined system of measures the country witnessed alternate seasons of temporary apparent prosperity, of sudden and disastrous commercial revulsions, of unprecedented fluctuations of prices and depression of the great interests of agriculture, navigation, and commerce, of general pecuniary suffering, and of final bankruptcy of thousands. After a severe struggle of more than a quarter of a century, the system was overthrown.

The bank has been succeeded by a practical system of finance, conducted and controlled by the Government. The constitutional currency has been restored, the public credit maintained unimpaired even in a period of a foreign war, and the whole country has become satisfied that banks, national or State, are not necessary as fiscal agents of the Government. Revenue duties have taken the place of the protective tariff. The distribution of the money derived from the sale of the public lands has been abandoned and the corrupting system of internal improvements, it is hoped, has been effectively checked.

It is not doubted that if this whole train of measures, designed to take wealth from the many and bestow it upon the few, were to prevail the effect would be to change the entire character of the Government. One only danger remains. It is the seductions of that branch of the system which consists in internal improvements, holding out, as it does, inducements to the people of particular sections and localities to embark the Government in them without stopping to calculate the inevitable consequences. This branch of the system is so intimately combined and linked with the others that as surely as an effect is produced by an adequate cause, if it be resuscitated and revived and firmly established it requires no sagacity to foresee that it will necessarily and speedily draw after it the reestablishment of a national bank, the revival of a protective tariff, the distribution of the land money, and not only the postponement to the distant future of the payment of the present national debt, but its annual increase.

I entertain the solemn conviction that if the internal-improvement branch of the ''American System'' be not firmly resisted at this time the whole series of measures composing it will be speedily reestablished and the country be thrown back from its present high state of prosperity, which the existing policy has produced, and be destined to witness all the evils, commercial revulsions, depression of prices, and pecuniary embarrassments through which we have passed during the last twenty-five years.[58]

An early payment of the national debt was regarded by Polk to be of such transcending importance that he was loth to relinquish the helm without having made a beginning. With a view to influencing his successor, he told his Secretary of the Treasury that he desired, if possible, to purchase government stock, ''however small the sum might be''; and as soon as the department estimates had been submitted, he directed Walker to purchase half a million dollars' worth.[59]

Like the President's message, Walker's report was an ably written document and a strong vindication of the financial policy of the Polk administration. The predicted disasters had not followed in the wake of the tariff of 1846; instead, Walker had

---

[58] Richardson, *Messages*, IV, 657, 661.

[59] ''I informed him [Walker] that I desired to do this supposing it might exert some influence over the policy of my successor. I deem the speedy payment of the public debt of great national importance. If I commence its payment my successor may dislike to take the responsibility of reversing my policy in this respect'' (Polk, *Diary*, IV, 162, 195).

the satisfaction of informing Congress that even the manufacturers did not "desire the restoration of the tariff of 1842." He came out boldly as an advocate of free trade, and although his views were too radical for practical purposes, it would be difficult to find a better statement of the free trade theory. After an elaborate argument to show that nations as a whole, as well as all classes within them, were best served by unhampered trade, he arrived at the following conclusions:

Whenever the laws of nature are beyond the reach of man, there is perfect order under the direction of Almighty power; but whenever man can disturb these laws, discord and injury are sure to ensue. . . . The laws of political economy are fixed and certain. *Let them alone* is all that is required of man; let all international exchanges of products move as freely in their orbits as the heavenly bodies in their spheres, and their order and harmony will be as perfect, and their results as beneficial, as is every movement under the laws of nature, when undisturbed by the errors and interference of man.[60]

Even though the President declared Walker's report to be "one of his ablest papers," his own remark concerning the Secretary's report of 1847 was applicable to this, also—that it was "in the main sound in its doctrines" but "some parts of it speculative, and perhaps too highly wrought."[61] The two men were in substantial agreement on the fundamentals of economic and financial policy. Polk, however, always directed his attention to the attainable, for he was too conservative by nature to indulge in theoretical discussions.

The specter of improvements—both external and internal—haunted the President to the closing hours of his official term. In January, 1849, he expressed to his cabinet a determination to veto a bill pending in Congress which proposed to pay Aspinwall and others $250,000 annually for twenty years, to enable them to construct a road across the Isthmus of Panama. He opposed the measure first of all on constitutional grounds; in addition,

---

60 Walker, *Annual Report*, Dec., 1848 (*H. Ex. Doc.* 7, 30 Cong., 2 sess.).
61 Polk, *Diary*, III, 299, IV, 224.

he regarded it as "little better than a proposition to plunder the Treasury." On the very last night of his administration he went to the capitol armed with a veto which was to be applied to *any* internal improvement bill. No bill of the kind was presented for his signature, but he regarded the unused veto message as "one of the ablest papers I have ever prepared."[62]

Among the bills signed on the last night of his official term was the one which established the Department of the Interior. "I had serious objections," says the *Diary,* "but they were not of a constitutional character and I signed it with reluctance." He feared that such a department, in its practical operations, would draw power from the states and extend, unduly, the jurisdiction of the national government. Had he been a member of Congress, he would have voted against the measure.[63] Walker, therefore, and not Polk, deserves the credit for this important achievement. It was the child of his fertile brain,[64] and the passage of the bill was due in no small degree to his personal influence.

Those who have been most bitter in their condemnation of Polk's foreign policy have found little to criticize in his internal administration. When he withdrew to private life all industries were in a flourishing condition, and not even the victorious Whigs cared to repeal the "great measures" of his administration. None except Clay was fatuous enough to dream of reviving the obsolete "American System."[65]

---

[62] Polk, *Diary,* IV, 314, 364.

[63] *Ibid.,* 371–372.

[64] Walker had, in his report, urged the creation of such a department, and it was his hand that drafted the bill. See Vinton's statement in *Cong. Globe,* 30 Cong., 2 sess., 514.

[65] See comments on his Ullmann letter in Schurz, *Henry Clay,* II, 299.

CHAPTER XXIV

THE "POLK DOCTRINE" AND MINOR DIPLOMATIC QUESTIONS

In a commencement address delivered before the Yale law school in 1903, Whitelaw Reid attached the name of "Polk Doctrine" to President Polk's declarations concerning European interference in American affairs. Although Reid himself condemned the doctrine, yet the very name given to it acknowledges Polk's important contribution to the great American policy of resisting European intermeddling with the affairs of the western hemisphere. Moreover, despite Reid's criticisms and his statement that it originated "in an intrigue of the slave power,"[1] the Polk Doctrine has been approved and continued by the American people; and Presidents chosen by the party which overthrew slavery, and of which Reid himself was a leading member, have increased rather than diminished the scope of its application.

Polk's first public declaration on the subject appeared in his first annual message of December 2, 1845, and referred to Oregon; but nearly three months before this he had applied the doctrine to the Hawaiian Islands, and certainly not in the interest of slavery. In September, 1845, Anthony Ten Eyck was sent as agent to the islands, and his instructions prepared under the President's order contained the following significant paragraph:

Your mission, under existing circumstances, is one of great importance. The United States have a deep stake in the continued independence of the Hawaiian Islands. They present one of those commanding commercial positions which Great Britain, judging from her past history, would be anxious to annex to her dominions. To promote the prosperity and secure the independence of these Islands, is therefore the clear policy as well as

---

[1] Reid, *The Monroe Doctrine, the Polk Doctrine and the Doctrine of Anarchism*, 7.

the duty of the Government of the United States. We could not view with indifference their transfer to or their dependence upon any European Power.[2]

This is a noteworthy addition the doctrine of Monroe: acquisition of the islands by Great Britain could hardly be regarded as colonization, and the question of suppressing representative government was, of course, not involved. The reason why the transfer could not be viewed with indifference was that it would affect, detrimentally, the commerce of the United States.

It was, however, the Oregon question, and his desire to obtain California, that gave the President the best opportunity to develop his policy of resistance to foreign influence in American affairs. Pakenham's rejection of his offer to fix the Oregon boundary at the forty-ninth parallel made it necessary for him to make recommendations to Congress, and, on October 24, he discussed the subject with Senator Benton. He told Benton that he was strongly inclined to reaffirm Monroe's declaration against permitting foreign colonization, "at least so far as this Continent is concerned." "I remarked," said he,

that Great Britain had her eye on that country [California] and intended to possess it if she could, but that the people of the U. S. would not willingly permit California to pass into the possession of any foreign monarchy, and that in reasserting Mr. Monroe's doctrine, I had California & the fine bay of San Francisco as much in view as Oregon.

The conversation then turned to Cuba and the two men agreed that

as long as Cuba remained in possession of the present Government we would not object, but if a powerful foreign power was about to possess it, we would not permit it. On the same footing we would place California.[3]

There was of course nothing new in Polk's stand on the Cuban question. From the beginning of our national existence Cuba had been regarded as essential to our commercial prosperity, and consequently within the sphere of American influence. His

---

[2] Buchanan to Ten Eyck, Sept. 10, 1845 (Buchanan, *Works*, VI, 255 ff.).
[3] Polk, *Diary*, I, 71.

attitude was the same as Jefferson's,[4] that its possession by Spain might be tolerated, but that it must not pass to a strong maritime power. Although he later attempted to purchase Cuba, Polk was not desirous of acquiring insular possessions, except as a safeguard to American interests. This fact is shown by his refusal, a short time before his conversation with Benton, to purchase from Sweden the island of Saint Bartholomew. In reply to the offer made by the king of Sweden, the President directed Buchanan to state that "the acquisition of distant insular possessions, for Colonial dependencies, has never been deemed desirable or expedient by the United States."[5] In a word, Polk was not an imperialist, albeit he was a most ardent expansionist.

Rumors of British and French designs on California induced Polk to take early steps to prevent their success. Six weeks before Congress had assembled he instructed Buchanan to notify Thomas O. Larkin, American consul at Monterey, that the President could not view with indifference the transfer of California to Great Britain or any other European nation, for "the system of colonization by foreign monarchies on the North American continent must and will be resisted by the United States." The government, he said, did not intend to interfere between Mexico and California, but "it would vigorously interfere to prevent the latter from becoming a British or French Colony."[6] In a communication written during the following month Slidell, also, was given a statement concerning the policy of his government. After speaking of the beneficial results of the Monroe Doctrine, Buchanan said that

The nations on the continent of America have interests peculiar to themselves. Their free forms of Government are altogether different from the monarchical institutions of Europe. The interests and independence of these sister nations require that they should establish and maintain an American system of policy for their own protection and security, entirely

---

[4] See Henry Adams, *History of the United States*, IV, 342–343.

[5] Buchanan to Ellsworth, July 28, 1845 (Buchanan, *Works*, VI, 212).

[6] Buchanan to Larkin, Oct. 17, 1845 (Buchanan, *Works*, VI, 275–276). The original is in the *Larkin Papers*, Bancroft Library.

distinct from that which has so long prevailed in Europe. To tolerate any interference on the part of European sovereigns with controversies in America; to permit them to apply the worn-out dogma of the balance of power to the free States of this continent; and above all, to suffer them to establish new Colonies of their own, intermingled with our free Republics, would be to make, to some extent, a voluntary sacrifice of our independence. These truths ought everywhere, throughout the continent of America, to be impressed on the public mind. . . . . Liberty here must be allowed to work out its natural results; and these will, ere long, astonish the world.[7]

So far, the expression of the President's sentiments had been confined to secret instructions, but his message of December 2, 1845, announced to Congress and to the world the policy which he meant to pursue. He told Congress that certain European nations, in order to check the territorial expansion of the United States, were attempting to extend to America the "balance of power" doctrine which had long been maintained in Europe. But the United States, he said,

can not in silence permit any European interference on the North American continent, and should any such interference be attempted will be ready to resist it at any and all hazards.
. . . . Existing rights of every European nation should be respected, but it is due alike to our safety and our interests that the efficient protection of our laws should be extended over our whole territorial limits, and that it should be distinctly announced to the world as our settled policy that no future European colony or dominion shall with our consent be planted or established on any part of the North American continent.[8]

In this pronouncement Polk professed to be reiterating the Monroe Doctrine, but it differed in two particulars from the declaration of Monroe. In the first place, Polk forbade *any European interference;* and in the second, he spoke only of North America. His statement that "we must maintain the principle that the people of this continent alone have the right to decide their own destiny" evidently applied only in cases where a people desired to join the United States, for his views with respect to Cuba and Hawaii would seem to preclude a transfer of

---

[7] Buchanan to Slidell, Nov. 10, 1845 (Buchanan, *Works*, VI, 295).

[8] Richardson, *Messages*, IV, 398–399.

possessions, even with the consent of the inhabitants. In each case it was the commerce of the United States which he sought to protect, and not the civil rights of the people of those islands. Polk's declaration was, also, much more definite than that of his predecessor; in fact it was a contingent declaration of war.

Some of the London papers were severe in their criticism of the President's message. They perverted it into a declaration of intention to absorb all of North America. "The President advises Congress," said the *Spectator,*

to arm and organize the militia that they may be prepared to receive all communities already settled on the North American continent into the bosom of the Union, and prevent the colonization of any part of the continent by European nations.

Only a part of this statement was true. The *Times* professed to see in the message not merely a bar to future colonization, but "we must infer from the language of the President that existing rights and settlements are held by a questionable tenure."[9] There was, of course, no occasion for this inference, for Polk had stated explicitly that existing rights should be respected.

On January 14, 1846, Senator Allen, chairman of the Committee on Foreign Relations, asked leave to introduce a joint resolution relating to the subject of foreign interference in American affairs. It followed closely the language of the President's declaration, and its object was to reënforce that declaration by giving it the formal approval of Congress. Calhoun objected even to the introduction of the resolution on the ground that a discussion of the subject would stir up enmities and would lead to no possible good. He resented, he said, such outrageous interference as that undertaken by France and England in the affairs of Buenos Ayres, but

the great question presented by this resolution was, whether we should take under our guardianship the whole family of American States, and pledge ourselves to extend to them our protection against all foreign aggression.[10]

---

[9] Quoted by Cass in *Cong. Globe*, 29 Cong., 1 sess., 240.
[10] *Cong. Globe*, 29 Cong., 1 sess., 197.

Allen's motion for leave to present his resolution was sent to the table, but on January 24 the vote was reversed. The main supporters of the resolution were Cass and Allen, the former asserting that the President's declaration would be barren of results "unless adopted by the national legislature." We could not, he said, permit the United States to be "belted round by the fleets, armies, and territories" of England; "Oregon and California, if gained, and Mexico influenced, if not ruled, would complete the circle" of British domination. In opposing the resolution, Calhoun characterized it as "vaporing bravado." He deplored the attempt to lay down general rules, and held that each question should be settled on its merits. For example, the machinations of Great Britain and France in Texas should, if necessary, be resisted by war, for they "would have as much right to induce a member to go out of the Union as to prevent one coming in."[!] The resolution was referred to the Committee on Foreign Relations, from which it never emerged; Polk's declaration, like that of his predecessor, remained a mere dictum of the executive.

Throughout the year 1846 there were persistent rumors of European designs to establish a monarchy in Mexico. As early as January 17 McLane wrote from London that

a favorite scheme of the leading powers of Europe is to compose the Mexican troubles by giving her a settled monarchical form of Government, and supplying the monarch from one of their own families.

There were many protests, he added, against Polk's allusions to the Monroe Doctrine.[11] However groundless such rumors may have been, their recurrence could hardly fail to cause apprehension on the part of the administration.

In March, Buchanan informed Slidell that "we have received information from different quarters, in corroberation of your statement[12] that there may be a design on the part of several

---

11 McLane to Polk, Jan. 17, 1846, *Polk Papers.*

12 Slidell had written on February 6 that "for some time past, rumors have been rife of the establishment of a monarchy in the person of a foreign prince" (*H. Ex. Doc. 60*, 30 Cong., 1 sess., 58).

European Powers to establish a monarchy in Mexico." It is supposed, said he, that the clergy would welcome such a change, and that continued revolution may induce the people to accept it as a means of security and protection. "Indeed, rumor has already indicated the King, in the person of the Spanish Prince Henry, the son of Francisco de Paula, and the rejected suitor of Queen Isabella." While Buchanan believed these rumors to be idle speculations, nevertheless Slidell was instructed to use the utmost vigilance in ascertaining whether such a plot really existed.

Should Great Britain and France attempt to place a Spanish or any other European Prince upon the throne of Mexico, this would be resisted by all the power of the United States. In opposition to such an attempt, party distinctions in this country would vanish and the people would be nearly unanimous.[13]

Apparently, the President did not believe that foreign nations would actually attempt to set up a monarchy in Mexico, for his diary is silent on this subject. Still, he was ever on the alert, and determined, if necessary, to resist such an attempt. In December, he denied Donelson's request for a leave of absence from Berlin, because "a project has been suggested, of establishing a monarchy in Mexico and placing a foreign Prince upon the throne." Although Prussia, said he, had no special interest in the matter, she probably would be committed, therefore Donelson should be in Berlin to meet the issue. Whatever the facts might be,

Should such a project be attempted, it must be resisted by this Government, at any hazard. This was shadowed forth in a mild manner in my late message to Congress.[14]

Rumors of the Mexican monarchy proved to be, as Mark Twain said of the report of his own death, "greatly exaggerated"; but in asserting that he would resist such a project, Polk can not

---

[13] Buchanan to Slidell, March 12, 1846 (Buchanan, *Works*, VI, 404–405).
[14] Polk to Donelson, Dec. 29, 1846, "Polk-Donelson Letters," *Tenn. Hist. Mag.*, III, No. 1, 72.

be charged with inventing a new doctrine, for this case at least fell clearly within the declaration of Monroe against the activities of the Holy Alliance. It is well known, of course, that at a later date France was compelled by the United States to withdraw her support from the Emperor Maximilian.

None of President Polk's utterances against foreign influence in America has met with so much criticism as his message relating to Yucatan. During the Mexican war this department maintained, as far as possible, a neutral position which necessarily deprived it of the protection of Mexico. In March, 1848, Justo Sierra, Yucatanese commissioner in Washington, applied to Buchanan for military assistance, stating in his application that the white inhabitants were threatened with extermination by the Indians. Buchanan and Walker were in favor of sending them arms and ammunition, and after some hesitation the President consented to authorize Commodore Perry to supply the white inhabitants with ammunition, if he could be assured that it would not find its way to other parts of Mexico.[15]

After several rather unsatisfactory conversations with both Buchanan and Polk, Sierra, on April 25, presented a formal communication from the governor of Yucatan. The governor requested aid against the Indians and stated that the people of the department "were ready to surrender their country & the sovereignty over it to any Government which would protect & save them from extermination." He stated, also, that a similar offer had been made to Great Britain and Spain. Prospect of foreign domination called for prompt action, and Polk informed his cabinet that

we could never agree to see Yucatan pass into the hands of a foreign monarchy to be possessed and colonized by them, and that sooner than this should take place the U. S. should afford the aid & protection asked, but that this could only be done by the authority of Congress.[16]

Without delay, the President began the preparation of a message on the subject of Yucatan. The preliminary draft was

---

[15] Polk, *Diary*, III, 374.   [16] *Ibid.*, 433–434.

shown to the cabinet and to various members of Congress, all
of whom approved the sentiments which he had expressed. As
submitted to Congress on April 29, 1848, the message, after calling attention to the deplorable conditions in Yucatan, stated
that the department had offered to transfer the "dominion and
sovereigny of the peninsula" to the United States, and that
similar offers had been made to both England and Spain.

Whilst it is not my purpose, [said he], to recommend the adoption of any
measure with a view to the acquisition of the "dominion and sovereignty"
over Yucatan, yet according to our established policy, we could not consent
to a transfer of this "dominion and sovereignty" either to Spain, Great
Britain, or any other European power.[17]

While the president alleged that he was restating the "established
policy" announced by Monroe, which "applies with great force
to the peninsula of Yucatan," it is obvious that the question
under consideration was not covered by either declaration of the
Monroe Doctrine. Monroe had spoken of colonization, and of
forcible interference with established governments; Polk asserted
that we could not consent to a transfer of "dominion and
sovereignty," even at the solicitation of the inhabitants. But to
show that the Yucatan question did not fall within the purview
of the Monroe Doctrine does not prove that Polk should not have
announced his own much-criticized doctrine. Monroe dealt with
the threatened dangers of his own time; was it presumptuous in
Polk to declare, in similar manner, his policy for dealing with
new phases of foreign domination? Indirectly, there was a close
connection between the Polk Doctrine and that of Monroe. The
purpose of the anti-colonization declaration of Monroe was to
shut out, for the future, undesirable neighbors; this, also, was
the purpose of forbidding the transfer of Yucatan to any European nation. In neither case was any thought given to the wishes
of the actual or the prospective inhabitants; the sole consideration was the welfare of the United States. Moreover, Polk's

---

[17] Richardson, *Messages*, IV, 581–582.

announcement regarding Yucatan was quite in line with that of his predecessors with respect to Cuba, and the degree of importance does not affect the principle involved. For example, when Secretary Clay, by order of President Adams, notified France and other powers that we could not consent to the occupation of Cuba and Porto Rico "by any other European power than Spain under any contingency whatever,"[18] he was thinking of the transfer *per se* and of the effect upon the United States, and not of the wishes of the Cubans.

In his message, President Polk made no specific recommendations, but left it "to the wisdom of Congress to adopt such measures as in their judgment may be expedient to prevent Yucatan from becoming a colony of any European power." There was no intimation that he desired to take permanent possession of the territory or that he had any other object in view than to prevent it from falling into the hands of a foreign nation; still, we know from his diary that he was ready to annex the department rather than see it become a possession of Great Britain.[19]

As soon as the message was read in the Senate, Calhoun asserted that the "broad and dangerous principle" announced in it could not possibly be deduced from the Monroe Doctrine. It was, however, referred to the Committee on Foreign Relations, from which, on May 4, Hannegan reported an act to enable the President to "take temporary military occupation of Yucatan." The debate which followed elicited widely divergent opinions, both as to the President's meaning and the expediency of occupying the territory. It is unnecessary to dwell on this discussion, for before it had proceeded far dispatches arrived bearing the news that a treaty had been concluded between Yucatan and the Indians. Calhoun's remarks, however, are worthy of note, on

---

[18] Clay to Brown, Oct. 25, 1825 (*Am. State Pap., For. Rel.*, V, 856).

[19] "Mr. Walker was in favour of its ultimate annexation to the United States, & Mr. Buchanan opposed it. I concurred with Mr. Walker rather than see it fall into the hands of England" (*Diary* (May 6, 1848), III, 444–445).

account of his peculiar interpretation of the Monroe Doctrine.
It consisted, he said, of friendly declarations, with "not a word
in any one of them in reference to resistance." But Polk, he
continued, "seems to hold these declarations as imposing a
solemn duty on him as Chief Magistrate to resist on all occasions;
and not only to resist, but to judge of the measure of that resistance."[20] As construed by Calhoun, the sole survivor of
Monroe's cabinet, the famous "doctrine" became a harmless
declamation—a simple statement of our desires, and not a warning to the European alliance. Hannegan, the chief supporter of
the bill, disclaimed any desire to annex Yucatan, although, like
the President, he was ready to do so if this should prove to be
the only means of saving it from British domination. That
country, in his opinion, would never neglect an opportunity to
strengthen her hold on the Gulf of Mexico: "Cuba was said to
be the key, and with Yucatan she would have both lock and key,
and control the whole outlet of the vast Mississippi." It was
control of the Gulf region, and not the desire to possess additional
southern territory, that led the President and his supporters to
resist a possible extension of British domination over the department of Yucatan. British activities in Texas had, justly or unjustly, convinced Polk that England was ever ready to deal a
blow at the commercial prosperity of the United States.

Discussion of the Yucatan question, and of the alleged attempt
of Great Britain to make the Gulf of Mexico a *"mare clausum,"*
naturally revived interest in the destinies of Cuba. That island
had always been regarded as the key to the Gulf, and administrations of all parties had agreed that its control must never pass
to a strong maritime power. As noted above, Clay, under Adams'
instructions, had, in 1825, asserted that "we could not consent
to the occupation of those islands by any other European power
than Spain under any contingency whatever." In similar

---

[20] Printed in full in Calhoun, *Works,* IV, 454 ff.

language Webster, in 1843, informed the United States consul at
Havana that his government "never would permit the occupation
of that island by British agents or forces upon any pretext whatever," and that the entire naval and military resources of the
United States would be employed to prevent it.[21]

At the first session of Congress under the Polk administration
resolutions were offered in both houses for the purpose of authorizing the President to purchase Cuba, provided the consent of the
inhabitants could be obtained. Nothing resulted from these resolutions, for more pressing questions soon absorbed the attention
of both Congress and the executive. But when, in 1847, certain
British statesmen urged their government to seize Cuba as
security for the interest on Spanish bonds held in England, the
American press began to discuss the advisability of purchasing
the island. For example, the New York *Sun* came out strongly
in favor of annexation. It stated in an editorial that Spain
would sell Cuba for $100,000,000, and that the Cubans were so
eager to join the United States that they would raise the necessary money if given a week's notice(!)[22] There is no evidence,
however, that the President gave serious thought to the subject
until the summer of the following year when the importance of
acquiring the island was urged upon him by John L. O'Sullivan,
editor of the *Democratic Review* and of the New York *News*.

In his diary for May 10, 1848, Polk mentioned a visit from
O'Sullivan and Senator Douglas. They had come, apparently at
the instance of the former, for the purpose of exhorting the
President to take immediate steps to buy the island from Spain.
As usual, he declined to give them his own views on the subject,
although his decision had already been made. "Though I expressed no opinion to them," is the comment in his diary, "I
am decidedly in favour of purchasing Cuba & making it one of

---

[21] Webster to Campbell, Jan. 14, 1843 (Wharton, *Int. Law Digest*, I,
372).

[22] Quoted in *Niles' Reg.*, LXXII, 338 (July 31, 1847).

the States of [the] Union.'' A few weeks later he wrote that
it was O'Sullivan ''who first suggested to me the idea of purchasing Cuba.''[23]

Late in the month, when consulting his cabinet on the advisability of making an offer to Spain, Polk emphasized the
danger of the island's falling into the hands of Great Britain.
Walker and Mason were in favor of making an offer, and were
willing to go as high as $100,000,000. Johnson objected to in-
corporating the territory into the Union, while Buchanan feared
that any agitation of the subject might injure the party in the
Presidential election.[24] Two days later Buchanan received an
''important despatch'' from the American consul at Havana
which said that on account of impending revolution the creoles
were in favor of annexation. O'Sullivan told the President that
an agent of wealthy Cuban planters had informed him of a
scheme of his employers to overthrow Spanish authority for the
purpose of hastening annexation. O'Sullivan said, also, that a
distinguished American general,[25] now in Mexico, had agreed to
resign his commission at the close of the war and to embark for
Cuba with discharged American troops. But Polk was too cir-
cumspect to indulge in filibustering schemes:

> I at once said to Mr. O'Sullivan that if Cuba was ever obtained by
> the U. S., it must be by amicable purchase, and that as President of the
> U. S. I could give no countenance to such a step, and could not wink at
> such a movement.[26]

When consulted on the subject, Cass expressed himself as
heartily in favor of purchasing Cuba, but Buchanan still maintained that the proposed acquisition was the ''gravest & most
important'' question that had ever been submitted to the cabinet.
At the next meeting he predicted that war with England and

---

[23] Polk, *Diary*, III, 446, 493. The fact that O'Sullivan was a ''Barnburner'' and an enthusiastic supporter of Van Buren is evidence that the
project was not prompted by a desire to extend the slaveholding area.

[24] *Ibid.*, 468–469.

[25] Probably Quitman.   [26] Polk, *Diary*, III, 475–477.

France would follow an attempt to acquire the island; but Polk nevertheless decided that R. M. Saunders, our minister at Madrid, should be instructed to buy it if he could. Buchanan petulantly demanded specific instructions as to contents of the dispatch to Saunders. Evidently he was preparing to disclaim responsibility in case the project should turn out to be politically unwise.

In order to forestall filibustering schemes, General Butler was instructed to prevent our troops from taking part in a Cuban expedition, and the American consul at Havana was told that the United States would "preserve national faith with Spain." On Walker's suggestion, it was decided that copies of these instructions should be forwarded to Saunders at Madrid, with directions to communicate them to the Spanish government. Indeed, Saunders was to make it appear that the presentation of this evidence of good will on the part of his government was the main object of his interview with the Spanish minister; he was then to say that the United States would make an offer to purchase the island, if such an offer would be agreeable to Spain. Walker's happy thought caused Buchanan to withdraw his objections, and he announced to that he "would cheerfully prepare the necessary instructions to Mr. Saunders."[27]

The dispatch to Saunders, in which Buchanan had incorporated the President's views, was formally approved at a cabinet meeting held on June 17, 1848. He stated that the United States had no reason to complain so long as Cuba should continue to be a colony of Spain,

But we can never consent that this Island shall become a Colony of any other European power. In the possession of Great Britain or any strong naval power, it might prove ruinous both to our domestic and foreign commerce, and endanger the Union of the States. The highest and first duty of every independent nation is to provide for its own safety; and acting upon this principle we should be compelled to resist the acquisition of Cuba by any maritime State with all the means which Providence has placed at our command.

---

[27] *Ibid.*, 487.

Having thus definitely stated the policy of his government
and the determination to enforce it, the Secretary of State proceeded to show the necessity for such a policy and to give reasons
for believing that American interests were already menaced by
the designs of Great Britain. Incidentally, these reasons had an
important bearing on the President's recent message relating to
Yucatan. Cuba, said Buchanan, is situated between Florida and
Yucatan, and its possession would give England command of
both inlets to the Gulf. In time of war she could effectively
blockade the mouth of the Mississippi and sever the connection
between the Gulf states and those on the Atlantic.

As reasons for believing that England had ambitious designs,
Buchanan cited first

her uniform policy throughout her past history to seize upon every valuable commercial point throughout the world whenever circumstances have
placed this in her power.

Under the mask of protector of the Mosquito Indians, "she is
endeavoring to acquire permanent possession of the entire coast
of the Carribean Sea from Cape Honduras to Escuda de Ver-
agua"—and this, too, in violation of her treaty of 1786 with
Spain. By a similar violation, a simple permission to cut log-
wood and mahogany had led to the establishment of the British
colony at Belise. She had taken forcible possession of the harbor of San Juan de Nicaragua with the evident purpose of obtaining control over all communication between the Atlantic and
Pacific oceans. Inability of Spain to pay the interest on securities held in England had given her a much more plausible pretext for seizing Cuba than she had for assuming the protectorate
of the Mosquito Indians, and the threatening utterances of Lords
Bentinck and Palmerston indicated a disposition to make use of
this pretext. Indeed, the recent dismissal of the British minister
at Madrid had made a rupture between the two nations almost
inevitable; should it come, "no doubt can be entertained that
Great Britain would immediately seize Cuba."

Saunders was then told that, in the opinion of the President, a crisis had arrived which made it desirable for the United States to purchase the island. He was, therefore, to conclude a treaty, if possible, paying as a maximum the sum of $100,000,000. He was instructed to make the offer orally, and not until he had made it plain to the Spanish government that the United States had been moved wholly by a desire to prevent Cuba from passing to another power.[28]

The hope[29] of the President to crown his work of expansion by annexing Cuba to the United States was doomed to disappointment, for the traditional reluctance of Spain to part with her West Indian possessions could not be overcome. After an exasperating delay the Spanish foreign minister replied that it was

more than any minister dare to entertain any such proposition; that he believed such to be the feeling of the country, that sooner than see the island transferred to any power, they would prefer seeing it sunk in the ocean.

After all, this statement amounted to a pledge that Spain would retain Cuba; and so long as the pledge could be maintained, it effected the main purpose which Polk had in view. Fear of British control of the Gulf had prompted his offer, and such control could not be obtained so long as Spain retained possession of the island.

A letter dealing with Central American affairs, similar to the one sent to Saunders, had already been transmitted to Elijah Hise, who had recently been made *chargé d' affaires* at Guatemala. The dissolution of the Central American confederacy, said Buchanan, had encouraged British encroachments on the Mosquito coast, therefore Hise was to promote a revival of the

---

[28] Buchanan to Saunders, June 17, 1848 (Buchanan, *Works*, VIII, 90-102). Polk, *Diary*, III, 493.

[29] A person who represented himself to be a financial agent of the Spanish queen told Dallas that he had been instructed to ascertain whether the United States would be willing to buy the island. Apparently his story was pure fabrication. See Polk, *Diary*, IV, 4-5.

confederacy. The Secretary was not yet prepared to say what course the United States would pursue with respect to the British protectorate over the Mosquito Indians, but

> To suffer any interference on the part of the European Governments with the domestic concerns of the American Republics and to permit them to establish new colonies upon this continent, would be to jeopard their independence and to ruin their interests. These truths ought everywhere throughout this continent to be impressed on the public mind.[30]

Hise concluded a general commercial treaty on the last day of Polk's term of office, but nothing was accomplished in the way of reuniting the Central American states. The Taylor administration adopted a more conciliatory attitude toward England the result of which was the conclusion of the well-known Clayton-Bulwer treaty of 1850.

Early in the Polk administration an event, unimportant in itself, very nearly caused a break in our diplomatic relations with Brazil. On October 31, 1846, Lieutenant Alonzo B. Davis, of the United States ship *Saratoga,* went on shore at Rio Janeiro to apprehend deserters from his vessel. As Davis was about to take them to his ship, the Brazilian police interfered and imprisoned both Davis and the sailors. Henry A. Wise was then minister to Brazil, and, to use his own expression, he played "old Hickory on them" by demanding the immediate release of the prisoners. He wanted, he said, "to make these Spanish & Portugese Mongrells in S. America understand that *the U. States* MUST *be respected.*"[31] All except one of the prisoners were set free, and the affair might have been dropped had not Wise and Commodore Rousseau of the American squadron not wounded the pride of the Brazilian court by further Jacksonian contempt for diplomatic punctilio.

A fortnight after the prisoners had been released, Wise ignored an invitation to the baptismal ceremonies of the Imperial Infanta, and Commodore Rousseau neglected to fire the customary

---

[30] Buchanan to Hise, June 3, 1848 (Buchanan, *Works*, VIII, 78–84).
[31] Wise to J. Y. Mason, Nov. 6, 1846, *Polk Papers*.

salute. A little later, when the Emperor's birthday was being celebrated, Rousseau neither fired a salute nor hoisted the flag on his ship, while Wise (not invited this time) made a speech on shipboard which was anything but complimentary to the Brazilians. Brazil now requested the recall of both men and asked for an apology from the United States. The apology was claimed on the ground of discourtesy to the Emperor and the more serious charge that Davis had denied the sovereignty of the empire by resisting the police—conduct which had been approved and supported by Wise.

When the complaints were presented in Washington by Lisboa, the Brazilian minister, Polk instructed Buchanan to say that he would neither apologize nor recall Wise and Rousseau; recall of the minister would imply dissatisfaction with his conduct, whereas it was highly approved by the President. Buchanan added, however, that since Wise had, before the trouble had arisen, asked to be relieved, the President would grant his request; Rousseau, also, would soon be sent to another port. With this understanding, Buchanan and Lisboa agreed to let the matter drop; but the Brazilian government recalled Lisboa, demanded an apology, and declared that a successor to Wise would not be received until this had been made.

The new demand for an apology was presented by the *chargé de affaires*, Leal, in the summer of 1847. The only question of importance was Lieutenant Davis's alleged resistance of the authority of the police in Rio Janeiro, and everything hinged on whether Davis or the police first had the sailors in custody. The evidence seemed to show that Davis had apprehended them before the police arrived on the scene. While it was admitted that the jurisdiction of any nation is absolute within its own borders, custom permitted naval officers to go on shore to arrest their own sailors. As this was all that Davis had done, he had, in Polk's opinion, committed no "infractions of police regulations," consequently Wise was justified in demanding his release from prison.

The threat to reject a new minister was resented as "dictating terms" to which Brazil "could not have expected submission"; but, said Buchanan, "the President will take no decisive steps" until he shall have learned that Brazil has actually refused to receive him.[32] This firm but reasonable declaration had the desired effect, and the new minister, David Tod, was received courteously by the Emperor. Wise returned to the United States filled with gratitude for the man whom he had once called a "petty tyrant" and whom he had tried to goad into fighting a duel. "I learn," wrote the President, after Wise had called to pay his respects,

that he returns to the U. S. my friend, & his expressions of gratitude to me to-day were as strong & decided as human language could make them, so that I have lived to conquer the hostility of at least one of my political opponents & persecutors. This I have done by performing my duty in a magnanimous and liberal manner.[33]

Zeal of naval officers to protect American rights nearly involved the government in difficulties with another South American state. In January, 1845, Buenos Ayres attempted to invest Montevideo with an absolute blockade; and because this was forcibly violated by French vessels, a United States naval officer, G. J. Pendergrast, demanded exemption for his own vessels. The authorities at Washington, however, held that an offense committed by one nation did not entitle another to disregard belligerent rights, and the officers were instructed to respect the blockade.

Before this question had been adjusted, British and French naval officers announced a blackade of the whole coast of Buenos Ayres and allowed other neutrals only forty-eight hours to withdraw their vessels from the harbors. Pendergrast entered a vigorous protest on the ground that neutrals[34] have no right to

---

[32] The most important letter (written to Leal on Aug. 30, 1847) is printed in Buchanan, *Works*, VII, 388–404. Nearly all of the correspondence relating to this affair may be found in *Sen. Ex. Docs. 29, 35*, 30 Cong., 1 sess.   [33] Polk, *Diary*, III, 192.

[34] England and France had not declared war on Buenos Ayres.

establish a blockade, and that even a belligerent has no right to declare an entire coast to be blockaded. United States vessels were given time to discharge their cargoes and withdraw from the ports, and, since no seizures were made, nothing more serious resulted than caloric speeches in Congress.[35]

On December 12, 1846, Benjamin A. Bidlack, acting without instructions,[36] concluded a commercial treaty with New Granada, one article of which provided for transit across and guaranteed the neutrality of the Isthmus of Panama. Doubtless Bidlack was moved to take this unauthorized step by Buchanan's letter of June 23, 1845, which instructed him to use his influence to prevent New Granada from granting transit concessions to European powers, and which stated that "the United States have strong motives for viewing with interest any project which may be designed to facilitate the intercourse between the Atlantic and the Pacific oceans."[37] Nevertheless, the arrival of the treaty in Washington took the President completely by surprise. At first, Polk doubted that he could approve this "entangling alliance."[38]

In general this document followed the usual form of commercial treaties, and only the thirty-fifth article merits special comment. Among other things, it stipulated that

The Government of New Granada guarantees to the Government of the United States that the right of way or transit across the Isthmus of Panama upon any modes of communication that now exist, or may be hereafter constructed, shall be open and free to the Government and citizens

---

[35] See correspondence, *H. Ex. Doc. 212*, 29 Cong., 1 sess.

[36] While this treaty was on its way to Washington, Buchanan, on January 2, 1847, authorized Bidlack to negotiate a commercial treaty. See Buchanan, *Works*, VII, 183–186.

[37] Buchanan, *Works*, VI, 180–181.

[38] "As a commercial Treaty it was liberal & in all respects satisfactory, but in addition to its commercial provisions it contained an article giving the guaranty of the U. S. for the neutrality of the Isthmus of Panama, and the sovereignty of New Granada over the territory. Serious doubts were entertained whether this stipulation was consistent with our long-settled policy to 'cultivate friendship with all nations, entangling alliances with none'" (Polk, *Diary*, II, 363).

of the United States, [and that] . . . . the United States guarantee, positively and efficaciously to New Granada, by the present stipulation the neutrality of the before-mentioned isthmus, with the view that the free transit from the one to the other sea may not be interrupted or embarrassed in any future time while this treaty exists; and, in consequence, the United States also guarantee, in the same manner, the rights of sovereignty and property which New Granada has and possesses over the territory.

The treaty was to remain in force for twenty years, and then indefinitely, unless terminated by twelve months' notice from either party.[39]

A few days of deliberation overcame Polk's scruples regarding the entangling alliance and convinced him that the transit agreement was too important to be rejected. On February 10 he submitted the treaty to the Senate with a message which stated that "the importance of this concession to the commercial and political interests of the United States can not easily be overrated." He advised ratification because

The treaty does not propose to guarantee a territory to a foreign nation in which the United States will have no common interest with that nation. On the contrary, we are more deeply and directly interested in the subject of this guaranty that New Granada herself or any other country.

Besides, the purpose was commercial, not political, and it was expected that England and France would join in the guaranty. The guaranty of sovereignty was, in his opinoin, indispensable to neutrality and to the protection of property rights; and assurance of New Granada's permanent sovereignty would remove cause for jealousy on the part of maritime powers.[40] Misgivings respecting the thirty-fifth article and pressure of other business caused a postponement of action until the next session of Congress, but in June, 1848, the Senate finally gave its approval. Although the extent of our obligation to insure the "neutrality" and the "sovereignty" of New Granada has been subject to different interpretations, the subsequent history of this treaty is

---

[39] Malloy, *Treaties and Conventions*, I, 302 ff.

[40] Richardson, *Messages*, IV, 511–513.

not within the purview of the present volume.[41] However, it may be said in passing that a forced construction of the thirty-fifth article was utilized by President Roosevelt to prevent Colombia from suppressing the Panama insurrection and to facilitate the process of "taking" the canal zone.

In the last year of his administration President Polk appointed the first diplomatic agent ever sent from the United States to reside at the capital of Ecuador and diplomatic relations were opened wtih the republic of Bolivia.[42] In both cases assurances were given that foreign interference would be resisted, and emphasis was laid on the identity of interests of the American republics.

One of the last diplomatic events of Polk's official term was the ratification of a postal convention with Great Britain. Success in its negotiation was due to the untiring efforts of George Bancroft, and its importance consisted in removing vexatious discriminations against United States mails. Of it the President said in his diary:

It places our own steamers and packets upon an equal footing with the Brittish and relieves our merchants, naturalized citizens, and others from a heavy discriminating charge of postage on letters and other mailable matter conveyed in American vessels. This change has been effected by the policy of the administration. Had it occurred under other circumstances & when so many other great events had not been crowded into a single Presidential term, it would have attracted more public attention and been regarded as an important achievement.[43]

It was, in deed, an important achievement, for it established reciprocal privileges and deprived the Cunard steamers of a virtual monopoly in carrying the mails.[44]

---

[41] See Latané, *Diplomatic Relations of the United States and Spanish America*, 182–188.

[42] Buchanan to Livingston, May 13, 1848; same to Appleton, June 1, 1848 (Buchanan, *Works*, VIII, 64, 74).

[43] Polk, *Diary*, IV, 271–272.

[44] See Buchanan to Bancroft, July 27, 1847, in which he speaks of the "conduct of the British Post Office, in charging the same postage on letters carried on our steamer, the Washington, to Southampton, at the

Polk's remark concerning the postal convention applies equally well to a number of minor diplomatic achievements which were overshadowed by the Mexican and Oregon questions; in a peaceful period they would have attracted more attention and redounded more to the credit of the man who directed our foreign policy. His vigilance in safeguarding American interests prevented foreign nations from gaining additonal influence on this continent. While the original Monroe Doctrine has long ceased to have any practical application, the "Polk Doctrine" has been an active force in our history down to the present day. It has not, indeed, been an unmixed blessing, for it has brought us burdens as well as prestige. But whether we approve or condemn the doctrine, it was Polk who first declared that the United States would not permit any interference, solicited or otherwise, in American affairs, by European monarchies. In general, his doctrine has been indorsed by the people of the United States.

---

expense of the United States, as though they had been carried there by a British steamer, at the expense of the British Government'' (Buchanan, *Works*, VII, 375).

CHAPTER XXV

CLOSE OF CAREER

Despite the one-term pledge included in his letter accepting the Presidential nomination, there were many who believed that Polk would stand for a second term. Some of the Democratic leaders *feared* that he might do so, while certain of his friends *hoped* that he might be induced to accept another nomination. Both fears and hopes were wholly unwarranted, for the President never swerved from his determination to retire at the end of four years. Notwithstanding Claiborne's disparaging remark that "no one but himself dreamed of his re-election,"[1] nothing in contemporary documents indicates that Polk indulged in such dreams; on the contrary, there is abundant evidence to show that he longed to retire from public life.

As early as December, 8145, Senator Benton expressed the belief that certain Tennessee politicians were planning to run Polk for another term. When told of this the President noted in his diary that there was not the slightest foundation for such a belief: "My mind has been made up from the time I accepted the Baltimore nomination, and is still so, to serve but one term and not be a candidate for re-election." In January, 1847, he rejoiced "that with my own voluntary free will & consent I am not to be again a candidate. This determination is irrevocable."[2]

During the course of his administration political leaders frequently suggested to the President that he ought to (sometimes must) run again. On all occasions his answer was the same—that under no circumstances would he again be a candidate.

---

[1] Claiborne, *Life and Correspondence of John A. Quitman*, I, 235.
[2] Polk, *Diary*, I, 142, II, 328.

In 1848, when commenting on Buchanan's scheming for the nomination, the President wrote in his diary:

> The truth is, I have no doubt, though I cannot prove it, that Mr. Buchanan has become apprehensive that in the contest for the nomination between Gen'l Cass, Mr. Woodbury, and himself the Democratic party may ultimately be forced to look to me for re-election. He knows that I have no such views & that I have constantly declared to all who have introduced the subject to me that I would retire at the end of a single term, but notwithstanding this he fears that a state of things might arise in which the party might require me against my will to be placed before the country for re-election.[3]

On May 13, 1848, the second anniversary of the declaration of war against Mexico, the President read to Cave Johnson a letter in which he formally declared that he would not stand for reëlection. It was addressed to Dr. J. M. G. Ramsey, a Tennessee delegate to the Democratic national convention, and was "to be by him presented to the convention if, as has been often suggested to me it might be, my name should be brought before the convention for nomination." Inasmuch as he was determined to retire, he deemed it "proper to relieve the Convention of any embarrassment which the presentation of his [my] name might produce." Subsequently the letter was shown to several of the delegates who had stopped in Washington on their way to Baltimore, and to personal friends. All regretted his determination to retire. Rhett, of South Carolina, and Venable, of North Carolina, went so far as to say that Polk could carry their respective states, but that Cass would be unable to do so. While he could not fail to be gratified with such expressions of approval, the President adhered to his original purpose, and his letter to Ramsey was read to the convention before the balloting had begun.[4]

Not only did the President decline another nomination, but from first to last he had refused to lend his influence to any

---

[3] *Ibid.,* III, 354–355.

[4] Polk, *Diary,* IV, 448–463, *passim.* The letter itself is printed in Jenkins, *Life of James Knox Polk,* 307.

aspirant of his party. Not even in his diary does he express a distinct preference, although there are indications that he probably preferred Cass. He made his appointments and shaped his policies with a view to the success of his own administration. To aspirants and to the public he made it clear that he would affiliate with no faction of the party; he would support the candidate chosen by the representatives of the people, whoever that candidate might be. He even tolerated the Barnburners until they had openly seceded from the party.

The Democratic national convention assembled at Baltimore on May 22, 1848, and its greatest difficulty proved to be the solution of a knotty problem presented by the delegates from New York. Two sets of delegates from this state appeared, and each claimed the right to seats in the convention. On the first day the credentials committee decided tentatively to admit neither faction unless it would agree to abide by the nomination. This decision was regarded as a victory for the Hunkers and as advantageous to Cass, and the Barnburners refused to submit to interrogations. When reporting this to Polk, J. Knox Walker wrote that "Your true position before the Convention will be presented immediately before any balloting." Two days later he reported much bitterness and confusion, and that the convention probably would admit both delegations.[5] This course was adopted eventually, as the convention did not care to assume the responsibility of deciding between the two factions.

The Barnburners, who favored the Wilmot proviso, were dissatisfied and retired from the convention. They met at Utica in June and nominated Van Buren for President. In August, at a convention held in Buffalo, they joined with Whigs and Abolitionists in nominating Van Buren and Charles Francis Adams on a "Free-soil" ticket.

The secession of the New York delegation from the Baltimore convention and their subsequent affiliation with old-time enemies

---

[5] Walker to Polk, May 22, 24, 1848, *Polk Papers.*

were regarded by the President as little short of party treason. He lost no time in removing from office B. F. Butler and other active Barnburners. When news of the nominations made at Buffalo reached Washington, he remarked that "Mr. Van Buren is the most fallen man I have ever known."[6]

Party schism and ill health overcame temporarily the iron will of the President, and he yielded to despondency—almost to despair. Schism mean the probable success of the Whigs and the reversal of his cherished policies. Ill health portended an early termination of his earthly career. On November 2, his fifty-third birthday, he confided to his diary:

It will be 21 years on to-morrow since my father died. My mother is still living. Upon each recurrence of my birthday I am solemnly impressed with the vanity & emptiness of worldly honors and worldly enjoyments and of [the wisdom of] preparing for a future estate. In four months I shall retire from public life forever. I have lived three fourths of the period ordinarily allotted to man on earth. I have been highly honoured by my fellow-men and have filled the highest station on earth, but I will soon go the way of all the earth. I pray God to prepare me to meet the great event.

The news, a week later, that Taylor had probably been elected President called forth another melancholy comment:

Should this be so, it is deeply to be regretted. Without experience in civil life, he is wholly unqualified for the station, and being elected by the Federal party and the various factions of dissatisfied persons who have from time to time broken off from the Democratic party, he must be in their hands and under their absolute control. Having no opinions or judgment of his own upon any one public subject, foreign or domestic, he will be compelled to rely upon the designing men of the Federal party who will cluster around him, and will be made to reverse, so far as the Executive can reverse, the whole policy of my administration, and substitute the Federal policy in its stead. The country will be the loose [loser] by his election, and on this account it is an event which I should deeply regret.[7]

The defection of the Barnburners, which augured Democratic defeat in November, made the President all the more determined

---

[6] Polk, *Diary*, IV, 36–37, 67.   [7] *Ibid.*, 177, 184–185.

to achieve new victories while his own party remained in power. During the summer of 1848 he busied himself with what proved to be a hopeless attempt to acquire Cuba, and with extending the influence of the United States in South and Central America.

When Congress convened in December, Taylor had been elected and there remained but one short session of Democratic rule. Polk's four great policies[8] had been carried through successfully, but the problem of slavery in the Mexican cession still remained to be solved. Defeat of his party at the polls did not deter the President from urging once more his own solution— the extension of the Missouri Compromise line. His persistency led Collamer, of Vermont, to compare him with the lawyer who, being reprimanded for contending against the opinion of the judge, replied that he "was not rearguing the case, *but damning the decision.*"[9]

Judged by standards of the period which was just closing, the solution offered by the President's message seemed both natural and reasonable. Even so shrewd a politician as Polk did not seem to realize that the days of King Compromise were numbered and that conscience and abstract principles had become the dominating factors in the slavery question. Influential leaders of both North and South were now more interested in constitutional rights than in rquare miles of territory, and the rank and file were rapidly falling into line. To be sure another compromise law was recorded in the statute books in 1850, but Clay's famous omnibus turned out to be Pandora's box in disguise. During the debate on this bill, Calhoun gave warning that disunion would surely result from further agitation against slavery on the part of the North. In reply, Seward announced his "higher law" doctrine which served as a battle-cry in renewed onslaughts upon the "peculiar institution."

---

[8] California, Oregon, Tariff, and the Independent Treasury.

[9] Coleman, *Life of John J. Crittenden,* 328.

Naturally, Polk was chagrined because the slavery question remained unsolved at the close of his administration, and, as we have seen in a preceding chapter, he left Washington harboring the fear that California would become an independent state.[10] Still, he had little cause for discouragement on account of failure in this particular. The most ambitious executive might well be satisfied with the achievements of his administration.

During the course of his official term Polk renewed amicable relations with nearly all of his political antagonists. Bailie Peyton was the first to seek a reconciliation, and in September, 1845, in response to an inquiry, the President said that he "would receive him courteously & respectfully."[11] Peyton was subsequently given a miltiary appointment during the war with Mexico. Wise, as we have seen, was completly won over by the loyal support which the President gave him while he was minister to Brazil. John Bell was the last to seek a renewal of friendly relations, but in January, 1848, he, too, offered the pipe of peace. As the two men had not spoken since the Speakership contest in 1835, the first interview was somewhat embarrassing, especially so on the part of Bell. The President's "manner and conversation," however, "soon put him at his ease."[12] With Clay, the President always maintained cordial personal relations. Clay was a dinner guest at the executive mansion on several occasions, and, according to Foote, he tendered his services to the President in overcoming Whig opposition to the treaty with Mexico.[13]

Polk left office harboring greater resentment for individual Democrats than for members of the opposition party. Blair and Benton had proved themselves to be "unprincipled," and the

---

10 See above, page 655.   11 Polk, *Diary*, I, 32.

12 "I said to him that I was glad to see him, and that so far as I was concerned I was willing to let bye-gones be bye-gones, to let the past be forgotten, and to renew with him our personal intercourse. He said that was his desire, that we were to live neighbors when we retired from public life, and that he desired to be on terms of friendship. I expressed similar desires on my part" (Polk, *Diary*, III, 284–285).

13 Polk, *Diary, passim*. H. S. Foote, *Casket of Reminiscences*, 22.

"baseness" of Wilmot could not "be adequately described." For the opposition party as a whole, his feelings had undergone no change. As late as February 20, 1849, he recorded that

The Whigs & abolitionists in Congress pursue me with a malignity and a bitterness which can only be accounted for because of their chagrin at the success of Democratic measures during my administration.14

Determined to uphold Democratic principles so long as the power rested in his hands, he went to the capitol on the last evening of his official term prepared to veto the Wilmot proviso and any internal improvement bill that might be presented. As we have seen in the preceding pages, he was not called upon to use the veto power, although Congress would in all probability have passed the obnoxious bills if the President's determination to veto them had not become known.

The delight caused by the thought of retirement is recorded by the President on February 13, 1849, the fourth anniversary of his arrival in Washington:

I am heartily rejoiced that my term is so near its close. I will soon cease to be a servant and become a sovereign. As a private citizen I will have no one but myself to serve, and will exercise a part of the sovereign power of the country. I am sure I will be happier in this condition than in the exalted station I now hold.15

General Taylor arrived in Washington on February 23, and immediately an annoying question of etiquette presented itself. Buchanan and other members of the cabinet were planning to call upon the President-elect, and one of them consulted Polk concerning the propriety of their doing so. Polk and Taylor had never met; but since their relations during the Mexican war had been mutually distrustful, the President was not at all certain that Taylor would call upon him to pay his respects. He told the members, therefore, that "if my Cabinet called on Gen'l Taylor before he called on me, I should feel that I had been

---

14 Polk, *Diary*, IV, 227, 343–344.
15 *Ibid.*, 331–332.

deserted by my own political family.'' All except the Secretary of State agreed with the President; Buchanan threatened to disregard Polk's wishes, but did not carry out his threat. Taylor removed the cause for embarrassment by calling at the White House on February 26, after which Polk gave a dinner in his honor and treated him with the utmost cordiality.[16] As they rode to the capitol on inauguration day, Polk found his successor to be well meaning, but ''exceedinglly ignorant of public affairs''; he added to the general's difficulties by *absconding* with the Executive Journal so that poor Taylor did not know what officers he was expected to appoint![17] When reporting to Polk this joke of the season, Cave Johnson said that the new President knew less about public affairs than even his opponents had believed.

On the evening of March 5[18] Polk boarded the steamboat and began his journey homeward. In response to invitations from southern cities, he traveled via Richmond, Charleston, and New Orleans, thence up the Mississippi river. During his whole Presidential term he had suffered much from chronic diarrhoea, and the fatigue of the journey caused its recurrence in an acute form. Medical attention gave temporary relief, and the ex-President reached Nashville much weakened yet apparently on the road to recovery. After a brief rest he was able to visit his mother at Columbia and Mrs. Polk's mother at Murfreesborough.

About a year before he left Washington he disposed of his home in Columbia and purchased the Nashville residence of the late Senator Grundy. It was renamed Polk Place, and under the personal supervision of Mrs. Polk the house was enlarged and refurnished, and the grounds beautified. The President

---

16 *Ibid.*, 349–359.

17 ''The old Genl himself says that by some accident or mistake *you* had taken off the *Executive Journal* & therefore he had been dilitory in presenting his nominations—he could not know what offices he had to fill on that acct!'' (Johnson to Polk, Washington, March 17, 1849, *Polk Papers*). Johnson remained in the Post Office Department for a few days after Taylor's inauguration.

18 As the 4th fell on Sunday, Taylor was not inaugurated until the 5th.

longed for the day to arrive when he might put aside the cares of state and enjoy the quiet of a private citizen, although many of his utterances indicate that he believed the end to be near.

For a time, after his arrival in Nashville, he was more cheerful. The enthusiastic welcome accorded by his neighbors and the interest which he took in supervising the improvements being made at Polk Place restored temporarily his old-time vigor. Whenever he undertook the performance of a task it was his habit to expend his energies freely; and in his present state of health, his storehouse of energy was rapidly exhausted. The labor of arranging the books in his library caused a recurrence of the malady from which he had suffered on his homeward journey, and it was soon apparent that he could not recover.

The Polk family as well as Mrs. Polk were Presbyterians, but the ex-President was not a member of any church. He went regularly with his wife to the church of her choice, although his preference was for the Methodist denomination.[19] A few days before his death his aged mother came from Columbia bringing her own pastor in the hope that her son might accept baptism and unite with the Presbyterian church. But the son recalled a promise once given to Reverend McFerren, of the Methodist church, that, when he was ready to join the church, McFerren should baptize him.[20] Having thus formally embraced Christianity, he felt prepared "to meet the great event."[21] He died on June 15, 1849, in the fifty-fourth year of his age. He was buried in the garden at Polk Place. In 1893 his body, with that of Mrs. Polk, was removed to the grounds of the state capitol. On his tomb is the following epitaph, prepared by A. O. P. Nicholson:

---

[19] "Mrs. Polk being a member of the Presbyterian Church I generally attend that Church with her, though my opinions and predilections are in favor of the Methodist Church" (Polk, *Diary*, I, 86).

[20] Chase, *History of the Polk Administration*, 474–475.

[21] See above, page 716.

By his public policy he defined, established, and extended the boundaries of his country. He planted the laws of the American union on the shores of the Pacific. His influence and his counsels tended to organize the national treasury on the principles of the Constitution, and to apply the rule of freedom to navigation, trade, and industry.

This eulogium by no means exaggerates the national service rendered by President Polk. Indeed, Nicholson might have added that he had made the American continents "safe for democracy" by repelling with vigor all interference by European powers.

Seldom in our history has such an ambitious and so varied a program been carried into effect in the brief space of four years. It was a program conceived, for the most part, by the President himself, and his dogged persistence was an important factor in procuring the legislation necessary for putting it in operation. And yet, as Schouler has truthfully said, when commenting on the ex-President's death:

After this brief-spaced decent tribute Polk's name was seldom publicly mentioned. Over the fruits, sweet and bitter, which his administration had cast so abundantly into the lap of the people, there sprang up very soon sectional quarrel and contention, but the gatherer of those fruits was very soon forgotten.[22]

And, in a great measure, he remained "forgotten" notwithstanding the fact that his tariff policy led to prosperity; that his "constitutional treasury" proved to be successful; that his "Polk Doctrine" has been approved and extended; and that his expansion policy added over five hundred thousand square miles of territory and gave the United States free access to the Pacific.

The acquisition of Louisiana, with its abundant resources and its value as a home for America's surplus population, has commonly been accredited to the statesmanship and farsightedness of Thomas Jefferson. When the centennial of this event was celebrated at St. Louis in 1904, Jefferson's part in the transaction was commemorated by medals struck in his honor. At a

---

[22] Schouler, *History of the United States*, V, 127.

similar exposition held in San Francisco in 1915 to celebrate the opening of the Panama canal, one listened in vain for any mention of the name of the man who had acquired the ground on which the exposition was being held, although days were dedicated officially to many individuals who had contributed little or nothing to the acquisition of the canal or to the prosperity of the Pacific coast. Possibly, many who attended the exposition could not have answered the campaign cry of 1844, ''Who is James K. Polk?'' And yet, every one who is familair with our history knows that Louisiana was purchased without Jefferson's knowledge or consent, and that a vast empire (including California) on the Pacific coast came into the possession of the United States as the result of a policy conceived by President Polk and consummated despite vigorous opposition, both at home and abroad.

Why, then, has this man's name been enveloped in comparative obscurity? Why has he not received full credit for his achievements? Undoubtedly one reason is that he possessed little personal magnetism, while his uncompromising independence dissatisfied all factions; and, consequently, he had no personal following to sound his praises and perpetuate his memory. The excerpt from Schouler, above quoted, suggests incidentally a more potent reason, although Schouler lays the chief emphasis on the fact that Polk was ''soon forgotten.'' As he says, ''there sprang up very soon sectional quarrel and contention,'' and unquestionably this sectional discord had much to do with attaching odium to the Polk administration and with consigning the President's memory to oblivion.

The introduction of the Wilmot proviso precipitated a real crisis in our history. The debate which it elicited presented new phases of the slavery question and rendered the sectional conflict truly ''irrepressible.'' The determination of the anti-slavery forces to exclude the institution from all territories called forth a counter-determination on the part of the South that the "rights" of the slaveholding states must be guaranteed and protected. Henceforth the slavery question overshadowed all others. Little thought was given to the "sweet fruits" which Polk had gathered. Debates on topics wholly unrelated to slavery inevitably drifted into a discussion of this fatal subject, and all attempts made to solve the problem increased rather than diminished sectional bitterness.

Since the conflict at first[23] concerned the territories acquired from Mexico, Polk's expansion policy was represented to be a conspiracy to extend slavery. But the President was not even given the credit usually accorded to a successful conspirator, for he was alleged to be the mere tool of more capable intriguers. On the other hand, the protagonists of slavery had no gratitude for the man who was charged with being their agent in the plot to extend slavery. His unswerving independence, his refusal to approve the extreme southern program, and his advocacy of an extension of the Missouri Compromise line, made him, in their eyes, a traitor to southern interests. As we have noted elsewhere, Polk's policy of compromise was the policy of a period which had just closed. Total exclusion of slavery from the territories had become the watchword of one of the parties to the all-absorbing contest; unrestricted admission of "slave-property" was demanded by the other. As the advocate of the traditional method of adjusting the slavery question Polk satisfied neither side, and he was charged by each with being weak and temporizing. The achievements of his administration and his valuable services as chief executive were obscured by the focusing of public attention on the slavery question in its new and more acute form. Leaders of more extreme views won the approval of their respective sections. Conservatives like Polk were remembered only to be condemned. In the earlier histories of the Mexican War the writers have derived their information mainly from Whig sources

---

23 It was not until the introduction of the Nebraska bill in 1854 that territories in the Louisiana Purchase were included in the discussion.

and from distorted accounts written by dissatisfied Democrats like Senator Benton.[24] Very naturally, therefore, Polk has been caricatured as the pliable instrument of the slave power, and little attention has been given to the constructive policies of his administration. More recently, however, much valuable material has been made available, and investigators have approached the subject with minds unprejudiced by the obsolete sectional controversy. They have found—and it is believed that the preceding pages have shown—that Polk was neither a conspirator nor a weakling, but that he was a constructive statesman, an unusually able executive, and a sound patriot. No other President took his task more seriously nor spent his energies more freely for his country; and few, indeed, have done more to increase the power and prestige of the nation.

---

[24] Especially his *Thirty Years' View*.

BIBLIOGRAPHY

PUBLIC DOCUMENTS

Abridgment of the Debates of Congress from 1789 to 1856, edited by Thomas H. Benton. New York, 1857.

American State Papers, Foreign Relations, Vol. V. Washington, 1858.

Congressional Globe. Washington, 1834–1873.

Executive Register of the United States, 1789–1902, compiled by Robert Brent Mosher. Baltimore, 1903.

Hansard's Parliamentary Debates, LXVII, LXXIX. London, 1843, 1845.

House Executive Documents
    212, 29 Congress, 1 sess.
    4, 29 Congress, 2 sess.
    6, 30 Congress, 1 sess.
    41, 30 Congress, 1 sess. (Emory, *Notes of a Military Reconnoissance.*)
    60, 30 Congress, 1 sess.
    7, 30 Congress, 2 sess.

House Reports
    312, 23 Congress, 1 sess.

Register of Debates in Congress. Washington, 1834–1856.

Senate Executive Documents
    1, 29 Congress, 1 sess.
    107, 29 Congress, 2 sess.
    1, 30 Congress, 1 sess.
    29, 30 Congress, 1 sess.
    35, 30 Congress, 1 sess.
    52, 30 Congress, 1 sess.
    65, 30 Congress, 1 sess.

Tennessee
    House Journal, 1839–40.
    House Journal, 1841–42.
    Senate Journal, 1839–40.
    Senate Journal, 1841–42.

Texas

> *Diplomatic Correspondence of the Republic of Texas,* edited by George
> P. Garrison. 3 vols. *In* American Historical Association, *Annual
> Report, 1907–1908.* Washington, 1908–1911.

> *Treaties, Conventions, International Acts, Protocols and Agreements, be-
> tween the United States of America and Other Powers, 1776–1909,*
> compiled by William M. Malloy. 3 vols. Washington, 1910.

MANUSCRIPTS

BUCHANAN, JAMES. *Papers:* Library of Historical Society of Pennsylvania.
CRALLÉ, RICHARD K. *Papers:* Library of Congress.
CRITTENDEN, JOHN J. *Papers:* Library of Congress.
GREEN, DUFF. *Letters:* Library of Congress.
JACKSON, ANDREW. *Papers:* Library of Congress.
JOHNSON, ANDREW. *Papers:* Library of Congress.
LARKIN, THOMAS O. *Papers:* Bancroft Library, University of California.
MCLEAN, JOHN. *Papers:* Library of Congress.
PIERCE, FRANKLIN. *Papers:* Library of Congress.
POLK, JAMES K. *Papers:* Library of Congress.
POLK, Col. WILLIAM. *Papers:* Library of Congress.
TRIST, NICHOLAS P. *Papers:* Library of Congress.
VAN BUREN, MARTIN. *Papers:* Library of Congress.
WELLES, GIDEON. *Papers:* Library of Congress.

PUBLISHED DIARIES AND CORRESPONDENCE

ADAMS, JOHN QUINCY. *Memoirs of John Quincy Adams, comprising portions of his diary from 1795 to 1848,* edited by Charles Francis
Adams. 12 vols. Philadelphia, 1874–1877.

BROWN, AARON V. *Speeches, Congressional and Political, and Other Writings.* Nashville, 1854.

BUCHANAN, JAMES. *The Works of James Buchanan, comprising his
speeches, state papers, and private correspondence;* collected and
edited by John Bassett Moore. 12 vols. Philadelphia and London,
1908–1911.

CALHOUN, JOHN C. *Correspondence,* edited by J. Franklin Jameson. *In*
American Historical Association, *Annual Report, 1899.* Washington,
1900.

CALHOUN, JOHN C. *The Works of John C. Calhoun,* edited by Richard K.
Crallé. 6 vols. New York, 1851–1870.

HEISS, JOHN P. "Papers," *Tennessee Historical Magazine,* II, No. 2.

LAUGHLIN, SAMUEL H. "Diary," *Tennessee Historical Magazine,* II, No. 1.

LINCOLN, ABRAHAM. *Complete Works,* compiled by John G. Nicolay and John Hay, edited by Francis D. Tandy. 12 vols. New York, 1905.

POLK, JAMES K. *The Diary of James K. Polk,* edited by Milo Milton Quaife. 4 vols. Chicago, 1910.

"Polk-Donelson Letters," *Tennessee Historical Magazine,* III, No. 4. Letters of James K. Polk and A. J. Donelson, edited by St. George L. Sioussat.

"Polk-Johnson Letters," *Tennessee Historical Magazine,* I, No. 3. Letters of James K. Polk and Cave Johnson, edited by St. George L. Sioussat.

"Polk-Pillow Letters," *American Historical Review,* XI, No. 4. Edited by Jesse Siddall Reeves.

TAYLOR, ZACHARY. *Letters of Zachary Taylor from the Battle-Fields of the Mexican War,* edited by William K. Bixby. Rochester, N. Y., 1908.

NEWSPAPERS

Baltimore
> *Niles' Weekly Register.*
> *Sun.*

Nashville
> *Democratic Statesman.*
> *Daily Republican Banner.* Daily and triweekly.
> *Union.* Semiweekly and triweekly.
> *Whig.*

San Francisco
> *Alta California*

Washington
> *Gazette.*
> *Globe.*
> *Madisonian.*
> *National Intelligencer.*
> *Spectator.*

PERIODICALS

American Historical Magazine. 9 vols. Nashville, 1896–1904. Contains Mary Winder Garrett's "Pedigree of the Polk Family," also letters of Jackson and other statesmen.

Democratic Review. New York, 1838–1859.

ARTICLES IN PERIODICALS

BOURNE, EDWARD G. "The United States and Mexico, 1847–1848," *American Historical Review*, V, No. 3.

SCHAFER, JOSEPH. "British Attitude toward the Oregon Question, 1815–1846," *American Historical Review*, XVI, No. 2.

SIOUSSAT, ST. GEORGE L. "Some Phases of Tennessee Politics in the Jackson Period," *American Historical Review*, XIV, No. 1.

BOOKS AND PAMPHLETS

ADAMS, EPHRAIM DOUGLAS. *British Interests and Activities in Texas, 1838–1846.* Baltimore, 1910.

ADAMS, HENRY. *History of the United States.* New York, 1891–1898.

AMBLER, CHARLES HENRY. *Thomas Ritchie.* Richmond, 1913.

BANCROFT, HUBERT HOWE. *History of California*, Vol. 5. San Francisco, 1886.

BENTON, THOMAS H. *Thirty Years' View.* New York, 1862.

BIRNEY, WILLIAM. *James G. Birney and His Times.* New York, 1890.

CHASE, LUCIEN B. *History of the Polk Administration.* New York, 1850.

CLAIBORNE, J. F. H. *Life and Correspondence of John A. Quitman.* 2 vols. New York, 1860.

COLEMAN, ANN MARY BUTLER. *The Life of John J. Crittenden, with selections from his correspondence and speeches.* 2 vols. Philadelphia, 1873.

CURTIS, GEORGE TICKNOR. *Life of Daniel Webster.* 2 vols. New York, 1870.

CURTIS, GEORGE TICKNOR. *Life of James Buchanan.* 2 vols. New York, 1883.

FOOTE, HENRY S. *Casket of Reminiscences.* Washington, 1874.

FREMONT, JOHN CHARLES. *Memoirs of My Life.* Chicago and New York, 1887.

GALLATIN, ALBERT. *The Oregon Question.* New York, 1846.

GARRISON, GEORGE PIERCE. *Westward Extension.* New York, 1906.

GRANT, U. S. *Personal Memoirs.* 2 vols. New York, 1885–1886.

GRAY, W. H. *A History of Oregon, 1792–1849.* Portland, 1870.

HITCHCOCK, ETHAN ALLEN. *Fifty Years in Camp and Field,* edited by W. A. Croffut. New York and London, 1909.

HOLST, Dr. H. VON. *The Constitutional and Political History of the United States,* translated by Alfred B. Mason and Paul Shorey. 8 vols. Chicago, 1881–1892.

HOLST, Dr. H. VON. *Verfassungsgeschichte der Vereinigten Staaten von Amerika.* 4 vols. Berlin, 1878–1884.

HOWE, M. A. DE WOLFE. *The Life and Letters of George Bancroft.* 2 vols. New York, 1908.

JAY, WILLIAM. *A Review of the Causes and Consequences of the Mexican War.* Philadelphia, 1849.

JENKINS, JOHN S. *The Life of James Knox Polk.* Auburn, 1850.

JONES, ANSON. *Memoranda and official correspondence relating to the Republic of Texas, its history and annexation. Including a brief autobiography of the author.* New York, 1859.

LATANÉ, JOHN H. *Diplomatic Relations of the United States and Spanish America.* Baltimore, 1900.

LEARNED, HENRY BARRETT. *Some Aspects of the Cabinet Meeting.* Washington, 1915.

MANN, MARY TYLER. *Life of Horace Mann.* Boston, 1865.

MEADE, GEORGE GORDON. *The Life and Letters of George Gordon Meade.* 2 vols. New York, 1913.

MEIGS, WILLIAM MONTGOMERY. *The Life of Thomas Hart Benton.* Philadelphia and London, 1904.

NELSON, ANSON and FANNY. *Memorials of Sarah Childress Polk.* New York, 1892.

PARTON, JAMES. *Life of Andrew Jackson.* 3 vols. Boston, 1876.

PHELAN, JAMES. *History of Tennessee.* Boston, 1889.

PORTER, VALENTINE MOTT. *General Stephen W. Kearny and the Conquest of California.* Los Angeles, 1911.

PRENTISS, GEORGE LEWIS. *Memoir of S. S. Prentiss.* New York, 1855.

REEVES, JESSE SIDDALL. *American Diplomacy under Tyler and Polk.* Baltimore, 1907.

REID, WHITELAW. *The Monroe Doctrine, the Polk Doctrine and the Doctrine of Anarchism.* New York, 1903.

RIPLEY, R. S. *The War with Mexico.* 2 vols. New York, 1849.

RIVES, GEORGE LOCKHART. *The United States and Mexico, 1821–1848.* 2 vols. New York, 1913.

SCHOULER, JAMES. *History of the United States.* 6 vols. New York, 1880–1899.

SCHURZ, CARL. *Life of Henry Clay.* 2 vols. Boston and New York, 1887.

SCOTT, NANCY N. *A Memoir of Hugh Lawson White.* Philadelphia, 1856.

SCOTT, WINFIELD. *Memoirs of Lieut.-General Scott, LL.D.* Written by himself. Usually cited as *Autobiography.* 2 vols. New York, 1864.

SHEPARD, EDWARD M. *Martin Van Buren.* Boston and New York, 1889.

SMITH, ASHBEL. *Reminiscences of the Texas Republic.* Galveston, 1876.

SMITH, JUSTIN H. *The Annexation of Texas.* New York, 1911.

SUMNER, WILLIAM GRAHAM. *Andrew Jackson.* Boston, 1888.

TEMPLE, OLIVER P. *Notable Men of Tennessee, from 1833 to 1875. Their Times and Contemporaries.* New York, 1912.

THOMPSON, WADDY. *Recollections of Mexico.* New York and London, 1846.

TYLER, LYON G. *Letters and Times of the Tylers.* 3 vols. Richmond, 1884–1896.

WHARTON, FRANCIS. *A Digest of the International Law of the United States.* 3 vols. Washington, 1887.

WILSON, J. G. *The Presidents of the United States.*

YOAKUM, H. *History of Texas, 1685–1846.* 2 vols. New York, 1856.

INDEX

Aberdeen, Lord, 417; and Oregon, 563, 574, 584.

Abolition vote, 279–280.

Adams, C. F., ''Free-soil'' nominee (1848), 715.

Adams, J. Q., 46, 304; opposes Polk, 44, 97, 122; slavery petitions, 109, 126; opposes annexation of Texas, 117, 126; declines to attend Polk's inauguration, 319; supports Polk's diplomatic appropriation, 443; agrees with Polk on ''all Oregon,'' 443, 590; death, 545; and Cuba, 699.

''Alabama letters,'' 271.

Alexander, A. R., 208.

Allen, E., 357, 371.

Allen, William, 403, 561, 585; on Oregon, 599; resigns, 609; desires congressional ''Polk Doctrine,'' 694.

Almonte, J. N., 354, 445, 465.

''American System,'' Polk's opinion of, 656 ff.; defeated, 678; Polk's able message on, 686; obsolete, 689.

Ampudia, Pedro de, 411.

Anaya, P. M., President ad interim, 521; appoints peace commissioners, 522.

Anderson, Alex., Senator, 169, 271.

Archer, W. S., 313, 441, 581.

Arista, Mariano, 412.

Armstrong, Robert, 152, 273, 286, 574; informs Polk of election, 283.

Ashburton, Lord, boundary mission, 558.

Ashmun, George, 467.

Astor, John J., 556.

Atchison, David R., 346, 586, 596.

Atherton, C. G., 126.

Atocha, A. J., advises Polk on Mexican policy, 396–399, 465; 472, 487; suggests bribery, 534.

Aristain, Miguel, peace commissioner, 522.

Badger, G. E., 631.

Bagby, A. P., 674.

''Balance of power,'' opposed by Polk, 693.

Baldwin, R. S., 631.

Bancroft, George, works for Polk's nomination, 237 ff., 272; Secretary of Navy, 298; instructions to Taylor, 375; order relating to Santa Anna, 439; his postal treaty with Great Britain, 711.

Bank of the United States, asks for recharter, 28; sale of stocks, 30.

''Bank war,'' importance of, 26; Polk's part in, 26–46.

Bankhead, Charles, British minister in Mexico, 506, 514.

Baranda, Manuel, desires peace with United States, 506.

Barnburners, convention (1848), 633; removed by Polk, 643.

Bayly, T. H., 305.

Beach, Moses Y., would make treaty without authority, 538.

''Bear flag'' episode, 426.

DUE

NOV 22 '66
NOV 22 '67
SEP 25 '68
OCT 9 '68

AY 6 '70
DEC 8 '71

OCT 16 '72
FEB 26 '73
NOV 8 '73
NOV 21 73
DEC 5 '73
NOV 13 74
NOV 19 '74

NO 21 '77

DEC 11 '85
DEC 11 '85

GAYLORD   PRINTED IN U.S.A.